SAFETY-CRITICAL COMPUTER SYSTEMS

SAFETY-CRITICAL COMPUTER SYSTEMS

Neil Storey

ADDISON-WESLEY

Harlow, England · Reading, Massachusetts · Menlo Park, California · New York
Don Mills, Ontario · Amsterdam · Bonn · Sydney · Singapore
Tokyo · Madrid · San Juan · Milan · Mexico City · Seoul · Taipei

Addison Wesley Longman Limited
Edinburgh Gate
Harlow
Essex CM20 2JE
England

and Associated Companies throughout the World.

Published in the United States of America by Addison Wesley Longman Inc.,
New York.

Cover designed by Chris Eley Design, Reading
and printed by The Oxted Colour Press Ltd, Oxted
Cover photographs supplied by British Aerospace, British Nuclear Fuels Ltd
and Railtrack
Illustrations by PanTek Arts, Maidstone
Typeset by CRB Associates, Norwich
Printed in Great Britain by T. J. Press Ltd., Padstow, Cornwall

First printed 1996

ISBN 0-201-42787-7

British Library Cataloguing-in-Publication Data
A catalogue record for this book is available from the British Library.

Library of Congress Cataloging-in-Publication Data is available.

To Jill, Emma and Jonathan

Preface

Increasingly, computers are being used in applications where their correct behaviour is vital. This includes not only obvious examples within fly-by-wire aircraft and nuclear shutdown systems, but also more commonplace applications within vehicles and domestic appliances. Failure of an engine management system or an anti-lock braking system could be potentially disastrous, as could the failure of a microwave oven to turn off the power when the door was opened. In fact, any system that controls significant amounts of power has safety implications for its design and use. This includes almost all industrial equipment and many domestic appliances.

If the safety of humans is entrusted to a computer-based system it is essential that it operates correctly. Unfortunately, the task of ensuring safe operation is an intractable one. Crucial systems, such as those in the Space Shuttle, use not one computer but several, arranged so that if one should fail another can take over. However, this form of *hardware redundancy* tackles only part of the problem. In many ways the failure of hardware components presents fewer problems than those of producing correct software. Duplicated computers running identical programs provide no protection against software faults. Many engineers see safety-critical system design to be concerned predominantly with producing *safe* software.

In reality one cannot totally separate the hardware and software aspects of safety. Both are necessary for the operation of the system, and faults in either could result in harm to individuals or the environment. Our primary concern then is *system safety*, and all aspects of the design process that impinge upon it. This will include considerations of both hardware and software, both of which are *safety critical.* Unfortunately, the production of a safe system is not restricted to its design. Mistakes in the production or installation of a system could render it dangerous, as could problems associated with its use or decommissioning. In practice, considerations of safety have implications for all phases of a product's life, from its conception to its demise.

The production of highly critical systems is very time consuming and expensive, and should not be undertaken lightly. Before undertaking any project it is necessary to study the safety implications of the system, and to balance these against its benefits. This requires an analysis of the hazards and risks associated with the system, and will determine the level of integrity required. This in turn will influence all aspects of the project, including the hardware architecture adopted, the software development methods used, and the degree of testing required.

Systems must not only *be* safe, they must be *shown* to be safe. In highly critical systems it may be necessary to convince an independent authority that a system is safe before it can go into service. This need for certification imposes tight constraints on the design and development methods that can be used, and each industry has its own standards and codes of practice.

Until recently, safety was seen as a specialist topic not relevant to most computer engineers. However, the increasing use of computers within real-time embedded control systems is changing this perception. More and more of the work of both hardware and software engineers is aimed at products that are now seen as being safety-related. This being the case, it is now essential that all computer engineers have a grounding in the various disciplines that are fundamental to the production of safe systems.

Until a few years ago, there were no books on the safety aspects of computer systems. More recently, the importance of the subject has led to the production of several authoritative texts covering various aspects of the subject. However, these are largely collections of papers by various authors, and generally lack a consistency of style and of assumed knowledge. The books are also aimed at professional engineers who are working or researching in this area, and who have considerable experience in the computer industry. For these reasons the available books are not ideal as student texts, nor for engineers with little experience in this field.

This book aims to fill this gap by providing an introduction to the various topics involved, within a single-author text, at a level appropriate to university and college courses and to practising engineers who require a grounding in safety.

Safety-critical systems form part of a group of applications that go under the general heading of *high-integrity systems*. Such systems are required in any application where failure has severe consequences, and this includes situations where failure could result in damage to the environment or large financial loss, as well as to applications that are safety critical. Examples of applications that require high integrity but are not directly safety critical include telephone exchanges and communication satellite systems. In each case the financial penalties for failure are extreme. Clearly the needs of all forms of high-integrity system are related, and the material within this text is, in most cases, equally relevant to any critical computer system. However, this text emphasizes those aspects that are of particular relevance to safety, as these are largely excluded from other texts that look at the design of high-integrity systems.

Who should read this book

This text is intended for both engineering and computer science students, and for practising engineers within computer-related industries who have had little or no training in safety.

When used as a student text it is suitable for final-year undergraduate and master's degree level courses within electrical engineering, electronics and computer science departments. The material presented provides a basis for courses on safety-critical computer systems and other high-integrity systems. It could also form a useful addition to courses on related topics such as fault tolerance, reliability engineering, formal methods and real-time system design.

Most engineers working within industry have had no formal training in the specialist skills needed to produce safety-critical systems. This text provides an insight into the requirements of such applications, and is presented in such a way that it is accessible to engineers with a broad range of skills. It is therefore suitable not only for engineers who are specialists in either hardware or software design, but also for those who consider computers at a systems level.

Assumed knowledge

The reader is assumed to have a basic understanding of computer operation, digital electronics and programming. Such a knowledge should be satisfied by the early years of any conventional electrical engineering, electronics or computer science course, or by experience within a computer-related industry. No knowledge of any specific computer system or programming language is assumed. Although the treatment is largely non-mathematical, an elementary knowledge of engineering mathematics is also assumed.

While the book does not assume any specific industrial background, those who have industrial experience will no doubt find that this enriches their understanding of the material.

Presentation of the material

The field of safety-critical systems covers a multitude of diverse topics. To guide the reader through this mass of information, and to aid comprehension, the material is presented using a 'top-down' approach. The book starts by looking at the use and requirements of safety-critical systems before considering the general principles of designing such systems. Detailed aspects of design are then covered, before turning to methods of establishing the success of the design process. A number of real-life safety-critical systems are discussed to illustrate the issues covered within the text. Worked examples are given where appropriate, and problems are provided at the end of each chapter to allow readers to assess their understanding of the material. Answers to the numerical problems are given in Appendix C. Where relevant, references are included to allow the reader to find additional information on the topics covered. A list of further reading is also included at the end of each chapter for those who wish to take their studies further.

Chapter contents

Chapter 1 begins by looking at the increasing use of computers in critical applications. It then defines some key issues in the production and use of such systems, and considers the costs and benefits involved.

Chapter 2 is concerned with the requirements of safety-critical systems. The important characteristics of a computer system vary considerably with its use, and this chapter identifies various criteria for judging system performance. It then considers the relevance of these factors in diverse applications such as shutdown systems and continuous control applications.

Chapters 3 and **4** look at the related topics of hazard analysis and risk analysis. The former explains the concept of hazard, and looks at various ways of identifying and analysing the hazards associated with an application. The latter considers the consequences of failure, and explains the need for varying levels of integrity in system design. This chapter also considers society's view of risk and ethical considerations.

The design and development of safety-critical systems are discussed in **Chapter 5**, which considers the development process throughout its various stages. Topics covered include requirements documents, specifications, top-level design and both hardware and software issues.

Fault tolerance is the subject of **Chapter 6**. Many consider fault tolerance to be synonymous with safety, and while this is not necessarily true, it is an issue of great importance. The chapter starts by discussing the nature of faults, and looks at methods of modelling these faults to simplify analysis. It then discusses the various forms of redundancy that form the heart of fault-tolerant systems. Hardware and software fault-tolerant techniques are then discussed, and the chapter ends by providing guidance on the selection of techniques for different applications.

Analysis of the effects of fault tolerance on the reliability of the system is left until **Chapter 7**. This starts by looking at the basic definitions used within reliability engineering, and then moves on to show how reliability models can be used to investigate the various system configurations discussed in the previous chapter. Both combinational and Markov modelling techniques are described, and the strengths of these two approaches are outlined. Reliability prediction is then studied for both hardware and software components, and the chapter ends by looking at methods of assessing the reliability actually achieved within critical systems.

The next three chapters look at various aspects of the implementation of safety-critical systems. The first of these, **Chapter 8**, looks at safety-critical *hardware*, and considers aspects such as design faults, the choice of a microprocessor for a given application, and the important topic of electromagnetic compatibility (EMC). **Chapter 9** then discusses safety-critical *software*, including issues such as the choice of a programming language and methods of software design. **Chapter 10** is concerned with the use of programmable logic controllers (PLCs) as a means of implementing critical systems.

One approach to the production of highly dependable systems relies on the use of powerful mathematical techniques that go under the general heading of *formal methods*. **Chapter 11** looks at these techniques, and discusses their contribution to the production of high-integrity systems.

Having looked at the requirements and design of safety-critical systems, the emphasis of the book then moves towards the evaluation and production phases. **Chapter 12** is concerned with testing, verification and validation, and includes consideration of both static and dynamic testing. **Chapter 13** then looks at quality management, and discusses the various civil and military standards that relate to work in this area. At the end of the development phase of a safety-critical project it is often necessary to obtain certification of the system from a regulatory authority. In **Chapter 14** the process of certification is discussed in the light of the various guidelines and standards used.

The final chapter looks at several commercial safety-critical applications with reference to the material already presented. This section helps to place the content of the earlier chapters in context, and illustrates the application of the various design and development techniques. Three Appendices are provided at the end of the text. The first is a list of acronyms used within this field, and the second illustrates the generation of test cases for use in dynamic testing. The last appendix gives the answers to the numerical problems within the text.

To the instructor

Teaching courses on safety-critical computer systems has previously been difficult for the instructor. Texts in this area tend to cover only isolated topics such as fault tolerance, reliability, software engineering, formal methods or the design of real-time systems. Some subject areas, such as hazard analysis, risk analysis and other safety related topics, are very poorly represented in books suitable for students. The result is that to provide even a partial coverage of the subject requires a large number of set texts. This book aims to solve this problem by providing a single volume that covers all the key issues involved in the production of safety-related systems. It is hoped that by providing such a resource it may encourage more institutions to teach courses in this very important area.

The material is presented in a way that should be accessible to students with a range of backgrounds and abilities. The treatment is largely non-mathematical, and concentrates on the key issues rather than the intricacies of design. Worked examples are used where appropriate within the text to reinforce the points made, and an extensive set of problems is given at the end of each chapter. These may be used by students for self-assessment, or by the instructor as set exercises.

A comprehensive **instructor's guide** is available for this text. This gives guidance on course preparation and content, and suggests how material may be selected to meet the needs of students with different backgrounds. The guide also gives fully worked solutions to all the numerical problems within the book, and key points for the non-numerical exercises. Instructors adopting this book as a course text should contact the publishers to obtain a complimentary copy of this guide.

Aims and objectives

This book aims to provide a unified treatment of a topic of great importance that is currently poorly represented within existing texts.

It is hoped that the provision of a comprehensive, though easily accessible textbook will prompt universities and colleges to consider providing courses in this area. In so doing they will provide for the next generation of computer engineers an insight into the special problems involved in the design of safety-related systems. If this book plays even a small part in increasing the awareness of the importance of this subject, then the effort that has gone into its production will have been worthwhile.

Acknowledgements

I would like to express my gratitude to the many people who have provided information and help during the preparation of this book. In particular, I wish to acknowledge the assistance of John Cullyer, who was a constant source of information and encouragement throughout its production. John was kind enough to read through both the initial and the final drafts of the text, and provided many useful suggestions for improvements. I would also like to thank Brian Wichmann, who was extremely supportive of the work, and provided a great deal of very useful technical data. Thanks also go to a number of people who provided data or feedback for particular chapters. These include Audrey Canning, Denton Clutterbuck, Graeme Parkin, Felix Redmill and David Whitehouse. I would also like to thank the various referees who commented on the manuscript for the publishers.

I would specifically like to thank those companies and individuals who provided material for the case studies in Chapter 15. I am indebted to the Health and Safety Executive for their permission to reproduce material within Section 15.2 (Crown copyright is reproduced with permission of the Controller of HMSO), and to Ron Bell for his assistance with that material. Thanks go to Airbus Industrie and Aerospatiale for supplying material for Section 15.3 (with special thanks to Airbus Industrie for the photograph), and to Peter Potocki and Marc Cambet for their useful feedback. I am also grateful to Ontario Hydro for providing the photograph and several of the diagrams for Section 15.4, and to David Parnas for his very helpful feedback on that section.

Tables 4.1 and 9.3 are taken from the RTCA/EUROCAE standard DO-178B/ED-12B, and are reproduced with the permission of RTCA. Tables 4.2, 4.3, 4.4 and 4.5 are taken from Defence Standard 00-56, and the Crown copyright is reproduced with the permission of the Controller of HMSO.

Table 4.12 is reproduced with the permission of the Engineering Council. Table 5.1 is Crown copyright, and is reproduced with permission of the Controller of HMSO. Figure 9.7 is reproduced with kind permission of Elsevier Science – NL, Sara Burgerhartstraat 25, 1055 KV Amsterdam, The Netherlands. Figure 10.1 is taken from IEC 1131-3 : 1993 and is reproduced with the permission of the British Standards Institution (complete copies of this standard may be obtained from BSI Customer Services, 389 Chiswick High Road, London W4 4AL, UK). Figures 11.10, 11.11 and 11.12 are adapted from a paper by Graeme Parkin (full bibliographic details are given in the text) and are Crown copyright, reproduced with the permission of the Controller of HMSO. Figures 15.21 and 15.22 are reproduced with the permission of the authors. I would also like to thank the British Computer Society Specialist Interest Group in Software Testing for their permission to reproduce the material within Appendix B.

Tables 4.6, 4.7, 4.10, 12.2, 12.4 and 12.5 and Figures 4.3, 5.2 and 5.3 are taken from Draft International Standard IEC 1508, and are reproduced with permission. Copies of this document may be obtained through national standards bodies. By their very nature, draft standards are transitory documents and are subject to change and modification. Readers are reminded to treat the extracts from IEC 1508 with due care.

Finally, I would like to express my heartfelt gratitude to my family for their support during the writing of this book. In particular I would like to thank my wife Jill, without whose support this text would never have been completed.

Neil Storey
Warwick, 1996

Publisher's note

Contents

1 Introduction

CHAPTER CONTENTS

1.1 Computers in critical applications

Since the invention of the microprocessor in the early 1970s the cost of computer-based technology has fallen steadily. This has led to a dramatic increase in the use of computers, to a point where they now outnumber the humans on our planet. The majority of microprocessors are not used in desktop computers or other applications conforming to our traditional image of a computer. Instead, they are in the form of 'embedded systems', where the presence of the processor is largely invisible to the outside world. The range of such applications covers a vast spectrum, from sophisticated aircraft flight control systems to washing machines, and from nuclear shutdown systems to antilock brakes. Automotive and domestic products represent the highest-volume areas, with production being measured in millions. At the other extreme are dedicated industrial control systems that may be unique.

A major distinction between embedded systems and the applications normally associated with general-purpose machines relates to the likely consequences of incorrect operation. Although it may be extremely annoying if a word processor crashes, it is unlikely that the operator will suffer any direct harm as a result. However, the failure of many embedded systems can result in direct, and possibly very serious, harm to one or more people. In some instances the importance of correct operation is clear: failure of the control system of a nuclear reactor could endanger the lives of thousands, if not millions of people, and could have implications for the global environment. On a smaller scale, failure of a critical avionics system could potentially cause an air crash killing hundreds of people. Similarly, failure of an automotive engine management or braking system could risk the lives of several people. In these cases the likely consequences of failure are obvious and the industries concerned have, over many years, developed methods of dealing with the risks involved. Many of these techniques form the basis of the later chapters of this book. Unfortunately, in many cases the consequences of failure of an embedded system are less clear, leading to an assumption that its operation has no implications for the safety of its users or the public. Many domestic appliances come into this category. In practice, any system that controls even modest amounts of power has the capacity to do harm. If, for example, the controller of a washing machine or a pop-up toaster fails in such a way that the heater is left on, this could result in a fire that could kill. Although such an event might seem unlikely, experience shows that, because of the large numbers involved, domestic appliances are a significant cause of personal injury.

From the above discussion it is clear that the operation of many embedded computer systems has a direct influence on the safety of their users and the public. Such systems are often referred to as **safety-related systems**, or sometimes as **safety-critical systems**.

1.2 Safety

Before looking in detail at the use of computers in safety-related systems it is important to discuss the more general topic of **safety**. Definitions of safety vary considerably. A sufficient definition for our needs is:

> ***Safety*** *is a property of a system that it will not endanger human life or the environment.*

From this definition we can more completely define the term safety-related system as follows:

> *A* ***safety-related system*** *is one by which the safety of equipment or plant is assured.*

This definition covers a wide variety of equipment, from a microswitch that ensures that a guard is closed before a machine may be operated, to a nuclear shutdown system. It also encompasses systems whose primary role is to ensure safety, and equipment that must provide safety while carrying out some other function. An example of the latter might be an aircraft autopilot.

The term **safety-critical system** is normally used as a synonym for a safety-related system, although in some cases it may suggest a system of high criticality.

Having defined terms relating to safety and safety systems, it is important to note that no system can be absolutely safe. Our goal in designing a system is to make it adequately safe for its given role. Unfortunately, determining an adequate level of safety inevitably involves personal judgement and opinion. This is complicated by the fact that safety is an emotive subject and people's perceptions of it are both varied and illogical. It is often observed, for example, that many people are afraid of flying, despite the fact that statistically they are safer in the air than when driving to the airport.

Although decisions on the appropriate level of safety for a given application require judgement, there are several techniques of analysis that can be used to assist in these decisions. The implications of failure vary greatly between applications, and this leads to the concept of **levels of integrity** that reflect the importance of correct operation. Once a project has been assigned a **safety integrity level**, this will determine the methods of design and implementation used for the system. We shall return to look at the meaning of 'integrity' in Chapter 2, and will discuss the various integrity levels in Chapter 4.

As many embedded computer systems are safety related it is prudent to begin *all* computer-based projects by investigating their safety implications. In the UK, Ministry of Defence standards require such an analysis to be carried out on all military software (MoD, 1991), and there is good reason to follow this practice for computer systems as a whole, for civil as well as military applications. If a system is found to have safety implications it must be allocated an integrity level reflecting its level of criticality. This will then determine the methods used for the design, construction and testing of the unit. The techniques used to investigate the safety implications of a system come under the headings of hazard analysis and risk analysis. The former looks at the identification of situations that could endanger human life or the environment, and the latter considers the risks associated with these events. These topics are discussed in Chapters 3 and 4 respectively.

The scope of safety

Considerations of safety have implications for the complete system, and for all stages of its life, from inception to decommissioning.

Safety can only be assured by considering all aspects of a system, including both hardware and software. We shall see in later chapters that software often plays a pivotal role in ensuring system safety. However, software alone cannot provide such assurance, as its correct operation is dependent on the system hardware. Similarly, in many cases hardware alone cannot satisfy requirements of safety, and an integrated approach to safety is essential. Consideration must be given to all aspects of the system, including sensors, actuators, cabling, connectors, communications links and power supplies. Human operators or users should also be considered as part of the overall system and their possible actions examined.

Safety cannot be produced simply by good design. The behaviour of any system may be upset by mistakes made during its production, installation or use. Failure to fit a component correctly or the use of an incorrect part may invalidate protective features within the design, and so compromise its safety. Similarly, installing or using a system inappropriately may result in a dangerous situation that is beyond the scope of the original design. Safety is very closely linked with **quality management**, and this very important topic will be discussed in Chapter 13. Safety issues continue throughout the working life of a system, and may include considerations of its eventual decommissioning. This has particular relevance in the nuclear industry.

Because safety considerations affect all the stages of a system's life, they also affect everyone who is connected with it, either directly or indirectly. This relationship is illustrated in Figure 1.1. Those affecting the safety of the system include the customer, the designers and those responsible for production and installation. Maintenance staff, and the operator or user of the system, may both affect and be affected by the safety of the system. Also to be considered are the general public, who might suffer the effects of any failure of the system. In extreme cases, as we have seen in the case of nuclear accidents, this group can potentially include the population of the entire world.

The safety aspects of a computer system may be divided into a number of categories. The first of these represents what might be termed the **primary safety** of the system itself. This includes dangers from electrocution or electric shock, and from burns or fire caused directly by the computer's hardware. The second class represents the **functional safety** of the system. This covers aspects concerned with equipment that is directly controlled by the computer, and is related to the correct functioning of the computer hardware and its software.

A third category represents what might be termed **indirect safety**, as in the case of **safety-related information systems**, and relates to the indirect consequences of a computer failure or the production of incorrect information. These considerations are of relevance in a wide range of systems, such as medical imaging and patient records systems. A well-known example illustrating such matters was the implementation of the London Ambulance Service

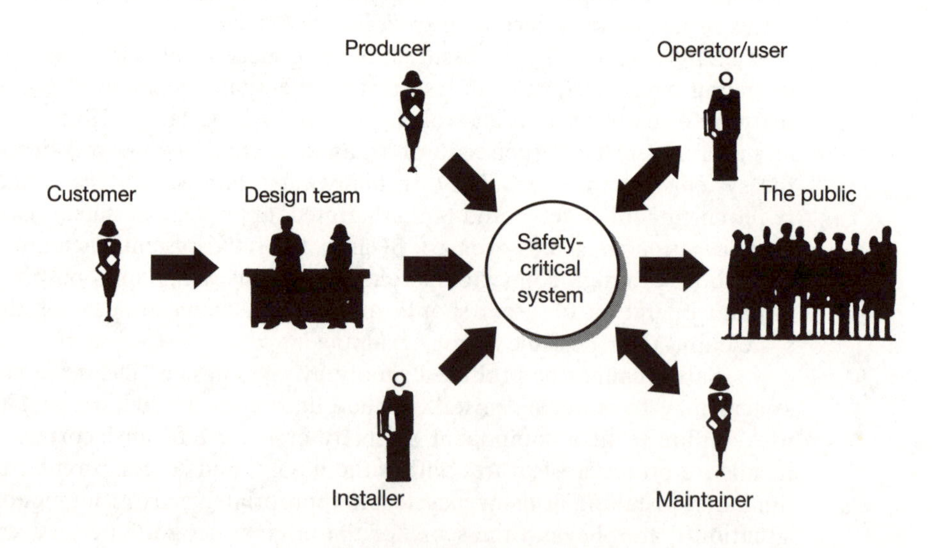

Figure 1.1 A safety-critical system.

dispatcher. When first installed, this system, which routes 999 phone calls to the appropriate emergency services, caused very long delays in dealing with emergencies. The safety implications of such delays are very clear. Other examples from this category relate to automated tools that are used in the design of safety-related equipment. Faults within such tools could lead to incorrect designs, that could in turn endanger life. From this example it is clear that the use of computer packages such as databases, finite element analysis utilities and even word processors could be considered to have safety implications. The hardware of the computers used to run these packages must also be considered, as a system fault could also lead to incorrect data.

Whereas safety is all-encompassing this text cannot be, and is restricted to considerations of functional safety. We shall therefore consider only those aspects of safety related to the direct effects of computer-controlled equipment. This restriction is in line with the definitions of safety and safety-related system given earlier in this section.

Forms of safety-related system

In most cases the safety-related systems that fall within the scope of this book may be categorized as being either control systems or protection systems.

Control systems are used to determine the operation of some form of equipment or plant. In some cases these control functions have no safety implications. This might be because the system being controlled is not capable of dangerous actions, or because safety is managed by some other system or subsystem. Alternatively, the control system may perform a dual role of controlling the equipment and providing safety functions.

Protection systems use sensors to detect fault conditions and produce outputs to mitigate their effects. In many cases the action of the protection system is to shut down the equipment concerned. Such systems are often called **shutdown systems**.

In the case of both control systems and protection systems the overall system configuration is similar, as shown in Figure 1.2. The equipment or system with which the application is concerned is often termed the **equipment under control** or **EUC**. This will have inputs from, and outputs to, the environment through which it performs its designed function. The EUC could be a complete process or production facility, such as a power station or chemical plant, or it could be a relatively small piece of equipment, such as a domestic appliance or an automotive component. In some industries the EUC is normally referred to as the **plant**. The control or protection system interacts with the EUC through **sensors** and **actuators** (or **effectors**) that are used to monitor and control certain parameters. The operation of the control or protection system is determined by the functions or algorithms implemented within it. Control systems are not always safety related but protection systems, by their very nature, usually are.

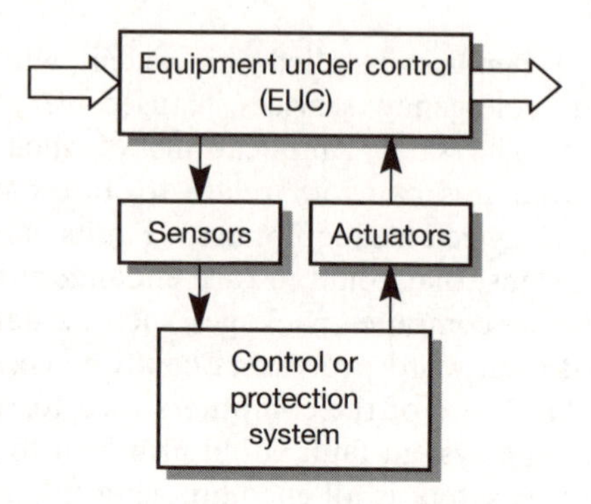

Figure 1.2 A typical control or protection system configuration.

Computers in safety-related systems

Within the field of industrial control it is common to use the term **programmable electronic system (PES)** to represent all forms of computer-based equipment. This term includes not only conventional computers and microcontrollers, but also other software-controlled units such as **programmable logic controllers (PLCs)**.

Clearly, not all control or protection systems are computer based. Indeed, we shall see as we discuss the various topics within this book that there are many cases where non-programmable methods have considerable advantages. If, for example, the temperature of a liquid can be kept to safe levels using a thermostat, this is preferable to using a complex and hence expensive microcomputer system to achieve the same end. However, there are many cases where a programmable electronic system is advantageous, or even essential, to achieving the control and safety features required.

When a computer-based system is adopted, the control or protection system will have two major components: hardware and software. Both are essential, and both directly affect the safety of the system. This arrangement is shown in Figure 1.3.

Advantages of computer-based systems

The most obvious advantage of computer-based systems is their processing power, which allows them to perform complex control functions that might be impossible by other means. They can take inputs from many sources, drive many outputs and perform complex calculations. Their operation is also characterized by high speed, low power consumption and a small physical size.

Modern digital devices are extremely reliable. Most systems based on such devices also possess a high degree of integration, resulting in a small number of components with relatively few interconnections. Such systems

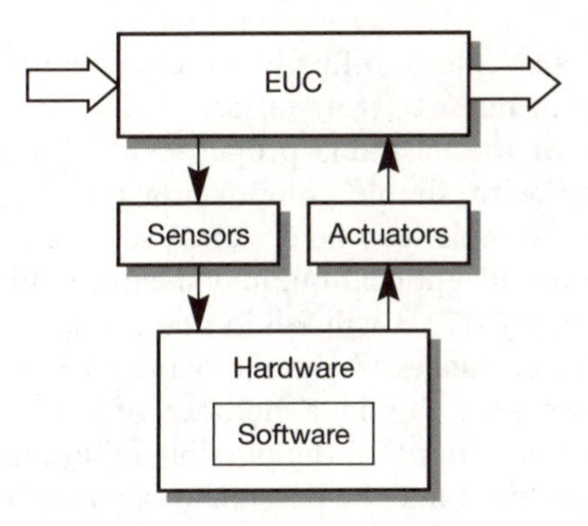

Figure 1.3 A computer-based control or protection system.

therefore tend to be highly reliable, both because of the nature of their components and because of the small number of interconnections, which are often a major cause of failure.

Another important property of computer-based systems is their flexibility: the system's characteristics may be drastically changed by modifications to the software without the need for hardware alteration. This often provides an efficient method of system upgrading at a relatively low cost.

In most cases the cost of implementing a programmable electronic control system is less than that of alternative methods. This is particularly true as the complexity of the required system increases. The additional benefit of software upgradability further increases the cost advantage. In low-volume projects development costs predominate, with software being responsible for the majority.

The availability of considerable processing power allows more sophisticated safety strategies to be implemented. These might include the use of self-diagnostic routines, condition monitoring, range checking and the implementation of interlocks.

Disadvantages of computer-based systems

The primary disadvantages of programmable electronic systems in safety-related applications stem directly from their inherent **complexity**.

By their very nature all computer-based systems are complex. Even minimal microprocessor arrangements have at their heart a component with hundreds of thousands of components and an extremely complex behaviour. Software too is associated with great complexity: even relatively simple programs may represent many thousands of possible execution paths.

Complexity is a major obstacle to safety. Complex systems are more difficult to design and are therefore more likely to contain design errors. They are more difficult to test and are thus more likely to contain undetected faults.

They are also more difficult to understand, and may therefore be more susceptible to human errors in installation or use.

One of the desirable properties of any safety-related system is **predictability**, and with simple components this is generally achievable. A simple switch, for example, can be designed so that it will normally 'fail safe', which, depending on the application, may mean to fail 'open' or to fail 'closed'. In any event it is likely that it will fail in one of these two modes, which are termed its possible **failure modes**. A simple arrangement of a small number of switches could conceivably fail in a number of ways, the number being determined by the combination of all the possible failure modes of the individual parts. By careful planning it may be possible to arrange a series of tests that would detect any of these patterns of failure, so providing an exhaustive test of the unit. It might also be possible to provide an alternative unit, so that if any of these failures were detected a backup could be provided.

In complex digital devices such as microprocessors the number of possible failure modes is so large that it may be considered to be infinite. In such cases it becomes impossible to devise exhaustive tests for such a device, and therefore the detection of failure will always be unreliable.

The problems associated with complexity are equally applicable to software. All but the simplest of programs are too complex to test exhaustively in any true sense. As in many safety-related systems much of the complexity is implemented within software, testing represents a serious problem.

1.3 Developing safety-related systems

Having identified not only advantages, but also disadvantages to the use of computers within safety-related systems, it is clear that a programmable solution will not always be ideal for a given application. However, in many cases the advantages outweigh the problems and a computer-based approach is adopted. In certain circumstances a computer-based system is the only viable method of producing the required functions.

The process of developing a safety-related computer system may be both involved and time consuming. Like all development projects it has various phases, and again as with all projects, these may be represented diagrammatically using a **lifecycle model**.

Various lifecycle models are used, each accentuating some aspect of the project. Thus some are more suitable for corporate planning, others for resource management or costing. Each technique has its advocates and its critics, and it is not within the scope of this text to discuss their merits. Figure 1.4 shows a typical development lifecycle model which has its origins in that given in the STARTS guide (1989). For obvious reasons this is often referred to as the 'V' lifecycle model. The model identifies the major elements of the development process and indicates the sequential nature of much of the

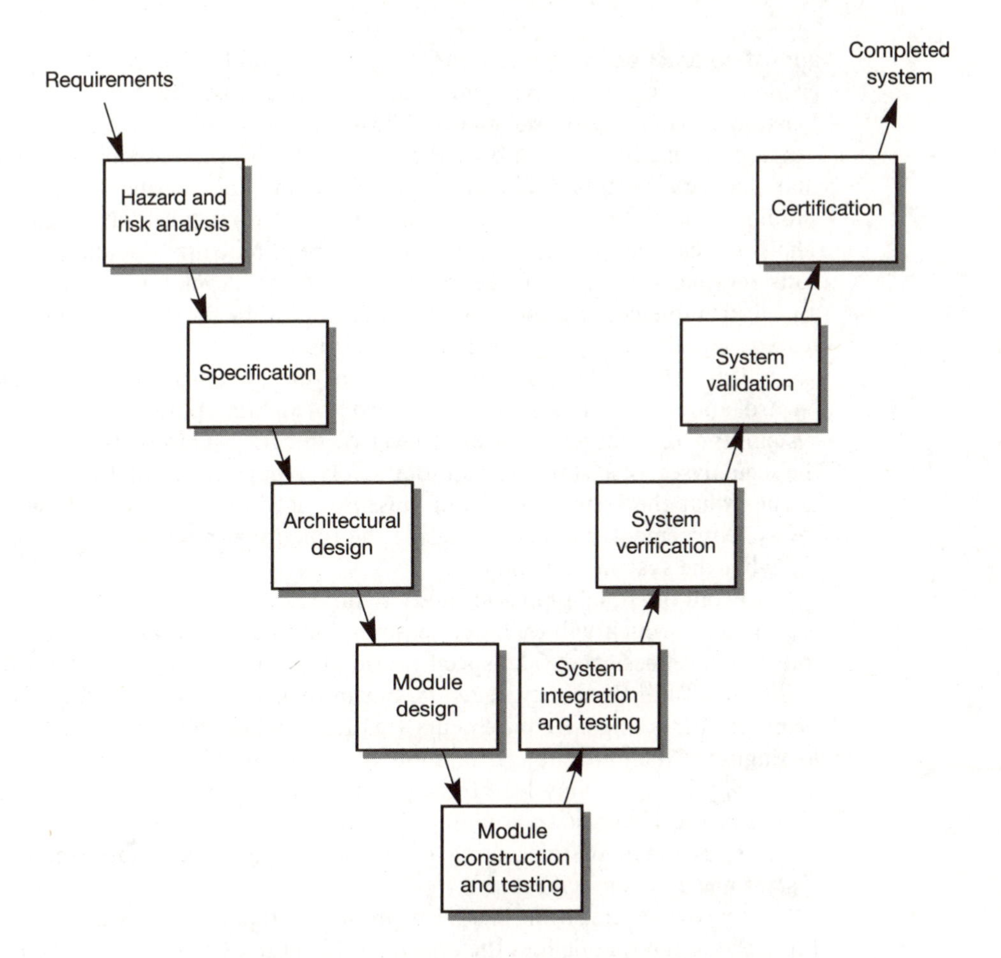

Figure 1.4 A typical development lifecycle model.

work. One of the attractions of this model is that its form emphasizes a 'top-down' approach to design (the left-hand arm of the diagram) and a 'bottom-up' approach to testing, as shown on the right-hand arm. Such models are only an approximation to the development process: in practice the various stages are not always performed in such a strictly sequential manner. Design often involves a great deal of iteration, with a series of operations being performed repeatedly until a satisfactory result is obtained. A degree of parallelism is also possible. Also missing from this simple model is any indication of information flow between the various stages. In practice, data from the specification stages of the work forms an input to the testing and verification stages of the project. We shall return to look at the use of lifecycle models in more detail in Chapter 5.

The starting point of any development project is determined by the **system requirements**. Generally, the term 'requirements' is taken to represent an almost abstract definition of what the system should do. Before the system can be implemented these abstract requirements must be formalized into a **functional requirements document**. This process is often referred to as the 'requirements capture' phase of the project. Using these definitions it is clear that the requirements documents are an attempt to describe what the system should do, and it is conceivable that they contain mistakes or are incomplete. The implications of limitations in the requirements documents may be considerable, as much of the remainder of the development programme is aimed at implementing the system described within these documents. For this reason, great care is taken in their preparation.

Once the functional requirements of the system have been established, hazard and risk analyses are performed to identify potential dangers in the system and to allocate an overall level of integrity. One of the outputs from these analyses is a statement of the **safety requirements** of the system. This defines what the system must and must not do, in order to ensure safety. The safety requirements then sit alongside the functional requirements in determining what the system must achieve.

From the functional and safety requirements of the system a specification is produced, which will include measures for safety assurance in line with the integrity level assigned. The specification attempts to define a system that will completely fulfil these requirements, but in reality it is possible for mistakes to be made at this stage. Requirements are often written in natural languages, such as English, which are subject to ambiguity. A misunderstanding of some aspect of the requirements may lead to a specification that is incomplete or incorrect. Errors of specification are a major problem in the production of highly critical systems, as much of the testing performed is aimed at establishing that the system meets this specification.

Once a specification has been produced, this is used as the basis for the top-level design that defines the system architecture. One of the major aspects of this process is to partition the system into hardware and software. This hardware–software trade-off is a vital part of the design phase and must take into account many diverse considerations, such as the volume of production and the operating speed. Safety requirements also play a large part in this process. The top-level design will inevitably split the project into a number of more manageable modules to simplify the design and testing processes. Specifications will then be produced for each module, these specifications being used later for module testing. Top-level design is followed by the detailed design of both the hardware and the software of each of the modules. When this design stage is complete the modules will be constructed and tested individually. This testing forms part of the process of verification which is used to establish that each module satisfies its specification. Verification continues throughout the development lifecycle and forms an important aspect of each phase. Verification techniques will be discussed in some detail in later chapters.

Once the various modules have been completed and verified, the process of system integration may begin. Methods of system integration vary considerably. In some companies integration is performed progressively, with more and more modules being combined and tested, producing an overall system of increasing complexity. In others a 'big-bang' approach is adopted where the complete system is assembled and tested as a whole. Both techniques have their positive and negative aspects, and these will be discussed in more detail in Chapter 5.

Once the system is complete and appears to be functioning correctly, the verification and validation of the entire system may begin. Note that these two terms are subject to very varied definition and many engineers seem unsure as to the distinction between them. Possibly because of this, the two functions are often grouped together as '**verification and validation**' or simply '**V & V**'. Within this text we shall adopt the most common distinction between the two terms, which is that

> ***Verification** is the process of determining that a system, or module, meets its specification*

and

> ***Validation** is the process of determining that a system is appropriate for its purpose.*

It can be seen from these definitions that verification seeks to show that the system corresponds to its specification. This is often performed at the module level initially, to show that each module performs its specified function. Validation, by contrast, sets out to determine whether the system as a whole accurately meets the requirements of the user. It therefore includes considerations of the correctness of the specification itself. We shall look at verification and validation in more detail in Chapter 12.

In many highly critical projects the final stage is to convince some external regulating body that the system is safe, and thereby to achieve **certification**. The process of certification varies considerably between one industry and another, although the general principles are common. In most cases standards and guidelines set out the design and development techniques that should be used in order to achieve certification. The nature of these guidelines, and the process of certification, are discussed in Chapter 14.

The lifecycle model of Figure 1.4 may be applied to the development of any system. In projects that are not safety related the hazard analysis phase may be performed only cursorily, although in order to establish that the project has no safety implications some form of analysis must be performed. For any system that is safety related a more detailed hazard and risk analysis phase is required in order to determine an appropriate integrity level for the project. This will then help to determine both the system design and the development methods adopted for the remainder of the project. For systems with few or no safety functions, formal certification is not normally required and the project will usually end with customer acceptance testing. Highly critical systems will generally go through a formal certification stage, determined by the standards used within that industry.

Faults, errors and system failures

In order to progress to looking at the production of safety-critical systems in more detail we need to define a few more terms. These are faults, errors and system failures, and are defined as follows:

> *A **fault** is a defect within the system.*
>
> *An **error** is a deviation from the required operation of the system or subsystem.*
>
> *A **system failure** occurs when the system fails to perform its required function.*

System **faults** may take a number of forms. For example, the failure of a hardware component represents a fault, as does a mistake within a piece of software. A mistake in the design of the system also represents a fault. The presence of a fault *may* lead to an **error**, which is the mechanism by which the fault becomes apparent. If, for example, a memory device within a computer were to fail the failure could go undetected for some time if that particular device were not accessed. The system would then possess a fault, but this would not have manifested itself by producing an error. Only when the device was used would its faulty operation cause an error, which could then affect the functioning of the system. Similarly, a software fault will only cause problems when the affected part of the program is executed. A software 'bug' may lie dormant within a rarely used subroutine for many years until a particular sequence of events satisfies the conditions required for its execution. During that period the system would have contained the software fault, but this would have had no effect on the system. However, when the code is finally executed, the fault *may* result in an error that could affect the system's operation. Such an error would take the form of a deviation from the intended operation of the system, for example the production of an incorrect value during a calculation, or the execution of an inappropriate routine.

If the presence of an error were to cause the system as a whole to deviate from its required operation, this would be termed a **system failure**. However, if the system were appropriately designed, it might be possible for it to continue to perform its required functions, even in the presence of one or more errors. One of the goals of a safety-critical system is that errors should not result in system failure. This could be achieved by interconnecting several modules in such a way that an error within one did not result in failure of the entire system.

It is useful to divide faults into two distinct classes. The first of these, termed **random faults**, are associated with hardware component failures. All physical components are subject to failure, and thus all systems are subject to random faults. When working within their correct operating environment, individual components fail randomly. However, statistical data gathered on large numbers of similar devices may enable predictions to be made concerning the probability of a component failing within a given period of time. This in turn allows the overall performance of the system to be predicted. Estimation of reliability on the basis of statistical data on individual components is discussed in Chapter 7.

The second class of faults are termed **systematic faults**. This covers many forms, including design faults and mistakes within the specification of the system. All software faults come within this category as they are faults within the design of the software. Systematic faults are not random and are thus not usually susceptible to statistical analysis. It is therefore more difficult to predict their effect on the reliability of the system.

Faults may also be categorized in other ways, for example by their duration. Some faults are permanent whereas others are transient in nature. All design faults and most random component failures are permanent, although their effects may not be visible at all times. However, some hardware faults are transient, such as the effects of a noise spike, or an alpha particle hitting a memory device. Although the fault is transient in these cases, the errors they produce may remain in the system unless some action is taken to remove them. Further discussion of the nature of faults is given in Chapter 6.

A fault-free system would operate perfectly, as it would be free from all design and component faults. There would be no errors and therefore no system failures. Unfortunately, the complete elimination of faults is impossible, first because all components are subject to random failure due to wear, ageing or other effects, and secondly because it is not possible to achieve perfection in design. Therefore faults are inevitable.

From the above discussion it is clear that much of the process of producing safety-critical systems is concerned with 'fault management'. In non-critical systems good design and the use of good-quality components can often produce acceptable performance. In highly critical systems additional measures must be taken to overcome the effects of faults. Broadly, these measures may be divided into four groups of techniques:

- fault avoidance
- fault removal
- fault detection
- fault tolerance.

Fault avoidance techniques aim to prevent faults from entering the system during the design stage. Fault avoidance is the primary aim of the entire design process, and various aspects of this topic are covered throughout the text. Of specific interest is the use of formal methods, as discussed in Chapter 11.

Fault removal methods attempt to find faults within a system before it enters service. These include both hardware and software testing techniques, which are discussed in Chapter 12.

Fault detection techniques are used during service to detect faults within the operational system so that their effects may be minimized. Fault detection is discussed in Chapter 6.

Fault tolerance techniques are designed to allow the system to operate correctly in the presence of faults. These techniques are described in Chapter 6.

Unfortunately, none of these methods is completely effective, and in highly critical applications a combination of these techniques is used so that system failures are kept to an acceptable level.

1.4 Costs and benefits

Safety is expensive. The goal of any project is therefore to achieve an appropriate compromise in terms of cost and safety. Experience shows that the cost of employing a systematic approach to achieving adequate safety is invariably far less than that incurred in the rectification of problems following an accident (HSE, 1993).

The costs of increasing the safety of a system must be balanced against the additional expenditure that will be required. Inevitably this will involve making value judgements concerning the value of human life and suffering. It is tempting to say that human life is beyond price and that no expenditure is too great if it might save a single life. However, such arguments fly in the face of logic.

It is well known that we could make vehicles safer by reducing their speed. It is estimated that a reduction in road speed of one mile per hour would reduce accidents by 5%. If we halved the maximum speed allowed on our roads we would cut fatalities considerably. This being the case, would we be prepared to accepted increased journey times and greater congestion on our roads in order to save lives? Should we return to requiring a man with a red flag to walk in front of all cars? Ultimately we have to make a value judgement as to what level of safety is acceptable. Similar decisions have to be made on financial grounds. We could no doubt increase the safety of buses and trains by increasing spending on safety features. We could, for example, insist on seatbelts and safety airbags for all passengers. If this move doubled the cost of the vehicles so that travelling costs increased (perhaps encouraging people to use less safe methods of transport) would this be justified? Again, value judgements are required.

Ultimately we have to put a value on human life, in both financial and other terms. We are clearly prepared to put people's lives at risk in order to bring benefits to the population as a whole. If this were not the case, then no large-scale civil engineering projects would be possible. Planning in many industrial sectors is done on the basis of assigning an actual monetary value to each life lost. Given that this is true, where do we draw the line? How much risk is acceptable and what benefits are necessary to justify them?

One of the considerations involved in the assessment of acceptable levels of risk is linked to the questions 'Who gains from the system' and 'Who is put at risk by the system'? If the person at risk stands to gain some form of benefit, then this may be a more acceptable situation than if a system benefits one individual but places others at risk. For example, it might be acceptable for a person to race a car on a racetrack and risk his life for the sake of the excitement involved, but it is less likely to be acceptable for him to race on the open road where others are put at risk.

There are no simple answers to questions concerning the acceptability of risk: ultimately it is matter of personal judgement. However, in order to assess the issues it is useful to be able to quantify the risks and benefits involved. Such an assessment makes use of hazard analysis and risk analysis, as discussed in Chapters 3 and 4.

Legal aspects

Having considered some of the social and moral implications of safety it is also necessary to look at another major consideration, that of legal liability.

The manufacturer of a product or system that causes harm to individuals or to the environment may be liable to either criminal or civil prosecution, or both (Davis, 1994; Wichmann, 1992). Criminal liabilities arise from legislation on both **safety at work** and **consumer protection**. Civil liabilities are centred on contract law and **sale of goods** legislation. In both cases the various laws vary considerably between countries, with major differences between, for example, Europe and North America. Successful prosecutions could result in fines or the imprisonment of the employees responsible.

Although it is not within the scope of this book to give any form of legal advice, it is perhaps worth making a few observations on the problems involved. First, we have seen that there is no such thing as absolute safety. Various techniques are available to help us to increase our confidence in the safety of a system, but no manufacturer can be absolutely sure of the safety of his products. Secondly, if a manufacturer is found to be responsible for human casualties, the financial implications may be enormous. This leaves the manufacturer in a very difficult position in knowing how to fulfil his moral, ethical, legal and commercial responsibilities.

Faced with these problems there are several steps that a manager may take to protect himself and his organization. Obvious measures include providing insurance against civil claims, although it is becoming extremely expensive to provide adequate cover against public liability. The use of proper labelling and warning signs may also help to divert liability away from the manufacturer towards the user of a system. However, the greatest responsibility of the manufacturer is that he should take adequate care in the design and manufacture of his products.

As it is unreasonable to expect any system to be perfect, a manufacturer may be able to defend the failure of one of his products by establishing that the system was as safe as could reasonably be expected, given the '**state of the art**'. In order to establish this, it will be necessary to demonstrate that appropriate design and development techniques were followed. Given the complexities of the processes involved in developing safety-critical systems it seems likely that a good way to establish that one has followed such practice is to show that the development was performed in line with appropriate guidelines and standards. Where such guidance exists within an industry, non-conformance with these recommendations might make justification of the correctness of the development extremely difficult.

The designer's obligations

Designers of safety-critical systems share, with other members of the company, a responsibility for the systems they produce. These responsibilities include professional, social, moral, financial and legal considerations. In order to discharge these obligations designers must be aware of the implications of the work they do, and ensure that others within their organizations are similarly informed. It is also their responsibility to ensure that they are familiar with the various techniques and development tools that may assist them in their work. It is every designer's duty to make all systems as safe as is reasonably possible.

The material within this text is not sufficient to enable an engineer competently to design highly critical systems. It does, however, provide grounding in the techniques used and may at least enable engineers to establish whether their work requires additional attention to safety. It may also encourage some to go on to specialize in this interesting and highly rewarding field of engineering.

REFERENCES

Davis D. (1994). Safety critical systems – legal liabilities. *Computing and Control*, **5**(1), 13–17

HSE (1993). *The Costs of Accidents at Work*. HS(G)96. London: Health and Safety Executive

MoD (1991). Interim Defence Standard 00-55 *The Procurement of Safety Critical Software in Defence Equipment*. Glasgow: Directorate of Standardization

STARTS Purchasers' Group (1989). *The STARTS Purchasers' Handbook: Software Tools for Application to Large Real Time Systems* 2nd edn. Manchester: National Computing Centre Publications

Wichmann B.A., ed. (1992). Legal liability for software in safety-related systems. In *Software in Safety-Related Systems*. (Wichmann B.A., ed.), pp. 27–33. Chichester: John Wiley

FURTHER READING

Bennett P., ed. (1993). *Safety Aspects of Computer Control*. Oxford: Butterworth-Heinemann

Hazards Forum (1995). *Safety-Related Systems: Guidance for Engineers*. London: The Hazards Forum

Redmill F. and Anderson T., eds (1993). *Safety Critical Systems: Current Issues, Techniques and Standards*. London: Chapman & Hall

PROBLEMS

1.1 Which industrial sectors are responsible for the highest-volume use of microcomputers? Give examples of some very high-volume products.

1.2 Which industrial sectors manufacture computer-based systems in very low volumes? Give examples of such systems.

1.3 Under what circumstances are the operations of a computer system likely to be safety related?

1.4 Give examples of safety-related computer systems within five distinct industrial sectors.

1.5 List four examples of computer-based domestic appliances where the controller is safety related.

1.6 Define the term 'safety'.

1.7 Explain the meanings of the terms 'safety-related system' and 'safety-critical system'.

1.8 How may a system be made absolutely safe?

1.9 Why is it appropriate to assign integrity levels to projects? Give examples of applications that might be assigned a high level of integrity, and others that might be assigned a lower level of integrity.

1.10 Explain the functions of hazard analysis and risk analysis.

1.11 What factors would be considered in the assignment of an integrity level for an application?

1.12 Distinguish between the terms 'primary safety', 'functional safety' and 'indirect safety'.

1.13 Explain the meanings of the terms 'control system' and 'protection system'. Which of these systems is safety related?

1.14 What is meant by the initials PES? What systems are encompassed by this expression?

1.15 List the advantages and disadvantages of computer-based systems.

1.16 Why is complexity a barrier to safety?

1.17 Why are computer systems less predictable than simpler systems?

1.18 Sketch a simple lifecycle model to describe the development of a safety-critical system.

1.19 Describe the meaning and importance of 'requirements capture'. What is the output of this process?

1.20 Suggest a possible cause of errors in the specification of a system. Why are such errors important?

1.21 How are the individual modules of a system integrated during the development process?

1.22 Define the terms 'verification' and 'validation'. How do the processes of verification and validation differ in terms of their scope and objectives?

1.23 What process generally forms the final phase of system development in highly critical systems?

1.24 Which aspects of the development lifecycle model of Figure 1.4 are common to all systems and which are unique to safety-critical systems?

1.25 Define the terms 'fault', 'error' and 'system failure'.

1.26 Explain the distinction between 'random' and 'systematic' faults and give examples of each.

1.27 Explain how faults may be classified by their 'duration', giving examples of each class.

1.28 Why are value judgements inevitable in the assessment of safety requirements?

1.29 Why are there legal implications to the design of safety-critical systems, and how may a company protect itself from prosecution?

1.30 Why are standards and guidelines of relevance to the legal liability of a company?

2 Safety Criteria

CHAPTER CONTENTS

2.1 Introduction

All engineering projects begin with a perceived need. This takes the form of a set of **requirements** for a system to perform a given task. Often these are termed the **customer requirements** for the project. In order to develop a system to meet these requirements they must first be documented by the preparation of a **requirements document**, which attempts to set out the needs of the customer in an unambiguous manner. Once completed this document forms a basis for the remaining stages of the design process.

The requirements for a given system will clearly include the functions to be performed by that system and will vary considerably from one application to another. For example, the requirements for an autopilot might include a need to measure accelerations and to compute relative positions, whereas those for a washing machine controller would be quite different. In addition to these **functional requirements** there are several more general characteristics which will be of importance in the final system. These **non-functional requirements** include such considerations as ease of maintenance, size and cost.

In safety-related systems, safety issues also form part of the requirements. Because of the importance of these safety considerations it is common to produce a separate **safety requirements document**, which sets out what is required of the system to ensure adequate safety. This document details what the system must do, and what it must not do, to achieve safety, and also lists other issues of importance. For example, in a laser control system it might define that a safety guard must be closed if the laser is active, and that the laser must not be activated while a door is open. The safety requirements document will also specify more general system characteristics that have implications for the safety of the system. These include considerations such as its reliability and its failure modes. Other requirements might relate to the positioning of the unit, the physical protection required or necessary administrative procedures.

The various functional, non-functional and safety requirements of the system result in a list of system-specific properties, together with a set of more general system characteristics. This latter category might include considerations of:

- reliability
- availability
- failsafe operation
- system integrity
- data integrity
- system recovery
- maintainability
- dependability.

In the next two sections we look first at various system characteristics that have particular importance in safety-related systems, and then at the form of safety requirements. The final section considers the safety case that is used to document the safety aspects of a system for external certification or assessment.

2.2 System requirements

There are many characteristics that are advantageous in almost all engineering systems. These include low cost, high reliability and ease of maintenance. However, the relative importance of these attributes, and the necessity for other characteristics, varies greatly between applications. In this section we look at a number of factors that are of particular relevance to safety-related systems, and discuss their importance in a range of applications. The various topics may be seen as 'design aims' for a particular system.

Reliability

As with almost all the terms discussed in this section, the term reliability may be defined in a number of ways. Here we will adopt the following:

> ***Reliability*** *is the probability of a component, or system, functioning correctly over a given period of time under a given set of operating conditions.*

Here, 'functioning correctly' is taken to mean 'operating as defined within its specification', and it is assumed that the unit was functioning correctly at the beginning of the period in question and that no maintenance is carried out during this period.

It can be seen from the above definition that the reliability of a component or system varies with time. A system might have a certain probability of working correctly over a period of one month, and a much lower probability of operating correctly for a year. When assessing reliability it is therefore very important to consider the performance of the system over an appropriate length of service. The period used will vary considerably, depending on the application. In situations where maintenance is expensive or impossible, a unit might be required to operate without maintenance for several decades. Examples might include communications satellites, robot spacecraft or cardiac pacemakers. In other situations the period of use might be much shorter. In military applications the period of interest might be limited to the duration of a particular 'mission' and might be as short as a few hours, or even a few minutes.

Reliability is of particular relevance in applications where continuous, uninterrupted operation is essential to the maintenance of safety. An example of such a system is a flight-critical aircraft system, where the safety of the aircraft is dependent on the system functioning correctly throughout its flight. However, reliability is an issue of great importance in all engineering systems, and we shall return to discuss this topic in more detail in Chapter 7.

Availability

This term may be defined as follows:

> *The* ***availability*** *of a system is the probability that the system will be functioning correctly at any given time.*

Like reliability, the availability of a system varies with time. However, unlike reliability, the availability of a system relates to a particular point in time, rather than to a given period.

Another way of looking at availability is that it represents the fraction of time for which a system is functioning correctly. For example, if within a period of 1000 hours a system is out of operation for a total of one hour owing to several periods of failure, its average availability during the period is 999/1000 or 0.999.

High availability is a very common design goal in many systems that are not directly safety related. Time-sharing computers, banking systems and telephone exchanges are all examples of systems where revenue is lost while the system is inoperative. In such cases availability is often more important than reliability, as a system failure may not itself be a problem provided that the system can be repaired quickly. Telephone exchanges are often specified to have a total 'downtime' of a few hours throughout their lifetime of several decades.

Availability may also be of great importance in safety-critical systems. This is often the case in situations where the system in question is not used continuously. A typical example might be a nuclear reactor shutdown system. This is employed relatively infrequently, and the safety of the plant is affected by the probability that it will work correctly when needed. In this case availability is of greater importance than reliability.

For safety-critical systems the requirements for availability are high and the numerical values are consequently very close to unity. For this reason it is common to describe such systems in terms of their **unavailability**, this being obtained by subtracting the availability from one. Thus a system with an availability of 0.999 has an unavailability of 0.001, or 10^{-3}.

Clearly, availability is closely linked to issues of reliability but the two terms are not synonymous. We will look in more detail at factors determining reliability and availability in Chapter 7.

Failsafe operation

Some systems have the highly desirable characteristic of possessing a set of output states that can be identified as being 'safe'. In such circumstances the system can be designed to 'fail safe' by ensuring that it adopts these outputs in the event of failure and inability to recover. An example of a failsafe arrangement might be a railway signalling system. Here the failsafe state corresponds to all the signal lights being red (the 'stop' condition), with all the points locked in their previous positions. This should bring all the trains safely to a halt. In systems that possess failsafe states it is often appropriate to adopt this state if there is any doubt as to the correct operation of the system.

Unfortunately, many systems do not possess failsafe states. For example, in a fly-by-wire aircraft there is no combination of the various outputs from the avionics computers that will maintain safety – the only safe state for the aircraft is on the ground! Under these circumstances the system must continue operating to maintain safety.

System integrity

This term may be defined as follows:

> *The **integrity** of a system is its ability to detect faults in its own operation and to inform a human operator.*

Here the main emphasis is on fault detection rather than fault tolerance. System integrity is of particular importance in critical systems that possess failsafe states. In such circumstances the system may be designed so that it will enter its failsafe state if there is any uncertainty about the system's correctness. Examples of systems where high integrity is important include the railway signalling example cited above, and systems such as aircraft autopilots. In this latter example the pilot, and no doubt the passengers, would prefer that the aircraft be flown manually if there was any doubt about the correctness of the autopilot's operation.

Over the years the word **integrity** has become widely used in expressions such as **high-integrity system** and **safety integrity level**. When used in these ways integrity takes on a much broader meaning, encompassing considerations of reliability, availability and other factors associated with critical systems. In many ways integrity is here being used as a synonym for **dependability**, as defined later in this section. This diverse use of the term can sometimes lead to misunderstanding and is symptomatic of the problems of varied definitions within this field.

Data integrity

In many applications the data held within the system is of great importance for a variety of reasons.

> ***Data integrity*** *is the ability of a system to prevent damage to its own database and to detect, and possibly correct, errors that do occur.*

Although data integrity is of great importance in almost all applications, there are numerous applications where it is vital. Examples that are not safety related include banking and insurance company systems, where the financial value of the data is very high. Data integrity may also be of importance in safety-related systems where, for example, the current state of the system is deduced and stored rather than measured directly. A corruption of this data could destroy the system's image of its own state and thus affect its operation.

System recovery

Although every effort may be made during the design process to produce a system that will tolerate faults, it cannot be guaranteed that a system will not fail. This might be due, for example, to a transient fault such as a noise 'spike' on the power supply or the effects of a lightning strike nearby. In many applications, particularly those that do not have failsafe states, it is vital that the system can detect the failure and restart itself quickly. Depending on the nature of the application, the recovery process may need to determine the current status of the system, to take appropriate action to continue operation, and to maintain safety.

Maintainability

It is useful to define two terms at this point:

> ***Maintenance*** *is the action taken to retain a system in, or return a system to, its designed operating condition.*

> ***Maintainability*** *is the ability of a system to be maintained.*

Maintainability may be treated in a qualitative or a quantitative manner. When the latter approach is adopted it is often expressed in terms of the **mean time to repair (MTTR)** the system in the event of a failure. Its relevance to safety is clear, as the availability of a system depends not only on how often the system fails, but also on the time taken to restore it to operation. In Chapter 7 we shall discuss the relationship between these factors in more detail.

The maintenance of safety-critical systems is greatly affected by the nature of the application. In some cases maintenance may be performed while the system is in service. This may entail performing repairs or preventative maintenance on a 'live' system, or shutting it down temporarily. Alternatively, maintenance may only be possible between periods of service. This latter situation usually exists in aerospace or avionics applications, where maintenance is only possible at the end of a flight.

One aspect of maintenance that is often overlooked is the problem of **maintenance-induced failures** (HMSO, 1992). Unfortunately, experience shows that it is not reasonable to assume that all repairs will be completely successful, and it is quite possible for a repair to produce separate, apparently unrelated, faults.

Considerations of maintainability play an important part in the design of safety-critical systems (Whetton, 1994) and we shall return to this issue when we consider design in more detail in Chapter 5.

Dependability

This term covers considerations of reliability, availability, safety, maintainability and other issues of importance in critical systems.

> ***Dependability*** *is a property of a system that justifies placing one's reliance on it.*

Dependability is quantified in terms of the various factors, such as reliability and availability, that combine to produce a dependable system. Dependability is of great importance in all critical systems, although the importance of the various factors that contribute to it will vary between applications.

Conflict between system requirements

We have seen that the requirements of a safety-critical system take many forms. There are certain characteristics that are invariably beneficial in the design of a system. These include high reliability and high availability. However, the relative importance of these factors will vary between applications. Unfortunately, in some cases there are conflicts between the various requirements of a system.

Some conflicting requirements are self-evident and exist in all engineering disciplines. For example, it is common to have a conflict between a desire for high performance and a desire for low cost. Opposing pressures from other factors, such as considerations of size and functionality, are also likely.

Requirements associated with safety may likewise conflict with other system requirements. It is clear from the definitions given above and in Chapter 1 that reliability and safety are not synonymous. Indeed, there are instances where reliability and safety place conflicting requirements on a system. In any application that has a failsafe state the system can guarantee safety by remaining in that state, thereby satisfying its safety requirements. However, this system would not satisfy its functional requirements and would have zero reliability and zero availability. It could be argued that while such a system is active it is less safe than when it has failed, since its failsafe condition guarantees safety whereas its active state may not. Therefore, safety must be reduced in order to achieve a functional system. Ultimately a compromise is required between the functionality of a system, perhaps quantified in terms of its reliability or availability, and its safety performance. If we take as an example a nuclear shutdown system, the cost of shutting down the reactor is very high and consequently false trips of the protection system are to be avoided. Faced with an uncertain situation the designer must decide whether the system will shut down the reactor or continue in operation. Such a decision is clearly a trade-off between considerations of safety and those of performance.

In circumstances as described above it is tempting to deduce that safety is incompatible with reliability. This is incorrect. It is true that these two requirements place opposing pressures on the designer, but the final design must satisfy *both* requirements in order to be acceptable. In such cases the hazard analysis and risk analysis phases of the project must identify *acceptable* levels of safety and reliability, and the final design must achieve both objectives. As in all engineering projects, some compromises may be required in order to achieve a realizable specification.

2.3 Safety requirements

In addition to the system requirements discussed in the previous section a safety-critical system will have to satisfy certain specific safety requirements relating to its function and characteristics. In order to determine these system-specific requirements a series of tasks must be performed. The main stages of this process may be categorized as follows:

- identification of the hazards associated with the system;
- classification of these hazards;
- determination of methods for dealing with the hazards;
- assignment of appropriate reliability and availability requirements;

- determination of an appropriate safety integrity level;
- specification of development methods appropriate to this integrity level.

In order to determine the characteristics that a system must have in order to be safe, it is necessary to understand the ways in which the system could harm people or property. A computer-based system has the capability of doing harm through the various components it controls. For each component that has the potential to do harm it is necessary to identify all actions that could be dangerous. This in turn shows the system outputs that have safety implications. The capability to do harm to people, property or the environment, is termed a **hazard**, and in Chapter 3 we look at the process of hazard analysis which is used to identify potential dangers associated with the system.

Having identified the hazards associated with a system it is useful to classify them by their severity and their nature. The **severity** of a hazard is related to the consequences of any accident that might occur as a result of that hazard. The **nature** of a hazard has considerable impact on the manner in which it may be controlled. In some cases hazards arise as a consequence of factors that are under the direct control of the system. For example, a laser control system may be able, instantly, to turn off a source of radiation that can harm an individual. The situation may be more complicated if there is a delay between the control system selecting a safe condition and the equipment entering that state. Examples of such an arrangement would be a high-voltage source associated with some capacitance, or a moving part with considerable inertia. In each case the equipment could remain hazardous for some time after the control system turns off the source of the hazard. There are also cases where the relationship between the control function and the source of danger is less direct and the control system has only a limited influence on the source of potential harm. An example of such an arrangement might be a set of road traffic signals. Here the hazards are associated with cars and pedestrians, which are not under the direct control of the system.

The importance of a hazard is related to both its severity and its frequency of occurrence. These two factors are combined within the concept of **risk**, which is discussed in some detail in Chapter 4.

Having identified all the hazards within the system it is then necessary to identify methods of dealing with each of them. For each action that the system can perform it is necessary to decide the conditions for which that action is safe. Clearly, if a particular action is never safe the system must be redesigned to preclude that action. Once appropriate conditions for safety have been established, these become part of the safety requirements of the system. For hazards that are under the direct control of the system, defining conditions of safety is usually straightforward. For example, in the laser control system mentioned earlier the conditions for safe operation might be expressed as follows:

do not turn on the laser until it is 'safe'
turn off the laser if it is 'unsafe'

where the term 'safe' would be clearly defined. The definition of safe would certainly include consideration of the presence of people within the danger area. Mechanisms which ensure that potentially hazardous actions are only performed at times when they are safe are termed **interlocks**. In cases where delays are present, some form of **guard** would be necessary to keep people away from dangerous parts of the system until they had become safe. These guards might take the form of safety cages on machine tools or automatic barriers on railway crossings. The operation of the guard mechanism might be controlled by a condition of the form

keep people away from the equipment until it becomes 'safe'

where the presence of a safe condition would be detected by the system in some way. In applications where the system has only indirect control over the source of the hazard, guards can be used to detect dangerous conditions and to keep people away from hazardous areas while they persist. For example, a gas sensing system for a coal mine cannot control the levels of gas within the mine, but it can use warning signs and alarms to prevent people from entering the danger area if high levels of dangerous gases are present.

It can be seen that the design of safety-critical systems is based on the identification and control of the potentially dangerous actions (or inactions) of the system. One aspect of the control of hazards is based on the use of interlocks, which prevent dangerous operations from being performed unless it is safe to do so, and guards, which keep people away from the system while it is hazardous. Interlocks use **sensors** to detect the state of the system in order to detect dangerous conditions, and guards use **actuators** to prevent exposure to danger. The safety requirements documentation must identify the potential hazards of a system and, where appropriate, define an interlock mechanism that will ensure its safety.

In some cases the hazards associated with a system are not related to dangerous actions that may be controlled by the use of interlocks and guards. For example, if a computer is used at the heart of an aircraft flight control system, the failure of the computer itself represents a hazard that cannot be treated in this way. Safety requires that the computer function correctly, and considerations of reliability, availability and other issues form an essential part of the safety requirements of the system.

Where interlock and guard mechanisms are used, they may also have implications for the reliability and availability requirements of the computer system. Wherever possible, interlocks and guards should be provided by simple, non-programmable means that remove the processor from the task of ensuring safety (Leveson, 1991). Where this is not possible, these interlock mechanisms will themselves rely on the correct functioning of the computer and the dependability of the system must be appropriate to provide adequate safety. The requirements of the system in this respect will be determined by considerations of the associated risks. Risk analysis is discussed in some detail in Chapter 4.

Having assigned appropriate reliability and availability requirements to the system it is then useful to assign it to an appropriate **safety integrity level**.

This is used to distinguish between systems requiring different levels of dependability, or 'integrity', and determine the development methods to be adopted. Systems that are assigned a high integrity level will be subjected to much more rigorous design and testing methods than could be justified for less demanding applications. The assignment of integrity levels will be described in Chapter 4, and the choice of appropriate development techniques will be discussed in Chapter 5 and elsewhere within the text.

The role of standards

Within many industrial sectors a great deal of experience has been gained in the use of computer systems in safety-critical applications. Much of this knowledge is encapsulated within numerous standards and guidelines that are used to provide assistance to engineers working within these areas, and to help them to achieve uniformly high levels of quality and safety. Standards fulfil several important roles, including:

- helping staff to ensure that a product meets a certain level of quality;
- helping to establish that a product has been developed using methods of known effectiveness;
- promoting a uniformity of approach between different teams;
- providing guidance on design and development techniques;
- providing some legal basis in the case of a dispute.

In some industries all systems must conform to specific standards that stipulate both system requirements and the development methods to be used. In these industries certification of the final system depends on adherence to these standards and meeting the acceptance criteria that they define. In other areas the use of standards is more flexible, with regulating authorities negotiating with system designers on appropriate design and development techniques. Here a company may seek certification by claiming conformance to a particular standard, or may suggest alternative methods. The regulating authority may accept alternatives to those given within the standards, but is likely to be biased in favour of the established techniques. Generally companies will opt to follow an established standard, but may seek permission from the certifying body to deviate from it in certain areas where its requirements are seen to be inappropriate.

In addition to formal standards there are several **guidelines** and **codes of practice** that provide advice. These may be used to give guidance on how a system may be produced in order to satisfy a particular standard. Alternatively, they may provide more general information that is not related to projects within a specific industry. Some standards provide both requirements and guidelines within a single document. Perhaps for this reason, the term 'standard' is often used to refer to both formal standards and more informal guidelines.

Sector-specific standards and guidelines, such as those in the aerospace, nuclear or mining industries, identify and discuss the major hazards found within those industries. Levels of risk are associated with requirements for reliability and availability that will be considered acceptable by the regulatory authorities and by the industries themselves. As such, the standards provide a basis for the production of safety requirements for projects within those industries. More generic standards and guidelines have also been developed to provide more general guidance of relevance to all industrial sectors (HSE, 1987a, b; IEC, 1995). In Chapter 14 we shall return to the issue of standards when we consider the process of certification.

2.4 The safety case

In many industries highly critical systems will require certification by a regulating authority before they may be put into service. As part of the certification process, the operator of the system will be required to produce a **safety case** that sets out the safety justification for the system. This describes the design and assessment techniques used in the development of the system. The safety case is sometimes referred to as a **safety argument**, a **safety justification** or a **safety assessment report**. Even in situations where a safety case is not a formal requirement of a regulatory authority or customer, the provision of such a document is accepted as good engineering practice.

The argument within the safety case is normally based on engineering judgement rather than strict formal logic. This is generally supported by some form of probabilistic risk assessment, using techniques that will be discussed in later chapters.

It is not the purpose of the safety case to prove that the system in question is safe – such a proof is a theoretical impossibility since no system is absolutely safe. The safety case does, however, provide evidence that the risks associated with the system have been carefully considered and that steps have been taken to deal with them appropriately. The document must identify all matters significant to the safety of the system and show how these issues have been addressed. It must also give evidence of precautions taken to ensure safe operation. The safety case is concerned not only with design issues, but also with considerations of assessment and project management.

We shall look in more detail at the process of certification in Chapter 14.

REFERENCES

HMSO (1992). *Dangerous Maintenance*. London: Her Majesty's Stationery Office

HSE (1987a). *Programmable Electronics Systems: An Introductory Guide*. Health and Safety Executive. London: Her Majesty's Stationery Office

HSE (1987b). *Programmable Electronics Systems: General Technical Guidelines*. Health and Safety Executive. London: Her Majesty's Stationery Office

IEC (1995). Draft International Standard 1508. *Functional Safety: Safety-Related Systems*. Geneva: International Electrotechnical Commission

Leveson N.G. (1991). Software safety in embedded computer systems. *Comm. ACM*, **34**(2), 34–46

Whetton C. (1994). Maintainability and its influence on system safety. In *Technology and Assessment of Safety-Critical Systems* (Redmill F. and Anderson T., eds), pp. 31–54. London: Springer-Verlag

FURTHER READING

Terry G.J. (1991). *Engineering System Safety*. London: Mechanical Engineering Publications

PROBLEMS

2.1 How are the safety aspects of the system requirements documented?

2.2 Define the term 'reliability' and explain why this factor varies with time. In what kind of application is high reliability of particular importance? Give two examples, not mentioned in the text, where reliability is of paramount importance.

2.3 Explain the meaning of the term 'availability'. What factors affect the relative importance of availability and reliability? Suggest two applications, not given in the text, where availability might be of more importance than reliability.

2.4 What is meant by the term 'unavailability'? Illustrate your answer with a numerical example.

2.5 Discuss the characteristics and advantages of 'failsafe' operation. Give two examples, not mentioned in the text, of systems that utilize failsafe states. Why do some systems not possess failsafe states?

2.6 Explain the meaning of 'system integrity'. In what classes of applications is integrity of great importance? Give two examples, not given in the text, of systems where high integrity is vital.

2.7 What is meant by 'data integrity'? Give an example to illustrate the importance of this characteristic.

2.8 Under what circumstances is system recovery a vital feature of a critical system? Give examples of applications where the ability to recover from a system crash is important.

2.9 Explain the meanings of the terms 'maintenance' and 'maintainability'. How are these factors related to safety? How is maintainability usually quantified?

2.10 What is meant by the term 'dependability'? How is this factor measured?

2.11 Give examples of conflicts that may exist between various aspects of a system's requirements. How can these problems be overcome?

2.12 Why are considerations of high reliability sometimes in conflict with requirements for safety? Under what circumstances could an unreliable system be safe?

2.13 What is meant by the term 'hazard'? Give some simple examples of hazards.

2.14 What factors combine to determine the risk associated with a hazard?

2.15 Give an example, not cited within the text, of a hazard that is under the direct control of a computer system.

2.16 Give an example, not given in the text, of a hazard that persists after the controller has selected a 'safe' state.

2.17 Give an example of a hazard, not cited in the text, where a controller has only indirect control over a hazard.

2.18 Explain, with the aid of examples, how interlocks and guards are used to control hazards.

2.19 Why is it preferable to implement interlocks and guards using simple, non-programmable components wherever possible?

2.20 What is meant by the term 'safety case'? What aspects are covered by a safety case?

3 Hazard Analysis

CHAPTER CONTENTS

3.1 Introduction

Probably the most important mechanism for improving the safety of a system is to identify the ways in which it can cause harm. Once these problem areas have been located, their importance can be assessed and, if they are found to be significant, appropriate steps may be taken to remove them or to mitigate their effects.

Situations that can cause harm are termed hazards, and we define the term as follows:

> *A **hazard** is a situation in which there is actual or potential danger to people or to the environment.*

From this definition we can identify several hazards associated with everyday life. For example, we could be stung by an insect while walking in the country; we could be knocked down by a car while walking in the city; or we could be struck by lightning while walking outside during a thunderstorm. If any of these incidents were to occur, we would term such a event an **accident**. However, the *potential* for such an accident to occur represents a hazard.

Associated with each of these hazards is a certain **risk**. This is related to the likelihood of the event occurring and to its likely consequences. When deciding on the advisability of a particular course of action we obviously consider the hazards associated with that activity and the risks associated with those hazards. It is clearly impossible to make an informed judgement on the acceptability of the risks if we are unaware of all the hazards.

When attempting to consider the potential problems associated with a particular system it is instructive to look at the experience that has been gained with the use of similar systems, or systems with common characteristics. Of particular interest are publications by Kletz (1995), Leveson (1995) and Neumann (1995) which look specifically at problems associated with computer-based systems.

Within this chapter we will look at several methods of analysing the hazards associated with a system. In the next chapter we look at the process of assessing the risks associated with those hazards, and at the task of deciding on the acceptability or otherwise of those risks.

3.2 Analytical techniques

Hazard analysis is not one, but a range of techniques, each providing a different insight into the characteristics of the system under investigation. Some methods have evolved within particular industries and have limited use in other areas. Others, although having origins within a specialist area, have found broad acceptance throughout many industrial sectors. Among the most widely used techniques are:

- failure modes and effects analysis
- failure modes, effects and criticality analysis
- hazard and operability studies
- event tree analysis
- fault tree analysis.

It is not appropriate within this text to look in detail at all the methods of hazard analysis given above. However, it is useful to have a basic understanding of the nature of these techniques. We shall therefore look briefly at each approach, and then, in the following sections, look in more detail at some of the more important methods.

Failure modes and effects analysis (FMEA) considers the failure of any component within a system and tracks the effects of this failure to determine its ultimate consequences. The process makes assumptions about the failure modes of the components and then determines their effects on the complete system. The analysis can be performed at a hardware component level, or at a functional level using a modular approach. Because it considers all component failures this approach is particularly good at detecting conditions where a single failure can result in a dangerous situation. However, the technique does not normally consider multiple failures. Unfortunately, because the analysis looks at the effects of all component failures, much work is associated with failures that do not result in hazardous conditions. FMEA involves much detailed, demanding work and is therefore expensive to apply to large complex systems in their entirety. Often FMEA is used at a late stage in the development process, when it is applied to critical areas rather than to the complete system.

Failure modes, effects and criticality analysis (FMECA) is an extension of FMEA that takes into account the importance of each component failure. This is done by considering the consequences of particular failures, and their probability or frequency of occurrence, in order to identify those sections of the system where failures are most important. This allows effort to be directed at the areas of greatest need.

HAZard and OPerability studies (HAZOP) use a series of 'guide words' to investigate the effects of deviations from normal operating conditions during each phase of a system's operation. HAZOP were originally developed within the chemical industry and are particularly powerful in demonstrating the effects of parametric changes and out-of-range values on safety. The studies rely on determining answers to questions of a 'what-if' nature, for example 'What would be the effect of an increase in temperature?' or 'What would happen if the oil pressure were reduced?' Although HAZOP can be computer assisted, they rely heavily on expert input. They can be very effective but are also very tedious and time consuming.

Event tree analysis (ETA) takes as its starting point the events that can affect the system and tracks them forward to determine their possible consequences. These events include both those associated with the expected operation of the system, such as a valve opening or closing, and fault conditions, such as the failure of a component. For complex systems this results in very large trees, as both hazardous and normal operations are considered. The basic form of an event tree may be understood by reference to a simple example, as shown in Figure 3.1. This shows an event tree for a small subsystem concerned with an alarm function. Here a pressure sensor is used to detect the presence of sufficient coolant pressure to maintain safe operation of a chemical plant. If the pressure drops below some predetermined value the sensor should detect this and activate an alarm relay, which in turn sounds a siren to warn the operators. The event tree begins on the left-hand side of the diagram with the event corresponding to a failure of coolant pressure. The tree then splits to represent the two possible immediate outcomes of this event. First, the pressure sensor could operate correctly, as shown by the upper branch, or secondly it could fail, as represented by the lower branch. For each of these eventualities we now consider the possible action of the next element in the chain, the alarm relay. In either case it could operate correctly or it could fail, leading to four possible paths. Lastly, the action of the siren is considered for each of these paths. As each event causes a branch of the diagram, a tree with N events will have 2^N branches. On the right-hand side of the diagram we see the possible responses of the system to the original event. It can be seen that if all the elements in the chain function correctly the alarm will sound, but if any element fails it will not. Perhaps in this simple example this result is not too surprising. The power of event tree analysis is that, in more complex arrangements, it allows the outcomes of events to be investigated in situations where their consequences are much less obvious.

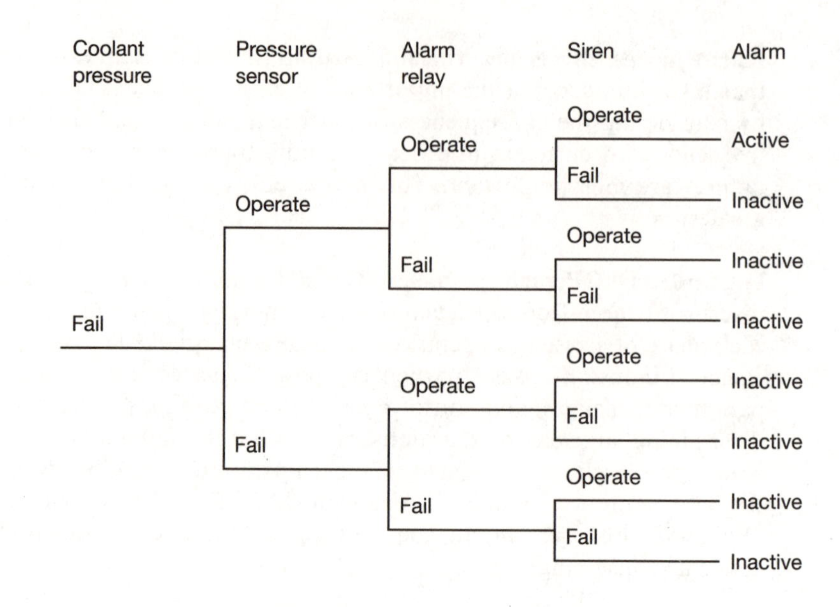

Figure 3.1 A simple event tree.

Fault tree analysis (FTA) differs from the use of event trees in that it tackles the problem in the reverse direction. Event trees start with all possible events and work forward to determine their outcomes. Consequently, much of the analysis is concerned with operations that have no safety implications. Fault tree analysis, in contrast, starts with all identified hazards and works backwards to determine their possible causes. In applications where information is available from similar systems already in service, data from earlier accidents, or incidents, may also be used as a starting point for the analysis. Logical operators, similar to those used in Boolean algebra, are used to combine the effects of events to determine relationships between cause and effect. Concentrating on events that are known to lead to hazards results in a simpler tree structure than that needed for event tree analysis.

Probabilistic hazard analysis

Although in this chapter we are primarily concerned with the *identification* of hazards, rather than their quantification, it should be noted that several of the techniques so far described can also be used to obtain some measure of the frequency of occurrence, or the probability, of a failure. This is termed **probabilistic hazard analysis**, and forms a major part of the overall process of hazard analysis. This approach is commonly used within FMECA, where a measure of criticality is applied to each possible failure mode. This allows the analysis to concentrate on those areas of greatest importance. Event tree and fault tree techniques may also be used to provide probability information. This is done by assigning probabilities to each branch of the tree corresponding to the probabilities of that path. This allows the overall probability of failure to be obtained by combining the probabilities of the various branches. An example of the use of probabilistic methods in event tree analysis, based on our earlier example, is given in Figure 3.2.

The essential structure of the tree of Figure 3.2 is similar to that given earlier, except that probabilities have now been added to each branch. It can be seen, for example, that the pressure sensor has a probability of operating correctly of 0.95 and a probability of failing of 0.05. Note that at each branch the sum of the probabilities is unity, as one or other of the two events must occur. The probability of following the path to any of the branches on the right-hand side of the diagram is simply the product of the probabilities of taking the appropriate branches along the route. By summing the probabilities associated with a particular outcome it is then possible to determine its likelihood. In this example the probability of the alarm operating correctly is approximately 0.84, and of it failing, 0.16. Again, these probabilities must sum to unity.

Although it is very attractive to be able to calculate the probability of a particular outcome, it must be remembered that the resultant figure is only as valid as the numbers used within the event tree. In some cases the probabilities associated with particular branches may have been obtained from historical data that has a sound statistical basis. In other cases it may have been necessary to estimate probabilities based on engineering judgement. In assessing the significance of any calculated value the assumptions made must be carefully examined.

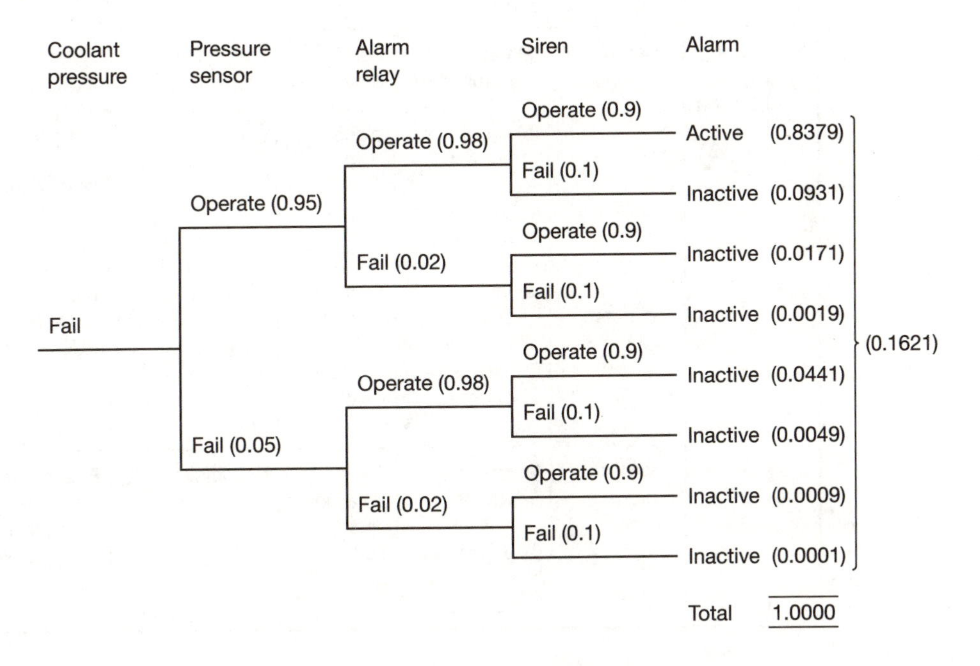

Figure 3.2 Probabilistic analysis applied to an event tree.

3.3 Failure modes and effects analysis (FMEA)

FMEA progressively selects the individual components or functions within a system and investigates their possible modes of failure. It then considers possible causes for each failure mode and assesses their likely consequences. The effects of the failure are determined for the unit itself and for the complete system, and possible remedial actions are suggested (IEC, 1985).

The technique may be applied at various stages of a development project. It is often used at a functional level early in the lifecycle, when it can be useful in the determination of the required safety integrity level. It can also be applied at a fairly late stage, after much of the design work has been done. Here it may be applied at either a component or a functional level. A simple example of FMEA is shown in Figure 3.3.

FMEA may be applied at several levels to refine the analysis. For example, a preliminary analysis might look at the effects on an aircraft of engine failure. This could be followed by looking at a component within the engine, such as a fuel pump, and then a component within the pump, such

FMEA for a microswitch						
Ref No.	*Unit*	*Failure mode*	*Possible cause*	*Local effects*	*System effects*	*Remedial action*
1	Tool guard switch	Open-circuit contacts	(a) faulty component (b) excessive current (c) extreme temperature	Failure to detect tool guard in place	Prevents use of machine – system fails safe	Select switch for high reliability and low probability of dangerous failure Rigid quality control on switch procurement
2		Short-circuit contacts	(a) faulty component (b) excessive current	System incorrectly senses guard to be closed	Allows machine to be used when guard is absent – dangerous failure	Modify software to detect switch failure and take appropriate action
3		Excessive switch-bounce	(a) ageing effects (b) prolonged high currents	Slight delay in sensing state of guard	Negligible	Ensure hardware design prevents excessive current through switch

Figure 3.3 A simple FMEA chart.

as a valve. There is much to be gained by performing this analysis within a team of perhaps four to eight engineers.

The analysis can include a probabilistic element by including probability and criticality information within the chart. As with other forms of analysis, its effectiveness is controlled by the judgement and experience of the engineers involved. FMEA is often used to provide input data for fault tree analysis, the two methods being largely complementary.

3.4 Hazard and operability studies (HAZOP)

The HAZOP technique was developed by ICI in the 1960s as a method of analysing hazards within chemical and process control plants. It was later developed and publicized by the Chemical Industries Association, and is now widely used within the chemical process industry (CIA, 1987). In recent years it has also come to be accepted as a powerful technique within other sectors, and is now used in a range of applications, including those based on the use of computers (Kletz, 1995).

The study is typically conducted by a team of from four to eight engineers, including experts in the application area as well as those directly concerned with the design of the system. The leader of this group would normally be an engineer with extensive training in the use of this and other hazard analysis techniques. The team starts from the basic specified operation of the system and investigates the effects of deviations from this normal operation. For each deviation the team sets out to answer a series of questions to decide whether the deviation could occur, and if so, whether it could result in a hazard. Safety features designed to control hazards are also considered. Where potential hazards are detected further questions are asked to decide when it might occur, what can be done about it, and when any corrective work must be done.

The HAZOP study begins by identifying the interconnections between components within the system and determining the corresponding interactions. These interactions may consist of the physical flow of material from one component to another, as in the case of a chemical plant, or may represent the flow of electricity, signals or data. Such flows are referred to as 'entities'. Each entity possesses certain properties or 'attributes' which determine the correctness of the system's operation. For example, the exchange of data between two components might have attributes related to the 'value' of the data exchanged and the 'bit rate' of its communication. Deviations from the design values for these attributes may have implications for the correct operation of the system.

The study is based on a rigorous and systematic investigation of possible deviations from each of the identified attributes. In order to structure the assessment process a series of 'guide words' is used to define particular types of deviation. In the chemical industry a generic list of guide words has been used for some time. These are:

no
more
less
as well as
part of
reverse
other than.

Experience has shown that this list is also useful when dealing with other systems, such as those based on the use of computers. However, additional guide words are necessary to cover timing considerations. Common additional words are:

early
late
before
after.

The various guide words will be given varied interpretations depending on the industry concerned and where they are applied. For this reason the meaning, or meanings, of each guide word must be defined as part of the study. Table 3.1 illustrates that guide words are likely to be interpreted differently between different applications, and Table 3.2 shows a range of possible meanings for two particular guide words, when applied to a range of attributes.

When applied simply, each attribute of each interaction within the system would be investigated by determining the effect of each relevant guide word. In practice, experience is used to guide the choice of questions for each area. The overall HAZOP process is illustrated in Figure 3.4.

The results of the study are recorded in a table that shows the findings and the recommendations of the team. Figure 3.5 shows a simplified example of a HAZOP study for a temperature sensor.

The final stage of the HAZOP process is to prioritize the results to identify areas that justify further investigation. Once hazards have been identified it may be useful to present the data using fault trees.

The HAZOP technique can also be applied to software (Chudleigh and Catmur, 1992). In this case, suitable attributes might include 'data value', 'pointer value', 'algorithm' and 'timing', and suitable guide words might include 'incorrect', 'too fast' and 'too slow'. In computer-based systems it is suggested that the analysis is initially directed at the installation as a whole. This is followed by a more detailed study of the components of the computer and its software.

Interest in the use of HAZOP studies in connection with computer-based systems has been increased by the publication in the UK of a draft military standard in this area. Draft Interim Defence Standard 00-58 is entitled *A Guideline for HAZOP Studies on Systems Which Include a Programmable*

Table 3.1 Possible guide word interpretations in different applications.

Guide word	*Chemical plant*	*Computer-based system*
No	No part of the intended result is achieved	No data or control signal exchanged
More	A quantitative increase in the physical quantity	A signal magnitude or a data rate is too high
Less	A quantitative decrease in the physical quantity	A signal magnitude or a data rate is too low
As well as	The intended activity occurs, but with additional results	Redundant data sent in addition to intended value
Part of	Only part of the intended activity occurs	Incomplete data transmitted
Reverse	The opposite of what was intended occurs, for example reverse flow within a pipe	Polarity of magnitude changes reversed
Other than	No part of the intended activity occurs, and something else happens instead	Data complete but incorrect
Early	Not used	Signal arrives too early with reference to clock time
Late	Not used	Signal arrives too late with reference to clock time
Before	Not used	Signal arrives earlier than intended within a sequence
After	Not used	Signal arrives later than intended within a sequence

Table 3.2 Possible guide word interpretations for a range of attributes.

Attribute	*Guide word*	*Possible meaning*
Data flow	More	More data is passed than expected
	Less	Less data is passed than expected
Data rate	More	The data rate is too high
	Less	The data rate is too low
Data value	More	The data value is too high
	Less	The data value is too low
Repetition time	More	The time between output updates is too high
	Less	The time between output updates is too low
Response time	More	The response time is longer than required
	Less	The response time is shorter than required

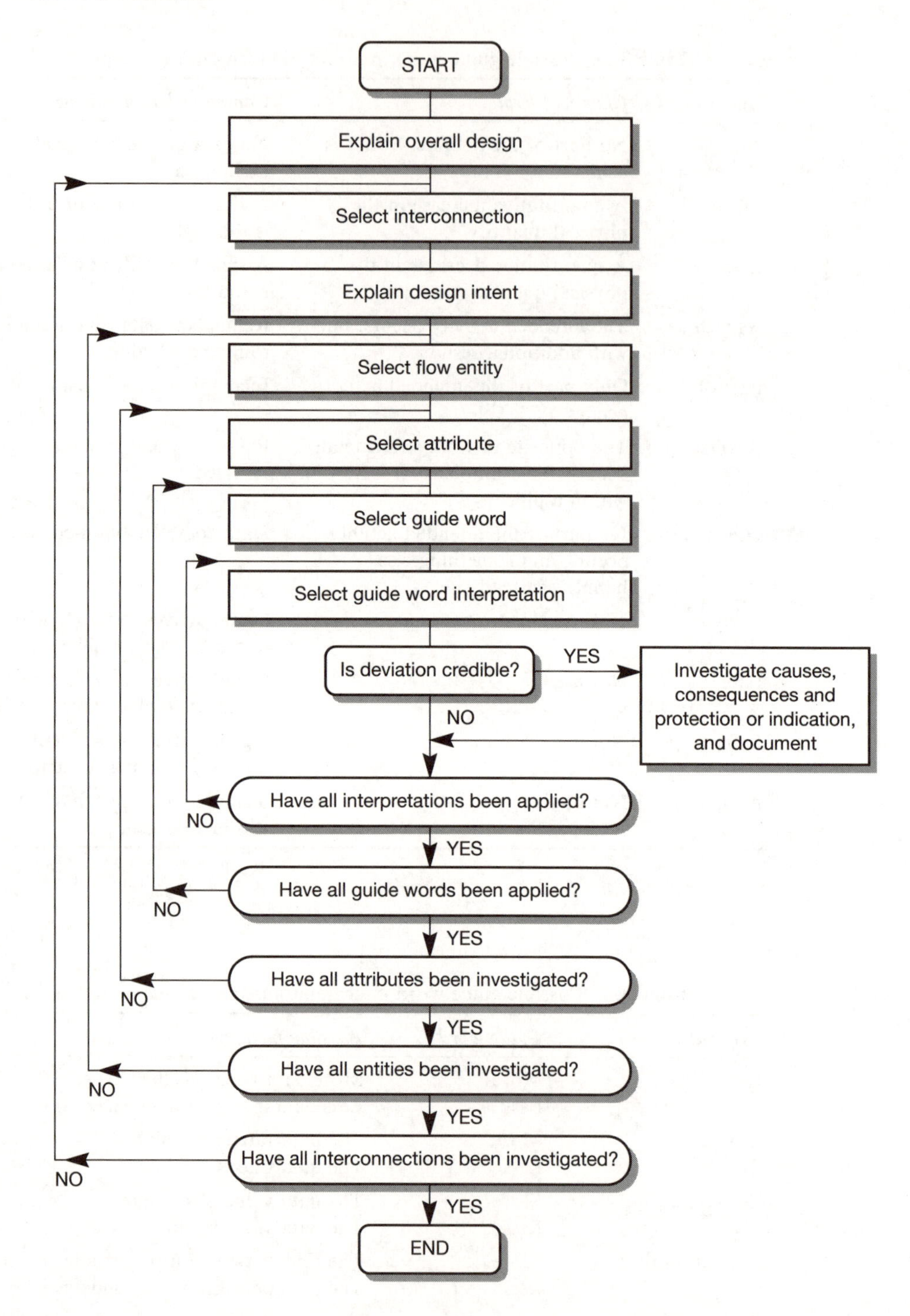

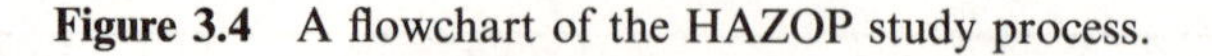

Figure 3.4 A flowchart of the HAZOP study process.

Item	*Inter-connection*	*Attribute*	*Guide word*	*Cause*	*Consequence*	*Recommendation*
1	Sensor supply line	Supply voltage	No	PSU, regulator or cable fault	Lack of sensor signal detected and system shuts down	
2			More	Regulator fault	Possible damage to sensor	Consider overvoltage protection
3			Less	PSU or regulator fault	Incorrect temperature reading	Include voltage monitoring
4		Sensor current	More	Sensor fault	Incorrect temperature reading, possible loading of supply	Monitor supply current
5			Less	Sensor fault	Incorrect temperature reading	As above
6	Sensor output	Voltage	No	PSU, sensor or cable fault	Lack of sensor signal detected and system shuts down	
7			More	Sensor fault	Temperature reading too high – results in decrease in plant efficiency	Consider use of duplicate sensor
8			Less	Sensor mounted incorrectly or sensor failure	Temperature reading too low – could result in overheating and possible plant failure	As above

Figure 3.5 Part of a simplified HAZOP results table for a temperature sensor.

Electronic System. This was issued for comment in March 1995 (MoD, 1995b). As well as standardizing the terminology the document outlines the procedures involved and provides a series of useful examples.

3.5 Fault tree analysis (FTA)

Fault tree analysis is a graphical method that starts with an event directly related to an identified hazard, the 'top event', and works backwards to determine its cause. Intermediate events related to the top event are combined using logical operations such as AND or OR, and the process is repeated, working back to the basic events that are the root cause of the hazard. The graphical nature of the analysis simplifies interpretation, and FTA is often used to represent dependencies identified using other hazard analysis techniques such as FMEA and HAZOP.

Events are combined using logical operations that are represented using a set of symbols. These symbols are covered within the IEC 1025 international standard (IEC, 1990). This defines two notations that are referred to as 'preferred' and 'alternative'. Examples of these symbols are shown in Figure 3.6.

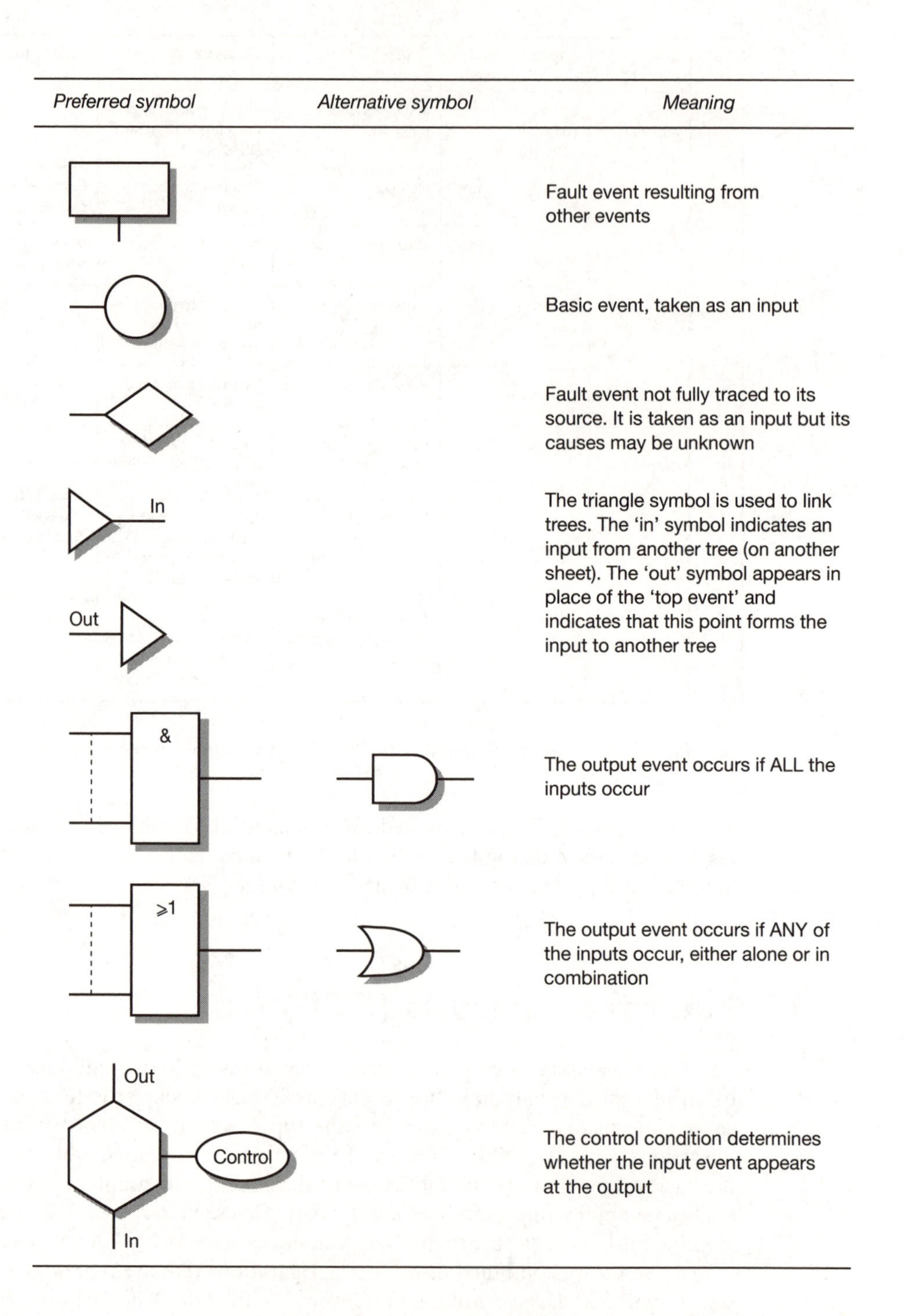

Figure 3.6 Fault tree symbols from IEC 1025.

Using the preferred symbols from IEC 1025 trees are conventionally drawn with the top event on the right-hand side of the diagram. A simple example of a fault tree using this notation is shown in Figure 3.7. This shows the conditions for failure of a heating system that can use either liquid or solid fuel. This system requires an electrical supply for the control system and a fan. It can be seen that the system will fail if the electrical supply fails or if both sources of fuel are lost.

When using the 'alternative' symbols from IEC 1025 the top event is usually drawn at the top of the diagram. Using this notation the symbols are very similar to those of conventional electronic logic diagrams, making the tree simple to interpret for anyone familiar with electronic circuits. Figure 3.8 shows the fault tree of Figure 3.7 represented in this way.

Despite the recommendations of IEC 1025, a majority of engineers draw fault trees using a notation similar to the 'alternative' notation given in the standard. We shall therefore follow this example for the remainder of this book.

When constructing a fault tree it is useful to differentiate between faults of various classes. Faults may be classified as primary, secondary or command faults (Vesely *et al.*, 1981). A **primary fault** occurs when a component fails while operating in an environment, and under conditions, for which it was intended. Thus a resistor rated at 1 W that fails while dissipating less than this power has suffered a primary failure. A **secondary fault** occurs when a component fails under conditions that are outside its designed operating range. If our 1 W resistor fails because it is dissipating 10 W, this would constitute a secondary failure. As the name suggests, secondary faults are caused by effects outside the component concerned. A **command fault** corresponds to a component performing its designed task correctly, but under inappropriate circumstances. If, for example, a solenoid operates correctly in response to an incorrect control signal, this is a command fault, the cause of which is related to the source of the inappropriate signal.

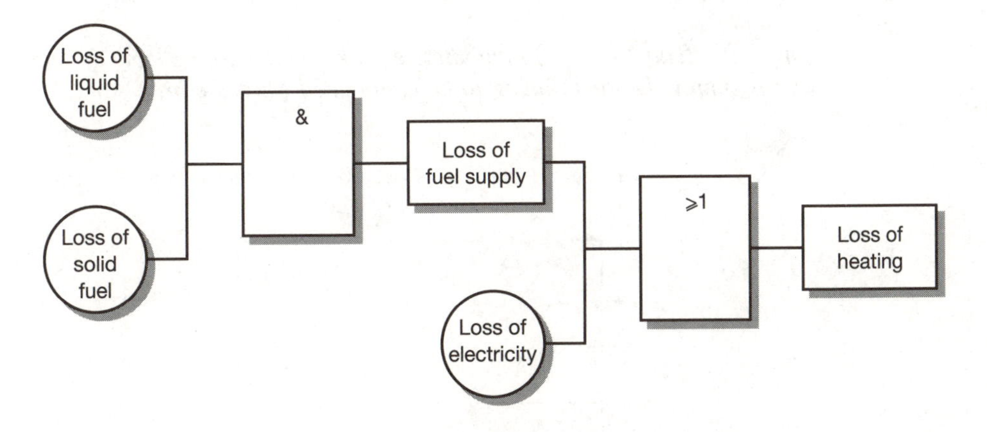

Figure 3.7 A simple fault tree.

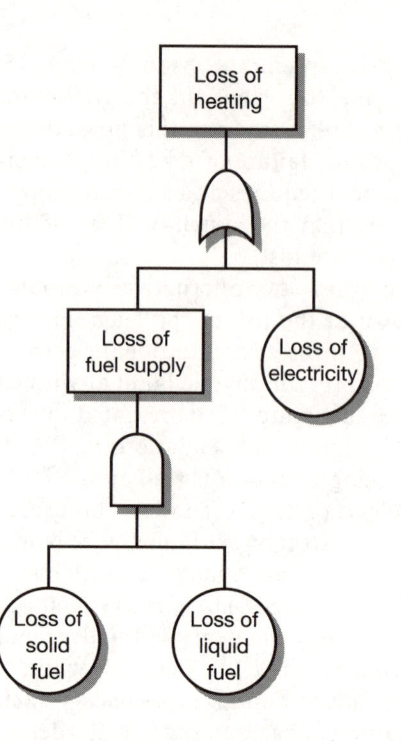

Figure 3.8 The fault tree of Figure 3.7 drawn using the alternative symbols of IEC 1025.

Perhaps the easiest way of understanding the construction of a fault tree is to look at some examples.

Example 3.1

Construct a fault tree for an automotive brake fluid warning lamp system. The top event is simply the lamp failing to be illuminated when the brake fluid level is low.

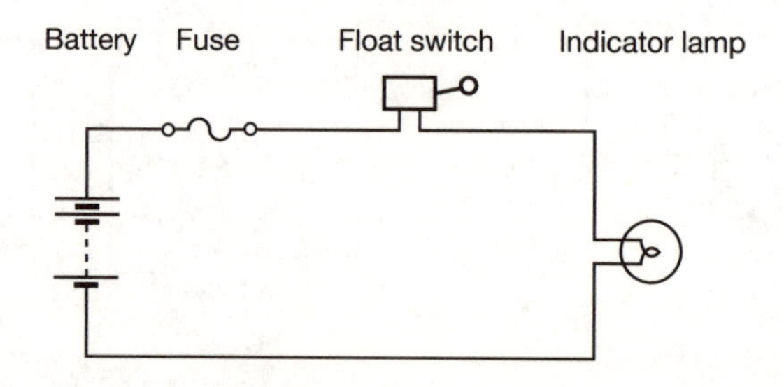

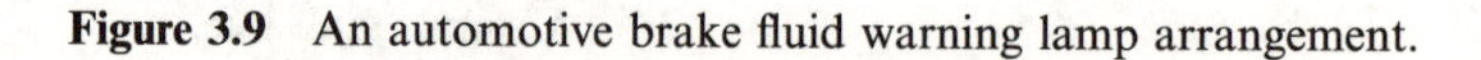

Figure 3.9 An automotive brake fluid warning lamp arrangement.

A circuit representation of this arrangement is shown in Figure 3.9. This shows a series combination of the battery, a fuse, a float switch used to detect the brake fluid level and the warning lamp. The circuit also includes cabling and connectors that are not included in this diagram.

A possible fault tree for this arrangement is shown in Figure 3.10. The tree shows that the lamp will fail to be illuminated if either of two conditions exists. The first is that there is a primary lamp failure, such as a broken filament. The second is that, for some reason, a voltage is not applied to the

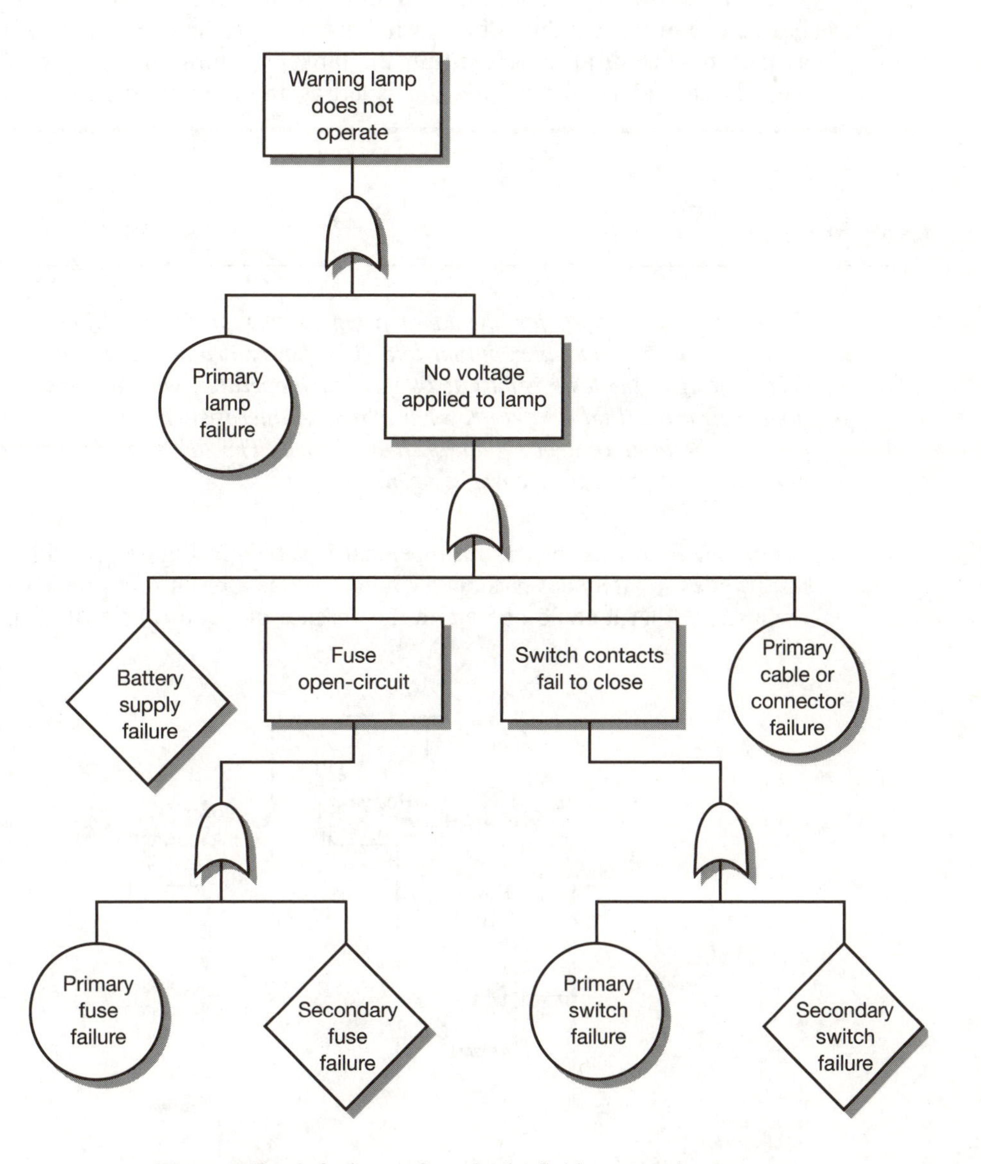

Figure 3.10 A fault tree for a brake fluid warning lamp system.

lamp. This latter condition is further analysed and four possible causes are identified. These are: failure of the battery supply; an open-circuit fuse; a switch failure; or a primary cable or connector failure. Failure of the battery supply could be caused by a number of factors, and the tree leaves this as an event not traced to its source. Failure of the fuse could be due to either a primary or a secondary failure. Here primary failure represents a fault within the fuse, causing it to blow under normal operation, and secondary failure represents a fuse failure caused by an excessive current. The cause of this large current is left as an event not traced to its source. Failure of the switch contacts to close could be due to a primary failure of the switch itself, or to some secondary effect, such as the presence of an object within the tank preventing it from operating. As with the secondary fuse failure, this is left as an event not traced to its source.

Example 3.2

Construct a fault tree for the laser firing system in Figure 3.11. The laser is controlled from a computer output line via a power driver and an electromagnetic relay. Firing of the laser is initiated by a human operator, who first ensures that the area is clear and that a safety cover is closed. A microswitch connected to the cover disables the laser control signal when it is open. The top event is the laser being activated while the safety cover is open.

A possible fault tree for this arrangement is shown in Figure 3.12. Firing of the laser while the safety cover is open could occur as a result of a primary failure of the laser, in that it could operate in the absence of a control signal. This event is

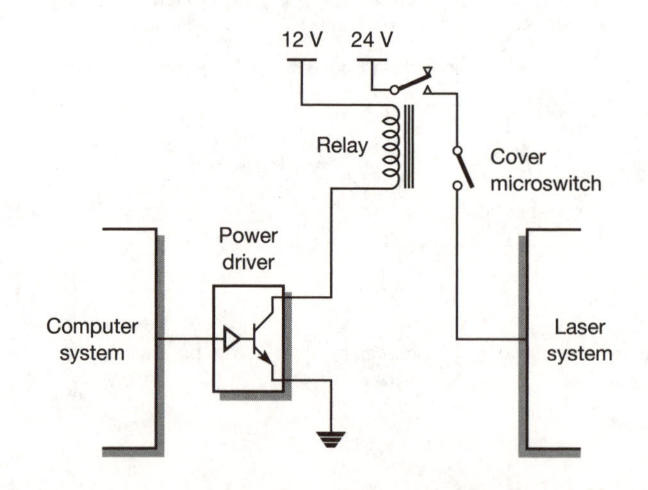

Figure 3.11 A laser control system.

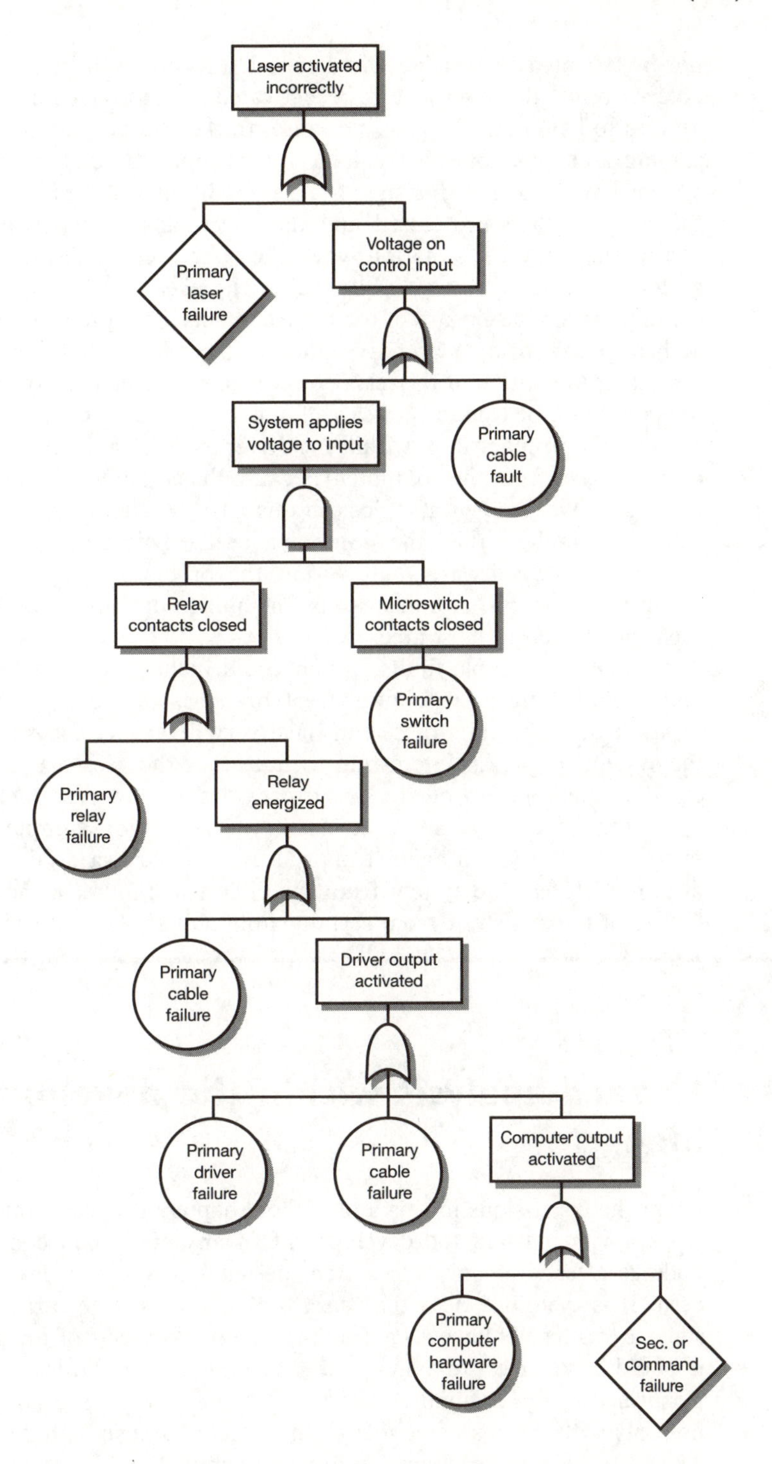

Figure 3.12 A fault tree for a laser control system.

not investigated further here, and so is left as an event not traced to its source. Alternatively, the laser could be activated because a control signal has been applied to its input. The possible causes of the latter event are that some form of cabling fault has applied a voltage to the input, or that other elements of the system have supplied this signal. This condition will be brought about if both the relay contacts are closed and the cover microswitch is closed. As we are considering only the situation when the laser fires while the cover is open, the switch contacts will only be closed in the event of a primary switch failure. Conditions for the closure of the relay contacts are more complicated. This could be brought about by a primary failure of the relay or because the relay coil was activated. Activation of the relay coil can be produced by activation of the driver, but could also be caused by a cable fault. The driver in turn could be activated as a result of a primary fault within the driver itself, a cable fault, or as a result of a control signal from the computer. Because the computer should not fire the laser while the cover is open, if it does so this must be due to a primary, secondary or command fault within the computer itself. This could be in the form of a hardware or software fault within the processor, failure of some external hardware or system, or a mistake by the human operator. This is again left as an event not traced to its source.

Note that cable faults, which could include faults within connectors or joints, contribute a large number of branches to the tree. Depending on the location of such faults these can have very diverse effects on the operation of the system. It is also interesting to note that the presence of the microswitch on the safety cover of the laser provides a powerful **interlock** preventing operation of the system as a result of human or computer error. It also safeguards the system against many forms of hardware failure. However, this does not protect the system from the effects of failure of the laser itself, from failure of the switch or from certain cable faults. No interlock is perfect.

3.6 Hazard analysis within the development lifecycle

From the discussions in this and earlier chapters it is clear that hazard analysis plays a vital part in the development of any embedded computer system. Its findings affect not only the system design but also the development methods used. It is therefore clear that hazard analysis must be carried out at an early stage, as its results have a great influence on all aspects of the project. However, it would be incorrect to assume that the analysis of hazards is a 'one-off' process performed at the beginning of the project. In fact, hazard analysis is concerned not only with the characteristics of the system but also with details of the design. Therefore, when a preliminary analysis shows that a system is safety related, hazard analysis will normally continue throughout the development process. The nature of this work, and the effort involved, will be determined by several factors, including the level of risk associated with the system, as identified by the early stages of hazard analysis.

The ongoing task of identifying and analysing hazards consists of a number of phases that occur at various stages in the development process. The names given to these activities differ widely, and here we will adopt a well accepted, though not universal, terminology (MoD, 1995a). The major hazard analysis activities for a typical project concerned with the development of a safety-critical system are shown in Figure 3.13.

Preliminary hazard identification (PHI)

The presence of significant hazards has considerable consequences for the design, development and use of any system. It is therefore essential to identify hazards at a very early stage so that appropriate action may be taken. Such action may involve redefining the nature of the system to remove or reduce the hazard, or designing the system in a manner appropriate to the severity of the hazard. The importance of this process dictates that *all* embedded computer systems should be subjected to a preliminary hazard identification process to identify any areas of concern. This should be carried out at an early stage in the development of a system – usually during project conception. A systematic study of both operational and fault conditions should be performed using proven methods, such as HAZOP. In applications where other similar systems are already in existence, data relating to previous accidents or incidents may be available to provide an important input to the hazard identification task.

The results of the PHI phase are recorded in the preliminary hazard list. In applications that are found to have significant hazards this document will form an input to later stages of hazard analysis. If the study identifies no important hazards then no further hazard analysis is required, as the system is clearly not safety critical. In this case the preliminary hazard list should be retained as evidence that the hazard identification process has been performed.

Preliminary hazard analysis (PHA)

The preliminary hazard analysis phase takes the hazards identified in the PHI phase and subjects them to a detailed study using HAZOP or some other systematic technique. Each hazard is considered in association with the functional requirements of the system to identify safety implications and to evaluate design alternatives. All the hazards identified are recorded in the **hazard log**, which represents an ongoing record of the safety issues of the system.

In addition to the identification of hazards, this analysis also attempts, as far as is possible at this early stage, to classify the severity of the hazards and to assign an integrity level requirement to each major function. Considerations of hazard severity and integrity levels will be discussed in Chapter 4.

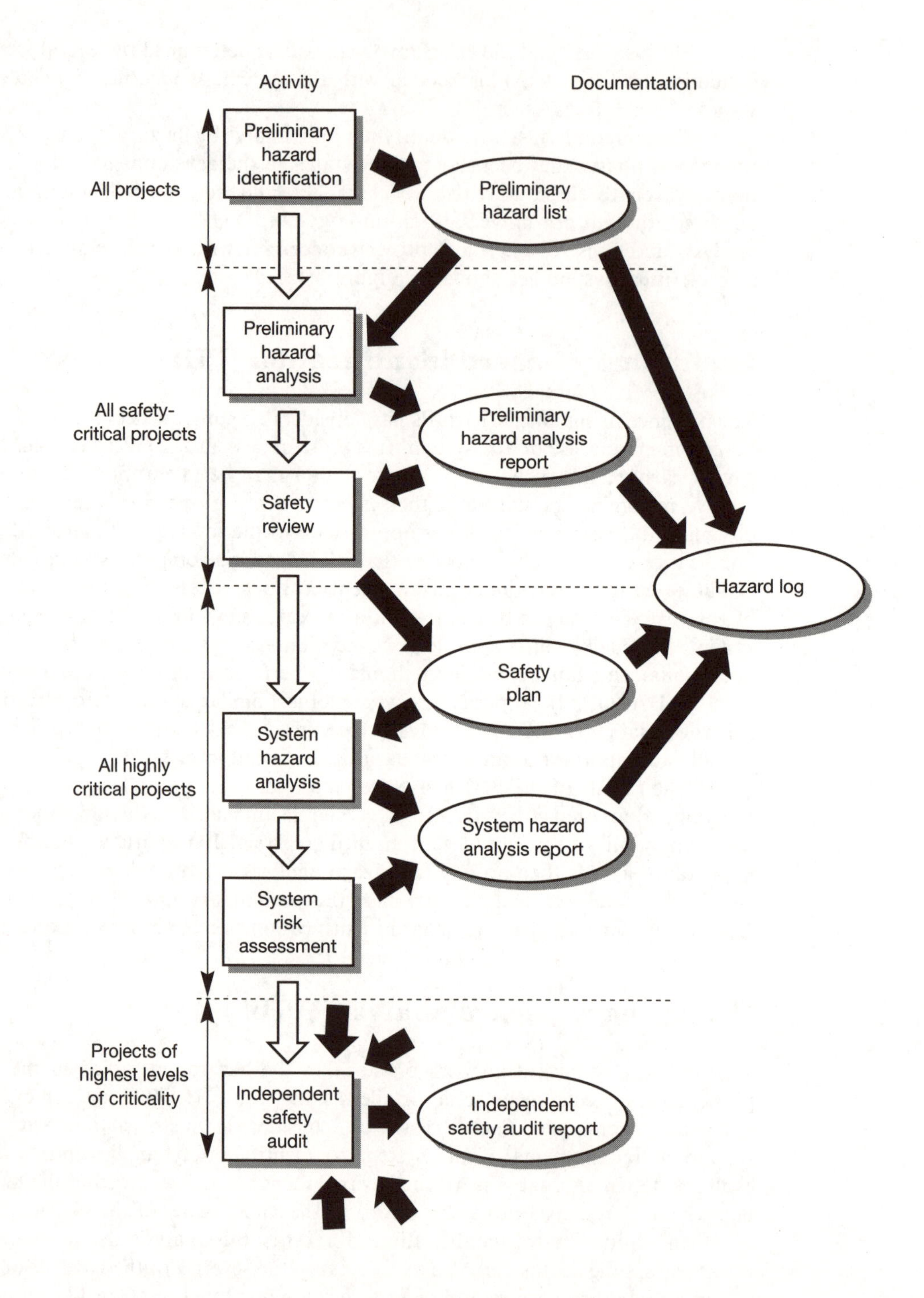

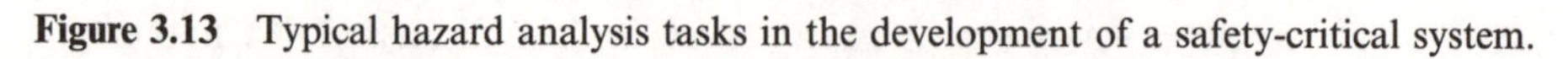

Figure 3.13 Typical hazard analysis tasks in the development of a safety-critical system.

The findings of the PHA are documented in the **preliminary hazard analysis report**. This provides a great deal of background information on the system and its hazards, including:

- a brief description of the system and its environment;
- an overview of the system's function and its safety features;
- the safety objectives of the system;
- justification of the risk and integrity level assignments made;
- target failure rates and safety levels;
- sources of any data used within the analysis;
- a bibliography of all documents used.

Preliminary hazard analysis is used as an input to the safety requirements phase and also to guide early decisions on system architectures and techniques. PHA will also guide later hazard and safety analysis activities.

Safety reviews

Throughout the development process the project is subjected to a number of reviews which look at all aspects of safety. These take data from the various reports and analyses and record their findings in the hazard log for future reference. The first of these safety reviews often comes after the PHA phase. Safety reviews are also carried out as part of project design reviews in the later stages of the development.

One of the tasks performed within the preliminary hazard analysis phase is an assessment of the integrity requirements of the system. If this analysis, and subsequent safety reviews, shows the system to be of relatively modest criticality, it is likely that further, more detailed, hazard analysis will not be necessary or economically justifiable. In this case development will continue using methods appropriate to the assigned level of integrity.

Safety plan

For all systems that have been shown to be of a moderate or high level of criticality, a safety plan is produced, setting out the manner in which safety will be achieved and defining the management structure responsible for further hazard and risk analysis. The safety plan may also identify key staff by name. This is of particular importance in assigning responsibilities within projects performed by large companies or consortia.

The safety plan is used to document the detailed safety planning of a project and the control measures that will be employed. It will include a record of the various standards and codes of practice to be followed, with details of how the requirements of these documents will be achieved. The plan is maintained throughout the project.

System hazard analysis

Systems shown to require a high level of integrity will be subjected to additional study in the form of a system safety analysis. The objectives of this work are to extend and refine the findings of the preliminary hazard analysis by considering the detailed functions of the system and the components that implement them. Initially the analysis takes its input from the system requirements and the findings of the PHA. As the project develops, the analysis becomes more concerned with the components and subsystems designed to meet these requirements.

In most cases a selection of hazard analysis techniques will be required to provide a comprehensive coverage of possible hazards. In addition to the techniques discussed earlier in this chapter, analysis may also be performed using other techniques, such as Markov modelling and the use of reliability block diagrams. These are discussed in Chapter 7.

System risk assessment

Data from the system hazard analysis is used as the basis of a risk analysis to investigate the consequences of the various hazards and their likely rates of occurrence or probabilities. The analysis is also used to assign integrity levels to the various components of the system.

Details of the system hazard analysis and the associated system risk assessment are documented in the **system hazard analysis report** and in the hazard log.

Independent safety audit

In projects concerned with systems of the highest levels of criticality an independent team of assessors is employed to perform a safety audit. This team takes data from the hazard log and the various hazard analysis reports and independently verifies the thoroughness of the work and the correctness of the findings. The outcome of the audit is documented in the **independent safety audit report**, which will form a vital part of the safety case used to achieve certification.

The use of independence in assessment is also recommended when developing systems of more modest levels of criticality. In such cases it is useful to identify different degrees of independence between the person carrying out the assessment and those performing the development work. These may be classified as:

(1) independent person

(2) independent department

(3) independent organization.

Increased levels of independence help to increase our confidence in the correctness of a system. However, the degree of independence will often be limited, for economic reasons. The various international standards give guidance in this area and we shall return to look at this issue in more detail in Chapter 12.

The use of an independent team of assessors places great importance on the completeness of the documentation for the project, and requires good discipline from all the staff involved. All results and analysis given within the various documents must be traceable back to its source to allow independent verification. This provision is termed an **audit trail**.

REFERENCES

Chudleigh M.F. and Catmur J.R. (1992). Safety assessment of computer systems using HAZOP and audit techniques. In *Safety of Computer Control Systems (Safecomp '92)*. Oxford: Pergamon Press

CIA (1987). *A Guide to Hazard and Operability Studies*. London: Chemical Industries Association Limited

IEC (1985). International Standard 812 *Analysis Techniques for System Reliability: Procedures for Failure Mode and Effect Analysis*. Geneva: International Electrotechnical Commission

IEC (1990). International Standard IEC 1025 *Fault Tree Analysis (FTA)*. Geneva: International Electrotechnical Commission. (Within Britain this standard is also available as British Standard BS 5760: *Reliability of Systems, Equipment and Components*. Part 7. *Guide to Fault Tree Analysis*)

Kletz T. (1995). *Computer Control and Human Error*. Rugby: Institute of Chemical Engineers

Leveson N.G. (1995). *Safeware: System Safety and Computers*. Reading, MA: Addison-Wesley

MoD (1995a). Draft Defence Standard 00-56 Issue 2 *Safety Management Requirements for Defence Systems Containing Programmable Electronics, Part 1: Requirements*. Glasgow: Directorate of Standardization

MoD (1995b). Draft Interim Defence Standard 00-58 *A Guideline for HAZOP Studies on Systems Which Include a Programmable Electronic System*. Glasgow: Directorate of Standardization

Neumann P.G. (1995). *Computer-Related Risks*. New York: ACM Press

Veseley W.E., Goldberg F.F., Roberts N.H. and Haasl D.F. (1981). *Fault Tree Handbook*. Washington, DC: US Nuclear Regulatory Commission, NUREG-0492

FURTHER READING

HSE (1995). *Out of Control*. London: Health and Safety Executive

Kletz T. (1995). *Computer Control and Human Error*. Rugby: Institute of Chemical Engineers

Lewis E.E. (1987). *Introduction to Reliability Engineering*. New York: John Wiley

Neumann P.G. (1995). *Computer-Related Risks*. New York: ACM Press

PROBLEMS

3.1 Define the term 'hazard'.

3.2 Suggest several hazards that are associated with your work or study.

3.3 Explain the meaning of the term 'risk'.

3.4 What factors contribute to risk?

3.5 Why is the identification of hazards important in the design of safety-critical systems?

3.6 List five techniques commonly used in hazard analysis.

3.7 Why is hazard analysis required at the beginning of all projects involving embedded computer systems? What aspects of the project are affected by this initial analysis?

3.8 Explain briefly the fundamentals of failure modes and effects analysis.

3.9 Why is much of the analysis performed in FMEA not directly related to safety?

3.10 How does FMECA differ from FMEA? What are its advantages when considering safety-critical systems?

3.11 Explain the principles of hazard and operability studies.

3.12 What are the characteristics of an event tree?

3.13 Construct an event tree for an emergency braking system for a moving machine. The system consists of a push-button, an air compressor and a pneumatic braking system.

3.14 Construct an event tree for a water temperature alarm system comprising a temperature sensor, two alarm relays connected in parallel and two sirens, one connected to each relay. The event tree should begin with an event corresponding to the water temperature failing by going too high. The final event to be considered is the activation of an alarm.

3.15 How does a fault tree differ from an event tree?

3.16 What is meant by the term 'probabilistic hazard analysis'? How may this process be used in association with FMECA?

3.17 In the braking system of Problem 3.13 the push-button has a probability of working correctly of 0.95; the air compressor has a probability of working correctly of 0.9, and the pneumatic brake has a probability of working correctly of 0.98. Construct an event tree of this arrangement and determine the probability of the braking system operating when the push-button is pressed.

3.18 In the water temperature alarm system of Problem 3.14 the probability of correct operation of the sensor is 0.98; each relay has a probability of correct action of 0.97; and each siren has a probability of correct operation of 0.95. Construct an event tree for this arrangement and determine the probability of at least one siren sounding in the event that the temperature goes above safe limits.

3.19 Explain the meanings of the terms 'guide words' and 'attributes' when applied to HAZOP studies. Give examples of suitable guide words and attributes for the analysis of a programmable system.

3.20 Distinguish between the meanings of the rectangle, circle and diamond symbols in a fault tree.

3.21 Why are fault trees often used in association with FMEA and HAZOP?

3.22 Construct a simple fault tree for an automatic lighting system. The lights are turned on by a light-activated switch. In the event of power failure a standby generator should start automatically to maintain power. The top event is the failure of the lights.

3.23 Construct a fault tree for the following arrangement.

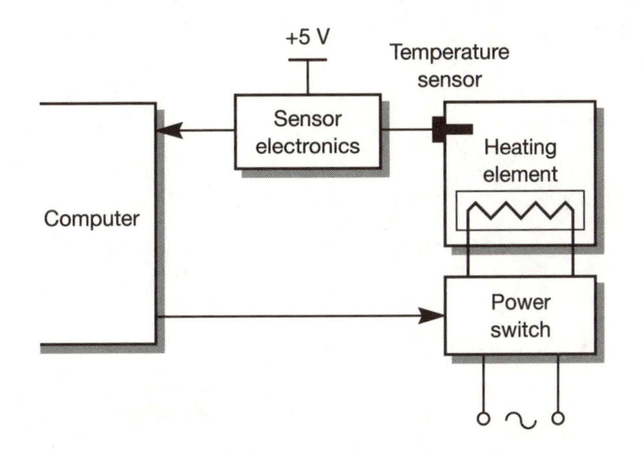

The diagram shows a heater controller for a tank of toxic liquid. The computer controls the heater using a power switch on the basis of information obtained from a temperature sensor. The sensor is connected to the computer via an electronic interface that supplies a binary signal indicating when the liquid is up to its required temperature. The top event of the fault tree is the liquid being heated above its required temperature.

3.24 How is the safety of the system in the last problem affected by the polarity of the control and monitoring signals used?

3.25 During what phases of project development is hazard analysis normally performed?

3.26 How are hazard analysis activities affected by the criticality of a system?

3.27 What hazard analysis activities are relevant to all embedded computer system development projects?

3.28 For each of the primary hazard analysis phases identify the principal sources of data and the main form of documentation.

3.29 Explain the use of the hazard log.

3.30 What is meant by the term 'safety review'?

3.31 What is the function of the safety plan?

3.32 How does the system hazard analysis differ from the preliminary hazard analysis?

3.33 What information is used as the basis of an independent safety audit? How is this activity documented?

3.34 What is meant by the term 'audit trail'?

4 Risk Analysis

CHAPTER CONTENTS

4.1 Introduction

In the previous chapter we noted that hazards are present in all aspects of our everyday life. Associated with these hazards are certain 'risks', which determine their relative importance and enable us to judge their acceptability. The *possibility* of being struck by a meteorite represents a hazard, as does the *possibility* of being stung by a mosquito or electrocuted by a wrongly wired appliance. However, the risks associated with these potential dangers may be very different. A large part of our lives is spent in assessing risks and our survival is closely linked to our abilities at this task.

In order to understand the nature of risk it is useful to consider the relationship between hazards and events that result in harm to an individual or the environment. It should be remembered that hazards represent situations of *potential* danger. When a hazard results in an event that causes actual harm, this occurrence is commonly termed an **accident**. In fact, safety engineers formally define an accident as *an unwanted and unexpected release of energy*, a definition that excludes some harmful occurrences such as exposure to dangerous chemicals. This has led some engineers to use the term **mishap** to include both accidents and other causes of harm (Leveson, 1986). In this text we will adopt the more common use of the term 'accident' that is synonymous with the term 'mishap':

> *An **accident** is an unintended event or sequence of events that causes death, injury, environmental or material damage.*

Much of the process of hazard analysis is aimed at identifying sequences of events that may lead to an accident. These trains of events are often termed **accident sequences** or **accident scenarios**. Only by investigating these sequences can the true significance of individual hazards be determined.

A great deal of useful information can also be gained by looking at events that might be considered as 'near misses'. These are often referred to as incidents:

> *An* ***incident*** *(or* ***near miss****) is an unintended event or sequence of events that does not result in loss, but, under different circumstances, has the potential to do so.*

The importance of a hazard is related to the accidents that may result from it. Two factors are of significance here, namely:

- the potential consequences of any accident that might result from the hazard;
- the frequency (or probability) of such an accident occurring.

The risk associated with a hazard is determined by these two factors and may be defined as follows:

> ***Risk*** *is a combination of the frequency or probability of a specified hazardous event, and its consequence.*

This definition allows risk to be treated in either a qualitative or a quantitative manner. If the latter approach is adopted, numerical estimates of both frequency and severity may be combined to produce a single measure of risk. This is shown in Example 4.1.

Example 4.1

Failure of a particular component is likely to result in an explosion that could kill 100 people. It is estimated that this component will fail once in every 10 000 years. What is the risk associated with this component?

One failure in every 10 000 years represents a failure rate of 0.0001 failures per year. Therefore, the risk is given by:

$$\begin{aligned} \text{Risk} &= \text{severity} \times \text{frequency} \\ &= 100 \times 0.0001 \\ &= 0.01 \text{ deaths per year} \end{aligned}$$

Risk may also be expressed in terms of its effects on individuals. This is of particular relevance when society as a whole is at risk. This might be the case when considering the global implications of environmental hazards, or simply when considering hazards that affect a great many people. This approach is shown in Example 4.2.

Example 4.2

In a country with a population of 50 000 000 approximately 25 people are killed each year by lightning. What is the risk associated with death from this cause?

The fraction of the population killed per year is simply $25/50\,000\,000 = 5 \times 10^{-7}$. The associated risk may be expressed by saying that each individual has a probability of 5×10^{-7} of being killed by lightning in any given year. Alternatively, we could say that the population as a whole is exposed to a risk of 5×10^{-7} deaths per person-year.

In some cases measures of severity and frequency are divided into classes to simplify the use of guidelines and standards. Recommendations, or requirements, are then based on these classes rather than on numeric values for these quantities. The classifications used vary greatly between industries, and the definitions of the various classes are very closely linked to the areas in which they are used. In the following sections we look at some of the classifications used within specific industrial sectors.

4.2 Consequences of malfunction – severity

All safety-related industries classify hazards in terms of their severity. Inevitably, the classifications used tend to be closely related to the nature of the relevant industry, thereby making comparisons difficult. In this section we look at a few examples of the classes used within particular areas.

Avionics

Civil aviation standards within Europe and the US categorize hazard severity as shown in Table 4.1 (RTCA/EUROCAE, 1992). It can be seen that the severity is defined in terms of the effects on the aircraft and its crew, as well as the likely influence on the safety of the occupants. Military avionics standards follow similar lines.

Table 4.1 Hazard severity categories for civil aircraft.

Category	*Definition*
Catastrophic	Failure condition which would prevent continued safe flight and landing
Hazardous	Failure conditions which would reduce the capability of the aircraft or the ability of the crew to cope with adverse operating conditions, to the extent that there would be: (1) a large reduction in safety margins or functional capabilities (2) physical distress or higher workload such that the flight crew could not be relied on to perform their tasks accurately or completely (3) adverse effects on occupants, including serious or potentially fatal injuries to a small number of those occupants
Major	Failure conditions which would reduce the capability of the aircraft or the ability of the crew to cope with adverse operating conditions to the extent that there would be, for example, a significant reduction in safety margins or functional capabilities, a significant increase in crew workload or in conditions impairing crew efficiency, or discomfort to occupants, possibly including injuries
Minor	Failure conditions which would not significantly reduce aircraft safety, and which would involve crew actions that are well within their capabilities. Minor failure conditions may include, for example, a slight reduction in safety margins or functional capabilities, a slight increase in crew workload, such as routine flight plan changes, or some inconvenience to occupants
No effect	Failure conditions which do not affect the operational capability of the aircraft or increase crew workload

Military systems

The UK Ministry of Defence has defined the techniques to be used for hazard analysis and safety classification for military computer-based systems in Interim Defence Standard 00-56 (MoD, 1995). This defines four levels of hazard severity, termed 'accident severity categories', as outlined in Table 4.2. It can be seen that here the definitions are more generally applicable, with the emphasis on death and injuries to individuals.

Proposed international standard – IEC 1508

In 1995 the International Electrotechnical Commission (IEC) issued a draft of a proposed international standard that is intended to form a generic basis for standards in all industrial sectors (IEC, 1995). Although this standard is only in draft form at the time of writing, its importance is such that its contents are

Table 4.2 Accident severity categories for military systems.

Category	*Definition*
Catastrophic	Multiple deaths
Critical	A single death, and/or multiple severe injuries or severe occupational illnesses
Marginal	A single severe injury or occupational illness, and/or multiple minor injuries or minor occupational illnesses
Negligible	At most a single minor injury or minor occupational illness

discussed in several sections of the book. The standard is also discussed in more detail in Chapter 14.

The proposed standard adopts a four-level system for categorizing the severity of hazards using classes with names identical to those given in Table 4.2. The document does not explicitly define the four classes, but it is likely that definitions similar to those given above are appropriate. When generating industry-specific standards, different industries will undoubtedly adopt class definitions to match their needs.

4.3 Probability of malfunction – frequency

The probability, or frequency, of a hazardous event may be expressed in a number of ways, and may be given quantitatively or qualitatively. Sometimes the rate is expressed in terms of the number of events per hour or per year of operation. Alternatively, it may be given as the number of likely events during the lifetime of the unit. In systems that are used intermittently, such as emergency shutdown systems, it is common to express the information in terms of the number of **failures on demand**, that is, the number of failures expressed as a fraction of the total number of times it is called upon to operate. It is perhaps worth noting that it is common to see failure probabilities given as a single probability figure *without units*. This practice can be very confusing, as the significance of the figure is clearly very different if it refers to 'failures per year', 'failures per hour' or 'failures on demand'. Unfortunately, even standards are not immune from this weakness.

Avionics

Within standards for aircraft systems the frequency, or probability, associated with hazards is normally expressed in terms of the number of occurrences that might be expected per hour of flight. Similar definitions are used within Europe (JAR, 1994) and in the US (FAR, 1993). The range of probabilities is divided

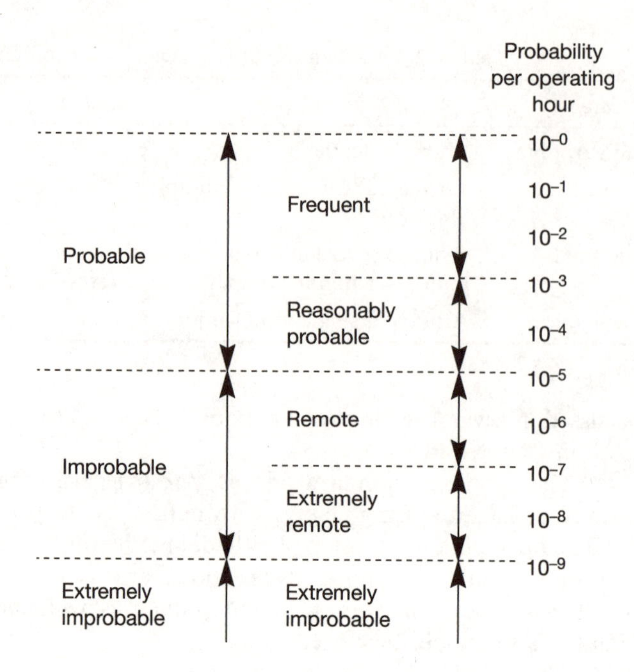

Figure 4.1 Hazard probability classes for aircraft systems.

into three main classifications: probable, improbable and extremely improbable. These three basic ranges are then subdivided into five classes. The definitions of these classes are shown in Figure 4.1.

Military systems

Interim Defence Standard 00-56 defines six categories of hazard probability, as shown in Table 4.3 (MoD, 1995).

Table 4.3 Accident probability ranges for military systems.

Accident frequency	*Occurrences during operational life considering all instances of the system*
Frequent	Likely to be continually experienced
Probable	Likely to occur often
Occasional	Likely to occur several times
Remote	Likely to occur some time
Improbable	Unlikely, but may exceptionally occur
Incredible	Extremely unlikely that the event will occur at all

Proposed international standard – IEC 1508

The draft of the proposed IEC standard adopts a six-level system for classifying the frequency of a hazard, using names for the classes identical to those given in Table 4.3. The classes are not defined within the standard, but it is likely that definitions similar to those used above would be appropriate in many cases. The definitions used for any particular applications are likely to reflect the nature of the hazards associated with the relevant industry.

4.4 Risk classification

We have seen that where quantitative methods are used to describe the severity and frequency of a hazard, it is possible to produce a numerical value for the associated risk by combining these two values. Examples 4.1 and 4.2 demonstrated this process. However, when qualitative measures are used to describe severity or frequency, as, for example, in Tables 4.1 and 4.3, direct calculation of risk is not possible. In such cases severity and frequency data must be combined in some less mechanical way (Figure 4.2). The result of this process is a classification of the risk associated with a particular hazard. This classification is sometimes called a **risk class**, a **risk level** or a **risk factor**. In fact, the use of risk categories is common even where numerical values are used for the severity and frequency of hazards, as their adoption simplifies the use of guidelines. Most standards define a number of risk classes and then set out development and design techniques appropriate for each category of risk. Unfortunately, there is little consensus on the naming or definition of the various classes. In this section we shall look at a few examples.

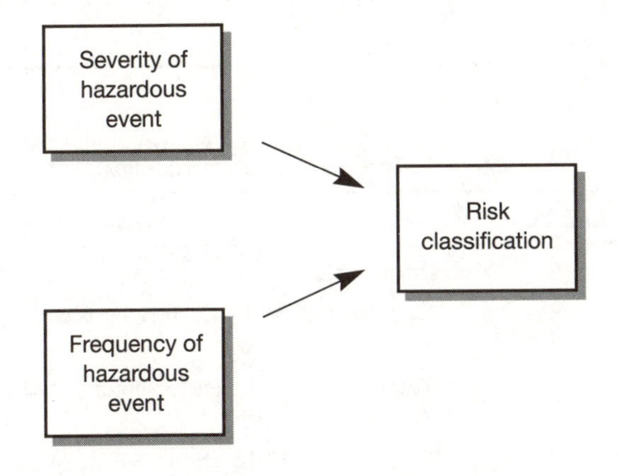

Figure 4.2 Determination of risk classification.

Military systems

Interim Defence Standard 00-56 (MoD, 1995) defines four accident risk classes which are given the symbols A, B, C and D, where A represents the most serious event and D the least serious. Table 4.4 shows the relationships between the various risk classes and the severity and frequency of the hazard. Table 4.5 gives the definitions of the four classes.

Proposed international standard – IEC 1508

The draft of the proposed IEC standard defines four risk classes which are given the symbols I, II, III and IV, where I corresponds to the most serious accident and IV the least serious. The suggested relationship between the risk classes and the severity and frequency of the hazard is shown in Table 4.6. However, the standard states that the actual form of this relationship will be sector dependent and will depend on the definitions used for the various frequency and consequence classes. The definitions of the risk classes are given in Table 4.7.

Table 4.4 Accident risk classes for military systems.

	Consequences			
Frequency	*Catastrophic*	*Critical*	*Marginal*	*Negligible*
Frequent	A	A	A	B
Probable	A	A	B	C
Occasional	A	B	C	C
Remote	B	C	C	D
Improbable	C	C	D	D
Incredible	D	D	D	D

Table 4.5 Interpretation of risk classes for military systems.

Risk class	*Interpretation*
A	Intolerable
B	Undesirable, and will only be accepted when risk reduction is impracticable
C	Tolerable with the endorsement of the Project Safety Review Committee
D	Tolerable with the endorsement of the normal project reviews

Table 4.6 Risk classifications from draft IEC 1508.

	Consequences			
Frequency	*Catastrophic*	*Critical*	*Marginal*	*Negligible*
Frequent	I	I	I	II
Probable	I	I	II	III
Occasional	I	II	III	III
Remote	II	III	III	IV
Improbable	III	III	IV	IV
Incredible	IV	IV	IV	IV

Table 4.7 Interpretation of risk classes from draft IEC 1508.

Risk class	*Interpretation*
I	Intolerable risk
II	Undesirable risk, and tolerable only if risk reduction is impracticable or if the costs are grossly disproportionate to the improvement gained
III	Tolerable risk if the cost of risk reduction would exceed the improvement gained
IV	Negligible risk

It can be seen that the assignment and definition of risk classes in military systems is directly equivalent to that found in the proposed IEC standard. This similarity reflects the great efforts being made to harmonize standards and guidelines throughout the world.

Tables 4.4 and 4.6 clearly illustrate the advantages associated with the use of risk classes. They allow standards and guidelines to deal with a small number of risk classes rather than to attempt to provide guidance for each combination of severity and frequency.

4.5 The acceptability of risk

The definitions of risk classes given in the previous section show that some levels of risk are simply not acceptable. It is clearly not satisfactory to have a hazard that could have catastrophic consequences and that could occur frequently. However, it may be acceptable to have a situation where an accident with negligible consequences could occur frequently, or where a potentially critical or catastrophic accident is improbable or even remote. The acceptability of a given level of risk is determined by the benefits associated with that risk, and by the amount of effort that would be required to reduce it.

The draft of IEC 1508 divides levels of risk into three ranges, as shown in Figure 4.3. The uppermost band of this diagram represents hazards where the risk is so great that it is deemed to be intolerable and cannot be justified on any grounds. In contrast, the lowermost band represents hazards where the risk is so small that it can generally be neglected. Between these two bands lies a third classification where a risk, though not insignificant, *may* be acceptable under certain circumstances. The criterion for acceptance of a particular risk is based on a decision as to whether it is **as low as is reasonably practicable** (ALARP), bearing in mind the benefits of the system and the costs of any further risk reduction. A risk level satisfying this criterion is termed the **tolerable risk** for the given application. A risk within the ALARP band is never acceptable if it can be easily reduced. Therefore a proposed system that poses even a very small risk may be judged unacceptable if that risk is unjustifiable. Conversely, a system that has a significant risk may satisfy the requirement if it offers sufficient benefits, and if further reduction of the risk is considered impracticable.

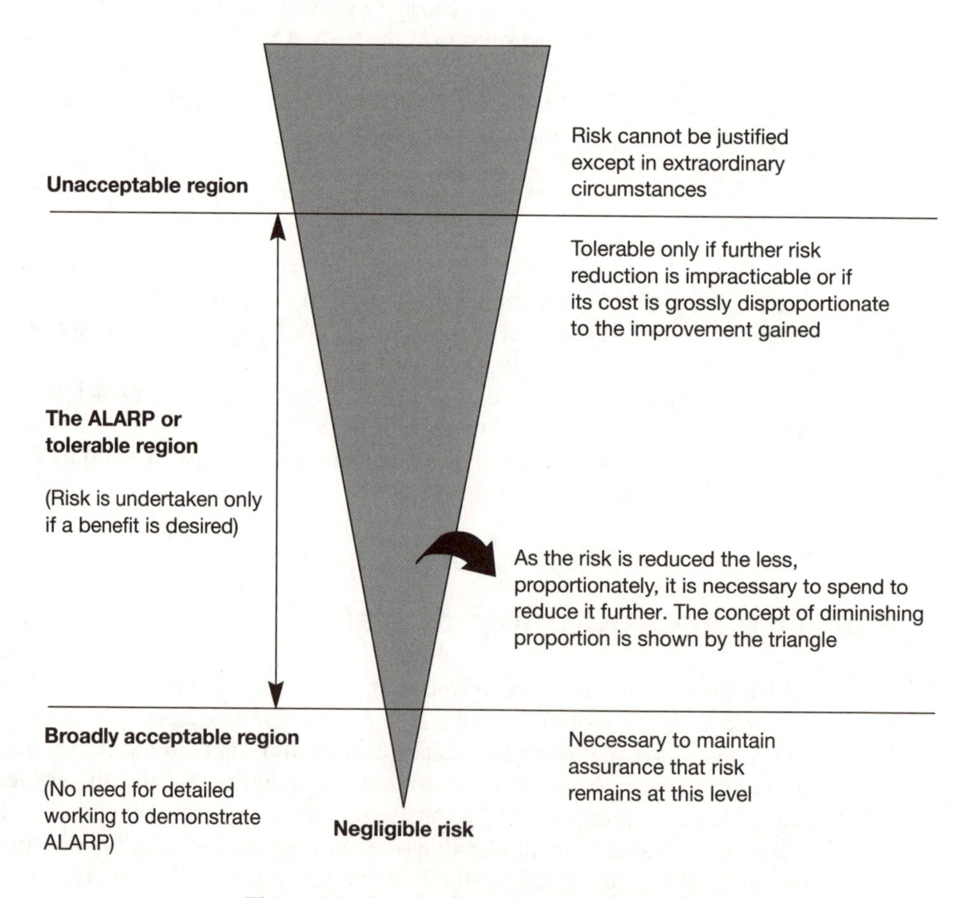

Figure 4.3 Levels of risk from draft IEC 1508.

The ALARP region of Figure 4.3 may be thought of as a zone where a system may be acceptable provided that it is possible to show that the risk is ALARP. Inevitably, a decision as to whether it is practicable to further reduce the risk associated with a particular application is a matter of professional judgement. In highly critical applications, it is the certifying authority that ultimately determines the acceptability of a given system. In reaching their decision they are likely to take into account the standards used within their industry, as well as the arguments put forward by the design team. In applications where the risks are high, those responsible will be expected to expend great effort, and possibly money, in reducing that risk. In lower-risk applications the effort that is expected from the developers is proportionately less. This concept is represented in Figure 4.3 by the width of the triangle.

If Tables 4.5 and 4.7 are considered together with Figure 4.3 it is clear that in each case the most serious risk class corresponds to the region of intolerable risk; the least serious risk class corresponds to the region of negligible risk; and the two remaining classes correspond to the upper and lower bounds of the ALARP region.

The task of producing a safety-critical system can be seen as a process of **risk management** or **risk reduction** (Bell and Reinert, 1993). The equipment under control can be considered to represent a certain level of risk in the absence of any protective measures taken by the system designer. If this level of risk is so low that it may be considered to be negligible, then no further action is required to reduce it further. If this is not the case, safety features must be incorporated within the design to reduce the risk to a level at or below that judged to be tolerable for the application. This process is illustrated in Figure 4.4.

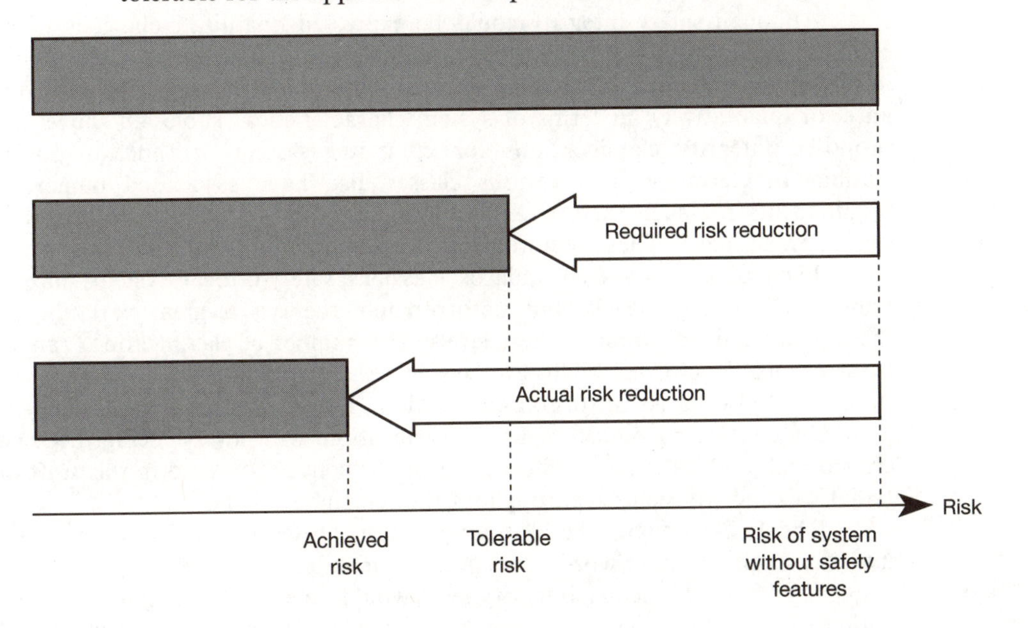

Figure 4.4 The process of risk reduction.

4.6 Levels of integrity

From the discussions in this and earlier chapters, it is clear that the importance of safe operation differs widely between applications. Although safety is always significant, the relative importance of safety in different situations is clearly related to the risks involved. Both an electric toaster and a nuclear reactor protection system should be adequately safe, but the definition of 'adequate' would be different in these two cases.

One could view the differing safety requirements between projects in terms of the level of risk reduction required. In projects associated with potentially high-risk situations a great deal of risk reduction is required in order to achieve a tolerable level of risk. In order to provide a high degree of risk reduction, the risk management mechanisms must themselves be highly dependable. In situations where a relatively low degree of risk reduction is needed, the requirements of the safety systems are less stringent. In such a situation financial considerations will inevitably preclude many techniques that might be appropriate for a more demanding application.

Differing requirements for safety systems lead to the concept of **levels of integrity** for safety-critical systems. In this context the word 'integrity' is concerned with 'safety integrity', which may be defined as follows:

> ***Safety integrity*** *is the likelihood of a safety-related system satisfactorily performing the required safety functions under all the stated conditions within a stated period of time.*

Although safety integrity could be expressed quantitatively, it is more common to allocate a system to one of a number of safety integrity levels. These in turn may be defined either quantitatively, in terms of measures of performance, or qualitatively, in terms of system characteristics. Table 4.8 shows the proposed integrity classifications for computer systems in nuclear power stations in Germany. The various classes also have associated numerical requirements for such factors as 'failures per year' and 'failure probability during an accident'. These requirements are illustrated in Table 4.9.

Each of the various standards classifies safety-critical systems into a number of integrity levels, but unfortunately there is a great variation in the number and definition of these levels. The number of classifications ranges from a single level to an eight-level system, and the numbering or naming of these levels also varies in form and direction. The international community is gradually converging on a four-level classification, with level 1 being the least critical and level 4 the most critical. This is the convention used in the draft of IEC 1508, and will be used throughout the remainder of this text.

The IEC standard sets out target failure rates for each of the safety integrity levels. In other words, it defines the maximum number of times that a system built to a particular integrity level would be expected to fail in a given period of time. In doing so the standard differentiates between two classes of system that are used in different ways. The first class covers systems that

Table 4.8 Proposed integrity classifications of computer systems in nuclear power stations in Germany.

Class	*Functional requirement*	*Systems involved*
I	Highest requirements of nuclear safety	Systems that release automatic actions for protection of human life and environment
II	High requirements of nuclear safety	Systems that act for the protection of human life and environment by • guiding safety variables under abnormal conditions • causing operator actions deterministically
III	Normal requirements of nuclear safety	Systems that • limit plant variables to specific values • avoid scrams • report disturbances in systems of class I and II
IV	High requirements of plant safety	Systems that • release actions automatically for protection of persons in the plant • protect important parts of the plant
V	High requirements of plant availability	Systems that • increase plant availability • protect normal parts of the plant
VI	High functional requirements	Systems that serve for optimal plant operation, e.g. with respect to efficiency or manœuvrability
VII	Component-related control	Systems for simple requirements

Table 4.9 Proposed requirements for the integrity classes of nuclear systems in Germany.

Class	*I*	*II*	*III*	*IV*	*V*	*VI*	*VII*
Maximum unavailability	10^{-5}	10^{-4}	10^{-2}	10^{-4}	10^{-2}	10^{-1}	10^{-1}
Maximum unavailability for safety-related systems	10^{-7}	10^{-5}	10^{-4}	10^{-5}			
Maximum failure probability per year	10^{-4}	10^{-2}		10^{-2}			
Maximum probability of dangerous failure per year	10^{-7}	10^{-5}	10^{-4}	10^{-5}			
Maximum probability of failure during an accident	10^{-6}	10^{-4}	10^{-3}	10^{-4}	10^{-2}		

operate in a 'continuous mode'. Failure rates for this group are expressed in **failures per year**, although discussion documents produced during the development of this standard gave rates in failures per hour. The difference between these two sets of units represents a factor of approximately 10^4, and so a knowledge of the units being used is vital. The second class covers systems that operate in what is termed a 'demand mode'. This classification includes applications such as shutdown systems, which are called upon only when needed. Failure rates for this group are expressed in terms of **failures on demand**, referring to the probability that the system will fail to operate when called upon to do so. Discussion documents for the standard referred to the two classes as 'continuous control systems' and 'protection systems', but later versions have adopted more precise definitions. Target failure rates for the four safety integrity levels are given in Table 4.10. It can be seen that the chosen sets of units have the characteristic that the numerical values of the ranges for the two classes are identical. This fact should not be allowed to mask the distinction between these two figures.

In Chapter 1 we noted that the production of safety-critical systems may be considered as a problem of fault management. We also saw that faults may be classified as random, as in the case of random hardware failures, or systematic, as in hardware or software design faults. When determining the safety integrity of a system it is necessary to consider its performance in respect of both these areas. We may therefore identify two elements that contribute to the overall safety integrity of the system:

> ***Hardware integrity*** *is that part of the safety integrity relating to dangerous random hardware failures.*
>
> ***Systematic integrity*** *is that part of the safety integrity relating to dangerous systematic failures.*

Systematic integrity covers all aspects of the design of the system and therefore includes considerations of hardware and software. However, in some cases it is appropriate to look at the software in isolation, leading to a third classification:

> ***Software integrity*** *is that part of the safety integrity relating to dangerous software failures.*

Table 4.10 Target failure rates for the safety integrity levels of draft IEC 1508.

Safety integrity level	*Continuous mode of operation (probability of a dangerous failure per year)*	*Demand mode of operation (probability of failure to perform its designed function on demand)*
4	$\geqslant 10^{-5}$ to $< 10^{-4}$	$\geqslant 10^{-5}$ to $< 10^{-4}$
3	$\geqslant 10^{-4}$ to $< 10^{-3}$	$\geqslant 10^{-4}$ to $< 10^{-3}$
2	$\geqslant 10^{-3}$ to $< 10^{-2}$	$\geqslant 10^{-3}$ to $< 10^{-2}$
1	$\geqslant 10^{-2}$ to $< 10^{-1}$	$\geqslant 10^{-2}$ to $< 10^{-1}$

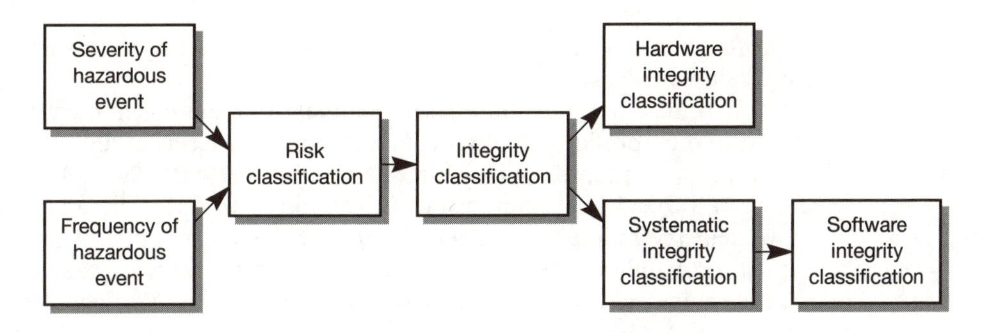

Figure 4.5 Assignment of integrity levels.

The assignment of an integrity level to a system, or part of a system, is based on the classification of the risks associated with it. Following the assignment of an overall system safety integrity level to a system or subsystem, individual integrity levels may be assigned to different aspects of the unit. For example, a software integrity level might be assigned to define the importance of the correctness of the software elements. This in turn will determine the development methods used and the level of testing performed. The process of assigning integrity levels is illustrated in Figure 4.5.

Clearly, the assignment of safety integrity levels is related to the risk class associated with an application. However, it is important to remember the distinction between these two classifications. *Risk* is a measure of the likelihood, and consequences, of a hazardous event. *Safety integrity* is a measure of the likelihood of the safety system correctly performing its tasks.

Allocation of integrity levels

The various standards give useful guidance on the process of assigning integrity levels to systems, or subsystems, that are safety critical. Draft IEC 1508 gives target failure rates for the various integrity levels but does not specify how these should be allocated to specific applications. This is because the IEC standard is intended to be generic in nature, rather than tied to any particular industry. The standard does, however, give guidance on the design and development techniques appropriate for each integrity level.

The process of assigning integrity levels to particular applications is considered within industry-specific standards. Being concerned with only a single application area, these can give detailed information on the relevant classifications for typical system components. This process was illustrated in Table 4.8, which shows how integrity classifications are assigned to various systems within nuclear power stations in Germany. Once an integrity level has been assigned to a system, its design and method of development must ensure that it meets the needs of that level. In many cases the standards define the requirements of the various integrity levels in a manner appropriate to the particular industry (as in Table 4.9), and set out development methods that must be used for each level.

In some cases standards specify an integrity requirement directly in terms of a maximum probability of failure, rather than in terms of an integrity level. This practice is adopted in civil aircraft standards (FAR, 1993; JAR, 1994), as shown in Table 4.11. Comparison of this table with Table 4.1 and Figure 4.1 shows that the failure requirements represent the specification of an allowable hazard probability class for each of the hazard severity categories. The requirements could therefore be expressed as 'any failure that could result in a catastrophic condition must be extremely improbable; any failure that could result in a hazardous condition must be extremely remote;' and so on.

The requirements set out in Table 4.11 define the performance that a civil aircraft equipment manufacturer must achieve if his products are to be acceptable. From this it can be seen that if failure of a piece of equipment could result in a 'major' incident, it must be expected to fail at most once in every 100 000 hours of service. If, on the other hand, its effects could be 'catastrophic', resulting in loss of the aircraft, it must be expected to fail not more than once in every 1000 million hours. This latter figure represents less than one failure in every 100 000 years of operation. Note that even in this most critical situation the standard does not say that the equipment must not fail. No system can guarantee freedom from failure. The standard simply defines acceptable levels for the dependability of the system.

Table 4.11 Relationship between the severity of an effect and its allowable probability for civil aircraft systems.

Category	*Severity of effect*	*Maximum probability per operating hour*
Normal		10^{0}
		10^{-1}
Nuisance		10^{-2}
Minor	Operating limitation; emergency procedures	10^{-3}
		10^{-4}
Major	Significant reduction in safety margins; difficult for crew to cope with adverse conditions; passenger injuries	10^{-5}
		10^{-6}
Hazardous	Large reductions in safety margins; crew extended because of workload or environmental conditions. Serious injury or death of a small number of occupants	10^{-7}
		10^{-8}
Catastrophic	Multiple deaths, usually with loss of aircraft	10^{-9}

Although the maximum probability figures for civil aircraft are normally expressed in failures per hour of operation, as in Table 4.11, it is interesting to compare the various ranges of probabilities with the integrity levels defined in the draft of the IEC 1508 standard. If allowance is made for the different units used (failures per hour as against failures per year), it can be seen that events that could result in a 'major' incident must have a probability corresponding to the failure of a system of category 1, those resulting in a 'hazardous' incident must have a probability corresponding to category 3, and those that could be 'catastrophic' must fall within the high range of category 4.

Achievable levels of integrity

We have seen that the allocation of an integrity level to a system or subsystem imposes requirements upon it in terms of its dependability. In later chapters we shall look at several methods that may be used to increase the dependability of a system in order to meet these targets.

In developing a safety-critical system it is necessary not only to achieve a high level of integrity, but also to be able to demonstrate that this has been done. Unfortunately, the latter often proves to be difficult, or perhaps even impossible, in highly critical systems. We have seen, for example, that aircraft systems are often required to have a probability of failure corresponding to less than one failure in every 100 000 years of operation. At present we know of no method of testing a system to demonstrate this level of performance. It is therefore surprising that some engineers, such as those responsible for components of the Paris Métro system, have claimed to have achieved failure rates 1000 times better than this value (Guiho, 1990).

As the highest level of integrity of IEC 1508 is itself beyond our current abilities to demonstrate dependability, it can be argued that any system that requires a system of greater performance is simply too dangerous. It is therefore becoming generally accepted that it is inappropriate to specify systems requiring an integrity above this level. We shall return to look at methods of investigating the dependability of a system in Chapter 12.

4.7 The view of society and ethical considerations

Whereas the process of hazard analysis is a logical, mechanistic procedure, the study of risks inevitably involves the use of judgement and opinion. When one assigns an integrity level to a system, or defines a tolerable failure rate, one is defining how much effort should be expended in improving the safety of the arrangement. In so doing, one is placing a value, either monetary or otherwise, on human life or suffering. Decisions on such matters are not simply a matter of engineering judgement – they must reflect the view of society.

Unfortunately, society's views on matters relating to safety and risk are not straightforward. Our opinions are often unpredictable and 'illogical'. However, they are no less valid because they are not based on an identifiable set of rules.

It is well known that the value placed on a human life can vary enormously, depending on the situation. If we consider the compensation awarded by courts to the dependants of people killed in accidents, we see that the legal system does not consider all lives to be equally valuable. The monetary value of such a payment is likely to be very different in cases where the victim is a baby; a child; a young adult; a breadwinner; or a senior citizen. The courts often use some kind of formula to determine the compensation to be paid in a particular case. This allows a value to be calculated on the basis of predetermined criteria and helps to provide a system that appears consistent and 'fair'. Factors considered within such calculations might include an estimate of lost income or the victim's commitments. The use of such a formula appears to remove the need for value judgements in determining appropriate levels of compensation. In fact, the formula simply formalizes a particular set of value judgements that were made by its creators.

There are also large differences in the value placed on the *preservation* of life in different circumstances. If one looks at decisions that have been made that have safety implications it is possible to determine the value being assigned to the preservation of life. Thus, a decision to spend a certain amount of money in order to protect a given number of people gives a minimum 'monetary value' to their lives. Similarly, a decision not to perform work that would protect a given number of people because it is too expensive, places a maximum value on those lives. Looking at examples of such cases it is possible to assess perceptions of human worth in a number of areas. Such estimates of the monetary value placed on a life give values that vary by a factor of more than 1000.

Society's perception of risk is greatly affected by the nature of that risk. Accidents in which large numbers of people are killed simultaneously are seen as being more serious than those in which a similar number of people are killed individually. Thus a train or air crash causes great discussion and media coverage, whereas a larger number of people being killed on the roads goes unreported and largely unnoticed.

One of the factors affecting our fear of events relates to our ability to control the situation. Many people are horrified by the possibility of a nuclear accident that might pollute the surrounding area for many miles. The much larger risk of being knocked down by a car usually produces much less concern. In the latter case we feel (often incorrectly) that we are in control of our own destiny. In the former case we feel helpless to protect ourselves.

An additional influence on society's view of the importance of a given event is related to its emotional impact. An accident that results in the death of a child is always tragic, but if it occurs in front of a television camera its emotional impact might be felt throughout the nation. A similar effect relates to projects that are the subject of great national interest. The failure of a space shuttle flight probably risks fewer lives than that of a commercial airliner, but the loss of the former would be seen as a national disaster.

It is clear that the assessment of risk is not a straightforward process. In many cases the issues are beyond the scope of engineering and must take into account considerations of emotions and ethics. It is for this reason that the various standards and guidelines are indispensable, for although they do not absolve the engineer of responsibility in this area, they do provide valuable guidance. Various learned institutions have also produced documents that offer guidance in this area. Of note are those from the Institution of Electrical Engineers (IEE, 1992), the Royal Society (1992) and the Engineering Council (1993). The last of these provides a 10-point 'code of professional practice' on risk issues, as shown in Table 4.12. The document gives guidance on each of the points within this table, as well as other matters related to risk.

Absolute safety is not an option. If the elimination of all hazards was seen as a necessary requirement, then no vehicles would move, no structures would be built and no appliances would be sold. Our goal is to produce a system that is *adequately safe*, given the benefits that it offers. In many cases minimum levels of integrity are set out in standards relating to the products concerned and are enforced by some regulatory authority. For the engineer these minimum requirements for integrity form a baseline for decisions on the adequacy of the safety of systems being designed. However, the engineer also has a professional and moral responsibility to make systems *as safe as is reasonably possible*. The remainder of this text discusses methods of achieving this goal.

Table 4.12 The Engineering Council's code of professional practice on risk issues.

1	Professional responsibility	Exercise reasonable professional skill and care
2	Law	Know about and comply with the law
3	Conduct	Act in accordance with the codes of conduct
4	Approach	Take a systematic approach to risk issues
5	Judgement	Use professional judgement and experience
6	Communication	Communicate within your organization
7	Management	Contribute effectively to corporate risk management
8	Evaluation	Assess the risk implications of alternatives
9	Professional development	Keep up to date by seeking education and training
10	Public awareness	Encourage public understanding of risk issues

REFERENCES

Bell R. and Reinert D. (1993). Risk and system integrity concepts for safety-related control systems. *Microprocessors and Microsystems*, **17**(1), 3–15

Engineering Council (1993). *Guidelines on Risk Issues*. London: Engineering Council

FAR (1993). *Federation Aviation Regulation 25.1309: Equipment, Systems and Installations*. USA: Office of the Federal Register National Archives and Records Administration

Guiho G. (1990). *The Vital Coded Processor*. Presentation to the meeting of the IFIP Working Group 10.4, Martinique

IEC (1995). Draft International Standard 1508 *Functional Safety: Safety-Related System*. Geneva: International Electrotechnical Commission

IEE (1992). *Safety-Related Systems: Professional Brief*. London: Institution of Electrical Engineers

JAR (1994). *Joint Aviation Requirements 25.1309: Equipment, Systems and Installations*. Cheltenham: Civil Aviation Authority

Leveson N.G. (1986). Software safety: why, what, and how. *ACM Comput. Surv.*, **18**(2), 25–69

MoD (1995). Draft Defence Standard 00-56 Issue 2 *Safety Management Requirements for Defence Systems Containing Programmable Electronics, Part 1: Requirements*. Glasgow: Directorate of Standardization

Royal Society (1992). *Risk: Analysis, Perception and Management*. London: Royal Society

RTCA/EUROCAE (1992). *Software Considerations in Airborne Systems and Equipment Certification*. RTCA/DO-178B; EUROCAE/ED-12B. Washington: Radio Technical Commission for Aeronautics. Paris: European Organisation for Civil Aviation Electronics

FURTHER READING

Brazendale J. and Bell R. (1994). Safety-related control and protection systems: standards update. *Comput. Control Eng. J.*, **5**(1), 6–12

Leveson N.G. (1995). *Safeware: System Safety and Computers*. Reading, MA: Addison-Wesley

PROBLEMS

4.1 Explain the difference between the terms 'hazard' and 'risk'.

4.2 What is meant by the term 'accident' and how do definitions of this term vary? How is an accident different from a mishap?

4.3 What factors contribute to the risk associated with an accident?

4.4 Failure of a particular component could result in the collapse of a building and the death of 50 people. It is estimated that the component will fail once in every 2000 years. Give a numerical estimate of the risk associated with this component.

4.5 A disease claims the lives of 100 people per year out of a population of 300 million. What is the probability of being killed by the disease? What is the risk to the society as a whole?
4.6 What is the purpose of dividing severity and frequency measures into classes? How is this process achieved?
4.7 Why do the severity and risk classes differ between the various standards?
4.8 What is meant by a 'catastrophic' event in a civil aircraft? How does this differ from the meaning of the same term, when used within military systems standards?
4.9 Define the term 'failures on demand'. To what form of system is this measurement usually applied?
4.10 What units are usually adopted to express the frequency of failure of avionics systems?
4.11 The frequency of failure of an avionics system may be divided into a number of classes. List these classes and give the failure rates corresponding to each.
4.12 In military systems the frequency of failure is often defined by classes that are defined qualitatively. What is meant by 'improbable' and 'incredible'?
4.13 How does the draft of the IEC 1508 standard define the six levels of hazard frequency?
4.14 What is the function of a 'risk class' (risk level or risk factor)?
4.15 Describe the risk classification system given in the draft of the IEC 1508 standard. How does this system relate to that used within military systems?
4.16 What factors determine the acceptability of risk?
4.17 Explain the meaning, and significance, of the term 'ALARP'.
4.18 Define the term 'tolerable risk'.
4.19 Explain the concept of risk reduction.
4.20 Define the term 'safety integrity'.
4.21 Describe the classification of integrity used within the draft of IEC 1508.
4.22 Identify the two main elements that contribute to the overall safety integrity of a system.
4.23 Explain the distinction between risk classes and safety integrity levels.
4.24 Why is it thought to be inadvisable to specify systems requiring levels of integrity greater than those defined within the draft of IEC 1508?
4.25 Discuss the role of engineering judgement in the determination of acceptable levels of risk and integrity.
4.26 Why is the view of society as a whole of importance in determining the acceptability of risk? What problems does this produce?
4.27 Why is it necessary to place a value on human life and suffering? Who determines this value?
4.28 What factors affect our perceptions of risk?
4.29 How do standards assist in decisions associated with the acceptability of risk?
4.30 What is the engineer's responsibility with regard to safety?

5 Developing Safety-Critical Systems

CHAPTER CONTENTS

5.1 Introduction

In previous chapters we considered the identification and evaluation of the hazards associated with a proposed system, and the generation of safety requirements. Following these phases of a project it is necessary to implement the system so as to minimize risk and to achieve these requirements. System safety can be achieved in a number of ways and there exists an order of precedence for applying various design techniques (Leveson, 1986).

The preferred method of ensuring a safe design is to produce a system that is **intrinsically safe**. Such a system is incapable of releasing sufficient energy to cause harm, or of causing harmful exposure to radiation or chemicals, during either normal or abnormal operation. In many cases an intrinsically safe system is not possible, or is impractical. In such a situation the next best solution is to adopt design techniques that prevent or minimize the occurrence of hazards. This approach includes the use of automatic control techniques and the use of **interlocks** and **guards**, as described in Chapter 2.

Next in the order of preference is an approach that seeks to control hazards when they occur. Such techniques include the use of failsafe devices, damage control and containment. Last in our order of precedence come design techniques that aim to reduce the impact of hazards. These include the use of warning devices and the training of staff in emergency procedures.

Invariably, the production of an intrinsically safe system is closely linked with the nature of the process itself and is not within the scope of the computer engineer. This being the case, most of the material within this chapter, and the remainder of this book, is concerned with techniques that seek to prevent or minimize the associated hazards through the use of appropriate design techniques.

This chapter begins by looking at the lifecycle of a typical safety-critical system and at different methods of modelling its various stages. It then describes the impact of safety considerations on each development phase by considering the 'safety lifecycle' of the system. Methods appropriate to the production of a critical system are then discussed, with particular emphasis being placed on the importance of the specification phase. 'Designing for safety' forms the next major topic, which includes an overview of both top-level and detailed design methods. This section also includes a description of hierarchical design techniques. One of the issues to be considered in the design of any system is maintainability. Here we look at the implications of designing a system for ease of maintenance, and at some of the possible conflicts between maintainability and other system requirements. A topic closely related to safety concerns the characteristics of the people associated with the development and use of critical systems. In this chapter we look briefly at the vast subject of 'human factors', and consider some implications for system design and development methods. Having considered various factors affecting the design of safety-critical systems, the chapter concludes by discussing safety analysis and the role of management within the development process. This includes a look at management structures and at training requirements for safety-critical system developers.

5.2 Lifecycle models

In Chapter 1 we looked briefly at the use of lifecycle models as a means of describing the development of a safety-critical system. We will now look in more detail at such models and discuss their uses and importance.

Over the years a number of models have been devised to describe the various phases of a development project. The models identify the various components of the project and may indicate interdependencies or interrelationships. Each of the models has its own characteristics and advantages, and often different models are used for different purposes.

An example of a widely used development lifecycle model is the 'V' diagram, which was shown in a simplified form in Chapter 1. This model may be expanded to indicate the outcome of each phase – the 'deliverable'. It may also show the flow of information between phases. An example of a relatively simple diagram is shown in Figure 5.1. This shows that although the primary flow of information follows a simple progression from one phase to another, data from early phases is used at a later stage. For example,

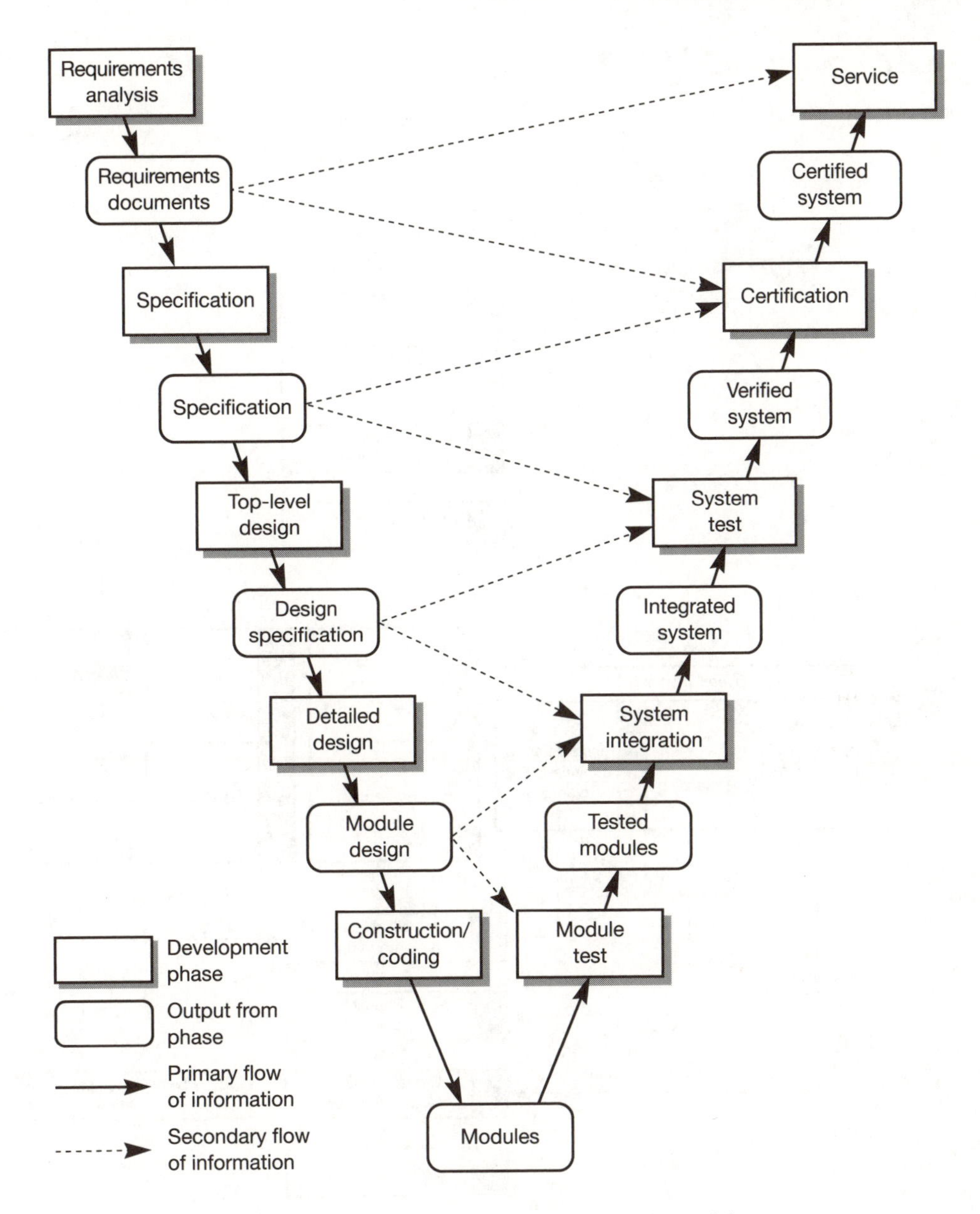

Figure 5.1 A 'V' development lifecycle model.

information from the specification forms a vital part of the testing and certification activities. Similarly, module design information is required in module testing and the system integration phase.

Companies often evolve a development model that is based on a 'V' diagram, but which is tailored to match their development methodology. However, the diagram is always a simplification of the actual development

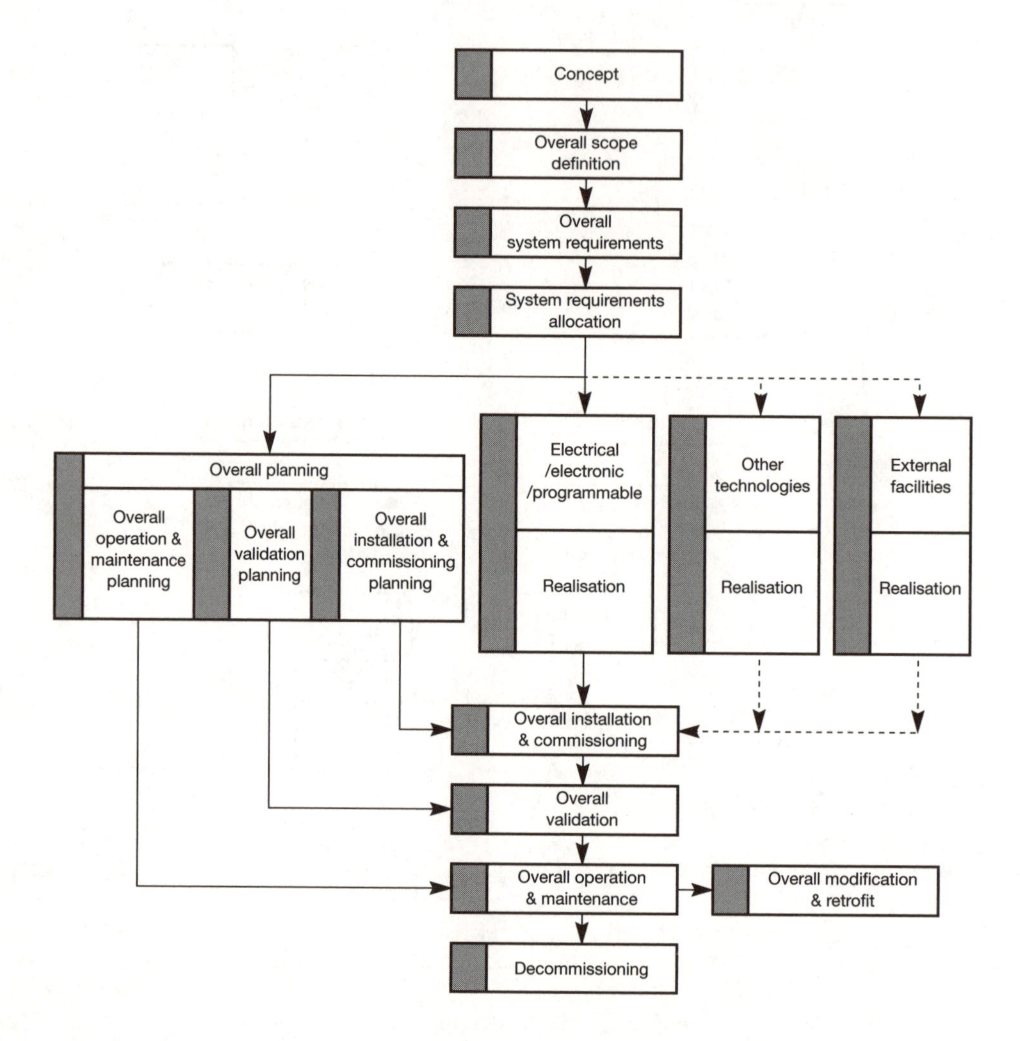

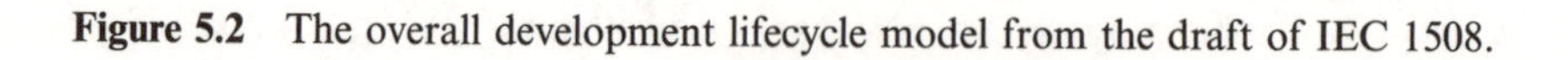
Figure 5.2 The overall development lifecycle model from the draft of IEC 1508.

process, as it does not show the inevitable iteration that occurs within and between lifecycle phases. Models have been developed in an attempt to indicate this iteration, but often these become too complex to be useful.

The 'V' model clearly illustrates the outcome of each phase of the development process, and also indicates the flow of information between phases. However, it does not show the amount of work involved in each stage or when that effort will be required. It also tends to divide the project into discrete stages and does not cope well with activities that occur simultaneously or take place throughout many phases.

Another widely used lifecycle model is that given in the draft of IEC 1508 and shown in Figure 5.2. This standard is primarily concerned with those aspects of the system that are based on electrical, electronic or programmable electronic technologies. However, it also considers sections that rely on other technologies (such as mechanical or hydraulic components) and facilities that are external to the system (the significance of these facilities will become clear in the next section). The model separates the realization of the system into three sections to represent these aspects of the implementation. It also clearly identifies various activities related to the planning of the later stages of the development process. These tasks are correctly shown as taking place in parallel with the realization phases of the project.

The IEC model covers all aspects of a project, from the conception of a system to its eventual decommissioning. It also considers the impact of modifications during the system's life. The standard describes in detail the activities to be performed during each phase of the lifecycle and outlines the inputs and outputs of each phase.

The use of lifecycle models is well established within project management and as a tool for quality assurance. In safety-critical applications such models may also be used to focus attention on the safety aspects of the project by using a model that concentrates on these elements.

5.3 The safety lifecycle

In addition to the overall lifecycle model described in the previous section, the draft of IEC 1508 also describes an overall safety lifecycle, as shown in Figure 5.3. This again covers all aspects of a system's life, from conception to decommissioning, and also considers the diverse aspects of its realization. The form of the safety lifecycle is very similar to that of the overall system lifecycle, with the addition of a phase concerned with hazard and risk analysis. The various phases of the safety lifecycle may be mapped on to the corresponding phases of the system lifecycle, with the additional hazard and risk analysis phase forming part of the overall system requirements phase. As with all such models it is a simplification of the real development process, and in particular 'assessment' and 'verification' activities are not included for reasons of clarity. Such activities take place within all phases of the safety lifecycle. Boxes 10 and 11 of the figure

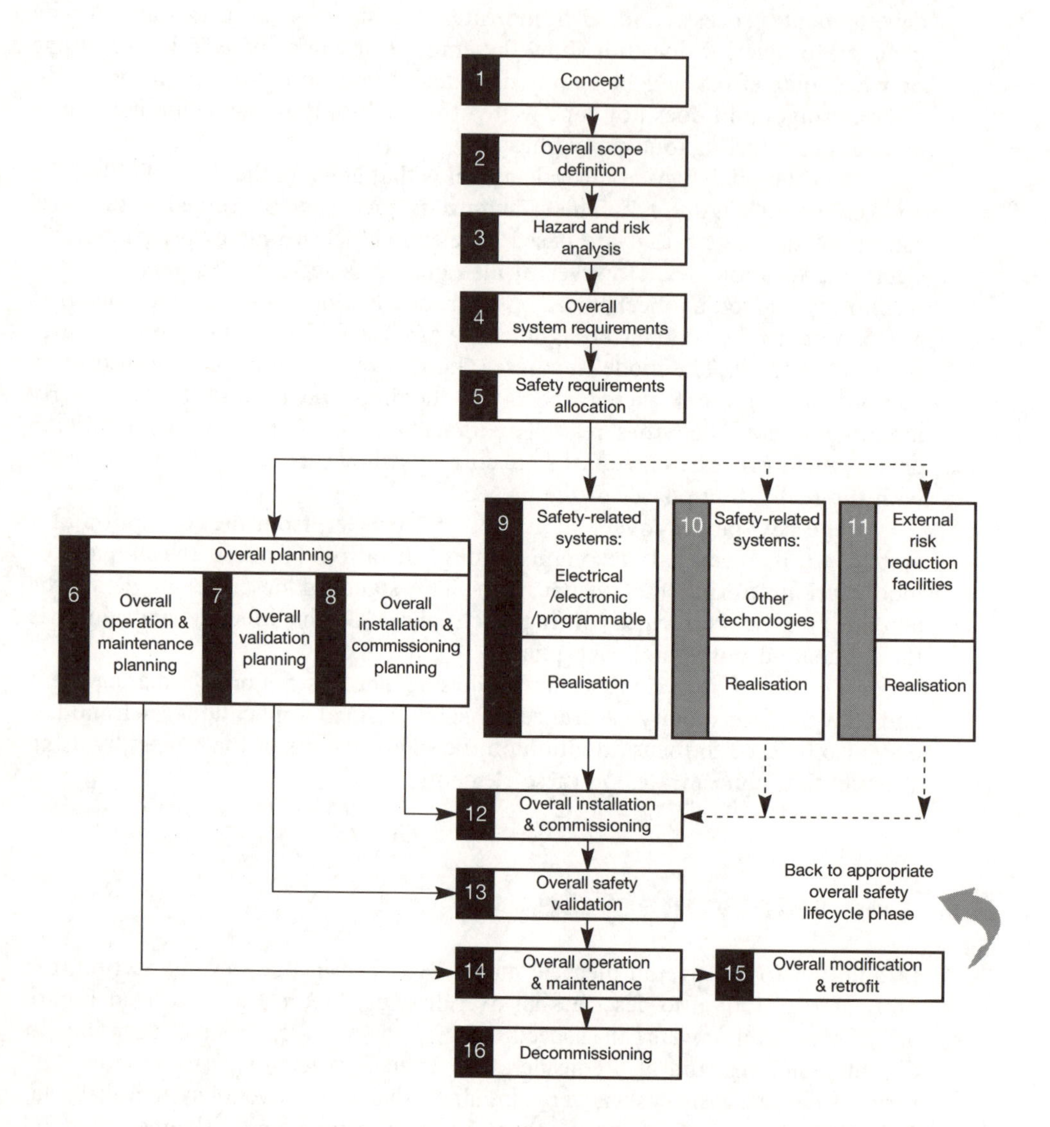

Figure 5.3 The overall safety lifecycle.

are shaded differently from the others to indicate that the standard does not deal in detail with these phases.

The importance of the safety lifecycle is that it focuses attention on the safety aspects of each phase of the development process. The standard defines the lifecycle as:

> *'The necessary activities involving safety-related systems, occurring during a period of time that starts at the concept phase of a project and finishes when any safety-related systems are no longer available for use.'*

The various phases of the safety lifecycle are represented by numbered rectangular boxes within the diagram. Each phase has an input, a defined function and an associated output or 'deliverable'. The deliverable from one phase represents the input to the next. Each phase also has an associated set of safety activities. Verification and assessment take place within each phase to ensure that these activities are performed correctly. One of the key features of this approach is that it provides a mechanism for verifying the results of each of the activities relevant to the safety of the system. For simplicity, the model shows hazard and risk analysis as a single phase near the beginning of the project. This phase corresponds to the preliminary hazard and risk analysis process. From our discussions in Chapters 3 and 4 we know that hazard and risk analysis is a continuing activity that goes on throughout the development process.

So far within this text we have concentrated on the activities corresponding to phases 1–4 of Figure 5.3. These are concerned with determining the overall characteristics of the system and looking at its safety implications. The model promotes a 'risk-based' approach to system development, whereby the results of the preliminary hazard and risk analysis determine the techniques adopted within the other parts of the project. Conceptually, the hazard and risk analysis associated with phase 3 of the model is used within phase 4 to determine the appropriate integrity level for the system. This will in turn determine the form of the other phases of the model. Thus, although the model can be used for developing systems of differing levels of integrity, the activities represented by the boxes may be very different.

Phase 5 of the model corresponds to the 'top-level design' aspects of the project. Within this phase the various safety requirements identified in phase 4 are allocated to appropriate safety-related systems. It should be noted that in general these will include systems based on a variety of technologies. This text is primarily concerned with safety-critical systems based on the use of programmable electronic systems (PESs). However, much of the material is also of relevance to systems that use non-programmable electronic and electrical techniques. We will see in Chapter 6 that there is a strong argument for using the simplest technology possible for providing safety features. Therefore, if a particular function can be achieved using simple non-programmable electronics rather than a computer-based system, this would be the preferred option. This does not imply that software itself is undesirable, but simply that software-based systems are inherently complex. High complexity should be avoided wherever possible, whether that complexity is in the form of hardware or software.

In some cases, a safety feature is best provided by a mechanical or hydraulic arrangement rather than an electronic approach. Consequently, phase 5 involves the task of allocating safety features to the most appropriate subsystems, which in general will include a combination of both electronic and non-electronic technologies. Also within this phase is the task of identifying other techniques that could be used to reduce the risks associated with the application. These might include, for example, the erection of a fence to keep people away from a dangerous area, or the posting of warning notices. Within IEC 1508 such activities are referred to as **external risk reduction facilities**.

The safety of a system is determined not only by its design and development, but also by how it is installed, used and maintained. For this reason an overall strategy for commissioning, operation and maintenance is established at an early stage in the development process, at a time when it can influence the detailed design of the system. These activities correspond to phases 6 and 8 of the model. Also at an early stage a scheme is devised for validating the completed system, and this is included within the model as phase 7.

Boxes 9, 10 and 11 of the safety lifecycle are concerned with the design and implementation of the various safety-related systems and features. The diagram in Figure 5.3 divides this phase into three components: box 9 deals with safety-related systems that are based on electrical, electronic or programmable technologies; 10 deals with safety-related systems based on other technologies; and 11 covers external risk reduction techniques. In this text we are primarily concerned with systems that fall within the first of these three categories, and in later chapters we will be considering various aspects of the design and implementation of safety-related systems.

Following the implementation of the various safety-related systems and features, these are combined during installation (phase 12), and the complete system then begins a process of validation and, if necessary, certification (phase 13). The operation and maintenance stages of the system's life are covered by phase 14 and any modification or retrofitting by phase 15. The eventual decommissioning of the system is addressed by phase 16.

5.4 Development methods

The main elements of the development of a safety-critical system are, in general, similar to those of less critical units. However, in critical applications the development process is dominated by a need to produce and demonstrate dependability. Consequently, each phase is carefully structured and documented to ensure that it is performed correctly.

In earlier sections we looked at the various elements of the development lifecycle of a safety-critical system and considered methods of modelling this process. The models described may be applied to the complete project, or to selected aspects of the work. This section attempts to give an overview of the techniques involved and, where appropriate, detailed discussion of topics will be left until later chapters.

Requirements and hazard analysis

During the project initiation phase it is normal to produce a statement describing the broad characteristics of the proposed system. This document is often referred to as the **customer requirements**, or the **user requirements**. Some engineers call it a **user requirements specification**, although this use is unfortunate as it may lead to confusion between this document and the system specification. The requirements documentation sets out the desired functions of the proposed system and also defines any required safety features. These features, which are also termed **safety invariants**, will have been identified by a **preliminary hazard analysis**, as described in Chapter 3. These safety requirements may impose constraints on the implementation of the system at an early stage. Hazard analysis activities then continue throughout the development process.

Specification

The specification aims to define, in an unambiguous manner, the precise operation of the system. This will include not only the functionality and performance of the arrangement, but also its interaction with other systems and its operators. The specification should state the safety invariants of the system and indicate any constraints that these place on the design.

In cases where elements of the design work are subcontracted, rather than performed in-house, the specification is normally produced by the supplier in response to a requirements document supplied by the customer. The specification would normally be produced as a result of considerable consultation between the two organizations, and usually forms the basis of a legal agreement between them. At the end of the development phase the supplier will need to demonstrate that the terms of the specification have been met in all respects. In order for this to be possible, the specification must be written such that there can be an objective assessment of whether the system satisfies the specification, and therefore (hopefully) the requirements. It should also be remembered that in the case of a disagreement between the customer and the supplier, the specification may become the basis of litigation.

An ideal specification should have a number of characteristics, including that it should be:

- correct
- complete
- consistent
- unambiguous.

The importance of the correctness of a specification is perhaps self-evident, but it is also vital that it is complete. Often a system fails simply because the specification does not say what it should do in a particular situation. Such omissions are usually associated with circumstances that were not foreseen when the specification was written. An example of such a situation is illustrated below:

> *A carriage moves vertically along a guideway between two end-stops. On each end-stop is a limit switch that should prevent further travel. If neither limit switch is closed the system should allow the carriage to move in either direction under the control of other routines. If the upper limit switch is closed the system controlling the carriage should ensure that it can only move downwards and hence away from that end-stop. Similarly if the limit switch at the bottom is closed the system should ensure that the carriage can only move upwards. This arrangement is shown in Figure 5.4.*

At first sight this description would appear to describe an arrangement that, if correctly implemented, would ensure that the carriage would be safely prevented from running into either end. Indeed, it is quite likely that in many cases hardware or software produced to implement this requirement would function correctly. However, the fragment is not complete, in that it does not state what the system should do if *both* limit switches are closed simultaneously. The reason for this oversight is clear, in that under normal circumstances the carriage cannot be at both ends at once, and hence at most one switch should be activated at any time. Unfortunately, the system may not always be functioning under normal circumstances. It is interesting to consider what happens if one of the switches fails. For safety reasons the switches would be

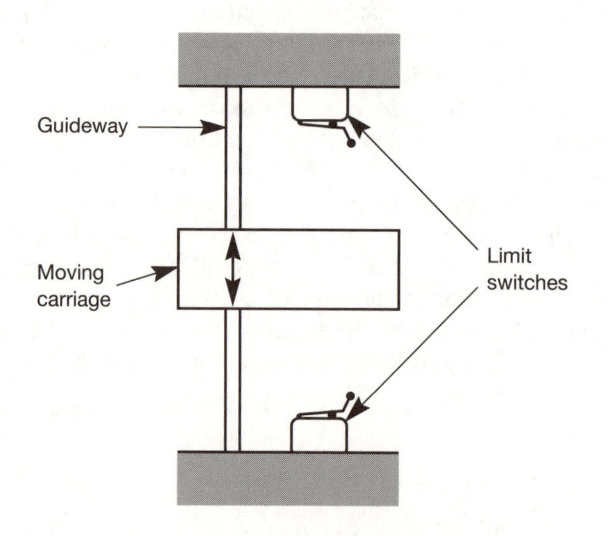

Figure 5.4 A moving carriage arrangement.

selected so that they would preferentially fail in the closed position, as this would normally be the safer option. If a switch fails closed the system would prevent the carriage from moving towards that switch, but would permit it to move in the opposite direction. If at some later time the carriage reaches the other end of the guideway, both switches will be closed simultaneously. If the system cannot deal with this circumstance, its behaviour may be unpredictable and possibly unsafe.

In this example it is quite possible that a system written to meet this specification would be safe, as it would simply prevent motion in either direction if both switches were closed. However, one can also conceive of several ways of implementing this function that are not safe. It should also be noted that simply stopping the carriage is not perhaps the best option in this situation. Should the system not take some special action in response to what is obviously a system failure? Clearly it should stop the carriage, but in most cases it should also report the fault condition.

Returning to our list of the desirable characteristics of a specification, we see that it should be 'consistent' and 'unambiguous'. The first of these simply says that it should not say different things in different places, which is self-evident. The latter requirement is also clear, but is extremely difficult to achieve.

Most specifications are written in a natural language such as English, together with necessary mathematical equations or notations. Here the term 'natural' is used to exclude other forms of communications, such as computer programming languages. Unfortunately, it is very difficult to write in a completely unambiguous way in any natural language, and examples of possible misunderstandings are common. For example:

Here is a picture of a man eating lion.

The problems associated with ambiguities within natural languages, and the inappropriateness of using English as a means of specifying the actions of a computer, are discussed in some detail by Hill (1972). This informative and highly amusing article lists numerous instances of ambiguities taken from diverse sources, including an Act of Parliament; the Book of Common Prayer; various 'official documents'; and a restaurant menu.

The ambiguity of natural languages makes it difficult to use automated methods to check specifications for components that are incorrect, incomplete or inconsistent.

The problems associated with the production of unambiguous specifications may be tackled in a number of ways. These range from techniques that provide a structured framework for the specification, to approaches based on the use of formal mathematical methods. Here we shall look briefly at some of the less formal procedures and leave formal methods until Chapter 11.

Over the years a number of **structured techniques** have been developed to reduce the problems associated with the unbridled use of natural language specifications. These techniques are often described as **semiformal**, as they lack the mathematical rigour associated with formal methods. These techniques may use textual or graphical notations, or a combination of both. The semantics of these methods restrict the variability and ambiguity of the statements used by limiting the range of expressions that may be adopted. The use of diagrams often reduces ambiguity, but may not in itself guarantee completeness.

Some computer-based tools are also available to assist in the specification phase of a project. These include **CORE**, a specification package developed by British Aerospace and System Designers (STARTS, 1989). This assembles information and allows a specification to be progressively subdivided to produce a structured, hierarchical definition of the system. This technique can be extended to provide input into the detailed design phase if required. CORE has facilities to assist in consistency checking, and can also be used to check for consistency between the final design and the specification.

Animation of the specification

We shall see in Chapter 6 that faults within the specification represent one of the greatest problems in the development of safety-critical systems. Such faults can arise from inadequacies in the requirements documents, or because the specification does not accurately reflect their intent. In either case the specification is incorrect, and if this deficiency is not corrected the final system will be flawed. Unfortunately, weaknesses in the specification of a system are often not apparent until the system is complete, when rectification can be extremely expensive.

One method of tackling this problem is through the use of **software animation** of the specification, an approach also known as **prototyping**. This technique is used to illustrate various characteristics of the system defined by the specification. In general, animation sets out to investigate particular aspects of the system rather than to satisfy the complete specification. For example, it might be used to look at the implementation of internal logic functions, or at a man–machine interface. The prototype would not normally be required to satisfy timing constraints, or to implement features such as fault tolerance or built-in self-testing. Because prototype software will not be used in the final system, it may be produced using less rigorous development methods than would be required for operational software.

A great advantage of software animation is that it allows the engineers responsible for the requirements documents to investigate the implications of their decisions. If they decide at this stage that there are errors in these documents, these can be corrected before the design is finalized. This process also highlights any misunderstanding of the requirements which may result from ambiguities.

It is important to appreciate the distinction between the use of a software animation and the use of **simulation** during system testing. Simulation is often used during the development of a system to study the performance of a trial design. On the basis of information gained through this process, the design may be modified and retested. This allows the success of the design to be investigated without going to the expense of constructing a physical prototype. Animation can be seen as a simulation of the specification, rather than a simulation of the design. Consequently, its purpose is to validate the specification of a system and not its design.

Top-level design

Often the first stage of design involves the partitioning of system functions between those features that are to be produced within hardware and those that will be implemented using software. When this has been done, the architecture of the hardware and software can be defined. This involves the **decomposition** of the system into manageable modules, the determination of the interfaces between these modules, and the specification of the functions and safety features associated with each module. It also involves the identification of the major data structures within the software. The top-level design process often produces a hierarchical structure in which high-level modules depend for their correct operation on lower-level components. We shall look at the hierarchical design process in more detail later in this chapter.

Detailed design

Following the process of decomposition performed in the top-level design phase comes the detailed design of the various functions of each module. Often the process of decomposition is iterative, with modules being broken into successively smaller submodules, each with its own specification. In Chapter 8 we shall look at various aspects of the design of the hardware of safety-critical systems, and in Chapter 9 we will consider software design.

Module implementation

After the detailed design stage comes the task of constructing circuits to implement hardware modules and writing programs to implement software components. One of the decisions to be made at this point concerns the choice of the programming language to be used. This will be determined not only by the characteristics of the language, but also by considerations of the availability of support tools and the experience available within the development team. We shall look at the choice of programming languages in more detail in Chapter 9.

Module test

Following the implementation of the individual modules, these must be tested to show conformance with the module specifications. Testing methods may be divided into what are termed 'dynamic' and 'static' techniques.

Dynamic testing involves operating or executing the module to investigate its characteristics. In the case of hardware this might involve operating the module within some form of a hardware **test harness**, which applies appropriate input signals and monitors the outputs. In the case of software modules it might involve the use of a software test harness that supplies and accepts data. Dynamic testing allows many aspects of a system's operation to be investigated, including temporal characteristics such as its speed of response.

Static testing, which is often termed **static analysis**, looks at the characteristics of the component without executing it. Static methods include such activities as design reviews and code walkthroughs. Software techniques include several procedures that are collectively referred to as **static code analysis**. Static testing plays an important role in establishing the characteristics of the system over its entire operating range – a function that cannot be performed using dynamic methods because of the infinite number of tests that would be required. However, static methods cannot be used to investigate all system properties. Some characteristics, such as its timing performance, must be investigated dynamically.

Module testing invariably requires a range of methods, including both dynamic and static techniques. Selection of the methods to be used, and the planning of the testing process, requires considerable skill, and the various standards give some guidance in this area. The British Computer Society is currently developing a standard covering the dynamic testing of software components which defines a generic testing process that is equally applicable to both hardware and software modules (BCS, 1995). This process is shown in Figure 5.5.

The testing process begins with a planning phase that establishes the techniques to be employed, and documents these within a **test plan**. Factors to be covered within the plan include:

- the techniques to be adopted in determining the **test cases** to be used;
- methods to be used in assessing the adequacy of the testing process;
- the degree of independence of the engineers selecting test cases from those responsible for the design of the system under test;
- the environment in which testing is to be performed;
- the criteria used to determine test completion.

Following the planning phase, individual test cases are then specified by defining:

- the initial state of the component under test,
- a set of inputs,
- the expected outputs corresponding to these inputs.

The various test cases are then executed and details of the tests are recorded to allow evaluation of the results. Any discrepancies between the actual and the expected outcomes are analysed to determine the source of the error. Upon completion of the test cases the test records are studied to see if

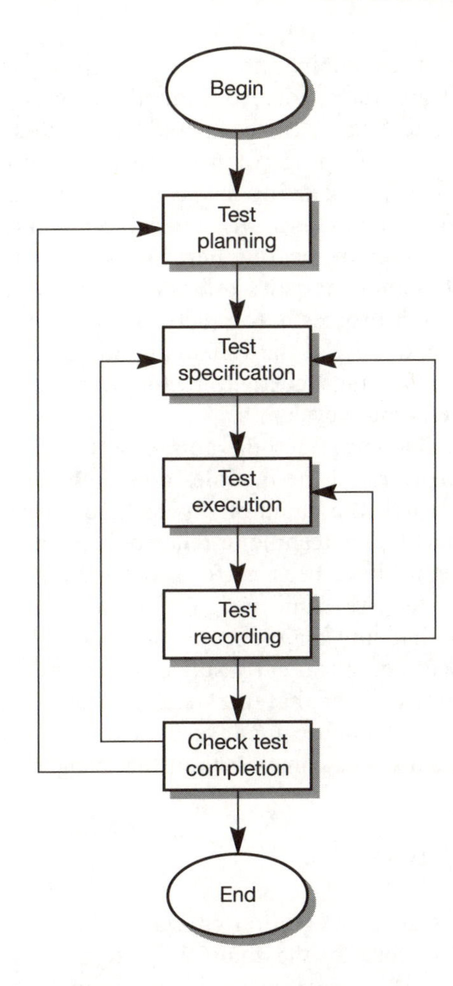

Figure 5.5 A generic test process.

they satisfy the test completion criteria within the test plan. If these are not met, the deficiencies are analysed and earlier testing phases are repeated.

We shall return to look at testing in more detail in Chapter 12.

System integration

System integration involves assembling the complete system from its component modules and performing initial testing to verify its functionality before progressing to full system testing and validation. A range of methods are used to achieve integration, although two main techniques can be identified. These are referred to as the 'progressive integration' method and the 'big bang' approach.

Progressive integration is the more traditional approach to integration and is in keeping with the 'bottom-up' school of testing. Here a small number of modules are combined to make a minimal system, which is then tested and any problems removed. Additional modules are then added successively, performing testing at each stage. This process continues until the system is complete. The advantage of progressive integration is that testing is initially performed on a system of low complexity, thereby simplifying the checking task. As further modules are added the incremental changes are small, hence reducing the task of locating new faults. The major problem with this method is that the characteristics of the complete system are not visible until the integration process is complete. This means that faults associated with the overall functionality of the system are not apparent until a very late stage. Such problems are the most costly to rectify, particularly when they are identified late in the development cycle.

The **big bang** method adopts a totally different approach to system integration. Here all the modules are combined immediately and the complete system is tested, the name of this technique suggesting a possible outcome of this approach! This technique relies on the expectation that, if the design and module testing have been performed competently, the system should function adequately to give some insight into its characteristics. This has the great advantage that any major problems within the requirements or specification may be identified at an early stage, thereby reducing the costs of rectification. The disadvantage is that the testing task is more difficult, because of the complexity of the unit being investigated. Perhaps as a result of these problems, this approach is less common than the 'progressive integration' method.

System test

Following system integration comes the task of system testing, which aims to show conformance of the complete system to its specification. As with module testing, this will normally require a combination of both dynamic and static techniques.

Testing of the complete system may sometimes be possible within its normal operating environment. However, in many instances this is impossible or undesirable, for safety or other reasons. In such cases testing will need to be performed using a simulation of the system's operating environment. Various aspects of testing, including the use of environmental simulation, are discussed in Chapter 12.

Certification

Where certification is necessary this will require an independent assessor to verify that all stages of the development have been performed with adequate care and competence. This will necessitate the provision of documentary evidence to support all aspects of the work, and full details of the tests used and their results. For this reason the certification process must be planned at the beginning of the project. The various standards and guidelines describe the documentation required at each stage of the development process, and these requirements must be built into the project at an early stage. We shall look at the process of certification in Chapter 14.

5.5 Designing for safety

Within models of the development lifecycle, such as those discussed in Section 5.2, we often represent design activities by a small number of distinct phases. In practice, however, design tasks are performed throughout the lifecycle. In order to produce a cost estimate for the development of a system some rudimentary design must be performed so that the complexity of the system and the amount of hardware and development effort required can be estimated. Often this work is based on the results of some form of feasibility study. The main design activities fall within the 'top-level' and 'detailed' design phases, but later phases may also contain a significant design component. The detailed design will not represent a complete and ideal solution to the problem, and later stages will involve making modifications and improvements to overcome deficiencies found during testing. Even during the maintenance phase it is likely that design modifications will be required for system upgrading and to remove 'bugs'.

Although design is clearly an ongoing process, it is convenient to consider it as a separate activity rather than as a component of each phase. Here we consider the nature of design without concerning ourselves with its timing within the lifecycle.

The design process may be divided into four activities (STARTS, 1987). These are:

- **abstraction**: the operation of generalizing, of identifying the essentials;
- **decomposition**: the process of reducing an object into a number of simpler, smaller parts; analysis of interactions, interfaces and structures; modularization;
- **elaboration**: the operation of detailing, adding features;
- **decision making**: identification and selection of alternative strategies.

In Chapter 1 we noted that the task of producing safe systems may be thought of as a process of fault management. In Chapter 6 we shall look in more detail at the nature of faults, but for the present it is sufficient to note that the faults associated with a system may be categorized into a number of groups, namely:

- errors in the specification of the system,
- random hardware component failures,
- systematic faults in the design (including software faults).

We noted earlier that these problems may be tackled through a combination of techniques to avoid, remove, detect and tolerate faults. When considering the design aspects of a project we can identify three approaches to fault management that are particularly relevant.

System architecture: The system architecture has an enormous effect on the ability of the system to tolerate faults within it. It can provide some protection against random hardware faults and some forms of systematic errors, but does not usually reduce the impact of specification errors. The architecture of the system relates to both the hardware and the software, and includes any non-electronic components. In Chapter 6 we shall consider the design of fault-tolerant systems and consider both hardware and software aspects of such systems. Chapter 9 will look at the design of safety-critical software.

Reliability engineering: Reliability engineering is primarily concerned with the susceptibility of a system to hardware component failures. However, it has been suggested that calculations of reliability may also be used in an attempt to predict the effects of some systematic failures, such as those due to software, on the failure rate of a system. Reliability is discussed in Chapter 7.

Quality management: Considerations of quality cover all aspects of a system's life, from conception through to decommissioning. They are therefore concerned with faults of all types. We shall look in more detail at this topic in Chapter 13.

We saw in Figure 5.3 that one of the early phases of the design process involves the allocation of safety features to appropriate subsystems. This includes **partitioning** the system into those functions to be performed within programmable elements and those to be implemented using non-programmable, or non-electronic, components. For the programmable elements of the system, a further partitioning is required between those features to be provided by hardware and those that will be produced within software. Decisions as to the nature of the final system will often be made using criteria that are somewhat different from those that might be applied in the design of non-critical systems.

In an undemanding application considerations of unit cost and development cost usually dominate the choice of implementation technique for a given function. Within safety-critical applications these factors are also of importance, but wherever possible the designer will tend to opt for the less complex solution to a problem, even if this is not necessarily the least expensive. Here the motivation is to minimize the total **cost of ownership** of the system, which includes considerations of possible future liabilities. This difference of perspective will often give rise to design decisions that would seem unnatural in a non-critical system. A designer might, for example, choose a combination of logic gates in preference to a programmable solution that requires less hardware, simply in order to reduce the problems of demonstrating the safety of the arrangement.

Hierarchical design

Once the system has been partitioned into its hardware and software components, the design of these sections may begin. One approach to this task is based on the principle of **hierarchical design** (Neumann, 1986). This technique, which is used for both hardware and software, divides the system into a series of layers. Modules within the higher layers depend for their correct operation on the correct functioning of lower-level components. These in turn depend on modules within lower levels. This process is illustrated in Figure 5.6, where the boxes represent modules within the safety-critical system under development. These modules may represent hardware or software, or a combination of both. Modules within the top layer of the diagram are dependent for their correct operation on the performance of modules in layer B, which in turn are dependent on modules in layer C, and so on. In practice the lower levels might represent processors, control devices or sensors, and the high-level modules might correspond to applications-level software or logic hardware implementing high-level features. The intermediate layers isolate these two extremes, and would include such components as communications software and device drivers.

One of the principles of hierarchical design is to enforce some form of *downward-only functional dependence*. This results in layers of **abstraction** that allow the functioning of lower levels to be hidden from those above them. In safety-critical applications this can prevent high-level sections of the system from directly activating potentially dangerous functions, except through the use of dependable lower-level modules that are used to ensure safe operation.

In the model in Figure 5.6 the lower layers would normally include relatively simple and trusted software or hardware modules to control the various actuators within the system. Where incorrect activation of an actuator could be potentially dangerous, it may be possible to include within this module a safety interlock to guarantee that it operates only when it is safe to do so. For example, a module to activate a machine tool might check that a mechanical guard is in place before applying power. If this is done, a fault within a higher layer of the system, perhaps resulting in the low-level module being called at the wrong time, should not result in a dangerous situation. In this case the

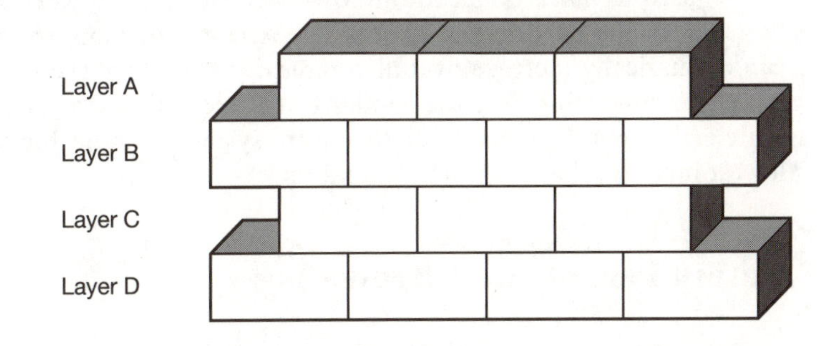

Figure 5.6 A layered approach to system design.

activating mechanism and the interlock mechanism have been **encapsulated** within a single module such that the former cannot be activated without the latter. In more complex systems interlocking may require signals from more than one low-level module. In this case higher-level modules are required to maintain safety, these being dependent on the correct operation of the modules 'below' them. In this way the hierarchy of the system is established, with more and more layers of abstraction separating the high-level operation of the system from the actual devices performing the safety-related functions.

A hierarchical structure can be used to divide a complex system into a number of modules, each with a manageable level of complexity. However, this is achieved at the expense of an increase in the total complexity of the system, because of the additional module interfaces created. Excessive use of modularization can also result in hardware and software that is harder to understand, as it tends to hide the form of the lower levels of the system. For these reasons the structure used must be chosen with care.

In some cases it may be possible to partition a system such that all safety-critical functions, including appropriate interlocks, are performed within low-level modules. It may also be possible to provide a degree of isolation between these modules, so that their operations are effectively independent. Where this is possible it has the advantage that only the relatively simple low-level routines require a high degree of integrity, whereas the more complex high-level routines are much less critical. This reduces the proportion of the system that needs to be produced to a high level of integrity and so reduces development costs. Unfortunately, this very attractive approach is not always possible, as in many cases high-level functions play an integral role in ensuring safety. The provision of adequate isolation also presents a problem, and we shall return to discuss this issue in more detail in Chapter 9 when we look at software partitioning.

A hierarchical structure may be arranged such that fault tolerance techniques implemented within the lower levels of the system are hidden from the higher layers by the levels of abstraction. This may enable the effects of failures of individual low-level modules to be masked from layers higher in the system.

The hierarchical approach to system design offers several potential benefits. It can separate system complexity into manageable partitions and can be used to mask faults within low-level routines. However, great care must be taken in the partitioning process as excessive or inappropriate partitioning can dramatically increase overall complexity and make the system unwieldy. It is also worth noting that the similarity between Figure 5.6 and a brick wall is quite significant. The safety of the entire system rests on the soundness of the lowest modules that form its foundation.

Safety kernels and firewalls

In some applications safety can be enhanced by the use of techniques such as safety kernels or firewalls.

A **safety kernel** consists of a relatively simple arrangement, usually a combination of hardware and software, that is used at the heart of a critical system. The small size and lack of complexity of the kernel allows it to be developed and tested to a point where it is trusted to ensure the safety of the system. A typical safety kernel might perform a set of safety-critical functions, or provide operating system components that perform critical tasks. The success of this approach will be determined by the ability of the designer to protect the kernel from outside influences that might interfere with its operation. This protection might be achieved physically, by the use of separate hardware, or logically, in the case of a software kernel, by providing software isolation. The problems of software isolation will be discussed in Chapter 9.

Within any safety-critical system there will be elements that are directly responsible for ensuring safety, and others that are far less critical. One approach to system design protects the critical elements by placing them behind a **firewall**. When considering hardware, this firewall may be a physical barrier to the dangerous effects of component failure. Alternatively, the firewall may take the form of a logical barrier within the system software. In this latter case, the barrier would aim to prevent failure of software outside the firewall from affecting the critical software within. To do this it must prevent unauthorized access or modification of the data and code within the protected region. In this respect, the problems involved are related to those of access control within applications aimed at achieving security rather than safety (Leveson, 1995).

5.6 Maintainability

The long-term safety of a system depends not only on its design and implementation, but also on the way in which it is used and maintained throughout its functional life. There are many factors that may degrade the system and cause its performance to differ from that envisaged at the design stage. Such factors include differences between the predicted and actual use of the system, and weaknesses in maintenance procedures.

Throughout all the phases of a system's life the key to safety is good management. During the development phases this task falls upon senior managers and members of the design team. Diligence by these staff is rewarded by the successful validation of the completed system, and perhaps by certification by a regulatory authority. Following the commissioning of the system the management of safety is less visible, and often its only outcome is the absence of events that were, in any case, thought to be unlikely. The long-term safety of the system requires a commitment by senior managers that continues throughout its life.

In Figure 5.3 we saw that the planning of an overall operation and maintenance strategy is performed in parallel with the design (or realization) phase of a project. This is essential to allow the requirements of both normal and abnormal operating modes to be addressed within the implementation. For example, it may be necessary to use the system during periods of maintenance while certain subsystems are inoperable. Once this strategy has been defined it will form an input to the design stage of the project.

Design for maintainability

In Chapter 2 we defined the term maintenance as 'the action taken to retain a system in, or return a system to, its designed operating condition'. We also defined maintainability as the 'ability of a system to be maintained'. Unfortunately, the requirements of maintainability vary considerably between applications. In some cases a system is regularly shut down between periods of use, allowing maintenance to be performed 'offline'. In such cases the goal of the design, from a maintenance viewpoint, is to minimize the cost of maintenance by reducing the frequency of servicing and the time required for any work to be done.

Computer systems that normally run continuously present a different problem for the design engineer. Here it may be possible to shut the system down temporarily while the necessary maintenance work is performed. In this case the time taken, and the frequency of the work, determine the availability of the system. Alternatively, the engineer might choose to design the system so that it can be maintained while in service. This can be done by utilizing some form of redundancy within the system, by having several modules capable of performing the same task. This latter approach results in a system of greater complexity because of the need to be able to power down some parts while others are active. It also results in a reduction in the safety levels of the system during maintenance, because its ability to tolerate failure of the functioning modules is reduced.

Maintenance activities can be either preventative or corrective in nature. **Preventative maintenance** aims to keep the system in good order and to remove the effects of wear and ageing before they result in a system failure. **Corrective maintenance** aims to restore the system to its designed state following some form of failure. Preventative maintenance may be performed at a time determined by some predetermined schedule, or be triggered as a result of monitoring of the system's condition. In either event it can be performed at a convenient time. This is often not possible with corrective maintenance, which usually has to be carried out at a time determined by the failure. In fault-tolerant systems a decision can be made to continue operating until it is convenient to carry out a repair, although during this time the system will be functioning at a lower level of safety. In modern aircraft it is normal to design certain systems so that the repair of a failed module can be delayed until the aircraft returns to its home base, while still maintaining acceptable levels of safety.

The maintainability of a system may be described qualitatively, by describing the relative ease or difficulty of the processes involved, or quantitatively, using statistics relating to maintenance activities. In the latter case it is common to specify the **mean time to repair** (MTTR), this being the mean time taken to return the system to its original state following a failure. Some engineers refer to this as the **mean corrective time**. In Chapter 7 we shall look at the relationship between the MTTR and the availability of the system.

Maintenance-induced failures

One aspect of the maintenance of safety-critical systems that is often overlooked is that of maintenance-induced failures. Evidence from a number of sources suggests that there is a significant probability that maintenance activities will not be completely successful (Whetton, 1994), and the effects of poor maintenance may be to produce new hazards within the system.

Much of the responsibility for maintenance-induced failures may well be attributable to weaknesses in the design of the system. A system that is difficult to maintain is likely to produce more problems in this area than one in which maintenance has been considered carefully.

Linked to the issue of maintenance-induced failures is the consideration of situations where attempts to improve the maintainability of the system may reduce its safety. An example of such a situation is the inclusion of built-in test equipment (BITE) within the system. BITE speeds maintenance by simplifying the task of locating faults. However, the inclusion of the additional hardware and/or software required inevitably increases the complexity of the system, and therefore reduces its reliability. Although reliability is not synonymous with safety, clearly a reduction in reliability is likely to reduce overall safety levels. Thus there is a trade-off between an improvement in maintainability, which in turn should increase the availability of the system, and a possible reduction in reliability. The consequences of these two factors need to be considered carefully at the design stage.

5.7 Human factors in safety

We observed in earlier chapters that wherever possible we should strive to make safety-critical systems as simple as possible. Unfortunately, in many cases the operating environment of such systems includes one or more highly complex entities, in the form of its human operators or users. When used as 'components' within critical systems, humans are often unreliable and unpredictable, and a great many accidents may be directly attributed to operator error. Computers are greatly superior in terms of speed and the ability to follow a predefined set of instructions. For this reason, it is normal to attempt to remove humans from tasks that can be implemented by following a well-defined set of rules.

Although humans cannot compete with computers in the implementation of simple control functions, there are areas where humans are pre-eminent.

Humans are flexible and adaptable, and are extremely good at dealing with unexpected events. These characteristics are often invaluable when a system strays from its normal operating regime and into uncharted territory. In such situations it may be only a human operator that can prevent an incident from becoming a catastrophe. Therefore the presence of humans within the operating sphere of a safety-related system brings both complications and potential benefits. Consideration of these issues is just one aspect of the important field of **human factors**.

To take advantage of the undoubted abilities of human operators the computer system must give up some of its 'authority'. For example, in an aircraft the pilot may override the automatic landing system by switching to manual control. This might permit the pilot to make mistakes that the computer system would avoid, but could allow the pilot to overcome faults within the aircraft. In this situation the human operator could be seen as directly implementing some of the safety requirements of the aircraft and acting as a backup system providing a form of fault tolerance.

Earlier in this chapter we discussed the partitioning of safety features into those to be performed by hardware and those to be implemented within software. From the above it is clear that in some cases safety features are implemented by what we might term **liveware**. This term has previously been applied to computer programmers, but here is taken to represent any human component within the system. It can be seen that appropriate partitioning of the safety features between hardware, software and liveware plays an important part in determining the overall safety of any system.

One of the consequences of using humans to implement safety features is that this inevitably increases the complexity of the overall system. Although a manually controlled system may appear simpler than an automated one, the inherent complexity of the human element within the resultant safety-related system has great implications for the safety of the arrangement. For this reason it is normal to attempt to remove operators and users from all responsibilities for safety. Unfortunately, this goal is not always realizable. This may be illustrated by considering examples within the railway industry.

The routeing of trains within the rail network is the responsibility of a number of signallers (often referred to as signalmen). Modern signal boxes employ large computer-based control systems that drive large track displays. The displays show the sections of track controlled by the relevant signal box and indicate the positions of trains and the states of the various points and signals. A signaller may select a route for a given train and set the associated points and signals appropriately. However, the safety features of the system should prevent him from routeing two trains onto the same track, or performing any other action that would result in a collision. If the control system functions perfectly the signaller should be incapable of causing a dangerous situation, regardless of his actions. The main responsibility of the signaller is therefore to perform what might be termed operational functions. However, the signaller does have a safety role within the system, as he has a responsibility to cope with faults and unforeseen events.

It is interesting to compare the responsibilities of a signaller with those of a train driver. The driver controls the speed of the train and is required to respond to signals and to environmental conditions. The driver of a conventional train is clearly directly responsible for its safety, since an accident could be caused by driving too fast or by not responding sufficiently quickly to signals. Because of the heavy burden that falls upon the driver various safety systems and warning devices are incorporated into modern trains. These range from the 'dead man's handle', which stops the train if the driver releases the controls (perhaps in the event of incapacity), to automatic systems that apply the brakes if the train goes through a stop signal. However, despite these facilities, drivers remain crucial to the safety of the rail network. In an attempt to remove the dependence on human operators several light rail networks now utilize automatic train systems that require no drivers. These depend heavily on computer-based systems to maintain train separation and to ensure passenger safety. Because of the consequences of failure, the integrity requirements for such control systems are very high.

Although it is often possible to remove humans from a direct responsibility for safety, this is not always practical and not always desirable. It has been suggested that we are now at a stage where it is feasible to consider replacing airline pilots with completely automated systems. However, no commercial airlines are considering this move at present. For all their human fallibility, pilots remain the most adaptable and dependable aircraft control system and are likely to remain so for many years. If improvements in aircraft safety are to be achieved, they are likely to come from systems that build on the pilot's strengths rather than trying to replace them.

We have seen that in some cases it is possible to produce critical systems where the responsibility for ensuring safety is completely removed from operators and users. However, this does not eliminate the influences of human factors on such systems. All safety-critical systems are designed and implemented by humans, and the development process will inevitably be affected by the characteristics of the engineers involved.

The task of developing a safety-critical system has many components. Some of these require great creativity, whereas others are mechanistic. Humans are often extremely creative but are less effective at executing complex, repetitive operations. Computers, on the other hand, are ideal for performing operations that can be defined by a set of rules, but are less successful at tasks requiring value judgements. It seems clear that effective development should take full advantage of both human and machine by utilizing the strengths of each.

One approach to allocating tasks between human and machine is to identify their relative strengths. This can be done qualitatively, by listing good and bad attributes, or quantitatively, by assigning performance figures. Any such comparison must take into account the range of tasks to be performed and the variety of environments in which they are to be carried out. This approach can be used to influence both the design of a system and the development methods to be used.

Human error

Following any major accident there is invariably an investigation to establish its cause and to assign blame. Although some events can be seen as 'acts of God', it is more likely that the cause will be attributed either to a failure of some form of safety system or to human error. From the discussion above we could consider this as a distinction between failures caused by either hardware or software, and failures due to liveware.

In reality any distinction between system failures and human error is inappropriate. Invariably, the dangerous failure of a system will reflect a weakness in its specification, design, implementation or maintenance, and will therefore represent a human error within its development. This being the case, all dangerous failures can be seen as resulting from some form of human error. The earlier distinction simply reflects whether the human concerned is a user or a developer.

The simplistic distinction between a system failure and human error is also unfortunate because it may mask the influence of the system's characteristics on the user's performance. If an aircraft crashes because the pilot does not notice that it has run short of fuel, then the competence of the pilot will be brought into doubt. If a number of planes were to crash in similar circumstances, then one would be forced to question the effectiveness of the display and warning systems of the aircraft.

Often a verdict of human error is welcomed by the developers of the equipment concerned as confirmation that they were not to blame for the incident. In many cases operators make mistakes because of a poorly designed **human–computer interface** (**HCI**), which hinders interaction. The design of HCIs, which are also called **man–machine interfaces** (**MMIs**), represents a major discipline that is outside the scope of this text. However, the importance of this topic should not be underestimated.

5.8 Safety analysis

In earlier chapters we looked at the use of hazard analysis and risk analysis as methods of determining the nature and importance of factors related to the safety of a system. In this section we consider **safety analysis**, which incorporates elements of both these topics together with consideration of the system's design. Safety analysis is the process of assessing the safety of a system by looking at the associated hazards and the methods used by the system to cope with them. The draft of IEC 1508 refers to this subject as **overall safety validation**.

In the UK the Health and Safety Executive (HSE) has published a framework for safety analysis (which it refers to as safety assessment), as shown in Table 5.1 (HSE, 1987). This outlines the various activities required to assess the overall safety of a system. Sections 1, 2 and 3 of the table relate to material

Table 5.1 The HSE safety assessment framework.

(1)	Analyse the hazards (a) identify the potential hazards (b) evaluate the events leading to these hazards
(2)	Identify the safety-related systems within the plant
(3)	Decide on the required level of safety integrity for the safety-related systems
(4)	Design the safety-related system using the safety integrity criteria appropriate for the specific application
(5)	Carry out a safety integrity analysis to assess the level of safety integrity achieved by the safety-related systems
(6)	Ensure, from the analysis of 5, that the integrity levels of 3 have been achieved

already covered within Chapters 2, 3 and 4 of this book. Sections 4, 5 and 6 are concerned with the design, analysis and validation of the system. These topics form the basis of later chapters.

From Table 5.1 it is clear that safety analysis is an ongoing task that continues throughout the development process. Hazard analysis is required at an early stage to guide system design and to provide a basis for risk analysis. This in turn is used to determine the safety integrity levels required for the various system components, and greatly affects the design and development methods adopted. As the design progresses, analysis is performed to determine the levels of integrity achieved for each component within the system. Following system integration, validation and, if necessary, certification will be dependent on the ability to demonstrate that the integrity levels achieved for the overall system, and the various subsystems, satisfy the requirements determined earlier.

5.9 Safety management

Safety is not achieved simply by following an appropriate set of development methods. It must be planned and built into the system by considering safety issues at all stages. As the safety of a system is determined by all aspects of its development and use, it follows that the achievement of safety requires specific attention by all concerned. **Safety management** is the planning, organization, monitoring and evaluation of the safety aspects of a project.

Because of the importance of safety management it is essential that a **safety culture** is encouraged *from the top*. A well-defined **safety policy** is essential to establish the working practices of the organization and to ensure that these are followed. A major component of safety management is the monitoring of safety performance. This should include both in-house and, where appropriate, independent assessments of safety systems and procedures.

The management structure adopted will vary considerably from one company to another, although it is likely that the main components of this hierarchy will be similar. Figure 5.7 shows the management structure recommended by Interim Defence Standard 00-55 (MoD, 1991). It can be seen that the **project manager** bears ultimate responsibility for the development of the system and its safety. However, much of the task of developing the system is delegated to a **project management team** appointed by the project manager. The standard refers to this team as the **design authority**, and at the end of the project an individual nominated by this team will be responsible for '**signing off**' the system on its behalf.

A primary responsibility of the project management team is administration of the safety aspects of the project. At each stage the team will perform hazard analysis and risk assessment, and will ensure that the various components are developed to an appropriate level of integrity. The team will also perform verification at each stage of the design, including, if appropriate, formal proofs of correctness. Along with their technical duties the project management team also bears responsibility for much of the documentation of the project. This includes the preparation and maintenance of the **safety plan** (as discussed in Chapter 3) and the **safety log**. The latter forms the main record of the safety activities of the project and contains the results of hazard analyses, design reviews and other similar documents.

The actual specification, design and implementation of the system are performed by the **design team**, which is appointed by the project management team and is responsible for carrying out duties in line with the various standards and codes of practice relevant to the project.

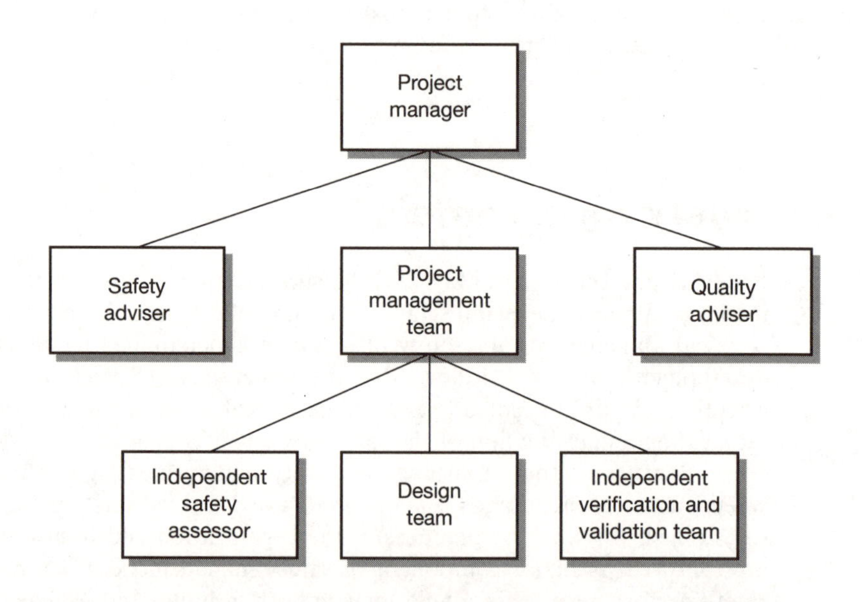

Figure 5.7 Safety management structure recommended by Int. Def. Stan. 00-55.

In addition to data from the design team, the management team takes information from at least two other sources. The **independent safety assessor** reviews and audits all the activities and documents of relevance to safety, and provides an independent check on the activities of the project management team. The **independent verification and validation team** (**IV & V team**) looks at the design at each stage, and provides a separate check on its correctness. In many cases the IV & V team will come from an external company that specializes in such work. This enhances independence and gives increased confidence in its findings. Information from these various sources is stored in the safety log, where it will be available for an independent safety audit if required.

As part of its work the project management team will carry out formal reviews of the specification, design and implementation of the system at various stages throughout the project. These reviews will be carried out by a committee that will normally include:

- members of the project management team,
- members of the design team,
- members of the IV & V team,
- relevant contractors and subcontractors,
- the independent safety assessor,
- representatives of the customer or system users,
- representatives of other interested parties.

The discussions of the review committee will be recorded in the form of minutes that will be added to the safety log.

The project manager will receive information on the development of the system from the project management team, but may also take advantage of advice from other sources. The safety and quality advisers provide a further level of independent assessment, by providing guidance directly to the project manager. This may include an assessment of the work of the management team and its subordinates.

Management issues

Although the safety management hierarchy may vary from one company to another, it is essential that a well-defined structure exists to formalize management responsibilities. This structure must assign duties and responsibilities to those associated with the project, and define the person to whom each member of staff should report.

Closely linked with issues of safety are the various considerations of quality management, such as configuration control. These matters also fall within the responsibilities of the project management team, but we shall leave discussion of such topics until Chapter 13.

Technical competence and training

An important factor in determining the success or failure of a project is the competence of the staff involved. In other areas of engineering a degree of competence may be demonstrated by the achievement of appropriate academic qualifications, and by appropriate recognized training. Unfortunately, in this developing field there are at present few established qualifications that satisfy the needs of an engineer working in the area of safety-critical systems.

In the UK a working party of the British Computer Society (BCS) has considered the requirements for post-experience education and training courses for the developers of safety-critical systems (McDermid, 1992). This working party looked at the principles, tools and techniques that should be taught, and made recommendations concerning course content, presentation and methods of assessment. It also looked at the formal qualifications that should be associated with such courses. The recommendations of the working party were that the level of training appropriate for an engineer would depend on his level of responsibility. It proposed that all staff should receive a basic level of specialist training, but that training should be an ongoing process over several years. Over this period the engineers concerned would develop the expertise needed to successfully manage projects concerned with the development of safety-critical systems. Some of the topics identified for inclusion within this training process are listed in Table 5.2. It can be seen that many of these topics are covered within this text, although clearly this table does not indicate the level of detail required for each topic.

Table 5.2 Topics for safety-critical system developers.

Hazard analysis
Risk analysis
Requirements
Techniques and technologies
General software and systems engineering issues
Architectural issues
Basic discrete mathematics
Formal specification
Formal approaches: principles and program verification
Testing
Validation
Fault tolerance
Psychology – the human–computer interface
Implementation
Management of safety-critical systems
Evaluation
Basic probability and statistics
Software reliability
Building safe systems
Integration of techniques

In 1995 the UK Institution of Electrical Engineers (IEE) published a proposed syllabus for postgraduate courses for professional engineers working in this area (IEE, 1995). These proposals cover courses leading to a Postgraduate Certificate, a Diploma or a Master's Degree, and cover topics broadly in line with those listed in Table 5.2. The UK Health and Safety Executive is also looking at the issue of adequate competence, and is funding work by the IEE and the BCS in this area (Storey, 1995).

REFERENCES

BCS (1995). *Standard for Software Component Testing*. Working Draft 3.0, British Computer Society Specialist Interest Group in Software Testing (BCS SIGIST) (standard in preparation)

Hill I.D. (1972). Wouldn't it be nice if we could write computer programs in ordinary English – or would it? *Comp. Bull.*, **16**(6), 306–12

HSE (1987). *Programmable Electronic Systems in Safety-Related Applications Vol. 2: General Technical Guidelines*. London: Her Majesty's Stationery Office

IEE (1995). *Safety-Related Systems Postgraduate Qualifications Syllabus Proposals*. Stevenage: Institution of Electrical Engineers

Leveson N.G. (1986). Software safety: why, what, and how. *ACM Comput. Surv.*, **18**(2), 25–69

Leveson N.G. (1995). *Safeware: System Safety and Computers*. Reading, MA: Addison-Wesley

McDermid J. (1992). Education and training for safety-critical systems practitioners. In *Software in Safety-Related Systems* (Wichmann B.A., ed.), pp. 177–207. Chichester: John Wiley

MoD (1991). Interim Defence Standard 00-55 *The Procurement of Safety Critical Software in Defence Equipment*. Glasgow: Directorate of Standardization

Neumann P.G. (1986). On hierarchical design of computer systems for critical applications. *IEEE Trans. Software Eng.*, **12**(9), 905–20

STARTS Purchasers' Group (1987). *The STARTS Guide: Vol. 1*, 2nd edn. Manchester: National Computing Centre Publications

STARTS Purchasers' Group (1989). *The STARTS Purchasers' Handbook: Software Tools for Application to Large Real Time Systems*, 2nd edn. Manchester: National Computing Centre Publications

Storey N. (1995). Safety through training. *Proc. Second Safety Through Quality Conference*, Cape Canaveral, FL, 23–25 October 1995, pp. 261–70

Whetton C. (1994). Maintainability and its influence on system safety. In *Technology and Assessment of Safety-Critical Systems* (Redmill F. and Anderson T., eds), pp. 31–54. London: Springer-Verlag

FURTHER READING

Pyle I.C. (1991). *Developing Safety Systems: A Guide Using Ada*. Hemel Hempstead: Prentice-Hall

Redmill F. and Rajan J., eds (1996). *Human Factors in Safety-Critical Systems*. Oxford: Butterworth-Heinemann

PROBLEMS

5.1 Describe, in order of precedence, the four main techniques for ensuring safety through design.

5.2 What is meant by the term 'intrinsically safe'?

5.3 Give two examples of techniques that may be used to prevent or minimize hazards.

5.4 Give examples of techniques for controlling hazards.

5.5 How may the impact of hazards be reduced?

5.6 What information is provided by the 'V' lifecycle model?

5.7 How does the form of the safety lifecycle model vary for systems of different levels of safety integrity?

5.8 What is meant by the term 'external risk reduction facilities'? Give examples of such activities.

5.9 Describe briefly the important characteristics of a system specification.

5.10 Describe a common cause of incompleteness within specifications. How can this situation cause problems?

5.11 Discuss the suitability of natural languages for the production of specifications. What alternative techniques are available?

5.12 What is meant by 'software animation' and what are its benefits? How does animation differ from simulation?

5.13 Explain the distinction between 'progressive integration' and the 'big bang' approach to system integration. What are the characteristics of these two methods?

5.14 Discuss the relevance of the choice of system architecture to fault management.

5.15 Describe the importance of partitioning in the production of safety-critical systems.

5.16 Explain the use of encapsulation in the implementation of safety interlocks.

5.17 Explain why different layers in a hierarchical design are normally associated with varying levels of complexity.

5.18 At what phase in a project is it advisable to establish a strategy for the operation and maintenance of the system? Why?

5.19 Discuss the characteristics of preventative and corrective maintenance.

5.20 Explain how improving the maintainability of a system might affect its overall safety.

5.21 What factors should be considered in allocating system safety features between hardware, software and liveware?

5.22 Discuss the role of human error in major accidents.

5.23 Describe the major components of the safety analysis process. At what stage of a project is this analysis performed?

5.24 Describe a typical structure for the management of a project concerning a safety-critical system.

5.25 Discuss the use of independence as a means of improving safety within the development of a critical system.

5.26 Why is establishing the competence of staff working on safety-critical systems somewhat more complicated than in other engineering disciplines?

Fault Tolerance

CHAPTER CONTENTS

6.1 Introduction

In Chapter 1 we discussed the meanings of terms such as 'faults', 'errors' and 'system failures'. We also noted that as faults are inevitable, in critical systems we use techniques to avoid, remove, detect and tolerate them. In this chapter we look at the last of these approaches.

The objective of the use of fault tolerance is to design a system in such a way that faults do not result in system failure. All methods of fault tolerance are based on some form of **redundancy**. This involves having a system which is more complex than that needed simply to perform the required task. This additional complexity may take various forms, and we will be looking at several methods of implementing redundancy later in this chapter.

Fault tolerance is not new. Computers as early as the EDVAC, designed in 1949, used duplicated arithmetic logic units (ALUs) to detect errors in calculations. Great strides were made in the 1950s, with much of the theoretical work being attributed to von Neumann (1956). In those early days fault tolerance was used largely to cope with failures in relatively unreliable hardware, which was then based on thermionic devices. As the computer industry evolved, hardware became much more reliable, but also far more complex. In modern computer-based systems much of this complexity is implemented within software. To be effective fault tolerance must provide protection against design faults, such as those in software, as well as against hardware faults. Today, fault tolerance is found at the heart of almost all critical systems, providing protection against a broad spectrum of faults. It is also widely used within complex components such as memory devices and microprocessors.

The motivation for using fault tolerance may vary markedly between one application and another. Characteristics that may be improved by using such techniques include reliability, availability, dependability and safety. Invariably these characteristics are interrelated, but often one demand predominates in a specific application. For example, fault tolerance might be used to achieve a long operating life in an undersea telephone repeater; to achieve high availability in a banking system; to increase likely mission success rates in a space shuttle; or to reduce or postpone maintenance in a communications satellite.

Within this text we are primarily interested in safety, although clearly this is closely linked with issues of reliability and dependability. In Chapter 2 we noted that under some circumstances requirements for safety may be at odds with achieving high reliability. In some systems safety can be achieved on the basis of fault detection and some mechanism for forcing the system to fail to a safe state. With effective fault detection methods such an arrangement could be safe even if the system had numerous faults and was unreliable. However, in all practical systems reliability is of great importance, and any system which is unreliable is likely to be unsuccessful even if it is safe. Fault tolerance can be used to prevent system faults from producing system failures, and can therefore be used to increase the reliability and availability of a system. Increased reliability is always beneficial and in many cases is a major issue in improving the safety of the system.

An important factor affecting the design of any fault-tolerant system is an assessment of the number of system failures that can be accepted within a given period of time. We noted in Chapter 4 that risk analysis is used to assign to the system a safety integrity level that reflects its required performance in this respect. The failure rate to be achieved by the system will guide the designer in the choice of the system architecture to be used. During the design process it will then be necessary to estimate the likely failure rate of the proposed system, to confirm that this will satisfy its requirements. In this chapter we shall look at the various techniques which are used to achieve fault tolerance, and leave analysis of the performance of these techniques until Chapter 7, where we look at reliability.

6.2 Types of faults

Faults may be characterized in a number of ways. For example, they may be distinguished by their nature, duration or extent.

Nature

The nature of a fault relates to its form. We noted in Chapter 1 that faults may be characterized as being either random or systematic. The primary cause of random faults is hardware component failure. All real components have a finite chance of failing over a period of time, and it is possible to build up statistics for similar devices that can be used to estimate failure rates. When simple components are assembled into modules the methods used to assemble the components, and the techniques used to interconnect them, may also result in failures, and again experience allows us to estimate the rates of such failures. Because of their random nature it is not possible to predict when a particular component or module will fail, but statistical analysis may make it possible to estimate the likelihood of it failing within a given period of time.

In addition to random hardware failures, systems are also subject to **systematic faults** of three main types: mistakes in the specification of the system; mistakes in the software; and mistakes in the hardware design. It is common to consider these as different forms of **design fault**. Systematic faults are more difficult to analyse than random faults and it is generally not possible to predict their effects on system performance. Much work has been aimed at the problem of predicting the likely effects of software faults on system performance, and we shall consider this topic in Chapter 7.

It can be seen that hardware faults may be due either to random component failures or to mistakes within the design. Software faults are always due to mistakes in the design of the system. There is no such thing as a random software fault.

Duration

Faults may also be classified in terms of their duration. Faults which remain in existence indefinitely, or until some corrective action is taken, are termed **permanent faults**. Design faults, including software faults, are always permanent, as are many hardware component faults. Some faults can appear and then disappear after a short time. These are referred to as **transient faults**. Examples of transient faults include the effects of alpha particle strikes on semiconductor memory chips. These events occur very infrequently, but can change the state of one or more bits within the memory plane without causing lasting damage to the device. Although the fault is transient, the error which it produces remains after the fault has disappeared, and steps must be taken to correct this error if system failure is to avoided. A third class of faults relates to those which are **intermittent** in nature. These faults appear, disappear and then reappear at some later time. Such faults may result from poor solder joints or corrosion on connector contacts, so that correct connections can be made at some times but not at others. Intermittent faults can also result from electrical interference and other EMC-related problems. (EMC (electromagnetic compatibility) is discussed in Chapter 8.) By their very nature intermittent faults are often very difficult to detect and remove, as the fault detection process must coincide with the existence of the fault. Unfortunately, many permanent faults *appear* to be intermittent because their effects are only apparent at certain times. For example, a software synchronization fault is permanent, as its code is always present, but its execution will only sometimes result in an error, depending on timing considerations. Such faults, having the characteristics of intermittent faults, are similarly difficult to locate.

Hardware component failures may be permanent, transient or intermittent, but design faults will always be permanent. However, it should be remembered that faults of any of these classes may result in errors that persist within the system.

Extent

A further classification of faults relates to their extent, in terms of the parts of the system that they affect. A **localized fault** may affect only a single hardware or software module, whereas a **global fault** has effects which permeate throughout the system.

Hardware faults

We have seen that hardware faults may be caused by random hardware component failures or design faults. They may also be permanent, transient or intermittent, and may have a local or global extent.

Regardless of the nature of the fault it is often useful to be able to model its effect on system behaviour. This can be done using one of a number of **fault models**. As with models used in other areas of engineering, these are not always perfect representations of the physical effect they attempt to depict. However, their use greatly simplifies analysis of complex systems, and can assist in the design of test procedures and in the simulation of fault conditions.

Fault models

The operation of a circuit may be considered at a number of levels. At the **atomic level** one looks at the individual components such as resistors and transistors, and their interconnections. At this basic level most faults can be seen as connections which are either open-circuit or are incorrectly joined to some other line. Examples of such faults are shown in Figure 6.1, which gives four possible fault conditions. (1) shows a break in a conductor. This could represent a physical break in a circuit track or wire, or an open-circuit terminal of a component such as a resistor or transistor. (2), (3) and (4) all represent incorrect connections between various nodes of the circuit. These could be between internal signal paths, as in (2), or between a signal path and one of the supply lines, as in (3) and (4). These conditions could represent physical short-circuits or bridges between

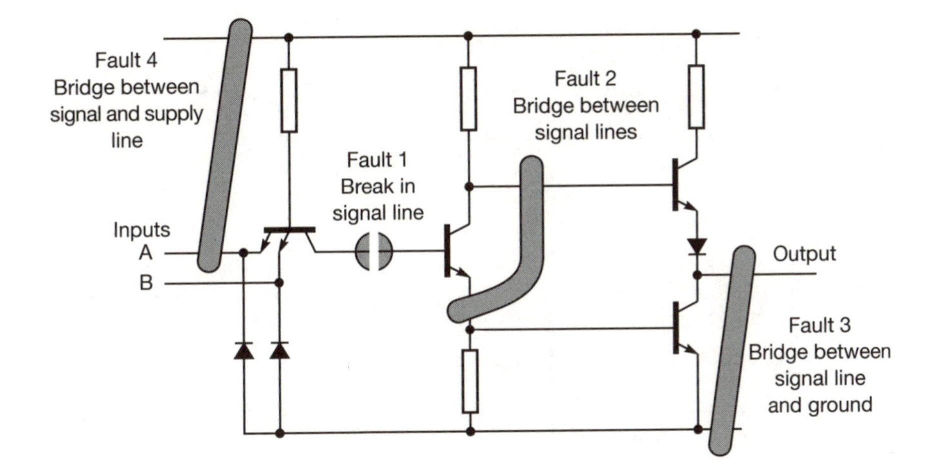

Figure 6.1 Typical component-level faults.

adjacent tracks within a circuit, or internal short-circuits within components. Clearly, not all fault conditions may be represented using these simple models, but in practice a large proportion of real faults may be adequately represented by one or other of these conditions.

Although the atomic-level model described above provides a good picture of the effects of faults on circuit behaviour, it can be seen that considering each component separately results in considerable complexity. One method of reducing this complexity in digital circuits is to look at the system at a modular, rather than an atomic, level. Typically the modules used would be gates or collections of gates.

Several fault models are used to represent different types of fault. Here we shall consider three forms:

- the single-stuck-at fault model
- the bridging fault model
- the stuck-open fault model.

The single-stuck-at model

One of the earliest, and also one of most widely used, fault models is the single-stuck-at model which has been used since the 1950s (Eldred, 1959; Kohavi, 1978). This makes no attempt to model the internal structure of a module but simply proposes that any failing module can be characterized by its external behaviour. The model assumes that a fault within a module will cause it to respond as if *one* of its inputs or outputs is stuck at a logic 1 or a logic 0. It also assumes that the basic functionality of the circuit is otherwise unaffected, and that the fault is permanent. An example of the model is shown in Figure 6.2, which shows the possible fault conditions associated with a module having three inputs and one

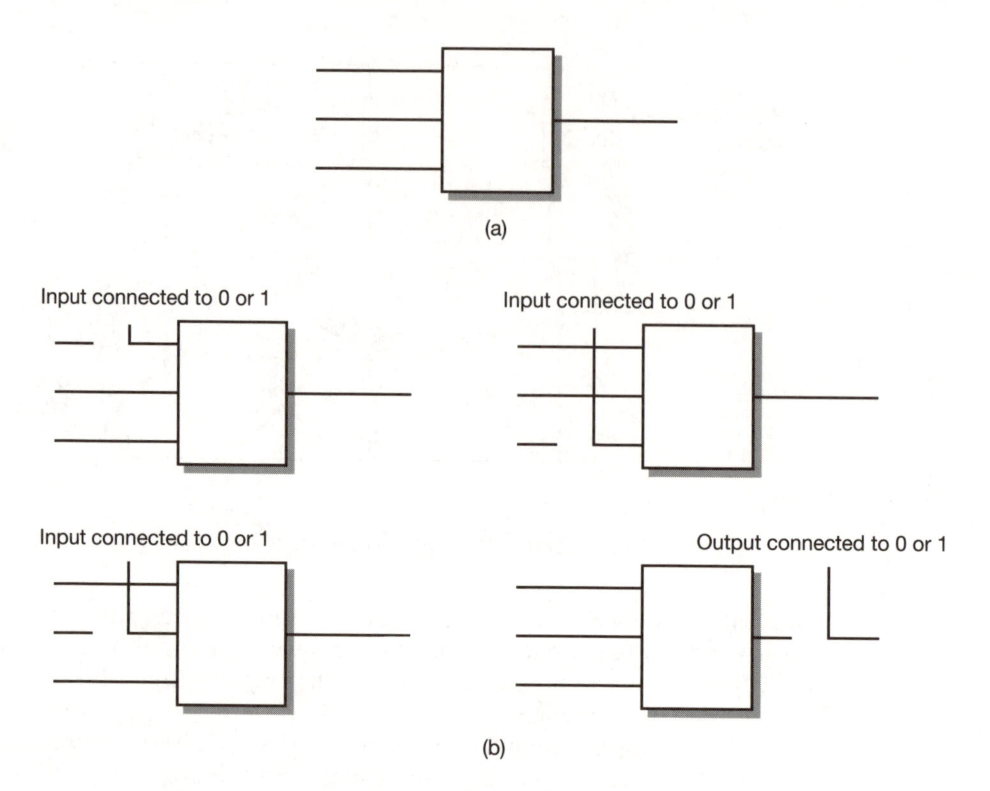

Figure 6.2 Examples of single-stuck-at faults: (a) the fault-free module; (b) possible single-stuck-at faults.

output. The single-stuck-at model cannot accurately represent all fault conditions. Indeed, it cannot represent transient or intermittent faults. However, it does permit a large number of faults to be modelled in a simple manner.

To illustrate the assumptions of the model consider the faults of Figure 6.1. Fault condition (1) would result in the output being continuously at logical 1, while (2) and (3) would result in the output always being at logic 0. Fault (4) would make the circuit behave as if its A input was permanently at logic 1. In fact, a majority of faults arising from broken tracks, open or short-circuit components and shorts between tracks can be represented by the single-stuck-at model.

The bridging model

A **bridging** or **short-circuit fault** occurs when two or more nodes in a circuit are accidentally joined together to form a permanent fault. Although such a fault may sometimes be represented by the single-stuck-at model, this is not always the case. When using positive logic the effect of such a fault is equivalent to the ANDing together of the lines concerned. When using negative logic the effect is equivalent to an OR operation. The result is an unintentional logic operation similar to a 'wired-AND' or 'wired-OR' function. An example of such a fault is shown in Figure 6.3, which represents a very simple form of bridging fault in which two input lines are joined. Often such a fault may be represented using the single-stuck-at model. More complex faults arise when a larger number of nodes are shorted together, or when the bridge represents a feedback path. In the latter case very complex circuit characteristics may be produced. Examples of such faults are shown in Figure 6.4.

A feedback bridging fault may convert a combinational circuit into a sequential arrangement, and may also result in instability or oscillation. The characteristics of the resulting circuit may be very complex.

The stuck-open model

The 'stuck-open' fault model is used to represent a class of faults associated with CMOS gates, which cannot be modelled by a 'stuck-at' representation.

The fault occurs when both the output transistors of a CMOS gate are turned off as a result of an internal open- or short-circuit. This causes the output to be pulled neither high nor low, producing an effect similar to

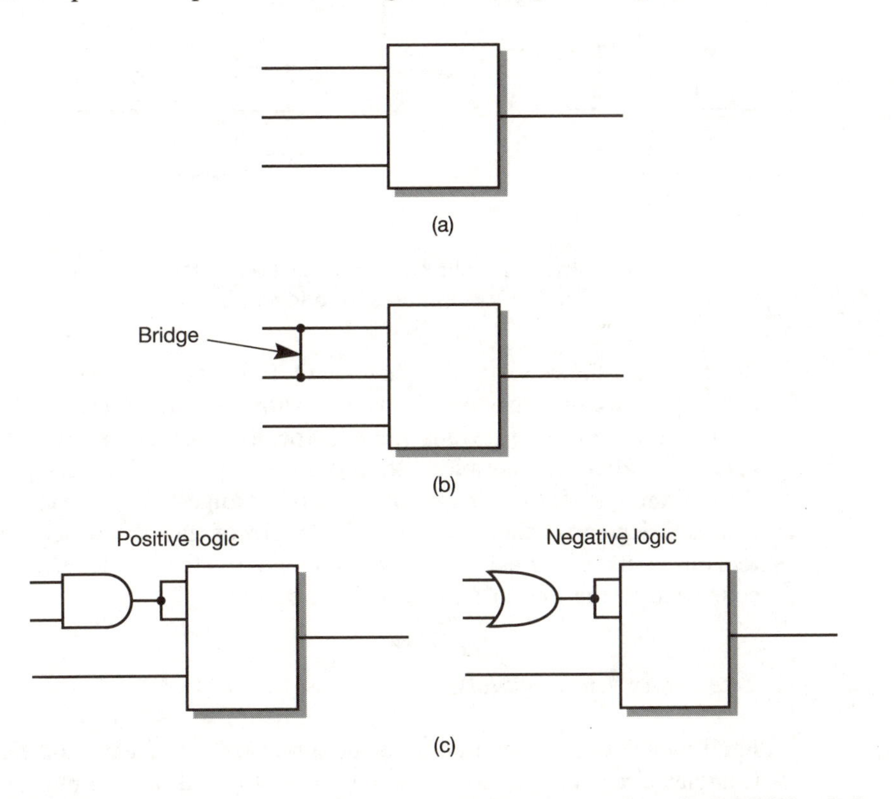

Figure 6.3 A single bridging fault: (a) the fault-free module; (b) a single bridging fault; (c) equivalent circuits.

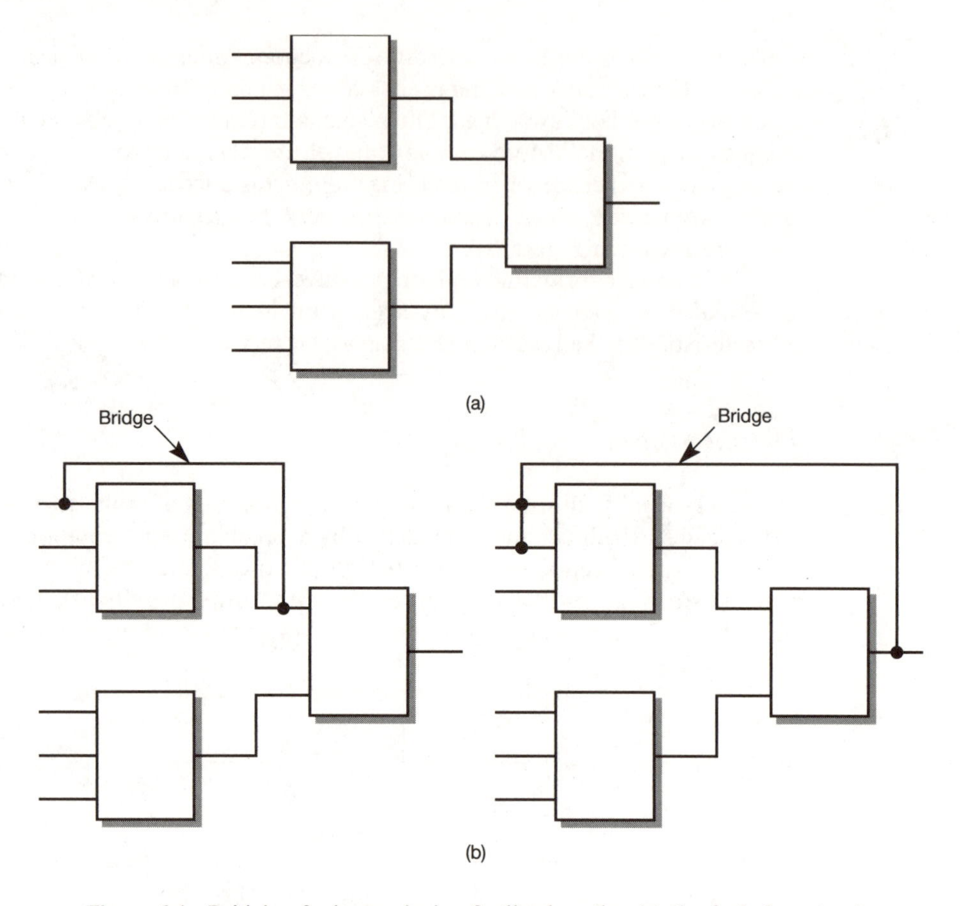

Figure 6.4 Bridging faults producing feedback paths: (a) the fault-free circuit; (b) possible bridging faults.

the high-impedance state of a three-state TTL gate. However, unlike the TTL case, here the capacitive load associated with the CMOS gate tends to maintain its output level at its previous value. Depending on the nature of the fault, the gate may alternate between driving the output and entering this 'output maintaining' state as the input pattern changes. This gives the circuit a complex sequential characteristic. The length of time for which the device will remain in its previous state is determined by the capacitance of the gates connected to the output and by leakage currents.

The use of fault models

Fault models are widely used in the design of testing schemes for digital systems. Complex circuits often have large numbers of inputs and outputs and very large numbers of internal components. Each component and each connection is the site of a potential fault, and the manufacturer is keen to know if the circuit meets its specification. In a simple combinational circuit it may be possible to test the circuit exhaustively by applying all the possible combinations of the inputs and checking the resulting outputs against its truth table. However, because the number of possible combinations increases exponentially with the number of inputs, the testing time increases rapidly with complexity. A circuit having 25 inputs could be tested in a few seconds; a circuit with 50 inputs might require some decades to test. The problem is even more intractable in sequential circuits, where checks would be required on transitions between all possible states.

Fault models provide a method of tackling this problem by characterizing the fault conditions that might exist within a system. A circuit with N nodes has $2N$ potential single-stuck-at faults. By identifying patterns of inputs that will detect each of these fault conditions it is possible to screen a circuit for faults without exhaustively testing its functionality. This is manageable even for circuits having tens of thousands of gates. The combinations of inputs used are termed **test vectors**, and determining a suitable set of such vectors is of great importance in system design.

One of the assumptions made in most testing schemes based on the use of fault models is that only a single fault is likely to exist within the circuit at any one time. The reason for this assumption is pragmatic, in that a circuit with N nodes can have $2N$ single-stuck-at faults but could have $3^N - 1$ multiple faults. Testing to locate all possible combinations of fault conditions would be impractical for all but the simplest circuits. Unfortunately, multiple faults can and do occur, because physical defects can affect more than one node. However, testing is limited to what is practical and the assumption of isolated faults is common.

Testing for the presence of bridging faults or stuck-open faults is even more difficult, first because the nature of the effects is more complex, making it more difficult to devise tests to detect them, and secondly because of the potentially large numbers of faults. We have seen that a circuit with N nodes has $2N$ potential single-stuck-at faults. However, there are $\binom{N}{M}$ possible bridging faults joining M out of N nodes. For example, there are of the order of N^2 potential bridging faults between two nodes, and approaching N^3 possible bridging faults between three nodes. These large numbers, combined with the complexity of the possible circuit behaviour, make exhaustive testing impractical in most cases. For these reasons it is common for testing schemes to disregard complex fault mechanisms altogether, and to hope that techniques designed to detect single-stuck-at faults will also uncover other faults.

For more than a quarter of a century the single-stuck-at fault model has been used with some success, particularly when applied to circuits containing relatively low-complexity devices such as TTL. Unfortunately, with the increasing use of LSI and VLSI components, predominately fabricated using MOS techniques, it has become apparent that this model is not always adequate (Wadsack, 1978; Banerjee and Abraham, 1984). One of the problems associated with the single-stuck-at fault model is its reliance on the use of gate-level representations of circuits. With complex integrated circuits a detailed knowledge of the internal logic is often not available to the test engineer. Also, as complexity increases the distinction between the physical circuit and its logical equivalent becomes more significant. Despite these problems this technique remains one of the most widely used methods for planning the testing of LSI and VLSI circuits. We shall return to the issue of testing in Chapter 12.

In safety-critical systems we are concerned not only with the presence or absence of faults, but also with their effects. Fault models may be used in association with **failure modes and effects analysis (FMEA)**, as discussed in Chapter 3, to determine which faults result in hazardous conditions. This can be used to influence the design so as to minimize the number of potentially dangerous failure modes.

In addition to their use in testing, fault models are also of importance in the production of fault-tolerant systems. In order to design a system capable of tolerating faults it is necessary to have a picture of what faults might be present. Fault models provide this insight, and also enable the designer to estimate the performance of the design by estimating the fraction of the possible faults within a system that can be tolerated.

Hardware design and specification faults

The fault modelling techniques described above can be used to represent physical defects within a circuit but are not concerned with the cause of these defects. Components operating within an appropriate environment exhibit random failures, and statistical techniques can often be used to make predictions about the likely rate of such failures. Fault models can then be used to design strategies to detect or tolerate these random failures. If a component is placed under increased stress owing to a mistake in the design of a circuit, it may fail more quickly than a statistical analysis would predict. If, for example, a resistor which is capable of dissipating one watt is made to dissipate two watts, it is likely that the circuit will work correctly for a period of time. However, the reliability of the resistor is likely to be lower than one would expect for a component operating within its specified rating. If as a result of this design fault the component were to fail, its effects would be indistinguishable from those caused by the random failure of the part. Therefore the fault modelling techniques outlined above are equally applicable to random component failures and parts which fail due to hardware design faults.

Although some failures produced by design faults may be modelled in this way, this is not always the case. Some mistakes in design do not result simply in increased stress being placed on a component, but may result in the operation of the system being incorrect. A mistake in logic design, for example, could mean that a system would give an incorrect output for a given combination of inputs. In some ways this fault may have similar characteristics to those caused by a component failure, in that some combinations of the inputs may produce correct outputs and other combinations produce problems.

However, unlike component failures such design faults cannot be simply modelled, and it is not feasible to construct a series of tests that will detect all possible design faults.

Errors in the specification of a system can manifest themselves as either hardware or software faults, and may cause even more daunting problems for the engineer. Most of the techniques used to achieve safety are aimed at ensuring that the system meets its specification. If this specification is incorrect then no amount of fault detection or fault tolerance will solve the problem. Errors in specification remain one of the most intractable problems within the field of fault tolerance. In general this area must be tackled by one or other of the fault avoidance techniques discussed in other chapters of this book, for example the use of **formal specification languages**, as discussed in Chapter 11.

Software faults

It is universally accepted that all but the most simple programs will inevitably contain 'bugs' – the colloquial term for software faults. Such faults may take an almost unlimited number of forms. Examples include:

- software specification faults
- coding faults
- logical errors within calculations
- stack overflows or underflows
- use of uninitialized variables.

Software does not fail randomly and does not degrade with age. Therefore all failures are systematic and are related to its design. As with hardware design faults, modelling of software faults is difficult because of their diverse forms. This, together with the complexity of most practical software, makes exhaustive testing impossible in almost all cases. In some circumstances a designer may specifically limit the complexity of a routine to make such testing feasible, but this is only possible in exceptional cases.

Faced with the certain existence of software faults, and the impossibility of locating, and hence removing, all of them, we must consider steps to tolerate their presence. However, we shall see later in this chapter that tolerating software faults is one of the more demanding requirements of a safety-critical system.

Fault coverage

We have seen that safety is achieved by a combination of fault avoidance, fault removal, fault detection and fault tolerance. In each case the success of these techniques can be measured by the **fault coverage** achieved, this being the fraction of possible faults that can be avoided, removed, detected or tolerated. In practice it is very difficult to make any numerical estimate of the success of fault avoidance, but in other areas fault models can be used to judge and compare design alternatives.

Fault removal coverage is a measure of the success in finding faults during the testing phase of system development. We noted earlier that fault models are used to select a set of test vectors to detect a maximum number of faults. The goal of testing may be to achieve 100% fault coverage by producing test vectors to exorcise all possible defects. However, the fault models themselves have deficiencies in that they do not include all possible faults. Most models are limited to single faults and do not consider transient or intermittent faults. Consequently, fault removal coverage is always less than complete, thus increasing the need for other techniques to mitigate their effects.

Many fault-tolerant architectures rely on detecting faults during operation. The success with which a system can perform this task is termed its **fault detection coverage**. Coverage can be estimated during the design phase using fault models, but this calculation is constrained by limitations in the models and by practical factors. The ability of a system to tolerate faults is described by its **fault tolerance coverage**.

The use of testing to measure the actual values achieved for the various forms of fault coverage is impractical for real systems, as this would require reproduction of all possible faults and combinations of faults. Estimates based on fault models give a picture of the effects that faults have on a system, but these should not be seen as numerical estimates of its likely reliability. The benefit of fault coverage analysis is that it allows alternative designs to be compared or the implications of changes to be investigated. In Chapter 7 we consider the effects of fault coverage on estimates of system reliability.

6.3 Redundancy

All forms of fault tolerance are achieved by some form of **redundancy**, that is, the use of some additional elements within the system which would not be required in a system that was free from all faults.

Most early fault-tolerant systems used duplicated hardware modules in such a way that failure of an individual module would not normally result in failure of the system. An example of such a system is the simple **triple modular redundancy (TMR)** system of Figure 6.5. The TMR arrangement uses three identical modules which each receive the same input signals. If all the modules are functioning correctly they will produce identical outputs, and any differences between their outputs indicates a module failure. A voting arrangement is used to remove the effects of any single failure by taking the majority view in the case of a disagreement and producing this at its output. The system can therefore tolerate the failure of any single module without this affecting the system's output.

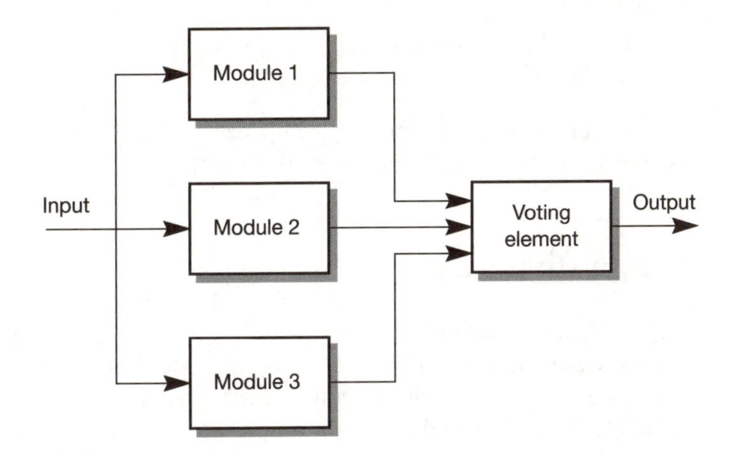

Figure 6.5 Triple modular redundancy.

Forms of redundancy

The TMR system described above is only one of a number of forms of redundancy, and it is convenient to distinguish between a number of basic types.

Hardware redundancy: The use of hardware in addition to that which would be required to implement the system in the absence of faults, with the aim of detecting or tolerating faults. The triple modular system described above is an example of this form of redundancy, and other forms are discussed in the section on hardware fault tolerance later in this chapter.

Software redundancy: The use of software in addition to that which would be required to implement the system in the absence of faults, with the aim of detecting or tolerating faults. Methods of software redundancy are discussed in the section on software fault tolerance later in this chapter.

Information redundancy: The use of information in addition to that required to implement a given function, with the aim of detecting or tolerating faults. Examples include the use of parity bits, error detecting or correcting codes and checksums. Information redundancy may be implemented using hardware or software techniques, and is widely used within communications and VLSI devices such as memories and processors. Various aspects of information redundancy are discussed later in this chapter.

Temporal (time) redundancy: The use of time in addition to that required to implement a given function, with the aim of detecting or tolerating faults. Temporal redundancy might involve repeating calculations and comparing the results obtained. This can be used to detect **transient faults**, and, if more than two calculations are performed, could allow a single faulty calculation to be ignored, thereby providing fault tolerance. Temporal redundancy can be implemented using hardware or software techniques.

Practical fault-tolerant systems use a judicious mix of techniques to provide protection against a range of possible faults.

Design diversity

The TMR arrangement described earlier gives some protection against random hardware component failure but none against design faults, as the identical modules are likely to exhibit similar problems. Failures as a result of similar faults in different redundant modules are termed **common-mode failures**. Providing protection against these faults is much more difficult than with random component failures. Such protection cannot be achieved simply by duplicating identical systems. The basic problem with design faults is that it is impossible to predict the nature or location of the fault. Most attempts to deal with such problems rely on redundancy combined with some form of **diversity**.

In diverse systems an operation is performed in different ways in the hope that the same fault will not be present in the different implementations. An example of such an arrangement might be similar to the TMR system described above, except that the redundant modules would be designed and manufactured by different teams to try to reduce the chance of identical problems occurring in the individual modules. This approach gives increased protection against common-mode faults in exchange for a large increase in design costs

Design diversity can be used in all forms of redundancy. In hardware systems this would involve using modules of different hardware design, whereas in software it would require different programs to implement the same function. It is often advantageous to adopt diverse technologies to implement the channels of a redundant system. For example, one channel might use a microcomputer-based system, whereas a parallel system could be based on a hard-wired approach. Where a non-programmable implementation is impractical a high degree of diversity can be achieved by using a microcomputer within one channel and a programmable logic controller (PLC) within another. The use of these two distinct approaches leads to widely different hardware and software within the two implementations.

In an ideal world a system incorporating both redundancy and diverse design would provide good protection against both random component failure and some forms of design faults. It would not, however, provide protection against mistakes within the specification, as even diverse systems will generally be attempts to implement the same specification.

Even discounting for the moment the problems associated with mistakes within the specification, the use of diversity cannot totally remove the possibility of common-mode failures. Research has shown that getting different teams to design a module does not remove the likelihood of similar faults in the implementations. One particular research project involved asking 27 engineers to independently implement a program from the same specification. The results showed that although the programs were each extremely reliable, they showed many common faults (Knight and Leveson, 1986). Despite this finding, it is generally accepted that diverse design has great value in reducing common-mode failures, although it cannot guarantee freedom from such problems (Bishop *et al.*, 1985). Diverse design has also been shown to be of benefit in locating ambiguities within the specification, as different teams usually adopt diverse interpretations.

6.4 Fault detection techniques

Many fault-tolerance techniques rely on the detection of faults. In practice faults are detected as a result of the errors they produce, and a purist might argue that we should therefore speak of error detection rather than fault detection. In some applications it is appropriate to consider errors rather than faults. This is particularly true when we consider transient faults that produce errors and then disappear. Any attempt to locate the fault itself will be futile, but it is important to deal with the consequences of the fault in terms of the resultant error. In areas such as communications, errors are often dominated by transient noise effects. Here it is common to be concerned with error detection and to use techniques such as error detecting and correcting codes to mitigate their effects. In other areas most faults are permanent, and it is important to locate the source of any errors so that appropriate steps may be taken to mitigate their effects. We are therefore primarily interested in the faults within our system, and for that reason we will here use the term fault detection.

As we have seen, faults may be associated with either hardware or software. Similarly, we may use either hardware or software techniques to locate faults of either type. Once a fault has been detected this information may then be used with an appropriate hardware or software form of fault tolerance. A great many fault detection schemes are used. Here we will consider some examples.

Functionality checking

Having noted that software techniques may be used to detect hardware problems, we start by looking at functionality checking. This involves the use of routines which check to see that the hardware of the system is functioning correctly. Common examples of this form of checking include memory, processor and communications checks.

Random-access memory (RAM) testing involves writing into and reading back from memory locations to verify their operation. In small systems it might be feasible to test all locations, but in most cases only a fraction of the memory space is tested. Some thought must go into the design of the algorithm used to test memory, as simply getting back the result written is not necessarily proof that the device is working correctly. It is possible, for example, that the memory location in question has a stuck-at fault on one of its bits but that the test pattern used matches the faulty bit. This can be detected by testing a location twice using a pattern and its ones complement. Even this test is not foolproof, however. In some cases testing a non-existent memory location using this technique will not detect the absence of the device. The capacitance of the floating bus lines is often sufficient to maintain the data word written, so that it is read back the next time the bus is accessed. Such problems can be tackled by interleaving writes and reads to different locations. Over the years several very efficient algorithms have been developed for testing large memory spaces in a short period of time, with reasonable fault coverage. These tests are often used to supplement parity checking or other forms of information redundancy. Read-only memory (ROM) may be tested by periodically calculating checksums and comparing these with values stored within the ROM.

The processor or processors within a system may be checked by executing a sequence of calculations and comparing the results with known values. The data and expected results for these calculations are stored in ROM. If the routine contains a wide range of processing operations this test verifies the operation of a large part of the system, including the processor, sections of the memory and the bus system.

In multiprocessor systems checks can be performed periodically to ensure that each processor can communicate with its neighbours. This verifies the communications paths, and also allows one processor to detect failure in another.

Consistency checking

Consistency checking uses some knowledge of the nature of the information within the system to test its validity. An example of this form of testing is **range checking**. This compares calculated or stored values for a variable with predefined values for its allowable range.

Signal comparison

In systems with redundancy it is possible to check the signals at similar points in the various modules to validate them. This process is simpler if the modules are identical, rather than of diverse design.

Checking pairs

Checking pairs are effectively a special case of the use of signal comparison. Here identical modules are designed to allow a comparison of multiple signals in an attempt to detect any discrepancies. If the modules produce identical signals it is assumed that both are fault free.

Information redundancy

Various forms of information redundancy can be used to detect faults. These include parity checking; *M*-out-of-*N* codes; checksums; cyclic redundancy codes; and error correcting codes. Each of these techniques uses additional redundant information that is used to check the validity of the data. These techniques are described in many texts, including Guy (1991).

Instruction monitoring

Normal operation of a processor involves the repeated fetching and execution of instructions. An error during the fetching of an instruction may corrupt the operation code or the operand. In either case the correct operation of the program is likely to be disrupted.

Corruption of the operand of an instruction will generally produce a legal instruction, albeit an incorrect one. Modification of the operation code, on the other hand, will sometimes produce a meaningless value which the processor can detect as an error. The action taken by the processor in response to such as error varies greatly between devices. Some processors immediately raise an exception, allowing the error to be detected immediately before further damage is done. Others have less satisfactory responses, in that they simply fetch the next byte from memory, ignoring an obvious system fault. In many devices the action taken in these circumstances is undefined. Processors that do not take appropriate action in response to unimplemented instructions must not be used in safety-critical systems. The choice of processors for such applications will be discussed in Chapter 8.

Loopback testing

We saw when looking at single-stuck-at faults that many faults are associated with signal paths that are broken or shorted to other parts of the circuit. One method of detecting faults of this kind is the use of loopback testing. This verifies that signals leaving one point of a circuit arrive at their destination unchanged. This is achieved by providing an independent return path for the signal back to its source, and by comparing the outgoing and return signals to ensure equivalence.

Loopback testing is widely used on input/output lines, particularly in applications such as serial communications. It can also be used within the processor section itself, to ensure correct connections between the processor and its associated components. Bus lines, for example, may be constructed as loops so that they leave the processor, go to all relevant nodes of the circuit, and then return to the processor for verification. In multiboard systems a 'daisy-chain' arrangement may be used to ensure that all the boards are present. The effectiveness of this technique requires that great care is taken with the layout of the boards to ensure that the outward and return paths are never adjacent, to prevent the possibility of a short-circuit.

Watchdog timers

One of the simplest methods of detecting the 'crash' of a processor is to use a watchdog timer. The timer is arranged so that it will cause the system to reset if it is allowed to time out, but is prevented from doing so by specific processor activity. While the processor is operating normally the timer is periodically loaded with an appropriate value. The timer repeatedly decrements this number and, if undisturbed, would eventually reach zero and reset the system. However, the value loaded into the timer is chosen to ensure that it will be reloaded by the processor before it reaches zero. Even so, if the processor were to crash it would stop reloading the timer which would soon time out and cause the system to be reset.

Although easy to implement, the watchdog does have limitations. Following a system crash the processor will often continue to operate for some considerable time before the watchdog is brought into play. During this time the operation of the processor is unpredictable and potentially hazardous. Although the watchdog will normally respond within a few milliseconds, this may not be fast enough to ensure safety or to prevent considerable damage to the system's database. It is also conceivable that the system could crash in such a way that the watchdog would still be reset periodically, thereby preventing its intervention.

Bus monitoring

A more sophisticated method of checking the operation of the processor is the use of bus monitoring to check the range of the addresses being accessed by a program. Each bus address is compared with the allowable range for that program, and any out-of-range value will result in an error being reported to the processor.

Power supply monitoring

Many modern electronic components operate over a fairly narrow range of supply voltages. Fortunately, the absolute maximum voltage permitted for such components is considerably greater than their nominal operating voltage. Consequently, a well-designed power supply, together with overvoltage protection, can normally protect components from damage due to excessive supply voltages.

Often more serious problems can arise when the supply voltage drops below that required for normal operation of the system. Although the power supply may protect the system from excessively high supply voltages, it cannot prevent the supply voltage from dropping below acceptable levels. This is inevitable when the system is first turned on and when it is turned off. It may also occur if the supply voltage fails or 'dips' during operation. Many processors behave unpredictably in these circumstances, even though memory and address decoding circuitry may be functioning correctly. This can result in large amounts of data being corrupted.

The adverse effects of power supply fluctuations may be reduced by the use of a power supply monitor. This detects a fall in the supply voltage before it reaches a dangerous level, and gives the processor time to take emergency action before the supply disappears. Data is protected by preventing the processor from operating during periods of low supply voltage – perhaps by holding it in its reset state. This condition is maintained until the supply returns to an acceptable level.

Some systems must operate continuously and cannot permit disruption by power supply failure. In such cases an **uninterruptible power source** must be used. These use large-capacity batteries which are charged continuously during normal operation, to provide power in the event of a supply failure.

6.5 Hardware fault tolerance

The most common method of achieving fault tolerance involves the use of redundant hardware. As the cost and size of electronic components have fallen, the use of replicated hardware has become progressively more attractive and is now increasingly used as a method of improving system reliability.

Hardware redundancy may take one of three basic forms, namely static, dynamic or hybrid. **Static** systems utilize **fault masking**, rather than fault detection, to achieve fault tolerance. They are designed to tolerate faults without requiring specific action by the system or its operator. **Dynamic** redundancy relies on the detection of faults and on the system taking appropriate action to nullify their effects. This involves the reconfiguration of the system to remove the influence of the faulty component. **Hybrid** techniques use a combination of these methods. A hybrid approach uses fault masking to prevent errors from being propagated within the system, and fault detection and reconfiguration to remove faulty units from the system.

Static redundancy

Static redundancy relies on the use of some form of voting mechanism to compare the outputs of a number of modules to mask the effects of faults within these units. The simplest version of this arrangement requires three modules and is termed a triple modular redundant system. Increased fault tolerance may be obtained by the use of additional redundant modules, and in general such schemes are termed *N*-modular redundant systems.

Triple modular redundancy

A simple triple modular redundant (TMR) system was discussed earlier and is shown in Figure 6.6. In such a system three modules receive identical input signals and should produce identical outputs. A voter compares the outputs from the three modules. If all three modules agree, their unanimous view on the appropriate output is produced by the voter. If, as a result of a single fault, the output of one of the units differs from those of its neighbours, the voter will produce an output corresponding to the majority view. This majority voting scheme therefore masks failure in any single module.

Here redundancy is used to prevent the failure of a single component causing the failure of the complete system – a so-called **single-point failure**. Triplication of the modules in Figure 6.6 protects against failures within the modules, but still leaves areas where single-point failures could occur. One such area is the source of the input signals. If these come from a single sensor, then failure of this sensor would affect inputs to all of the modules and thus negate the effects of the redundancy. In critical systems it is normal to duplicate, or perhaps triplicate, the sensors in order to remove this possible source of a single-point failure. It is not uncommon to use diverse sensors in such cases to reduce the likelihood of a systematic fault within the sensors causing common failures.

Unfortunately, using multiple sensors can sometimes lead to other problems. This is particularly true in the case of analogue signal sources, or sensors which have variability in their speed of response. When analogue

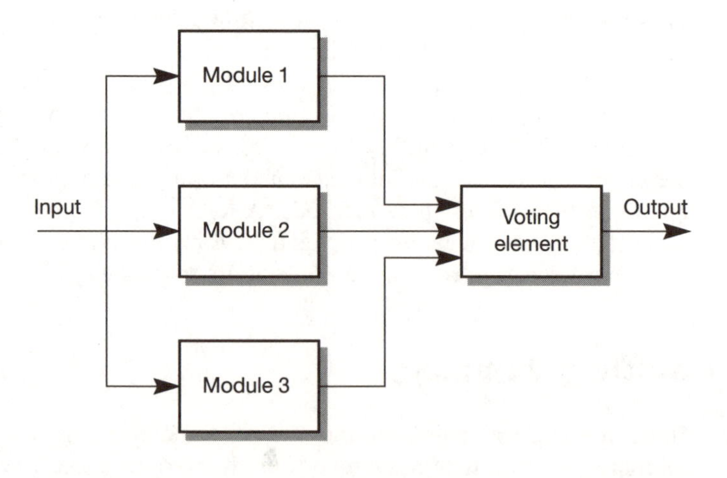

Figure 6.6 A simple triple modular redundancy arrangement.

signals form an input to a digital system they must be digitized using an analogue-to-digital converter. To avoid a possible source of single-point failure it is desirable to duplicate not only the analogue sensors, but also the digital-to-analogue converters associated with them. Unfortunately, quantization errors mean that in general these converters will not always produce identical outputs, which greatly complicates the task of comparing the module outputs. Sensors with variable response speeds produce similar problems. As duplicated sensors must be physically separate, they will generally be activated at slightly different times. Because of the high speed of digital systems, the differences between the sensor outputs could result in disagreements at the module outputs if steps are not taken to deal with transient differences.

The other area vulnerable to single-point failure is the voting arrangement. One approach to this problem is to design the voter to be dependable. The function of the voter is not complex and it may therefore be possible to produce a simple, reliable unit which will meet the overall performance requirements of the system. This approach is described later in this section. An alternative technique is to replicate the voting mechanism, as shown in Figure 6.7.

Triplication of the voting element removes a source of single-point failure and produces three independent outputs that will *all* be correct provided that no more than a single module fails. Several such stages may be cascaded, using the three outputs from one stage to drive the three inputs to the next. Failure of a single voting element will result in a single output failure, the effects of which should be removed by the next TMR stage. Such an arrangement is shown in Figure 6.8.

It is clear that the TMR system cannot provide protection against simultaneous failure of two of its three modules. Use of this techniques relies on the assumption that failure of two modules is significantly less likely than failure of a single module. In the case of random hardware component failures

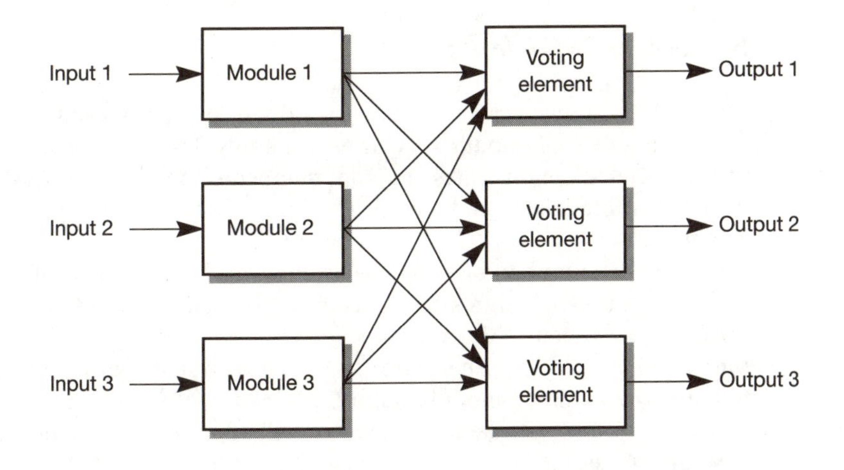

Figure 6.7 A triple modular redundancy system with triplicated voting.

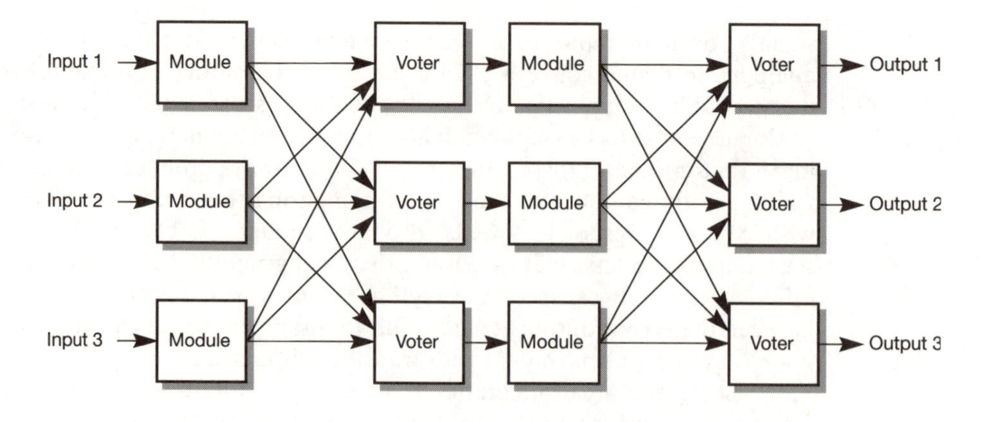

Figure 6.8 A multistage TMR arrangement.

this is likely to be the case, but systematic failures, such as hardware design or software failures, may affect all similar modules at the same time. Hardware redundancy using identical modules provides little protection against such systematic faults.

Static hardware redundancy provides fault tolerance by masking the effects of module failure. Faults are therefore tolerated without any specific action being required of the system. However, once a module has failed the ability of the system to tolerate further faults is reduced, and in a TMR system may be non-existent. It is therefore vital that the presence of a faulty module is noted so that it can be repaired or replaced. This may be of particular importance in the case of intermittent or temporary faults, which may not be noticed during regular maintenance. A system which logs every disagreement between modules will provide much useful data for detecting unreliable module or system operation.

N-*modular redundancy*

The TMR arrangement may be generalized by considering an arrangement of any number of modules. This is generally termed ***N*-modular redundancy (NMR)**, and in many cases an odd number of modules is used to enable a majority voting scheme to be used. The form of such an arrangement is shown in Figure 6.9.

As the number of modules is increased the ability of the system to withstand module failures also increases. In general, module failure will not result in a system failure provided that a majority of the modules are functioning correctly. Therefore, although a system with three modules can tolerate only a single module failure, a system with five modules may tolerate two failures and a system with seven will tolerate three module failures. In general the system will tolerate the failure of $(N-1)/2$ modules without producing a system failure. The advantages of using large numbers of

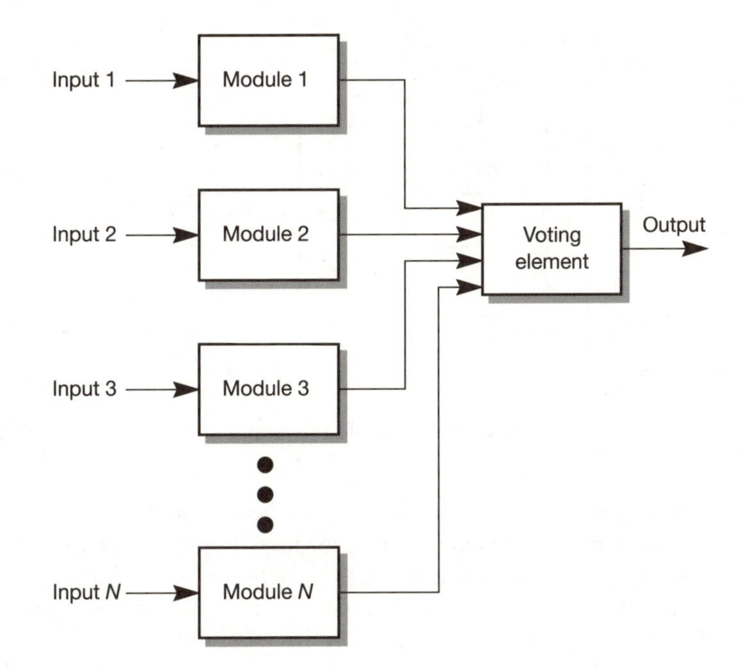

Figure 6.9 An N-modular redundant system.

redundant modules is clear. However, the disadvantages are also self-evident in that it results in high cost, size, weight and power consumption. In practice the number of identical modules is rarely greater than four.

Although Figure 6.9 shows a single voting element, clearly there are advantages to the use of multiple voters, as discussed earlier for TMR systems.

Voting techniques

The voting operation may be performed either in hardware or in software and, as we have seen, may take place at several stages throughout a multiple-stage system.

Hardware voting elements may be very simple. Figure 6.10 shows an arrangement suitable for a TMR system. This compares its three inputs and produces an output of logical '1' if two or more of its inputs are '1', or logical '0' if two or more of its outputs are '0'. The truth table of the arrangement is shown to demonstrate the characteristics of the circuit. Because of the low complexity of the circuit (approximately that of a single MSI package) it may have a reliability much greater than that of the duplicated modules. In many cases modules produce many bits of output requiring several independent comparisons. This can be achieved by duplicating this simple circuit for each output bit. It can be seen that although the circuit itself is simple, for circuits producing large numbers of outputs the voter can represent a significant

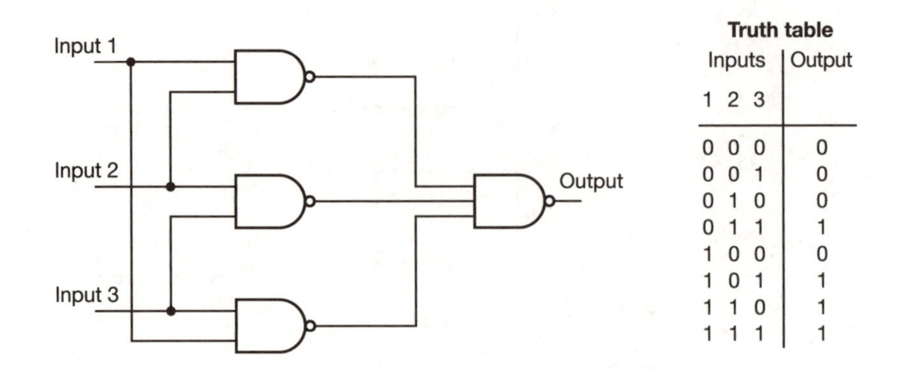

Truth table

Inputs 1	2	3	Output
0	0	0	0
0	0	1	0
0	1	0	0
0	1	1	1
1	0	0	0
1	0	1	1
1	1	0	1
1	1	1	1

Figure 6.10 A simple three-input, single-bit voting element.

amount of hardware. It should also be noted that this simple circuit has no mechanism for indicating or recording discrepancies for use during maintenance or for reliability assessment. Including such features within a hardware voter produces a considerable increase in its complexity and, as we shall see in Chapter 7, a corresponding fall in its reliability.

Performing voting in software removes the need for additional hardware. It also simplifies the collection of data relating to any disagreements between the inputs. This information is a form of fault detection and is invaluable in determining maintenance requirements. It should be remembered, however, that software is not a free resource and that any extra features implemented in software have their own costs in terms of development effort, speed of response and an increase in system complexity. Performing error monitoring in software increases its complexity, and therefore also has implications for its reliability.

One of the primary considerations in deciding between hardware and software voting schemes is the required speed of operation. Hardware voters operate very quickly, being limited only by the propagation delays of the gates within them. Software voting is much slower, as each comparison may represent many processor operations. In many cases the appropriate technique is chosen based on a trade-off between speed of operation and hardware costs.

Dynamic redundancy

Static systems achieve fault tolerance by **masking** faults, and in this way they prevent errors from propagating throughout the system. The price for this is very high levels of redundancy, with at least three modules being required to tolerate a single fault and five modules being needed to enable two faults to be accommodated. Dynamic systems adopt a different approach, using fault detection in place of fault masking. One unit is normally in use, with one or more **standby systems** being available in case this unit should fail. This approach reduces the amount of redundancy required, as only two modules are needed to cope with a single fault and three to cater for two faulty units. The success of this approach is largely determined by the effectiveness of the fault detection process.

As was noted earlier, fault detection schemes operate by detecting the errors produced by a fault. Consequently, errors must be produced within the system before a dynamic system can recognize the fault and take appropriate action. Dynamic systems do not mask faults, but rather they attempt to **contain** faults and then to reconfigure the system to achieve fault tolerance. For this reason dynamic redundancy is suited to applications that can tolerate temporary errors within their operation.

Standby spares

One of the most common dynamic redundancy systems is the 'standby spare' arrangement shown in Figure 6.11. Here one module is operated in connection with some form of fault detection scheme. While no fault is detected the single module drives the outputs through a switch arrangement which is controlled by the fault detection system. If a fault is detected, the switch will reconfigure the system so that outputs are taken from the standby module.

Reconfiguring the system following the detection of a fault effectively removes the faulty module from the system and thus removes its effects (though not necessarily any errors already produced). The process of reconfiguration will cause a momentary disruption of the system while outputs are switched. This disruption may be minimized by the use of a **hot standby** arrangement, where the spare is run continuously in parallel with the active unit. This allows a fast transfer of control with a minimum of delay. A disadvantage of this arrangement is that the standby unit increases the power consumption of the system. The standby unit is also subjected to the same operating stress as the active unit, which could be greater than that of an unpowered module.

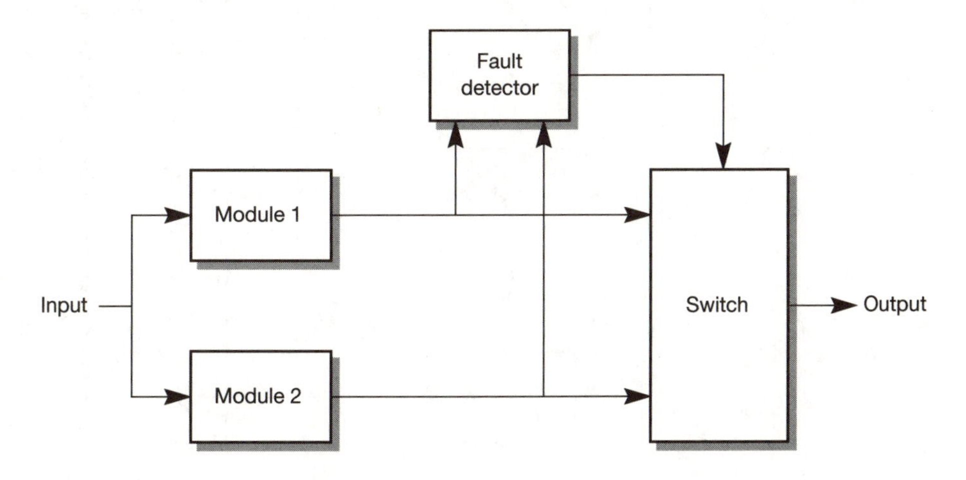

Figure 6.11 A standby spare arrangement.

An alternative approach is to use a **cold standby** arrangement, where the standby is unpowered until called into service. This reduces power consumption and reduces wear and tear on the backup module, but will generally cause more disruption at the changeover. Control cannot be switched to the replacement unit until it has come up to power and has carried out any initialization procedures.

The two-module system of Figure 6.11 can be extended to include any number of standby modules, as shown in Figure 6.12. As before, a single module determines the outputs at any one time, with fault detection circuitry switching to successive modules in the event of module failures.

The effectiveness of the standby spare arrangement depends very heavily on the performance of the fault detection techniques used. Fault detection was discussed in some detail in Section 6.4.

Self-checking pairs

Another example of dynamic redundancy is the self-checking pair arrangement. Here two identical modules are fed with the same input signals and their outputs

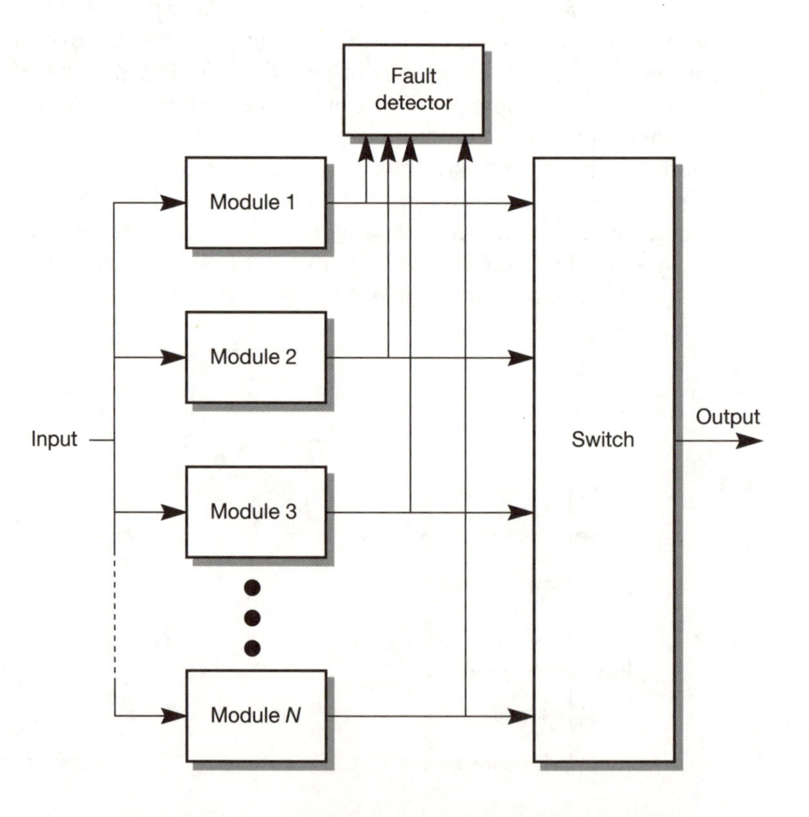

Figure 6.12 A standby sparing system with N modules.

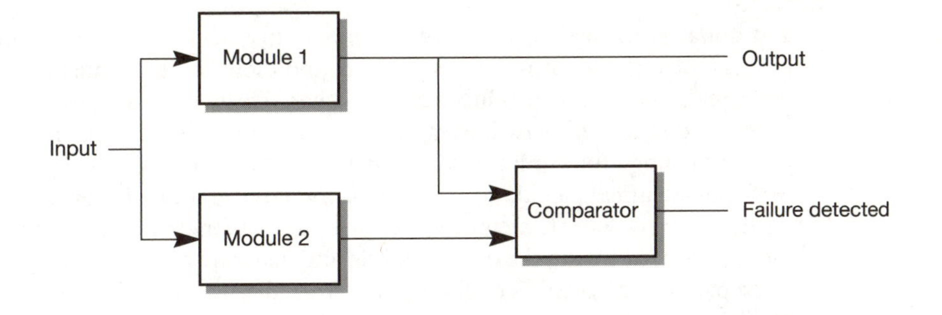

Figure 6.13 A self-checking pair.

are compared. The output from one of the modules is passed to the next stage and the output of the comparator is used as a failure detection signal. The arrangement is shown in Figure 6.13.

The comparator may be implemented in either hardware or software. A simple hardware comparator may be formed using a number of Exclusive-OR (XOR) gates (Figure 6.14). A single gate is used to compare each corresponding signal from the two modules. The output of the XOR gate will be '0' when the signals match and '1' when they are different. The outputs from a set of gates may then be inclusive-ORed together to produce a signal which is '1' if any of the comparisons have failed. This forms a 'failure detected' signal.

If each of the modules in the checking pair contains a processor the comparison may be performed in software, thus removing the need for

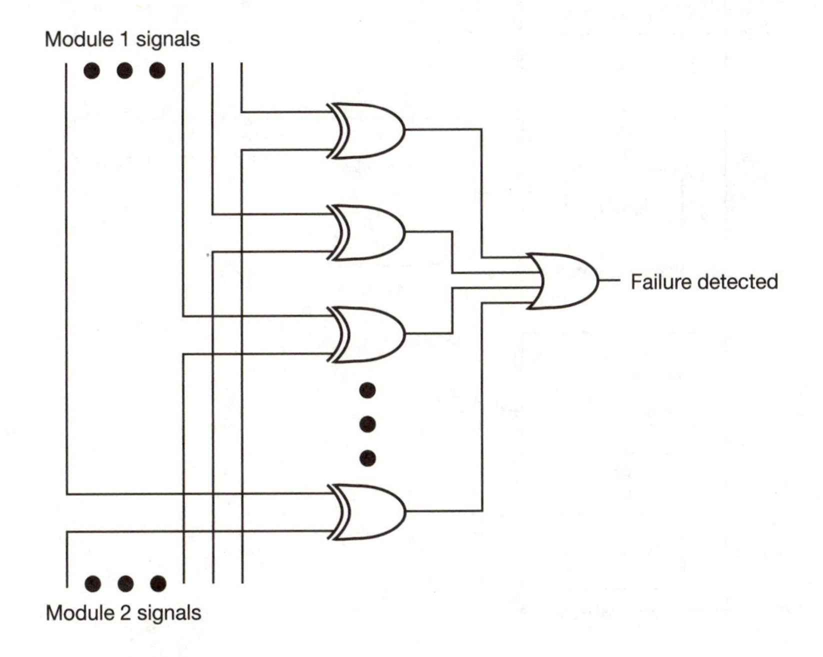

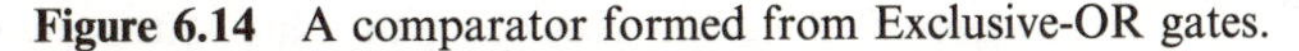

Figure 6.14 A comparator formed from Exclusive-OR gates.

additional hardware. To remove the possibility of a single-point failure both processors must perform the comparison, and therefore each must have access to the signals and results produced by the other. This can be achieved in a number of ways, one of which is illustrated in Figure 6.15. The circuit here uses dual-ported memory for communication between the two modules. Each processor performs identical calculations on the same input data and stores a copy of its results in the dual-port memory. The processors then compare their results with those produced within the other module and generate a 'fail' output signal if any discrepancy is detected. The fail signals from the two modules are combined by an OR gate, which will produce a 'failure detected' signal if either unit fails. Failure of the dual-port memory will normally be detected by both units, as this will result in discrepancies between the stored and calculated values.

The duplicated comparison provided in software in the above system may also be achieved within hardware, but at the expense of additional components. The provision of multiple comparisons reduces the likelihood that an error within a module will result in an incorrect output because of a comparator fault. The result of this duplication is the production of multiple signals indicating that a failure has been detected. In Figure 6.15 two such signals are combined using an OR gate. Failure of this gate could result in a loss of fault detection, despite duplication of the comparators. This weakness may be overcome as shown in Figure 6.16. Here the outputs from two independent comparisons control separate switches in series with the

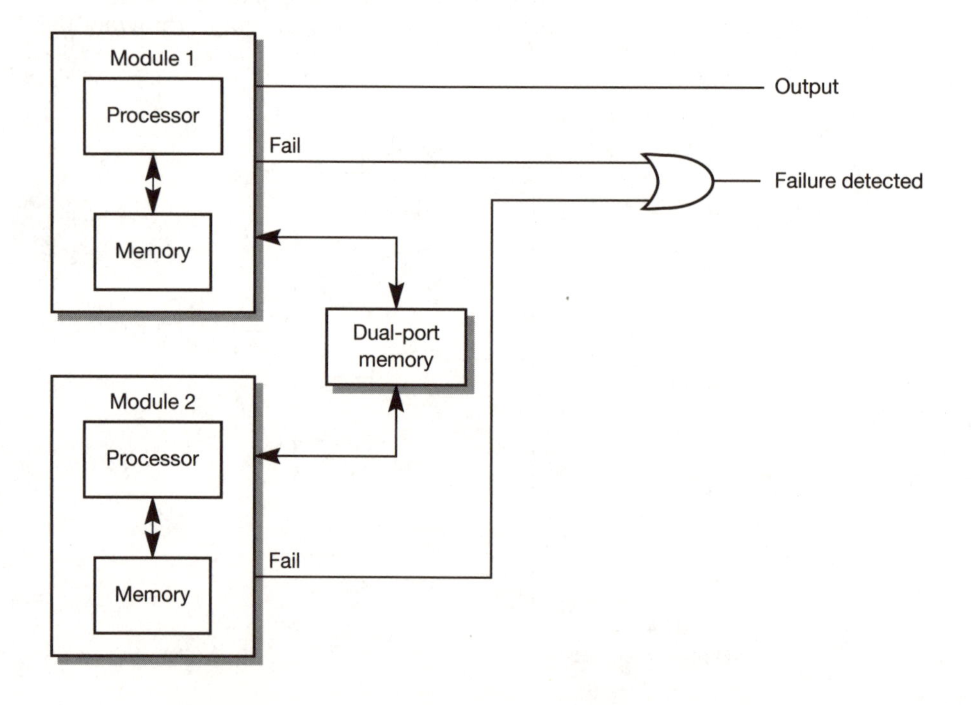

Figure 6.15 A self-checking pair using software comparison.

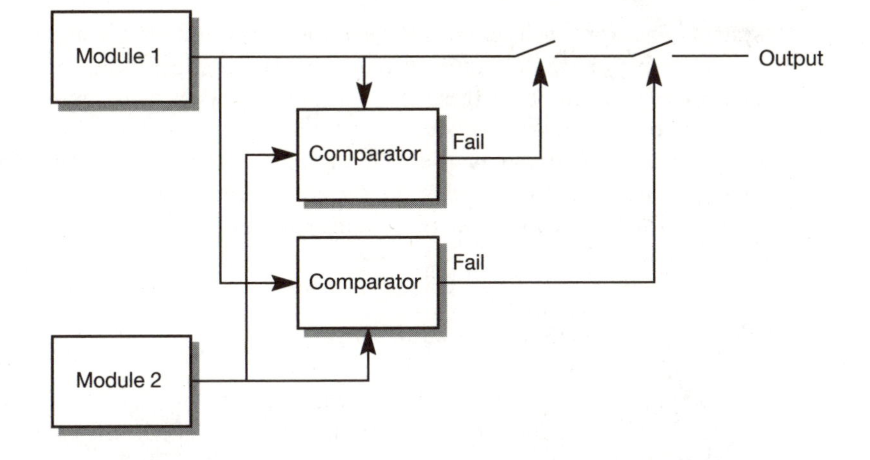

Figure 6.16 Combining failure detection signals using switches.

output of the active unit. If both comparisons show no discrepancies, the two switches are closed and the output of the active unit is applied to its destination. If either comparison shows disagreement between the modules, one of the switches will be opened and the output will be disconnected. Thus both modules must agree in order for an output to be generated. Failure of either comparator, or either switch, should not allow incorrect signals to be produced at the output, even in the event of a module failure. Such an arrangement is not suitable in all situations, but is of use where disconnecting the output causes the system to enter a safe state.

The self-checking pair arrangement does not in itself provide fault tolerance. It does, however, provide a powerful method of fault detection, which can be used to advantage in dynamic fault-tolerant systems. For example, a number of self-checking pairs could be used in a standby spare configuration, with the comparisons performed within the pairs forming the basis of the fault detection system.

We noted when considering static redundancy systems that analogue inputs and signals with variable response times make the voting process difficult, as the various modules do not always see the same inputs. Such inputs also cause problems for self-checking pairs for precisely the same reasons. Dealing with these problems can often lead to a considerable increase in system complexity.

Hybrid redundancy

We have seen that static redundancy uses voting to produce fault masking, but achieves this at the cost of large amounts of redundancy. Dynamic systems make use of fault detection and some form of switching to remove faulty units from the system. This approach requires less redundancy but does not mask faults, making it unsuitable in many applications where transient faults are unacceptable. Hybrid systems combine these techniques and may provide many of the benefits of the two approaches.

Hybrid redundancy uses a combination of voting, fault detection and module switching. Many techniques are used, although most can be generalized as some form of *N*-modular redundancy with spares.

N-*modular redundancy with spares*

This approach, as its name implies, embodies elements derived from the static technique of *N*-modular redundancy and dynamic methods based on the use of standby spares. A typical arrangement is shown in Figure 6.17.

The arrangement provides *N* active modules connected through a switching arrangement to a voter. In the absence of any module faults the voter will simply present the unanimous view of the modules as its output. Should one of the active modules fail, the voter will mask this fault by adopting the majority view of the correct output. However, the module which produced a diverse output is identified by the disagreement detector and this module is removed from the voting arrangement by the switch unit, its place being taken by one of the spare modules. The voting arrangement therefore gives tolerance of the first fault within the system. The faulty module is then removed to restore the fault tolerance capability of the arrangement. The number of faulty modules that can be accommodated is determined by the number of spare units provided.

Hybrid techniques require a level of redundancy between those associated with static and dynamic systems, and in many cases offer an attractive compromise, although great care must be taken in the design of the switch. The use of majority voting masks faults from the outside world, while fault identification and system reconfiguration maintain fault tolerance and guide maintenance.

Module synchronization and diversity in hardware redundancy

Many aspects of hardware redundancy are related to a comparison between the operation of different modules performing the same processing operations on supposedly identical inputs. In static techniques this comparison takes the form of voting, where modules which do not agree with the consensus view are ignored. Within dynamic systems fault detection is often performed by comparing the outputs, or internal signals, of different modules. In each case the comparison is much easier to perform if it can be assumed that the signals associated with each module should be identical at all times. In microprocessor-based systems this requires that the processors operate in exact synchrony. In practice this can only be accomplished by driving the processors from the same

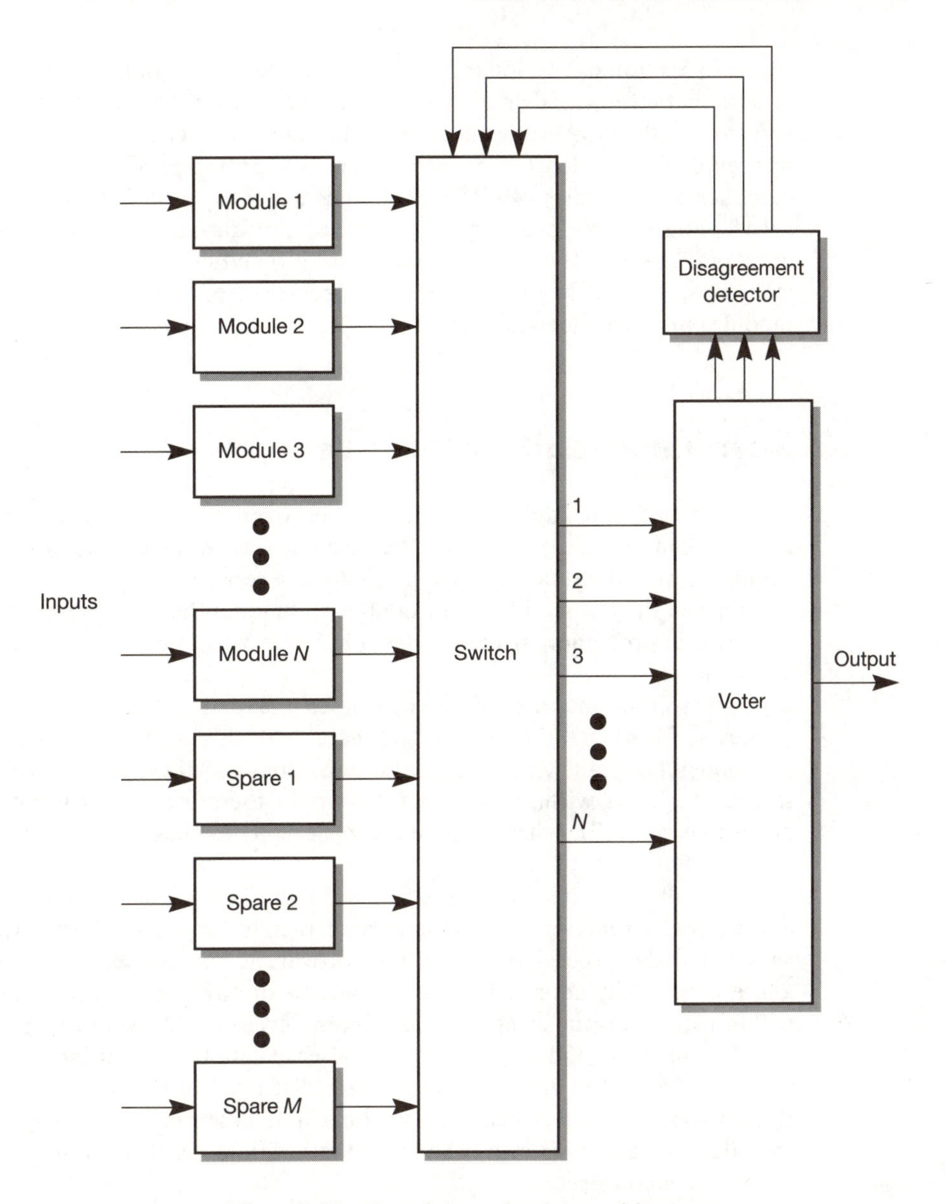

Figure 6.17 *N*-modular redundancy with spares.

clock signal. Under these circumstances the devices are said to be in **lock step**. One problem with this arrangement is that it requires that there is one circuit section – the clock – that is common to all modules. This makes this circuit a possible site for a single-point failure. In many cases it is not possible to operate all modules in lock step. In these circumstances the voting or comparison methods must allow for the timing differences which will inevitably occur between the modules.

In Section 6.3 we looked at the use of diverse design to combat the effects of systematic faults, such as those due to mistakes in the hardware design, the software or the system specification. Although diversity offers gains in terms of improved fault tolerance it can make the provision of redundancy more complicated. Modules of different designs are likely to differ in their response speeds, and so may produce temporary output disagreements even when they are working correctly. To overcome these difficulties voting or signal comparison must be synchronized with the operation of the system such that all modules produce identical signals

6.6 Software fault tolerance

The term 'software fault tolerance' can be taken to mean two distinct things. First, it can be used to mean 'the tolerance of software faults'. Using this definition we would include within this area several of the hardware techniques discussed in the last section. For example, techniques that use diverse redundancy will provide protection against systematic faults associated with software as well as hardware.

A second interpretation takes it to mean 'the tolerance of faults (of whatever form) by the use of software'. In this section we will look at techniques that fall within this definition. Some of these techniques are used to tolerate faults within software (and would therefore satisfy the first of our definitions as well), whereas others can be used to tackle both hardware and software faults.

In all computer-based systems software forms an essential component and normally represents a major part of their overall complexity. Experience shows that the process of generating software is very susceptible to mistakes, and it is generally accepted that all programs of any size have faults, or 'bugs', within them. Various techniques have been developed to avoid the introduction of software faults and to track down and eradicate those that circumvent these methods. Several of these techniques are discussed in other chapters. Despite these techniques, in critical applications it is essential to design systems to tolerate software bugs and other systematic faults, as their complete removal cannot be guaranteed.

When a hardware module containing a processor is duplicated to provide redundancy, any programs within the module must also be duplicated. If the software within each module is identical, then this duplication of the software does nothing to increase the system's ability to tolerate faults within this software – any fault within one version of the program will be present in all the copies. Duplication of the hardware provides protection against random component failures, as units will fail at different times. A problem within the software is likely to affect all identical modules at the same instant. In order to protect the system from software faults there must be diversity in the software. We will look at two of the more common methods of achieving fault tolerance through the use of software. These are the 'N-version programming' and the 'recovery block' methods.

N-version programming

As suggested by its name, this technique involves using several different implementations of a program (Chen and Avizienis, 1978; Avizienis, 1985). These versions all attempt to implement the same specification and therefore should produce the same results. The different versions may be run sequentially on the same processor, or in parallel on different processors. The various routines use the same input data and their results are compared. In the absence of disagreement between the software modules the unanimous answer is passed to its destination. If the modules produce different results the action taken will depend on the number of versions used. For a duplicated system ($N = 2$) the situation is analogous to that of the self-checking pair discussed earlier. Disagreement between the modules represents a fault condition, but the system cannot tell which module is incorrect. This problem might be tackled by repeating the calculations in the hope that the problem is transient. This approach would be successful if the error had been caused by a transient hardware fault which disrupted the processor during the execution of the software module. Alternatively, the system might attempt to perform some further diagnostics to decide which routine is in error. A more attractive arrangement uses three or more versions of the software. If $N = 3$ or more then it is possible to use some form of voting to mask the effects of faults. It is clear that such an arrangement is a software equivalent of the triple or N-modular redundant hardware system. Although large values of N have attractions from a functional viewpoint, the high costs involved usually make them impractical. In real applications it is extremely unusual to use a value of N greater than 2.

Through the use of diversity, N-version programming provides a degree of protection against the systematic faults associated with software. However, it should be remembered that diverse implementation does not guarantee the absence of common faults. The limitations of such design diversity were discussed at the end of Section 6.3.

The main disadvantages of N-version programming are its processing requirements and its cost of implementation. If a single processor is used the calculation time will be increased by a factor of more than N, compared to that of a single version implementation. The increase beyond a factor of N is caused by the additional complexity associated with the voting process. If N processors are used, this time overhead may be removed, with the cost of additional hardware. In either case, the software development costs tend to be increased by a factor of more than N, owing to the cost of implementing the modules and the voting software. This high development cost restricts use of the technique to very critical applications where the cost can be tolerated. Such applications include the primary flight control system of the Airbus A330/340 aircraft, which is discussed in Chapter 15.

Recovery blocks

The recovery block method was introduced in the early 1970s (Horning *et al.*, 1974; Anderson and Lee, 1990). It uses some form of error detection to validate the operation of a software module. If an error is detected an alternative software routine is used.

The recovery block scheme is based on the use of **acceptance tests**. These tests may have several components and may, for example, include checks for runtime errors (for example arithmetic errors, such as a divide by zero); reasonability (to confirm that the results obtained are reasonable); excessive execution time; and mathematical errors. This last category might involve reversing a calculation to check its validity. For example, a routine to calculate a square root could be checked by squaring its result to confirm that the original value is obtained. In Chapter 9 we shall see that in critical applications it is normal to divide software into manageable modules and to tightly specify the operation of each module. During software development it will be necessary to demonstrate that each module achieves the functionality set out in its specification. Such an approach can also be used to devise runtime tests which will demonstrate that a module has functioned correctly.

Systems using the recovery block approach require duplication of the various critical software modules. In each case a **primary module** is executed, followed by its acceptance test. Failure of the test will result in the execution of an alternative, redundant module, after which the acceptance test will be repeated.

primary module
acceptance test
secondary module
acceptance test

Any number of redundant modules may be provided to give increased fault tolerance. As soon as execution of one of the versions of the module results in a successful test, execution proceeds to the next software operation. If the system fails the acceptance test for all of the redundant modules, an overall software failure is detected and the system must take appropriate action.

One problem with the arrangement described so far is that execution of a faulty module can cause damage to the system state, which must be repaired before correct operation can be resumed. This is tackled by establishing a recovery point before execution of the module, to which the system can return in the event of a module failure. One could picture this operation as the taking of a 'snapshot' of the state of all variables within the system. If an error is detected at a later stage, all the variables can be reset to these values to remove the effects of the error. This process is an example of backward error recovery. In practice, taking a complete record of the entire system state at the beginning of every module is inefficient and more sophisticated techniques are employed.

An example is the recovery cache technique, which stores only those values that are about to be changed. It should be noted that the use of the word 'cache' in this context refers to its meaning as a 'hiding place', and is not related to its use to describe high-speed buffers.

The structure of the recovery block mechanism therefore consists of:

establish recovery point
primary module
acceptance test
alternative module 1
acceptance test
alternative module 2
.
.
.
alternative module n
acceptance test

An alternative method of describing this structure uses a small number of keywords to represent the various stages of the process (Anderson and Lee, 1990). The acceptance test is identified by the keyword **ensure**. This is placed at the beginning of the structure as it is common to all versions of the module. This is followed by the primary module, identified by the keyword **by**, followed by any number of alternative modules each preceded by **else by**. The module is terminated by an **else error** clause, representing the condition that all the modules fail to satisfy the acceptance test.

ensure ⟨*acceptance test*⟩
by ⟨*primary module*⟩
else by ⟨*alternative module 1*⟩
else by ⟨*alternative module 2*⟩
.
.
.
else by ⟨*alternative module n*⟩
else error

This syntax does not indicate the establishment of a recovery point, but this operation is implied at the beginning of each block.

Comparison of hardware and software fault-tolerant techniques

It is apparent that there are very strong parallels between the software fault tolerance methods outlined above and the hardware techniques described in the previous section. *N*-version programming provides fault masking in a manner similar to *N*-modular redundant hardware arrangements, the comparison of results in the former being equivalent to the voting arrangement in the latter. The recovery block approach uses error detection to switch between primary and backup software modules, and is clearly similar to techniques used in dynamic hardware redundancy schemes.

All forms of hardware fault tolerance require the provision of redundant hardware resources. Software redundancy also requires an increase in resources to achieve the same functionality. In the case of *N*-version programming several forms of the module must be executed, with an additional overhead for the voting operation. In the recovery block scheme duplicated calculation is only required when a module fails, but the overhead associated with acceptance testing is likely to be appreciably greater than that associated with voting. In an application where timing is critical it is essential that time is available to execute not only the primary, but also the alternative modules.

A major distinction between hardware and software techniques of fault tolerance is that duplication of identical hardware modules can be used to provide tolerance of some forms of hardware faults, whereas duplication of identical software modules has little benefit. Repeatedly executing an identical software module can provide protection against transient faults, but provides none against software design faults. Software redundancy is therefore invariably associated with diverse design of the software modules. Because of the high cost of this process, this form of fault tolerance is usually reserved for highly critical applications.

6.7 Selecting fault-tolerant architectures

In this chapter we have discussed a large number of fault-tolerant arrangements with varying degrees of sophistication. Selecting an appropriate architecture for a given application requires both skill and experience. Often much guidance can be obtained from standards and guidelines used within the industry in question.

Within this text we are primarily interested in computer-based systems, and this chapter has concentrated on arrangements of programmable modules. In some applications it may be possible to provide some aspects of the system using non-programmable elements. This has the advantage that such subsystems are usually less complex than computer-based modules. Complexity is a great enemy of safety, and is avoided wherever possible in systems that are safety critical. Thus if the functions of a module can be achieved using a non-programmable arrangement this is likely to be preferred for a safety-related application.

In many control systems the required functions are too complex to be implemented using non-programmable techniques. However, it may be possible to separate the control and safety aspects of the system to allow a relatively simple, non-programmable element to guarantee the safety of the system. A simplified example of such an arrangement is shown in Figure 6.18, which shows a storage tank that feeds a toxic liquid to some chemical process. In this imaginary example the process requires the liquid to be supplied at a variable pressure, and this is achieved by controlling the height of the liquid within the tank. To achieve this control function a depth gauge senses the height of the liquid and a computer-based control system uses information from this sensor to control a pump, which pumps liquid into, or from, this tank to obtain the required head of liquid. Let us not concern ourselves with whether this arrangement is a sensible method of achieving this function, but simply accept that this is the selected method of control.

In the arrangement described by Figure 6.18 the computer-based control system is safety critical. If the system were to fail the pump could be activated in such a way that it overfilled the tank, resulting in spillage of the toxic liquid. The criticality of the system would depend on the consequences of such a spillage. Depending on the criticality level, it might be necessary to provide fault tolerance within the control system and to employ the various other techniques described within this text to achieve a high-integrity system. If the consequences of spillage were great, then the cost of implementing the control system would be very high.

Consider instead the arrangement shown in Figure 6.19. Here the computer-based control system still has responsibility for controlling the height of the liquid in the tank, but a separate, non-programmable system provides additional safety protection. Failure of the computer system should not now cause a spillage of liquid, and the integrity level of this part of the system is

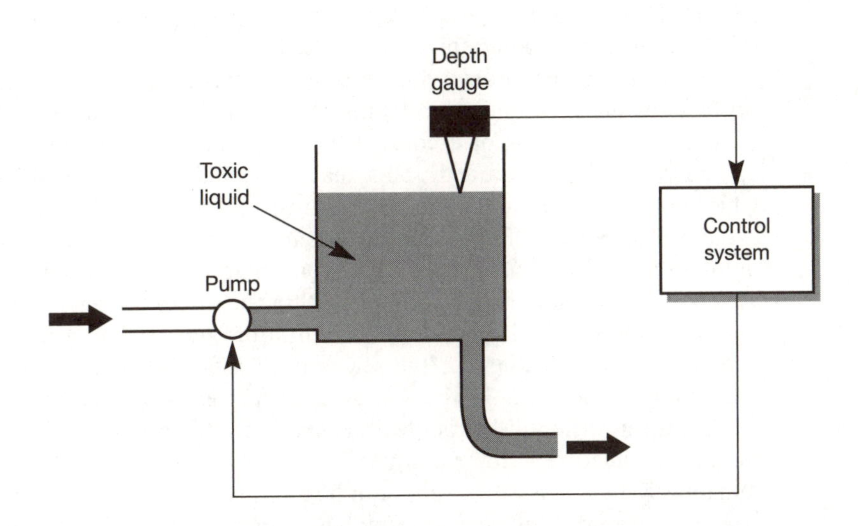

Figure 6.18 A safety-critical control system.

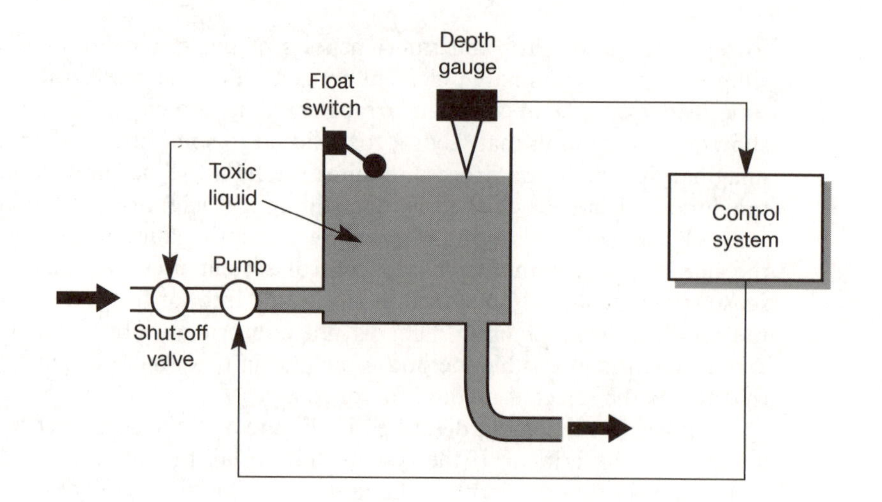

Figure 6.19 Use of a non-programmable safety channel.

reduced. The integrity required of the float switch and shut-off valve may be high, but these are simple systems and are more predictable. If increased integrity is required, two independent, non-programmable safety systems could be used in parallel.

Unfortunately, it is not always possible to separate the control and safety functions of a system. For example, in an aircraft autopilot it is not practicable to provide a simple non-programmable system that will ensure the safety of the aircraft if the computer-based system fails. However, where possible it is always preferable to maintain safety using simple systems rather than to rely on an inherently complex computer-based system.

The fault-tolerant systems described in this chapter all use redundancy to prevent the malfunctioning of a subsystem from producing a system failure. In some applications loss of a control function may be acceptable provided that system safety is maintained. This may be achievable using arrangements in which some redundant channels are non-programmable. Table 6.1 shows some examples of possible fault-tolerant systems. Within this table computer-based modules are given the acronym PES, which stands for programmable electronic system – this notation is widely used within the safety industry. Non-computer-based modules are designated as NP – non-programmable. Table 6.1 does not aim to set out guidelines for the selection of a fault-tolerant architecture for a particular application. Rather, it gives a few examples of the form systems might take at different levels of integrity. The table does not indicate the detail of the architecture – for example, it does not suggest whether a static or a dynamic system is used – it simply indicates an appropriate level of redundancy. It can be seen that non-programmable channels often replace computer-based modules where this is possible.

Table 6.1 Examples of fault-tolerant arrangements.

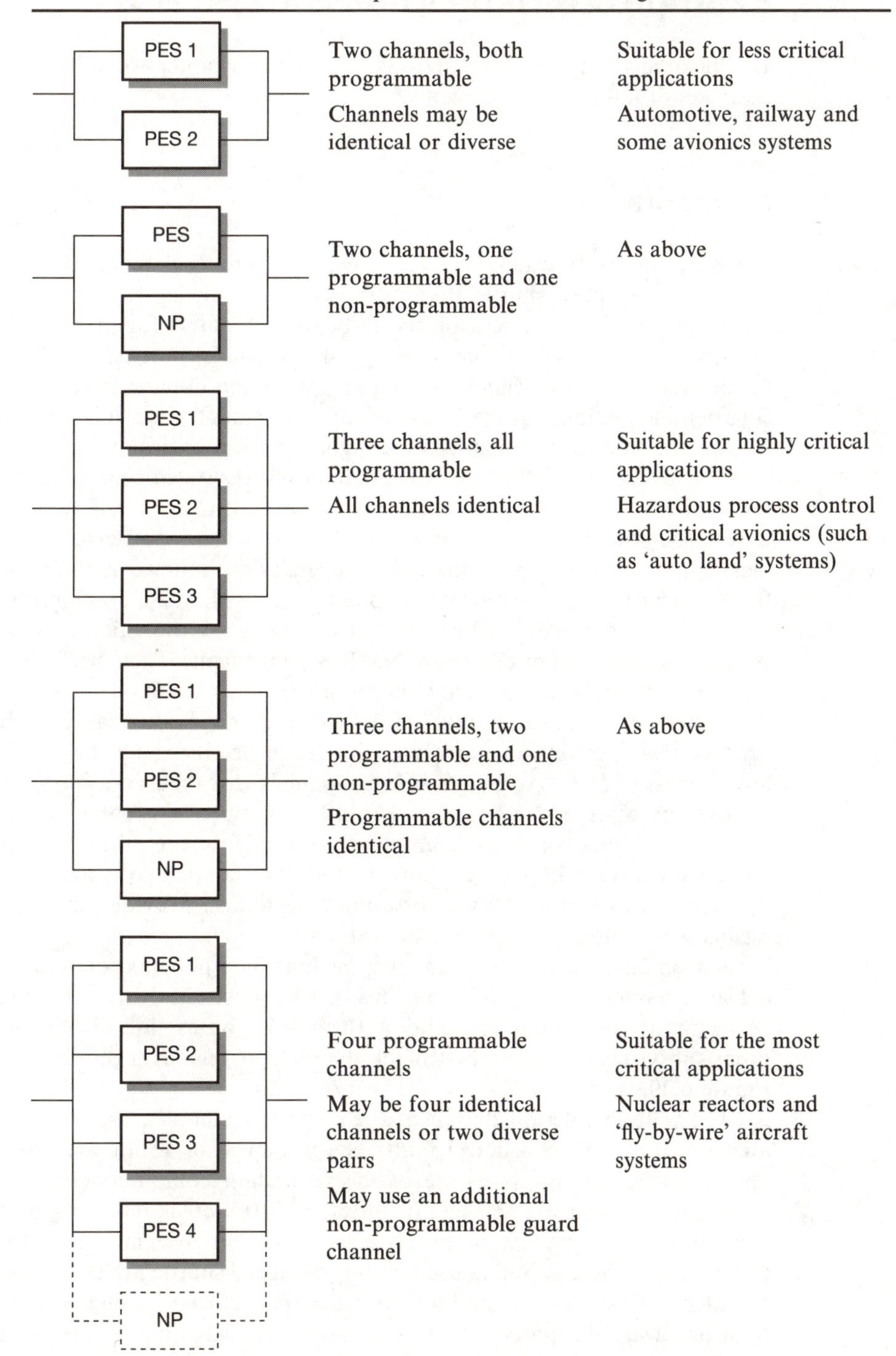

Arrangement	Description	Application
PES 1, PES 2	Two channels, both programmable Channels may be identical or diverse	Suitable for less critical applications Automotive, railway and some avionics systems
PES, NP	Two channels, one programmable and one non-programmable	As above
PES 1, PES 2, PES 3	Three channels, all programmable All channels identical	Suitable for highly critical applications Hazardous process control and critical avionics (such as 'auto land' systems)
PES 1, PES 2, NP	Three channels, two programmable and one non-programmable Programmable channels identical	As above
PES 1, PES 2, PES 3, PES 4, NP	Four programmable channels May be four identical channels or two diverse pairs May use an additional non-programmable guard channel	Suitable for the most critical applications Nuclear reactors and 'fly-by-wire' aircraft systems

6.8 Examples of fault-tolerant systems

To illustrate the principles discussed within this chapter we will look at some examples of fault-tolerant systems.

Space shuttle

Probably the most widely known example of fault tolerance is that used by NASA in the space shuttle (Sklaroff, 1976). At various stages of a flight the shuttle is entirely dependent on its on-board computers for many flight-critical functions. Failure of the computer systems could risk not only the lives of the astronauts, but also a vehicle costing several billion dollars. It is also clear that considerable national pride rests on the success of each mission. For these reasons the computer system has the highest level of criticality.

The nature of the application imposes very stringent requirements in terms of reliability, integrity, availability and fault tolerance. The space shuttle uses a combination of redundancy, hardware and software voting, fault masking, fault detection and design diversity to achieve high integrity and fault tolerance. Five identical computers are used, their configuration being under software control. During critical phases of the mission four of the computers are configured in an NMR arrangement. They perform identical operations on similar input data and broadcast their results. Hardware voting is performed by the various actuators to provide fault masking, but each processor also compares its result with those produced by its neighbours. If any processor detects a disagreement it signals this fact, and voting is used to remove the offending computer. The fifth computer normally performs non-critical functions such as communications. However, this computer also contains a diverse implementation of the flight control software produced by a different contractor. This diverse implementation provides some protection against systematic faults within the software.

Communication between the various components of the system is achieved using an array of serial buses. Five buses are used to communicate between the five computers and a further 23 buses link the computers to other subsystems. A simplified block diagram of this arrangement is shown in Figure 6.20.

The fault-tolerant design of the computer complex uses hybrid redundancy to both mask and detect faults. Several levels of voting are used to mask any faults within the hardware of the redundant computers. Each computer also provides extensive self-test facilities, with full error reporting to the crew. This allows faulty units to be removed from the system before they cause problems. As the computers used within the space shuttle are conventional 'off-the-shelf' units, most of the fault detection is performed using software rather than hardware techniques. However, hardware watchdog timers are provided within each computer to detect crashes.

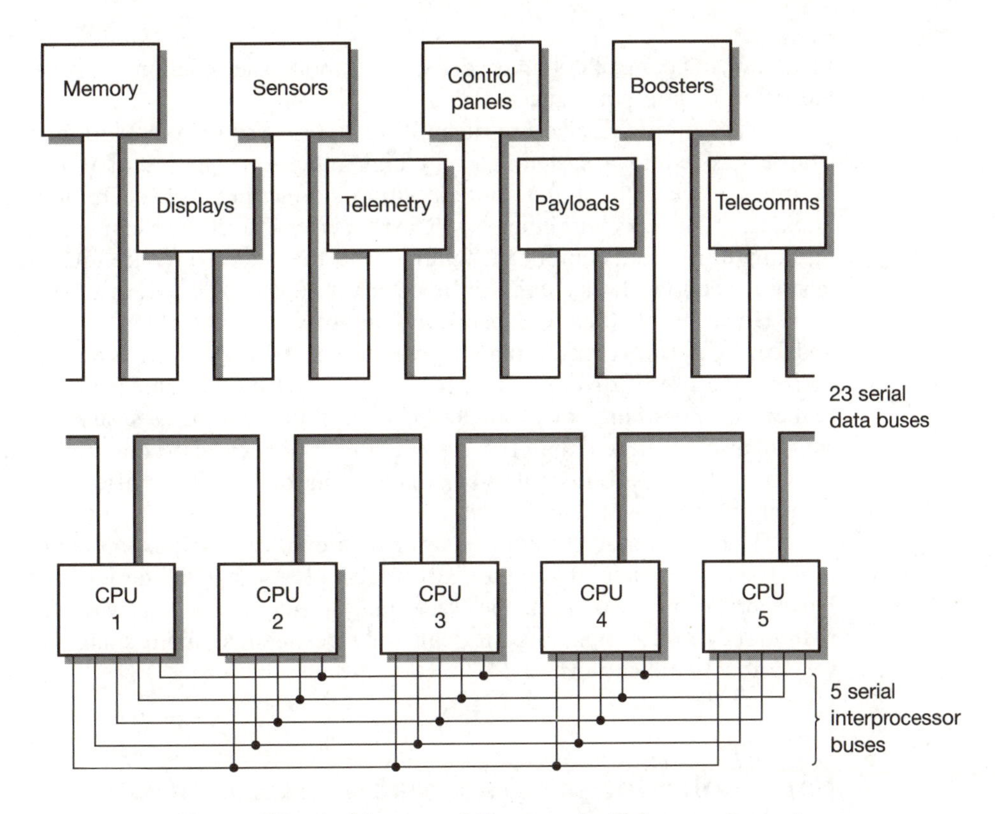

Figure 6.20 Architecture of the space shuttle's computer systems.

Failure of one of the four computers in the NMR set is masked owing to both hardware and software voting techniques. When such a failure is detected the computer concerned is switched out of the system, leaving a TMR arrangement. Failure of a second computer can also be tolerated as voting will again detect and mask its effects. Following this second failure the system is switched into a duplex mode, where the two remaining computers compare their results in order to detect any further failure. In the event of a third failure the system will report inconsistencies to the crew and will attempt to use fault detection techniques to identify the offending unit. The system can therefore effectively detect and tolerate the failure of two of its main computers, and can provide detection and limited tolerance of failure of a third unit. In extreme cases the fifth on-board computer can take over critical functions. This unit has diverse software and could be used if a systematic fault was discovered in the software within the other four machines. At all times the crew are informed of the status of the system. Ultimate authority for the configuration of the computer complex always resides with the crew and the controllers on Earth. Although the system can operate satisfactorily following the failure of one or more of its computers, in such circumstances the crew or controllers may decide to abort the mission because of the reduction in safety margins.

The comprehensive use of multiple hybrid redundancy within the space shuttle has led to a system of very high integrity, capable of tolerating the failure of several of its computers without affecting safety. The use of four identical computers within an NMR arrangement gives excellent tolerance and masking of random component failures, and the use of software fault detection techniques allows faulty units to be detected and removed from the configuration. However, the heavy dependence on software for voting, fault detection and configuration control places great importance on the correctness of its design. The use of diverse software within the fifth computer is an attempt to reduce the possibility of a single software fault causing a system failure. It should also be noted that the system uses five identical computers, thereby allowing the possibility of a systematic hardware fault affecting all the computers simultaneously.

The space shuttle computer systems are an excellent example of a highly fault-tolerant system that takes advantage of a range of design techniques. However, it is clear that the very high costs associated with large-scale redundancy and design diversity can only be justified for a small number of very critical applications.

Fault-tolerant programmable logic controllers (PLCs)

Programmable logic controllers (PLCs) are increasingly being used as the basis of low-volume control systems. These are mass-produced embedded computers that are available with a variety of input and output modules to suit a range of applications. Originally, PLCs were thought of as simple replacements for existing non-programmable control hardware, and as such they were often used to replace systems based on large numbers of relays. For this reason, early PLCs were usually programmed using ‘ladder logic’, a diagrammatic programming technique often used to design relay circuits. Today, a range of programming techniques are available for PLCs, including the use of more conventional programming languages.

Over the past few years much attention has been given to the use of PLCs within safety-related applications (Goring, 1994; Greenway, 1994). Some PLCs use fault-tolerant techniques within their design to increase their reliability. A typical unit would use three identical processors within a TMR arrangement, with duplicated or triplicated input and output modules. Such an arrangement is shown in Figure 6.21.

The TMR configuration provides both tolerance and masking of random hardware failures within the processors and the ancillary components. This, together with built-in fault detection facilities, results in a system that is considerably more reliable than a comparable design using a single processor.

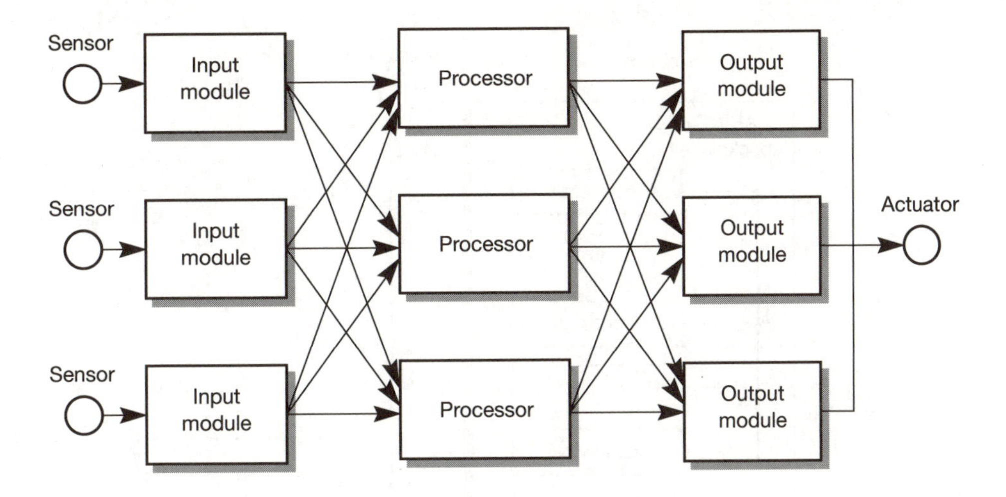

Figure 6.21 A typical arrangement for a high-reliability PLC.

However, the use of identical hardware modules, each with identical software, provides no protection against systematic faults. We shall return to look at the use of PLCs within safety-critical applications in Chapter 10.

Fault-tolerant avionics systems

Work is currently being directed towards the development of a standardized, modular computer architecture for use in commercial aircraft (Cook, 1992). One of the organizations looking at standardization in this area is Aeronautical Radio Inc. (ARINC). This corporation has the United States airlines as its principal stockholders, and sponsors the Airlines Electronic Engineering Committee (AEEC) which proposes standards for aircraft equipment and systems. A proposed system uses a number of standard cabinets that contain replaceable modules, which may be either processors, power supply units or bus gateways. Communication between the modules within a cabinet is achieved using a backplane bus conforming to the ARINC 659 standard. The cabinet is linked to the outside world by a gateway module that is connected to an external serial data bus. This bus conforms to the ARINC 629 standard and is used for communications between cabinets, and for communications between the cabinets and the aircraft's actuators and sensors. A block diagram of this arrangement is shown in Figure 6.22. Some actuators and sensors have a degree of intelligence and can interface directly to the ARINC 629 data bus. Simpler devices are connected to the bus by a data concentrator.

The modular approach provides a reduction in design cost because of the standardization of processor hardware. It also has advantages in terms of reduced wiring complexity and weight. Maintenance is also simplified by the

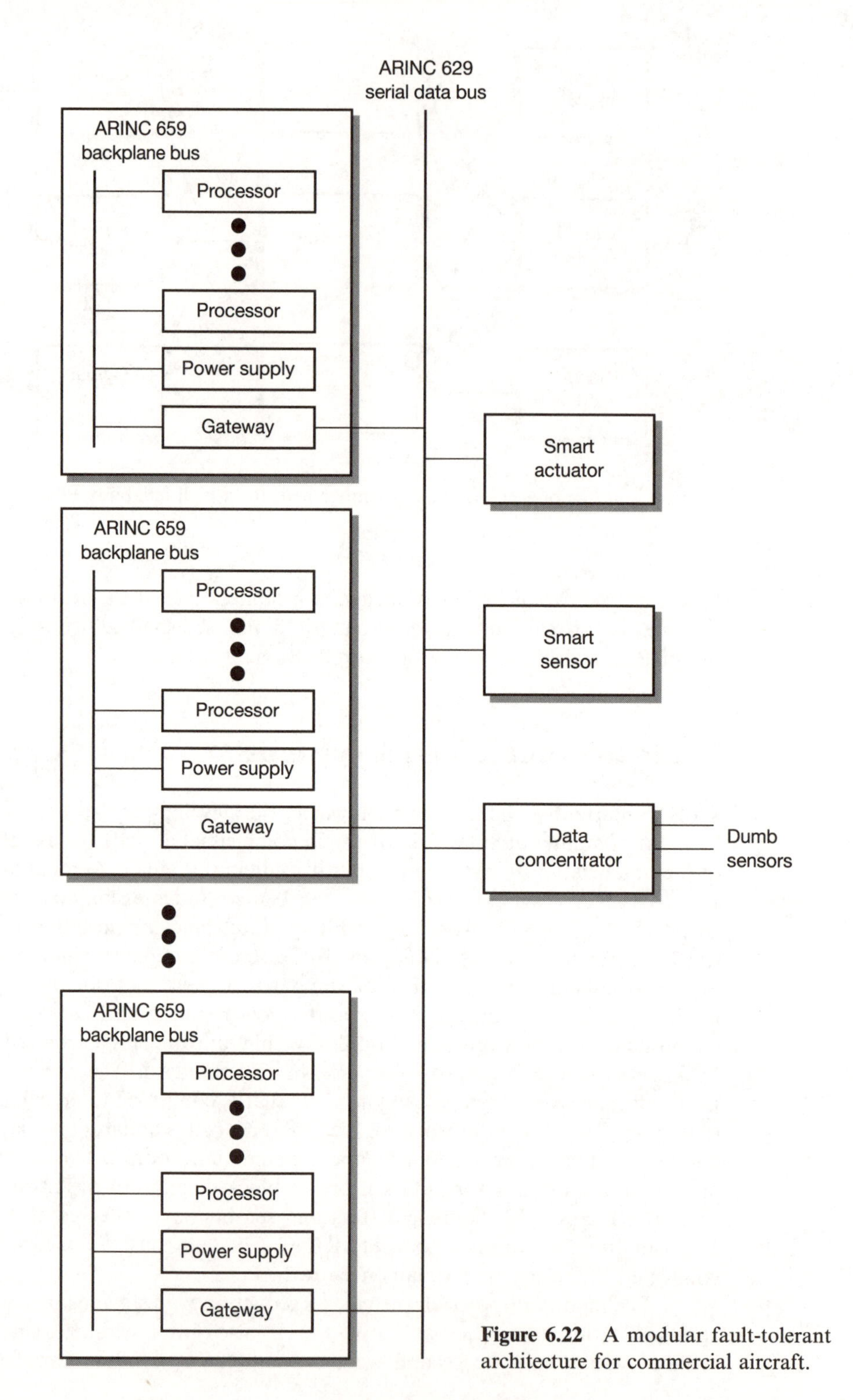

Figure 6.22 A modular fault-tolerant architecture for commercial aircraft.

modular approach and the reduction in wiring. From a safety viewpoint, the arrangement increases safety margins by increasing the amount of redundancy within the system. The centralized bus structure allows any processor to communicate with any sensor or actuator. However, the arrangement places great importance on the integrity of the ARINC 629 data bus that forms the heart of all system communication.

In Chapter 15 we shall look in more detail at the architecture and design used in several commercial safety-critical systems.

REFERENCES

Anderson T. and Lee P.A. (1990). *Fault Tolerance: Principles and Practice*, 2nd edn. New York: Springer-Verlag

Avizienis A. (1985). The N-version approach to fault-tolerant software. *IEEE Trans. Software Eng.*, **11**(12), 1491–1501

Banerjee P. and Abraham J.A. (1984). Characterisation and testing of physical failures in MOS logic circuits. *IEEE Design and Test*, **1**(3), 76–86

Bishop P.G., Esp D.G., Barnes M., Humphreys P., Dahll G. and Lahti J. (1985). PODS – a project on diverse software. *IEEE Trans. Software Eng.*, **12**(9), 929–40

Chen L. and Avizienis A. (1978). N-version programming: a fault tolerant approach to reliability of software operation. In *Proc. 8th Ann. Int. Conf. on Fault-Tolerant Computing*, Toulouse, France, 21–23 June, pp. 3–9. New York: IEEE

Cook A. (1992). Certification of digital systems in commercial avionics applications. *Safety of Computer Control Systems 1992 (SAFECOMP'92)*, pp. 179–84. Oxford: Pergamon

Eldred R.C. (1959). Test routines based on symbolic logic statements. *JACM*, **6**, 33–6

Goring A. (1994). Methods and techniques of improving the safety classification of programmable logic controller safety systems. In *Technology and Assessment of Safety-Critical Systems* (Redmill F. and Anderson T., eds), pp. 21–30. London: Springer-Verlag

Greenway A. (1994). A user's perspective of programmable logic controllers (PLCs) in safety-related applications. In *Technology and Assessment of Safety-Critical Systems* (Redmill F. and Anderson T., eds), pp. 1–20. London: Springer-Verlag

Guy C.G. (1991). Errors, reliability and redundancy. In *Digital Systems Reference Book* (Holdsworth B. and Martin G.R., eds), ch. 1.16. Oxford: Butterworth-Heinemann

Horning J.J., Lauer H.C, Melliar-Smith P.M. *et al.* (1974). A program structure for error detection and recovery. In *Proc. Int. Symp. on Operating Systems*, Rocquencourt, France, 23–25 April, pp. 171–87. Berlin: Springer-Verlag

Knight J.C. and Leveson N.G. (1986). An experimental evaluation of the assumption of independence in multiversion programming. *IEEE Trans. Software Eng.*, **12**(1), 96–109

Kohavi Z. (1978). *Switching and Finite State Automata Theory*. New York: McGraw-Hill

Sklaroff J.R. (1976). Redundancy management techniques for space shuttle computers. *IBM J. Res. Devel.*, **20**(1), 20–8

von Neumann J. (1956). Probabilistic logics and the synthesis of reliable organisms from unreliable components. *Automata Studies, Annals of Mathematical Studies*, Princeton University Press, **34**, 43–98

Wadsack R.L. (1978). Fault modelling and logic simulation of CMOS and NMOS integrated circuits. *Bell Syst. Tech. J.*, **57**(5), 1449–74

FURTHER READING

Anderson T. and Lee P.A. (1990). *Fault Tolerance: Principles and Practice*, 2nd edn. New York: Springer-Verlag

Johnson B.W. (1989). *Design and Analysis of Fault Tolerant Digital Systems*. Reading, MA: Addison-Wesley

PROBLEMS

6.1 What system characteristics may be improved by the use of fault tolerance? Give examples of applications where each of these characteristics is of primary importance.

6.2 What were the primary objectives of most early applications of fault-tolerant techniques? How has the role of fault tolerance changed over the years?

6.3 Distinguish between random and systematic faults. Give examples of each type.

6.4 Explain how faults may be characterized by their duration. Gives examples of faults that fall within different categories of duration.

6.5 What is the function of a fault model?

6.6 What problems are associated with the use of atomic fault models?

6.7 Explain the assumptions of the single-stuck-at fault model.

6.8 Why does the single-stuck-at model allow more complex systems to be investigated than is possible using an atomic model?

6.9 What is the relationship between the number of nodes within a circuit and the number of potential single-stuck-at faults?

6.10 When planning testing, what assumptions are normally made as to the number of single-stuck-at faults that might exist within a system? What is the justification for this assumption?

6.11 A system may be considered to have 100 nodes. How many possible single-stuck-at faults need to be investigated assuming that only single faults are considered? How many fault conditions need to be considered if multiple faults are allowed?

6.12 What problems arise when using the single-stuck-at model with complex integrated circuits fabricated using MOS techniques?

6.13 Why are fault models more suited to some forms of fault than to others?

6.14 What is meant by the term 'fault coverage'? Describe the various forms of fault coverage measures.

6.15 Define the term 'redundancy'.

6.16 Explain what is meant by 'common-mode failure'. How can the problems of common-mode failure be tackled?

6.17 What forms of fault may be tackled by the use of design diversity? What forms of fault are not susceptible to this approach?
6.18 Why does the use of design diversity not totally remove the problems associated with common-mode failures?
6.19 Explain, with the use of examples, the meaning of the term 'functionality checking'.
6.20 Why is great care needed in the design of routines to test the operation of RAM?
6.21 How is 'consistency checking' used to detect faults?
6.22 Discuss the use of signal comparison as a method of fault detection.
6.23 Give four examples of information redundancy which are used for fault detection.
6.24 Explain briefly what is meant by the terms 'instruction monitoring', 'loopback testing', 'watchdog timer', 'bus monitoring' and 'power supply monitoring'.
6.25 Explain the difference between static and dynamic fault tolerance.
6.26 Why are simple TMR systems susceptible to single-point failures? How may this problem be overcome?
6.27 Why do analogue signal inputs cause problems for TMR and similar systems?
6.28 In an *N*-modular redundant system containing *N* modules, how many module failures can be tolerated before a system failure occurs?
6.29 Design a simple five-input single-bit voting element.
6.30 What factors must be considered in deciding between hardware and software voting techniques in a static fault-tolerant system?
6.31 What are the advantages and disadvantages of dynamic fault tolerance compared to static methods?
6.32 Describe the standby spare fault-tolerant technique. What is meant by cold and hot standby? What are the characteristics of each technique?
6.33 What methods may be used to perform the comparison in a self-checking pair arrangement? Discuss the merits of each.
6.34 What is meant by the term 'software fault tolerance'?
6.35 Describe the *N*-version programming approach to software fault tolerance.
6.36 Explain the use of recovery blocks in software fault tolerance. Describe the basic structure of the recovery block mechanism.
6.37 Why is duplication of identical software modules of no benefit in providing tolerance of software faults?
6.38 Why is the use of non-programmable modules attractive in safety-critical systems? Give examples of systems where non-programmable modules might be used to provide safety features. Give examples where this is not feasible.
6.39 What aspects of the design of the space shuttle's computer complex provide protection against random hardware failure?
6.40 How does the design of the space shuttle's computer system tackle the problems of systematic faults?
6.41 How does the architecture of the high-reliability PLC described in this chapter provide protection against software faults?
6.42 The fault-tolerant avionics system described in this chapter provides a method of linking several processors, actuators and sensors. How may this arrangement be used to reduce the system's susceptibility to random hardware faults and systematic faults? What weaknesses does this approach have in comparison with that used within the space shuttle computer complex?

System Reliability

CHAPTER CONTENTS

7.1 Introduction

Background

It can be argued that the field of reliability engineering was established largely as a result of problems experienced during the second world war. The vast resources allocated to military equipment resulted in previously unknown levels of production. However, much of the equipment failed very quickly, often before reaching service. Many of the problems could be attributed to the failure of electronic components that often had a functional lifetime of only a few hours. The American government was particularly concerned about the implications of these problems, and during the 1940s a number of research groups were established in the US in an attempt to improve the reliability of electronic components. This work was concerned with the electrical properties of the components, and also environmental factors such as vibration and shock. In 1950 the US Department of Defense set up an ad hoc group to look at the reliability of electronic equipment for the army, navy and air force, and this produced its final report in 1952. In August 1952 the US Department of Defense joined with representatives of the electronics industry to form the Advisory Group on Reliability of Electronic Equipment (AGREE). This began a five-year project that resulted in the production of a wealth of advice concerning the assessment of reliability during the manufacture of electronic systems. On the basis of this work, and much that followed, the US military issued a series of specifications for their suppliers, covering the reliability of electronic components. During the 1950s the material covered in these documents became established as good working practice within industry in both the military and civil sectors.

In the postwar years the increased reliance on complex electronic systems emphasized the need for high-reliability systems. The race into space, trans-oceanic telephone links, communications satellites, avionics and nuclear power, are all examples of emerging technologies that were heavily dependent on the use of sophisticated electronics that had to be reliable. In parallel with these needs were the equally important considerations of economics. Products that were unreliable would not sell. In order for electronics to fulfil its role within high-volume consumer products, components had to be dependable throughout the lifetime of the product.

Over the years the reliability of electronic components has increased enormously and in most consumer products greatly exceeds that of the other components. However, our increasing reliance on computer-based systems in critical applications pushes the requirement for reliability to the limit.

Applicability

In Chapter 6 we looked at several architectures that could be used to prevent a fault within a single component from producing a system failure. A reduction in system failures results in increased reliability, and in this chapter we look at methods of defining and quantifying reliability. High reliability is normally a necessary, but not sufficient, condition to guarantee safety.

We have seen in earlier chapters that systems may fail for a variety of reasons. In particular, faults may be random or systematic in nature. Random component failures can occur at any time, and it is not possible to predict when a particular device will fail. However, by observing a large number of similar devices it may be possible to perform a statistical analysis to allow an estimate to be made of the probability of failure within a certain time period. Failures caused as a result of systematic faults are not random in nature and therefore do not lend themselves to statistical analysis. Such failures may be predictable to some extent. For example, an overstressed device could fail whenever a particularly high load is applied, or a software fault might manifest itself at a set time. Once a systematic fault has been identified its likely effect on the reliability of the system may be studied, and in most highly critical applications any identified systematic faults would be removed. However, unidentified systematic faults represent a serious problem, as their effects are unpredictable and are not normally susceptible to statistical analysis. In computer-based systems the most common form of unidentified systematic fault is the software 'bug'.

Reliability engineers are divided on how to approach the problems associated with systematic faults such as those within software. Some say that since software faults are predictable, in that a fault will occur each time the code is executed, statistical analysis cannot be used. This leads to the view that we cannot apply a figure to the reliability of software. An alternative view is held by engineers who feel that it *is* appropriate to use statistical methods with software. They argue that because of the complexity of the software within a typical application, faults could take an almost limitless number of forms. The complex process involved in generating software means that faults could be randomly distributed throughout the code. The effects of these faults cannot be predicted and thus may be considered to be random in nature. Engineers who belong to this camp maintain that unknown software faults *are* sufficiently random to allow statistical analysis to be applied. It is important to note, however, that once a software bug has been identified it can no longer be considered to be random.

Faced with these two views of this issue it is difficult to give a definitive treatment to this topic. Unfortunately, those who decry the use of analytical techniques for software faults are unable to provide an alternative quantitative method of assessing their effects on reliability. Faced with this problem we shall turn our attention to the analysis and modelling of random failures. All engineers are happy with this method of treating random component failures. Some also believe that such methods may have a place in the analysis of software faults.

Reliability

Components that fail as a result of non-systematic faults will fail at a random time. For a given device it is not possible to predict the time of failure, but it *is* possible to quantify the rate at which members of a family of components will fail. Therefore, our definition of reliability is based on the probability of a device functioning correctly for a given period of time. In fact, reliability may be defined in a number of ways, some qualitative and others quantitative. Here we will take reliability to be the probability of a component or system functioning correctly over a given period of time under a given set of operating conditions. Clearly, by this definition reliability is a function of time and it is normally given the symbol $R(t)$.

If we consider a set of N identical components, all of which begin operating at the same time, then at some later time t, the number of components functioning correctly is $n(t)$, where

$$R(t) = \frac{n(t)}{N}$$

One may also define the term **unreliability**, which is the probability that a system will not function correctly over a given period of time. This term is given the symbol $Q(t)$ and is also called the probability of failure.

If the number of components to have failed during a time t is given the symbol $n_f(t)$, then

$$Q(t) = \frac{n_f(t)}{N}$$

and, from the definitions of reliability and unreliability, it is clear that

$$Q(t) = 1 - R(t)$$

Failure rate

Closely related to the reliability of a component is the rate at which such devices fail. The failure rate of a device or system is the number of failures within a given period of time. For example, if a device fails, on average, once in every 1000 hours of operation, it has a failure rate of 1/1000 failures per hour. The failure rate of a component normally varies with time and is given the symbol $z(t)$.

Failure rate may represent the frequency of the repeated failure of a single device, or the combined failure rate of a number of units. In the latter case the failure rate is the instantaneous rate at which components are failing, as a fraction of the number of devices still functioning. Thus

$$z(t) = \frac{1}{n(t)} \frac{\mathrm{d}n_{\mathrm{f}}(t)}{\mathrm{d}t}$$

Experience shows that the failure rate of electronic components normally exhibits distinctive characteristics, as shown in Figure 7.1. For obvious reasons, this characteristic is normally described as a 'bathtub' curve. Initially, components exhibit high 'infant mortality' owing to the presence of manufacturing faults that were not detected during the testing stage of their manufacture. As time passes the number of components containing these defects diminishes and the failure rate drops to a fairly constant level. At some later time the effects of ageing become apparent and the failure rate again rises as the devices 'wear out'. Manufacturers normally aim to use components only during the relatively constant part of this curve, and this is normally termed their 'useful life period'. In critical applications extended soak testing is used before systems are installed to catch any early failures. This is often in the form of 'accelerated life testing',

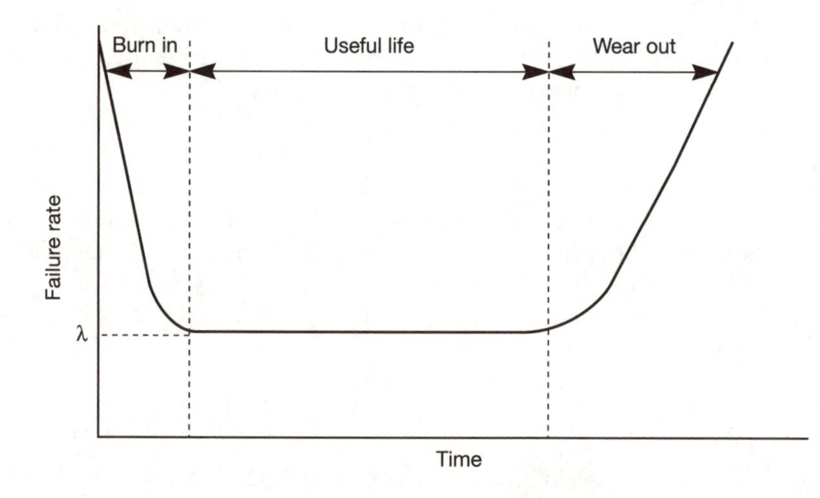

Figure 7.1 Typical variation of failure rate with time for electronic components.

using a more hostile environment than would be experienced by the unit in service. Such testing is often termed the 'burn-in' phase. This aims to produce faults in a few hours or days, that might take years to appear in normal operation. Critical systems would normally be replaced before their reliability falls to unacceptable levels owing to the effects of ageing. The relatively constant failure rate throughout the useful life of the unit is given the symbol λ.

It can be shown that during the useful-life stage the failure rate is related to the reliability of the device by the expression

$$R(t) = \mathrm{e}^{-\lambda t}$$

The exponential relationship between reliability and time is known as the **exponential failure law**. This indicates that for a constant failure rate reliability falls exponentially with time. Thus the probability of a system working correctly throughout a given period of time decreases exponentially with the length of this time period.

Time-variant failure rates

The exponential failure law described above assumes a constant failure rate. This relationship is widely used and is a good model for the random failure of hardware components. However, software failures are due to design faults and in some circumstances may be located and removed during the lifetime of the product. In this case the number of failures will tend to decrease with time and the constant failure rate model is no longer appropriate. This form of failure behaviour may be modelled by the Weibull distribution (Siewiorek and Swarz, 1982), which results in an expression for reliability of the form

$$R(t) = \mathrm{e}^{-(t/\eta)^{\beta}}$$

where β is the shape parameter and η is the characteristic life. It can be seen that for certain values of β the reliability increases with time, and approaches unity as t tends to infinity.

Although time-variant failure rates are of importance in the modelling of software and other systematic faults, the majority of reliability analysis is based on an assumption of a constant failure rate. For this reason the remainder of this chapter assumes this relationship.

Mean time to failure

Another way of describing the reliability of a system is to give its mean time to failure (MTTF), that is, the expected time that a system will operate before the first failure occurs. It can be shown that

$$\mathrm{MTTF} = \int_0^{\infty} R(t)\mathrm{d}t$$

and therefore, for the period where the failure rate is constant,

$$\text{MTTF} = \int_0^\infty e^{-\lambda t}\, dt = \frac{1}{\lambda} \tag{7.1}$$

This leads to the very simple result that the MTTF is the inverse of the constant failure rate of the system. Thus a system with a constant failure rate of 0.001 failures per hour will have a mean time to failure of 1000 hours. It is important to note that it is *not* reasonable to assume that such a system will operate correctly for 1000 hours. The reliability of a system at a time t is given by

$$R(t) = e^{-\lambda t}$$

and thus at a time $t = 1/\lambda$ (that is, at a time equal to its MTTF), the reliability is

$$R(t) = e^{-\lambda(1/\lambda)} = e^{-1} = 0.37 \tag{7.2}$$

Thus any given system has only a 37% chance of functioning correctly for an amount of time equal to the MTTF, or conversely a 63% chance of failing in this period. However, for a large number of units the MTTF represents the average time for which they would operate before their first failure.

Mean time to repair

The mean time to repair (MTTR) is quite simply the average time taken to repair a system that has failed, and to get it operational. The figure includes the time taken to detect the failure, locate the fault, effect a repair and reconfigure the system. Often the MTTR may be estimated during the design stage to allow system performance to be predicted, but may need to be determined experimentally when the system is operational.

Just as we describe the reliability of a system using its failure rate λ, we can quantify the repairability of a system using its repair rate μ, which is the average time taken to repair the system. It has units of repairs per hour. Just as the MTTF is $1/\lambda$, the MTTR is $1/\mu$.

Mean time between failures

If it can be assumed that once a failed system has been repaired its performance will be equivalent to the original system, then it is possible to predict the mean time between failures (MTBF), which is simply given by

$$\text{MTBF} = \text{MTTF} + \text{MTTR}$$

In most cases the time taken to repair the system will be small compared with the time for which the system operates, so in practice the MTBF will be numerically similar to the MTTF.

Availability

The availability of a system is the probability that the system will be functioning correctly at any given time. In other words, it is the fraction of the time for which it is operational. This can be expressed in terms of previously defined terms as

$$\text{Availability} = \frac{\text{Time system is operational}}{\text{Total time}} = \frac{\text{MTTF}}{\text{MTTF} + \text{MTTR}}$$

In critical systems the availability will normally be close to unity, and it is sometimes more convenient to describe a system in terms of its **unavailability**, where

$$\text{Unavailability} = 1 - \text{Availability}$$

It was noted in Chapter 2 that high availability is of paramount importance in some applications. Its relevance in terms of safety depends on whether safety can be guaranteed when the system is inoperative. In applications that have failsafe states it may be possible to maintain safety even when the computer-based system is not operating. In such cases availability may not be primary to safety, but will still be of importance to the overall performance of the system.

7.2 Reliability modelling

In the previous section we discussed several ways of describing the reliability of individual components. During the design stage of a project it is essential to be able to predict the final reliability of a complete system containing many parts. In this section we look at the use of reliability modelling to estimate the reliability of complex systems. The two most common methods are the 'combinational modelling' and the 'Markov state modelling' approaches.

Combinational models

Combinational reliability models allow the reliability of a system to be calculated from the reliability of its component parts. The components in question could be subsystems or individual electronic devices.

The model distinguishes between the situation where failure of any one of a number of components will cause system failure, and the case where several components must fail simultaneously to cause a malfunction. These two situations are modelled by the series and parallel models respectively. The symbols within reliability block diagrams are described within the international standard IEC 1078 (IEC, 1991).

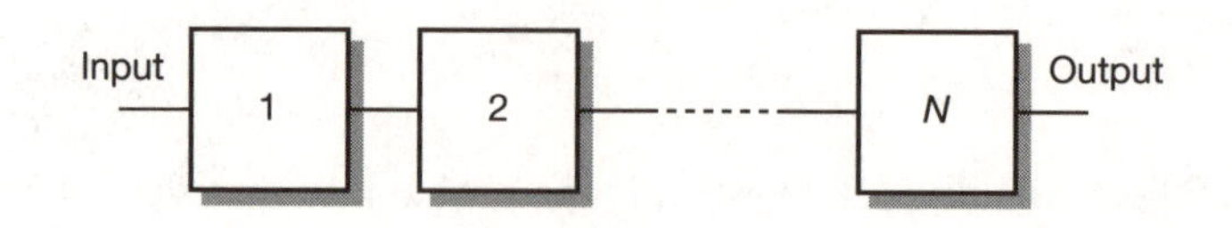

Figure 7.2 A series combination of components.

Series systems

Within any module that is not itself fault tolerant, it can be assumed that failure of any of its components may cause a system failure. Such an arrangement is represented in Figure 7.2. Here the components are shown in series, as any failure will prevent input data from correctly reaching the output. It should be noted that this representation is diagrammatic and does not correspond to the physical interconnection of the components. The model simply shows that failure of any of the components implies failure of the complete system.

As failure of any of the components will result in overall failure, the failure rate of a series system is equal to the sum of the failure rates of the individual components. If a system contains N components, and it may be assumed that failures in the various components are independent, then the system's failure rate λ, during its constant failure rate period, is given by

$$\lambda = \lambda_1 + \lambda_2 + \ldots + \lambda_N$$

where λ_i is the constant failure rate of the ith component. This may be rewritten as

$$\lambda = \sum_{i=1}^{N} \lambda_i$$

The reliability of the arrangement may also be expressed in terms of the reliability of the components. If $R_i(t)$ is the reliability of the ith component in the system, then the overall system reliability $R(t)$ is given by the expression

$$R(t) = R_1(t)R_2(t)\ldots R_N(t)$$

which may be written as

$$R(t) = \prod_{i=1}^{N} R_i(t) \qquad (7.3)$$

Example 7.1

A system is composed of 100 components and failure of any component will result in failure of the system. If the failure of the various components is completely independent, and each component has a reliability of 0.999, calculate the overall system reliability.

From Equation 7.3 we know that the reliability of a series arrangement of components is simply the product of their individual reliability. In this case, the reliability is therefore

$$R(t) = 0.999^{100} = 0.905$$

This example illustrates the relationship between component and system reliability. Here we see that the resultant reliability of the overall system is considerably worse than that of the individual components. If we consider the unreliability of the components $Q_c(t)$, we see that

$$Q_c(t) = 1 - R_c(t) = 1 - 0.999 = 0.0001$$

whereas the unreliability of the resultant system is

$$Q(t) = 1 - R(t) = 1 - 0.905 = 0.095$$

This represents an increase in unreliability by a factor of almost 1000.

Example 7.2

A series system containing 100 components is required to have a reliability of at least 0.999. Assuming that each of the components is equally reliable, what minimum reliability would they require to achieve the specified system performance?

If the reliability of the individual components is $R_c(t)$, then from Equation 7.3 we have

$$R(t) = R_c(t)^{100} \geqslant 0.999$$

This gives

$$R_c(t) \geqslant \sqrt[100]{0.999} \geqslant 0.99999$$

It can be seen that in order to achieve very high reliability using a series arrangement of many components, the individual components must themselves be extremely reliable.

Parallel systems

In systems that contain redundancy, failure of one component or subsystem need not result in failure of the complete system. Such an arrangement is described as a parallel system and is shown diagrammatically in Figure 7.3. In this arrangement it is assumed that the system will remain operational provided that at least one of the parallel elements is functioning correctly.

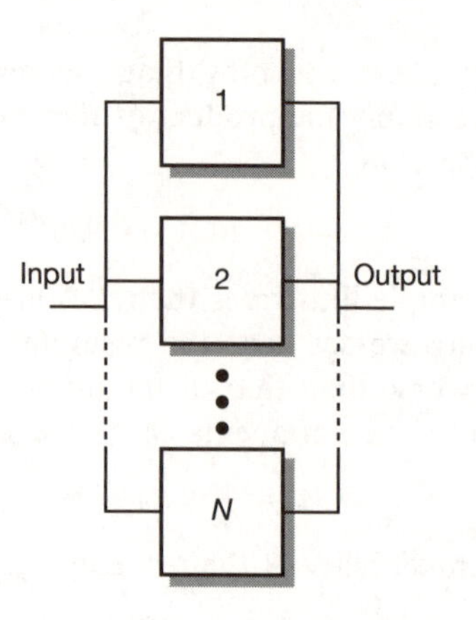

Figure 7.3 A parallel combination of components.

To determine the reliability of a parallel system we start by considering the probability of failure, first of an individual module, and then of the complete system. As the reliability of a component $R(t)$ is the probability of that component functioning correctly for a period of time t, then $[1 - R(t)]$ must be the probability of it failing within that time. You will recall that the quantity $[1 - R(t)]$ is termed the unreliability of the component and is given the symbol $Q(t)$. If a system contains N parallel modules, then the probability of all the units failing independently will be the product of the probabilities of each unit failing individually. Thus, the probability of failure of the system is given by

$$Q(t) = [1 - R_1(t)][1 - R_2(t)]\ldots[1 - R_N(t)]$$

where $R_i(t)$ is the reliability of the ith module. The reliability of the system is therefore

$$R(t) = 1 - Q(t) = 1 - [1 - R_1(t)][1 - R_2(t)]\ldots[1 - R_N(t)]$$

or simply

$$R(t) = 1 - \prod_{i=1}^{N}[1 - R_i(t)] \tag{7.4}$$

If, as is often the case, the parallel modules are identical, each with a reliability of $R_{\mathrm{m}}(t)$, this expression may be simplified. The system reliability then becomes

$$R(t) = 1 - [1 - R_{\mathrm{m}}(t)]^N \tag{7.5}$$

Example 7.3

A system consists of three identical modules and will operate correctly provided that at least one module is operational. If the reliability of each of the modules is 0.999, what will be the reliability of the complete system, assuming that the modules fail independently?

From Equation 7.5 the reliability is

$$\begin{aligned} R(t) &= 1 - [1 - R_{\mathrm{m}}(t)]^N \\ &= 1 - [1 - 0.999]^3 \\ &= 0.999\,999\,999 \end{aligned}$$

When dealing with systems that have a reliability that is very close to unity it is often more convenient to use a measure of unreliability. In this case the unreliability $Q(t)$ is $1 - 0.999\,999\,999$, or 1.0×10^{-9}. It can be seen that a parallel combination of reliable modules produces a system of very high reliability, even when the number of modules is low.

Example 7.4

A system requires a minimum reliability of 0.999. A module designed to fulfil the requirements of the system is found to have a reliability of only 0.85. If a parallel combination of these modules is used to implement the system, what is the minimum number of modules needed to achieve the required reliability?

From Equation 7.5 we have

$$R(t) = 1 - [1 - R_{\mathrm{m}}(t)]^N$$

and therefore

$$R(t) = 1 - [1 - 0.85]^N \geqslant 0.999$$

Rearranging gives

$$\begin{aligned} 0.001 &\geqslant [1 - 0.85]^N \\ N &\geqslant 3.64 \end{aligned}$$

Because N must take an integer value, the minimum number of modules required is four.

Example 7.5

A system is required to have a minimum reliability of 0.999 and is to be constructed using a parallel combination of modules each having a reliability of 0.65. What is the minimum number of modules required?

Repeating the analysis of the previous example we have

$$R(t) = 1 - [1 - 0.65]^N \geqslant 0.999$$

This gives

$$0.001 \geqslant [1 - 0.65]^N$$
$$N \geqslant 6.58$$

Because N must take an integer value, the minimum number of modules required is seven. It can be seen that producing high reliability using unreliable components implies large numbers of modules. In practice such an arrangement is rarely attractive, as the added complexity leads to a high implementation cost and a low MTTF.

Series–parallel combinations

In practice, real systems are often more complicated than the simple series and parallel combinations described above. However, all systems may be reduced to some combination of these two forms, which can then be reduced systematically to produce a single equivalent element. This process is illustrated in Figure 7.4. Figure 7.4(a) shows a system consisting of a series combination of parallel modules. The reliability of this arrangement can be calculated by first combining the parallel elements into a single module of equivalent reliability and then combining the resulting series elements into a single module. Figure 7.4(b) shows the first of these operations. Here module 10 has an equivalent reliability to the parallel combination of modules 1, 2 and 3. Similarly, modules 11 and 12 represent the effective reliability of the parallel combinations of modules 4, 5 and 6, and 7, 8 and 9 respectively. The overall reliability of the system is represented by that of module 13. This is determined by evaluating the series combination of modules 10, 11 and 12.

Parallel combinations of series elements may be analysed in a similar manner by first combining the series modules and then combining resulting parallel elements. Using these techniques, any combination of series and parallel units may be simplified and its reliability assessed.

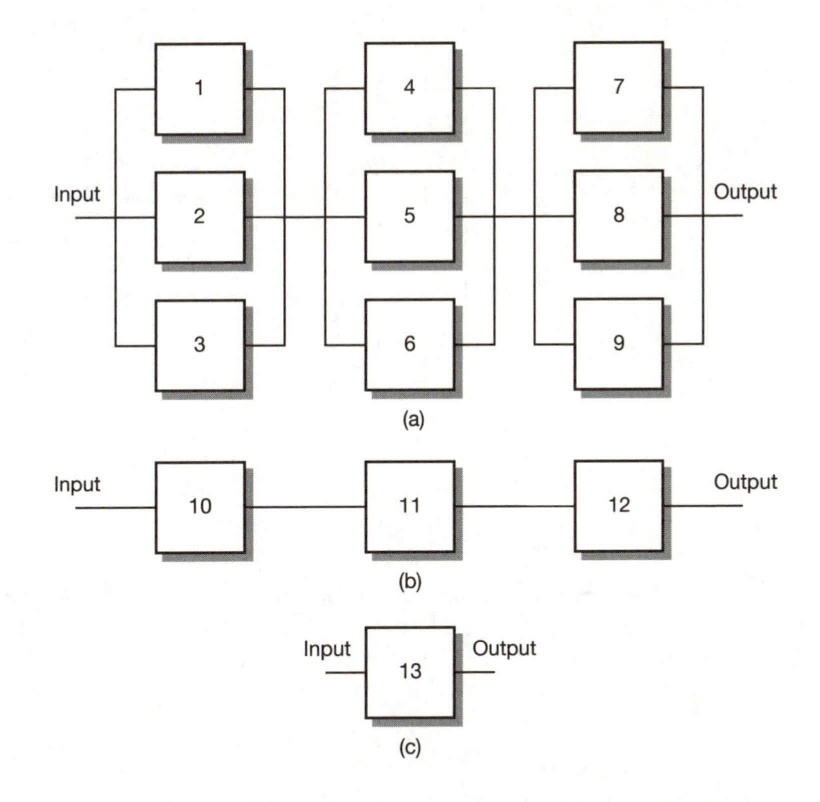

Figure 7.4 A series–parallel combination arrangement: (a) the original arrangement; (b) the result of combining the parallel modules; (c) the effect of combining the series elements.

Example 7.6

A system may be described by the reliability model shown at the top of the next page. Calculate the reliability of the system, given that the modules have the following values for their reliability:

Module 1	*0.99*
Modules 2, 3 and 4	*0.80*
Modules 5 and 6	*0.90*
Modules 7 and 8	*0.95*
Module 9	*0.94*

The reliability of the parallel combination of modules 2, 3 and 4 is given by

$$\begin{aligned} R(t) &= 1 - [1 - R_{\mathrm{m}}(t)]^N \\ &= 1 - [1 - 0.8]^3 \\ &= 0.992 \end{aligned}$$

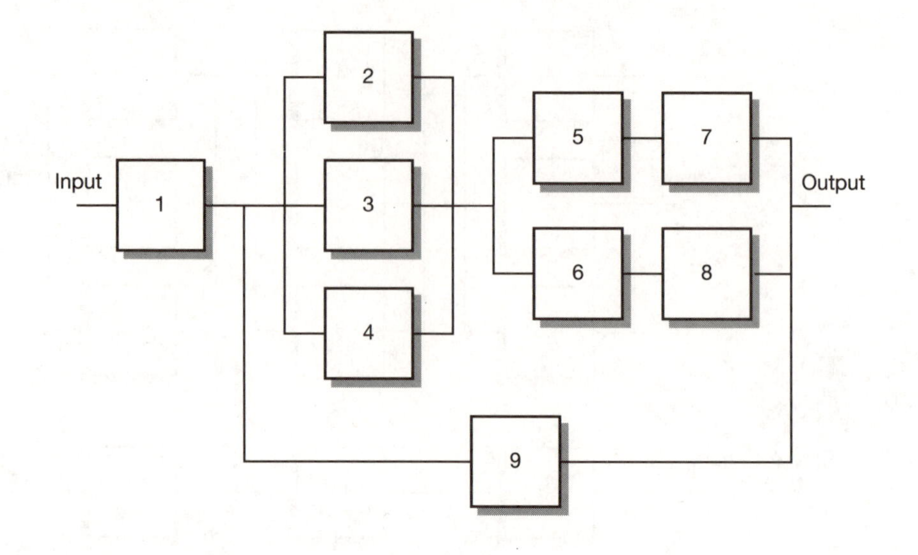

The series combinations of modules 5 and 7 and modules 6 and 8 each have a reliability given by the products of the reliability of the individual modules. Thus each pair has a reliability of 0.90×0.95, or 0.855. The parallel combination of these two paths is simply

$$\begin{aligned} R(t) &= 1 - [1 - R_{\mathrm{m}}(t)]^N \\ &= 1 - [1 - 0.855]^2 \\ &= 0.979 \end{aligned}$$

The system may therefore be represented by the simpler form:

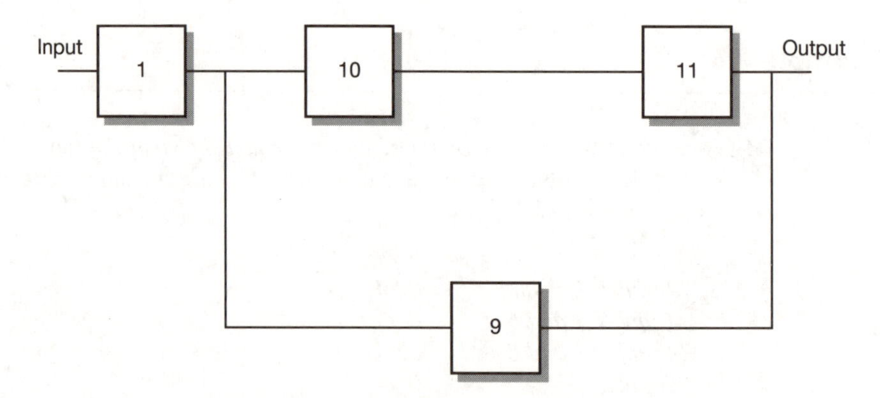

where module 10 represents the combination of modules 2, 3 and 4 and has a reliability of 0.992, and module 11 represents the combination of modules 5, 6, 7 and 8 and has a reliability of 0.979.

The series combination of modules 10 and 11 has a reliability of 0.992×0.979, or 0.971. This combination in parallel with module 9 produces an arrangement with a reliability given by

$$R(t) = 1 - [1 - R_1(t)][1 - R_2(t)]$$
$$= 1 - [1 - 0.971][1 - 0.94]$$
$$= 0.998$$

The reliability of the complete system is now the product of this figure and the reliability of module 1. Thus the system reliability is 0.998 × 0.99, that is 0.988, or approximately 0.99.

Triple modular and N*-modular redundancy*

In Chapter 6 we looked at several forms of static redundancy that may be used to achieve fault tolerance. The voting mechanisms used within these arrangements may be represented within reliability block diagrams, as shown in Figure 7.5.

The simplest of the static configurations, triple modular redundancy (TMR), uses three parallel modules and will function correctly provided that at least two modules are operational. If we ignore the effects of the voting mechanism, the probability of the system working correctly may be expressed in words as follows:

Probability of correct operation = Probability of no failures
+ Probability of only module 1 failing
+ Probability of only module 2 failing
+ Probability of only module 3 failing

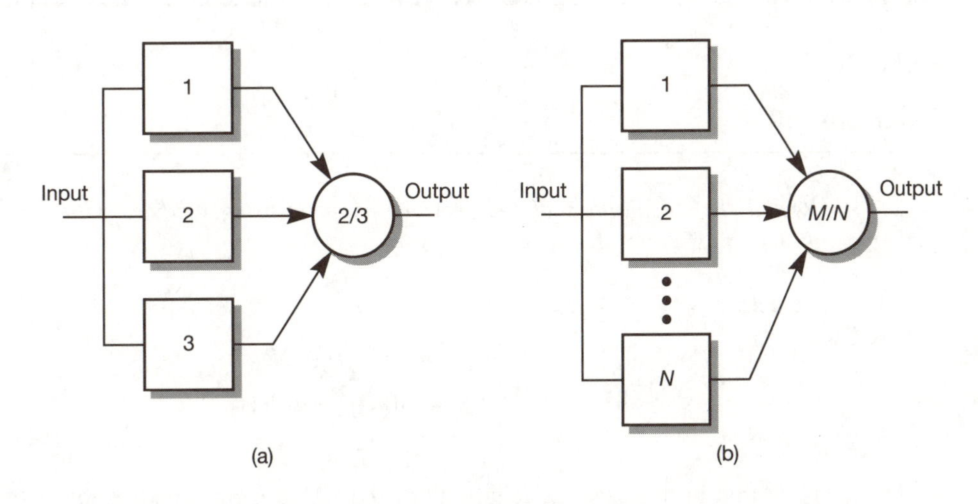

Figure 7.5 Representation of voting mechanisms within reliability block diagrams: (a) triple modular redundancy; (b) N-modular redundancy.

If the probability of a module working correctly is $R_m(t)$, then the probability of it failing is $[1 - R_m(t)]$, and the system reliability is given by

$$R_{TMR}(t) = R_1(t)R_2(t)R_3(t) + [1 - R_1(t)]R_2(t)R_3(t) + R_1(t)[1 - R_2(t)]R_3(t) + R_1(t)R_2(t)[1 - R_3(t)]$$

where $R_1(t)$, $R_2(t)$ and $R_3(t)$ represent the reliability of modules 1, 2 and 3 respectively.

If, as is often the case, the reliability of the three modules is identical, this simplifies to

$$\begin{aligned} R_{TMR}(t) &= R_m^{\ 3}(t) + 3R_m^{\ 2}(t)[1 - R_m(t)] \\ &= 3R_m^{\ 2}(t) - 2R_m^{\ 3}(t) \end{aligned} \tag{7.6}$$

Example 7.7

A TMR system consists of three identical modules each with a reliability of 0.95. Calculate the reliability of the resultant system, ignoring the effects of the voting arrangement.

From Equation 7.6 we have

$$\begin{aligned} R_{TMR}(t) &= 3R_m^{\ 2}(t) - 2R_m^{\ 3}(t) \\ &= 3(0.95)^2 - 2(0.95)^3 \\ &= 0.993 \end{aligned}$$

Example 7.8

Repeat the calculations of the previous example using modules with a reliability of 0.4.

As before,

$$\begin{aligned} R_{TMR}(t) &= 3R_m^{\ 2}(t) - 2R_m^{\ 3}(t) \\ &= 3(0.4)^2 - 2(0.4)^3 \\ &= 0.352 \end{aligned}$$

Note that in this case the reliability of the TMR arrangement is lower than that of an individual module. This illustrates that the use of redundancy does not necessarily increase the reliability of a system. It also shows that a system may be fault tolerant without being reliable. In a TMR arrangement the resultant reliability is only greater than that of the modules themselves if the module reliability is greater than 0.5. Reliability cannot be produced by combining unreliable modules.

A similar analysis to that given above can be applied to systems with N identical modules in which M modules must function correctly in order to prevent a system failure. This results in an expression for the reliability of the form

$$R_{M\text{-of-}N}(t) = \sum_{i=0}^{N-M} \left(\frac{N!}{(N-i)!\,i!} \right) R_{\mathrm{m}}{}^{N-i}(t)[1 - R_{\mathrm{m}}(t)]^{i} \tag{7.7}$$

Substituting values of 3 and 2 for N and M respectively yields a result equivalent to that derived above for the TMR arrangement.

Example 7.9

An N-*modular redundant system consists of five identical modules each with a reliability of 0.95. Calculate the reliability of the resultant system, ignoring the effects of the voting arrangement.*

From Equation 7.7 we have

$$\begin{aligned} R_{3\text{-of-}5}(t) &= \sum_{i=0}^{2} \left(\frac{5!}{(5-i)!\,i!} \right) R_{\mathrm{m}}{}^{5-i}(t)[1 - R_{\mathrm{m}}(t)]^{i} \\ &= R_{\mathrm{m}}{}^{5}(t) + 5R_{\mathrm{m}}{}^{4}(t)[1 - R_{\mathrm{m}}(t)] + 10R_{\mathrm{m}}{}^{3}(t)[1 - R_{\mathrm{m}}(t)]^{2} \\ &= 10R_{\mathrm{m}}{}^{3}(t) - 15R_{\mathrm{m}}{}^{4}(t) + 6R_{\mathrm{m}}{}^{5}(t) \\ &= 10(0.95)^{3} - 15(0.95)^{4} + 6(0.95)^{5} \\ &= 0.9988 \end{aligned}$$

So far in our discussions of static redundant systems we have ignored the effects of the voting mechanism. As the voter is usually a very simple circuit (as described in Chapter 6) it is possible that its reliability may be sufficiently high to allow a single, non-redundant voter to be used. Such a system may be modelled as a series combination of the M-of-N arrangement described earlier, with a single element representing the reliability of the voter. In more critical applications a fault-tolerant voting arrangement will be needed. Such a voting arrangement will then represent a parallel combination of elements in series with the M-of-N network. This series–parallel combination can then be reduced and analysed as discussed earlier.

Dynamic redundancy and fault coverage

In Chapter 6 we looked at various forms of dynamic redundancy. These use some form of fault detection to switch between a number of redundant modules. This arrangement may be modelled as a parallel combination of elements as described above, in which correct operation will be maintained provided that at least one of the modules functions correctly. This may be represented within a reliability block diagram, as shown in Figure 7.6.

Dynamic systems may function in many ways. In a standby spare configuration a primary module is used exclusively unless fault detection circuitry determines that there is a problem with this unit, when control will switch to a standby module. Thus in the arrangement of Figure 7.6, module 1 would be used exclusively unless a fault were detected, when control would switch to module 2. The success of such an arrangement is critically dependent on the effectiveness of the fault detection circuitry.

The system will function correctly if module 1 is fault-free. Alternatively, it will function correctly if module 1 fails provided that the fault circuitry detects this fault and module 2 is fault-free. This may be expressed in probability terms as

$$R(t) = R_1(t) + [1 - R_1(t)]C_1 R_2(t)$$

where $R(t)$ is the system reliability, $R_1(t)$ and $R_2(t)$ represent the reliability of module 1 and module 2 respectively, and C_1 is the fault coverage of module 1. The fault coverage represents the probability of a fault within the module being detected. For modules with identical reliability $R_m(t)$ and fault coverage C_m, this becomes

$$R(t) = R_m(t) + [1 - R_m(t)]C_m R_m(t) \tag{7.8}$$

If we assume perfect fault coverage, that is $C_m = 1$, this reduces to

$$R(t) = 1 - [1 - R_m(t)]^2$$

which is equivalent to the expression obtained earlier in Equation 7.5.

It is interesting to note that if we assume a fault coverage of 0, the expression of Equation 7.8 reduces to $R_m(t)$ and the reliability of the system

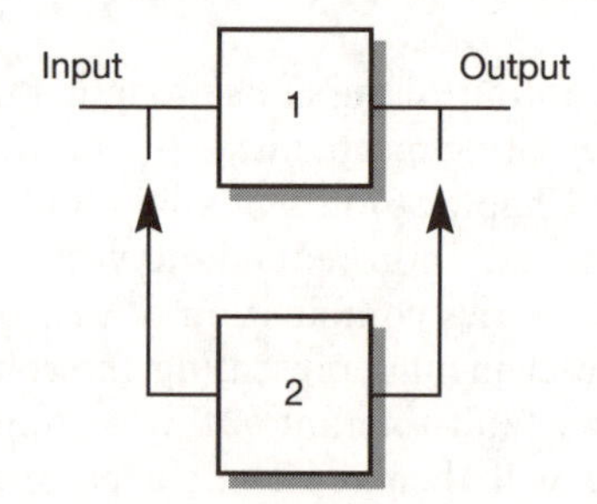

Figure 7.6 A simple dynamic redundant system.

becomes simply the reliability of the primary module. Clearly nothing is gained by having redundant modules if faults are never detected to bring them into service.

Alternative dynamic configurations, such as the use of self-checking pairs, use different methods of fault detection, resulting in slightly different reliability models. Hybrid systems combine the features of static and dynamic systems and again result in variations on the models given above. However, the basic techniques outlined in this section may be used to model all the various fault-tolerant architectures.

Cut and tie sets

Networks that consist entirely of active elements arranged without feedback may be analysed using cut and tie sets (Bansal *et al.*, 1982). These methods do not give an exact value for the reliability of the system, but give upper and lower bounds for its value. This is often useful when dealing with complex arrangements where exact calculation would be difficult.

Cut sets are formed by drawing lines through the reliability block diagram to represent combinations of elements in which simultaneous failure would lead to system failure. Of particular interest are **minimal cut sets**, which represent cut sets in which no subset will result in system failure. Examples of minimal cut sets are shown in Figure 7.7(a). Here it can be seen that failure of component 1 will result in a system failure, whereas failure of component 2 must be accompanied by failure of either 3 or 4 to affect the overall system.

The overall reliability of the complete system may be approximated by considering the influence of each of the minimal cut sets separately. Each cut set

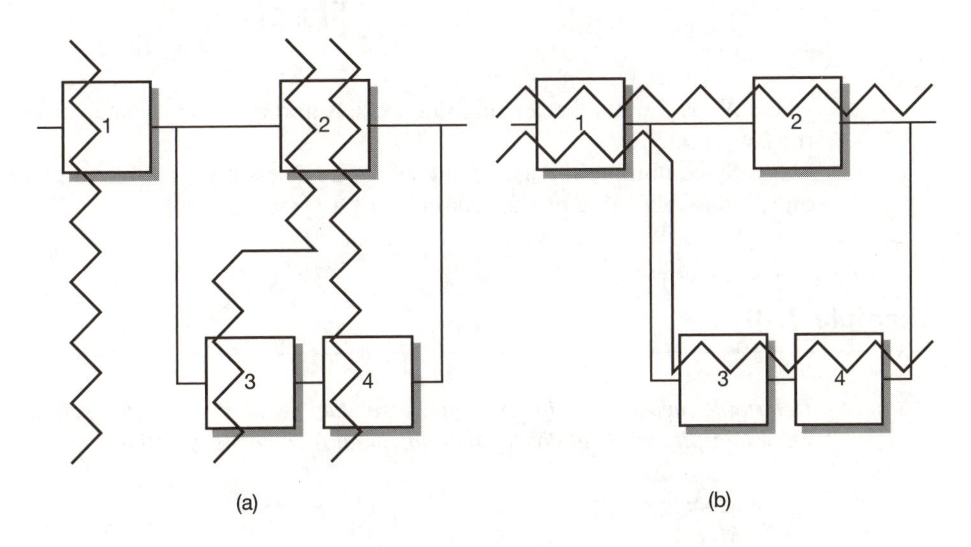

Figure 7.7 Minimal cut and tie sets: (a) minimal cut sets; (b) minimal tie sets.

represents a parallel combination of components, and from Equation 7.4 we know that the reliability of this combination is given by

$$R(t) = 1 - Q(t) = 1 - [1 - R_1(t)][1 - R_2(t)] \ldots [1 - R_N(t)]$$

or simply

$$R(t) = 1 - \prod_{i=1}^{N}[1 - R_i(t)]$$

By combining the influences of all the minimal cut sets it can be shown that the overall reliability must be greater than a value given by the expression

$$R(t) > 1 - \sum_{j=1}^{N_C} \prod_{i=1}^{n_j}[1 - R_i(t)] \tag{7.9}$$

where N_C is the number of minimal cut sets and n_j is the number of elements in the jth cut set.

Tie sets (or path sets) are formed by drawing lines through the reliability block diagram to represent groups which, if all the elements were working, would guarantee the functioning of the system. **Minimal tie sets** represent tie sets in which no subset will perform this function. Figure 7.7(b) illustrates the concept of minimal tie sets.

By combining the effects of all the minimal tie sets it is possible to place a maximum value on system reliability. This is given by the expression

$$R(t) < \sum_{j=1}^{N_T} \prod_{i=1}^{n_j} R_i(t) \tag{7.10}$$

where N_T is the number of minimal tie sets and n_j is the number of elements in the jth tie set.

By combining the use of cut sets and tie sets it is possible to place bounds on the possible value of the reliability of a system.

Example 7.10

Determine upper and lower bounds to the reliability of the arrangement of Figure 7.7, if the reliability of the individual modules is as follows:

Module 1	*0.8*
Module 2	*0.7*
Modules 3 and 4	*0.9*

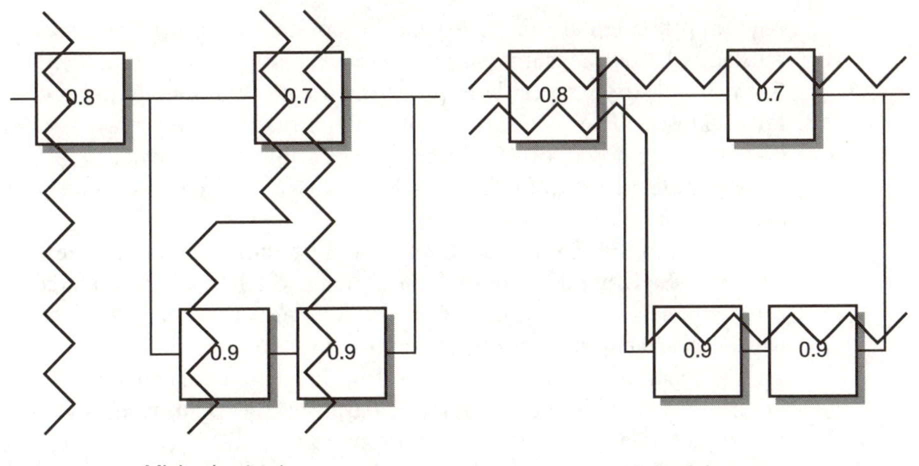

Minimal cut sets   Minimal tie sets

From Equation 7.9 we have

$$\begin{aligned} R(t) &> 1 - [1 - R_1(t)] - [1 - R_2(t)][1 - R_3(t)] - [1 - R_2(t)][1 - R_4(t)] \\ &> 1 - [1 - 0.8] - [1 - 0.7][1 - 0.9] - [1 - 0.7][1 - 0.9] \\ &> 0.74 \end{aligned}$$

and from Equation 7.10 we have

$$\begin{aligned} R(t) &< [R_1(t)][R_2(t)] + [R_1(t)][R_3(t)][R_4(t)] \\ &< [0.8][0.7] + [0.8][0.9][0.9] \\ &< 1.208 \text{ (that is, } <1.0) \end{aligned}$$

In this case the actual value of the reliability is given by

$$\begin{aligned} R(t) &= R_1(t)\big(1 - [1 - R_2(t)][1 - R_3(t)R_4(t)]\big) \\ &= 0.8\big(1 - [1 - 0.7][1 - 0.9 \times 0.9]\big) \\ &= 0.7544 \end{aligned}$$

Cut and tie set analyses would not normally be used for arrangements as simple as that in the above example. However, in complex systems the calculation of an exact value for the reliability may be impractical. In such cases, an estimate based on cut and tie sets may represent a sufficient and efficient method of assessing reliability. As the complexity of the arrangement increases, the values obtained from the two approaches tend to converge, this convergence being more rapid when the reliability of the individual blocks is high. In practice, analysis often uses only a cut set approach to obtain a lower limit on system reliability.

Although cut and tie set methods are usually simpler than obtaining an exact value for system reliability, they may themselves involve a considerable amount of calculation. A system of moderate complexity may result in a reliability block diagram containing several millions of minimal cut and tie sets. Such complexity inevitably requires the use of computer-based tools to perform the analyses. The estimations of reliability produced may be improved by systematic removal of the multiple counting of elements. This is a process ideally suited to automation, making this approach particularly suitable for computer-based tools.

Minimal cut sets that contain only a single element represent potential sites for **single-point failure** of the system. Such sets are referred to as 'first-order' cut sets. If the failure of two components can result in system failure this will be represented by a cut set containing two elements – a second-order cut set. Analysis of the system can be simplified by considering only certain low-order cut sets. This simplification is based on the assumption that simultaneous failure of a large number of components is unlikely and can therefore be neglected. The validity of this assumption will depend on the reliability of the components concerned.

In addition to their use with reliability block diagrams, cut and tie sets may also be used in the analysis of **fault trees**. Here minimal cut sets represent combinations of events that can result in the top event of the tree.

Reliability and MTTF

In this section we have often referred to a numerical value for the reliability of a module and used this figure to calculate system reliability. It is important to remember that reliability is a function of time, and that these figures depend on the time for which the system must operate. Different applications place varying constraints on the system designer in terms of reliability and length of service. In some military situations mission duration might be measured in hours, whereas in other situations equipment might have to operate dependably for several decades. Thus one designer might be looking for a reliability of 0.999 for a period of only 24 hours, whereas another might require a reliability of 0.99 for 10 years.

By contrast, the mean time to failure (MTTF) of a system is a fixed characteristic that does not change with time. It might seem logical that reliability and a high MTTF would go hand in hand, but this is not necessarily true. Adding redundancy to a system may increase its reliability over a given time period, but by increasing its complexity it may also reduce its MTTF. As the period of service of a module approaches its MTTF its reliability falls. We noted earlier in the case of a TMR system that adding redundancy only increases the system's reliability if the module reliability is greater than 0.5. In Section 7.1 we saw, in Equation 7.2, that the reliability of a system at a time equal to its MTTF is only about 0.37. Therefore, when the period of service of a unit is comparable with its MTTF, adding redundancy will not increase the overall reliability.

In highly critical systems we normally wish to achieve high levels of reliability. This is usually achieved by using redundant, fault-tolerant designs with modules that are operated for periods which are short compared with their MTTF.

Independence of failures

In the analysis of series and parallel systems given above it has been assumed that all failures are independent. This assumption is normally valid in the case of random component failures, but is not so for systematic faults. Consider, for example, the case of a parallel system consisting of three identical modules each containing a software fault. In this situation, because each module receives the same input data, it is likely that all the modules would fail simultaneously, thereby removing any benefit from the redundancy. Design faults of other kinds are also likely to produce correlated faults in different modules, resulting in common failures. Similarly, intermittent faults may be caused by interference or other transient events that affect more than one module, leading to simultaneous failures.

Because faults of these kinds produce correlated errors in a number of modules, the assumptions made in the analysis within this section are invalid. For these reasons the combinational modelling techniques described above are frequently restricted to the analysis of random component failures.

Markov models

The combinational modelling techniques described above determine the overall reliability of a system by using measured or predicted values for the reliability of its constituent parts. An alternative approach is to assign various states to a system and to determine the probability of being in any of these states. This is termed Markov modelling (Lewis, 1996). As an example, one might assign two possible states to a system, representing the working and not working conditions. The probability of being in either state would then indicate the availability of the system. One of the advantages of this approach is that it provides a more powerful way of modelling systems that are repairable, allowing variables such as the time taken to repair a system to be incorporated. A detailed treatment of Markov modelling is beyond the scope of this text. However, it is instructive to consider a simple example.

Discrete Markov modelling

Consider a simple two-state system as shown in Figure 7.8. In this system the two states are assigned the designations 1 and 2, and the model assumes that the probabilities of leaving or remaining in a particular state are constant for all time, at the values indicated in the diagram. Transitions between states occur in discrete steps, and thus this is termed a discrete Markov model of the system. The

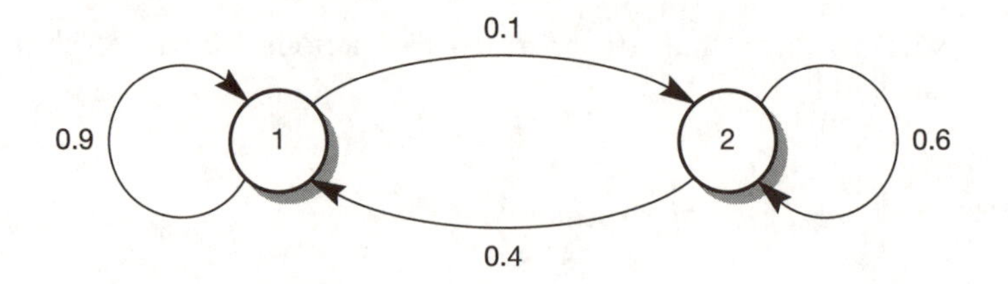

Figure 7.8 A two-state system.

two states could represent any aspects of the system and could, for example, represent working and non-working states.

If we assume that the system is initially in state 1, the diagram shows that at the end of the first time interval it has a probability of 0.9 of remaining in state 1 and a probability of 0.1 of leaving state 1 and entering state 2. Note that the sum of these probabilities is unity, as the system must follow one of these courses of action. Therefore, at the beginning of the second time interval it has a probability of 0.9 of being in state 1 and of 0.1 of being in state 2. At the end of the second time interval the probabilities of leaving or remaining in its current state are again defined by the diagram, and this process continues for successive time steps. The possible sequences of transitions taken by the system, together with the probabilities of following each route, can be represented in a tree diagram, as shown in Figure 7.9.

It can be seen that from the end of the second time interval onwards there are several ways of ending up in either state. The probability of being in each state is therefore the sum of the probabilities of each route leading to that state. If we sum these probabilities at the end of each time interval we quickly see a pattern emerging, as shown in Table 7.1.

Clearly, at the end of each time interval the sum of the probabilities of being in each state must equal unity, as the system must be in one or other state. However, as time progresses the probabilities of each state tend to particular values, depending on the transition probabilities. In this example the probability of being in state 1 tends towards a value of 0.8, and that of being in state 2 tends to a value of 0.2. Within just a few transitions the state probabilities are very close to their limiting values.

The state probabilities shown in Table 7.1 are determined by the transition probabilities between the states, and also by the initial conditions

Table 7.1 Successive state probabilities for the two-state system.

	Time interval				
	1	*2*	*3*	*4*	*5*
State 1	0.9	0.85	0.825	0.8125	0.806 25
State 2	0.1	0.15	0.175	0.1875	0.193 75

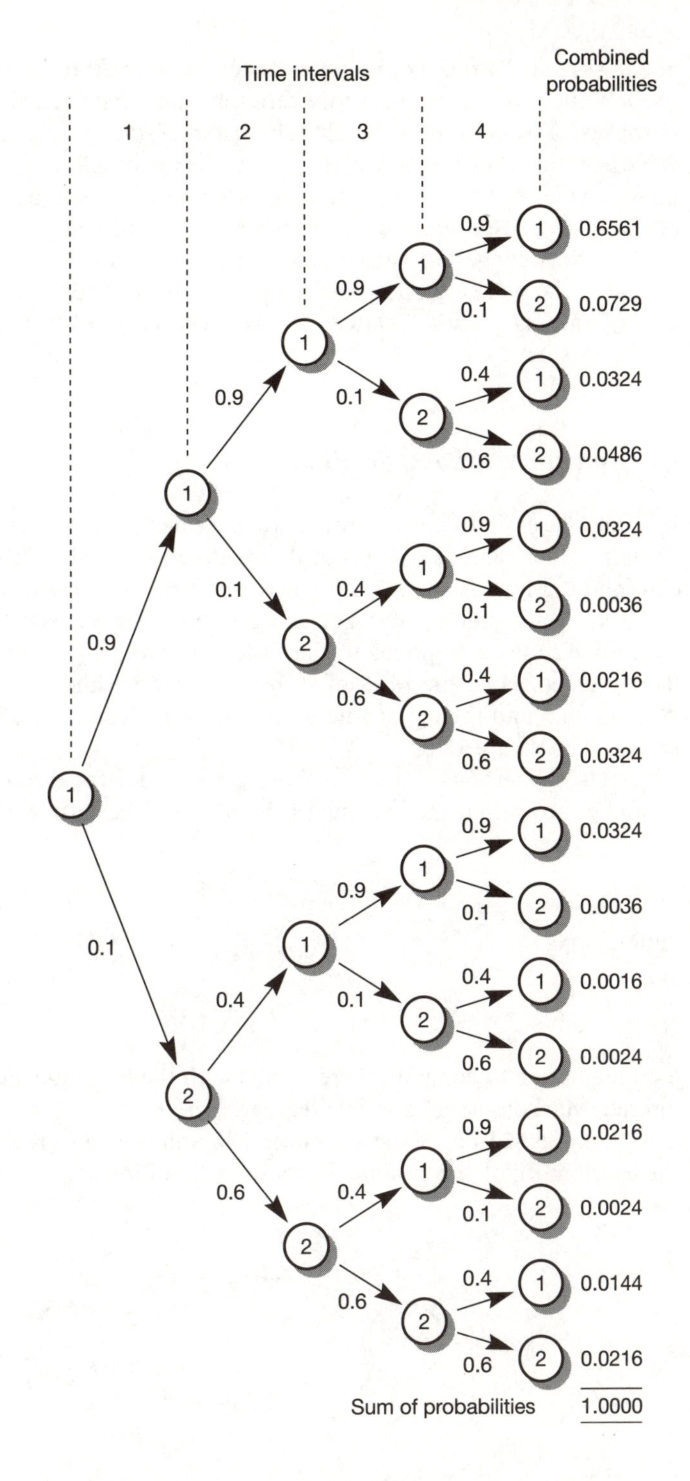

Figure 7.9 A tree diagram of the two-state system.

of the system. In this example the system started from state 1; the initial state probabilities would be markedly different had it started from the other state. However, a very important characteristic of this model is that the limiting values of the state probabilities are independent of the initial conditions, as these have only a transient effect. In other words, the long-term characteristics of the system are not affected by its initial conditions.

It was suggested earlier that the two states of our simple system could represent the working and failed states. In this case the probability of being in either state is clearly related to the reliability of the system and to its availability.

Continuous Markov modelling

In many cases it is more sensible to consider a system in a continuous time domain rather than as a series of discrete time intervals. This can be done using continuous Markov modelling, where the probabilities of state transitions are replaced by transition rates. Let us again consider our simple two-state system, where one state corresponds to the system working correctly and the other to its having failed. Here the rates of transition between the two states represent the failure rate λ and the repair rate μ, as defined in Section 7.1. The resulting model is shown in Figure 7.10.

Using methods similar to those given above for discrete Markov models, it can be shown that the limiting probabilities of being in each state are given by

$$P_1 = \frac{\mu}{\lambda + \mu}$$

and

$$P_2 = \frac{\lambda}{\lambda + \mu}$$

You might like to compare these results with the limiting values obtained for the discrete Markov model obtained earlier.

As the MTTF of the system is $1/\lambda$ and the MTTR is $1/\mu$, P_1 represents the availability of the system; P_2 its unavailability.

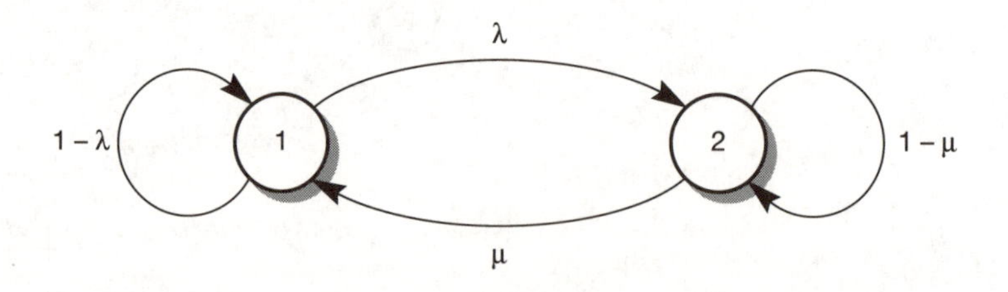

Figure 7.10 A continuous Markov model of the two-state system.

7.3 Reliability prediction

Any safety-critical system will have a certain requirement for reliability, and in Chapter 6 we discussed a range of system architectures that can be used to increase a system's tolerance of faults. In the previous section we saw how the reliability of a system may be modelled, and how this is related to the reliability of its component parts. Clearly, it would be useful to be able to predict the reliability of a system at the design stage. This would allow the design to be evaluated before going to the expense of building the system. Unfortunately, reliability prediction is not a straightforward process. We have seen that system failure can be caused by various types of fault. Some of these, such as hardware component failures, have a random nature and may be subjected to some form of statistical analysis. Others, such as design and specification faults, are systematic and analysis – and therefore prediction – is much harder.

Electronic component failure

The most widely used technique for predicting the failure rate of electronic equipment is based on the use of the United States Department of Defense military handbook MIL-HDBK-217 (DoD, 1992). This was first issued in 1965, but has been regularly revised to reflect refinements in the techniques and data used. The handbook provides models for the failure rate of various electronic components that have been obtained using experimental data on actual device behaviour.

The models and data within the standard aim to predict the failure rate of individual components from a knowledge of their form and their operating environment. Failure rates are given in terms of the number of failures expected within a million hours of operation. From a knowledge of the expected failure rates of individual components a figure can be produced for a complete system by combining their effects, as described in the previous section.

The models used differ between components to reflect their different failure mechanisms. For a single fixed resistor the model given is

$$\lambda_p = \lambda_b \pi_R \pi_Q \pi_E \text{ failures}/10^6 \text{ hours}$$

where λ_p is the part failure rate, λ_b is the base failure rate reflecting the electrical and thermal stresses on the part and the various π terms represent environmental and other effects. Here π_R models the importance of the resistor value, π_Q concerns the quality of its manufacture and π_E is an environmental factor.

Tables in the handbook give guidance on appropriate values for the various parameters for a given application and for different types of resistor. The base failure rate is determined by the ambient temperature of the resistor and a thermal stress factor. Here the stress factor is the ratio of the operating power to the rated power of the device. The handbook gives a table showing values of λ_b for different temperature and stress factors. It also gives an

Table 7.2 Resistance factor π_R for a fixed resistor.

Resistance range (ohms)	π_R
<0.1 M	1.0
>0.1 M to 1 M	1.1
>1 M to 10 M	1.6
>10 M	2.5

equation that can be used to calculate the parameter for situations not given within the table. For composition resistors, values for λ_b vary from 0.0007 to 0.0065 for the range of conditions given in the table.

The value of π_R varies with the resistance of the component. Table 7.2 shows examples of values of this parameter for a composition resistor. Thin-film wire-wound and network resistors have slightly different values. It can be seen that high-value resistors have a greater failure rate than those of a lower value.

The quality of manufacture is taken into consideration by the factor π_Q. For fixed resistors the value of this parameter ranges from 0.03 for devices manufactured and screened to the highest levels, to a value of 15 for commercial parts. For military-grade components the parameter has a value of between 1.0 and 5.0.

The environment in which a component is used will have a significant effect on its reliability. The handbook defines a number of environmental classes covering a broad range of applications. Because of the nature of the document these classifications are represented by typical military situations. These range from benign ground-based environments through more hostile airborne situations to the very severe conditions experienced by equipment during a rocket launch. The most hostile environment documented covers equipment shot from a cannon. The effects of these differing operating conditions are represented by the parameter π_E, which for a fixed resistor takes values from 1.0 for a benign ground-based application to 490 for a cannon launch.

From the tables it is possible to assign appropriate values to the various parameters and to calculate the predicted part failure rate for a given set of conditions. As an example, if we selected a commercial-grade composition resistor of 1 MΩ and used it in an ambient temperature of 70°C with a power dissipation of 10% of its rated power in a helicopter environment, the predicted failure rate would be approximately 0.02 failures per million hours of operation. This represents one failure in every 6000 years. If the same resistor were to be used in a benign ground-based application at an ambient temperature of 30°C, the failure rate would decrease by a factor of about 80.

For more complicated electronic components the calculation of predicted failure rate becomes more involved, with additional terms being required. The equation used for microcircuits, logic circuits, gate arrays and microprocessors is

$$\lambda_p = (C_1\pi_T + C_2\pi_E)\pi_Q\pi_L \text{ failures}/10^6 \text{ hours}$$

where

λ_p	is the part failure rate
C_1	is related to die complexity
π_T	is related to ambient temperature
C_2	is related to package failure rate and varies with construction methods
π_E	is determined by the operating environment
π_Q	is determined by quality issues
π_L	represents the learning factor and is determined by the number of years for which the device has been in production.

The parameters π_T, π_E and π_Q represent the same dependencies as in the model of the resistor discussed above, although their values will be different.

Semiconductor memory devices have a similar model to that given above for other microcircuits, with the exception that an additional term is added within the brackets:

$$\lambda_p = (C_1\pi_T + C_2\pi_E + \lambda_{cyc})\pi_Q\pi_L \text{ failures}/10^6 \text{ hours}$$

Here the terms have the meanings given above and λ_{cyc} represents the effects of the frequency of read/write operations. For all but EEPROM memory devices of certain types this parameter is zero, yielding a model identical to that given earlier for other microcircuits.

It is not appropriate here to list in detail the values associated with the various parameters and their interdependencies. However, as an example we could take a particular memory device and look at the values of the various terms in the expression for its failure rate. Let us consider a commercial-grade 32 kbyte NMOS static RAM in a 28-pin plastic package, used in an undemanding environment. Typical values for the various parameters would be:

C_1	0.016 for an NMOS static RAM
π_T	0.19 at 40°C
C_2	0.01 for a 28-pin plastic, dual inline package
π_E	0.50 for a benign ground-based environment
π_Q	10 for a commercial device
π_L	1.0 for a device which has been in production for more than two years
λ_{cyc}	0 for a non-EEPROM memory device.

These values result in a predicted failure rate of approximately 0.08 failures per million hours, or about one failure in every 1400 years. It should be remembered that although the examples we have considered yield very low failure rates, these relate to individual components. The predicted failure rate of a complete system might represent the combined effects of thousands of components, and could be much higher.

The reliability prediction methods discussed above are termed ‘parts stress analysis’, as they take into account the electrical, thermal and environmental stress experienced by a component. This form of analysis can only be performed on a system during the later stages of a design, once the hardware components have been specified. Often it is useful to perform a preliminary analysis of a system before the hardware design reaches this level of detail, to ensure that reliability predictions are going to be within acceptable bounds. For this purpose the MIL-HDBK-217 standard describes a second, less rigorous method of investigating reliability, based on a 'parts count' approach. This requires much less detailed information about the design, but uses data on part quantities, quality levels and environmental conditions. This approach is suitable for use at an early stage in a design or during the proposal phase. The parts count method generally produces a more conservative estimate of failure rate (that is, it suggests a higher likely failure rate) than the more detailed parts stress analysis method.

It is obvious from the above examples that determining the predicted failure rates of each component within a complex system would be time-consuming and error-prone if performed manually. Fortunately, a number of automated tools exist to speed up the process. These computer-aided engineering (CAE) tools take circuit design data in a form compatible with conventional CAD tools and combine it with data extracted from the reliability handbook. In many ways they perform a task similar to that of a circuit simulator, except that they determine the effect of each component on the failure rate of the circuit rather than analysing circuit behaviour.

Limitations on the prediction of device failure rates

Throughout the above discussion we have used the term 'predicted failure rate' rather than 'calculated failure rate'. It is very important to note that the methods described do not allow us to calculate with any accuracy the failure rate of any real system. Indeed, the MIL-HDBK-217 handbook states that its function is to provide a common basis for the comparison of competing designs, rather than to provide a numerical value for reliability. If two designs are subjected to the analysis outlined in the handbook, the figures may give some guidance as to which design is likely to have a greater reliability. The analysis may also indicate whether modifications to existing designs are likely to have a significant impact on system reliability. What is clear is that the values obtained cannot be considered as realistic estimates of the reliability that would be achieved if particular designs were constructed.

Software reliability prediction

Over the years a number of researchers have attempted to develop ways of predicting the reliability of software. These techniques are usually related to an estimate of the number of errors within a program. The goal of this work is to produce an estimate of the likely failure rate of a piece of software that could be used in a manner similar to the analysis of hardware component failures described in the previous section.

If one has two computer programs that implemented the same function and one's only knowledge of these two pieces of software is that the first is known to contain more errors than the second, then one might reasonably deduce that the second program would be *likely* to be more reliable than the first. However, this is by no means certain. It is not reasonable to assume that the reliability of the programs is directly related to the number of errors within them. It is possible, for example, that the first program contains a large number of errors within routines that are used very infrequently, whereas the second contains a single error within a routine that is run frequently. This scenario might result in the program with fewer errors exhibiting more system failures and a correspondingly lower reliability.

As a result of this observation we might modify our prediction of reliability by estimating not only the number of errors within our program, but also their distribution. We might, for example, weight the number of errors within a section of the program by the frequency with which this section of code is executed. This would give increased importance to errors in frequently used sections. Unfortunately, this approach also has significant problems. First, there is the difficulty in obtaining any realistic estimate of the number of faults within a piece of software, and secondly one must consider not only the presence of faults, but also their effects.

Estimating the number of faults within a piece of software is a difficult task. In any critical application one would assume that any software fault that was located would be removed, and so the number of known errors in the final system would normally be zero. However, as all software engineers know, there are always errors within pieces of software of any size, so the problem arises as to how we estimate how many faults we have not found. One method commonly used to estimate these undetected faults is to record the number of faults located throughout the development process. If the number of faults located within a fixed period of time, for example for each person-day of development effort, is plotted against time, we would expect to get a graph of the form shown in Figure 7.11.

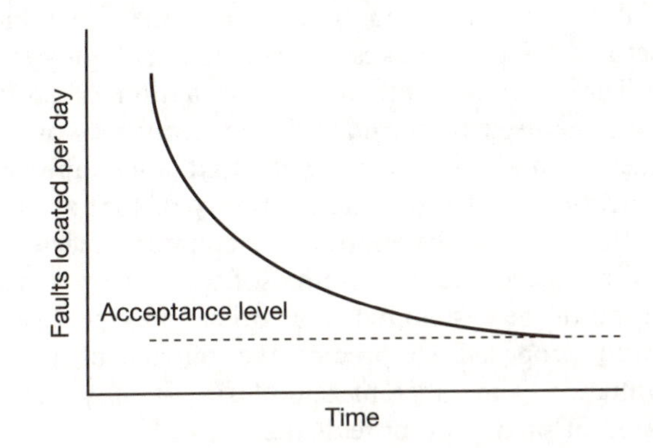

Figure 7.11 The variation of additional faults located with time.

If the number of faults located per day were directly proportional to the number of remaining faults we would expect the curve to be a decaying exponential. In practice, as more faults are located the remaining errors are more difficult to locate, and the rate of detection falls. Examination of the shape of the curve obtained allows it to be extrapolated and the area under the curve to be determined. This gives an estimate of the original number of errors in the code, and from a knowledge of the number located it is possible to estimate the number remaining. At some time the rate of detection of further faults becomes so low that a commercial decision is made to release the software. Although this method produces a numerical estimate of the number of faults remaining within a piece of software, its accuracy is uncertain. This is particularly true when highly critical systems are being developed, as one would like the number of remaining faults to be very small. Obtaining an accurate assessment of the number of remaining faults within each section of a program, so that this can be analysed in association with frequency of execution data, is normally an unrealistic goal.

Another approach to estimating the remaining errors within a program is based on the use of mutation testing (DeMillo *et al.*, 1978). This involves making minor changes (mutations) to a program and then testing the software using the same methods as for the original program. The success of the testing process in detecting the mutations then gives an estimate of the success of the testing procedures used. This in turn can be used to estimate the number of undetected errors from a knowledge of the number found. Problems associated with this technique relate to the vast range of possible mutations to be investigated, and also the inherent assumption that these mutations will have only minor effects on program operation. Mutations that cause major changes in the operation of the software allow little to be deduced about the nature of the original code.

Other methods of estimating the number of errors within programs are based upon experience of past projects. One could postulate that programmers working in a particular area tend to make mistakes at a fairly constant rate, and that the number of errors will thus be proportional to the program size. Although this relationship might give broad estimates of likely error rates, the variability of human programmers, and the inevitable differences between one project and another, makes any predictions highly suspect.

The second hurdle to the estimation of software reliability identified above is the need to consider the consequences of software faults rather than just their number. As it is accepted that some faults are likely to remain within the operational software, the reliability of that software will be determined by how often these faulty sections of code are executed, and whether execution results in a system failure. Some software errors may have little impact on the operation of the system, whereas others may be disastrous. No mechanism has yet been proposed to predict the impact of undetected faults on system performance. The inherent complexity of any software-based system makes this kind of prediction unrealistic.

Despite the enormous difficulties involved, much important work has been done on the prediction of software reliability. Most techniques recommended by the various standards are based on an assessment of the techniques used to develop and test the software, in addition to information on previous similar systems (Harris and Dale, 1982; Littlewood and Strigini, 1993; Musa *et al.*, 1987; Pyle, 1991). Unfortunately, work in this area is yet to receive universal acceptance by the software engineering community, and remains an area of intense academic research and debate.

7.4 Reliability assessment

Once a system has been designed and a prototype system produced it is necessary to demonstrate that it meets its reliability requirements. During the development phase predictions will have been made concerning failure rates and availability, but these will need to be confirmed by testing. The testing phase of product development is discussed in Chapter 12. There are, however, some aspects of testing specifically related to reliability, which will be discussed here.

Once a unit has been constructed its reliability may be investigated experimentally. This could make use of a single unit by measuring the times between successive failures to determine the failure rate or the availability. Although this approach is feasible, unless the unit fails very frequently it will take an inordinate amount of time to gather sufficient data for meaningful analysis. As the goal of most projects is to produce systems that fail infrequently, this method is rarely attractive. An alternative approach is to construct a large number of identical units and to determine the mean failure rate for the group. This will allow a meaningful estimate of the failure rate to be made in a time comparable to the MTTF. In low-cost applications requiring a relatively low reliability such an approach is quite feasible, particularly if accelerated life testing is used to reduce the testing times required. However, in critical systems this approach is rarely possible. Such systems are often very expensive and the production of large numbers would be prohibitive. Also, because such systems require very low failure rates, the necessary testing times would be long. Some very high-integrity avionics equipment is required to fail less than once in every 10^9 hours of operation. This represents a time to failure of over 100 000 years.

One of the implications of having a requirement for a very long MTTF is that it is generally impossible to demonstrate by testing that this requirement has been achieved. In such systems acceptance and certification are often based on reliability models for the hardware and the use of appropriate development techniques for the software. This situation is accepted within several standards governing the development of high-integrity systems in areas such as aeronautics. At present highly critical systems are specified to require a reliability that is several orders of magnitude better than can be demonstrated by testing.

REFERENCES

Bansal V.K., Misra K.B. and Jain M.P. (1982). Minimal pathset and minimal cutsets using search technique. *Microelectronics and Reliability*, **22**(6), 1067–75

DeMillo R.A., Lipton R.J. and Sayward F.G. (1978). Hints on data selection: help for the practising programmer. *IEEE Computer*, **9**(4), 34–41

DoD (1992). *Military Standardization Handbook: Reliability Prediction of Electronic Equipment*. United States Department of Defense MIL-HDBK-217F

Harris L.N. and Dale C.J. (1982). Approaches to software reliability prediction. In *Proc. Ann. Reliability and Maintainability Symp.*, Los Angeles, CA, 26–28 January, pp. 167–75. New York: IEEE

IEC (1991). International Standard 1078 *Analysis Techniques for Dependability – Reliability Block Diagram Method.* Geneva: International Electrotechnical Commission. (Also available in the UK as BS 5760: *Reliability of Systems, Equipment and Components. Part 9: Guide to the Block Diagram Technique* (1992). British Standards Institution)

Lewis E.E. (1996). *Introduction to Reliability Engineering* 2nd edn. New York: John Wiley

Littlewood B. and Strigini L. (1993). Validation of ultrahigh dependability for software-based systems. *Comm. ACM*, **36**(11), 69–80

Musa J.D., Iannino A. and Okumoto K. (1987). *Software Reliability Prediction and Measurement*. London: McGraw-Hill

Pyle I.C. (1991). *Developing Safety Systems: A Guide Using Ada.* Hemel Hempstead: Prentice-Hall

Siewiorek D.P. and Swarz R.S. (1982). *The Theory and Practice of Reliable System Design*. Bedford, MA: Digital Press

FURTHER READING

Billinton R. and Allan R.A. (1992). *Reliability Evaluation of Engineering Systems: Concepts and Techniques*, 2nd edn. New York: Plenum Press

O'Connor P.D.T. (1995). *Practical Reliability Engineering*, 3rd edn. Chichester: John Wiley

PROBLEMS

7.1 Define the terms 'reliability', 'unreliability' and 'failure rate'.

7.2 How does the failure rate of a typical electronic component or system vary throughout its life?

7.3 What is the relationship between the failure rate of a system during its useful life period λ and its reliability $R(t)$?

7.4 Define the term MTTF. How is the MTTF related to the reliability and the failure rate of a system?

7.5 Calculate the reliability of a system at a time equal to half of its MTTF.

7.6 A system is required to have a reliability of 0.99 for a period of five years. Assuming that the system follows an exponential failure law, what must be its MTTF?

7.7 A system has an MTTF of 1000 hours and an MTTR of five hours. Calculate the MTBF and the availability of the system.

7.8 A component has a failure rate of 0.005 failures per hour and a repair rate of 0.2 repairs per hour. What is the system's availability?

7.9 Determine the failure rate of the following system assuming that modules 1, 2 and 3 have failure rates of 0.7, 0.8 and 0.9 failures per hour respectively.

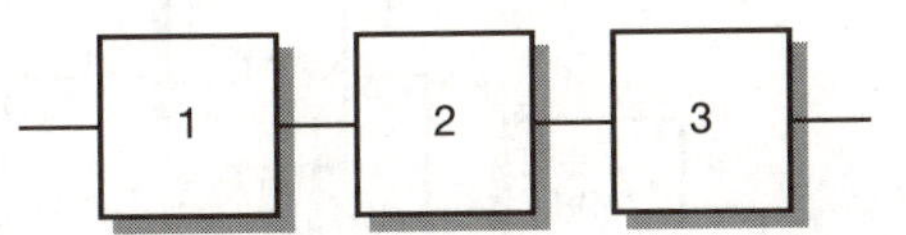

7.10 For an arrangement similar to that shown above, calculate the reliability of the system given that the reliability of modules 1, 2 and 3 is 0.7, 0.8 and 0.9 respectively.

7.11 A system is composed of 20 components and failure of any component will cause a failure of the complete system. If each component has a reliability of 0.97, calculate the overall system reliability.

7.12 A system contains 50 components and is required to have a reliability of 0.995. Assuming that failure of any component will cause a system failure, and that all components are equally reliable, calculate the minimum reliability required of the components to achieve the specified system performance.

7.13 A system may be represented by the following reliability model:

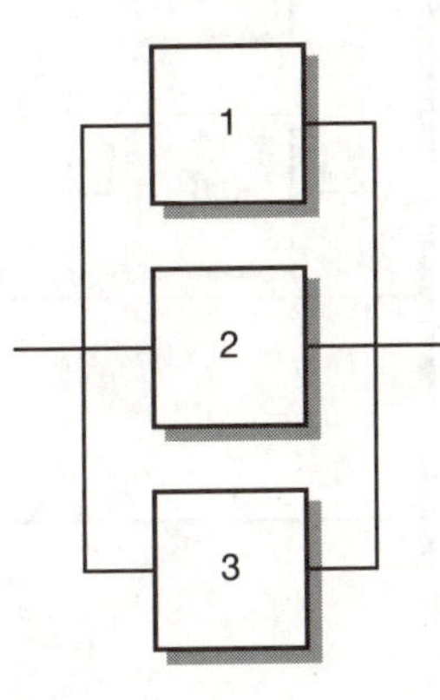

If the reliability of modules 1, 2 and 3 is 0.8, 0.9 and 0.95 respectively, what is the overall system reliability?

7.14 A module has a reliability of 0.9. How many such modules would be required in a parallel fault-tolerant combination to provide a system reliability of 0.998?

7.15 A system may be described by the following reliability model, where the numbers within the boxes represent the module reliability. Calculate the system reliability.

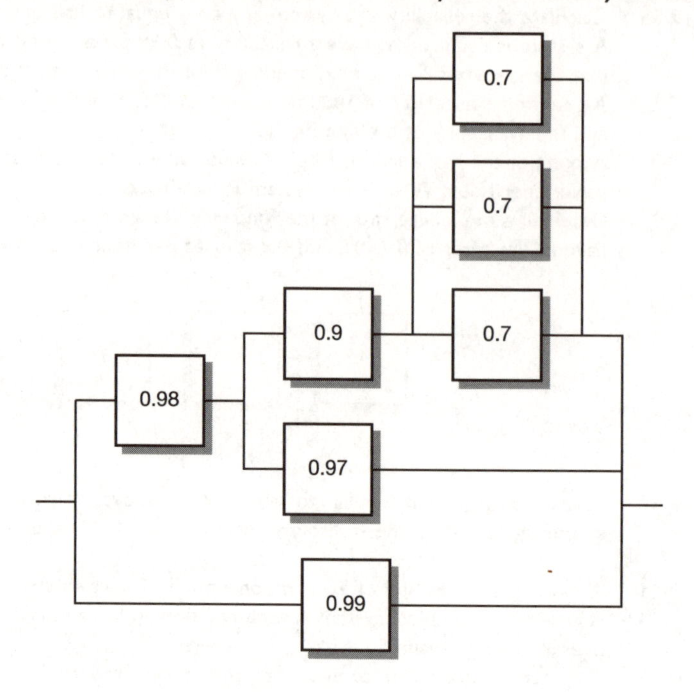

7.16 Repeat the calculation of the last exercise for the following system.

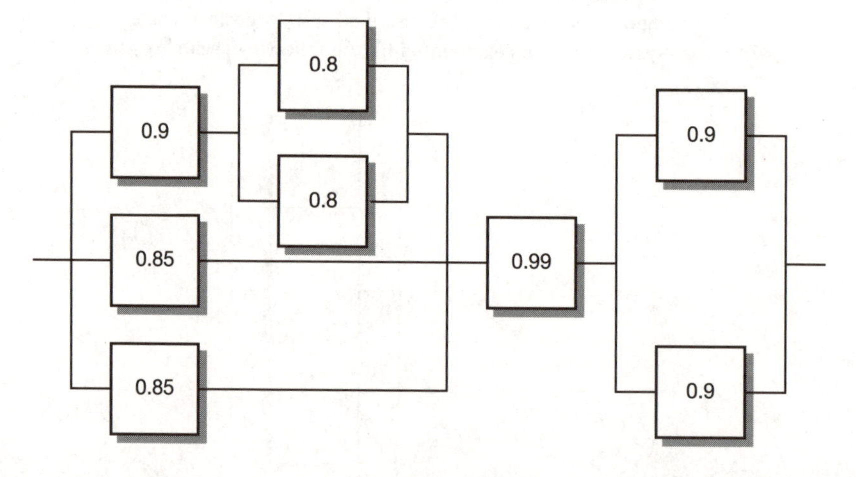

7.17 A TMR system contains three identical modules each with a reliability of 0.9. Calculate the reliability of the system, ignoring the effects of the voting arrangement.

7.18 Repeat the above analysis assuming a module reliability of 0.5.

7.19 A fault-tolerant system has five identical modules each of reliability 0.9. If the system will function correctly provided that a majority of the modules are working, calculate the reliability of the system.

7.20 A fault-tolerant system consists of two identical modules and employs dynamic redundancy. If the reliability of the modules is 0.95 and the fault coverage of the fault detection mechanism is 0.9, calculate the system reliability.

7.21 Use cut and tie sets to determine upper and lower bounds on the reliability of the system corresponding to the model given in Problem 7.15.

7.22 Repeat the calculations of the last exercise for the system described in Problem 7.16.

7.23 Explain why increasing the reliability of a system could result in a reduction in its MTTF.

7.24 Recalculate the data given in Figure 7.9 and Table 7.1 assuming that the simple two-state system was initially in state 2.

7.25 Determine the limiting values of the state probabilities of the following discrete Markov model.

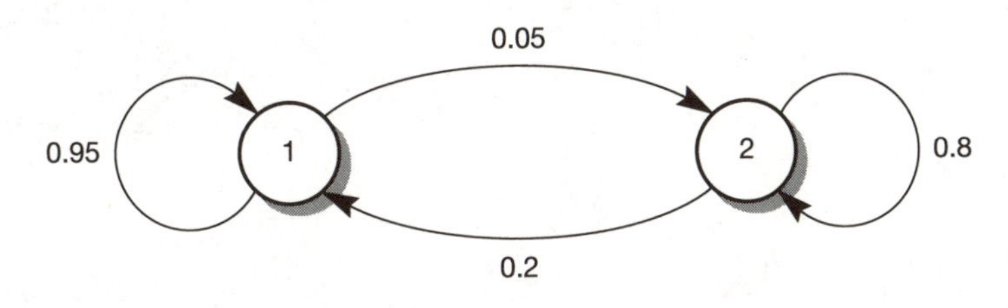

7.26 A system may be described by the following continuous Markov model, where state 1 represents the working state and state 2 the failed state.

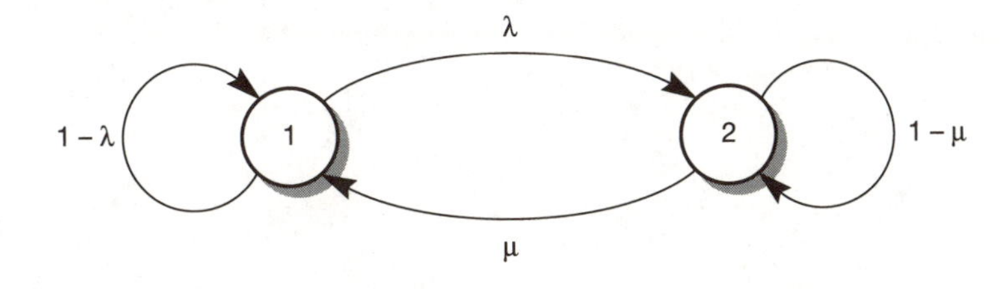

If the failure rate λ of the system is 0.002 failures per hour and the repair rate μ is 0.1 repairs per hour, calculate the availability and unavailability of the system.

7.27 What factors affect the failure rate of complicated electronic components such as microprocessors and memory devices?

7.28 Why can software failures not be predicted in the same way as failures due to the random failure of hardware components?

7.29 What methods are available to estimate the number of errors within a piece of software? What are the limitations of these methods?

7.30 How may the reliability of critical electronic systems be measured?

8 Safety-Critical Hardware

CHAPTER CONTENTS

8.1 Introduction

In Chapter 6 we looked at the effects of hardware architectures on fault tolerance and in Chapter 7 we considered their implications for system reliability. In this chapter we shall look at further topics related to hardware that have particular importance to safety. It is not the function of this chapter to describe the design of real-time computer systems as this topic is covered in great detail in many other texts. Rather, it sets out to discuss particular issues that are of great importance in critical applications. In some cases these issues receive little or no consideration in books on the general aspects of hardware design.

One of the most intractable problems associated with the design of critical computer-based systems relates to faults in the design of the microprocessor itself. Fault-tolerant techniques based on multiple identical channels provide protection against the failure of a processor, and against manufacturing faults, but provide no safeguards against design faults, as these will affect all identical channels. Because of the high dependability of modern microprocessors, and the high cost of diverse design, it is common to largely ignore this problem in systems of relatively low levels of integrity. However, in highly critical applications this issue must be addressed in order to minimize the possibility of system failure.

Closely linked to the issue of microprocessor design faults is the problem of choosing a microprocessor for a given safety-critical application. Such a decision must consider the performance of candidate devices, but must also look at other issues related directly to safety. Considerable work has been directed at the design of processors specifically for highly critical applications. Such devices would seem an obvious choice for safety-related systems, but unfortunately the issue is not straightforward. The restricted use of specialized components reduces the tool support available and provides limited industrial experience on which to assess their long-term dependability.

Many safety-critical systems are required to function in environments that would be described as 'hostile'. These may be characterized by wide fluctuations in temperature, humidity or vibration levels, or the presence of large amounts of electromagnetic interference. The physical aspects of a system's environment will affect its reliability, as described in Chapter 7, and must be taken into account in its design and construction. The electromagnetic environment of the system must also be considered to determine the required electromagnetic compatibility (EMC) performance of the unit. EMC is the ability of a system to operate correctly in the presence of external interference, and also involves its impact on other systems. EMC issues have implications for all phases of the development of a system, and clearly are of great importance to safety. However, at present the conventional training given to computer systems engineers gives little grounding in this area.

8.2 Microprocessor design faults

Despite the obvious relevance of microprocessor design faults to all forms of computer-based system, there is very little information published on this topic. Few textbooks mention the subject at all, and little is available in the research literature. One of the few papers to discuss such matters is the excellent but short paper by Wichmann (1993), which outlines several of the issues involved. Indications that there are problems to be solved in this area come from several sources. These include anecdotal evidence from workers in the field, and from such sources as the 'comp.risks' computer newsgroup (edited by Peter Neumann), which provides a catalogue of problems that have been experienced over the years.

Perhaps the first point to emphasize is that modern microprocessors are extremely dependable. For this reason, in most applications the probability of failure due to inherent defects within the chip is much less than that due to problems arising from other causes, such as software errors. It is therefore not surprising that design faults are largely ignored until a problem comes to light. In highly critical applications faults of all kinds need to be considered and, where possible, removed or tolerated. In such cases all forms of design fault represent particular problems, as they are not masked by the use of replicated identical channels.

We noted in earlier chapters that complexity is a major obstacle in the development of safety-critical systems, as it makes it difficult to both avoid and detect faults. Modern microprocessors are extremely complex, having perhaps several millions of gates. Such complexities are beyond the scope of our most rigorous methods of system development (these will be discussed in Chapter 11), forcing manufacturers to rely heavily on testing as a means of validating their designs. At the end of Chapter 7 we discussed the difficulties of demonstrating the reliability of a system by testing alone. Because of the relatively low cost of microprocessors it is quite feasible to perform prolonged tests using large numbers of identical devices. Tests of this sort can be used to demonstrate a failure rate that is quite acceptable for the range of non-critical applications for which most commercial microprocessors are intended. Unfortunately, extended testing only investigates the susceptibility of the device to random hardware component failures, and to design faults that affect the rate of such failures. This form of testing will not uncover design faults that are outside the scope of the test programs used. Let us assume, for example, that a certain processor performs incorrectly for a given sequence of instructions. If the program used to test this device contains this sequence it will fail the first time the program is executed. If, however, the test program does not contain this sequence it will work correctly indefinitely, and running the program more than once does not increase our confidence in its correctness. In order to locate all such problems we would need to perform a wide range of different tests that cover all possible sequences of instructions. Unfortunately, such **exhaustive testing** is impossible in a device of this level of complexity, because of the vast number of instruction sequences that are possible. We will return to this topic in Chapter 12.

Forms of design fault

Design faults within microprocessors may take a number of forms, but may be divided into two broad categories:

- failure of the circuit to correctly implement its intended function;
- failure of the documentation to correctly describe the circuit's operation.

It might seem at first sight that only the first of these groups represents what one would normally term a *design* fault, as the second is simply a weakness in the documentation. However, from the user's standpoint the **manual** of a microprocessor represents its 'definition', and any discrepancy between this and its actual operation has exactly the same effect as a functional error.

In most modern processors implementation errors may be caused by mistakes within the design of the physical hardware, or within the implementation of its **microcode**. In terms of their external characteristics there is no clear distinction between these two forms of fault, and there seems no reason to differentiate between them here.

It is often said that when designing critical systems one should assume that 'whatever can go wrong, will go wrong'. Applying this philosophy it is clear that the potential for mistakes in the design of a microprocessor is enormous. This being the case, the problems that appear within real devices will be those that are most likely to avoid detection during the testing process and during actual use. Experience shows that early versions of processors have significantly more problems than later releases, as the manufacturer progressively corrects faults located in the field.

In complex processors some instructions see very limited use and faults may go undetected for some time. Because most applications are programmed in high-level languages, much of the development testing is performed using vast test suites of compiled programs. As some compilers do not use particular machine code instructions, such testing is far from exhaustive. Wichmann (1993) reported that a particular processor's operations were completely incorrect for certain instructions that were not generated by the associated C compiler. He also cited a case where a processor's 64-bit integer operations were incorrect. When notified, the manufacturer of the device simply removed them from the documentation!

This last example raises the issue of the completeness of the documentation provided for most microprocessors. It is widely known that many processors have several undocumented instructions. Sometimes these features are added by the manufacturer for testing purposes and are not intended for general use. Alternatively, they may be instructions which, for one reason or another, the manufacturer is not prepared to acknowledge. The writers of safety-critical code would obviously avoid such undocumented features, but may have less control over the action taken by compilers. The presence of undocumented instructions represents a deficiency in the definition of the processor provided by the user manual, and therefore limits the ability of the designer to predict its actions.

Faults that are particularly difficult to detect include those that occur only in exceptional circumstances. An example quoted by Wichmann relates to the indirect jump instruction in the 6502 processor. This operates incorrectly if the indirect address happens to straddle a page boundary. The widely publicized divide problem in the Pentium processor was related to a fault within a rarely executed arm of a case statement in the microcode. Similar problems relate to the interaction between asynchronous events, such as interrupts, and particular instructions. An example of such a problem might be where a particular instruction or sequence of instructions performs incorrectly if it is interrupted. Because of the asynchronous nature of interrupts, and the vast number of possible instruction sequences, complete testing for such problems is impossible. It is significant that in recent years we have seen several instances of major companies recalling chips after their release, because of problems related to exception handling.

Fault rectification

As manufacturers become aware of faults within their microprocessors they adopt a range of responses, depending on the perceived importance of the defect. In some cases they will see the problem as insignificant and will simply ignore it. In other situations they will acknowledge the effect as a 'feature' of the device and will modify the documentation accordingly. In severe cases they may modify the mask of the chip in order to remove the effect, often without notifying users of the change to the design. In extreme circumstances, usually as a result of external publicity, they may acknowledge the problem, modify the device and recall existing circuits.

Each of these actions may have unsatisfactory consequences for the designers of safety-critical systems. Where no action is taken, a known 'bug' is left in place for successive design teams to find (or perhaps not find) by testing. Manufacturers are reluctant to publicize known faults within their devices for commercial reasons.

Changing the documentation of a device is preferable to ignoring the existence of a problem, but is not an ideal solution. Although the manual may be changed, the manufacturer is unable, and would probably be unwilling, to notify past and present users of the device. Manuals and data sheets tend to stay in circulation for many years, and most manufacturers do not highlight changes from earlier versions. Thus an engineer would be unlikely to notice a change from an earlier version unless he had occasion to refer to the relevant item. For these reasons, simply changing the documentation might remove the liability of the manufacturer in the event of an incident but may have relatively little impact on the underlying problem.

Where a major flaw is discovered within the operation of a processor the manufacturer will normally modify the mask in order to remove the effect. Unfortunately, experience shows that such modifications may also introduce spurious effects, including other, perhaps seemingly unrelated, faults. Regardless of the success or otherwise of the corrective action, the result is the generation of a variant of the processor, with different characteristics but an identical part number. This could result in a processor that fails in the field being replaced with a seemingly identical device that has subtly different characteristics. Such a change would nullify all the testing and validation performed during the development process. In order to avoid this situation it is necessary to ensure that any replacement devices are of the same mask type (revision) as that used during development. Unfortunately, manufacturers do not normally mark devices with their revision number unless they are manufactured to meet certain military standards that require it (for example MIL-STD-883D).

Tackling design faults

In earlier chapters we considered the development of safety-critical systems as a process of **fault management** and, as with other issues, the problems of processor design faults may be tackled in a number of ways. In Chapter 6 we looked at the use of **fault tolerance** and **fault detection** as means of combating faults. We noted that design faults could be tackled by the use of **diversity**, as a means of reducing the probability that redundant channels would fail simultaneously. This approach can be used to tackle the problems of microprocessor design faults by using different processors within the various redundant subsystems. This approach is used in some highly critical applications, such as crucial avionics systems, but the high cost of replicating the design makes it inappropriate for all but the most exacting application.

Fault removal, in the form of testing, is also of great importance in combating design faults although, as was noted earlier, the complexity of modern microprocessors places limits on the effectiveness of this approach.

Perhaps the most important weapon in the fight against processor design faults is the use of **fault avoidance** techniques. Microprocessor manufacturers have a vested interest in making good products and a considerable amount of effort is directed at producing designs that are correct. However, the goal of such work is normally to produce devices of sufficient integrity for the wide range of non-critical applications for which they are primarily intended. Unfortunately, this level of integrity is generally far below that which is desirable for safety-critical systems. Over the years a great deal of effort has been directed at the development of highly dependable microprocessors that are intended specifically for critical applications. Notable among such work has been the development of the VIPER microprocessor in the UK (Cullyer, 1988) and the development of the FM8502 processor in the USA (Hunt, 1986). These projects have taken advantage of formal methods in an attempt to produce devices that can be *proved* to be free from design faults. At present, work in this area must be considered to be at the research stage and such devices are not being used commercially. We shall return to look at the development of dependable microprocessors in more detail when we look at formal methods in Chapter 11.

It is clear that there are several impenetrable problems associated with the production of processors that are free from major design errors. However, in many cases chip manufacturers have the ability to improve the situation considerably for the developers of critical systems. Unfortunately, because safety-critical applications represent a very small part of the sales of commercial microprocessors, manufacturers do not see the production of devices suitable for high-integrity systems as a major consideration. Consequently, developers of such systems do not have the economic influence required to encourage manufacturers to take the necessary steps to solve their problems. In fact, many of the difficulties are related to the availability of information rather than any inherent problems with the available devices. Steps that would improve the situation include:

- the publication of lists of known design faults within microprocessors;
- the provision of a subscription facility to allow developers to automatically receive bug reports;
- the labelling of chips with their revision numbers and the issuing of details of each revision, and how it relates to known faults.

It would seem reasonable for developers to pay a fee to cover the costs of these facilities, and it is likely that many companies would wish to take advantage of such information were it available. However, at present manufacturers have little motivation to instigate such mechanisms and feel that the publication of data highlighting faults within their equipment is not in their best interests. The market for safety-critical systems is small, and the responsibilities, and possibly the liabilities, are great. It seems likely that it will require government action to improve the situation, perhaps by insisting that such facilities must be available for all devices used within military applications. This would ensure that all suppliers of military-grade components would provide this information, and would also allow developers of civil systems to benefit.

8.3 Choice of microprocessors

The choice of microprocessor for any real-time application will clearly be determined by a number of factors, including the processing power and architectural features of the available devices. Within this chapter we are not concerned with such issues, but consider only those characteristics that are of particular relevance to safety. In highly critical applications the integrity requirements may play a large part in determining the processor to be used, whereas in less critical situations they represent less of a constraint. In all cases such considerations will be appropriately weighed alongside other factors.

One area to be considered in the choice of a microprocessor relates to the issue of design faults, as discussed above. In the previous section we looked at some of the difficulties associated with the use of commercial microprocessors within safety-critical projects. It is clear that in many cases these problems are not the result of fundamental limitations in the technologies involved, but simply reflect the fact that these devices are not primarily intended for such applications. Indeed, it was noted that it is often a lack of information that causes the greatest difficulties, as manufacturers are reluctant to divulge data on design errors or to publicize characteristics that are known to cause problems.

In order to overcome these problems some system developers have resorted to designing their own microprocessors, specifically for critical applications. An example of such a device is the AAMP2 processor, which is manufactured by Rockwell International (Best *et al.*, 1982). This device is used by the company's subsidiary, Collins Avionics, within a number of aircraft and other systems, there being about 30 such processors in every Boeing 747-400. The AAMP2 is one of a family of processors that have been designed and manufactured by Rockwell for use in critical systems. We shall be returning to look at another member of this family in Chapter 11, when we consider the use of formal methods in the development of microprocessors. The production of a custom microprocessor allows a manufacturer to implement a device of an appropriate level of integrity, and also gives access to all the available data on that device. However, few companies have the resources to undertake such work, and fewer still manufacture critical systems in sufficiently large numbers to justify such a development effort.

Although the development of custom microprocessors allows them to be tailored to the needs of critical projects and provides access to the necessary data, it does not in itself provide a total solution to the problems of processor design faults. One of the disadvantages of the use of such devices it that they are inevitably used in a smaller number of applications than are commercially available components. This reduces the experience gained in operational use and the likelihood of uncovering dangerous faults. This disadvantage is shared by any device that is made specifically for critical projects.

Microprocessors that are dedicated to critical applications also tend to have problems associated with software support. Any device that seeks to overcome the problems of specification weaknesses will tend to have its own unique instruction set. This means that compilers and other software tools must be custom made for the processor, and will therefore be expensive. Such tools are also likely to see relatively little industrial use, hence reducing our confidence in them. In Chapter 9 we will see that it is preferable to use compilers that are validated by an approved centre and which have seen considerable industrial use. It is unlikely that such compilers will be available for custom or specialist microprocessors.

When selecting a commercial processor for a critical application, the presence of design faults is not the only issue of importance to safety. Certain microprocessors have characteristics that make them unsuitable for any safety-related application, although these are not the result of faults as defined earlier. For example, some simple microprocessors have a very unsatisfactory method of dealing with the situation where they fetch and attempt to execute an illegal opcode. Certain microprocessors deal with this situation by fetching the next byte from memory and attempting to execute that byte. This means that the processor simply ignores an obvious system error and attempts to continue executing what may be random locations. The situation is even worse in some other devices, where the action taken in response to illegal opcodes is undefined.

Weaknesses also exist in relation to test instructions, as some microprocessors have undocumented instructions with potentially dangerous effects. An example of such a processor is the Motorola 6801, which has a test instruction that fetches an infinite number of bytes from memory. This produces a regular, easily identified pattern on the address bus, which aids fault identification. However, if the instruction is executed inadvertently, perhaps as a result of a jump garbled by noise, its effects are dramatic. Because interrupts are processed only at the *end* of an instruction, this infinitely long instruction represents a 'black hole' that is impervious to both maskable and non-maskable interrupts. The only method of escape from the effects of this instruction is to reset the processor. Clearly, a watchdog timer connected to the reset line would rescue the system from this situation. However, as this instruction is undocumented a designer could be forgiven for connecting the watchdog timer to the non-maskable interrupt to enable a unique handling routine to be used. A watchdog timer connected in this way would be totally ineffective if a system crash resulted in the execution of this particular instruction. Because the 8-bit opcode has only 256 possible combinations, and because several hundred instructions might be executed before the watchdog takes effect, this is not a possibility that can be ignored.

Processors that possess potentially dangerous characteristics should clearly not be used in critical applications. However, there is very little guidance available to assist in the choice of commercially available processors for such situations. Often problem areas are uncovered as a result of unpleasant experiences with a particular device, but this data is often not disseminated for reasons of commercial confidentiality. Companies that have experience in this field will have amassed their own data to guide them in the selection of processors for new projects. Companies with little background in this field are well advised to be guided by the choices made by others. However, even this information is in short supply.

The development of safety-critical computer systems requires some very specialized tools that are often specific to a particular microprocessor. When selecting a processor it is therefore important to consider the availability of support tools, as this may greatly influence the success of the project. Because the tool manufacturers are themselves subject to market forces, it follows that the availability of tools for a given processor will reflect the use of that processor within critical projects. Tool availability may therefore give some guidance on the perceived suitability of a particular microprocessor for safety-related projects.

Microprocessors being used in industry

At present there is very little reliable data to indicate industrial trends in the selection of microcomputers for use in safety-critical applications. From the above discussion it is clear that a small number of companies are using their own devices, or processors that have been specifically developed for critical applications. However, the majority of companies are using conventional microprocessors from established manufacturers.

Many military applications require processors that can withstand the severity of battlefield conditions. Other systems, including examples from the aerospace and nuclear sectors, are also subjected to hostile environments, such as the presence of high levels of electromagnetic radiation. Such projects require the use of devices that are radiation hardened, and currently the 1750A processor is being widely used in such applications. This processor is defined by MIL-STD-1750A, and its widespread use in critical projects has led researchers to look at its architecture to investigate its suitability for high-integrity systems (Cullyer, 1992). Such work has increased our understanding of the device and has highlighted potential problems that may be avoided by appropriate software design. The experience gained from using these processors in a number of critical projects has resulted in the 1750A, and the more recent 1750B, becoming *de facto* standards in many current military and space applications.

Safety-critical systems that operate in less demanding situations tend to use more general-purpose microprocessors. In applications within the scope of 8-bit processors, the Motorola 68HC11 is quite widely used, particularly in the automotive industry. Projects of this type are often of a relatively low level of criticality, and the processor is usually chosen for reasons associated with functionality and software support, rather than for considerations directly related to safety. However, the 68HC11 provides several features that are useful in the production of dependable systems. These include the provision of protected control registers; a watchdog timer; a clock monitor; an illegal opcode trap; and the inhibiting of test instructions during normal use.

Critical projects requiring more processing power use devices selected from a wide range of processors from several manufacturers. This being said, the Motorola 68020 is proving to be a popular choice within a wide range of industries. This device is far from the 'state of the art', being in the middle of the current 68000 series. Later members of this family achieve an improved performance by providing larger caches and through memory management and pipeline techniques. However, the 68020 has sufficient performance for a large proportion of real-time control applications, and its architecture forms the core of a range of integrated processors that are designed specifically for embedded systems. The extensive use of the 68020 within critical applications has resulted in good tool support and has increased our confidence in its suitability for such tasks. It has also prompted researchers to look in detail at its characteristics to identify potential problem areas (Cullyer and Scales, 1995). The findings of such work, combined with experience gained from its extensive industrial use, enhance our ability to use the device safely for critical projects.

8.4 Electromagnetic compatibility (EMC)

Electromagnetic compatibility is the ability of a system to work correctly in the presence of interference from other electrical equipment, and to not interfere with other equipment or other parts of itself. Examples of the problems associated with EMC are shown in Figure 8.1. Part (a) of this figure shows the situation where interference from an external noise source affects the operation of a critical system. This is most often caused by electromagnetic radiation, or by coupling through common power lines. Part (b) shows the situation where there is undesirable interaction between sections of the system. This can be brought about by a number of mechanisms, including electric, magnetic or electromagnetic coupling, power supply variations and ground currents. Part (c) of the figure represents the case where interference produced by the safety-critical system affects another critical system. As in example (a), this is usually associated with electromagnetic radiation or power line coupling.

Clearly, the safety implications of EMC are enormous. Critical equipment that is susceptible to external interference may be unpredictable and therefore potentially dangerous. Equipment that generates excessive interference could affect the operation of nearby equipment that may also have safety functions. Unfortunately, being inherently random in nature, interference is difficult to characterize and its effects are very difficult to predict.

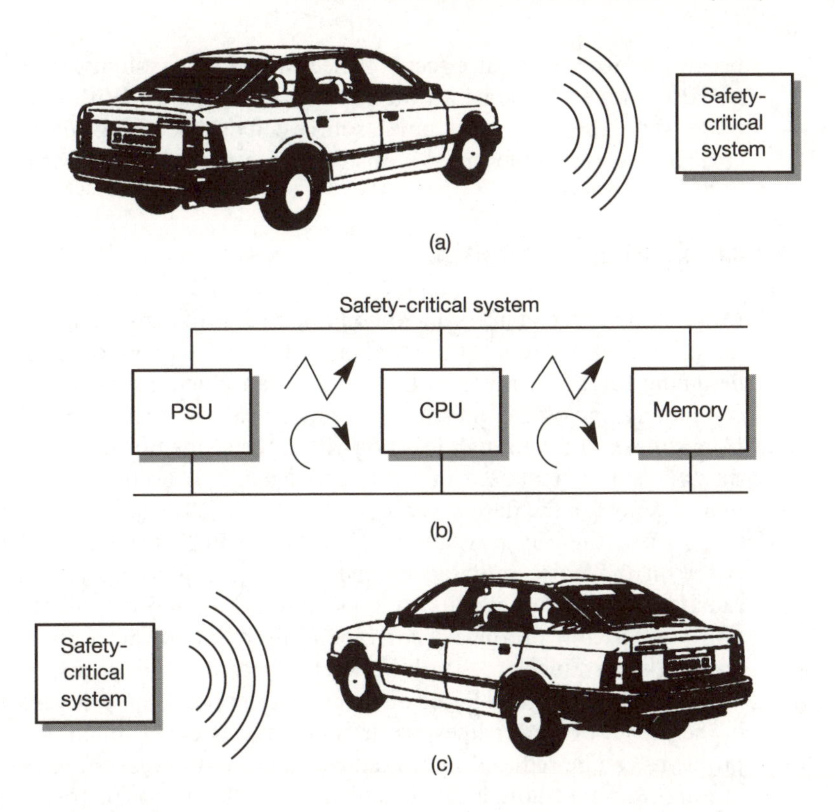

Figure 8.1 Examples of EMC problems: (a) an external source interferes with a safety-critical system; (b) one section of a safety-critical system interferes with another; (c) a safety-critical system interferes with another critical system.

Some safety-related systems are used in environments that are very hostile, not only in terms of their temperature or humidity but also in terms of electromagnetic interference. An example of such a situation is the engine compartment of a car. When observed from a distance of several miles, our major cities resemble large electromagnetic noise sources, and in certain parts of the spectrum the dominant noise source is the ignition systems of cars. This perhaps suggests how 'unpleasant' it must be within the metal screening of the engine compartment itself. Other industries also have their share of unpleasant environments, such as in close proximity to jet engines, nuclear reactors or high-power electric motors. Clearly, equipment that is used in such hostile conditions must be designed to cope with the rigours of its surroundings. However, all critical equipment should be designed to provide adequate resilience in the wide range of conditions in which they may be used.

Certain pieces of equipment are well known as sources of EMC problems. Among these, mobile telephones are perhaps the best known. Many airlines ban their use during flight (or perhaps during take-off and landing) because of fears of their effects on electronic flight systems. Portable computers are also banned by some airlines, for similar reasons. With the proliferation of these and other potential noise sources, it is becoming vital that all safety-critical systems are designed with EMC as a major consideration.

Designing for EMC

Most electronic engineers have come across problems of interference at some point in their careers. Unfortunately, there is a common misconception that designing for EMC involves little more than placing sensitive equipment inside conducting enclosures and using screened cables throughout. The truth is far from simple, and although it is not within the scope of this text to cover in detail the causes and treatment of EMC problems, it is useful to look at some of its implications for the design process.

First, the physical layout of the printed circuit board (PCB) has a large effect on the noise radiated by the circuit. Long tracks act as antennas that radiate and pick up signals. A good design can reduce radiated emissions by up to 20 dB, and produce a corresponding reduction in noise sensitivity. Long tracks also produce cross-talk between adjacent signal paths.

Loops built into PCBs also act as antennas. This causes severe problems in the layout of power lines, as these invariably cover much of the board. Such problems can be reduced by routeing a return path adjacent to the outward path of long tracks, although this has obvious implications for tracking densities.

The use of ground planes within multilayer PCBs greatly reduces emissions from boards, but the track above a ground plane represents an impedance mismatch at any abrupt change in direction. In order to reduce this effect it is normal to break right angles into pairs of 45° turns.

Conductors that leave the enclosure provide an access route for noise, and it is normal to provide filtering on all such lines. Filters must be positioned adjacent to the aperture, so that the cable does not radiate within the enclosure before reaching the filter.

One of the largest sources of electrical noise within the system is often the power supply, particularly if this is of a switching variety. Adequate screening of the PSU must be provided and the outputs should be filtered where they leave this inner enclosure. Most digital logic chips give poor power supply rejection at high frequencies, and so extensive use of decoupling capacitors is essential. It is normal to use a fairly large capacitor of about 100 μF at the power input to each board, and smaller capacitors of 0.01 to 0.1 μF positioned as close as possible to each chip.

Much of the noise associated with digital systems is concerned with the transients caused when devices change state. Because of the high speed of modern circuits the resultant waveforms resemble square waves, and consequently have components at very high frequencies. One approach to reducing radiated emissions is to increase the rise and fall times of waveforms within the circuit, as shown in Figure 8.2.

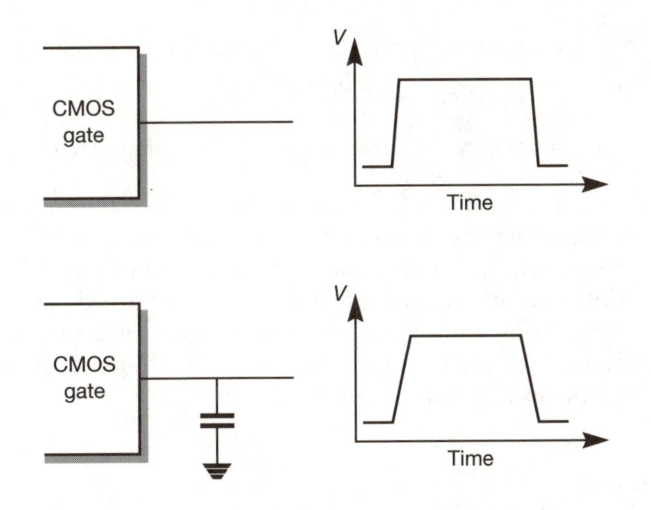

Figure 8.2 Increasing the rise and fall times of digital signals.

Adding capacitance to the output of a CMOS gate increases its switching time and reduces the high-frequency components within its output signal. However, this approach cannot be incorporated into conventional designs without a great deal of thought. Increasing the switching time increases the power consumption of the system, and will affect the timing of related components. However, we are starting to see devices specifically designed to use this technique. Philips is marketing a version of the 8051 8-bit microcontroller family that has been specifically designed to improve its EMC performance. These devices have increased parasitic capacitance in their output buffers to increase rise and fall times, and also employ other techniques, such as disabling external clock signals when they are not being used.

The task of designing a system to optimize its EMC performance is not an easy one. Fortunately, a range of automated tools is becoming available to assist the engineer in assessing the success of his design. Various computer packages are available that aim to predict the EMC performance of systems at the design stage. This allows comparison of alternative designs and should greatly reduce the cost of prototyping and testing.

Achieving good EMC performance

Good EMC performance cannot be achieved simply by good design. The best design could be compromised by, for example:

- incorrect assembly of a component using plastic rather than metal washers,
- painting or plating a bonding surface before assembly,

- incorrect procurement or storage of components,
- incorrect assembly of gaskets,
- changes of components during maintenance.

From the above examples it is clear that all aspects of development, manufacture and maintenance can potentially affect a product's behaviour. For this reason, in common with consideration of quality, and indeed safety itself, EMC can only be achieved as a result of a dedicated commitment by senior management and the enforcement of strict codes of practice for all staff. This is clearly very closely linked with considerations of quality management, which will be discussed in Chapter 13.

Legislation

In Europe, legislation effective from 1 January 1996 imposes very strict rules on the performance of electrical products and equipment in respect of EMC. The directive covers the whole range of electrical and electronic equipment that is capable of producing electromagnetic interference or being affected by it. The 'essential requirements' of the directive are that:

'The apparatus shall be so constructed that:

(a) The electromagnetic disturbance it generates does not exceed a level allowing radio and telecommunications equipment and other apparatus to operate as intended.
(b) The apparatus has an adequate level of intrinsic immunity to electromagnetic disturbance enabling it to operate as intended.'

Although this legislation relates to the EU, it is likely that similar laws will come into effect in North America within the next few years, and in other parts of the world soon after.

Although these new laws impose considerations of EMC on the producers of all electrical equipment, providers of safety-critical systems have for some time had an obligation to consider these effects under more general health and safety legislation (Brown, 1994). It is unlikely that any system that would fall foul of the new EMC rules would be of sufficient integrity to be suitable for highly critical applications. In fact, the new laws perhaps assist the designers of safety-critical systems by attempting to control the rapid rise in interference sources in the environment. However, although the new legislation places some constraints on the design of electrical and electronic equipment, it is unlikely that the problems posed by EMC for safety-related systems will disappear.

REFERENCES

Best D.W., Kress C.E., Mykris N.M., Russell J.D. and Smith W.J. (1982). CMOS/SOS microprocessor. *IEEE Micro*, August, 11–25

Brown S. (1994). Dangers of interference: EMC and safety. *IEE Rev.*, **40**(4), *EMC Supplement*, 11–13

Cullyer W.J. (1988). Implementing safety-critical systems: the VIPER microprocessor. *VLSI Specification, Verification and Synthesis*, Calgary, 12–16 January, pp. 1–25. Brentford: Kluwer Academic Press

Cullyer W.J. (1992). *Application of Formal Methods to Highly Reliable Software for Spacecraft and for the DSN*. NASA Jet Propulsion Laboratory Report, May

Cullyer W.J. and Scales W.J. (1995). Irregularities in the behaviour of the 68020 processor. *High Integrity Systems*, **1**(3), 301–11

Hunt W.A. (1986). *FM8502: A Verified Microprocessor*. Technical Report 47, Institute of Computing Science, University of Texas, Austin

Wichmann B.A. (1993). Microprocessor design faults. *Microprocessors and Microsystems*, **17**(7), 399–401

FURTHER READING

Chatterton P.A. and Houlden M.A. (1992). *EMC Electromagnetic Theory to Practical Design*. Chichester: John Wiley

PROBLEMS

8.1 What are the implications of microprocessor design faults for the effectiveness of fault-tolerant arrangements?

8.2 Why are processor design faults normally ignored in the development of non-critical systems?

8.3 Discuss the problems involved in testing a microprocessor. What forms of design fault are most likely to escape discovery?

8.4 As testing can be used to demonstrate the long-term reliability of microprocessors, why does this not uncover all forms of design fault?

8.5 Describe the two broad categories of microprocessor design fault.

8.6 Why do documentation faults have similar effects to design faults?

8.7 Describe the problems caused by interrupts when attempting to test a processor.

8.8 Describe the various actions taken by chip manufacturers in response to processor design faults. What are the implications of these actions?

8.9 How could chip manufacturers reduce the adverse effects of microprocessor design faults? Why are they often reluctant to take these steps?

8.10 What factors should be considered when selecting a microprocessor for a safety-critical application?

8.11 Discuss the advantages and disadvantages of using processors that are specifically designed for critical applications.

8.12 Some manufacturers design their own microprocessors specifically for critical projects. What are the advantages of this approach and why do more companies not follow this route?

8.13 What part does tool availability play in the selection of a microprocessor?

8.14 Which system requirement restricts the choice of components in many military and space projects? Give an example of a processor that satisfies this requirement.

8.15 Components for critical systems must satisfy functional as well as safety requirements. As new components usually have an improved performance compared to established devices, are these an obvious choice for use in safety-related systems?

8.16 Discuss the influence of printed circuit-board layout on the EMC performance of a system.

8.17 How may the problems associated with 'loops' within PCB tracks be reduced?

8.18 How may problems associated with power supplies and power line noise be reduced?

8.19 Why do PCB ground planes produce EMC problems for circuit layout? How may these be tackled?

8.20 Why is the switching time of devices related to EMC performance? How may this relationship be used to improve a system's performance?

8.21 Why is it not possible to achieve good EMC performance simply through good design?

8.22 Give examples of non-design activities that might affect a system's EMC performance.

8.23 How does recent EMC legislation affect the designer of safety-critical systems?

Safety-Critical Software

CHAPTER CONTENTS

9.1 Introduction

All programmers know that getting even a simple program to work correctly can be difficult. Programs rarely work correctly first time, and usually several iterations of writing, testing and modification are required to produce a 'working' solution. In non-critical applications this cycle of development ends when the program stops failing the series of tasks being used to test it. Thus the 'dependability' of such a program is determined almost exclusively by how it is tested.

Unfortunately, testing software is notoriously difficult. The testing process usually involves executing the software in a series of situations that represent its expected range of operation. The effectiveness of this process is determined by the ability of the test routines to predict the range of inputs that the program will receive. Inevitably, this method will tend not to detect faults that occur in unusual or unexpected situations. For this reason, even 'well-tested' commercial software will fail periodically when a user does something out of the ordinary. To overcome this problem it would be attractive to use some form of **exhaustive testing** that reproduces all the possible conditions the software will encounter in operational use. Unfortunately, in computer-based systems this is almost always impossible, as the number of possible sequences of events is vast. We shall discuss this problem in Chapter 12, when we look at testing in more detail.

Although we cannot test software exhaustively, testing still plays a vital role in the production of all computer-based equipment. When producing a critical system this testing is used not only to locate faults within the software, but also as part of the assessment process to gain certification. Much of this testing involves executing the software or its components within its target environment, or in some cases within a simulation of that environment. This is termed **dynamic testing**, and its function is to demonstrate that the code is functionally correct – that is, that it does what the specification says it should.

Critical code is also subjected to **static testing**, in which the structure and properties of the software are studied. This testing, which is also called **static code analysis**, is 'static' in the sense that the code is not executed but is simply analysed. Various techniques come within this area, and these may be categorized in terms of their *nature* and their *depth* (Wichmann *et al.*, 1995). Here nature relates to the broad objectives of the analysis and could be concerned with specific properties, such as portability. Depth, in this context, is concerned with the analytical depth of the technique. A very shallow technique might look at the layout of a program, whereas a deeper analysis might consider its internal structure. The deepest forms of analysis are concerned with formal proofs of the correctness of the software.

Static code analysis tools may be used to study the form of programs to investigate characteristics such as control flow, data use and information flow. This analysis can detect some classes of errors within a program, such as the use of previously undefined variables or the accessing of inappropriate memory locations. It can also detect some obviously dangerous structures, such as infinite loops – the software equivalent of 'black holes'. Many static code analysis tools are not concerned with the functionality of a program, but simply with its structure. They cannot therefore determine whether a program does what it should, but can detect characteristics that indicate or suggest the presence of some kinds of fault. We shall look at several such tools in Chapter 12, when we look at testing techniques. Deeper forms of static analysis tools look at the defined functions of the software and can be used to verify that the software implements these features correctly. We shall look at such techniques in Chapter 11, when we consider formal proofs of correctness.

Unfortunately, although the various forms of static code analysis offer many advantages to the system developer, they also impose some constraints. First, the use of such techniques places several restrictions on the programming languages that may be used and on the structures used within these languages. Secondly, the analytical methods are not simply a case of running a computer package: they require highly skilled and experienced staff to carry out the work and to analyse the results. In some areas, such as the use of formal proofs of correctness, there is a shortage of engineers with the necessary expertise.

In Chapter 1 we identified four basic techniques for the production of highly dependable systems:

- fault avoidance
- fault removal

- fault detection
- fault tolerance.

None of these techniques, used in isolation, can produce systems of the highest integrity, but used together they can be highly effective. In Chapter 6 we looked at the use of fault tolerance and fault detection in combating both hardware and software faults, and we shall return to consider some of these techniques later in this chapter. Fault removal is concerned with the use of testing to detect and hence eliminate faults, and we shall be looking at this activity in Chapter 12. Fault avoidance involves the use of design techniques that reduce the likelihood of faults occurring. Several techniques come within this category, including the use of 'formal methods', as described in Chapter 11.

When designing safety-critical software it is necessary to incorporate techniques associated with each of these **fault management** strategies. A given piece of software might include one or more of the fault-tolerant techniques discussed in Chapter 6, together with appropriate methods of fault detection. Its designer should also take steps to **design for testability**, implying the use of techniques that will simplify the application of both dynamic and static testing methods. Throughout the development process the designer should also follow a systematic strategy of fault avoidance.

Many engineers see the production of dependable software as the most important element in the creation of safety-critical systems. In fact, many talk of '**software safety**' as if this were a distinct discipline. Others, however, are very concerned at the separation of the hardware and software aspects of system design. Some insist that the very term 'software safety', and the similar phrase '**safe software**', is logically incorrect. They argue that software in isolation can harm no-one, and that it is only when it is linked with hardware that a safety-critical system is formed. They therefore maintain that it is meaningless to talk of software safety or hardware safety, but that we must consider only system safety. Although this argument has a certain logic, it adds very little to our understanding of the problems involved. A similar argument could presumably be used to deny the existence of unsafe drivers, as it is the vehicle that causes harm, not the person driving it. Clearly, software is critical to the safety of many computer-based systems and software faults *can* result in people being killed. It is therefore reasonable to talk of 'safety-critical software', and it seems pedantic to get excited about the use of similar widely accepted expressions.

Within this chapter we look at development methods used in the production of software for safety-critical systems. However, we shall for the moment postpone consideration of the use of formal methods, which are covered in detail in Chapter 11. We shall consider the choice of programming languages for such work, bearing in mind the requirements for both static and dynamic testing, but leave a detailed study of these testing techniques until Chapter 12. We shall then look at the design methods used to implement safety features within the software of a system. This chapter does not attempt to cover all aspects of software engineering, but concentrates only on those aspects of particular relevance to safety.

9.2 Choice of programming languages

In safety-critical systems the choice of programming language is of great significance and several researchers have looked at this very important topic (Carré *et al.*, 1990; Cullyer *et al.*, 1991). In choosing a language one must consider a number of factors, including:

- the functional characteristics of the language,
- the availability and quality of support tools,
- the expertise available within the development team.

We shall look briefly at each of these aspects.

The characteristics of the language

When considering the suitability of a language for a critical application its characteristics must be considered from a number of viewpoints. Carré has identified six factors that influence the suitability of a programming language for use in high-integrity systems (Carré *et al.*, 1990). These are:

- *Logical soundness*: is there a sound, unambiguous definition of the language?
- *Complexity of definition*: are there simple, formal definitions of the various language features? Complexity in these definitions results in complexity within compilers and other support tools, which can lead to errors.
- *Expressive power*: can program features be expressed easily and efficiently?
- *Security*: can violations of the language definitions be detected before execution?
- *Verifiability*: does the language support verification, that is, proving that the code produced is consistent with its specification?
- *Bounded space and time requirements*: can it be shown that time and memory constraints will not be exceeded?

No standard programming language performs well in all of these areas. Indeed, many perform badly in respect of several of these considerations. This is because most widely used languages were not created explicitly for critical applications. Because safety-critical software represents a relatively small proportion of the world's total programming effort, it follows that most programming languages will favour commercial considerations such as productivity and ease of use, rather than their suitability for use in safety-critical systems.

The programming language Ada *was* written specifically for use in critical applications, and has a great many features that assist in the creation of highly dependable software. However, even Ada does not represent an *ideal* language for such applications. This is partially because many of the factors listed above are in conflict. For example, languages that have great expressive power also tend to be complex, increasing the problems of verification and security. Other limitations come from the fallibility of those responsible for the definition of the language. Programming languages are often extremely complex, and are susceptible to design faults like any other man-made entity.

When comparing programming languages for critical applications it is tempting to describe some as being 'safer' than others. Such a comparison is inappropriate, as no language can be inherently safe or unsafe – only the programs that they produce (or perhaps more precisely the systems in which they function) can have such attributes. However, some languages are definitely more suitable than others for the production of critical software because they make it easier to produce dependable code – and to demonstrate its freedom from certain forms of error. Note that the responsibility for producing 'safe' software still rests with the programmer.

Over the years a great deal of experience has been gained concerning the nature of commonly occurring software faults. Clutterbuck (1992) lists four common problems that may occur within programs written in a number of languages:

- *subprogram side-effects*: where variables in the calling environment may be unexpectedly changed;
- *aliasing*: where two or more distinct names refer (possibly inadvertently) to the same storage location. This means that changing one variable will also change a seemingly different variable;
- *failure to initialize*: where a variable is used before it has been assigned a value;
- *expression evaluation errors*: such as those caused by the use of an out-of-range array subscript, an arithmetic divide-by-zero or an arithmetic overflow.

With certain programming languages the compiler will detect some of these faults or potential faults and notify the operator. With others the responsibility rests with the programmer to avoid such pitfalls. In general the amount of checking increases with the level of sophistication of the language. Low-level languages, such as assembler, provide no checking and allow the programmer substantial freedom to innovate. This is one of the reasons why several standards oppose the use of assembler in critical software. An early draft of the UK Defence Standard 00-55 (MoD, 1991) banned the use of assembly code in software for military safety-critical systems, although this is now seen as unrealistic.

Another consideration when selecting a programming language is the **portability** of the code. Here we are primarily concerned not with the ability to transfer the code between target machines, but rather with any differences between the **development environment** and the **target system**. It should be remembered that software development is often performed on a different computer from the one to be used for the final application. Problems may occur, for example, when the software is transferred from a powerful work-station to a more modest single-board computer. In such a situation memory restrictions on the target might result in a stack or heap overflow that would not occur on a more powerful machine. It is also important to have a mechanism for ensuring that programs execute in the same way in both environments.

Another potential problem area relates to the arithmetic associated with the language. It is perhaps surprising that programming languages differ considerably in the definition of their arithmetic operations. This means that even a simple integer calculation may produce a different result when performed in different languages. This is not to imply that there is any disagreement as to the sum of two and two, or to the product of seven and four. The differences occur when exceptional circumstances occur. A typical situation may arise when the result of a multiplication or a division is larger than the maximum integer that may be represented by the word length of the variable used (an overflow). This may occur as a result of a division by zero. In some languages the result will correspond to the largest allowable number, whereas in others a separate code is used to represent an infinite number. The difference between these two representations becomes clear if we now assume that the result is used for further calculations where we subtract a large number from it. In the first case we obtain a real number, whereas in the second we still have infinity (since $\infty - N = \infty$). It is clearly vital that a programmer knows the nature of the arithmetic operations that he is using. Unfortunately, in many languages the models used for arithmetic are poorly defined, and in some cases the language definitions do not specify what the output should be under certain conditions. This may cause compilers from different manufacturers to produce dissimilar results.

With floating point arithmetic the issues are even more complicated. In one way the problem is more severe, as the greatly increased complexity allows greater scope for mistakes. For this reason some standards consider that floating point arithmetic should be avoided altogether in systems of the highest levels of criticality. However, in many programming environments floating point calculations are checked for overflow, whereas integer calculations are not. It has also been observed that with Ada fixed point calculations are more vulnerable to compiler errors than those associated with floating point. For these reasons, the choice between integer and floating point methods is far from straightforward.

Cullyer *et al.* (1991) compared the characteristics of six programming languages to investigate their suitability for use in high-integrity systems. These were assembler; C; CORAL-66; Pascal; Modula-2 and Ada. They looked at 11 factors:

- *Wild jumps*: can it be shown that the program cannot jump to an arbitrary memory location?
- *Overwrites*: are there language features that prevent an arbitrary memory location being overwritten?
- *Semantics*: are the semantics of the language defined sufficiently for the translation process needed for static code analysis?
- *Model of maths*: is there a rigorous model of both integer and floating point arithmetic?
- *Operational arithmetic*: are there procedures for checking that the operational program obeys the model of the arithmetic when running on the target processor?
- *Data typing*: are the means of data typing strong enough to prevent misuse of variables?
- *Exception handling*: if the software detects a malfunction at runtime, do mechanisms exist to facilitate recovery?
- *Safe subsets*: does a subset of the language exist which is defined to have properties that satisfy these requirements more adequately than the full language?
- *Exhaustion of memory*: are there facilities to guard against running out of memory at runtime?
- *Separate compilation*: are facilities available for separate compilation of modules, with type checking across the module boundaries?
- *Well understood*: will the designers and programmers understand the language sufficiently to write safety-critical software?

Conventional assembly code programming provides very few of the desirable features suggested by these questions. Assemblers allow unconstrained use of any operation within the instruction set of the processor, and it is the programmer who is responsible for the arithmetic and the program structure. To reduce the burden placed on the programmer, several **structured assemblers** have been produced. These provide some high-level language constructs but still translate one-for-one into machine code. Because of the advantages of this form of assembler in the production of safety-critical software, the survey considered no other forms of assembler. The results of the analysis are shown in Table 9.1. This lists the six languages covered by the survey and indicates their performance in respect of the various topics outlined above.

It is not within the scope of this text to look in detail at the data provided in Table 9.1. However, it is clear that none of the languages listed provides all the features required of a programming language for the generation of safety-critical software. Of the languages listed, probably Modula-2 provides the most impressive set of characteristics. Unfortunately, as we shall see later, the comparatively limited industrial use of this language reduces its attractiveness in many applications.

Table 9.1 A comparison of computer programming languages (from Cullyer *et al.*, 1991).

	Structured assembler	*C*	*CORAL 66*	*ISO Pascal*	*Modula-2*	*Ada*
Wild jumps	*	?	?	?	?	*
Overwrites	?	X	X	?	?	?
Semantics	?	X	?	?	*	?
Model of maths	?	X	?	*	*	?
Operational arithmetic	?	X	X	?	?	?
Data typing	?	X	?	?	?	*
Exception handling	X	?	X	X	?	*
Safe subsets	?	X	X	X	?	X
Exhaustion of memory	*	?	?	?	?	X
Separate compilation	X	X	?	?	*	*
Well understood	*	?	?	*	*	?

X – the facility is not provided, and this may result in equipment that is unsafe
? – the language provides some protection, but there remains a risk of malfunction
* – sound protection is provided, and good design and verification should minimize the risk of serious incident

The table suggests that by far the least suitable language for dependable computing is C. This is unfortunate, as it is probably the most widely used systems programming language in the world. The problems associated with C are numerous. These include the widespread and unrestricted use of pointers, which makes it impossible to demonstrate that access and assignment operations are safe, and the lack of a sound definition of the semantics. This latter problem results in great variations in the operation of the language between versions. Several aspects of the language are simply not defined, such as the action to be taken in the event of an integer overflow. C++ provides some improvements in terms of the structure of the language, but does not remove many of the inherent problems.

Several attempts have been made to develop new languages for use in critical applications. Notable examples of this approach are NewSpeak (Currie, 1989) and Euclid (Lampson *et al.*, 1977). Unfortunately, there are several disadvantages with this strategy. Perhaps the major problem is that the field of critical computing is relatively small, and thus the number of potential users of the language is limited. This means that the enormous development costs associated with the necessary compilers and support tools are spread over a restricted user base, making the products expensive. Staff training is also an issue, as expertise cannot be transferred from less critical applications. Another important concern is that the limited use of the software tools will reduce the amount of effort that can be justified in their development, and reduce the number of 'bugs' found by users in the field. These factors combine to reduce the overall dependability of the support tools.

An alternative approach to the problem of language selection attempts to remove many of the deficiencies associated with existing, widely used languages.

Many of these problems stem from a small number of isolated features, and it is often possible to identify a **subset** of the language that reduces these weaknesses. Unfortunately, as indicated in Table 9.1, no internationally standardized subsets currently exist for most of the programming languages discussed above. However, widely used subsets do exist for several of these languages, and some of them are listed in Table 9.2. SPADE-Pascal is a widely used subset of ISO Pascal produced by Program Validation Limited (now Praxis) (Carré and Debney, 1985). In the last few years a great deal of effort has been directed at the development of subsets of Ada for use in critical applications. Of note is SPARK (Carré *et al.*, 1990), which is one of the few languages to possess complete formal semantics. Unfortunately there are no suitable subsets of C or C++, as it is impossible to effectively check pointers within these languages.

The subsets are formed from the full versions of the languages by removing any features or constructs that prevent verification. They also make use of **annotation** to aid in the verification process. Annotation involves adding formal comments to a program to define its function and operation. These comments would include information on the inputs, outputs and function of a particular module, as defined in its specification. These annotations may then be used as an input to the verification tools associated with the language.

It can be seen from Table 9.2 that in each case the subset provides a considerable improvement when compared to the performance of its parent language. For this reason these subsets, which are often referred to as **safe subsets**, are preferred for all safety-critical applications.

Table 9.2 A comparison of computer programming languages (from Cullyer *et al.*, 1991).

	CORAL subset	*SPADE-Pascal*	*Modula-2 subset*	*Ada subset*
Wild jumps	*	*	*	*
Overwrites	*	*	*	*
Semantics	*	*	*	?
Model of maths	?	*	*	*
Operational arithmetic	?	*	?	*
Data typing	?	*	*	*
Exception handling	X	X	?	*
Safe subsets	?	*	*	?
Exhaustion of memory	*	*	?	?
Separate compilation	?	?	*	*
Well understood	*	*	*	*

X – the facility is not provided, and this may result in equipment that is unsafe
? – the language provides some protection, but there remains a risk of malfunction
* – sound protection is provided, and good design and verification should minimize the risk of serious incident

The support tools

In addition to the functional characteristics of a language, one must also consider the development tools available to support its use. In recent years a number of dedicated tools have been produced for use with the subset languages used in safety-critical systems. These include good support for SPADE-Pascal and the SPARK subset of Ada.

One of the most important issues related to language choice is the quality of the available compilers. The sophistication of modern programming languages results in compilers of great complexity. Consequently, verification of a compiler for languages such as Ada or Pascal is beyond the current state of the art, and is likely to remain so. For certain languages, centres have been established to investigate the performance of commercially available compilers. The results of tool evaluations are generally published, and compilers that satisfy a certain set of tests are said to be **validated** by that institution. It is important to remember that the process of validation is performed to determine conformity to the (international) language standard, rather than to establish quality or performance. Such validation does not guarantee the correctness of the code generated by the compiler under all circumstances. For safety-critical applications validation should be seen as a necessary, but not always sufficient, requirement of the compiler. Validated compilers are available for a range of languages, including Ada and Pascal.

Wherever possible widely used compilers and development tools should be used, as the widespread use of a tool increases the chances of errors being noticed and corrected. We are therefore likely to have less confidence in a new product than in a mature one. This consideration also implies that it is better to adopt a widely used language than a novel one, since the use of the various tools is likely to be greater in the former. This factor has implications for the use of languages such as Modula-2. From Table 9.2 it is clear that a suitable subset of Modula-2 has many of the attractive attributes associated with safety-critical software. However, the comparatively little use of this language within this field is a distinct disadvantage. Some safety-critical applications are using Modula-2 (for example, the SACEM project within the commuter train network in Paris), and perhaps, in time, sufficient experience will be gained to allow it to become a preferred language in this area.

Those readers familiar with Ada may be aware than one of the requirements 'written in stone' for this language is that there should be no compilers that support only a subset of the language. This requirement stems from a desire to keep the language pure, preventing manufacturers from implementing some, but not all, of the features. The requirement ensures that only compilers supporting the complete language can be called Ada compilers. This doctrine would appear to contradict the discussion earlier in this section relating to the use of 'safe subsets' of the language. The explanation of this apparent inconsistency is that the use of subsets relates to the aspects of the language that are actually used, not to the scope of the compiler. When developing a critical system an engineer will use a subset of the language to produce the software, but will then compile the programs using a validated compiler that supports the complete language. The use of a restricted compiler would not only go against the doctrine of Ada, but would also remove the advantages associated with widely used commercial software tools. Such considerations are also of relevance when using other programming languages. For example, when using a subset of Pascal it would be normal to use a validated ISO Pascal compiler.

Despite the considerable effort that goes into the development and testing of a validated compiler, like any other complex piece of software it will contain faults. The effects of a compiler fault are to introduce errors into the resulting object code. In many ways the effects of these object code errors are identical to those caused by mistakes in the source code. Fortunately, the number of faults in validated compilers is very small. Work on the Sizewell nuclear reactor primary protection system (PPS) suggests that typical compiler faults produce an effect equivalent to the presence of an undetected fault in every 50 000 lines of code (Pavey and Winsborrow, 1993). In all but the most critical of projects such error rates would pale into insignificance compared to other sources of software error. However, in highly critical systems their effects cannot be ignored, particularly as they occur at a stage after any static code analysis or other testing has been applied to the source code. In some cases analysis of the object code, rather than the source code, may be used to trap these faults.

A compiler feature that causes some concern when producing critical systems is **optimization**. Some compilers follow the code generation stage with a process that 'optimizes' the object code by removing what it considers to be redundant or inefficient operations. In some cases this simplification can greatly assist the task of static code analysis by removing unnecessary components within the program. Unfortunately, the process involved is both complex and varied, and can sometimes have unforeseen side-effects. For this reason many consider that it is safer to disable the optimization function altogether. The issue of the advisability of using optimization is open to some debate, and engineers and compiler manufacturers differ in their recommendations. However, it should be remembered that changing compiler options may have dramatic effects on the code produced and its functioning. For this reason, options should not be selected during testing and then disabled to produce operational code.

Available expertise

A major consideration in the selection of a programming language for any application is likely to be the expertise available within the design team. Programmers working in a familiar language are likely to be more productive and to make fewer mistakes. However, this consideration cannot be allowed to predominate over other factors. Engineers working outside the safety-critical area are often most familiar with C, but this is not a sufficient reason for selecting this language for a safety-critical application.

Programming languages being used in industry

An informal survey by Rowe (1994) provides some indication of the languages being used in safety-critical projects in various industries. The survey looked at several industrial sectors, including aerospace, air traffic control, land vehicles, ships, railways and nuclear reactors. No distinction is made between projects of different levels of integrity, and the use of subsets of languages is not identified. However, the results suggest that Ada is becoming established as the most popular language for such applications, with assembler the next most common.

Activities in the aerospace sector are well represented in the survey, which gives an interesting insight into working practices. Boeing, for example, appear to be working primarily in Ada, with additional code in assembler. However, other languages such as FORTRAN, Jovial, C and C++ are also used. This diversity of languages no doubt reflects the wide range of applications within the company. For example, the seat-back entertainment system of the 777 aircraft uses C++. What is perhaps more surprising is the range of languages used. The survey suggests that approximately 140 languages were used in the development of the 757/767, and about 75 were used in the 747-400.

The European Space Agency, a consortium of companies from various European countries, mandates the use of Ada in all mission-critical systems. The NASA Space Station also uses Ada, possibly with some assembler. The space shuttle uses Hal/s and Ada in addition to other languages, but at least one shuttle experiment uses C++. The Northrup B2 bomber control system also uses C++, and some air traffic control systems in the US, Canada and France use Ada.

Automotive systems appear to make extensive use of assembler, with C, C++ and Modula-2 also being used. Lucas use their own control language, Lucol, in addition to C++ and assembler.

The survey suggests that the railway sector has adopted Ada as a *de facto* standard in many situations. It is used for switching systems by European Rail, and by Eurotunnel for parts of the Channel Tunnel system. Ada was also adopted for work on the extension to the London Underground.

Software for the Denver Airport baggage handling system was written in C++, but there is no suggestion that the initial problems experienced by this system were directly related to the choice of programming language.

Choice of language for a given application

In many safety-critical applications the programming language to be used is specified by the customer or by codes of practice within the relevant industry. For example, much of the work commissioned by the American Department of Defense must be performed in Ada. In applications where this is not the case the choice of language will be affected by the various factors discussed earlier, and also by commercial considerations.

In projects that are assigned a high level of integrity, the programming language must satisfy the requirements outlined above. For this reason the most suitable languages are probably a safe subset of Ada or a safe subset of Pascal. A safe subset of Modula-2 might also be considered, but the limited use of this language within safety-critical applications makes it less attractive than suitable subsets of Ada or Pascal.

In projects that are assigned a low level of integrity, rigorous verification and the use of static code analysis is not justifiable on economic grounds. Under these circumstances restrictions placed on the choice of language may be eased, and it might be appropriate to consider Ada, ISO Pascal, Modula-2 or structured assembly languages.

Within the safety-critical community it is generally agreed that in applications where safety is concerned unstructured assembly language and C or C++ should *not* be used.

In recent years more and more companies are turning to Ada for all their critical applications. This includes military projects such as the European Fighter Aircraft, and civil applications such as the signalling in the Channel Tunnel. This has led to a great deal of work being directed at identifying the remaining weaknesses of the language (Wichmann, 1989) and the provision of much useful guidance on the use of Ada in safety-critical systems (a good example being the book by Pyle given in the Further Reading list at the end of this chapter). The latest version of the language, Ada 9X (Barnes, 1993; Wichmann, 1994), provides improved visibility of the object code and simplifies the task of validation. Because of the ongoing developments of this already very good language, companies not yet committed to a programming language would be well advised to strongly consider adopting Ada for all projects requiring a high integrity, with a suitable subset being used for the most critical applications.

9.3 Software design

Software design is a highly creative and iterative process that progressively refines the information given within the specification of a system, to produce a detailed implementation. The task may be divided into two main activities, namely the top-level design and the detailed software design.

Top-level or architectural design

The architectural design phase of a project forms the first stage in the process of transforming the abstract specification into a concrete implementation. It includes the tasks of selecting the methods to be used to achieve the various functional requirements of the system, and of deciding upon the techniques appropriate to implement the various safety features. Fault detection and fault-tolerant features will need to be incorporated into the architecture of the system at this stage, as discussed in Chapter 6. The designer must also consider the need for assessment, both during development and for the purposes of certification.

An early task within the top-level design phase is to partition the system into those components to be implemented in hardware and those that will be achieved using software. When this has been done the architectural design of the software may begin. This involves the production of a complete specification of the software architecture, its components and its data structures, together with specifications for the interfaces between the various components. As the system is progressively partitioned the number of interfaces grows, and the nature of these interfaces plays a increasing part in determining the system's behaviour. This process is illustrated in Figure 9.1.

The specification of each module within the system must include details of its interaction with other modules. This interaction may be formalized in an interface design specification (IDS), which sets out the data or messages sent between units, and any protocols used. Because the system interacts with the

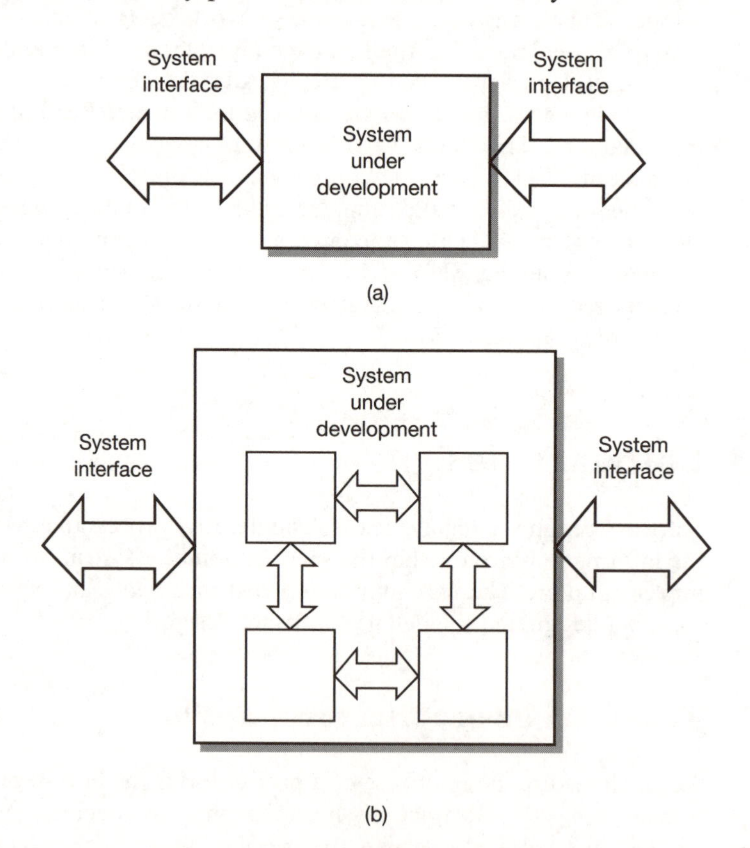

Figure 9.1 System partitioning: (a) the complete system; (b) partitioned system showing module interaction.

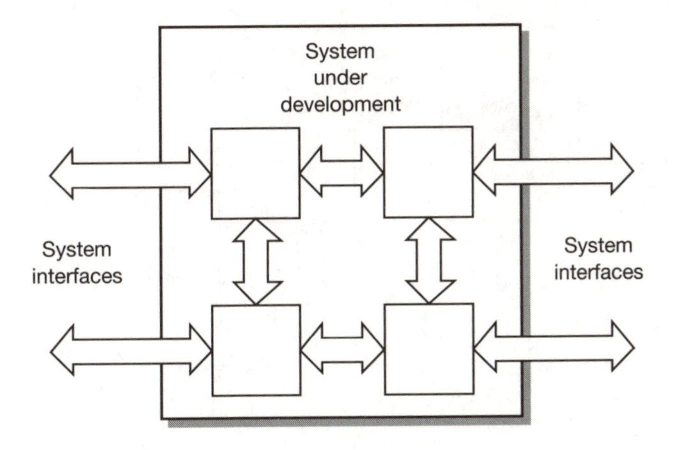

Figure 9.2 A system interacting with its environment.

'outside world', it follows that some of the modules within the system will have interfaces not only with other modules, but also with external systems. This is shown in Figure 9.2.

Sometimes the interaction with external systems may be relatively simple. For example, a module might turn *ON* or turn *OFF* an external actuator, or sense an external switch. In other cases the interaction may be more complex, either because of the nature of the information being passed, or because of inherent complexity in the external system. Often the most complex interfaces involve human operators. This is because such human–computer interfaces (HCIs) are often required to pass a great deal of information to the operator, and also because the operator, being a highly complex system, is inherently unpredictable. The design of the HCI will determine the ease of use of the system, and can also greatly affect its safety (as discussed in Chapter 5).

Partitioning is an iterative process, with larger modules being progressively subdivided, as shown in Figure 9.3. For each module a specification is produced that sets out its function, software architecture and data structures. An interface design specification is also produced for each module to define its interaction with other modules and the outside world. A test plan should be produced for each module at this time. Planning the testing process at an early stage forces the designer to think about how the module can be verified and encourages 'design for testability'. It also prevents the designer from defining a system that cannot be tested. Because interaction with the user is likely to be a key factor in the success of a system, it may be appropriate to produce drafts of user manuals during this phase of the development. These can be passed back to the customer, to obtain early feedback on the likely acceptability of the design, and may also highlight any HCI problems.

The architectural design phase of a project refines and partitions the specification as a step towards its implementation. In so doing it is likely to uncover inconsistencies or inadequacies within the specification that must be

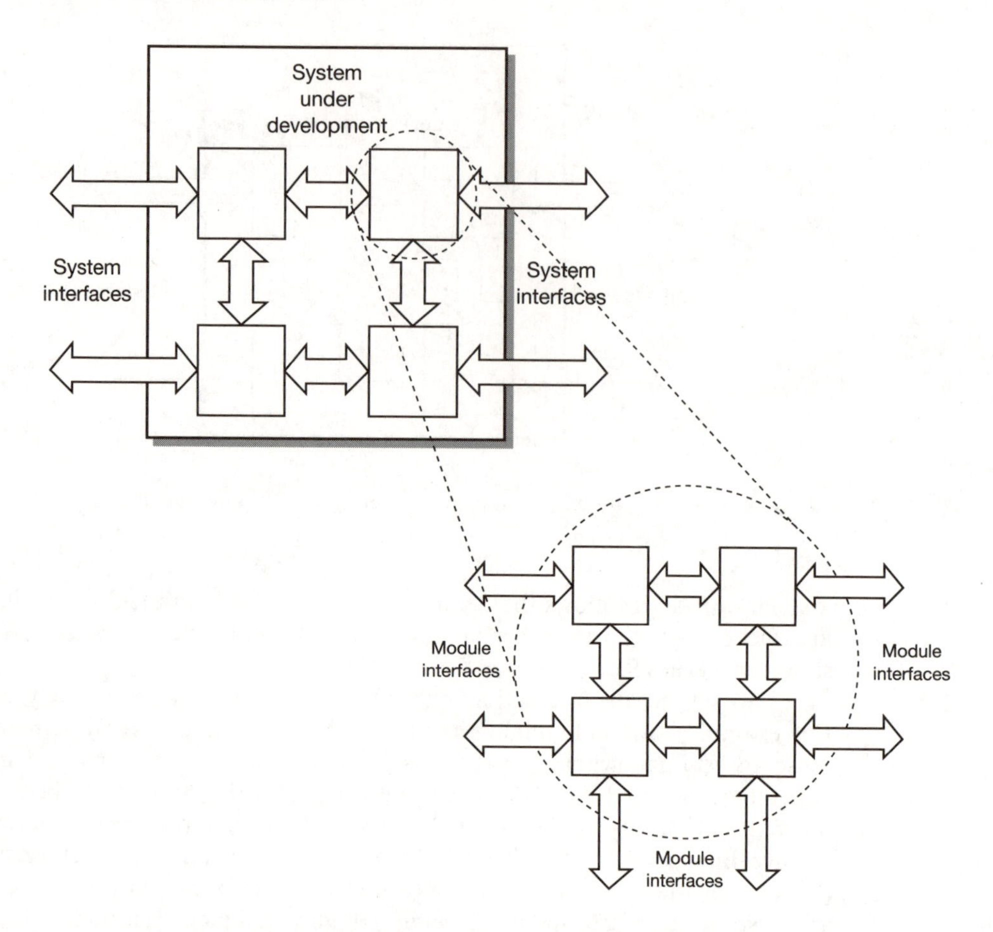

Figure 9.3 The process of repeated partitioning.

rectified. This leads to a gradual evolution of the specification through a series of iterations that continue throughout the development process. However, this does not mean that the designer may make changes to the specification at will, simply to ease its implementation. Any changes must be agreed by all parties concerned, including the project management team and the customer. Changes to the specification must be controlled under some form of change control system, which forms part of the quality assurance scheme for the project. This will document the nature of the modifications, their justification and any consequences. Quality assurance will be discussed in some detail in Chapter 13.

Because the architectural design represents the first step towards implementation of the system, mistakes made at this stage will affect its overall correctness and safety. In all safety-critical projects the architectural design process must be verified to ensure that the resulting top-level design is a true representation of the specification. We shall look in more detail at the process of verification in Chapter 12.

Software partitioning

Although partitioning of software is considered to be good practice for any software project, in critical software it is fundamental to the provision of safety.

One of the important characteristics of partitioning is that it aids **comprehension** of the software. Large monolithic programs are inherently difficult to understand, and are therefore more likely to conceal errors. They also make checking and verification more difficult for both manual and automated methods. Well-partitioned programs are broken down into a number of modules that are each easy to read and assimilate. This aids understanding of both the detail and the overall design.

A second aspect of partitioning is that it provides a level of **isolation** between software functions. This can be used to contain faults and is fundamental to the provision of software fault tolerance. The ability to isolate modules also simplifies the process of verification, as it allows the sections of code to be dealt with individually. Isolation also permits the various modules to be assigned different levels of integrity dependent on their criticality, as discussed in Chapter 4. This integrity level will determine the development and verification methods used for that module. Where the operation of one module is critical to the correct operation of another, the criticality of each routine will be at least as great as any routine that depends on it.

In general the partitioning of software will produce a layered structure, as shown in Figure 9.4. The upper layers of this arrangement represent the modules of the software responsible for the overall control and command functions. These routines will call lower-level routines to implement the various features of the software. At the lowest level are the input/output routines and the device drivers.

Clearly, the correct operation of a given module is dependent not only on its own soundness, but also on the proper functioning of the modules with which it interacts. Conceptually this suggests that the upper-level modules of Figure 9.4 will be dependent for their correct operation on those below them. With this in mind, it is interesting to view this figure in relation to the various methods of **fault management** discussed earlier. Fault avoidance and fault

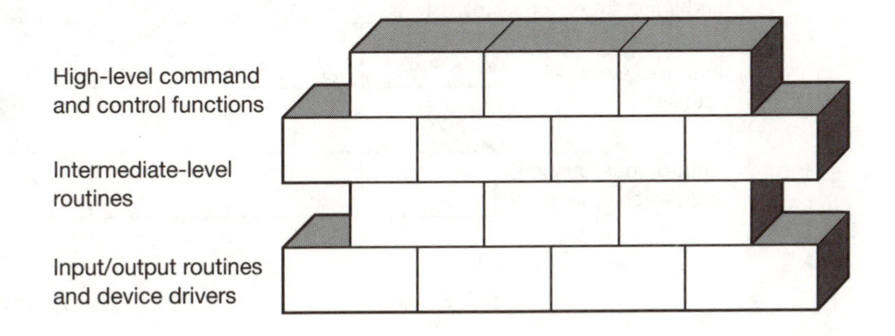

Figure 9.4 The layered structure of software.

removal aim to improve the dependability of the individual modules and hence the overall system. If the modules can be seen as isolated units, then effort can be concentrated on the more critical areas, thereby increasing the efficiency of the development process. Fault detection and fault-tolerance techniques can be used to contain faults, preventing them from propagating throughout the system and reducing their effects. For example, if a low-level routine detects a fault in its own operation, or with an associated I/O device, it could pass this information to any calling module, allowing it to take this fault into account. This calling module might choose to take data from an alternative I/O device, thereby containing the fault and providing fault tolerance.

Because a fault within one module may affect the operation of another, the way in which the system is partitioned is of great importance to the safety of the system. To illustrate this point, consider the system of Figure 9.5. In Chapter 2 we discussed the use of **interlocks**, which use one or more sensors to ensure that the situation is safe before an actuator is operated. In this figure a switch, perhaps connected to some form of safety gate, must be closed before the actuator is permitted to operate. The arrows within the diagram represent the flow of data within the software, and it can be seen that information from the input routine for the switch communicates with a high-level module through a number of intermediate-level routines. When the high-level module wishes to operate the actuator it will use this information to determine whether it is safe to do so. If it is, it will send a command to the output routine, again through a number of intermediate modules.

A consequence of the structure of the system represented by Figure 9.5 is that failure of any of the modules concerned could result in dangerous operation of the actuator. A fault in the input module, or any of the modules carrying input data to the high-level module, could result in the system believing that the switch was closed when it was not. This would allow the high-level module to operate the actuator, thinking that it was safe to do so. Alternatively, failure of the high-level module itself, the output module, or any

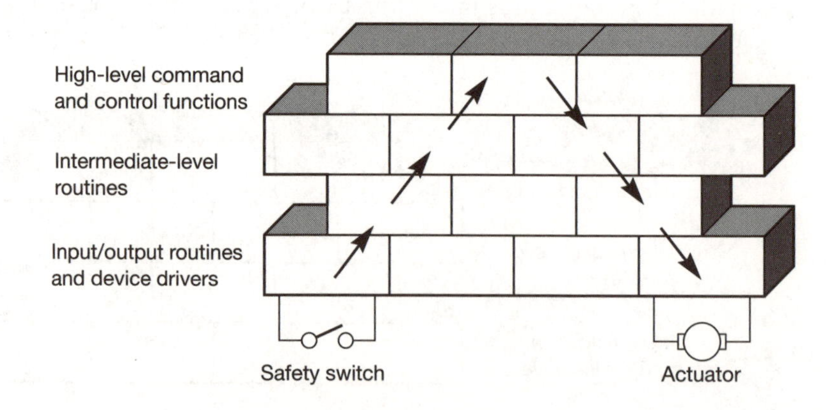

Figure 9.5 A poorly structured system.

of the associated intermediate modules, could cause the system to operate the actuator despite the absence of an appropriate signal from the switch. This again could lead to a dangerous situation. As each of the modules associated with this mechanism could potentially cause an unsafe situation, all are safety critical. If failure of this arrangement could result in a serious accident, then each of the associated modules would need to be allocated a high level of integrity, resulting in a very expensive system. Indeed, the situation is more complicated than this simplified picture would suggest, as the complexity of the modules tends to increase as we move upwards. The low-level input/output routines are normally relatively simple and can be written and verified easily. In contrast, the high-level routines are often complex in nature, as they implement the command and control structures of the system. In some cases a rigorous verification of these top-level routines would be extremely difficult – or perhaps impossible.

An alternative method of partitioning our system is shown in Figure 9.6. In this arrangement the input and output functions associated with the interlock are performed by a single module which receives instructions from higher-level routines. The low-level module now has complete responsibility for implementing the interlock function, and is the only module that needs to be of a high integrity. Instructions from the high-level routines are now interpreted as 'switch on the actuator *if* it is safe to do so', and the low-level routine will not operate the device unless the switch is closed.

There are several advantages to this arrangement. First, failure of the high-level routine or the intermediate modules will not result in incorrect operation of the actuator, and thus these routines are no longer safety critical (at least in respect of this actuator). Secondly, the one remaining critical module is a low-level routine and is therefore likely to be of low complexity, thereby reducing the problems of verification. A further advantage is that the verified

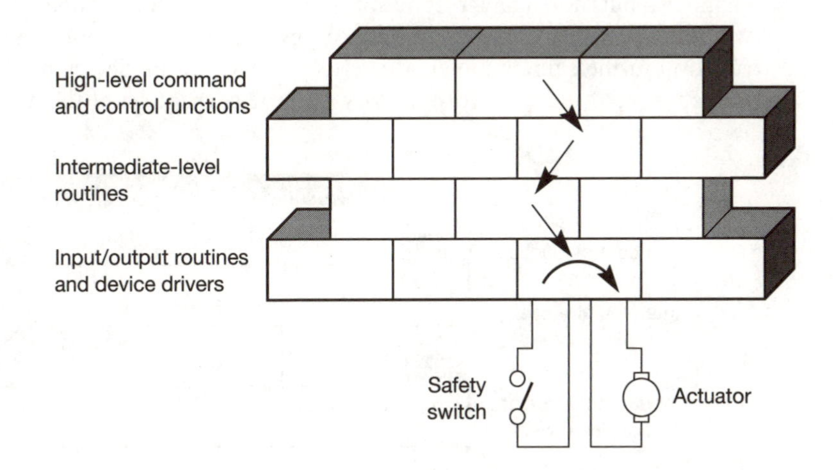

Figure 9.6 An improved method of software partitioning.

module and its associated hardware can be viewed as a *trusted* subsystem, reducing the criticality of higher-level modules and simplifying the design. In practice, in safety-critical applications the modules responsible for initiating and transmitting potentially dangerous commands would also be allocated an appropriate level of criticality to provide a duplicate safety mechanism in case of failure of the interlock arrangement.

The above example illustrates two aspects of the design of safety-critical software:

(1) The safety-critical routines should be kept as small and as simple as possible.

(2) Adequate isolation should be achieved between the software modules.

The second of these requirements is necessary because any verification of the individual routine is pointless if an external module can interfere with its operation.

Isolation is also of great importance when considering the provision of fault tolerance within software. Figure 9.7 represents a possible implementation of a fault-tolerant arrangement based on the use of N-version programming, as discussed in Chapter 6. Here two routines, referred to as 'Version A' and 'Version B', represent diverse implementations of a common function. A third module, labelled 'Fault detector', supplies common data to these two routines and compares their results to enable fault detection. In the event of a disparity being produced this module would perform further analysis in an attempt to determine which module was incorrect, in order to 'tolerate' the fault.

From our study of fault tolerance in Chapter 6 it is clear that redundancy provides protection against faults that are induced independently in the various channels, but not against common-mode faults. Thus if one of the modules within the system were to influence the operation of both versions of the function in the same manner, this effect would not be detected. This undesired influence might take the form of a systematic corruption of the data used by the

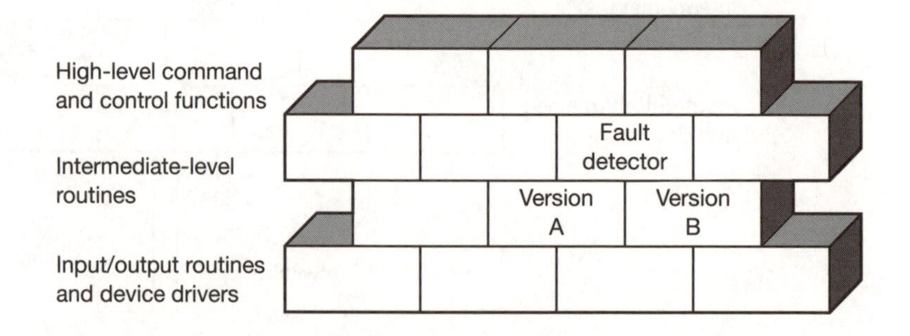

Figure 9.7 The use of partitioning in software fault tolerance.

routines, or some other common effect. The goal of isolation is to guarantee that no module can affect the operation of any other module, thereby removing this and other problems.

It can be seen that the property of adequate isolation between modules represents a major advantage in the design of safety-critical systems. Indeed, if perfect isolation could be achieved the task of developing software would be greatly simplified, as only critical modules would need to be verified. Faults within non-critical modules would be relatively unimportant, as they could not affect the parts of the system responsible for safety. Unfortunately, despite its obvious advantages, absolute isolation between software routines is impossible. To see why this is true, we need to consider the ways in which one piece of software might upset the operation of another.

Software isolation

Some programming environments provide no meaningful isolation between software modules. Programs written in assembly code, for example, running on a 'bare' processor (that is, without any form of memory management) cannot be protected from the effects of other rogue routines. One module might function impeccably, but if a second routine modifies memory locations that it is using, the operation of the module will be compromised.

In order to ensure that one routine will not affect the operation of another, several factors need to be considered. One consideration, as we have seen, is that we need to ensure that the routines do not overwrite inappropriate memory locations. You may remember that this was one of the factors considered in Section 9.2, when we looked at the choice of programming languages. When using conventional assembly code (that is, using non-structured assemblers) and languages such as C, it is not possible to provide such protection and it is thus impossible to provide adequate isolation.

Overwriting data is not the only way in which one routine may affect another. If a safety-critical routine must function within a given time to be effective, it can be upset by a routine which 'hogs' the processor, delaying its operation. In an extreme case a routine might enter an infinite loop and 'hang' the processor until a watchdog timer is activated. Again, in Section 9.2 we identified 'bounded space and time requirements' as an issue in language selection.

In non-critical applications isolation between programs is often managed by an operating system that is responsible for allocating time to a series of concurrent tasks, preventing any single task from taking too much of the processor's time. Operating systems often make use of memory management hardware to limit a program's access to memory, and should thus prevent overwriting of data. Unfortunately, in highly critical real-time applications the use of an operating system is not acceptable. Even simple operating systems are far too complex to be verified using currently available techniques, and their highly asynchronous nature makes them difficult to analyse. There is little point in having carefully verified application software if the operating system managing the system may be undependable.

In smaller systems some of the functions of an operating system are often provided by a runtime kernel that includes a task scheduler. The presence of such a kernel simplifies the production of software modules, as these can now be treated as isolated tasks. As with the use of operating systems, the integrity of the arrangement is greatly affected by the dependability of the kernel itself. Fortunately, runtime kernels can be of relatively low complexity, making it feasible to perform full verification. At present a great deal of effort is being directed at the production of verified kernels for such languages as Ada. Recently, the Alsys CSMART Ada kernel has been certified for flight-critical systems such as those within the Boeing 777 aircraft. However, at present the use of kernels is normally reserved for systems of a lower level of criticality. For highly critical systems verified code is usually run on a 'bare' processor, allowing the development engineer total control and visibility of the operating code.

When software is written to run without the use of a task scheduler isolation between the various modules must be provided by the programmer, using the facilities of the programming language. We have seen that languages such as unstructured assembly code and C do not facilitate the construction of well-isolated modules, but this is not true of all languages. For example, the 'safe subsets' discussed in Section 9.2 can be used, together with appropriate static code analysis techniques, to provide modules with adequate levels of isolation for most applications.

Perhaps the most effective language for the development of well-isolated modules is Ada. Here software is constructed as a number of **Ada packages**, with the compiler maintaining appropriate independence between these components. Ada also provides a mechanism for dealing with separate **tasks** by directly implementing a task scheduler within the operational code. For low and medium levels of integrity this approach offers many advantages, but despite the high dependability of validated Ada compilers, the use of Ada tasks is not recommended for systems of the highest levels of criticality. In such cases it is preferable to implement a simple cyclic execution scheme, written directly in the Ada language, rather than to use the much more complex task scheduler provided by the compiler. Ada is a comparatively new language and is still the subject of considerable development work (Wichmann, 1994). In time it is possible that enhancements to Ada, combined with confidence gained from extensive use, will make the use of Ada tasks preferable to the use of simpler schedulers that do not have a proven track record.

Despite the great strengths of languages such as Ada, it is never possible to guarantee *complete* isolation between software modules. One reason for this is that such a situation would require a perfect compiler and, as we have noted earlier in this chapter, real compilers do occasionally make mistakes. However, even if such a perfect compiler were available this would not solve the problem completely. In order to see why this is true it is useful to note that the model we have been using to represent the modular structure of our system is incomplete.

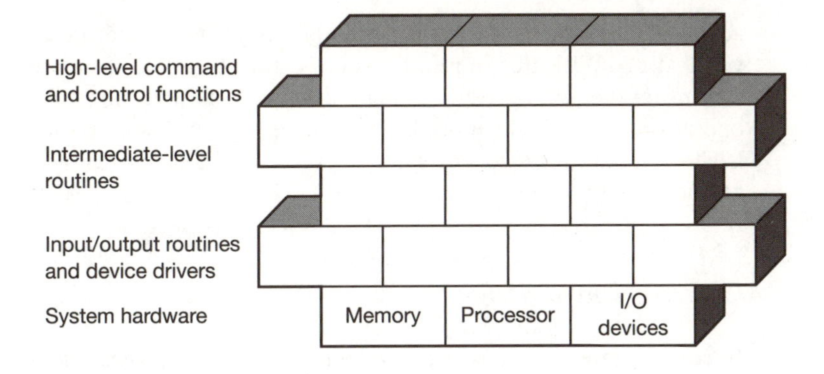

Figure 9.8 The relationship between system software and hardware.

For a better understanding of the problem we should extend our model, as shown in Figure 9.8. This shows not only the software of the system, but also the hardware necessary for its execution. In this simplified diagram the term 'I/O devices' is taken to represent not only the interfacing components, but also the sensors and actuators of the system.

Because the execution of the software is dependent on the actions of the system hardware, the behaviour of this hardware will clearly influence its operation. Thus even perfect code could be upset by limitations or faults within the various physical components.

Limitations of the hardware might include restrictions to the amount of memory space or processing time available. If one routine uses too much RAM or places too much data on the stack, other routines might be adversely affected. Many programming languages allow the system designer to place constraints on memory usage, or at least to establish the maximum memory or stack space required for a given routine. Similarly, the designer must ensure that no routine takes so long to execute that others are ignored.

Faults within the hardware are usually more difficult to predict and to cope with. The range of problems that could arise is almost limitless, but a few examples will illustrate some of them. Perhaps the most obvious fault, and also the easiest to neglect, is that the processor could simply stop. This would prevent all the routines from executing and any redundancy gained by multiple versions or other techniques would be worthless. At a more subtle level, faults within the processor or the memory devices could affect the bus system, causing data or addresses to be corrupted. This could lead to instructions or data being read from or written to incorrect locations. This could result in a hardware equivalent of the 'wild jumps' or 'overwrites' identified earlier as potential problems within programming languages. As with the software case, such problems could destroy the operation of a routine, or could cause one routine to affect the operation of another. The use of ROM, rather than RAM, for program storage has clear advantages in reducing the risk of corruption.

It is clear that although complete isolation is an enviable goal it is not an achievable objective in a practical system. However, adequate isolation can be achieved for most purposes, greatly simplifying the task of testing and verification. With this in mind it is important to note that as complete isolation can never be guaranteed, system designers should not rely on the correct operation of a single module to achieve safety, even if that module is well trusted. As in all aspects of safety, several *independent* means of assuring safety are preferred.

Object-oriented design

In recent years there has been an increasing use of object-oriented techniques in the production of all forms of software. Many engineers meet these methods for the first time using languages such as C++, but they are also associated with languages such as Ada and Modula-2.

Object-oriented design (OOD) differs from functionally or data-oriented approaches in that functions and data are treated as indivisible elements which collectively form **objects**. Software components are arranged as collections of interrelated data and procedures. They are accessed only through their defined interfaces, and their components are neither visible nor directly accessible.

The process of object-oriented design may be represented as a series of stages:

(1) Define the problem.

(2) Develop an informal strategy for the solution of the problem.

(3) Identify the *objects* used in the informal strategy.

(4) Identify the *operations* used in the informal strategy.

(5) Partition the system into a set of modules and establish their interfaces.

(6) Implement the data structures and procedures within these modules.

It can be seen that there are few differences between this approach and the techniques of system partitioning discussed earlier in this chapter. However, the use of a language that supports an object-oriented approach allows the modules to be defined as **abstract data types**. This allows the problem to be mapped into appropriate abstractions, rather than being forced into structures defined by the programming language.

One of the key features of object-oriented design is the use of **inheritance**, which allows an object to inherit attributes and operations from other objects. This is often used as a means of reducing the effort required to implement new functions, and can be seen as a means of reusing software (we shall look at software reuse later in this section). The use of inheritance has great implications for the understandability of the software concerned. It can be used to hide design details, making programs easier to read, but may have the effect of masking the true nature of the operations performed.

The data hiding and encapsulation features of object-oriented design provide good separation between the definition of a system and its ultimate implementation. This allows attention to be directed at the design of the various modules without being concerned with their eventual construction.

Although an object-oriented approach offers many potential benefits, some of the features associated with OOD languages must be avoided when developing safety-critical systems. One such problem area is linked with the use of dynamic dispatching, which requires that certain operations are determined at runtime. This feature causes great problems for verification and validation of the system's operation. Languages such as Ada 95 fully support OOD, but provide facilities to turn off options such as dynamic dispatching.

Trial software

Often during the process of software design an engineer will need to experiment to investigate various ideas. This will involve the writing of trial software to demonstrate the success or otherwise of design alternatives.

The function of trial software is to demonstrate the suitability of a particular design, not to form the basis of operational code. Consequently, the techniques used for the production of such programs are often far less formal than would be required for material that will form part of the ultimate system. It is also acceptable to use programming languages that would not be suitable for the production of the final software.

It is important to note the distinction between the various forms of software that are produced during the development process but do not form part of the final system. In particular, confusion may arise between trial software and that used for animation or simulation. **Animation** (or **prototype**) software is used to illustrate the characteristics of the specification, and to demonstrate that this is a true representation of the customer's requirements. **Trial software** is used to investigate design ideas before they are implemented, and so aid the engineer in the choice of techniques. **Simulation software** is used to represent the behaviour of the system or its environment, to allow the performance of the chosen design to be investigated, usually during the testing phase of the project. We shall look at the use of simulation in more detail in Chapter 12, when we consider testing. Unfortunately, although the use of these three kinds of software is widespread, the terminology used for the various forms is subject to some variability.

Detailed software design

When the architectural design process has reduced the system to modules of a manageable size, work may begin on the detailed design phase that precedes the task of implementing (programming) the software. In practice the division between these two levels of design is often indistinct, although a milestone is usually inserted between them to form the focus of a design review.

The first stage of the detailed design process is to gather together information and to make some initial decisions related to the form of the relevant module. Much of the required information will come directly from the specification document for the module. At this stage we are concerned with determining *what* the module is to do rather than *how* this will be achieved. The data to be gathered may be categorized as follows:

Purpose: The functions to be performed by the module must be identified, including both primary and secondary requirements. The design must also define what the module should do in exceptional circumstances, such as at power-up, in the event of power failure, and in the event of error messages from other modules.

Data use: The inputs and outputs should be identified, along with any internal data shared between multiple functions within the module. Any external data values read or modified by the module should also be noted.

Performance: The required speed of operation of the module should be determined for each of its various functions. Resource requirements must also be assessed in terms of program and data space, and use of the system stack (or stacks).

Fault conditions: Every form of failure that might occur within the module and its associated I/O devices should be listed. For each failure mode the conditions under which that fault could occur should then be identified.

Integrity level: For each of the failure modes identified above, the implications should be assessed in order to determine an overall integrity-level requirement for the module. This will in turn dictate the methods appropriate for its development.

Testing: When the module has been implemented it will need to be tested to show that it satisfies its requirements. At the design stage it is appropriate to define what the module must do in order to be accepted. These acceptance criteria will form the basis of later test plans.

Once the various pieces of information have been assembled the detailed design can begin. This involves an iterative process of functional decomposition that continues until directly implementable procedures, subroutines and data types are identified.

The techniques used for the detailed design phase will be greatly affected by the overall development methods and tools being used for the project. For example, the use of formal methods may permeate all phases of system development, including those concerned with design. We shall look at the use of formal methods in Chapter 11. Several special-purpose design tools or methods may also be used to facilitate the design process. These include such techniques as Yourdon (Yourdon and Constantine, 1979), Jackson (1983) and

Mascot (RSRE, 1987). The programming language used is also likely to influence design methods. Well-structured languages such as Ada and Pascal greatly simplify the design process, as they naturally support an iterative approach to functional decomposition. Ada in particular is often considered to be a **design language** rather than simply a programming language. Using Ada, the architectural design is described directly within the constructs of the language, and later stages of design refine this information, progressively adding more detailed material. When complete, the design can be automatically implemented as code by an Ada compiler.

The detailed software design phase results in a specification for each software component that describes its function, parent routine, data structures, interfaces, algorithms and assumptions. It also gives estimates or limits for the size of the module and states any constraints on its implementation. As with the architectural design phase, the overall detailed design must be verified to show that it is a true representation of the system. The need for such an analysis must be considered throughout the design process, and must also be reflected within the documentation. As before, we shall leave discussion of the process of verification until later chapters.

Design description

The primary output of the software design process is the **design description**. This is a definition of the software architecture and the low-level requirements derived from the software specification. The information to be included within the design description is normally defined within the standard being used for the project. Table 9.3 shows the form of the design description required by the aerospace standard DO-178B (RTCA/EUROCAE, 1992).

It can be seen from Table 9.3 that the design description includes details of all aspects of the software design, including restrictions imposed by the hardware on which it will execute. The partitioning of the system is included, together with the methods used to guarantee isolation (to prevent breaches of the partitioning).

The reference to **deactivated code** in Table 9.3 refers to sections of the software that are physically present but which are intentionally not executed. Typically this might include test software used for debugging purposes that is not executed in the final version. It can be argued that it is better to leave this software in place and deactivated, than to recompile or relink to remove it, so drastically changing the memory map of the system. This ensures that the final code is as close as possible to the code used during testing. Counter-arguments say that it is better to remove any non-executing segments to reduce the complexity of the code and to remove the chance of it being executed inadvertently. Deactivated code should not be confused with **dead code**. This refers to sections of unexecuted code that are created unintentionally. These may be formed as a result of modifications to the program which leave remnants of code that are no longer required. Alternatively, they may be

Table 9.3 Requirements for the design description from DO-178B.

(a)	A detailed description of how the software satisfies the specified software high-level requirements, including algorithms, data structures, and how software requirements are allocated to processors and tasks
(b)	The description of the software architecture defining the software structure to implement the requirements
(c)	The input/output description, for example a data dictionary, both internally and externally throughout the software architecture
(d)	The data flow and control flow of the design
(e)	Resource limitations, the strategy for managing each resource and its limitations, the margins, and the method for measuring those margins, for example timing and memory
(f)	Scheduling procedures and interprocessor/intertask communication mechanisms, including time-rigid sequencing, pre-emptive scheduling, Ada rendezvous and interrupts
(g)	Design methods and details for their implementation, for example software data loading, user-modifiable software, or multiple-version dissimilar software
(h)	Partitioning methods and means of preventing partition breaches
(i)	Descriptions of the software components, whether they are new or previously developed, with reference to the baseline from which they were taken
(j)	Derived requirements from the software design process
(k)	If the system contains deactivated code, a description of the means to ensure that the code cannot be enabled in the target computer
(l)	Rationale for those design decisions that are traceable to safety-related system requirements

formed due to logical mistakes within the construction of the program that make some paths through the code unreachable. In any event, the presence of dead code indicates some weakness in the program that should be addressed. Static code analysis should detect any code that *cannot* be reached during the execution of a program, but cannot always find sections that are not used for reasons associated with the input data of the system.

Reuse of software

Because of the high cost of software development, particularly for critical applications, the reuse of existing software from other projects is commercially very attractive. There are also very sound engineering reasons for reusing tried and tested software components. As confidence increases with use, well-established code is likely to be more dependable than that which is newly created.

Where software components are to be taken from other projects it is vital that these have been developed to an appropriate level of integrity, or that appropriate steps are taken to make them comply with the requirements of the current project. Full documentation of the development and verification of the components will be required, and this will need to be reviewed in the light of their change of use. Guidelines on the reuse of software are included in many of the standards used within this area, for example Interim Defence Standard 00-55 (MoD, 1991) and DO-178B (RTCA/EUROCAE, 1992).

9.4 Software implementation

The process of implementing the software design will vary greatly, depending on the programming language and development methods used. Programmers used to working in poorly structured languages may see this task as quite distinct from that of program design. Indeed, in such languages there is a radical change in the form of the program at this stage. Implementing software is often referred to as **coding**, this term perhaps suggesting that during this process the design becomes *concealed* within the intricacies of the language used. Clearly, any operation that masks the form of the design is undesirable as this will increase the likelihood of faults going undetected.

When using well-structured and formalized languages, such as Ada, the nature of the design is not masked and the programming task is an extension of the detailed design. It has been suggested that in such cases it is better to consider the language as a means of documenting the software design, for automatic conversion into code by the compiler (Pyle, 1991). Ada is therefore often viewed as a **software design language**, rather than simply a programming language (Goldsack, 1985). The language is used throughout the software design process, with more detail being added as the task progresses.

When writing critical software the emphasis is invariably on safety and *not* on efficiency. Programming 'tricks' that save a few bytes of memory, or a few microseconds of execution time, must be avoided in favour of standard techniques that are easily understood and easy to document.

It is not within the scope of this text to deal in detail with all the software engineering aspects of programming. Instead, we will consider only those elements of this process that have particular relevance to safety.

Defensive programming

In general, software routines implement algorithms that act on input data in order to determine their output. Invariably the algorithms make some assumptions concerning their input data, and the routine's output may be unpredictable if these assumptions are incorrect. For example, a simple calibration routine might adjust an incoming data value by dividing it by a scaling factor. The nature of the quantities involved might dictate that the scaling factor can never be zero, and a simple implementation of this function might therefore ignore this possibility. If, due to an error in the calling routine, the scaling factor were to be zero, such a routine might give an incorrect and potentially dangerous output when faced with the problem of dividing by zero.

Defensive programming involves defining the assumptions made by an algorithm and checking that these assumptions are satisfied before it is executed. If it is found that the assumptions are invalid, the routine can then be made to take some appropriate (safe) action. In the previous example, the programmer would first study the algorithm being used for the scaling operation to determine the limits imposed on the input values. An appropriate action would then be defined for use if these limits were exceeded. The calling program would be written to guarantee that only legal values could be passed to the routine, but as a further safeguard the calibration software would check the incoming data before executing the scaling operation. If the values were found to be inappropriate the defined alternative action would be performed, thus ensuring safety. We therefore try to guarantee the best, but cater for the worst.

Software annotation

We have seen that the design process results in a detailed description of each software component. This would include information on its function, inputs and outputs, data structures and algorithms. We have also seen that the algorithms make some assumptions concerning the nature of the data used by the component. This description is used to check the resulting implementation for conformance with the design, and as the basis of later testing. Automated tools may also be able to make use of this information, provided that it is in an appropriate form.

Annotations are a method of embedding information within a program so that it can be used for checking or verification. The annotations are 'hidden' within comments in the program, but use a syntax that allows analysis tools to detect and extract them. This permits the annotations to be invisible to the compiler, while allowing other tools to use them as required. An example of such a syntax is that used by the SPARK examiner, an analysis package for use with SPARK Ada. Within Ada a double minus sign (– –) indicates the beginning of a comment. When using the SPARK examiner, annotation may be added by beginning them with the pattern '– –#'. This permits both ordinary comments and annotations to be incorporated as needed. Examples of the information incorporated within annotations are:

- a list of global variables used;
- a list of dependencies – that is, how variables are interdependent;
- pre-conditions – the conditions assumed at entry;
- post-conditions – the conditions intended upon exit.

We shall consider the use of analysis methods in more detail in Chapter 12.

9.5 Software tools

A wide variety of software tools is available to provide assistance during each phase of the software development lifecycle. These may be broadly divided into those used for: program translation; testing and project management.

Program translation tools

The most important tools within this category are clearly compilers and assemblers. A wide range of such tools is available to suit the many programming languages used; the diversity of target processors; and a range of development platforms.

In all safety-critical applications validated compilers should be used whenever possible. In Section 9.2 we noted that these are extremely dependable, and that in most cases errors introduced by such compilers are likely to be insignificant compared with those introduced by other means.

Compilers and assemblers convert their input programs into another form, which may be executable or may require further translation. Compilers may produce executable or relocatable code directly, or may produce assembler source code as a form of intermediate language. This latter option may be useful in allowing static code analysis to be performed at the assembly code level, rather than at the high-level language source code level. Such an analysis could detect errors produced by the compiler that would not be found by analysing the original source code. This process has merit if you trust the relatively simple assembler needed to complete the translation more than the comparatively complex compiler. An alternative and more common solution to this problem is to perform the analysis directly on the object code, rather than the source program. This prevents faults within either the compiler or the assembler from circumventing the analysis. The process of static code analysis will be discussed in Chapter 12.

Program testing tools

A range of tools is available to assist in the testing of software-based systems. These include tools for performing static tests on the code without executing it (static code analysis) and tools that assist in dynamic testing. Some tools can assist in both of these areas. We will leave further discussion of the tools within this group until we look at testing in more detail in Chapter 12.

Project management tools

Because of the complexity of many software projects there is great scope for the use of automated techniques to assist in various aspects of project management.

The STARTS Guide (1987) lists a variety of such tools, which it subdivides under the headings:

- project management
- configuration management
- project infrastructure and project support environments
- requirements definition and design.

Some of the tools within these classifications are discussed in other chapters, but a full treatment of all the available tools is not within the scope of this text. Those requiring more information on the available tools are referred to the above guide.

Tool reliability

In many cases the automated tools used in the production of software-based systems are extremely complicated, and verification of such tools would be impossible. In any event, the primary use of these tools is often within commercial rather than safety-critical applications, and such verification would be economically unjustifiable. For these reasons we must assume that all such tools are imperfect. The problems associated with tool faults may be tackled in two main ways, first by attempting to use the most reliable tools available, and secondly by using a range of tools to achieve some form of independence.

Tool selection is a major problem for all companies, particularly for those with little experience in this field. Validated tools are clearly preferable where they exist, but these are not always available. It should also be remembered, as was mentioned in Section 9.2, that validated does not mean verified. Logic suggests that tools will become more reliable with use, and so mature tools are always preferable to novel ones. This is not to say that a given copy of a tool miraculously improves with age, but that feedback from customers allows manufacturers to remove bugs in successive releases. Various independent organizations provide guides to the tools available for particular functions. These give commercial information such as price and licensing details, but may also list the number of users, the years of use and the support available. An example of such a guide is the STARTS Guide (1987).

Even the use of validated or well-respected tools will not remove the possibility of tool errors. These must be tackled by the judicious use of **independence** and **diversity**. In some cases it may be possible to confirm the correct action of a tool by performing the same task using an alternative product. Alternatively, checks may be performed to investigate the correctness of the tool's operation. The functioning of compilers and assemblers, for example, may be checked by performing static analysis of the object code they produce. Verification tools can be investigated by duplicating tests using diverse techniques. This approach forms a normal part of most independent verification and validation activities, where the checking team will usually use tools different from those used during development. Although the use of diverse tools greatly increases one's confidence in the results of such tests, it is important to remember the problems associated with diversity, as discussed in Chapter 6. Even products from different companies *could* have the same faults. It is interesting to note that two of the most widely used software verification packages, SPADE and MALPAS, despite being developed and marketed by different companies, have common roots in a single MoD research establishment.

9.6 Safety-critical software – an overview

We saw in earlier chapters that the use of inherently complex, software-based systems is not our first choice when developing safety-critical applications. Wherever possible we would prefer to use simple, electromechanical or non-programmable electronic solutions to problems related to safety. However, the use of computers within safety-critical systems is increasing dramatically in almost all industrial sectors.

Figure 9.9 shows the amount of software used within a range of civil aircraft from a single manufacturer over a period of 30 years (Potocki de Montalk, 1993). The graph shows that the quantity of software, measured in

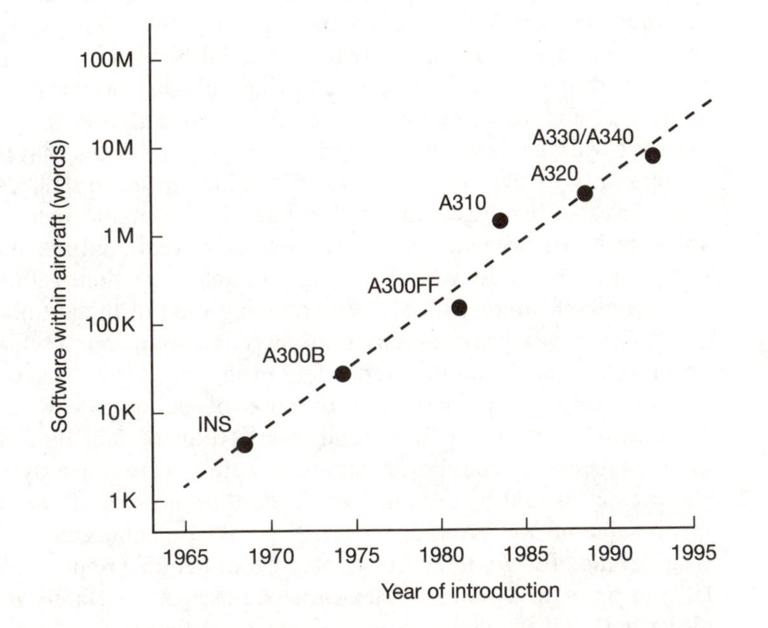

Figure 9.9 The use of software in civil aircraft.

words of executable code, has almost doubled for every two years of the period shown. If this trend continues, we would expect to see a further increase by a factor of about a 1000 over the next 20 years. Although not all the software in an aircraft is related to safety, a large proportion *is* critical and has a direct influence on the safety of the aircraft. This would suggest that safety-critical software will become even more important in civil aircraft as we move into the 21st century. It is interesting to note that over the period covered by the graph of Figure 9.9, the number of fatal accidents throughout the world, measured per million hours of flight, has fallen by a factor of nearly 10 for most classes of civil aircraft. Although it is not possible to conclude that this improvement is related to a greater dependence on software-based systems, it can be seen that the dramatic increase in the use of software has been achieved without an escalation in accidents.

The automotive industry is also moving towards an increased dependence on computer-based systems. Modern cars now use microcontrollers to perform a number of functions, such as engine management, antilock braking and sophisticated display control. In more advanced cars computers are being used within adaptive suspension units and power train management. As time passes, these advanced features tend to migrate towards lower-priced and higher-volume vehicles, and we will inevitably see a progressive increase in the use of software-based systems in all cars. The provision of ever more features has also resulted in a dramatic increase in the cost and weight of the wiring loom that carries power and control signals throughout the vehicle. In an attempt to solve this problem several manufacturers are introducing automotive bus networks to reduce the number of wires required. An example of such an arrangement is the **controller area network** or **CAN** bus (Arnett, 1987). This system typically uses two power conductors and a two-wire serial bus arrangement. The four wires travel throughout the vehicle, allowing all the electrical equipment to be controlled and to communicate. In many cases the devices connected to the network will be relatively simple input or output devices that interface switches or actuators to the bus. However, the ability to add intelligence to the nodes offers great advantages and will result in a dramatic increase in the use of software-based systems in cars. By their very nature, most automotive subsystems are safety related. We can therefore predict a dramatic increase in the volume of safety-critical software being used in the automotive industry.

Given our previous observations concerning our preference for simple, non-programmable solutions to safety problems, it is necessary to consider why industry is steadily increasing the use of computers within safety-critical systems. The reason for this trend stems from the fact that safety is only one of a number of system requirements. If safety were our only requirement then no software would be used in aircraft because no aircraft would fly. Planes are much safer on the ground, so safety would be enhanced by preventing them from taking off. We noted in Chapter 4 that people are prepared to take certain risks in order to achieve certain gains. Consequently, safety must be evaluated along with other system requirements in determining the acceptability of a system.

Clearly, there are many advantages associated with the use of computers within real-time control systems. They permit the implementation of sophisticated techniques that may be impossible by other means. They may also reduce the size or volume of the hardware required. Unfortunately, software-based systems bring with them considerable complexity, which increases the problems of ensuring adequate safety. As in all engineering projects the key to success lies in choosing an *appropriate* technology for the problem in hand. Experience shows that in systems of a relatively low level of criticality, the use of software-based systems often represents an efficient and cost-effective solution. However, in highly critical systems the cost of ensuring adequate safety makes the use of less complex solutions more attractive. Therefore, in such applications computers will tend to perform highly critical functions only when no other solution is possible.

REFERENCES

Arnett D.J. (1987). A high performance solution for in-vehicle networking – controller area network (CAN). *SAE 870823*

Barnes J.G.P. (1993). Highlights of Ada 9X. In *Ada Yearbook 1993* (Loftus C., ed.). Amsterdam: IOS Press

Carré B.A. and Debney C. (1985). *SPADE-Pascal*. Southampton: Program Validation Limited

Carré B.A., Jennings T.J., Maclennan F.J., Farrow P.F. and Garnsworthy J.R. (1990). *SPARK – The SPADE Ada Kernel*, 3rd edn. Southampton: Program Validation Limited

Clutterbuck D.L. (1992). Drive report: review of current tools and techniques for the development of safety-critical software. In *Software in Safety-Related Systems* (Wichmann B.A., ed.), pp. 145–75. Chichester: John Wiley

Cullyer W.J., Goodenough S.J. and Wichmann B.A. (1991). The choice of computer languages for use in safety-critical systems. *Software Eng. J.*, **6**(2), 51–8

Currie I.F. (1989). NewSpeak: a reliable programming language. In *High Integrity Software* (Sennett C., ed.). London: Pitman

Goldsack S., ed. (1985). *Ada for Specification and Design – Possibilities and Limitations*. Cambridge: Cambridge University Press

Jackson M. (1983). *System Design*. Englewood Cliffs, NJ: Prentice-Hall

Lampson B.W., Horning J.J., London R.L., Mitchell J.G. and Popek G.L. (1977). Report on the programming language Euclid. *ACM SIGPLAN Notices*, **12**(2)

MoD (1991). Interim Defence Standard 00-55 *The Procurement of Safety Critical Software in Defence Equipment*. Glasgow: Directorate of Standardization

Pavey D.J. and Winsborrow L.A. (1993). Demonstrating equivalence of source code and PROM contents. *Comput. J.*, **36**(7), 654–67

Potocki de Montalk J.P. (1993). Computer software in civil aircraft. *Microproc. Microsys.*, **17**(1), 17–23

Pyle I.C. (1991). *Developing Safety Systems: A Guide Using Ada*. Hemel Hempstead: Prentice-Hall

Rowe R. (1994). Safety-critical systems computer language survey results. Internet *comp.software-eng* newsgroup, November

RSRE (1987). *The Official Handbook of MASCOT* Version 3. Malvern: Computer Division, RSRE

RTCA/EUROCAE (1992). *Software Considerations in Airborne Systems and Equipment Certification*. RTCA/DO-178B; EUROCAE/ED-12B. Washington: Radio Technical Commission for Aeronautics. Paris: European Organisation for Civil Aviation Electronics

STARTS Purchasers' Group (1987). *The STARTS Guide: Vol. 1*, 2nd edn. Manchester: National Computing Centre Publications

Wichmann B.A. (1989). *Insecurities in the Ada Programming Language*. NPL Report DITC 137/89. Teddington: National Physical Laboratory

Wichmann B.A. (1994). Producing critical systems – the Ada 9X solution. In *Technology and Assessment of Safety-Critical Systems* (Redmill F. and Anderson T., eds), pp. 194–203. London: Springer-Verlag

Wichmann B.A., Canning A.A., Clutterbuck D.L. *et al.* (1995). Industrial perspective on static analysis. *Software Eng. J.*, **10**(2), 69–75

Yourdon E. and Constantine L. (1979). *Structured Design: Fundamentals of a Discipline of Computer Program and Systems Design*. Englewood Cliffs, NJ: Prentice-Hall

FURTHER READING

McDermid J., ed. (1992). *Software Engineer's Reference Book*. Oxford: Butterworth-Heinemann

Pyle I.C. (1991). *Developing Safety Systems: A Guide Using Ada*. Hemel Hempstead: Prentice-Hall

Wichmann B.A., ed. (1992). *Software in Safety-Related Systems*. Chichester: John Wiley

PROBLEMS

9.1 What factor tends predominantly to determine the dependability of general-purpose software? Why is this situation unacceptable in the case of critical software?

9.2 What restrictions are imposed on software development methods by the use of static code analysis?

9.3 Explain the meanings of the terms 'dynamic testing' and 'static testing'. How do the objectives of these two forms of testing differ?

9.4 Discuss the use of assembly code programming in safety-critical systems.

9.5 What aspects of software portability are of particular relevance to safety?

9.6 Describe the use of language subsets in the development of safety-critical software.

9.7 Discuss the problems associated with arithmetic in safety-critical software.

9.8 At what stage of the development process are fault tolerance and fault detection introduced into a system?

9.9 Explain how the use of interlock mechanisms affects the choice of partitions within safety-critical software.

9.10 Describe the importance of effective isolation within safety-critical software. Why is perfect isolation between software modules impossible?

9.11 Why is the use of a runtime kernel normally not recommended for projects of the highest levels of criticality? How may the execution of multiple tasks be managed in such systems?

9.12 How can system hardware affect the isolation between software components?

9.13 Describe the differences between trial software, animation software and simulation software.

9.14 Define and differentiate between the terms 'deactivated code' and 'dead code'.

9.15 What is meant by the term 'defensive programming'? Give examples of the use of defensive techniques within safety-critical software.

9.16 Explain the meaning and function of 'software annotation'.

9.17 Discuss the advantages and disadvantages of the reuse of software within safety-critical projects.

9.18 What is meant by the term 'validated' when applied to a compiler?

9.19 The tools used in the development of software are not perfect. How may imperfections within tools be overcome?

9.20 Discuss the *appropriateness* of using software-based systems within safety-critical applications.

10 Programmable Logic Controllers

CHAPTER CONTENTS

10.1 Introduction

Programmable logic controllers (PLCs) are self-contained microcomputers which are optimized for industrial control. They consist of one or more processors together with power supply and interface circuitry, within a suitable housing. A range of input and output modules is normally available to allow such units to be used in a wide range of situations, with 'off-the-shelf' hardware. Facilities are also provided for programming and for general system development.

Because PLCs are basically microcomputers within a box, much of the material within the hardware and software chapters of this book is of direct relevance to their use. However, the development of systems based on PLCs differs considerably from that of systems using more conventional computer hardware. Consequently, in this chapter we shall look at issues of particular relevance to systems built around this form of technology.

PLCs were introduced in the 1970s as a way of producing and marketing computers in large quantities, in an industrial area that is characterized by the diversity of its applications. At that time many simple control systems were based on the use of electromechanical relays, and PLCs were initially seen as a replacement for this form of circuitry. Designers working with relays were used to producing their designs using a graphic notation based on **ladder diagrams** (or **ladder logic**). To simplify the adoption of an alternative technology, manufacturers of PLCs added a user interface to their products which enabled them to be programmed in a manner that was intuitive to engineers familiar with ladder diagrams. Initially, the controllers had a functionality that was limited to the simple logic functions that could be produced using relays. As time passed more elaborate features were added to meet the diverse needs of the control engineer. These included sophisticated displays, and data logging and communication facilities.

From their inception PLCs have been used for machine and process control, and have therefore been widely used in safety-critical applications. For this reason, the units have been specifically designed for high reliability and dependability. Particular attention has been paid to hardware reliability, and modern designs promise extremely long MTBFs. In recent years we have also seen the production of PLCs specifically aimed at high-integrity applications. These use fault-tolerant techniques to achieve extremely high reliability, and one manufacturer claims a mean operating time without a dangerous failure of more than 7.8 billion years (Boothroyd, 1995)! Although one must judge this figure in the light of the problems associated with the assessment of reliability discussed at the end of Chapter 7, it would seem that units of very high reliability are available.

We shall see in Section 10.3 that modern PLCs may be programmed in a number of ways. In general, programming methods are aimed at minimizing development time rather than optimizing speed of execution. Most units are based on the use of a **system kernel** that provides a set of routines to interface to the various input/output modules. Simple PLCs execute code sequentially without any form of multitasking, but more complex devices may be much more sophisticated. The system kernel is provided as **firmware** and its source code is not normally available to the system developer. Use of the kernel simplifies the task of PLC programming and concentrates much of the complexity of the software into the trusted firmware. This reduces the likelihood of errors within the application program, but places great importance on the correctness of the system software.

In Chapter 8 we noted that when choosing a microprocessor for safety-critical applications it is preferable to choose a device that has seen considerable industrial use. Experience gained in this way increases our confidence in the device, both in its reliability and in its freedom from major design errors. In Chapter 9 we made similar observations concerning software development, with relevance to the choice of programming languages, compilers and other software development tools. We also noted, when considering software reuse, that software that has been used extensively is likely to be more reliable than newly created code. These considerations strongly support the use of PLCs in safety-critical applications. PLCs use standardized hardware that is likely to have seen far more industrial use than specialized single-board computers or custom equipment. System software is also likely to be well proven. A mature PLC design will have been well tested because of both its high volume of use and the variety of applications in which it has been used. This variety greatly increases the likelihood of uncovering obscure 'bugs'.

Unfortunately, not all aspects of the use of PLCs are so satisfactory. Although the hardware and software of PLCs are well tried, they are proprietary products and details of their design and development are not normally available to system developers. This makes it impossible for manufacturers of safety-critical systems to verify the hardware or software. To overcome this problem, the TÜVs (standards organizations) in Germany are now offering a certification service for PLCs. Under this scheme vendors provide details of both the hardware and the system firmware of the PLC, which are then independently assessed.

When using PLCs that have seen extended industrial use one may gain considerable confidence in the device from the experience of other users. If, for example, a particular type of PLC has accumulated some tens of thousands of years of operating time, spread across a number of units, this gives us a certain faith in its correctness. However, quantifying that faith is extremely difficult. Unfortunately, the system developer is usually wholly dependent on the equipment manufacturer for information on the use of the unit, and for details of its performance during its service. A manufacturer may claim a given number of satisfied customers, and perhaps estimate the number of hours of use seen by a device, but is less likely to give details of the faults that were found during that period or how they were rectified. Without such data it is very difficult to assess the PLC's performance. Even if such data was available, its interpretation would be extremely difficult. The value of previous experience with a given device will be greatly affected by the nature of the applications and the operating environments in which it has been used.

The availability of off-the-shelf hardware and interfacing software reduces development times and costs, and makes PLCs particularly suited to low-volume applications such as those in the process control industry. There is no doubt that a considerable amount of effort has gone into the development of modern PLCs, and this has resulted in devices that have extremely good hardware reliability. Units are also available that use multiple processors to achieve fault detection or fault tolerance, further enhancing their suitability for critical applications. However, hardware reliability is not the only requirement of safety-critical systems, and problems remain in terms of the verification and validation of systems based on PLCs.

10.2 PLC hardware

A typical programmable logic controller contains a single processor and a single power supply unit within a modular case. Input and output modules fit within this case, or plug into it with connectors. Some units are designed to mount onto a standard 'DIN rail', whereas others are designed for direct mounting. Input modules typically include general-purpose digital and analogue interfaces, and more specialized units for particular sensors, such as thermocouples. Output modules include digital units containing electromechanical or solid-state switches, analogue interfaces and drivers for stepper motors or displays. Modules for specialist functions such as communications and high-speed counting are also available. External connections to the modules are usually through terminal blocks or multiway connectors.

Most PLCs support various user interaction devices such as keyboards, keypads and display panels. These permit fairly sophisticated user interfaces to be constructed. Communications facilities are usually provided through one or more serial channels, and error detection is normally incorporated within these links. These can be used for remote access and to enable a unit to 'call for help' in the event of a hazardous situation. As many applications require the collection of large amounts of information, data-logging is normally provided, with the ability to download this information to a remote computer over a serial link. Many PLCs provide some form of **built-in self-test** (**BIST**), which may be activated at power-up and may also be used periodically during operation. Unfortunately, the coverage of such testing is usually poorly defined.

PLCs are normally programmed by downloading application software over a serial link. User programs are often stored in battery-backed RAM, although for safety-critical applications it is preferable to store such software in a form that is less easily corrupted, such as EPROM or EEPROM. Many PLCs provide this facility. Because PLCs are often used in electrically hostile environments, EMC is of great importance and manufacturers place great importance on this aspect of design and production.

In recent years we have seen the introduction of PLCs aimed specifically at highly critical applications. These include so-called 'failsafe' devices and fault-tolerant units. **Failsafe PLCs** are designed for use in applications that possess **safe states**, as discussed in Chapter 2. These PLCs usually contain two identical processors and a method of comparing their operation to detect any discrepancy. As the two channels receive the same input data, any difference between their operation must signal a failure. In this event, the system as a whole is made to shut down into its known safe state. Separate power supplies and input/output interfaces are normally used for each processor to minimize the risk of a single fault affecting both channels. This produces an arrangement in which it is extremely unlikely that a random hardware failure will result in a dangerous failure. However, as the two channels are identical this approach gives no protection against systematic failures, such as errors in the user or system software.

Fault-tolerant PLCs commonly employ three processors in a triple modular redundancy (TMR) arrangement, as described in Chapter 6. A typical controller uses identical processors with triplicated input and output modules. Separate power supplies are also used to minimize the possibility of common-mode failure. A voting mechanism compares the outputs of the three channels and effectively masks the effects of any single failure. This results in a level of fault detection that is comparable to the failsafe approach, but has the added benefit of **fault masking**. This allows such an arrangement to be used in critical applications that do not have failsafe states, as correct operation can be maintained even in the presence of a fault. The price to be paid for this facility is an increase in complexity and a resultant reduction in reliability.

10.3 PLC programming techniques

Many early PLCs were programmed using some form of graphical interface that allowed control functions to be described in a manner similar to that used to design relay circuits. This method, although familiar to many engineers, does not allow the use of structured techniques, and gradually manufacturers began to provide alternative programming facilities. Unfortunately, this evolutionary process resulted in an absence of any standardization in programming techniques.

In 1993 the International Electrotechnical Commission released a standard aimed at producing some uniformity in the field of PLCs. This is entitled IEC 1131: Programmable Controllers, and part 3 of this document relates to programming languages (IEC, 1993). Unfortunately, because of the prior existence of several well-established techniques, the standard's authors thought it necessary to incorporate several diverse programming methods rather than specifying a single preferred technique. The standard therefore describes two graphical and two text-based languages, plus a graphical technique that may be used to generate sequential structures. It concentrates on the syntax of the languages, but is often less definitive about their semantics. This may lead to problems of ambiguities and implementation differences.

The techniques defined within the standard are:

- **Ladder diagrams** (LD): A graphical method based on techniques used for the design of relay circuits. This approach gives very little support for structuring.
- **Function block diagrams** (FBD): A graphical technique that defines a program in terms of control blocks. It provides support for a hierarchical structure, allowing users to build up libraries of such blocks.
- **Instruction lists** (IL): This is a low-level text-based language similar to assembler. It provides no support for program structuring.
- **Structured text** (ST): A high-level, structured, text-based language.
- **Sequential function charts** (SFC): A high-level graphical method that can be used to structure program elements, written in one of the above programming languages, to perform sequential control functions.

Programs written using either a graphical or a text-based language require some form of declaration section to set out the variables used. The standard defines a common graphical declaration format that is used for both the graphical languages, and a common textual declaration format that is used for both text-based languages.

It is not within the scope of this text to describe in detail the programming languages defined in the standard. However, it is perhaps useful to show the form of these languages to illustrate their basic structure. Figure 10.1 gives an example taken from the standard. It shows a simple function 'WEIGH' as it would be represented in each of the four programming languages. The figure also shows the textual and graphical forms of the required declarations.

The function 'WEIGH'

> Function WEIGH provides the functions of BCD-to-binary conversion of a gross weight from a scale, the binary integer subtraction of a tare weight which has been previously converted and stored in the memory of the programmable controller, and the conversion of the resulting net weight back to BCD form, e.g. for an output display. The 'EN' input is used to indicate that the scale is ready to perform the weighting operation. The 'ENO' output indicates that an appropriate command exists (e.g. from an operator push-button), the scale is in proper condition for the weight to be read, and each function has a correct result.

A textual form of the declaration of this function is:

```
FUNCTION WEIGH : WORD  ( * BCD encoded * )
   VAR_INPUT ( * "EN" input is used to indicate "scale ready" * )
      weigh_command : BOOL ;
      gross_weight  : WORD ;  ( * BCD encoded * )
      tare_weight  : INT ;
   END_VAR

( * Function Body * )

END_FUNCTION                    ( * Implicit "ENO" * )
```

The body of function WEIGH in the IL language is:

```
            LD          weigh_command
            JMPC        WEIGH_NOW
            ST          ENO             ( * No weighing, 0 to "ENO" * )
            RET
WEIGH_NOW   LD          gross_weight
            BCD_TO_INT
            SUB         tare_weight
            INT_TO_BCD                  ( * Return evaluated weight * )
```

The body of function WEIGH in the ST language is:

```
IF weigh_command THEN
   WEIGH := INT_TO_BCD (BCD_TO_INT (gross_weight) - tare_weight) ;
END_IF ;
```

Figure 10.1 A comparison of PLC programming techniques.

Several manufacturers are now supporting, or are planning to support, the programming languages defined within IEC 1131-3. However, it will be several years before it is possible to assess whether the standard has achieved uniformity across the industry. Standardization between manufacturers would bring many advantages, but would also leave some problems unsolved. The most important of these relate to the nature of the various PLC languages and the availability of software development tools.

In Chapter 9 we looked at criteria for the selection of programming languages for safety-critical applications and made some observations

An equivalent graphical declaration of function WEIGH is:

```
                +-------------------------+
                |          WEIGH          |
       BOOL ---| EN                   ENO|--- BOOL
       BOOL ---| weigh_command  net_weight|--- WORD
       WORD ---| gross_weight              |
        INT ---| tare_weight               |
                +-------------------------+
```

The function body in the LD language is:

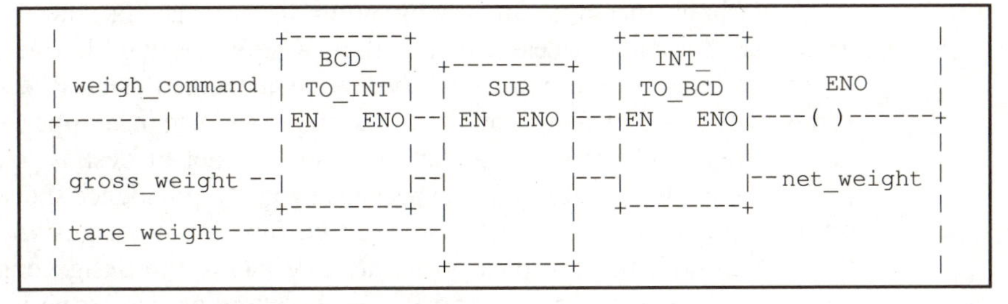

The function body in the FBD language is:

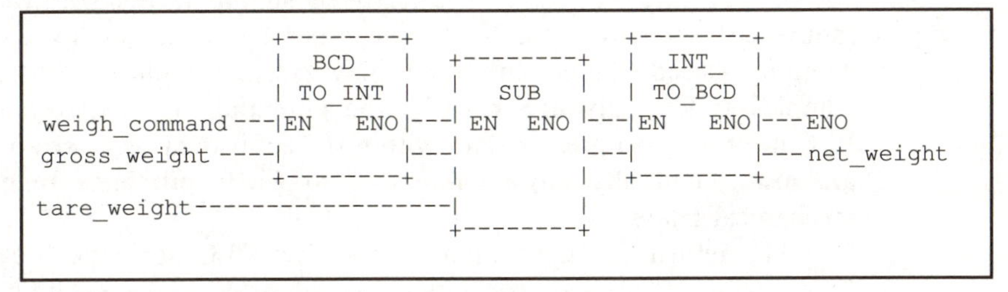

Notes on the graphical languages:

1. The graphic diagrams are produced using characters from a standardized set (ISO/IEC 646). Graphic and semigraphic representation is allowed but is not defined in this part of the standard.
2. The vertical lines on either side of the LD diagrams represent the power rails. The left rail may be considered as ON at all times.
3. The --| |-- symbol represents a pair of normally open contacts. These contacts are closed when the associated Boolean variable is ON.
4. The --( )-- symbol represents a relay coil. The state of the left side is copied to the associated Boolean variable and to the right side.

Figure 10.1 (*cont.*).

concerning currently available languages. Unfortunately, existing PLC languages do not satisfy many of the requirements of high-integrity software. In particular, it is often difficult to structure programs effectively and the widespread use of global variables makes effective isolation impossible. The various PLC languages are also poorly supported by software tools. Some tools are available to aid documentation and cross-referencing of variables, but support for software testing is very limited.

10.4 PLCs versus relays

Programmable logic controllers are often used in applications that might otherwise have been constructed using electromechanical relays, and are often used as replacements for existing relay-based systems. This being the case, it is perhaps relevant to compare these two technologies in terms of their suitability for use in safety-critical applications.

Perhaps the most surprising point to note is that the high-technology approach does not necessarily result in a safer system. If one compares the hardware reliability of equivalent systems constructed using PLCs and relays in terms of the rate of dangerous failures, their performance appears to be similar (Greenway, 1994). If we consider the likely impact of design errors on system performance we might also expect a broad equivalence between the two approaches, as the complexities of the two functional designs are comparable.

Although the complexity of the task facing the design engineer may be similar in the cases of relays and PLCs, the complexities of the resulting system will be very different. Relays are relatively simple devices with well-understood failure characteristics. PLCs, on the other hand, are highly complex microcomputer-based components that may contain millions of transistors and complex system software. Clearly, the potential for design errors within the PLC itself is much greater than within the equivalent relay arrangement. PLCs are also potentially more vulnerable to EMC problems than are electromechanical relays.

In return for their high complexity, PLCs provide greatly increased functionality. If used appropriately this will often enable safety to be enhanced by implementing mechanisms that would be impractical using relays. This might include such facilities as self-testing, error logging and remote fault reporting. Increased functionality may also allow an increase in the functional performance of the system, and may have other benefits unrelated to safety. PLCs offer increased flexibility and possibly a reduction in development time.

Because of the high dependability of modern PLCs, and their ability to implement superior architectures, it is likely that in many cases the benefits to safety of their adoption will greatly outweigh their disadvantages. Increasingly we are seeing PLCs being used in place of relays, and it is inevitable that this trend will continue. However, it is vital that the use of PLCs as a direct replacement for relays does not mask the underlying technology. One of the great benefits of a system implemented using relays is the complete independence of its various elements. An arrangement with several interlock mechanisms provided by relays is likely to give excellent protection against both random and systematic faults. However, the same arrangement implemented using a single PLC would be susceptible to a single-point failure within the controller. The independence of the 'virtual relays' provided by the PLC is an illusion provided by the user interface – this must not be mistaken for true independence of the hardware.

10.5 PLCs in safety-critical systems

PLCs have for many years been used in safety-critical systems, although until recently their use was restricted to applications requiring a relatively low level of integrity. Manufacturers are now producing controllers, such as the failsafe and fault-tolerant PLCs discussed above, that are clearly aimed at highly critical systems. In this section we look at the suitability of PLCs for such applications, and at some of their implications for system development.

When looking at system integrity requirements in Chapter 4 we differentiated between systems that provide a continuous control function and those that are used intermittently, as in a shutdown system. The requirements for these two configurations are very different, and below we look at the use of PLCs in each of these situations.

Shutdown systems

Shutdown systems are used in association with potentially dangerous processes that possess safe states. Such a system is often termed an **emergency shutdown system** or **ESD**. The function of a shutdown system is to drive a process into its safe state in a controlled manner, in the event of process parameters exceeding defined limits. Traditionally such systems have been implemented by hardwired techniques using electromechanical relays or logic circuits. Because of the lack of flexibility of these methods, developers have looked to PLCs to provide a more convenient solution (Halang and Scheepstra, 1993).

The various standards relating to safety-critical systems describe shutdown system architectures that are suitable for applications of different levels of integrity. For example, draft IEC 1508 provides guidance on the forms of redundancy that would be acceptable for each level of integrity, both for shutdown systems and for continuous control systems (IEC, 1995). Below are a few examples that illustrate ways in which the recommendations of the IEC standard for shutdown systems may be implemented using PLCs. It should be noted that the IEC recommendations are not specific to PLCs, and that the architectures recommended could be implemented using a range of technologies. However, the examples shown illustrate arrangements that are particularly suited to systems using PLCs, and are typical of those being used in industrial applications.

Integrity level 1

In applications of a low level of criticality a single-channel shutdown system may be acceptable, as such an arrangement provides two independent methods of ensuring safety, one within the control system and one within the shutdown system. Typical level 1 systems would use either a fairly sophisticated single-channel arrangement with some form of self-testing and monitoring, or a simple two-channel approach. Examples of these techniques are shown in Figure 10.2. In this figure, and the others in this section, the arrangements are shown in a simplified form, with the inputs and outputs represented by a single line in each case. The action of the shutdown system is depicted as the opening of a switch in series with the output, thus disconnecting its control action. The physical implementation of the systems would often be far more complex than the arrangements shown, which are meant simply to illustrate their basic form.

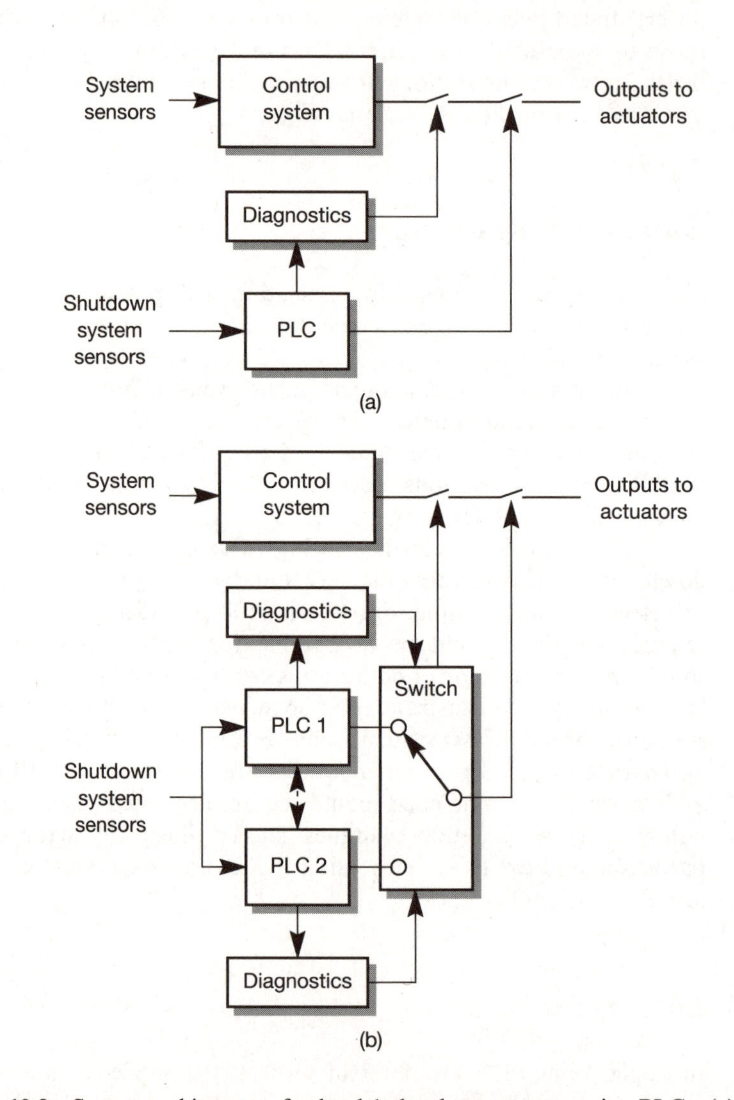

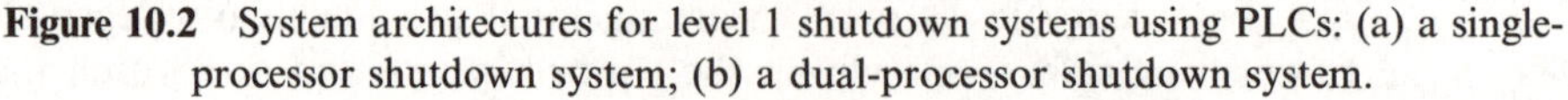

Figure 10.2 System architectures for level 1 shutdown systems using PLCs: (a) a single-processor shutdown system; (b) a dual-processor shutdown system.

In Figure 10.2(a), and several of the following figures, the PLC implementing the shutdown function is augmented by an arrangement performing diagnostics on its operation. The diagnostics function would normally include both hardware and software elements, and would include both self-checking performed by the PLC and hardware arrangements such as a watchdog. If the shutdown system detects that system parameters have gone outside their allowable limits it will take action to shut down the system, overriding the actions of the control system. Similarly, if the diagnostic unit detects that the shutdown system has malfunctioned, it will also shut down the system.

The two-channel arrangement of Figure 10.2(b) provides additional integrity by tolerating the failure of a single shutdown unit. Diagnostic information from each channel is used to control a switch that can isolate a single PLC in the event of its failure. Simultaneous failure of both units would cause the switch logic to shut down the system. Communication between the two PLCs allows their system states to be compared and permits each device to detect differences in their operation. Any such differences would indicate a fault within one of the PLCs, and would result in both units attempting to shut down the system. Thus the system will be shut down if either PLC detects a dangerous state, or if the diagnostic units detect that both channels have failed.

The IEC standard uses a notation for the various processor architectures that reflects the number of *independent* channels used and the number of those channels that must function correctly in order for the arrangement to perform its prescribed task. In the case of a shutdown system this task is to activate the shutdown mechanism. The arrangement of Figure 10.2(a) is termed a **1-out-of-1 (1OO1)** architecture, as it has a single shutdown channel and this must function correctly in order for the system to be shut down. Figure 10.2(b) represents a **dual 1-out-of-1 (1OO1D)** arrangement, as it comprises two channels that share input and output devices.

Integrity level 2

Applications with an integrity level of 2 would normally use at least two channels within the shutdown system, although the IEC standard does permit the use of appropriate single-channel arrangements. When using two channels these could use common input and output devices, as in Figure 10.2(b), or could employ diverse devices, as shown in Figure 10.3.

The arrangement of Figure 10.3 has two completely independent shutdown channels each taking their inputs from a separate set of sensors. The channels also employ different output devices, which in this case are connected in parallel. As a result, *both* channels must generate appropriate signals in order to shut down the system. The objective of this arrangement is to reduce the number of spurious trips. This configuration is often termed a

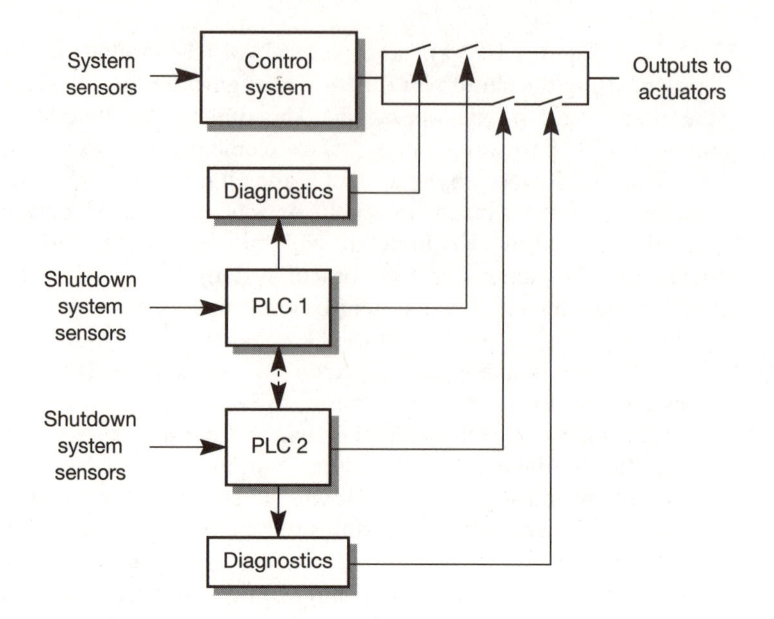

Figure 10.3 A dual-processor arrangement with dual I/O.

2-out-of-2 (2OO2) structure, as both of the channels must agree to shut down the system.

Integrity level 3

For level 3 systems the IEC standard requires a minimum of two independent channels within the shutdown system. It also requires that where two channels are used each channel must be able to independently produce a shutdown. This requirement precludes arrangements such as the 2OO2 arrangement described above, where both channels must agree to instigate a shutdown operation. A suitable arrangement may be formed by modifying the arrangement of Figure 10.3 so that the switches controlled by the two PLCs are in series rather than in parallel. This results in a system with two independent channels in which either may produce a shutdown (a 1OO2 arrangement). An alternative architecture, using three independent channels, is shown in Figure 10.4.

The triple processor configuration uses independent sets of sensors for each of the channels and has independent outputs arranged as a voting network. This results in an arrangement in which a shutdown can be produced by any two of the three PLCs – a **2-out-of-3 (2OO3)** architecture. This is an example of a triple modular redundant (TMR) arrangement, and provides safe operation even if one of the PLCs fails. By tolerating single faults it also

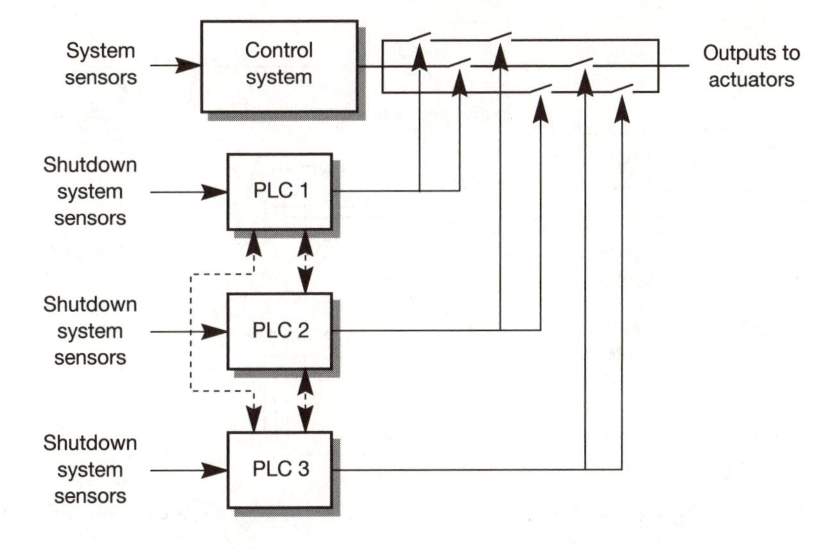

Figure 10.4 A triple-processor arrangement with triple I/O.

reduces the number of false trips. The TMR structure may be produced using separate PLCs, or by using a proprietary fault-tolerant PLC as described earlier.

Integrity level 4

The architectures described earlier in this section provide varying degrees of protection against random failure of components within the PLCs used in the shutdown system. However, because these arrangements use identical channels they provide no protection against systematic faults, such as errors in the application or system software.

For level 4 systems the IEC standard recommends that a detailed quantitative analysis is performed to determine the characteristics of target configurations. It makes no recommendations concerning specific architectures, but it is generally accepted that a degree of diversity is appropriate for systems of the highest level of integrity to reduce the likelihood of common-mode failures. A possible system employing diversity is shown in Figure 10.5 (Goring, 1994). Here two TMR units are used in parallel to reduce the probability of common systematic faults. This represents a **dual 2-out-of-3 (2OO3D)** configuration. In this arrangement the two TMR assemblies would come from different manufacturers and their software would be developed by separate teams. Although not eliminating the problems of common-mode failures (as discussed in Chapter 6), this approach has the potential to produce systems of very high integrity.

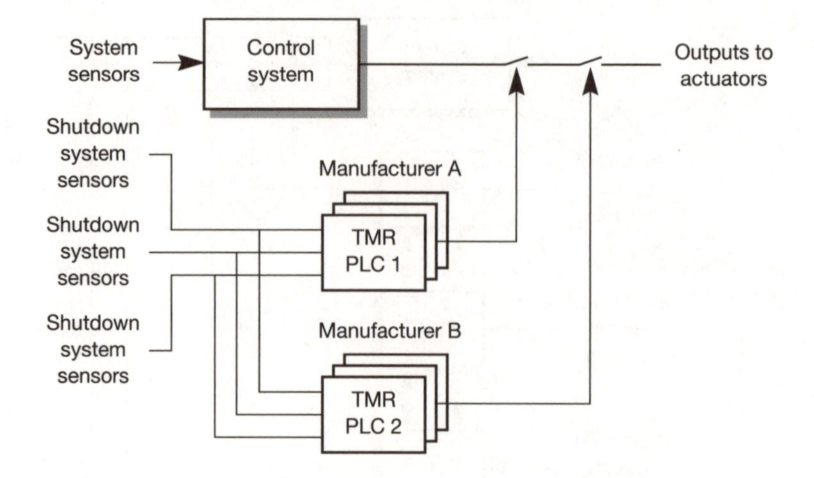

Figure 10.5 A dual triple-modular redundant shutdown system with diversity.

Continuous control systems

In addition to their use within shutdown systems, PLCs are also used in applications that require continuous control. The IEC standard describes architectures appropriate for continuous control systems of different levels of integrity, and gives guidance on methods of estimating their failure rates. For systems of integrity levels 1 and 2, a typical arrangement might use a 1-out-of-2 structure with self-test. This is an example of a two-channel system with dynamic redundancy, as discussed in Chapter 6. Level 3 systems would normally require a TMR system to provide both fault tolerance and fault masking. Systems requiring a safety integrity level of 4 would probably require an arrangement using an N-modular redundancy approach, with N being greater than 3. However, in practice few continuous control systems requiring the highest levels of integrity are based on commercial PLCs. The reasons for this are numerous and are largely concerned with the problems of verification and validation outlined in earlier sections of this chapter, and discussed below.

Developing safety systems using PLCs

Selection of an appropriate architecture is clearly not the only issue of importance in the development of a safety-critical system. In addition to defining system structures, the various standards also outline the design and development methods appropriate for systems of each level of integrity. Unfortunately, when using PLCs engineers are often unable to conform with the recommendations of these standards, particularly in the areas of verification and validation. Many of the techniques required depend on total access to details of the hardware design, the source code of the software and information on the development methods used. Such data is not normally available to system developers, as few PLC manufacturers would be prepared to provide information to a customer that would permit their products to be directly copied.

In the absence of detailed information on the design of a PLC, users must validate systems using results from their own testing, test data provided by the manufacturer and, where applicable, data from an independent assessment of the PLC. As has been noted several times before, validation on the basis of testing alone is extremely difficult, and even more so when the accuracy of the data may be unknown.

When producing a shutdown system the complexity of the functions to be implemented is often relatively low. This is clear from the fact that in many cases it would be feasible to implement these functions using hardwired logic. In such a situation it may be possible to obtain sufficient insight into the behaviour of the system to validate the user software. This being the case, for systems of a low level of integrity the experience gained from use of the PLC in other applications, combined with the manufacturer's assessment of its reliability, may be sufficient to validate the remaining parts of the system. A key point in such a validation is likely to be the fact that safety can be achieved at any time by driving the system into its safe state. Thus, for example, a self-checking pair of PLCs can achieve a safe situation if one of the channels fails, no matter what the cause of that failure. This gives very good protection against random hardware failure. However, for applications that require a high level of integrity it may be necessary to use a diverse implementation, as in Figure 10.5, to gain sufficient confidence in the system in respect of systematic errors within the PLC.

The validation of a continuous control system based on a PLC is often far more difficult. In general, the functions to be implemented in a control system are more complex than those required for a shutdown mechanism, making validation by testing more arduous. Also, as many control systems do not possess safe states, faults must be tolerated rather than simply detected. This places an increased importance on the ability of the developer to predict the likely failure modes of the system – a task made more difficult if data on one of its major components is not available. As a result of these difficulties, PLCs are rarely used in continuous control systems that require a very high level of integrity.

Future trends

At present, system developers are reliant on PLC manufacturers to provide much of the information needed for system validation. This situation can be greatly improved by incorporating some independence into the assessment of the controllers by employing appropriate external testing. Such an arrangement is currently in operation in Germany, where the TÜVs are now offering a certification service for PLCs. Unfortunately, the lack of standardization of both hardware and software complicates this process. This lack of standardization has also resulted in a shortage of development tools to support PLCs.

The recent publication of IEC 1131 may help this situation, but its adoption of a wide number of programming methods has done little to promote a unified approach. Work is under way on the development of more formal techniques of software production, and some of these will be discussed briefly in Chapter 11.

At the time of writing, a major research program is under way in the UK, with support from the Department of Trade and Industry (DTI) and the Science and Engineering Research Council (SERC). The project has the title 'Software Engineering Methods for Safe Programmable Logic Controllers' (SEMSPLC) and represents a major initiative in this area (Canning *et al.*, 1995). The four-year project aims to produce methods suitable for the development of application software for safety-critical PLC-based systems, using a language suited to industrial control. We await with interest the outcome of this work.

REFERENCES

Boothroyd D. (1995). Failsafe system gains the flexibility of the PLC approach. *Comput. Control Eng. J.*, **6**(1), 43–4

Canning A.A., Clarke S., Hatton S. *et al.* (1995). Guidance for the development of critical PLC and SCADA systems. *Proc. Second Safety Through Quality Conf.* Cape Canaveral, FL, 23–25 October, pp. 27–38

Goring C.J. (1994). Methods and techniques of improving the safety classification of programmable logic controller safety systems. In *Technology and Assessment of Safety-Critical Systems. Proc. Second Safety-Critical Systems Symposium, Birmingham* (Redmill F. and Anderson T., eds), pp. 21–30. London: Springer-Verlag

Greenway A. (1994). A user's perspective of programmable logic controllers (PLCs) in safety-related applications. In *Technology and Assessment of Safety-Critical Systems. Proc. Second Safety-Critical Systems Symposium, Birmingham* (Redmill F. and Anderson T., eds), pp. 1–20. London: Springer-Verlag

Halang W.A. and Scheepstra J. (1993). PLC-implementation of emergency shut-down systems. *12th International Conference on Computer Safety, Reliability and Security (Safecomp '93)*, Poznań-Kiekrz, Poland. London: Springer-Verlag

IEC (1993). International Standard IEC 1131 *Programmable Controllers – Part 3: Programming Languages*. Geneva: International Electrotechnical Commission. (In Europe this standard is also available as a normalized European standard – EN 61131-3)

IEC (1995). Draft International Standard 1508 *Functional Safety: Safety-Related Systems*. Geneva: International Electrotechnical Commission

PROBLEMS

10.1 Why is the widespread use of a controller of relevance to the designer of safety-critical systems?

10.2 How are user programs normally entered and stored within a PLC? Comment on the suitability of this storage method for safety-critical applications.

10.3 Describe the architecture used in a conventional failsafe PLC. What forms of fault are tackled by this approach?

10.4 Describe the construction of a typical fault-tolerant PLC. What are the advantages and disadvantages of such a system in comparison with a failsafe PLC?

10.5 How do sequential function charts differ from the graphical programming methods described in IEC 1131?

10.6 Why is the standardization of PLC programming methods of importance to developers of safety-critical systems?

10.7 Discuss the relative merits of relays and PLCs in the construction of simple safety-critical systems.

10.8 What pitfalls face an engineer when replacing a relay-based protection system with one based on a programmable logic controller?

10.9 What is the main function of an emergency shutdown system? Against what class of faults does such an arrangement provide protection?

10.10 Compare the characteristics of the dual 1-out-of-1 (1OO1D) shutdown system of Figure 10.2(b) with those of the 2-out-of-2 (2OO2) arrangement of Figure 10.3.

10.11 Compare the characteristics of a 1OO2 shutdown system configuration with those of a 2OO3 arrangement.

10.12 Discuss the problems associated with the verification and validation of systems based on programmable logic controllers.

10.13 Describe the difficulties involved in producing continuous control systems of very high integrity using PLCs.

10.14 Discuss the problems of independent validation of PLCs.

11 Formal Methods

CHAPTER CONTENTS

11.1 Introduction

The term 'formal methods' describes the use of mathematical techniques in the specification, design and analysis of computer hardware and software. In this chapter we shall look at the various forms of these techniques and see how they may be used to advantage in the development of safety-critical systems. We shall also consider the implications of the use of these methods, and look at some of the industrial experience with these techniques over the past few years.

We have seen that many of the problems associated with the development of safety-critical systems are related to deficiencies in their specification. In Chapter 5 we noted that a specification should be unambiguous, complete, consistent and correct. Documents written in natural languages are always susceptible to misunderstanding, as it is generally impossible to write in a way that cannot be misinterpreted. It is also difficult to ensure that such documents represent a full and correct description of the required system, or even to demonstrate that they are consistent. This is because any assessment of correctness, completeness or consistency must be performed on the basis of an engineer's understanding of both the specification and the requirements.

Over the years a great many techniques have been developed to tackle the problems associated with the production of unambiguous and precise specifications. These include a large number of CASE tools, and graphic or diagrammatic methods of describing the requirements or specification of a system. These techniques are often referred to as *formalized* methods (*not* formal methods), as they provide a systematic approach to the problem and thus help to promote a consistent method of development. Unfortunately, such techniques are only a partial solution as they still rely on the engineer to apply the techniques correctly and to interpret the results.

Formal methods are based on the use of formal languages that have very precise rules. This allows systems to be defined in a manner that can be interpreted unambiguously. It also permits specifications to be checked automatically for certain omissions and inconsistencies. Languages designed for this purpose are termed **system specification languages**, or sometimes **formal specification languages**, and their use offers many potential advantages in the development of critical systems. However, it would be wrong to assume that the use of formal methods is restricted to the production of unambiguous specifications. In fact, the use of formal methods may pervade all phases of the development lifecycle and, if used wisely, can greatly assist in the production of highly dependable systems.

One of the greatest advantages of describing a system in a formal, rather than an informal, manner is that automated tests may then be performed on this description. This allows software tools to check for certain classes of error, but also allows different descriptions of the system to be compared to see if they are equivalent. The development of any new engineering system involves an iterative process of transformation in which the requirements are abstracted through various stages of specification and design, to appear ultimately as a finished implementation. The requirements, the specification and the various levels of the design are all descriptions of the same system, and thus should be functionally equivalent. If each of these descriptions is prepared in a suitable form it should be possible to *prove* this equivalence, thereby greatly increasing our confidence in the development process.

In Chapter 1, and again in Chapter 5, we looked at diagrammatic methods of representing the lifecycle of a project. Figure 11.1 shows a simplified model that follows the main transformations of the definition of the system, as the project moves from its requirements through to its implementation phase. Within this diagram each descending arrow represents a conversion of the description of the system from one form to another.

Each transformation of the definition of the system provides the potential for error within the development process. When producing critical systems it is therefore necessary to confirm that each of these tasks has been performed correctly. This is known as **verification**, and must be performed whatever development methods are adopted. Verification will be discussed in detail in Chapter 12.

The process of verification is illustrated in Figure 11.2, which shows that each step of transformation is matched by the task of confirming that the activity has been performed correctly. This involves demonstrating that the description of the system which forms the input to that phase is functionally equivalent to that at its output (here the word 'functionally' is taken to include all the features of the system, including its safety aspects). If we look back at the 'V' diagram introduced in earlier chapters to represent the development

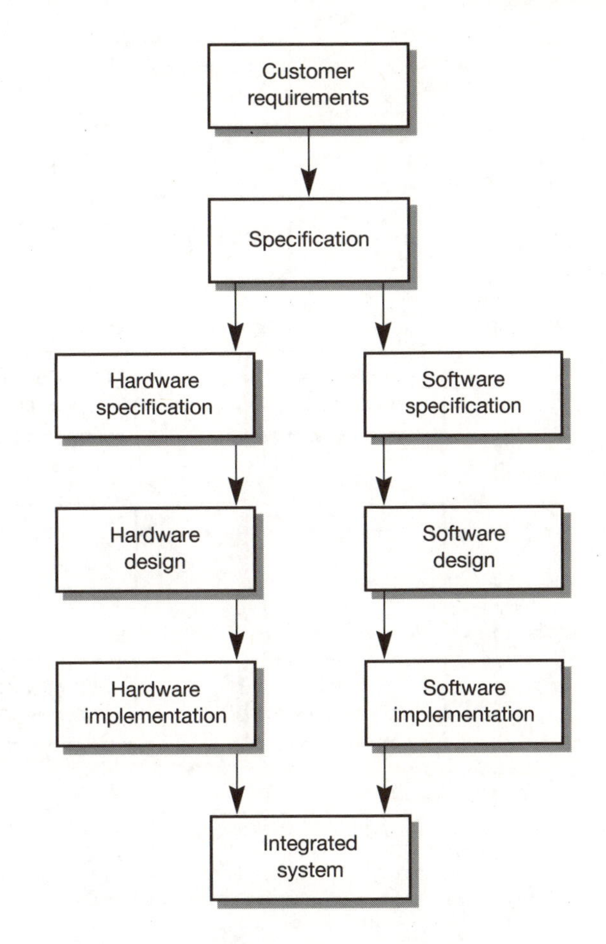

Figure 11.1 A simple project development model.

lifecycle, it is clear that the phases of Figure 11.1 represent the left-hand side of the 'V', and the ascending arrows of Figure 11.2 correspond to the right-hand side. As the customer requirements represent only an 'informal' description of the system, their transformation into a specification is capable of *validation* but not *verification*. We shall return to this point in Section 11.2 when we consider the extent of the application of formal methods.

In some cases systems are produced through a process of **incremental development**. Here, several versions of a system are produced sequentially, each with slightly different specifications. Usually this progression is planned from the outset, to allow a gradual enhancement of the system's capabilities. In this situation the development of a later version does not represent a transformation of the original specification, and verification of its operation must be performed against the modified definition of the system. Although much of the earlier verification work may be of relevance to later versions, the overall process of verification and validation must be performed separately for each revision.

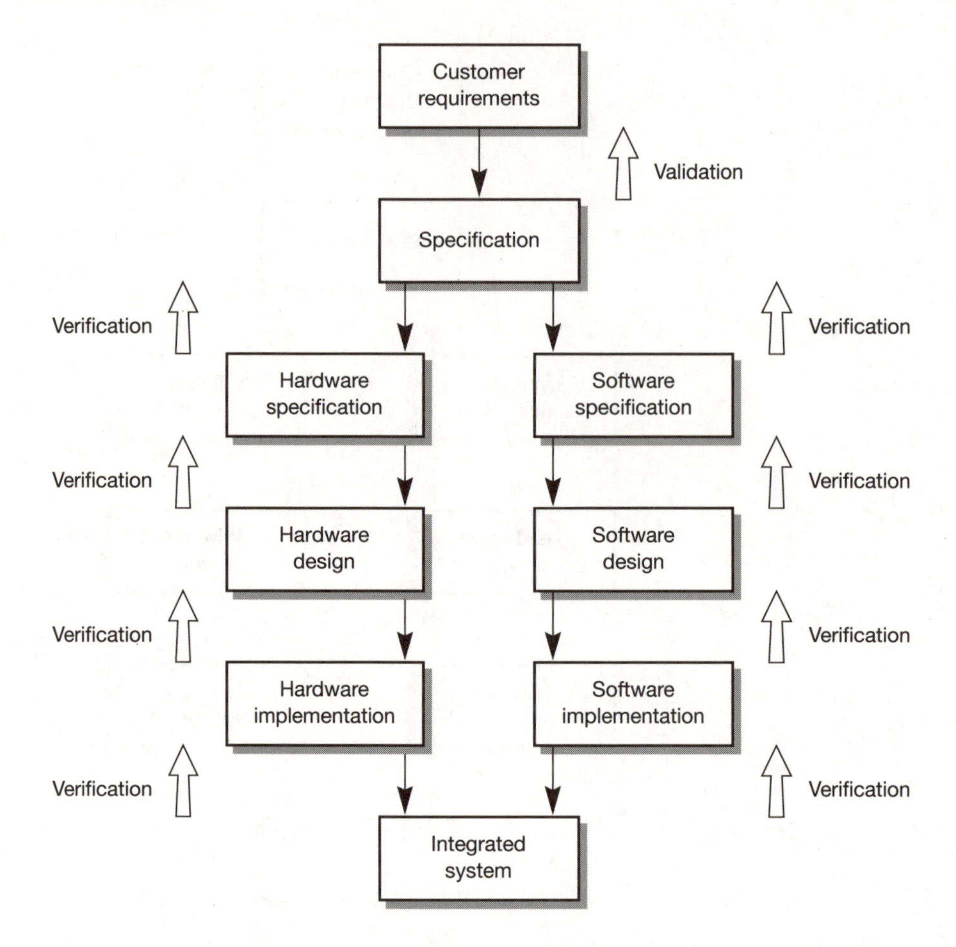

Figure 11.2 The formal verification process.

When a system is defined *informally* throughout its various phases of development, the process of verification relies heavily on engineering judgement and skill. If, for example, the top-level specification is written in a natural language, then considerable expertise will be required to demonstrate that this, together with all its possible ambiguities, is directly equivalent to the system defined by the hardware and software specifications. The use of formal methods offers a solution to this problem by defining the system at all levels in ways that allow functional comparison. The ultimate goal of formal methods is to allow the equivalence of each representation to be *proved*, thus demonstrating that the final system is a correct implementation of the original requirements. Various software tools are available to help in performing the various proofs required for verification; however, the process is far from automatic. Thus the use of formal methods does not remove the need for skilled engineers (far from it), but does change the form of the engineering judgements that are required. The main rationale for adopting a formal approach is that it can give greater confidence in the results of the verification process.

Another aspect of the use of formal descriptions for the input and output of each phase of development is the possibility of automating some of these development tasks. If we take, for example, the software development phases of the project, we see that the process starts with a software specification, which is translated into a software design and then into a software implementation. As the formal specification of the software defines precisely what the program should do, it would seem feasible to produce some form of translator that could convert the specification directly into code. What we require is a compiler that takes a design specification as its input. We could also imagine a hardware 'compiler' that would take as its input a hardware specification and produce a complete printed circuit board (PCB) or VLSI design. If we take this process one stage further we could conceive of a package that would take our original formal requirements documents and perform the complete software and hardware design for us.

Unfortunately, we are a long way from this Utopian situation, although automated tools can give a great deal of assistance. We noted when discussing Ada in Chapter 9 that this is often considered to be a **software design language**. Ada is a very 'formal' programming language, which goes some of the way to automating the software generation process by largely eliminating the 'programming' (implementation) phase. The input to the compiler is a description of the *design* of the software and the output is the executable code. Similarly, packages exist that greatly simplify the task of hardware design by translating hardware specifications directly into logic diagrams. These in turn can be converted into PCB or VLSI layouts to complete the implementation. It must be stressed that these tools do not complete these translations automatically, and that a great deal of ability is still required to produce a good design. However, they are an invaluable aid to a skilled design engineer.

Although offering several important advantages, the use of formal methods also imposes a considerable number of constraints on the development methods used. Because a chain is only as strong as its weakest link, formal proofs would need to be performed at each stage of the development to achieve maximum benefit. This has great implications for the design methods that can be used within the project. The use of formal proofs also relies heavily on the use of mathematical techniques that are foreign to many engineers. This may necessitate a considerable amount of retraining of staff to take full advantage of these techniques.

Because of the difficulties involved in performing formal proofs to show the equivalence of the various transformations of the specification of a system, recent work has looked at techniques aimed at proving particular properties of a system, rather than its complete correctness. Such techniques can be used to demonstrate that a system satisfies its safety requirements, without attempting to prove that all aspects of the system's implementation are correct. This more limited goal simplifies the problem considerably and allows the production of tools that can perform the necessary proofs quickly and largely automatically.

The history and importance of formal methods

The use of formal mathematical techniques in the design of computer-based equipment dates back to the early 1970s. The impetus for the work came not from considerations of safety, but from concerns over security. Even before the widespread phenomenon of 'computer hackers' governments were concerned about the security of sensitive information stored within their computers. Much work was done to develop so-called 'security kernels' that could be added on top of a conventional operating system to protect data from alteration or observation. This required a clear, unambiguous definition of the security regulations that defined the access rights to this data, and resulted in a 'security model' described in mathematical terms. This led on to the more widespread use of formal specifications as a means of removing the ambiguities associated with natural languages.

During the 1980s computers were increasingly used in real-time control and other situations where their failure could have serious consequences. In order to improve the dependability of these systems, mathematical techniques were borrowed from the security sector and new methods of design and verification were developed. At the forefront of this work were major research teams at the Universities of Oxford, Cambridge and Edinburgh, and at RSRE in the UK, and at MIT, Stanford, SRI and the University of Texas in the USA.

By the end of the 1980s the field of formal methods had advanced to a point where a number of well-respected tools and techniques had been developed. However, the industrial use of the techniques remained very limited and many developers still considered it an untried technology. This situation was brought into focus in 1991, when the UK Ministry of Defence issued Interim Defence Standard 00-55 (MoD, 1991), which made some aspects of formal methods mandatory for the software of all safety-critical military projects.

Industry's response to the new defence standard was hostile. Contractors considered that they were being forced to adopt a development methodology that was untested and too expensive. They collectively voiced the opinion that the necessary tools were either not available, or were too immature for use in critical projects. They also identified the shortage of trained staff as a major problem. Learned institutions such as the Institution of Electrical Engineers (IEE) and the British Computer Society (BCS) were drawn into the argument, with committees and special interest groups putting forward views for or against the mandatory use of formal methods. In response to the debate, the Ministry of Defence softened its position slightly by accepting the problems of tool availability, but saying that only by issuing such a standard could they encourage software suppliers to develop the necessary tools.

Standards produced since the publication of Interim Defence Standard 00-55 have been varied in their requirements concerning the use of formal methods. The draft of IEC 1508 recommends the use of formal methods, as does a recent standard from the European Space Agency (ESA, 1991). However, the civil aviation standard DO-178B (RTCA/EUROCAE, 1992) lists the use of such techniques under 'alternative methods', saying that at the time of its publication they were of 'inadequate maturity' or of 'limited applicability for airborne systems'. As a result of the comments within this standard the Federal Aviation Authority (FAA) and NASA in the USA provided funding for an investigation into the use of formal methods. The resulting report, produced by John Rushby (1993), concludes that

> 'Formal methods should be part of the education of every computer scientist and software engineer, just as the appropriate branch of applied maths is a necessary part of the education of all other engineers.'

However, he also observed that

> '... it will be many years before even a small proportion of those working in industry have been exposed to a thorough grounding in formal methods, and it is simply impractical to demand large scale application of formal methods in airborne software...'

By the start of 1996 it was possible to identify only a handful of industrial projects that had been developed using a *fully* 'formal' approach. The shortage of mature tools and of experienced staff remains a problem, and it seems unlikely that these difficulties will disappear in the near future. However, although relatively few companies have adopted a wholly formal approach, the introduction of certain formal methods within the lifecycle is now well established. Perhaps the most widely used of these are the techniques associated with the production of unambiguous requirements and specification documents. Also in common use are various automated tools that use formal methods to improve the dependability of the design process (particularly in the development of software). Techniques which are less often used include those associated with mathematical proofs of correctness. These methods require highly skilled staff with a particular flair for mathematics. They are also extremely time-consuming and expensive. For these reasons proofs of correctness are normally reserved for projects of the very highest levels of integrity.

A few years ago it seemed possible that the use of formal methods would come to dominate the development of safety-critical systems. The image of systems being designed semi-automatically from formal specifications to produce *proven* implementations was very appealing. However, formal methods have not yet lived up to this dream, and it seems unlikely that they ever will. The use of formal verification methods throughout the complete development of a system is extremely expensive, and is only justifiable in a small number of highly critical applications. However, in such projects these techniques represent the current state of the art in developing dependable systems. In less critical applications it is impractical to use formal design and verification techniques throughout the development process, although judicious use of selected methods can be very beneficial.

The widespread use of formal methods lies not in the rigorous proof of each aspect of the complete development of systems, but in the discriminating use of selected techniques. Many critical projects now make use of some form of formal methods, either in their specification or in their design, and this is likely to be an increasing trend. Within the remainder of this chapter we shall look at several aspects of the subject, but concentrate on those issues of most relevance to the majority of engineers. The author makes no excuse for this very long introductory section. Formal methods are much misunderstood and a grasp of the fundamental principles is essential. In the remainder of this introduction we shall look at the basis for the use of mathematics within engineering systems and at the restrictions imposed by the use of digital techniques. We shall then look briefly at the use of discrete mathematics and mathematical logic. The material within the remainder of this section is very elementary and readers with a basic understanding of these topics might like to go immediately to Section 11.2.

Why 'formal' methods?

'Conventional' mathematical techniques assume that quantities are **continuous**; that is, that they change smoothly from one value to another without any discontinuities. Most physical quantities, such as temperature, pressure and humidity, are continuous in nature, at least when viewed on a macroscopic scale. This enables many physical systems to be '**modelled**' by creating a mathematical analogy of their behaviour. Such models increase our understanding of a system's characteristics and allow us to predict what it will do in a range of circumstances.

The use of mathematical modelling is at the heart of all forms of control engineering. Figure 11.3(a) shows a simple model of a basic control system. Here an input signal, representing the desired output of the arrangement, is compared with the actual output to produce an error signal. This is fed to some form of **controller** that uses this signal, together with knowledge of the **process** being controlled (the **plant**), to produce appropriate control signals. If the system is designed correctly, the signals produced by the controller will drive the process so that its output will follow the input signal. The starting point for the design of the controller in this arrangement is the **transfer function** of the process being controlled, G_p. This is a mathematical representation of its operation, derived either from a knowledge of its form or by observation. Once the nature of the plant is understood, several standard design techniques are available to assist in the design of a controller to produce the desired operation. Where the process is essentially linear within the normal operating range of the system, the design of the controller is relatively straightforward. However, the presence of non-linearities or time delays within its characteristics make the design task more onerous.

The initial design of the control system takes the form of a second transfer function, G_c, representing the controller required. As the plant we are considering has a continuous nature, the controller will also be described by a transfer function that is continuous. The next stage of the design process is to decide on a method of implementing this transfer function to produce an

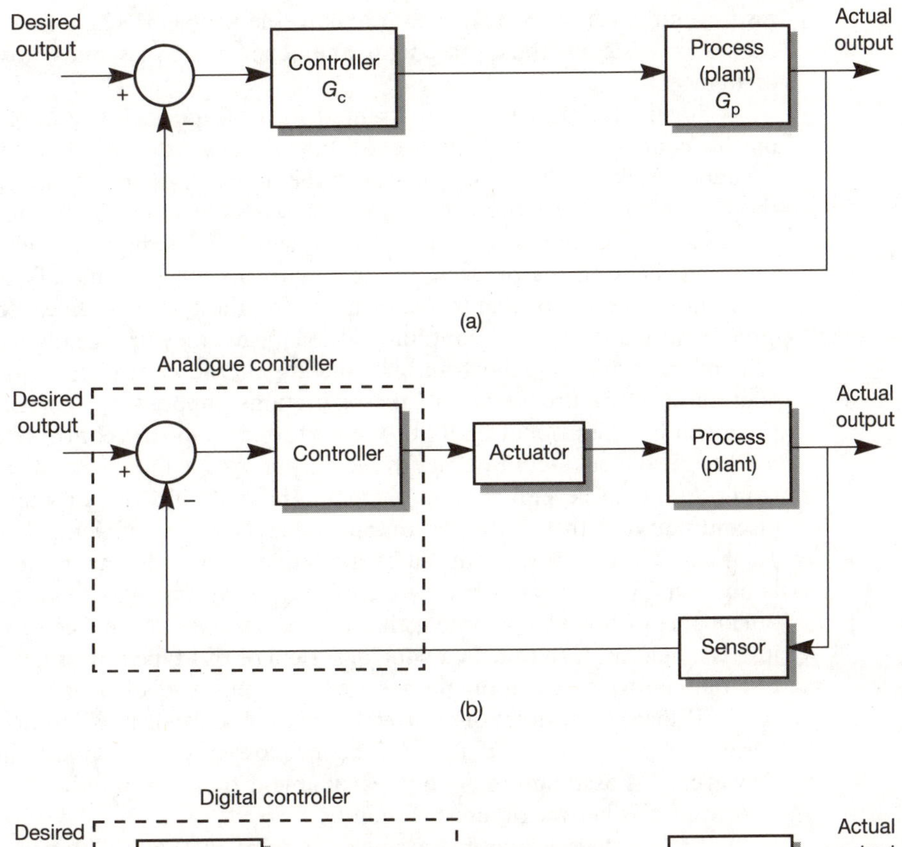

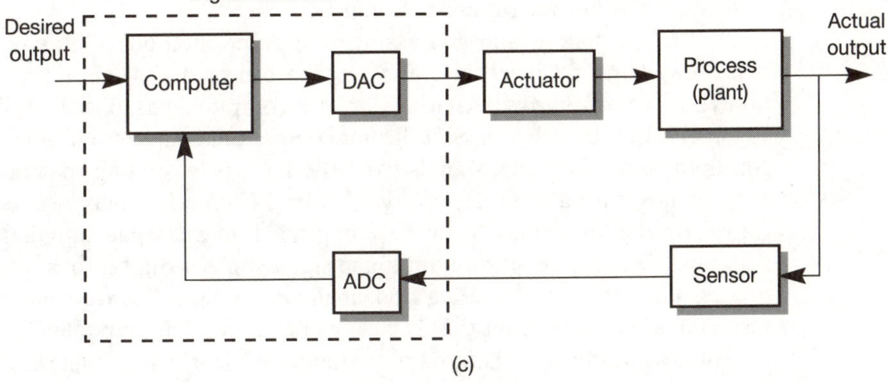

Figure 11.3 Analogue and digital control systems: (a) a model of a simple control system; (b) an analogue implementation; (c) a computer-based implementation.

operational system. In some cases it might be feasible to achieve the required features using mechanical, or perhaps hydraulic, components, but here we will restrict ourselves to electronic solutions to the problem. This allows two main classes of systems: those based on analogue techniques and those that are digital.

Figure 11.3(b) shows the essential form of an analogue implementation of the control system of Figure 11.3(a). It can be seen that the primary difference between these two figures is the addition of an actuator, by which the controller affects the process, and a sensor, by which it determines the plant's state. The presence of these components affects the relationship between the controller and the process, and it may be necessary to modify the transfer function of the controller to compensate for these effects. Because analogue circuits normally produce continuous waveforms, they are ideally suited to the task of implementing the transfer function of the controller, which is itself continuous in nature. Owing to the restrictions imposed by any real circuitry, there will be operational limits to the performance of the controller, but these need not produce discontinuities in the output. The avoidance of discontinuities is important for several reasons, perhaps the most obvious of which is that a discontinuity in the controller output suggests that a violent change in the plant's output could be produced by a relatively small change in the input. This is not usually the desired behaviour of such a system. A second, perhaps less obvious, reason is that a system that can be assumed to be free of discontinuities is much easier to test. In a control system of this type it would be normal to test the controller by applying a series of inputs spread over its operational range. If the system functions correctly at two closely situated points, it may be reasonable to assume that it will function correctly at all points in between. However, this assumption is only reasonable if there are no abrupt changes or discontinuities between these two points.

An alternative and increasingly popular method of implementing the control system of Figure 11.3(a) is by the use of digital circuitry. This might take the form of 'hardwired' logic, or of a computer-based system, as shown in Figure 11.3(c). In either case additional components are required to convert the continuous, or analogue, signals from the sensors (assuming that these produce such signals) into a discrete, or digital, form. Converters may also be needed to transform digital signals from the computer into analogue signals to drive the actuators. The conversion of analogue signals into a digital form is a two-stage process consisting of **sampling** and **analogue-to-digital conversion** (**ADC**). This results in a representation that is a series of discrete measurements separated by abrupt discontinuities. This data is therefore clearly no longer continuous in nature.

The discontinuous nature of a digital representation of the signals within our system does not prevent us from successfully producing the functions of our controller. Nyquist's theorem suggests that if we sample at a sufficiently high rate we need lose no information as a result of this sampling, and by digitizing to an adequate resolution quantization effects can be minimized. The various mathematical operations required to implement the transfer function required for the controller can also be achieved using the various techniques that are widely used in digital signal processing. Thus, by taking care in the design of our system we should be able to produce a controller in which the output signals are equivalent to those produced by an analogue system. Indeed, there are many advantages to the use of digital rather than analogue approaches, including such considerations as accuracy and repeatability. When the digital systems are computer based they also offer the advantages of flexibility and reprogrammability, among many others. However, when considering the many advantages of digital systems in such applications it is also important to note that they do have some disadvantages.

One of the primary problems associated with the use of digital techniques in critical applications is that testing becomes more difficult. We noted earlier that when testing a system that has a continuous nature we can perform tests at various positions within its operational range and make inferences about its operation between these points. Because digital hardware and software are discrete in nature, a slowly varying input signal need not produce a smooth variation at the output. To illustrate this point, consider the following assignment statement:

$$z = (2 * x * x)/(x - 27) - (54 * x)/(x - 27)$$

Given integer values of x, and assuming the numbers used are small enough to avoid an overflow, this statement will return a value equal to $2x$ for all values of x except 27, for which the output is indeterminate. For this unique value of x the output will depend on the language and possibly even the compiler used (the differences between languages in respect of arithmetic exceptions is discussed in Chapter 9). Although this example is somewhat contrived, it does illustrate that we cannot assume that small changes in the input to a program will result in small changes at the output.

If we cannot rely on evidence from samples within the input space to investigate the behaviour of our system, it would seem that we need to test its performance in response to all possible combinations of its inputs. To investigate the implications of such an approach, consider the arrangement of Figure 11.4. This shows a position control system that takes three inputs corresponding to X, Y and Z coordinates, and generates appropriate signals to drive some form of mechanism to that position. Feedback signals from sensors on the machine are used to guide the controller's actions.

It can be seen that the controller in Figure 11.4 has three 10-bit input signals plus a further three 10-bit feedback signals. Thus the number of unique input and feedback combinations is equal to 2^{60}, or about 1.15×10^{18}. If it were possible to perform a test to verify the output of one of these states in only one microsecond, it would take nearly 40 000 years to test all of the possible states. This test would not be sufficient, however, as it takes no account of the possible influence of the sequence of input states.

Faced with our inability to extrapolate from the behaviour of individual points, and the impracticability of exhaustively testing the complete input space, we clearly need another method of investigating the behaviour of digital

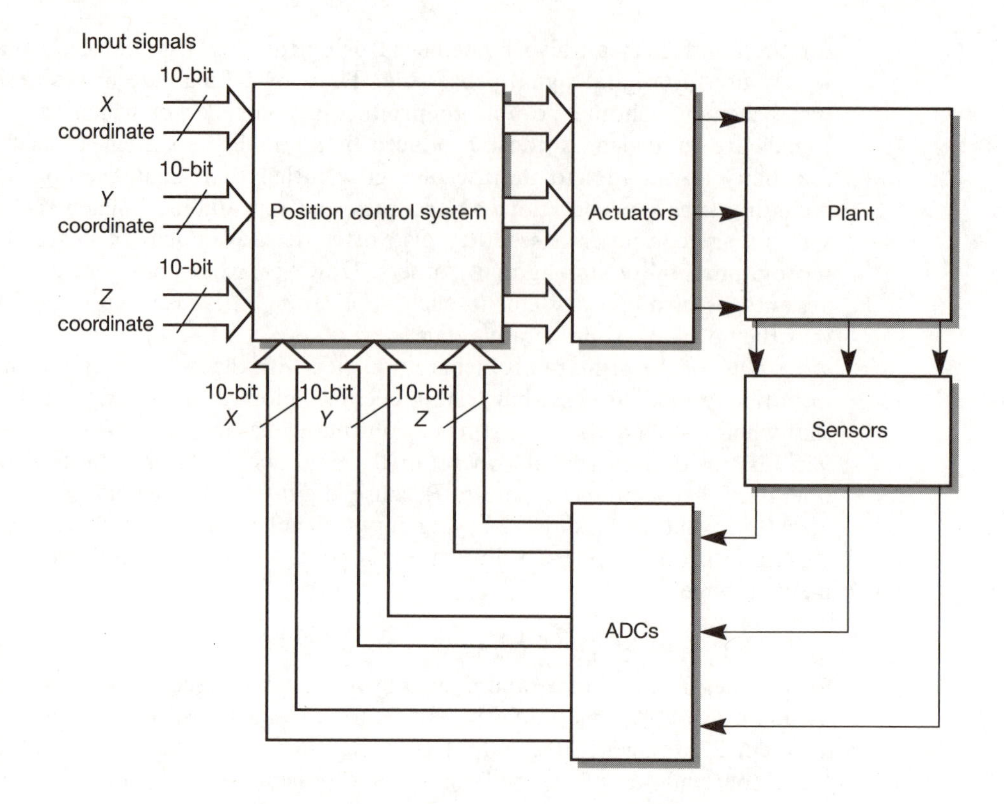

Figure 11.4 A three-coordinate positioning system.

systems. To achieve this we need to move away from the conventional mathematics that we use for continuous quantities, to **discrete mathematics**, which is specifically designed for this purpose.

Discrete mathematics

Whereas conventional 'continuous' mathematics is used to calculate numerical values for variables within mathematical models, discrete mathematics is used to prove theorems related to the characteristics of quantities. Thus instead of determining that a variable x has a value of 127, we might use a theorem to prove that for *all* values of y within a given range, x satisfies the condition that $125 \leqslant x < 130$. Using proofs based on mathematical induction it is possible to investigate the response of a system to a very large or even infinite number of discrete input states, thereby removing the need to make inferences from a limited number of observations.

Formal methods are based on the use of discrete mathematics and the use of mathematical logic. They allow digital systems to be described, or modelled, in a *complete* way, which makes no assumptions of continuity.

Mathematical logic

All formal methods are based on the use of mathematical logic, and although it is not within the scope of this book to fully describe this topic, it is perhaps relevant to mention some of the general concepts involved. Readers requiring more information might like to consider the excellent introduction given in the Appendix of John Rushby's paper on formal methods. This is listed as suggested further reading at the end of this chapter.

Logic may be defined as:

'The science of reasoning, proof, thinking or inference'

and we are all familiar with basic examples of logical reasoning, such as:

John is older than Jill.
Jill is older than Paul.
Therefore, John is older than Paul.

It is tempting to think that logic is in some way an absolute science, and that there would therefore be only one form of logic. However, we shall see that this is not the case.

Within formal methods we are primarily interested in 'formal logic' – that is, logic that is associated with the *form* of statements rather than their content. For example, if we look at the above example comparing the ages of John, Jill and Paul, we see that we can deduce the soundness of the statements without any knowledge of the three individuals concerned. However, in order to do this we *do* need to know the meaning of the term 'older'.

If we construct some alternative logical statements we can remove the need for a knowledge of the term 'older', for example:

A is a member of *B*.
All *B*s are members of *C*.
Therefore *A* is a member of *C*.

In this example we require no knowledge of the nature of *A*, *B* or *C* in order to realize the soundness of the reasoning. However, we do need to understand what is meant by terms such as 'all' and 'member'. We therefore have the scope to define a range of '**logics**' that each take a number of key words (such as 'all', 'and', 'or' and 'except') and assign to them very precise meanings. This similarly allows us to define a wide range of different formal methods.

Logics differ not only in the list of key words that they use, but also in the sophistication of the concepts they can represent. Although there are many formal systems used, many of the important techniques may be divided into a number of classes.

Propositional calculus

This is the simplest form of formal logic, allowing symbols to be combined using two basic 'connectives'. These represent the key words 'implies', which is normally represented by the symbol '$\supset$', and 'not', for which the symbol '$\neg$' is used. Strings of these symbols may be used to construct formulas, and well-formed, self-contained formulas are termed 'sentences'. Thus, if

Q represents a red sky at sun-set, and
R represents bad weather tomorrow

then a possible relationship between them could be written as

$$Q \supset (\neg R)$$

which would be interpreted as:

'a red sky at sun-set implies good weather the following day.'

Expressions may be combined to form more complex relationships and additional connectives can be formed, simplifying the representation of complicated propositions.

Predicate calculus (or first-order logic)

Propositional calculus is very limited in its ability to represent even quite simple logical relationships. In particular, it treats its various 'propositions' as being separate entities, making it impossible to represent connected events. Predicate calculus is an extension to this basic technique that allows the use of 'variables' which can occur in several propositions, greatly increasing its expressive power. The grammar of predicate calculus defines several additional symbols, and permits, for example, expressions of the form

$$\forall x : (\exists y : y = x + 1)$$

Here the symbol $\forall$ represents 'for all' and the $\exists$ symbol may be read as 'there exists'. The above expression may therefore be interpreted as

'for each x, there is some y such that $y = x + 1$'

We might also write expressions of the form

$$\forall z : \text{Prime}(z) \supset \neg\text{Prime}(z + 7)$$

which would be interpreted as

'for each z, if z is a prime number then, $z + 7$ is not'

First-order theories

There are a number of theories that add axioms and inference rules to the predicate calculus. These include theories related to equality (or identity), arithmetic, set theory and the use of data types. These extensions greatly enhance the expressive power of the calculus and provide many features that are essential to formal methods.

Higher-order logic

Higher-order logic, as its name implies, is a more sophisticated logic that allows the use of functions that can take other functions as their arguments, and which can return functions as their result. Higher-order logic is notationally complex, but has many properties that are convenient in the field of formal methods. Most of the more advanced formal verification techniques are based on the use of higher-order logic.

Mathematical logic and formal methods

The general term 'formal methods' covers a wide range of techniques based on the use of discrete mathematics and mathematical logic. These use logics of different types and of varying levels of sophistication. In the next section we shall look at some of these methods and discuss their characteristics and use.

11.2 Formal methods within the development lifecycle

Formal methods may be used in a number of ways within the development of a system. These may be categorized in terms of the rigour with which they are used and the sections of the system to which they are applied.

Rigour in the application of formal methods

Rushby (1993), in his paper on formal methods, identifies four levels of rigour in the application of formal methods:

Level 0 *No use of formal methods*
Documents are written in natural languages, pseudocode or a programming language, augmented with diagrams and equations. Verification is a manual process of review and inspection. Validation is based on testing that is determined by the nature of the requirements, the specification and program structure.

Level 1 *Use of concepts and notation from discrete mathematics*
Here some of the natural language components of requirements and specification documents are replaced with notations and concepts derived from logic and discrete mathematics. This does not represent a full adoption of a formal approach, and proofs, if any, are performed informally. The advantages gained by incorporating these elements of formalism into an otherwise informal approach include the provision of a compact notation that can reduce ambiguities. It also provides a systematic framework that can aid the mental processes involved.

Level 2 *Use of formalized specification languages with some mechanized support tools*
Specification languages provide a standardized notation for discrete mathematics and usually provide some automated methods of checking for certain classes of faults. At this level proofs are normally conducted informally, and are referred to as **rigorous proofs** (rather than formal proofs). However, several methods provide explicit formal rules of deduction that would permit formal proof, albeit manually.

Level 3 *Use of fully formal specification languages with comprehensive support environments, including mechanized theorem proving or proof checking*
The most formal of methods use specification languages that employ a strictly defined logic and that provide techniques for the use of **formal proofs**. The complete formalism of proving methods permits the use of mechanized techniques, including proof checkers and theorem provers. **Proof checkers** are used to check the steps of a proof produced by an engineer, whereas **theorem provers** attempt to discover proofs without human assistance. The advantages of the use of a fully formal approach are that it greatly increases the probability of detecting faults within the various descriptions of the system, and that the use of mechanized proving techniques effectively removes the possibility of faulty reasoning. Among the disadvantages associated with such methods are the considerable effort, and hence expense, involved in their use, and the fact that the languages involved are generally very restrictive and often difficult to use.

It can be seen that the term 'formal methods' may be applied to a wide range of techniques, from the introduction of some discrete mathematics to the use of a specification language with mechanized theorem proving. When engineers use the term they often discount techniques associated with levels 0 and 1 as described above, and consider only more rigorous approaches. In Europe the term is commonly applied to all methods within levels 2 and 3, whereas in North America the title is often reserved for the most formal techniques within level 3. Within this text we shall adopt a broader definition of the term, and look at techniques within all levels.

Decisions concerning the appropriate choice of development methods for a given application will be greatly affected by the integrity level of the application, and by the elements of the project concerned. Many development projects can be handled successfully without the use of formal methods, by using techniques classified above as level 0. Where the objective is simply to analyse the correctness of particular algorithms or mechanisms, the rigour associated with level 1 techniques may be appropriate. Alternatively, if the nature of the project suggests the use of a formalized specification together with manual review procedures, then level 2 methods might be suitable. Where an element of a highly critical system is crucial and contains many complicated mechanisms or architectures, the mechanized theorem proving of level 3 techniques might be suggested.

Extent of the application of formal methods

In Figure 11.2 we looked at the various transformations of the description of a system throughout its development. The figure also indicated the steps required to verify this process. Formal methods may be applied to none, some or all of the various transformation and verification activities. We may also choose to apply such methods to the complete system, or only to selected components or subsystems. Alternatively, we may decide to use formal methods to verify only certain characteristics of the system, such as those connected with safety. Having decided that a formal approach is relevant for certain aspects of the development, we must then decide on the appropriate level for each task. It may be necessary to adopt a number of different formal methods, perhaps of different levels, for the various aspects of the development process.

The use of different formal methods for the various stages of system development allows the most suitable techniques to be used for each aspect of the work. Some languages, for example, are ideal for describing the top-level characteristics of a system, whereas others are more suitable for performing the gate-level hardware design. However, when attempting to perform a complete, formal verification of a system using mechanized techniques at level 3, the use of different languages produces considerable difficulties. Although the proof-checking or theorem-proving facilities within the tools can be used to verify the equivalence of different descriptions of the system, this is only possible when they are written in the same language. If different languages are used the formal descriptions must be translated, creating a further process that requires verification. Experience shows that such translations are very difficult to verify. A solution to this problem would be to use a single language for all phases of the system's development. Unfortunately, no single language is suitable for such a broad range of tasks, and this difficulty remains a major barrier to the complete verification of systems.

The need for different development techniques within the various phases of a project is brought about by the differing nature of the information being manipulated at each stage. The first major transformation of the description of the system occurs during the **requirements analysis** phase. This involves taking the customer requirements and from them generating an unambiguous specification. The inputs to this process are the customer's perceived needs, which are, of necessity, not formally documented. Although several automated tools are available to assist in the task of **requirements capture**, there are limits to the degree of formality that may be introduced into this process. Ultimately, the specification must be reviewed by the customer to see that it fulfils the needs of the application, rather than the requirements document. Therefore, there is limited scope for the use of formal methods during this phase. For this reason, the process of generating a specification from the customer requirements is normally considered to be capable of *validation*, rather than *verification*. This distinction is indicated in Figure 11.2.

Formal methods are most widely used in the production of unambiguous specifications, but are also applied within later development phases. In the following sections we shall look at several aspects of the use of formal methods in the development of safety-critical systems.

11.3 Formal specification languages

Formal specification languages provide a precise vocabulary, syntax and set of semantics for the description of system characteristics. Such languages describe the system, not its design, and therefore impose very few constraints on the implementation of the system. They do not, for example, affect whether particular parts of the system are constructed using hardware or software techniques.

One of the most straightforward methods of specification is to define the relationships between objects algebraically. This approach is commonly used in association with abstract data types. One of the most widely used **algebraic specification languages** is **OBJ** (Futatsugi *et al.*, 1985). This is a formal, executable specification language that can be used to specify functional behaviour in terms of rules that are expressed as equations. It can also be used to add formality to object-oriented design, or for the specification of Ada packages. Although the use of executable languages such as OBJ is straightforward, the specifications produced are large and therefore difficult to check.

Alternatives to the use of algebraic techniques include **model-based specification languages**. These rely on the production of a model of the system, based on mathematical entities. This results in a specification that is only a fraction of the size of an equivalent specification written in a language such as OBJ. The best-known examples of the model-based approach are VDM and Z.

The **Vienna Development Method (VDM)** was originally developed at IBM's Vienna research laboratories in Austria (Jones, 1990). It comprises a formal language for specifying the behaviour of a system, along with techniques for producing designs and programs that conform to this specification. VDM specifications are composed of **operations** that each have a **state** consisting of external entities with which it interacts. It may also have **pre-conditions** and **post-conditions**. The basic form of a simple operation is shown below.

```
NAME
ext     < list of external variables >
pre     < list of pre-conditions >
post    < list of post-conditions >
```

External variables may be defined as being **read only** (rd) or **read and write** (wr). Operations may use values of read-only variables but may not change them. Variables that are defined as having read-and-write access rights may be used and modified by the operation. This declaration might take the form:

```
ext   rd   temperature : ℕ
      rd   pressure    : ℕ
      wr   control     : ℝ
```

The symbol $\mathbb{N}$ represents a standard **type** which contains all the **natural numbers** (that is, the positive numbers 0, 1, 2, 3...). Similarly, $\mathbb{R}$ represents the set of **real numbers** between positive and negative infinity. These types are not restricted in range (or, in the case of real numbers, in resolution) by limitations imposed by any physical implementation of the system. Such issues must be considered explicitly within the specification. Another standard type is the **Boolean** type, represented by the symbol $\mathbb{B}$. This can take only the values *true* and *false*.

Pre-conditions represent the assumptions that may be made concerning the state of the operation before its execution. These take the form of one or more **predicates**, that is, expressions that are either true or false. The predicates are expressions consisting of variables, operators, function names and curly brackets. The syntax of these expressions forms part of the definition of VDM. A typical precondition might be of the form:

```
pre    temperature > 0 and
       temperature < 255
```

The action taken by the system in the event that the pre-conditions are *not* met, is not defined by the specification.

Post-conditions define all the things that must be achieved by the operation during its execution, provided that the pre-conditions were met before it started. Post-conditions are also in the form of predicates written in the syntax of the method. These might look something like the following:

```
post   output = (temperature – offset)
       and
       error = (temperature – req_temperature)
```

VDM also permits the use of conditional predicates using, for example, WHILE or IF...THEN...ELSE structures.

```
post  if s1 = s2 then
        output1 = t1 and
        output2 = d1
      else
        output1 = t2 and
        output2 = d2
```

The notation provides a rich assortment of operators and quantifiers, allowing complex conditions to be expressed succinctly. A complete operation might look something like this:

```
HEATER

ext   rd  temp1         : ℕ
      rd  set_point     : ℕ
      wr  heat_control  : ℕ

pre   temp1 > 0 and
      set_point > 0

post  if temp1 > set_point then
        heat_control = 10
      else
        if temp1 > (temp1 – 20) then
          heat_control = 5
        else
          heat_control = 0
```

An operation may be defined in terms of an algorithm. This produces a definition that resembles a program but is used to *define* the system, not to *implement* it. Algorithms may also include other operations, allowing complex systems to be defined in a modular or hierarchical manner. Ideally these components should be largely self-contained, and should each represent a particular aspect of the system. In the following example DISPLAY_LEVEL and LOG_LEVEL are previously defined operations.

```
VALVE_CONTROL

ext   rd  level      : ℕ
      rd  min_level  : ℕ
      wr  valve      : 𝔹

begin
      if level < min_level
        valve = true
      else
        valve = false
      DISPLAY_LEVEL
      LOG_LEVEL
end
```

```
┌── Schema_name ─────────────────────────
│ Schema signature
├──────────────────
│ Schema predicate
└────────────────────────────────────────
```

Figure 11.5 The form of a Z schema.

Despite the simplicity of the examples given above, the notation of VDM is complex and makes use of several symbols that are unique to the language. Consequently it is seen by many as complicated and time-consuming to learn. VDM is also designed primarily to deal with sequential systems and, like conventional mathematics, has no concept of time. It can be extended to cope with temporal considerations but such techniques do not cope well with the concurrency present within complex control applications.

Z was developed at the University of Oxford and is based on typed set theory and predicate calculus (Spivey, 1992). It makes use of graphical techniques to increase the readability of the specification and permits the addition of explanatory text to enhance understanding. A specification in Z comprises a collection of **schemas**, where each schema defines relationships between specific entities. (It could be argued that one should use the word 'schemata' as the plural of schema, but most engineers (and most textbooks) refer to 'schemas'.) The basic form of a schema is shown in Figure 11.5. The name of the schema is followed by a section termed the schema 'signature', which declares the entities used. The next section is termed the schema predicate or body. This uses a form of predicate logic to define relationships between the entities declared within the signature.

An example of a simple schema is shown in Figure 11.6. This declares three quantities: *oil_pressure*, *min_pressure* and *max_pressure*, each of which are of type $\mathbb{N}$, the built-in type representing natural numbers. The body of the schema contains two predicates combined by the '$\wedge$' connective, which may be read as 'and'. The body may therefore be read as '*oil_pressure* is greater than *min_pressure* and *oil_pressure* is less than *max_pressure*'. This schema therefore simply states that the three entities represent positive, discrete quantities, and that the value of *oil_pressure* must lie between those of *min_pressure* and *max_pressure*.

```
┌── Oil ─────────────────────────────────
│ oil_pressure: ℕ
│ min_pressure: ℕ
│ max_pressure: ℕ
├──────────────────
│ oil_pressure > min_pressure ∧ oil_pressure < max_pressure
└────────────────────────────────────────
```

Figure 11.6 The Oil schema.

```
— Alarm ————————————————————————
level      :  ℕ
trip_level :  ℕ
siren      :  {off, on}
————————————
level > trip_level  ⟺  siren = on
————————————————————————————————
```

Figure 11.7 The Alarm schema.

A second schema is shown in Figure 11.7. This defines two entities of type $\mathbb{N}$, and a third, *siren*, which can take the values 'on' or 'off'. The body of this schema contains the '$\Longleftrightarrow$' connective. This represents an equivalence of the associated predicates. Thus the two predicates are either both true or both false. In this case it is clear that if *level* is greater than *trip_level* then the *siren* will be 'on'; if not, *siren* will be 'off'.

Once a schema has been defined it may be referenced within other schemas, as illustrated in Figure 11.8. This shows how a schema called *Oil_Check* may be formed using the two schemas already defined.

A specification based on previously defined schemas includes the signatures and predicates within those schemas. Thus a hierarchy of schemas may be assembled to simplify the construction of the complete specification. The hierarchical structure of Z allows the content of a specification to be divided into a number of manageable sections, in very much the same way as in VDM. Z is in many ways similar to VDM, and also has no predefined method of dealing with temporal issues. Again it is possible to extend the language to incorporate time, but the resulting notation is still limited in its ability to model concurrency.

Although both VDM and Z are widely used for sequential applications, both have difficulties with concurrent systems. Notations for expressing **concurrency** are normally based on **temporal logics** or **process algebras**. These are extensions to predicate calculus, or other logical techniques, that incorporate time. A great deal of research is currently under way in this area, but many problems remain to be solved and few languages have gained commercial credibility in this area.

```
— Oil_Check ————————————————————
Oil
Alarm
————————————
level        = oil_pressure
min_pressure = 0
max_pressure = 100
trip_level   = 70
————————————————————————————————
```

Figure 11.8 The Oil_Check schema.

The formal languages most commonly used within industry are probably VDM and Z for sequential systems and LOTOS (Bolognesi and Brinksma, 1987) and CCS (Moller and Tofts, 1989) for concurrent applications. All these methods would be classified as level 2 techniques, following the conventions outlined in Section 11.2. No level 3 techniques are widely used within industry, but this classification includes HOL, PVS and the Boyer–Moore theorem prover. HOL was developed at the University of Cambridge and is used primarily in the UK (Gordon and Melham, 1993). PVS was developed by SRI and is used primarily in the USA, including NASA (Owre *et al.*, 1992). The Boyer–Moore theorem prover was developed at the University of Texas and is used mainly in North America (Boyer and Moore, 1988).

Validation of formal specifications

The use of a formal language in the production of a specification does not guarantee its correctness. As the specification is based on an inherently informally defined customer requirement, there is always the possibility of the needs of the project being misunderstood. It is also conceivable that some mistake has been made in the construction of the specification.

In order to gain confidence in the correctness of a formal specification several types of testing may be employed. These may be divided into those that check the structure and form of the specification, and those that look at its functionality.

Most formal languages have associated tool sets that permit various forms of checking to be performed semi-automatically. Such tests would include an investigation of the internal consistency of the specification and some rigorous typechecking. The structure of the specification would also be analysed.

Although the specification can be tested largely automatically to confirm that it meets various structural and language rules, such tests do not show that the specification satisfies the requirements of the system. In order to achieve this, it is necessary to demonstrate that the functionality of the specification is correct. As it is not possible to *prove* the equivalence of a formal specification and an informal requirement, a more objective method of assessment is required.

Emulation of the specification

We noted in Chapter 9 the advantages of the use of **software prototypes** (or **animation**) as a method of validating the specification. When the specification is written in a natural language the process of animation requires a program to be written to emulate the system described within it. When a system is defined formally it may be possible to automate the process of producing an executable form of the specification.

Some specification languages are directly executable, the most widely used being **OBJ**. A specification written in such a language can be run on a suitable host machine to investigate its characteristics and to demonstrate its equivalence to the requirements. This emulation is used to investigate the functional properties of the system and does not attempt to replicate its timing characteristics. One advantage of this approach is that it allows the customer to confirm that the specification satisfies the requirements, even if the customer is not familiar with the formal language used. The emulation provides an early source of feedback, and can be invaluable in locating faults before implementation begins.

Despite the clear advantages of executable languages such as OBJ, they also have disadvantages. Executable specifications tend to be much larger than specifications written in VDM or Z. Consequently, they are more complex and harder to check. For this reason some workers discourage the use of executable languages in favour of specifications written in more conventional specification languages such as VDM (Wichmann, 1992). In order to produce an executable form of such a specification some translation must be performed. In VDM this may be achieved by replacing implicit specifications with executable equivalents (O'Neill, 1992). This represents the use of an *executable subset* of the language. Various tools are available to assist in this process and to translate the resulting document into an executable specification. Alternatively, specifications written in other languages may be translated into OBJ, or a conventional programming language, to produce an executable form for validation.

The use of formal specifications

Once a formal specification has been written and validated through the use of an executable version and by a process of review, it can be seen as a trusted, unambiguous representation of the required system. This specification will normally be used as an input to the design stage, and we shall be looking at this process in the following sections. In highly critical projects a formal specification may be used as the basis of formal proofs of correctness of the design and implementation of the system. However, as was mentioned earlier, few applications can justify the expense involved in such rigorous methods.

In some cases a formal specification is produced largely to provide an insight into the characteristics of the system and to help in the production of an optimized, informal specification. This informal document is then used as an input to later stages of the project.

11.4 Formal methods of design and implementation

The design process takes the system definition provided by the specification and transforms it into a form appropriate for implementation. The first phase of this, the architectural design, determines the overall structure of the required system and the nature of the interfaces between its various components. The output of this phase will include a series of specifications for the necessary hardware and software subsystems. A fundamental difference between the information contained within the architectural design and that within the specification is that the former describes how the system will be built, rather than what it should do.

In many cases there will be structural similarities between the architectural design and the specification. It may, for example, be appropriate to define a subsystem within the design to produce the functions associated with a given component of the specification. However, in general there will also be structural differences between the two descriptions of the system, because of constraints defined by the implementation. If, for example, the reliability requirements of the system dictate the use of fault tolerance, then a single function within the specification will map into multiple redundant subsystems in the design. Also, some design functions, such as those required for voting between redundant units, will not be represented within the specification at all. Structural changes may also be required for reasons of implementation efficiency, in terms of both cost and performance.

When formal methods are used within the design phases, the design techniques used will be greatly affected by the nature of the formal methods adopted. When using specification languages such as Z or VDM, design normally incorporates a series of **refinements**, as shown in Figure 11.9. Each refinement represents an incremental transformation of the definition of the system on its route to implementation. Several formal methods provide facilities for verifying the correctness of the relationships between the various specifications of the same system, although these techniques are less effective when there are significant structural changes between the specifications.

In order to simplify the verification process it would be advantageous to use a single formal language throughout the design process. However, formal specification languages, even if they are executable, are not suitable for the production of operational software. Similarly, such languages are normally inappropriate for the detailed design of hardware. For these reasons it is normal to perform the architectural design in the same language used for the formal specification, and, at some lower level, to translate the software and hardware specifications into other languages more suited to detailed design. The levels at which these translations are performed will be determined by the nature of the languages being used.

We noted in Chapter 9 that languages such as Ada may be considered as software design languages. When using such a language, the detailed design phase would be performed within the programming language and the process of implementation performed largely automatically by the compiler. Where less design-oriented languages are used, the detailed design may be performed separately from the process of coding that implements the software.

Detailed hardware design is normally performed using a hardware description language such as VHDL (Shahdad, 1986) or ELLA (Morison *et al.*, 1982). These often provide interfaces to computer-aided design packages

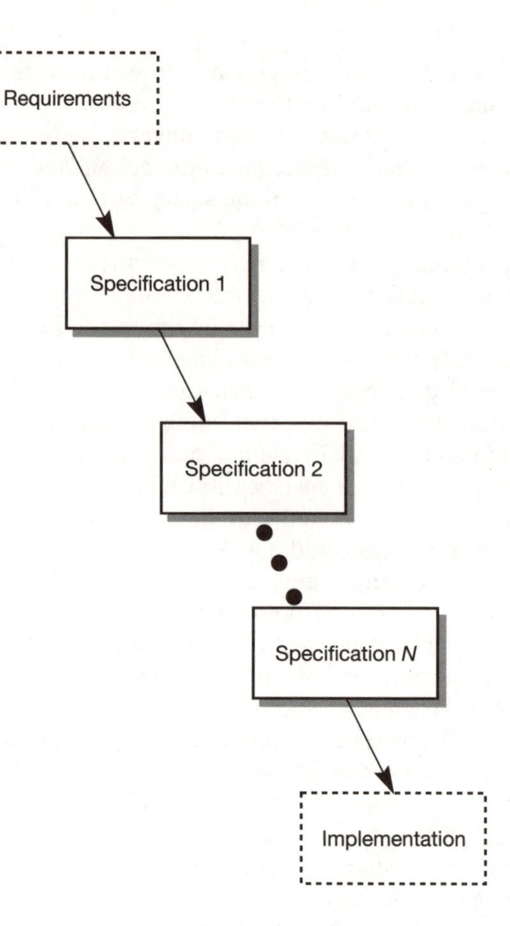

Figure 11.9 System design through repeated refinement of the specification.

for implementation in a PCB or VLSI form. Some formal methods, notably the Boyer–Moore approach, can be used for hardware design down to the gate level.

11.5 Formal methods and verification

When formal methods are used throughout the lifecycle of a system, **formal verification** can be used to prove that the resulting system satisfies the requirements set out in the specification. This process involves the use of mathematical **proofs** (which are often semi-automated) which are applied to each transformation of the specification. When completed, such verification gives great confidence in the correctness of the development process, and at present represents the 'state of the art' in development methods. Unfortunately, despite the use of automated tools, the process of formal verification is extremely time-consuming and requires a level of mathematical ability that is beyond the scope of many engineers. Thus, formal verification is reserved for projects of the highest levels of criticality that can justify the very large costs involved. It should also be noted that the use of formal proofs does not imply engineering perfection. Like any mathematical operation, proofs are only valid if they are performed correctly. It is possible for human error to invalidate the verification process as with any other method of assessment.

Because of the high costs involved it is unusual to apply formal methods throughout the development lifecycle. More commonly, such techniques are reserved for certain sections of the work where their use is thought to be appropriate. Formal verification can be used to prove the correctness of these aspects, although even when considering only part of the project, few projects can justify the costs involved. In most cases verification of the transformations between various formally defined stages is performed **rigorously** rather than formally. This might involve establishing the form that the necessary proofs might take, but would fall short of actually performing them. Such a verification might require an engineer to convince a review team that a formal proof *could* be performed, if required.

Using formal methods to prove system properties

An alternative to using formal methods to prove the correctness of a system is to use such methods to prove that a system has particular properties. Such an approach can sometimes be used to demonstrate the safety-related properties of a system in order to establish its overall safety. Unfortunately, given a general mathematical model of a system, such proofs are usually impossible.

A way of tackling this problem is to restrict the mathematical models used to those that will allow automated proofs. One method of achieving this is to use propositional logic, which consists of Boolean variables and connectives such as AND, OR and NOT. Using such models it is possible to prove particular properties, although the difficulty of the proofs increases with the complexity of the system being modelled.

Recently, a patented algorithm has been developed to tackle the problem of automating proofs in a range of industrial applications. This technique, known as Stålmarck's algorithm after its inventor, provides very fast proofs for problems that have a low 'degree of hardness' (Stålmarck and Säflund, 1990). This is determined by the least number of simultaneous assumptions involved. The hardness of a propositional formula is not determined by the number of variables involved, and thus a formula with over a million variables could still have a low degree of hardness and could therefore be proved quickly. Fortunately, industrial experience shows that people tend to design systems with a low degree of hardness, as this increases their understandability. Indeed, one could argue that all safety-critical systems should satisfy this requirement.

The use of propositional logic is best illustrated with the aid of a simple example. Here we will look at an example given by Parkin (1995) based on the use of **Prover**, a tool which implements Stålmarck's algorithm. The arrangement concerned is given in Figure 11.10, which shows a simple automotive circuit. Here a battery is connected to a radio and a brake switch through an ignition switch. An indicator light is illuminated when the brake switch is closed, provided that the ignition is *ON*. A separate switch can also activate this indicator, even if the ignition is *OFF*. A clear problem with this circuit is that there is a 'sneak path' whereby the radio will be activated when the ignition is *OFF*, if the brake and the switch are operated simultaneously.

The first stage of using Prover is to produce a description of the arrangement in propositional logic. To do this the items within the circuit are represented by the Boolean variables `Battery`, `Ignition`, `Brake`, `Switch`, `Radio` and `Indicator_light`. Thus, for example, the battery is *ON* when `Battery` is *True* and *OFF* when it is *False*. The interactions between the components may then be entered into the tool in a number of ways. In some cases the easiest method will involve use of Prover's graphical user interface (GUI), as shown in Figure 11.11. The resultant description of the circuit may be read very easily by anyone familiar with electronic logic circuits and shows, for example, that the radio will be *ON* if the battery and the ignition are *True*, or if the battery, brake and switch are all *True*.

An alternative method of describing the circuit is to use a text-based approach, as shown in Figure 11.12. Prover also allows the circuit to be described in other ways, such as through the use of system graphs.

Once the description of the system has been entered, Prover can be used to investigate required system properties. For instance, in the above example it might be appropriate to test the requirement that the radio is only on when both the battery and the ignition are *True*. This would be done by getting the tool to attempt to prove the relationship

```
(Radio <-> (Battery & Ignition))
```

In this case it would be unable to prove this relationship, because of the sneak path formed by the brake and the switch, which would be found using Stålmarck's algorithm.

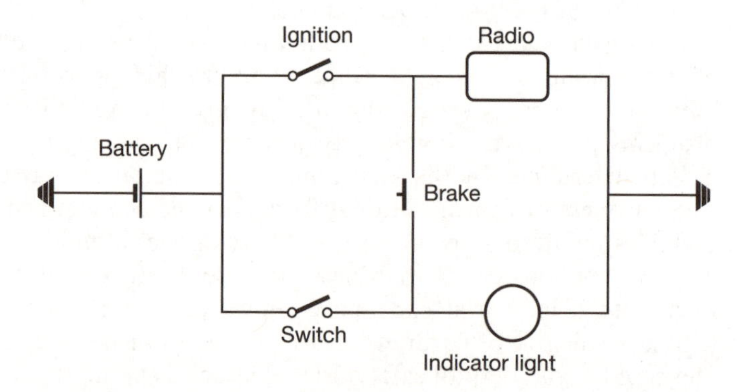

Figure 11.10 A simple car electrical circuit (with a sneak path).

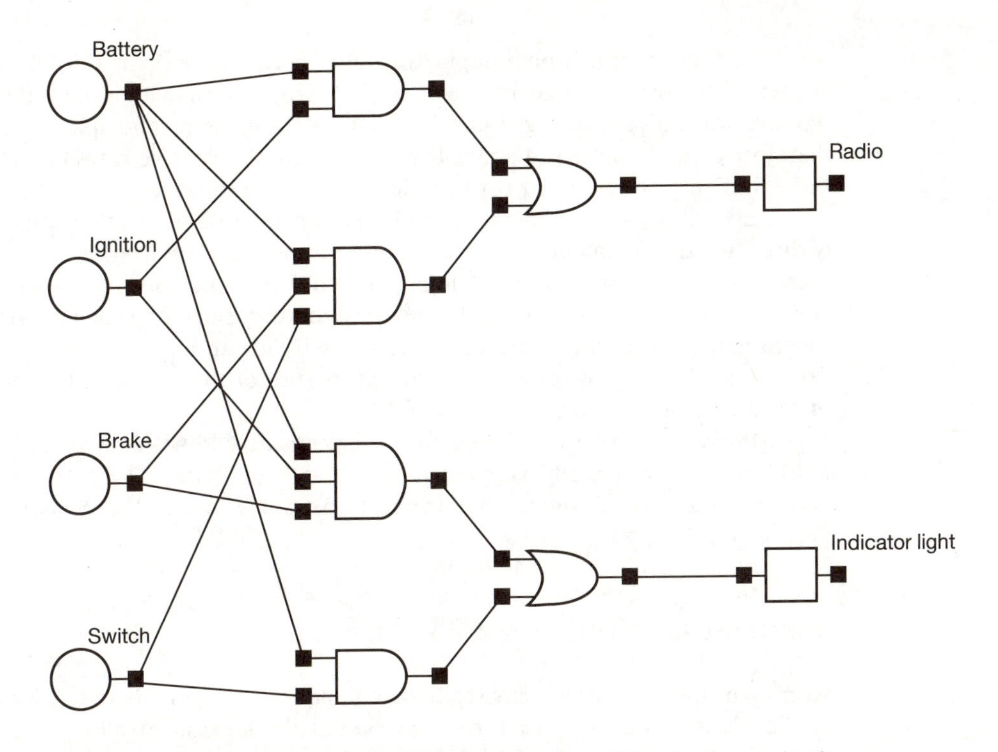

Figure 11.11 Prover GUI representation of the simple car circuit.

Although the above example is trivial it does demonstrate the steps required in the use of Prover, which are:

- model the system using propositional logic;
- write down the system requirements in propositional logic;
- prove the requirements with respect to the mathematical model.

An advantage of this approach is that the proofs are performed automatically and are fast. The tool can also handle large systems, and has

```
(Radio <-> ((Battery & Ignition) # (Battery & Brake & Switch)))
&
(Indicator_light <-> (Battery & Switch) # (Battery & Ignition & Brake)))

Symbols key:   &      AND
               #      OR
               <->    Equivalent to
```

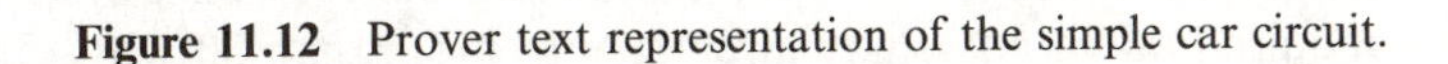

Figure 11.12 Prover text representation of the simple car circuit.

been used on propositional logic formulas with more than 100 000 logical elements. Its primary disadvantage is that propositional logic employs very basic relationships, making it unsuitable for a complete system specification. It therefore cannot be used to prove the correctness of a complete system, but can be very effectively used to prove particular system properties.

Like many formal methods tools, Prover may be used at various points within the development lifecycle. For example, by translating a system's specification into propositional logic, the tool may be used to assist in the validation of the specification by proving that it satisfies specific safety or functional requirements. Alternatively, if used with an appropriate translator, Prover may be used to prove the safety properties of the implemented software or hardware of a system.

Prover has been developed by Logikkonsult NP AB of Sweden, and is marketed and technically supported in the UK by NPL. The tool has been used in a number of commercial applications, some of which are discussed in Section 11.6.

Formal methods and PLCs

At present there are no commercially available formal methods that are directly applicable to systems based on programmable logic controllers. However, research work is under way on the use of formal techniques in the specification and verification of such systems. This includes the use of OBJ to model and verify systems using single PLCs prior to hardware implementation, and the use of LOTOS to model distributed systems involving several controllers (Fencott and Fleming, 1992). Work is also being directed at integrating graphical techniques with formal specifications for the construction and validation of PLC software (Halang and Kramer, 1992). Recent work has shown that it is feasible to model PLC programs using propositional logic for use with tools such as Prover. Translators for the various PLC programming languages could be used to allow semi-automatic use of such tools, although the lack of rigid semantics within IEC 1131-3 complicates the task of producing such translators.

11.6 Industrial applications of formal methods

Formal methods may clearly be important in the development of all forms of critical system. In this section we shall look at a few examples of the use of formal methods taken from a range of industrial sectors. Some of these are directly related to safety, whereas others are included because they illustrate the impact of formal methods on system development.

In the air transport sector, formal methods were used extensively in the development of the traffic alert and collision avoidance system (TCAS) which is required on all passenger aircraft with more than 30 seats. This aims to reduce the likelihood of midair collisions between aircraft. After flaws were found in the original standard for TCAS, formal methods were used to produce a new formal specification. The work employed no automated tools and the techniques used would correspond to level 1, as defined in Section 11.2. However, the resulting specification was widely thought to be a great improvement over corresponding English language and pseudocode versions.

A second project within the air transport sector to make use of formal methods was the development of the central control function display information system (CDIS), which was designed by Praxis for the UK Civil Aviation Authority (CAA). This is a distributed information system providing services to air traffic control staff. The hardware of the system includes a central processing system, a number of workstations and a local area network supporting a number of external connections. The central processing section uses three processors and has 40 Mb of memory. The unit provides fault tolerance through the use of duplicated hardware. The software for the system consists of some 80 000 lines of source code written in C. The requirements for the system were documented in three complementary models: a world model of the system in its environment based on entity-relationship analysis; a model of the processing requirements based on real-time Yourdon techniques; and a formal mathematical specification written in VDM. The central document was the core specification written in VDM, which gave a full and precise description of the data handled by the CDIS and the effects of all operations that could be carried out by users.

The Paris Métro signalling system was designed to reduce train separation and was the first safety-critical software system to be certified by the French railway authority (Gerhart *et al.*, 1994). The system, called SACEM, caters for 60 000 passengers per hour and made extensive use of formal methods for verification and validation. The software consists of about 21 000 lines of Modula-2, of which about two-thirds were deemed to be safety critical and were subjected to formal specification and verification. Here formal methods were not used to produce the operational code, but to validate it by a form of 'reverse engineering'. The specification was written in the B language (Abrial *et al.*, 1991), and the system was developed by GEC Alsthom, Matra Transport and CSEE (Compagnie de Signaux et Entreprises Électriques).

One of the most widely publicized applications of formal methods in recent years was the development by IBM of its CICS transaction processing system (Houstan and King, 1991). A new release of this software product contained over a quarter of a million lines of new code, of which 37 000 were produced from Z specifications, and a further 11 000 were partially specified in Z. The formal specifications were subjected to rigorous (rather than formal) verification. The company estimated that the use of formal methods reduced the number of problems per line of code by a factor of about 60%, and reduced the cost of production of the code by about 9%. The CICS project is considerably larger than would normally be acceptable for a system that was safety critical, but it serves to illustrate that formal methods can cope with relatively large pieces of software.

Another well-known project involving formal methods was performed by Inmos in association with the University of Oxford. This involved the development, in Z, of the floating-point unit for the T800 Transputer (Barrett, 1989). The work was so successful that it uncovered faults in the IEEE floating-point standard, and in other hardware implementations used for testing purposes. The company estimated that the development work was completed in less than 50% of the time that would have been required using informal methods.

A second project involving the use of formal methods in the development of a microprocessor was performed by Collins Avionics and SRI, with partial funding from NASA. This involved the formal verification of part of the Rockwell AAMP5 microprocessor. The AAMP5 is a derivative of the AAMP2 processor which was discussed in Chapter 8. The AAMP5 is one of the most complex microprocessors to which formal methods have been applied, its architecture being specifically designed for block-structured high-level languages such as Ada. It has a stack-based architecture and supports floating-point calculations that are implemented by microcode. The operation of the processor was specified in PVS at both the instruction set and the register-transfer level, and the PVS theorem prover was used to verify that the microcode correctly implemented the specified behaviour for a representative subset of instructions. The project demonstrated the feasibility of formally specifying a commercial microprocessor and formally verifying its microcode.

Prover has been used in a number of industrial projects, including railway, avionics and nuclear applications. ABB Signal in Sweden have used the tool in the production of computer-based railway interlocking systems. Here it is claimed that it reduced the time spent on verification by more than 90%, and that overall development time was cut by more than 20%. Saab Military Aircraft has also used Prover in commercial applications. These include an analysis of the landing gear of the Gripen multirole aircraft. Here hardware and software components were initially modelled separately, and then merged to enable study of the functioning of the complete system. This analysis was initially performed assuming all the components to be fault free, but was later extended to consider fault conditions.

Having identified a number of apparently successful projects it is only fair to point to an application where the use of formal methods proved to be less beneficial. This avionics application involved the flight warning computer (FWC) of the Airbus 330 and 340 aircraft (Garavel and Hautbois, 1993). The FWC comprises three Intel 80386 processors with software in Ada, PL/M and assembler. After the implementation of the system it was decided to perform a second implementation using formal methods to investigate the formal approach. The specification was written in LOTOS and comprised over 27 500 lines, this being about the same size as the existing Ada code. However, the development of the LOTOS specification took about 30% longer than that of the Ada program. The LOTOS design proved too large to be processed by the available formal verification tools, and was validated by simulation and testing. The LOTOS design was then used to generate an executable program, but this was several orders of magnitude slower than was required for the final system. This example serves to illustrate the importance of selecting suitable languages and appropriate goals for such projects.

In the examples cited above formal methods were used for only part of the development process. This use of formal techniques is representative of the way in which such methods are currently being used within industry. It is possible to identify applications that have used formal methods throughout the development lifecycle, but these are restricted to a small number of research projects. Perhaps the best known of these is the VIPER dependable microprocessor project (Cullyer, 1988). This work, which was performed by the Royal Signals and Radar Establishment (RSRE) with funding from the UK Ministry of Defence, set out to develop a microprocessor specifically for safety-critical applications. Formal methods were used throughout the development lifecycle, using a combination of languages and techniques. The top-level specification was performed in LCF-LSM, a language invented at the University of Cambridge and a forerunner of HOL. This was also used for the top-level design, which was then converted into ELLA, which was used for the circuit-level design. Marconi then used HILO to produce an implementation in CMOS, and Ferranti used FDL to produce a bipolar version. Extensive proofs were performed using a combination of level 1, 2 and 3 techniques, to establish the equivalence of each stage of the design and ultimately to verify that the final circuit was a true representation of the original specification. The overall architecture of the system was formally verified using the theorem proving features of HOL. In order to facilitate formal verification, a relatively simple 32-bit architecture was adopted that provides no interrupt facilities. Perhaps because of this lack of sophistication VIPER was never a commercial success, being used only in a handful of experimental projects. However, the work remains an important milestone in the use of formal methods.

In parallel with the work on VIPER, a similar project was performed at the University of Texas in the development of the FM8502 processor (Hunt, 1986). This is a 32-bit microprocessor of similar complexity to the processor of a PDP-11. It contains eight general-purpose 32-bit registers and supports a 32-bit address field. The FM8502 was developed using LISP and the Boyer–Moore theorem prover. The final specification amounts to fewer than 10 pages and can be proved automatically on a Sun workstation in about 7 hours.

11.7 Formal methods – the current situation

Over the past few years considerable experience has been gained of the use of formal techniques in the development of safety-critical systems in a wide range of industrial sectors (Bowen and Stavridou, 1993; Gerhart *et al.*, 1994). Many international standards in the area of safety now recommend or require the use of formal methods for certain aspects of the development of critical systems (Bowen and Stavridou, 1993). However, the use of formal methods has also been associated with a considerable amount of controversy. Supporters of this approach point to potential improvements in dependability and suggest that development times may be reduced. Opponents argue that benefits in dependability are unproven, and that in many cases the use of formal methods leads to a dramatic increase in development effort.

One of the major problems associated with the formal methods debate is that it is impossible to determine the effectiveness of such techniques in improving the dependability of critical systems. We noted in Chapter 4 that the integrity requirements of safety-critical systems considerably exceed our current methods of assessment. This being the case, we are not able to measure the effects of the use of formal methods on system integrity (Bowen and Stavridou, 1992). Many engineers believe that the use of appropriate formal techniques, alongside other methods, can improve dependability, but this belief is based on engineering experience and judgement, rather than definitive evidence.

In most cases it is inappropriate to use formal methods throughout the development lifecycle, and there are few industrial examples of such use. The use of automated theorem proving is also a very specialized process, and it is likely that such techniques will continue to see very limited application. However, there are situations where such expensive techniques might be justified, and as methods improve with maturity we may see these sophisticated approaches used in particularly critical applications. It is interesting to note that the two examples of the extensive use of formal methods cited above both relate to the production of dependable microprocessors. We noted in Chapter 8 that faults in microprocessors represent a particularly difficult problem to tackle, and that such faults invalidate many of the fault avoidance techniques used in software development. It is possible that in future years we will see an increased use of formal techniques in the development of critical sections of commercial processors (as in the case of the Inmos T800 Transputer and the Rockwell AAMP5). This may help to avoid the type of problems suffered by early versions of the Intel Pentium processor, which had an undetected fault within its floating-point division routine.

Although the use of machine-supported formal verification may remain a very specialized activity, it is clear that the application of other forms of formal methods is becoming common in safety-critical projects. In particular the use of formal specification languages is now widespread, and is becoming well understood. The availability of tools in this area is also increasing, although familiarity with them is limited. While it is not possible to measure the improvement in dependability achieved by the use of such techniques, it is generally agreed that these methods, when combined with accepted 'best practice', can help to increase safety. The recent development of tools such as Prover, which can be used to prove particular system properties, may also represent an important development. However, experience with such tools is currently very limited, and it is too early to judge their long-term significance in this area.

Although the debate concerning the advisability of adopting formal methods is far from over, there is much evidence to suggest that *mature* techniques can and should be used to produce safer systems. At present, few applications will justify the use of techniques corresponding to level 3 as defined earlier, but a judicious selection of techniques from levels 1 and 2 may represent an efficient and cost-effective way of improving the development process. For many projects this may correspond to the use of an appropriate formal specification language as a means of producing a simple and unambiguous description of the system. If this achieves nothing more than giving the designers a greater insight into the functioning of the system, then the use of formal methods may still have been justified.

In some ways there are parallels between the position of formal methods in the second half of the 1990s and that of the microprocessor in the early 1980s. At that time industry was being encouraged to embrace the new technology, but those companies that were first into the arena were faced with high development costs and poor development support. Many companies that were quick to take up the challenge paid a high price for their enthusiasm, but perhaps benefited in the long run by having gained experience that put them ahead of their competitors. At the present time many formal methods are relatively immature and have limited tool support. However, the benefits of certain techniques, such as the use of formal specification languages, is becoming clear. It is perhaps too early to judge the full impact of formal methods on the development of safety-critical systems, but it seems certain that all engineers should be aware of the potential benefits and pitfalls of their use.

REFERENCES

Abrial J.-R., Lee M.K.O., Neilson D.S. *et al.* (1991). The B-method. In *VDM '91: Formal Software Development Methods*, pp. 398–405. Berlin: Springer-Verlag

Barrett G. (1989). Formal methods applied to a floating-point number system. *IEEE Trans. Software Eng.*, **15**(5), 611–21

Bolognesi T. and Brinksma E. (1987). Introduction to the ISO specification language LOTOS. *Comput. Netw. ISDN Syst.* **14**, 25–59

Bowen J.P. and Stavridou V. (1992). Formal methods and software safety. *Proc. Safecomp '92: Safety of Computer Control Systems*. Zurich, October, Pergamon Press

Bowen J.P. and Stavridou V. (1993). Safety-critical systems, formal methods and standards. *Software Eng. J.*, **8**(4), 189–209

Boyer R.S. and Moore J.S. (1988). *A Computational Logic Handbook*. New York: Academic Press

Cullyer W.J. (1988). Implementing safety-critical systems: the VIPER microprocessor. In *VLSI Specification, Verification and Synthesis*, Calgary, 12–16 January, pp. 1–25. Brentford: Kluwer Academic Press

ESA (1991). *Software Engineering Standards*, ESA PSS-05-0. Paris: European Space Agency

Fencott C. and Fleming C. (1992). Practical formal methods for process control engineering. *Safety of Computer Control Systems (Safecomp '92)* Proc. of the IFAC Symposium, Zurich. Oxford: Pergamon Press

Futatsugi K., Goguen J.A., Jouannaud J.P. and Meseguer J. (1985). Principles of OBJ2. *Proc. 12th ACM Symp. on Principles of Programming Languages*, New Orleans, pp. 52–66

Garavel H. and Hautbois R.-P. (1993). An experience with the LOTOS formal description technique on the flight warning computer of the Airbus 330/340 aircrafts. *Proc. First AMAST Int. Workshop on Real-Time Systems*, Iowa City: Springer-Verlag

Gerhart S., Craigen D. and Ralston T. (1994). Experience with formal methods in critical systems. *IEEE Software*, January, pp. 21–39

Gordon M.J.C. and Melham T.F., eds (1993). *Introduction to HOL: A Theorem Proving Environment for Higher-Order Logic*. Cambridge: Cambridge University Press

Halang A.H. and Kramer B. (1992). Achieving high integrity of process control software by graphical design and formal verification. *Software Eng. J.*, **7**(1), 53–64

Houstan I. and King S. (1991). CICS project report: experiences and results from the use of Z in IBM. *VDM '91: Formal Software Development Methods, Proc. 4th Int. Symp. of VDM Europe*, Noordwijkerhout, Netherlands, 21–25 October, Vol. 1, pp. 588–96. Berlin: Springer-Verlag

Hunt W.A. (1986). FM8502: *A Verified Microprocessor*. Technical Report 47, Institute of Computing Science, University of Texas, Austin

Jones C.B. (1990). *Systematic Software Development Using VDM*, 2nd edn. Englewood Cliffs, NJ: Prentice-Hall

MoD (1991). Interim Defence Standard 00-55 *The Procurement of Safety Critical Software in Defence Equipment*. Glasgow: Directorate of Standardization

Moller F. and Tofts C. (1989). *A Temporal Calculus of Communicating Systems*. LFCS, December

Morison J.D., Peeling N.E. and Thorp T.L. (1982). ELLA: a hardware description language. In *Proc. IEEE Int. Conf. on Circuits and Computers*, New York, 28 September–1 October, pp. 604–7. New York: IEEE

O'Neill G. (1992). *Automated Translation of VDM Specifications into Standard ML Programs*, Report NPL DITC 196/92. Teddington: National Physical Laboratory

Owre S., Rushby J.M. and Shankar N. (1992). PVS: a prototype verification system. *11th International Conference on Automated Deduction (CADE)*, Saratoga, NY. Vol. 607 of *Lecture Notes in Artificial Intelligence*. Springer-Verlag

Parkin G.I. (1995). Complex systems proved and improved. *ERA Avionics Conference*, London, published by ERA Technology Ltd

RTCA/EUROCAE (1992). *Software Considerations in Airborne Systems and Equipment Certification*. RTCA/DO-178B; EUROCAE/ED-12B. Washington: Radio Technical Commission for Aeronautics. Paris: European Organisation for Civil Aviation Electronics

Rushby J. (1993). *Formal Methods and the Certification of Critical Systems*. Technical report CSL-93-7, SRI International, Menlo Park, CA

Shahdad M. (1986). An overview of VHDL language and technology. In *Proc. 23rd ACM/IEEE Design Automation Conf.*, Las Vegas, NV, 29 June–2 July, pp. 320–6. Washington: IEEE Comput. Soc. Press

Spivey J.M. (1992). *The Z Notation: A Reference Manual*, 2nd edn. Hemel Hempstead: Prentice-Hall

Stålmarck G. and Säflund M. (1990). Modelling and verifying systems and software in propositional logic. *IFAC SAFECOMP '90* London

Wichmann B.A., ed. (1992). A development model for safety-critical software. In *Software in Safety-Related Systems* (Wichmann B.A., ed.), pp. 209–23. Chichester: John Wiley

FURTHER READING

McDermid J.A. (1993). Formal methods: use and relevance for the development of safety-critical systems. In *Safety Aspects of Computer Control* (Bennett P., ed.), pp. 96–153. Oxford: Butterworth-Heinemann

Rushby J. (1993). *Formal Methods and the Certification of Critical Systems*. Technical report CSL-93-7, SRI International, Menlo Park, CA. (Also issued as *Formal Methods and Digital System Validation*, NASA CR 4551)

PROBLEMS

11.1 Explain how the development process may be understood in terms of diverse *definitions* and *transformations*. Discuss the process of verification with respect to this model.

11.2 What problems are associated with specifications written in natural languages? What qualities characterize a good specification?

11.3 What constitutes a formalized method and how do these differ from formal methods? Give examples of formalized methods.

11.4 How does a formal specification language differ from a computer programming language?

11.5 Why is the specification of a system susceptible to *validation* rather than *verification*? Differentiate between these two terms.

11.6 Why could the value returned by an expression within a program be dependent on the programming language used?

11.7 Devise a program assignment statement which, given integer values of y, returns a value of $10y$ for all values of y except $y = 20$.

11.8 A digital control system has four 16-bit parallel inputs. If a single test can be performed in 1 μs, how long would it take to test all possible combinations of the inputs?

11.9 How is it possible to have more than one form of logic?

11.10 How does usage of the term 'formal methods' differ between Europe and North America?

11.11 Which lifecycle phase has relatively limited scope for the use of formal methods? Why is this?

11.12 What is an algebraic specification language? Give an example of such a language.

11.13 Which are the most widely used model-based specification languages?

11.14 Describe briefly the structure of a specification written in VDM.

11.15 What is meant by an 'external variable' in VDM? What characterizes 'rd' and 'wr' variables?
11.16 What are natural numbers within VDM?
11.17 Define the terms 'pre-conditions', 'post-conditions' and 'predicates'.
11.18 Explain what is meant by a 'schema' in Z, and describe its basic form.
11.19 What forms of formal methods are normally used for concurrent systems? Give examples of such techniques.
11.20 To what level of rigour do techniques based on VDM and Z correspond? What languages may be used for applications that require a more rigorous approach?
11.21 What forms of checks can be performed semi-automatically to aid in the validation of formal specifications? What other aspects of the specification must also be investigated?
11.22 Why is it sometimes useful to produce a formal specification, even if later stages of the development lifecycle do not use a formal approach?
11.23 How do the languages used for the detailed design and implementation of a system differ from those used for the high-level design?
11.24 Explain what is meant by formal verification. How does this differ from rigorous verification?
11.25 Why does the use of formal proofs not guarantee a perfect implementation?
11.26 Discuss the advantages and problems of using a single formal language throughout the development lifecycle.
11.27 Describe the problems associated with determining the effectiveness of formal methods in improving safety.

12 Verification, Validation and Testing

CHAPTER CONTENTS

12.1 Introduction

In Chapter 11 we noted that the development of a new product may be considered as a series of transformations of its definition. Each lifecycle phase progressively changes this definition as the work proceeds from the customer requirements through to its complete implementation. Each phase therefore takes a description of the system as its input, and develops this to form the input to the next stage.

In order to have confidence in the final system, it is necessary to confirm that each phase of the development work has been performed correctly. This is achieved through a process of verification.

> ***Verification*** *is the process of determining whether the output of a lifecycle phase fulfils the requirements specified by the previous phase.*

The task of verification is to demonstrate that the output of a phase conforms to its input, rather than to show that the output is actually correct. If the input specification is wrong, the verification process will not necessarily detect this. Therefore, mistakes in early phases of a project may propagate through later stages without detection. This is of particular importance in the case of errors in the original customer requirements documents or the top-level specification.

In order to overcome these problems, verification is supplemented by a process of validation, which attempts to locate problems within the specification of a phase.

> ***Validation*** *is the process of confirming that the specification of a phase, or of the complete system, is appropriate and is consistent with the customer requirements.*

Validation may be performed on individual phases, but is more often used to investigate the characteristics of the complete system. It often looks at the behaviour of a prototype system, or a simulation, and determines whether this operates in a manner that satisfies the needs of the customer or user. Validation of the completed system demonstrates its suitability for use, and confirms the appropriateness of the original specification.

Verification and validation are achieved by performing various tests to investigate the nature of the different descriptions of the system.

> ***Testing*** *is the process used to verify or validate a system or its components.*

Results from the testing procedure may be used to assess the integrity of the system and to investigate specific characteristics such as its safety. Testing will also uncover faults that may then be removed, so increasing the system's dependability.

Testing is performed at various stages during the development of a system, and it is perhaps convenient to identify three major activities:

- module testing
- system integration testing
- system validation testing.

Module testing involves the evaluation of small, simple functions of hardware or software. Faults detected at this stage are usually relatively straightforward to locate and remove because of the simplicity of the components involved. **System integration testing** investigates the characteristics of a collection of modules and is generally aimed at establishing their correct interaction. Faults detected during this process are likely to be more expensive to correct than those discovered during module testing, as the arrangement is inherently more complex. **System validation testing** aims to demonstrate that the complete system satisfies its requirements. Any problems that are detected at this stage are likely to involve weaknesses in the customer requirements documents or in the specification. In either event they are likely to prove extremely costly to correct, as any modifications to these documents must propagate through the entire development process. Because the complexity and cost of correcting faults increase as we move from module testing towards system testing, it is clearly essential to locate faults as soon as possible within this progression.

Testing may take a number of forms, and in particular may be dynamic or static, or may be based on the use of mathematical models. **Dynamic testing** involves the execution of a system or component in order to investigate its characteristics. These tests may be carried out within the system's natural working environment or within a simulation of that environment. Dynamic tests may also be carried out using simulations of system components to allow evaluations to be made before hardware is available. Simulation can greatly reduce development costs by allowing alternative designs to be compared without the expense of building the units. When performed using actual system hardware, dynamic testing may allow all aspects of a system's performance to be investigated, including its temporal properties. However, tests using simulations do not always give complete information on system behaviour. For example, they may not provide real-time operation or give representative timing data.

Static testing investigates the characteristics of a system or component without operating it. Examples of such tests include reviews, inspections and design walkthroughs. Software methods include various tests that go under the general heading of **static code analysis**. Such tests investigate the form of software without execution. Many engineers use the word 'testing' to mean *dynamic* testing, and would refer to *static* testing as **analysis**. Within this text we use 'testing' to refer to both dynamic and static techniques.

Modelling involves the use of a mathematical representation of the behaviour of a system or its environment. The model is used to gain an insight into the likely characteristics of the system, and may be applied manually or using a computer. Modelling is usually employed at an early stage to investigate the basic nature of the proposed system or the environment in which it is to operate. Such techniques may also be used later, during integration testing and system validation. Animation of a formal specification is an example of modelling.

A typical development programme would include both static and dynamic testing, and would also make use of some form of modelling. However, the importance of the different techniques tends to vary throughout the lifecycle, as illustrated in Table 12.1 (CONTESSE, 1995). The choice of techniques will also be affected by the safety integrity level of the system.

Testing methods may also be categorized in respect of the information available to those performing the work. In **black-box testing** the test engineer has no knowledge of the implementation of the system and relies simply on information given in the specification. This approach is sometimes called **requirements-based testing**. Such techniques may be applied to individual modules, but are more commonly used with complete systems or self-sufficient subsystems. Black-box testing is perhaps the purest form of evaluation, as it

Table 12.1 Principal testing methods within the development lifecycle.

Lifecycle phase	*Dynamic testing*	*Static testing*	*Modelling*
Requirements analysis and specification		✓	✓
Top-level design		✓	✓
Detailed design		✓	✓
Implementation	✓	✓	
Integration testing	✓	✓	✓
System validation	✓		✓

simply checks whether the system does what the specification says it should. However, the invisibility of the internal structure prevents the test engineer from identifying and investigating individual modules, and may therefore complicate testing. Black-box testing provides the greatest level of independence between the developer and the evaluator, and is therefore of great benefit in independent validation. This approach is widely used in the validation of software tools such as compilers. Unfortunately, high-quality functional testing is often difficult and expensive.

In **white-box testing** the engineer has access to information concerning the implementation of the system and uses this to guide his work. Most testing methods adopt a white-box approach, although the amount of information available to a test engineer may vary. Such techniques are applicable to testing at all stages of development, and to both the hardware and the software aspects of a system. Knowledge of the internal structure of a unit greatly simplifies dynamic testing, as tests can be devised to investigate each module individually. Internal knowledge may also be used to assist in the choice of test conditions in an attempt to minimize the number of points needed.

Dynamic testing may be performed using black-box or white-box methods, and a typical development project would use a combination of these. Static testing, however, requires an insight into the design and implementation process and so can only employ a white-box approach. Mathematical modelling does not make use of system hardware or software and so the terms black-box and white-box are inapplicable.

We have identified ways of categorizing testing in terms of the elements of the system involved, the nature of the tests performed and the information available to the test engineer. We now turn our attention to the planning of the verification and validation activities, before looking in more detail at dynamic, static and modelling methods. The chapter then considers techniques for investigating the safety aspects of a system and various strategies for testing critical systems. We will then look at design techniques that can simplify the testing process, and at the various test tools and simulation methods that can be used. The chapter concludes by discussing the role of independent verification and validation in the development of safety-critical systems.

12.2 Planning for verification and validation

When developing safety-critical systems, the tasks of verification and validation represent a very large part of the required effort. Consequently, forward planning of such activities is essential both to estimate and to minimize costs. Because verification and validation are based on testing, **test planning** is an essential part of the development process. One aspect of this work is concerned with planning the module and system integration testing. Validation of the complete system is one of the last stages of system development, but the planning of this activity should be performed at an early stage. In Figure 5.3 we looked at the overall safety lifecycle of a safety-related system and noted that the process of validation should be planned early within the project, where such plans may affect the design. Taking account of the need for validation at this early stage may save considerable effort later in the development process.

In the classic 'V' lifecycle model of Figure 5.1, we noted a secondary flow of information from the early phases of a project to later stages (as shown by the broken lines). The right-hand side of this diagram represents the implementation and testing phases of the work. As the system is progressively transformed from an array of individual modules to a complete system, it must be verified against progressively earlier transformations of its specification. Thus, for example, the implementation of an individual module must be tested against its design, and the complete system must be compared with its specification. The planning involved in these activities may be incorporated within the V diagram, as shown in Figure 12.1. From this figure it is clear that for each phase on the left-hand side of the diagram, the production of a new transformation of the specification must be accompanied by the generation of a test plan describing how the implementation of this transformation may be verified.

The test planning at each stage must identify the features that need to be investigated and also the level of rigour appropriate for the testing process. This latter consideration is clearly affected by the safety integrity level of the unit, and raises issues of **test adequacy** and **test coverage** that will be considered later in this chapter.

Overall safety validation plan

System validation needs to consider all aspects of the system and all its possible modes of operation. These will include considerations of any safety mechanisms based on 'other technologies', such as mechanical or hydraulic arrangements, and external risk reduction techniques. Before the system is implemented its eventual validation should be considered, taking into account all factors that could affect its safety. The draft of IEC 1508 (IEC, 1995) outlines a series of requirements for the overall validation plan. These are summarized in Table 12.2, from which it is clear that the test plan must include a considerable amount of detail of the

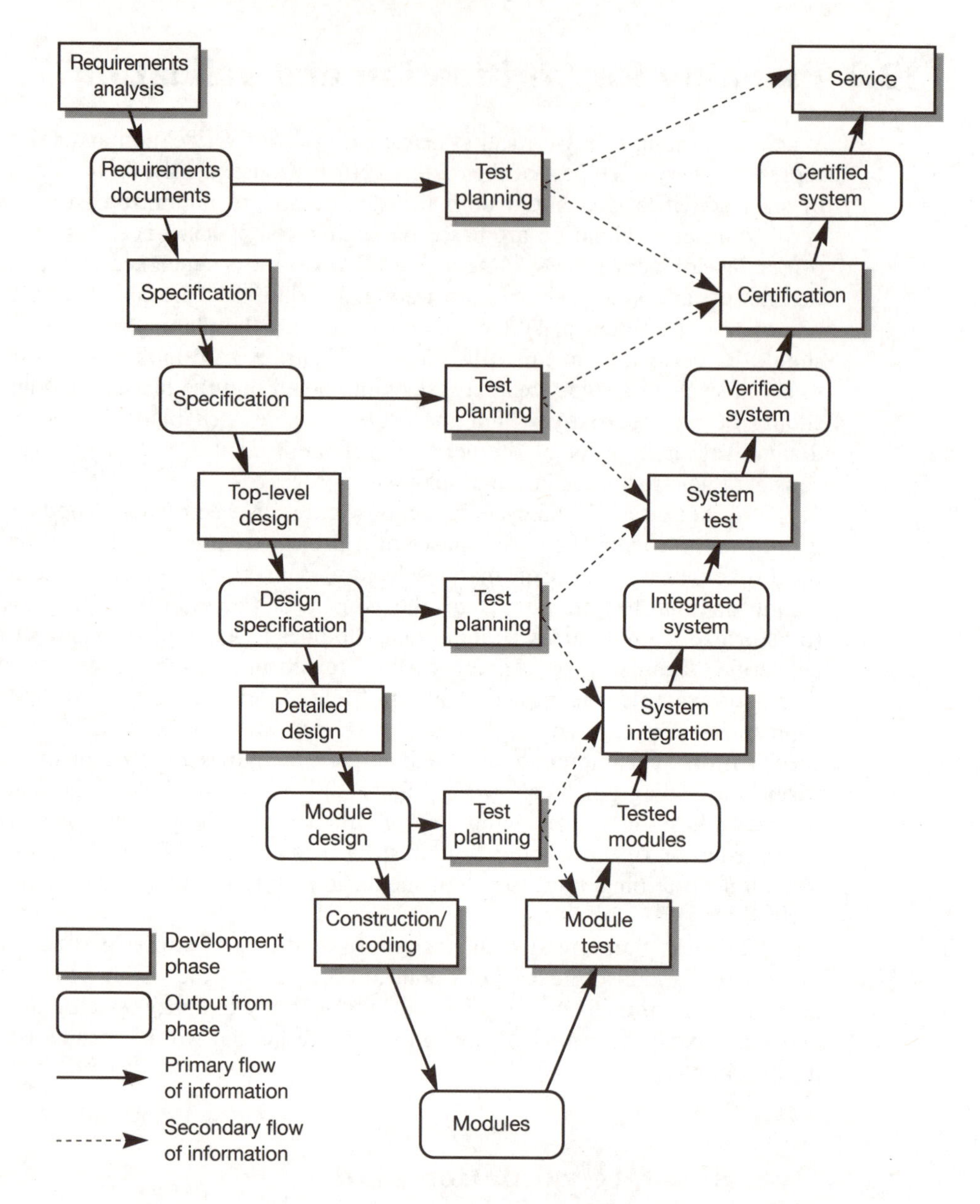

Figure 12.1 A 'V' development lifecycle model incorporating test planning.

validation process to be followed. Inevitably, such plans will require a qualitative assessment of alternative testing techniques in order to determine the methods appropriate for a given aspect of the work. The following sections describe a range of testing methods that may be applicable to various aspects of system development.

Table 12.2 An overall safety validation plan (from draft IEC 1508).

(a)	Details of when the validation shall take place
(b)	Details of who shall carry out the validation
(c)	Identification of the relevant modes of the system's operation, including: • preparation for use, including setting up and adjustment • start up • teach • automatic • manual • semi-automatic • steady-state operation • re-setting • shutdown • maintenance • reasonably foreseeable abnormal conditions
(d)	Identification of the safety-related systems and external risk reduction facilities that need to be validated for each mode of the system before commissioning commences
(e)	The technical strategy for the validation, for example whether analytical methods or statistical tests are to be used
(f)	The measures, techniques and procedures that shall be used to confirm that each safety function conforms with the overall safety requirements documents and the safety integrity requirements
(g)	The specific reference to the overall safety requirements documents
(h)	The required environment in which the validation activities are to take place
(i)	The pass/fail criteria
(j)	The policies and procedures for evaluating the results of the validation, particularly failures

12.3 Dynamic testing

Dynamic testing involves the *operation* of the system under test. This entails the execution of a number of **test cases** that investigate particular aspects of the system. Each test case comprises a set of input **test data**, a specification of the expected output and a statement of the function being tested. The input test data is often referred to as an **input vector** and the output data as an **output vector**. Test cases have associated **pre-conditions** that specify the required state of the system prior to execution of the test, and **post-conditions** that define the state the system must be in after the test. In some cases tests may be carried out to investigate the operation of the system in circumstances where the pre-conditions are not met, to determine its response to anomalous inputs.

Dynamic testing may be divided into a number of categories, determined by the manner in which test cases are selected. The most important of these are:

- functional testing
- structural testing
- random testing.

Functional testing

As the name suggests, functional testing sets out to identify and test all the functions of the system that are defined within its requirements. Specific test cases are devised to investigate each aspect of operation, although tests will often cover more than one function. This form of testing requires no knowledge of the implementation of the system and is thus an example of a black-box approach to assessment.

The way in which the various test cases investigate the required functions of the system may be represented in a test matrix, as shown in Figure 12.2. This allows a test engineer to confirm that all the requirements are covered by the tests performed.

Structural testing

Unlike functional testing, which makes no assumptions concerning the implementation of the system, structural testing uses a detailed knowledge of its internal structure to investigate its characteristics. It is therefore an example of a white-box approach. Structural testing identifies the internal organization of a

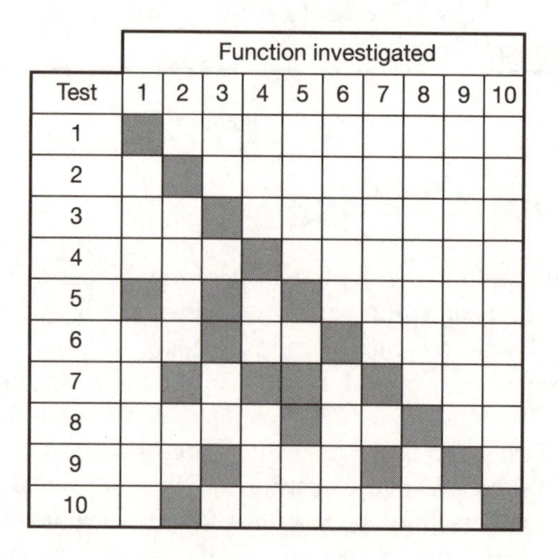

Figure 12.2 A test matrix.

system and uses this information to devise tests to check the operation of individual components and their interactions. In the case of hardware testing this might involve applying test signals to investigate particular modules within the system. When applied to software, tests might be devised to investigate the various routines and execution paths. A knowledge of the internal organization of the system allows critical conditions to be investigated, such as the effects of limiting values. Structural testing often attempts to investigate a large proportion of the possible conditions within the system. For example, when testing software it might attempt to test every branch or jump within a program. Such methods are often referred to as **coverage-based testing**.

Random testing

Functional and structural testing methods use sets of input data that are chosen to investigate some particular characteristic of the system under test. In contrast, 'random' testing involves the use of test conditions that are freely chosen from the range of possible inputs. This input range is often termed the **input space** of the system, where an arrangement with n inputs is considered to have an n-dimensional input space. Using this model, any particular combination of inputs represents a position within this multidimensional volume. The use of randomly chosen inputs aims to detect fault conditions that might be missed by more 'systematic' techniques. Test cases may be randomly sampled from within the input space, or may be given a probability distribution which matches that which would be expected in operation. In the latter situation, test cases may be derived from a simulation of the environment or from recorded measurements of a real environment.

Dynamic testing techniques

A wide range of dynamic testing techniques are used in the development of safety-critical systems. Although it is not within the scope of this text to describe all such techniques in detail, it is useful to outline some of the more important ones. More details of these techniques, and those in the following sections, may be found in a number of sources, including the *Software Engineer's Reference Book* (McDermid, 1992); the British Computer Society's draft *Standard for Software Component Testing* (BCS, 1995); and standards such as DO-178B and IEC 1508.

Test cases based on equivalence partitioning: Partitions the input and output values of the system or component into sets or ranges that can reasonably be expected to be treated in the same manner. Tests are then performed to investigate performance within each partition. Both valid and invalid values are partitioned and tested in this way.

Test cases based on boundary value analysis: Tests the performance of the system at the extremes of 'equivalent' partitions of the input and output ranges. Tests would normally be performed for values at, and either side of, each boundary. Both valid and invalid values are partitioned and tested in this way.

State transition testing: Investigates the performance of a system or component by considering its state transition model. Tests are performed to investigate the transitions between states, the events that cause these transitions, and the actions that result from the transitions.

Probabilistic testing: Testing aimed at determining the reliability of the system. Depending on the application, such tests might attempt to obtain figures for the failure rate in terms of failures over a given period of time, or failures on demand. For safety-critical systems the low failure rates required limit the ability of this form of testing to achieve its objectives.

Structure-based testing: This investigates individual components of the hardware or software, as discussed above.

Process simulation: This involves the production of a simulation of the process or equipment to be controlled by the system under development. Simulation may greatly aid the testing process by allowing a wide variety of situations to be reproduced quickly and safely. We shall look at simulation in more detail in Section 12.10.

Error guessing: Experienced test engineers can often predict input conditions that are likely to cause problems. Error guessing involves selecting such cases and adding them to the test schedule.

Error seeding: This involves the insertion of errors into the implementation of a system to see if they are detected by the testing procedures. This gives some indication of the effectiveness of the testing process, and may allow the number of unfound errors to be estimated.

Timing and memory tests: Investigates the response time and any memory constraints of the system.

Performance testing: Within the requirements of the system there will be various features that determine necessary levels of performance. For example, a given feature might require that a certain operation is performed within a given period of time. All such requirements are identified and tests are devised to ensure that each is satisfied.

Stress testing: This involves inflicting a very high workload on the system to ensure that it can cope with all normal circumstances.

Test case generation

Critical components of the testing process include the selection of an appropriate set of testing techniques and the generation of suitable test cases. Test case generation is perhaps most easily understood by considering examples, and an excellent source of such material is the BCS draft *Standard for Software Component Testing* (BCS, 1995). This illustrates the process for a range of testing techniques, and although the standard is concerned with the testing of software components, the techniques illustrated are also of relevance to other forms of dynamic testing. Appendix B reproduces two examples taken from this standard which are concerned with the generation of test cases relating to equivalence partitioning and boundary value analysis.

12.4 Static analysis

Static testing methods investigate the properties of a system without operating it. Some of these techniques are performed manually, others make use of automated tools. Manual techniques include walkthroughs, design reviews, various forms of inspection and the use of checklists. Automated methods include conformance tests for hardware, and the use of various forms of verification and analysis tools for software. Formal proofs of correctness are a form of static analysis, and may be performed either manually or using computer-based tools.

Many automated software testing packages come under the general heading of **static code analysis tools**. This term encompasses a range of techniques including:

- formal verification
- semantic analysis
- control flow analysis
- data flow analysis
- complexity measurement
- range checking.

Static techniques can be used to establish properties of software or hardware that are true under *all* conditions. This is generally not possible using dynamic testing, which can only demonstrate a system's characteristics for the limited number of conditions under which tests have been performed.

Static analysis techniques

Static techniques are diverse and numerous. In this section we shall look briefly at some of the more widely used techniques.

Walkthroughs/design reviews: These processes are forms of peer review and involve the systematic investigation of documents by a number of engineers. A **code walkthrough** requires an engineer to lead colleagues through the design or implementation of software, and to convince them of its correctness (Yourdon, 1989).

Checklists: A set of questions to stimulate a critical appraisal of all aspects of the system. Questions are usually general in nature and are thus applicable to many types of system.

Formal proofs: Formal proofs are used to show the correctness of some aspect of the design or implementation of a system using formal descriptions of different transformations of its definition. They therefore represent a form of static analysis. Formal proofs were discussed in Chapter 11.

Fagan inspections: This is a systematic audit of quality assurance documents aimed at finding errors and omissions (Fagan, 1986). The complete development process is investigated in five stages, namely planning, preparation, inspection, rework and follow-up.

Control flow analysis: An analysis of software to detect poor and potentially incorrect program structure. Programs are represented by a directed graph which is then progressively reduced. This process will identify several problem areas, such as inaccessible code, infinite loops and poor structure.

Data flow analysis: A diagrammatic representation of the flow of data throughout a program. Data flow diagrams show each data transformation distinctly, as information passes from the input to the output. This can be used to check the appropriateness of the operations being performed, and can also allow a comparison between the actual and the required data flow.

Symbolic execution: A method of checking for agreement between source code and its specification. Programs are run using algebraic variables in place of input data. Assignment statements do not produce numeric values, but instead are used to produce algebraic expressions for the variables concerned. The resultant formulas can then be compared with those predicted from the specification. The results of the analysis form a set of formulas for each possible path through the software. For all but the simplest programs the amount of information produced is too large to be assimilated, and usually some form of user interaction is required to direct the analysis to paths of interest. Some tools perform automatic simplification of the data to remove redundant information and to aid interpretation. Such tools are often termed **semantic analysers**.

Metrics: These methods evaluate certain properties of the software and relate them to desired attributes, such as reliability and complexity. Automated tools are normally required to perform the analysis, which may take several forms. Common examples include measures of:

- graph theoretic complexity – based on the complexity of the program control graph;
- module accessibility – the number of ways a module may be accessed;

- complexity measures – such as those due to McCabe, Halstead or Hennell;
- number of entry and exit points per module.

Experience with the use of these metrics is somewhat limited, and they are at present not fully endorsed by the control community. However, they are being used in certain applications, such as the checking of three million lines of software for the Channel Tunnel project.

Sneak circuit analysis: 'Sneak circuits' are latent conditions inadvertently designed into a system that can cause it to malfunction in certain circumstances. They may be physical 'paths', but may also take a variety of other forms, such as timing irregularities or ambiguous display messages. Sneak analysis aims to locate these weaknesses by looking at the basic topological patterns within the hardware and software.

The use of several software static analysis techniques is only possible when suitable programming languages are used. The availability of the numerous test tools also varies between languages. In Chapter 9 we considered the choice of programming languages for safety-critical applications and, from the material within this chapter, it is clear that the implications of static analysis may greatly influence this selection.

12.5 Modelling

Modelling is used most extensively during the early phases of project development and is of particular importance in the production of the specification and the top-level design. However, modelling is also used in later stages of the work, and often plays an important part in system validation.

Modelling techniques

A range of modelling methods are used in the production of safety-critical systems. Some are based on the use of mathematical models, whereas others are graphical in nature. Many require the use of computer-based tools, although some may be performed manually. Here we will look briefly at some of the more widely used techniques. As in the previous sections, more details of these methods may be found in a number of texts.

Formal methods: Formal methods may be used to model a system as an aid to implementation, verification and validation. The use of formal methods was discussed in Chapter 11.

Software prototyping/animation: Animation (or software prototyping) involves the production of a software model that represents the features of the specification. The characteristics of this model may then be investigated to validate the specification. The use of animation was described in Chapter 5, and its use with formal methods was discussed in Chapter 11.

Performance modelling: This technique aims to ensure that the working capacity of the system is sufficient to meet its requirements. A model is constructed of the system processes and their interactions. This is used to determine the requirements of each function for system resources such as processor time and memory space. From these requirements the total system demand is determined under average and worst-case conditions. This information is used to ensure that the system can always satisfy this demand, with some margin of safety. Data from the modelling process may also form an input into performance testing activities, as described in Section 12.3.

State transition diagrams: Control structures can often be described in terms of a finite number of discrete states and the combinations of input signals that cause the system to switch between them. Such a representation is termed a **finite state machine**, and the operation of such a system may be completely defined by a state transition diagram. This shows the various states and indicates how the system moves between them. The systematic form of this approach allows arrangements specified in this way to be checked for **completeness**, **consistency** and **reachability** (whether it is possible to get from one state to another by any sequence of inputs).

Time Petri nets: Petri nets are a form of graph theoretic model that can be used to represent information and control flow in systems with concurrent or asynchronous characteristics. Potentially hazardous conditions may be represented as states within this model, and analysis can then investigate the timing constraints necessary to avoid such states. This can be used to select appropriate runtime mechanisms, for example watchdog timers, to detect dangerous failures (Leveson and Stolzy, 1987; Bologna, 1993).

Data flow diagrams: These are a diagrammatic representation of the flow of data through a program. Information from data flow analysis is combined with implementation data to detect poorly structured, and potentially incorrect, programs. Errors that may be detected include:

- variables that are written more than once without being read;
- variables that are written but are never read.

These errors may suggest the omission of part of the program or the presence of redundant code.

Structure diagrams: Structure diagrams are in many ways complementary to data flow diagrams, in that they represent the program structure that implements this flow of data. Structure charts may be derived from data flow diagrams as a means of defining the hierarchical structure of the software, although such structures are not unique. The diagram, which is also called a structure chart, takes the form of a tree that reflects the relationship between program units.

Environmental modelling: Testing safety-critical systems within their operational environment is often inadvisable, or perhaps impossible. In such cases it is normal to test systems using a simulation of the operating environment. This has the added benefit that test conditions can often be generated more easily and quickly in this manner, allowing more complete and efficient testing. We shall look at the use of environmental simulation in more detail in Section 12.10.

12.6 Testing for safety

The testing of non-critical systems is primarily concerned with investigating performance with respect to functional requirements. In safety-critical systems such considerations are supplemented by a need to show that safety requirements are also satisfied.

The safety requirements of a system include both general and specific elements. General requirements includes the achievement of appropriate levels of safety integrity, reliability and quality, for the component modules and for the system as a whole. Specific requirements include mechanisms for dealing with the various hazards associated with the system that have been identified by the process of hazard analysis. The nature of safety requirements was discussed in Chapter 2.

The draft of IEC 1508 describes the task of ensuring conformance with the safety requirements as **overall safety validation**. The standard requires that this process be carried out in accordance with the overall safety validation plan, as outlined earlier in Table 12.2. The results of the validation are documented in an **overall safety validation report**. This must include full details of the work performed, together with its results and a discussion of any discrepancies between expected and actual results.

DO-178B incorporates the concept of **traceability**, in which key safety requirements should be traceable through the various stages of development to specific elements of the low-level implementation. This enables each safety requirement to be traced to a specific test or series of tests designed to investigate its implementation.

The safety validation process must consider the behaviour of all parts of the system, including sections based on non-electronic technologies and external risk reduction facilities. Validation of a system in respect of its specific safety requirements requires that tests be performed to show that each identified hazard has been effectively countered. In some cases it may be possible to demonstrate such properties by the use of dynamic testing, although static analysis or modelling techniques may be needed, as exhaustive testing of even simple responses is often impossible. Validation of the general safety requirements of a system will often require a combination of testing techniques. Properties such as reliability and failure rate have target values that are beyond our ability to demonstrate using dynamic testing (as discussed at the end of

Chapter 7). In such cases, validation is likely to require supporting evidence from a static analysis of the design, and from a study of the development methods employed.

12.7 Test strategies

In the introduction to this chapter we noted that the relative use of dynamic, static and modelling techniques differs considerably between the various lifecycle phases. In Sections 12.3–12.5 we looked at several testing methods, and Table 12.3 indicates the development phases in which these are most commonly used (CONTESSE, 1995).

A typical safety-critical project would make use of several testing methods in any given development phase. The choice of techniques is likely to be determined by a number of factors, including in-house expertise and the availability of tools. One of the key factors affecting the choice of techniques is the integrity of the unit being developed, and the various international standards give guidance on the methods that are appropriate for systems of differing levels of integrity. Table 12.4 shows an example of such guidance from draft IEC 1508. This lists various static analysis methods and indicates their suitability for systems of safety integrity levels 1–4 (SIL1–SIL4).

It can be seen that some of the techniques listed are deemed to be suitable for certain levels of integrity but not for others. For example, Fagan inspection is highly recommended for systems of integrity level 4, is recommended for systems of levels 2 and 3, but has no recommendation for level 1 applications. Here it is likely that the technique is judged to be unjustifiable for level 1 systems, on economic grounds. In some cases certain techniques are 'not recommended' for a given situation. This would be indicated by 'NR' within the relevant table. This indicates that the method is unsuitable for technical reasons, and its use in such cases would need to be justified to any independent assessor.

In addition to selecting appropriate techniques for the testing process, it is also necessary to determine the rigour with which these techniques should be applied. Testing alone cannot be used to achieve high integrity within a system, but appropriate testing forms a necessary part of the development task. In order to demonstrate that a system has been adequately tested, it is necessary to quantify the thoroughness of the testing performed.

Test coverage

One approach to quantifying the testing process is through the use of some form of **test coverage analysis**. This attempts to estimate the performance of the testing procedure as a percentage of some ideal value. Such analysis may be applied to a range of factors, including the number of possible input states, the number of

Table 12.3 Use of testing methods throughout the development lifecycle.

Static	*Dynamic*	*Modelling*
Requirements analysis and functional specification		
Walkthroughs		Formal methods
Design reviews		Software prototyping/ animation
Checklists		
Top-level design		
Walkthroughs		Performance modelling
Design reviews		State transition diagrams
Checklists		Time Petri nets
Formal proofs		Data flow diagrams
Fagan inspection		Structure diagrams
Detailed design		
Walkthroughs		Formal methods
Design reviews		
Control flow analysis		
Data flow analysis		
Symbolic execution		
Checklists		
Fagan inspection		
Metrics		
Implementation		
Static analysis	Functional testing	
	Boundary value analysis	
	Structure-based testing	
	Probabilistic testing	
	Error guessing	
	Process simulation	
	Error seeding	
Integration testing		
Walkthroughs	Functional testing	Environmental modelling
Design reviews	Timing and memory tests	
Sneak circuit analysis	Boundary value analysis	
	Performance testing	
	Stress testing	
	Probabilistic testing	
	Error guessing	
Validation		
	Functional testing	Environmental modelling
		Software prototyping/ animation

Table 12.4 Static analysis techniques – recommendations from draft IEC 1508.

Technique	*SIL1*	*SIL2*	*SIL3*	*SIL4*
1. Boundary value analysis	R	R	HR	HR
2. Checklists	R	R	R	R
3. Control flow analysis	R	HR	HR	HR
4. Data flow analysis	R	HR	HR	HR
5. Error guessing	R	R	R	R
6. Fagan inspections	–	R	R	HR
7. Sneak circuit analysis	–	–	R	R
8. Symbolic execution	R	HR	HR	HR
9. Walkthroughs/design reviews	HR	HR	HR	HR
One or more of the above techniques should be used				

HR = highly recommended, R = recommended, – = no recommendation

possible internal states, or some estimate of potential fault conditions. When using static techniques it is often possible to establish system characteristics that hold for all, or a defined range of conditions. With dynamic testing this is often impossible, and test coverage analysis gives an estimate of the fraction of all possible conditions that are studied.

Test coverage analysis may be applied to black-box testing by considering all the possible input states of a system. If the system is then tested by applying a certain number of test cases, the test coverage may be calculated by dividing the number of test vectors used by the size of the input space. An *ideal* test scheme might provide complete input test coverage, and would represent what is termed '**exhaustive testing**'. Unfortunately, this goal is almost always impossible. For simple combinational hardware it might be possible to investigate the complete input space, although this would only be possible for systems with a relatively small number of inputs. A system with a modest 40 binary inputs (perhaps five 8-bit analogue signals) has an input space of 2^{40}, or about 10^{12} combinations. At one test per millisecond this would take about 35 years to test. For sequential hardware the situation is far more complicated, as it is necessary to investigate the effects of sequences of input patterns. If these sequences involve more than a very small number of patterns, then exhaustive testing of this type is not only difficult, it is impossible, as the time required to perform the tests exceeds the age of the universe!

Computer-based systems are inherently sequential in nature, and here the input may consist of sequences of almost unlimited length. Under these circumstances it is not meaningful to consider exhaustive testing in terms of investigating all possible input patterns. An alternative way of looking at the problem is to take a white-box approach and to consider the system's internal states. When considering modelling techniques earlier, we noted that we can often describe a system in terms of a finite number of discrete states and the combinations of input signals that cause the system to switch between them – the so-called 'finite state machine' approach. Within a computer program the action taken at any time is determined by the values of various binary patterns. These patterns include input data from external signals, the contents of memory locations and internal registers, and machine status words that indicate the results of previous operations. At any instant the combination of all these binary patterns represents the '**system state**'. A brute force approach to testing the system might be to use individual tests to show that the system behaves correctly for selected system states. This being the case, we could calculate the test coverage of this process as the percentage of all the possible system states that are investigated. Exhaustive testing, in this context, would involve the use of tests to investigate all of the possible system states. To gain some insight into the magnitude of this task, it is interesting to consider a simple 8-bit microcomputer with 64 kbytes of memory. The number of individual bits making up the state of this arrangement is approximately $65\,000 \times 8$, or about 520 000. Therefore the number of possible states is about $2^{520\,000}$ or about $10^{160\,000}$. The time required to perform an exhaustive test of such a system exceeds the age of the universe by thousands of orders of magnitude. Consequently, the test coverage achievable using this approach will always be vanishingly small.

As it is impossible to investigate all possible input conditions or all internal states, it would seem sensible to tackle the problem from a different direction. In Chapter 6 we looked at the process of fault modelling as a means of predicting the ways in which a system might fail. We then considered fault detection coverage and fault tolerance coverage in respect of their relevance to the production of fault-tolerant systems. Fault modelling may also be used to assist in the design of testing methods. If we can predict all the ways in which a system might fail, it should be possible to devise tests to look at individual potential failures. As before, we could calculate the test coverage as the percentage of all possible failures that are investigated. Unfortunately, this approach also has problems. In Chapter 6 we looked at hardware faults, and noted that no modelling technique provides a perfect description of the physical effects it attempts to depict. We also noted that the number of possible single faults could be extremely large, and that multiple faults were so numerous that they could not be considered in any practical testing scheme. If, for example, we consider a microprocessor having a million transistors, this could have of the order of 10^{12} single bridging faults, but approaching 10^{18} bridging faults between three nodes. Considering the possible bridges between any number of nodes produces vast numbers of potential faults. Similarly, a system with N nodes may have $2N$ single-stuck-at faults, but $3^N - 1$ multiple faults. For a microprocessor this latter figure is enormous. In a computer-based system we also need to consider potential software faults. Although it is probably possible to place an upper limit on the number of possible software errors that could be incorporated within a program (given the limits imposed by the memory space of the system), for all practical purposes this value may be considered to be infinite. It is therefore clear that exhaustive testing based on any form of fault modelling technique is impossible, and that, as before, any realistic measure of fault coverage will be vanishingly small.

From the above discussion it is clear that exhaustive testing is not feasible for any practical computer-based system. It is also apparent that a 'brute force' approach to testing is doomed to failure. Effective testing is therefore reliant on the skill of the test engineer in defining a programme of tests that will yield meaningful data. As all the properties of a system cannot be tested, it is necessary to identify the features of importance and to determine an appropriate strategy to investigate them. Some forms of testing identify a number of situations to be investigated and then attempt to test an appropriate number of these cases. Such testing, which is often termed **coverage-based testing**, can take several forms.

Because the starting point of the design of any system is its requirements, it would seem sensible to perform tests to confirm that these have been satisfied. In a safety-critical system both functional and safety requirements need to be investigated. This may be achieved by devising individual tests to confirm that each aspect of the requirements documents is satisfied. The **requirements test coverage** is then the percentage of the functions within the requirements documents that are investigated, this being determined by a process of **requirements coverage analysis**. When considering the safety requirements of a system, any test scheme would *have* to achieve a test coverage of 100%. Similarly, the functional requirements would normally be completely investigated. System requirements testing can be performed using a black-box approach, relying only on what the system should do in order to check its characteristics. Module testing can follow a similar pattern by testing sections of the system against the functional aspects of their specifications.

A second form of coverage-based testing adopts a white-box approach and is termed **structure-based testing**. Here information on the internal structure of the system is used to devise tests to activate and test individual components. Such methods are often used for software testing, where the components are statements or distinct sections of code. Structure-based software testing may be applied with different levels of rigour depending on the integrity requirements of the application. Draft IEC 1508 identifies a number of program elements that may be tested. These include:

Statements: This is the least rigorous test, since it is possible to execute all code statements without exercising both branches of each conditional statement.

Branches: Both sides of every branch should be checked. This may be impractical for some types of defensive code.

Compound conditions: Every condition in a compound conditional branch (that is, conditions linked by AND or OR) should be exercised.

Linear code sequence and jump: This is a linear sequence of code statements that includes conditional jumps and which is terminated by a jump. It will often be infeasible to test all subpaths owing to constraints imposed on the input data by the execution of earlier code.

Entire path: This involves execution of all possible paths through the code. Complete testing is normally infeasible due to the large number of potential paths – indeed, in most non-trivial programs there are effectively an infinite number of paths.

Because execution of all possible tasks is impractical, the task of the test engineer is to select a set of paths to investigate the system effectively, using the smallest number of tests. In making this selection various techniques may be used, such as:

Data flow analysis: Execution paths are selected on the basis of data usage. For example, a path may be chosen because a particular variable is both written and read.

Call graph: A program is composed of subroutines that may be called from other subroutines. A call graph is the tree of subroutine invocations in the program. Tests may be designed to cover all invocations in the tree.

The percentage of all possible paths that are tested is termed the **structural test coverage**.

It should be noted that not only is complete test coverage impossible in some cases, it may also be inadvisable. If, for example, a testing regime required 100% statement coverage, this would impose restrictions on the programming methods that could be used to implement the software. Defensive programming techniques often result in sections of code that are never executed and thus cannot be tested dynamically.

Test adequacy

Because exhaustive testing of a computer-based system is impossible, it is necessary to decide the form and amount of testing required for a given application. This in turn will determine the level of confidence that can be placed on the testing process. Decisions on these matters are made with respect to a set of **test adequacy criteria** associated with the project.

Guidance on the selection of test adequacy criteria is given in the various national and international standards, such as DO-178B (RTCA/EUROCAE, 1992). Many of these mandate certain aspects of testing and would, for example, normally require complete coverage of the safety requirements within the dynamic testing. By requiring different adequacy criteria for systems of various degrees of criticality, the standards suggest the confidence that may be associated with the corresponding levels of testing.

Test adequacy criteria determine the number and form of the test cases used during testing, and also the manner in which the test results are obtained and analysed. A typical set of criteria will require the use of several testing methods and will necessitate both black-box and white-box techniques. Adequacy criteria may be divided into two main categories:

- requirements-based criteria
- structure-based criteria.

The former are normally associated with black-box testing, and take their information from the definition of the system. These are sometimes referred to as specification-based criteria, as the system specification forms the source of much of the data used for such testing. Structure-based criteria require white-box methods and use data on the structure of the system gained by analysing the detailed implementation.

An adequacy criterion is normally associated with an underlying testing technique that is required to satisfy it. For example, requirements-based criteria will necessitate particular requirements-based testing methods and will stipulate what such testing is to achieve. Structure-based criteria will require structure-based testing methods, and will specify necessary coverage levels where appropriate. Several requirements-based and structure-based testing methods were described earlier in this chapter, as were various forms of test coverage.

Although the various standards give guidance on the choice of test adequacy criteria, they do not give definitive, quantified requirements for the level of testing required for computer-based systems. One of the reasons for this is that there are currently no accepted metrics for the 'testedness' of software (Wichmann, 1993). There is now a widespread acceptance of the ISO 9000 series of quality assurance standards, and this has led to great improvements in software quality. However, these standards are largely procedural, rather than technical, and give no specific requirements for the amount of testing to be performed. Although several factors concerned with 'testedness' are extremely difficult to quantify, there are some measures, such as those related to structural testing coverage, that could form the basis of a useful testedness metric. Such a measure would not give a full picture of the quality of the testing process, but would at least quantify one aspect of it.

Timing aspects

Within this text we are primarily concerned with safety-critical systems that must operate in real time. Real-time systems may be divided into two groups, depending on whether they have 'hard' or 'soft' time constraints.

- Hard real-time systems have time constraints such that the response of the system to a given stimulus must always occur within a given amount of time.
- Soft real-time systems have time constraints such that the mean response time, over a defined period, is less than some specified maximum value.

The first of these categories represents a much more demanding requirement, and it is into this group that most embedded control systems fall.

Satisfying 'hard' real-time constraints represents one of the most demanding aspects of the generation of safety-critical systems. In particular, the task of demonstrating that these requirements have been met, poses particular problems. This process may be considered in two parts:

- establishing the timing constraints from the system requirements;
- demonstrating that these requirements have been satisfied.

The first of these tasks is often more difficult than it would seem, as many timing constraints are implied rather than explicitly stated. For example, a requirement that the power delivered to a particular actuator be controlled to an accuracy of 1% may not seem to impose any timing constraints on the system. However, if the rate of change of the output signal and the response time of the actuator are considered, it is clear that timing is of importance. If the output were produced using a pulse-width modulation technique, the update rate of this output would also need to be considered. When specifications are written in natural languages it is extremely difficult to identify and quantify all the timing implications within the system definition. One approach to this problem lies in the use of appropriate formal specification methods, as discussed in Chapter 11. Languages such as timed CSP or techniques such as time Petri nets may be used to produce an unambiguous specification of the timing requirements of a system.

When the timing constraints have been identified it is then necessary to verify that they have been satisfied. Investigating the temporal characteristics of the hardware aspects of a system is often fairly straightforward. Hardware analysis and simulation may be used to predict timing behaviour, and this may be confirmed by dynamic testing. Problem areas associated with hardware include asynchronous activities, such as those experienced in communicating with external systems or sensing quantities within the environment. Investigating the timing properties of software is often far more difficult because of the complexity of its behaviour. Dynamic testing, in the form of performance testing, is used to demonstrate that timing constraints are met, but cannot prove that this will be true under all circumstances. Performance modelling is also used to show that the system will function correctly, even in worst-case conditions. Performance testing was described briefly in Section 12.3 and performance modelling was outlined in Section 12.5.

The cost of testing

One of the most important considerations when selecting a test strategy is cost. In order to assess the success of a project in minimizing the costs associated with testing, it is useful to have a measure of test expenditure. One such metric is the **test cost factor** (CONTESSE, 1995). This is defined by the expression:

$$\text{Test cost factor (TCF)} = \frac{\text{Test expenditure}}{\text{Test expenditure} + \text{Design expenditure}}$$

The factor therefore represents the fraction of the entire design and testing cost that is associated with testing.

Values for the TCF will vary with the nature of the application, and it is likely that it will increase with both system complexity and the required integrity level. However, for systems of similar characteristics the value of the TCF reflects the ability of the development team to minimize testing costs. In practice, this reflects the success of the design team in producing a system that is easy to test. Experience suggests that the TCF has a typical range of 0.25–0.75 (CONTESSE, 1995).

Because test planning is performed at an early stage, it is also possible to produce an estimate of the TCF at this time. This value may then be compared with later estimates and with a final value calculated at the end of the project. Such data can be used as feedback to guide the estimation of testing costs for other applications.

12.8 Designing for testability

Because testing represents a major proportion of the effort involved in the development of safety-critical systems, it is prudent to adopt design techniques that simplify the testing process. Important system attributes in this regard are its:

- **controllability** – how easy it is to inject signals to drive the system to a particular state;
- **observability** – how easy it is to detect signals within the system that reflect its operation.

Design for testability is a vast topic and a detailed discussion is not within the scope of this text. However, it is appropriate to consider a few issues of direct relevance to this subject.

Structured and object-oriented design techniques

Structured design involves the decomposition of a system into a number of modules that each perform a particular task. This process simplifies testing by allowing the various modules to be investigated separately. This approach may be applied to both hardware and software components.

Object-oriented design (OOD) and the related object-oriented programming (OOP) offer similar advantages to structured design and programming, but go further in terms of the definition of the modules involved. If used appropriately these offer additional benefits, including the potential for reusability.

Choice of programming languages

In Chapter 9 we looked in some detail at issues relating to the choice of programming languages for critical applications. From that discussion it is clear that the language used has a great impact on the testability of the resultant system. Many static analysis techniques are only possible with languages that possess certain properties, and such considerations may also restrict users to specified subsets. The availability of tools is also of great importance, with good tool support being obtainable for only a small number of languages.

The programming language adopted will also affect the nature of the testing that is performed during development. For example, if programs were written in C it would be advisable to perform 'type checking' on the software. However, if more strongly typed languages were used, such as Pascal or Ada, such testing would be of little benefit.

System complexity

Simple systems are easier to test. Therefore, every attempt should be made to reduce the complexity of the hardware, software and data structures. A reduction in complexity also offers advantages in other areas, such as reliability and the cost of implementation.

Input/output methods

The techniques used to input and output data play a large part in determining the complexity of the overall system, and in particular dictate many of the intricacies of the timing constraints. Simple program-controlled techniques tend to produce characteristics that are relatively simple to investigate, whereas asynchronous methods, such as the use of interrupts, can be much harder to test. For this reason some standards prohibit the use of interrupts in highly critical systems.

More information on the choice of design techniques for safety-critical systems can be found in the *CONTESSE Test Handbook* (1995). This looks at a series of implementation schemes and compares them in terms of their testing attributes.

12.9 Development tools

The development of any computer-based system requires the use of a range of hardware and software tools. These are used at various stages of a project and take many forms. Hardware tools include a wide variety of pieces of test equipment, such as logic analysers, timing analysers, oscilloscopes and, of course, personal computers and workstations. In many cases the hardware tools used in the development of safety-critical systems are identical to those required in less demanding projects. Software tools also play a vital part in the development of all computer systems, with such packages as compilers, debuggers and editors being used universally. However, critical projects often place great emphasis on the use of specialized software tools that are not appropriate for less demanding applications. In this section we consider some aspects of the selection of development tools for such applications.

Typical safety-critical projects will make use of a wide range of software-based tools at all stages of their development. Figure 12.3 gives an overview of some of the most widely used packages, indicating their use within the development process. The figure divides the packages into those that are used throughout the development lifecycle (so-called horizontal tools), and those that are restricted to a small number of lifecycle phases (vertical tools). Members of the latter group often form part of a suite of test tools that share a common user interface and, possibly, a common data format. The objective of a unified data format is to allow information from one tool to be used by another.

Several of the tools represented within Figure 12.3 were discussed in earlier sections of the book. Design tools encompass the broad range of ECAD packages and include both hardware and software design aids. Coding tools include compilers and assemblers, although some of these also fulfil a design function. Static and dynamic testing tools were discussed earlier in this chapter, and hazard analysis tools were discussed in Chapter 3.

Simulation tools may be used to simulate the system under development to allow a trial design to be evaluated before construction. Alternatively, they can be used to provide an environment for the system that allows safe and more effective testing. We shall look at the use of environmental simulation in Section 12.10.

The remaining vertical and horizontal tools are primarily concerned with managing the large amounts of data required for a safety-critical project. Audit

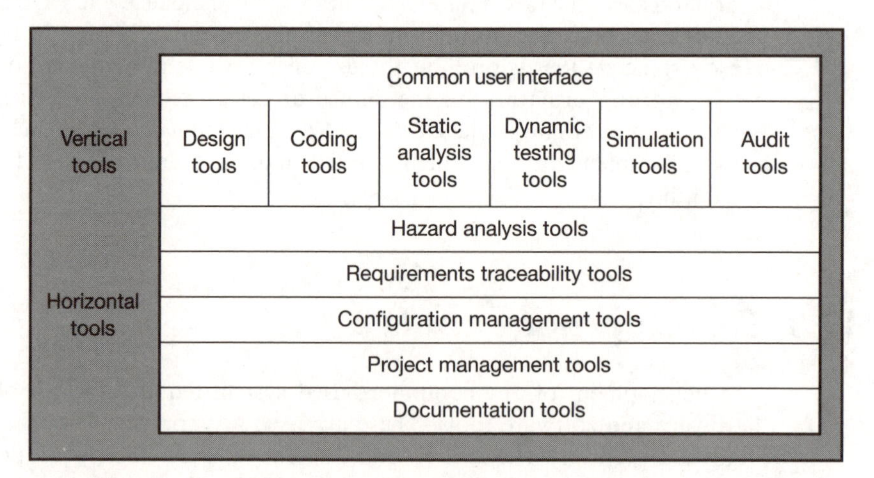

Figure 12.3 Classes of development tools.

tools are used to assist and formalize the auditing operations within the project. Requirements traceability tools are used to keep track of the various aspects of the requirements of a system throughout its development, and to ensure that each function is specifically investigated in the validation of the final implementation. Configuration management tools fulfil several functions concerned with the control and reporting of system configuration and various aspects of change control. Project management and documentation tools include a broad spectrum of packages covering many aspects of these tasks.

Of particular interest to the development of critical systems are the tools associated with static and dynamic testing. A recent survey of software testing tools for safety-critical systems (Cullyer and Storey, 1994) identified several problems associated with the available packages. It reported a general weakness in support for real-time dynamic testing and suggested that manufacturers' literature was often misleading in this area. Many tools investigate the dynamic performance of software by a process of 'instrumenting the source code'. This involves the addition of function and procedure calls to the program, as a basis for instrumentation and testing. In extreme cases the resultant software might be eight to ten times larger than the original program. Such testing provides much useful data on the functionality of the software, but gives no insight into its temporal properties. It will also have very different characteristics in terms of program and data storage. Perhaps one of the most disturbing findings of the report relates to the integrity of the testing tools. If the results of testing are to be used to support claims for the safety of a system, then the integrity of the tools used must also be considered. Recent standards require that tools are appropriate to the project in question. For example, Interim Defence Standard 00-55 (MoD, 1991) says that:

> 'All tools and support software used in the development of safety-critical software shall have sufficient safety integrity to ensure that they do not jeopardise the safety integrity of the SCS [safety-critical system].'

Although this condition would seem quite reasonable, it places the system developer in a very difficult position as few, if any, tool manufacturers claim any particular level of integrity for their products. This leaves the responsibility for determining the suitability of a tool clearly in the hands of the developer. Unfortunately, as we have seen, determining the integrity of any component or package simply on the basis of its observed performance is very difficult and extremely time-consuming. Also, as the packages themselves are often very expensive, evaluation of a number of competing products is usually prohibitive.

Apart from the difficulties of determining the level of integrity of any given product, there is also a general problem of the availability of highly dependable packages. A common 'rule of thumb' within industry is that the safety integrity level of the development tools should be no more than one level lower than that of the product being developed. Unfortunately, it is generally agreed that almost all software development tools have an integrity level that is at most level 1. A very few tools conform to the requirements of level 2, but there are currently no tools available that have been developed to the rigours of levels 3 or 4. Most tool manufacturers use development methods in line with established software quality standards, such as those of ISO 9000 TickIT, but this is not in itself sufficient to guarantee their suitability for a given project. When selecting tools developers must consider not only the supplier's claims for their products, but also the manufacturer's credibility and track record.

12.10 Environmental simulation

When developing safety-critical systems it is often inappropriate, or perhaps impossible, to test the system fully within its operational environment. For example, when testing a nuclear shutdown system it would be unwise to investigate its performance by taking a reactor into a potentially dangerous state. In such situations it is normal to perform testing using a **simulation** of the system's environment. This not only guarantees safety during the testing process, but may also allow a more efficient and complete investigation of the system's performance.

Forms of environment

It is self-evident that the environment of a critical system will vary greatly from one application to another. However, it is useful to differentiate between elements that are natural and those that are constructed.

Natural environmental factors

Some systems sense what one might term 'natural' environmental factors, such as temperature, pressure and humidity, and treat these as system inputs. For example, a temperature controller might measure each of these quantities and use them to determine its operation. Systems may also produce outputs that directly or indirectly affect external environmental factors. In addition to this intentional interaction with the real world, all systems affect, and are affected by, the physical environment in which they are situated. Any equipment will have a maximum and a minimum temperature at which it will function correctly, and will have permitted ranges for other physical quantities such as pressure and vibration. This interaction between the system and its environment is represented in Figure 12.4.

In some circumstances simulators will be required to reproduce only those quantities that are directly sensed or controlled by the system. In such cases it is assumed that other factors will be 'within allowable limits' and will therefore have negligible effects. In other situations it may be necessary for a simulation to reproduce a range of environmental factors that may have an incidental influence on the unit in question.

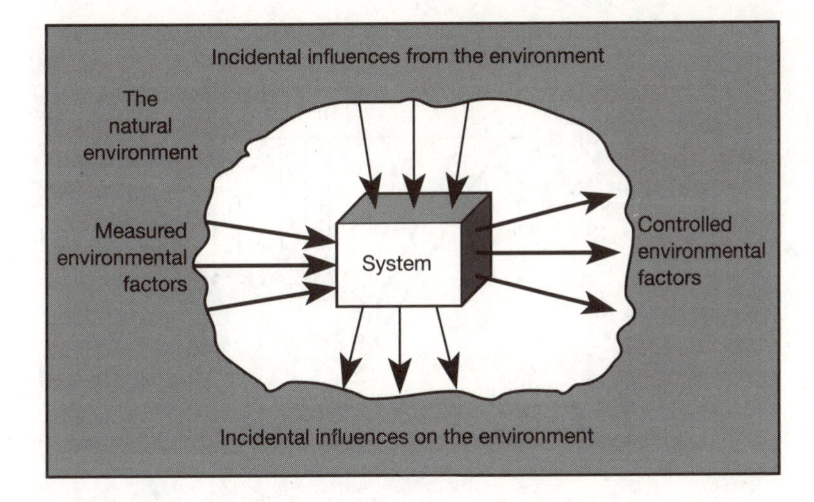

Figure 12.4 Interaction between a system and its natural environment.

One of the characteristics of natural environmental factors is that our knowledge of them is limited. Even seemingly simple quantities such as air temperature may be affected by highly complex mechanisms such as turbulence, which make accurate modelling very difficult.

Constructed environments

In most cases many of the input and output signals of computer-based equipment come from other constructed systems. In such cases the 'environment' of the equipment is the sum of the various components to which it is connected. As these components have been designed and manufactured, they tend to be better understood than elements within a natural environment. However, the behaviour of such units may be complex in nature. As with a natural environment, there may also be unintentional interaction between the system and the 'plant' to which it is connected. EMC is an obvious example of such an effect, where the plant may adversely affect the system or vice versa. This is illustrated in Figure 12.5.

Often the incidental interaction between the plant and the computer system is too unpredictable to be accurately simulated. Therefore a simulation of such an arrangement is likely to reproduce only the input and output signals of the system and ignore other effects. It is thus only a partial simulation of the actual environment.

Modules and their environment

Having considered the environment of a complete system, it is clear that we can adopt a similar approach to represent the environment of an individual module

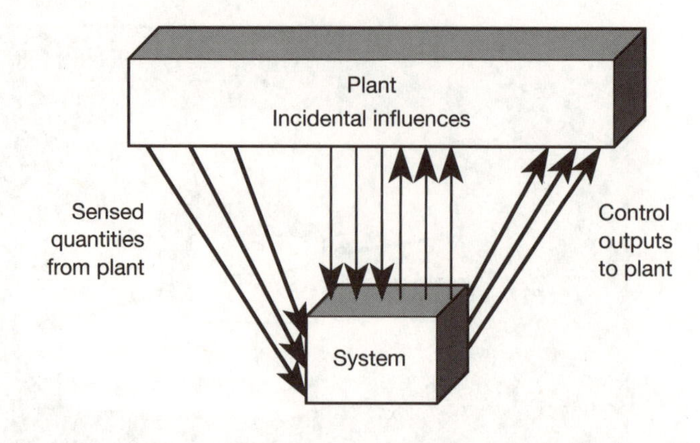

Figure 12.5 Interaction between a system and its constructed environment.

within that system. In Chapter 9 we looked at the partitioning of a system and at the interaction between the constituent modules. The various components have as their environment the other parts of the system, and possibly elements of the outside world. This situation is illustrated in Figure 12.6. If we consider module E in this figure we see that it interacts only with other parts of the system. Its environment is thus entirely constructed. Module F, on the other hand, communicates with elements of the outside world as well as with other modules. Therefore, depending on the nature of the external interface, this could have a partially natural environment.

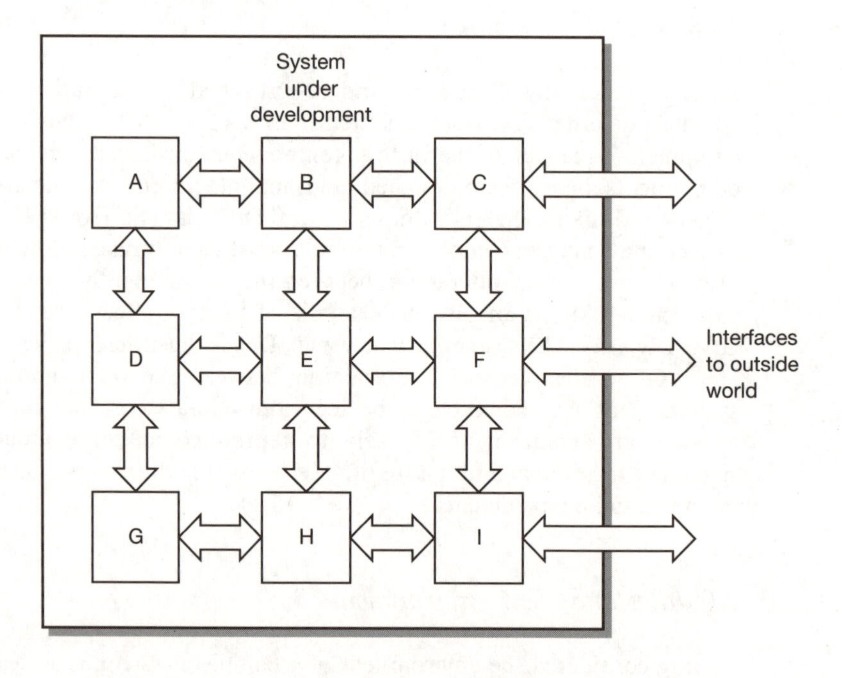

Figure 12.6 The interaction between modules of a system.

The modules of Figure 12.6 could represent hardware, software or some combination of the two. In any event, being constructed (and in this case, being made within the project in question) their characteristics should be well understood. This being the case, simulating their behaviour should be relatively straightforward. This would suggest that simulating the environment of any module that has no external interface would be straightforward, as the characteristics of all its external associated modules are known. Unfortunately, this overlooks the exchange of information between modules. Because module F interacts with the outside world, its characteristics, as seen by module E, will vary depending on the state of the external environment. Consequently, the response of module D to signals from module E will also be affected. Thus, although module D has no direct connection to the outside world, its environment is still affected by changes outside the system.

The human–computer interface

As was discussed in Chapter 5, a human operator represents one of the most complex components within any system. One may choose to consider the operator as part of the external environment of the system, or alternatively as one of the constituent modules. In either case, the modules that interact with the operator and, through the knock-on effect, other modules, have a complex entity within their environment. This greatly complicates the task of environmental simulation.

Forms of environmental simulator

Environmental simulators can take many forms and range from the very simple to the highly complex. Simulators may consist of hardware or software, or a combination of the two, and may be used at various points in the development process.

Generally the complexity of the simulator tends to increase with the level of integration of the unit being investigated. When testing at a modular level simulators are often extremely simple. In order to test a simple hardware input/output module it might be appropriate to connect to it a series of switches and lights to represent the unit's inputs and outputs. One might consider such a unit to be a basic environmental simulator, as it mimics the behaviour of its operational situation. Similarly, software routines are commonly tested by writing simple test programs to investigate their various functions by supplying and accepting data representing its normal operation. These simple pieces of test hardware or software are normally referred to as **test harnesses**, and although they share many of the characteristics of other forms of environmental simulator, they will not be discussed further.

Sometimes the testing of individual modules requires a greater level of sophistication than can be provided by a simple test harness. This is the case where the data exchanged between modules is complex, or has critical timing constraints. In such cases testing of the unit will require a more complete simulation of its external environment. However, in many cases it is not necessary to simulate the action of all the other components of the system, but simply to consider their interface to the module in question. This process is illustrated in Figure 12.7.

In Chapter 9 we discussed the partitioning of a system as part of the process of top-level design. At that time we noted that part of the task of defining each module is to prepare an interface design specification (IDS) that describes its interaction with other modules. Using the IDS of the module in question it is possible to simulate its interaction with other modules and so to reproduce its immediate environment. This process is known as **interface simulation**, and is shown in Figure 12.8. Here the environment of module E from the previous figure is being reproduced by simulating its interfaces with the other modules. Module E could represent a hardware module, in which case the various interfaces would also involve hardware. Alternatively the module could be a program element, when the various interfaces would be implemented in software. In this latter case, the simulator and the module being tested would coexist within the same computer. In some situations the interface controller is used manually to generate test signals in response to commands entered at a keyboard. Alternatively, the controller may be automated to reproduce a sequence of test situations.

As modules are combined to form more complex entities the sophistication of the simulators required to test them also tends to increase. Indeed, in

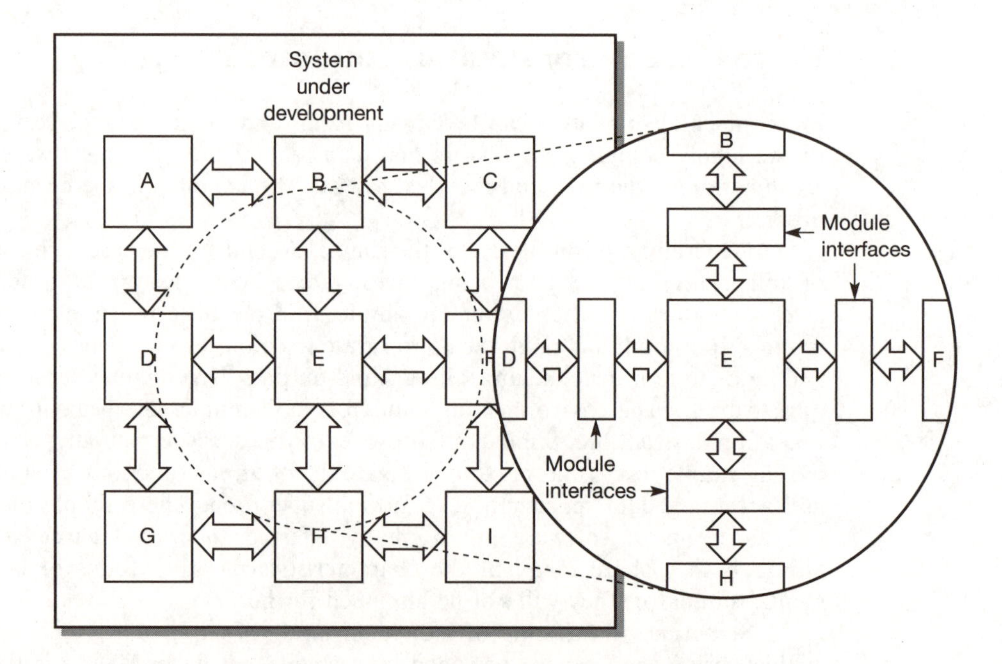

Figure 12.7 Module interface structure.

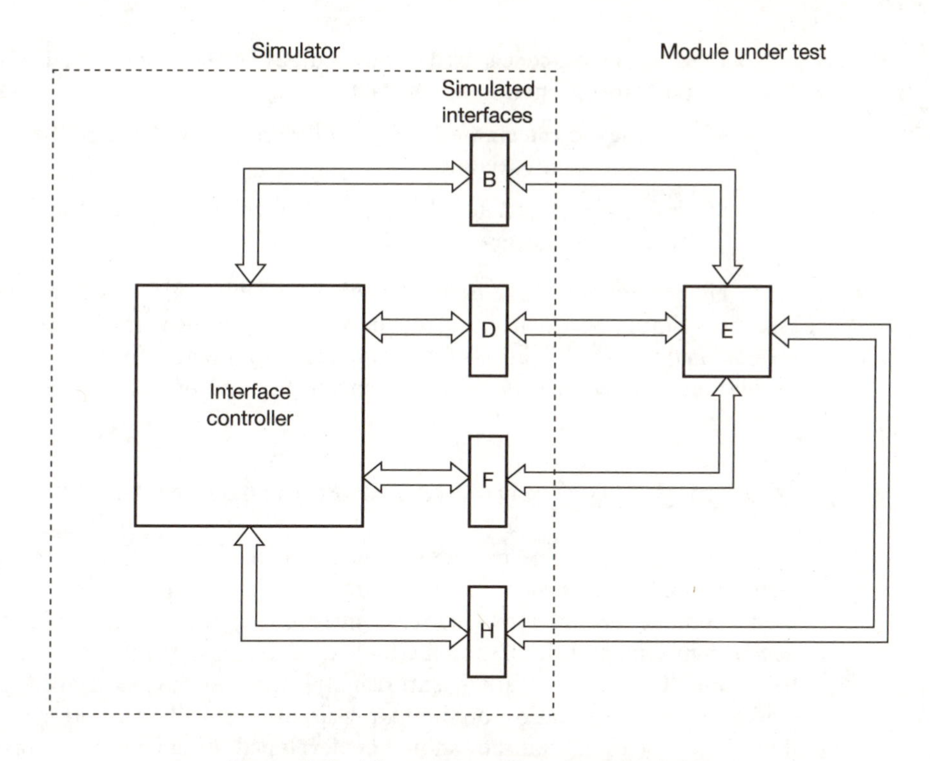

Figure 12.8 The process of interface simulation.

many cases the simulator required to imitate the environment of a component may be considerably more complex than the unit being tested. Take, for example, the case of a simple three-term controller used to control the flow of some dangerous material in a sophisticated chemical process. Here the controller itself is relatively simple, whereas the simulator required to represent the action of the entire chemical plant would be extremely complex.

Simulators used for final testing and for system validation are often extremely complex. For example, in the case of a controller for an aircraft engine this might include a testbed including actual sensors and actuators. For the final stages of testing of such a controller, an instrumented engine would normally be used.

Simulator requirements

If simulators are to be used to test critical systems then clearly our confidence in the test results will be affected by the fidelity of the simulation used. This raises the thorny issue of how we measure the quality of a simulation. Several factors are involved in this assessment, including:

- **variables simulated** – which environmental variables are included within the simulation and which are ignored;

- **accuracy of models used** – the accuracy of the models used to represent the various environmental factors;
- **accuracy of calculations** – the resolution and accuracy of the calculation used for each variable;
- **timing consideration** – the effects of calculation speeds and update rates on the simulation.

Unfortunately, there is no universally or even widely agreed method of assessing simulator quality, as the importance of the various factors differs greatly between applications. In practice, confidence in the fidelity of a simulation is based largely on value judgements and on experience.

Integrity requirements for environmental simulators

In safety-critical projects test results based on the use of simulators invariably play a major role in system validation and, where appropriate, in the safety case used to obtain certification. This raises questions concerning not only the fidelity of the environmental simulation methods used, but also the necessary integrity of the simulation tools. Rather surprisingly, the various standards give little guidance on the validation of simulators used in critical applications. However, it has been suggested that they should be developed using methods appropriate to a system with a safety integrity level that is one less than that of the system in question (Storey and Craine, 1994). This implies that simulators used in the production of highly critical systems must themselves be developed using very rigorous techniques. It is also recommended that such simulators should be developed quite independently from the system they are designed to test, to reduce the risk of common design faults. Unfortunately, such independence will inevitably increase development costs.

12.11 Independent verification and validation

Standards such as DO-178B and the draft of IEC 1508 give guidance on the degree of independence that should be adopted for various aspects of system development. These recommendations suggest that different levels of independence are appropriate for distinct phases of the work, and that these are dependent on the integrity level of the application. Table 12.5 shows an example of the recommendations given in the IEC standard. These relate to the task of software safety validation, and it can be seen that the degree of independence required increases with the integrity level. Where more than one degree of independence is recommended for a particular integrity level, the approach adopted will be determined by a number of factors specific to the application. These factors are discussed within the standard.

Table 12.5 Independence requirements for software safety validation.

Degree of independence required for validation	*SIL 1*	*SIL 2*	*SIL 3*	*SIL 4*
1. Independent person	HR	HR	NR	NR
2. Independent department	–	HR	HR	NR
3. Independent organization	–	–	HR	HR

HR = highly recommended, NR = not recommended, – = no recommendation

It can be seen from Table 12.5 that for systems of all levels of integrity it is recommended that some form of independence is included within the validation process. For level 1 systems, adequate independence may be obtained by involving other staff within the same department. For systems of higher levels of integrity it becomes vital to increase the level of independence by using staff from outside the relevant department, or from outside the organization. Increasing the independence between those involved in validation reduces the chance of common mistakes or common misconceptions.

Several companies and laboratories specialize in providing independent verification and validation services for safety-critical software or complete systems. Various bodies accredit such organizations in respect of the quality of their procedures and the international standards to which they conform. In the UK, the National Measurement Accreditation Service (NAMAS) has begun accrediting companies for testing the computer software used in safety-critical systems. The first such company (ERA) was accredited in 1994. The approved testing methods involve a suite of in-house procedures including both static and dynamic techniques. Accreditation implies adherence to internationally accepted standards, and it is likely that independent validation from an accredited laboratory will become a normal requirement in highly critical applications. Moves in this direction are being prompted by the increasing acceptance of standards such as DO-178B and IEC 1508 and the desire to reduce the risks of litigation.

12.12 The roles of testing

So far within this chapter we have looked primarily at the use of testing as part of the overall verification and validation process. It is appropriate at this point to note that testing has a number of roles, and that its objectives vary accordingly. Testing has three main purposes within safety-critical projects, these being:

- development testing
- validation testing
- production testing.

Development testing is aimed at *locating* faults within the system so that these may be removed. The goal of such testing is to find as many faults as possible, and a range of dynamic, static and modelling techniques may be used. Validation testing aims to demonstrate the absence of faults and to demonstrate other positive features. Here again, dynamic, static and modelling techniques are commonly used in this process. Both development and validation testing are used to investigate the characteristics of the design and implementation of a system, and are carried out during the development phase. Such testing is applied to both the hardware and the software aspects of the system.

Production testing is used to test an individual implementation of a system, rather than its design. It therefore aims to detect any defects within a particular unit as a result of a manufacturing or component fault. What is being tested here is the accuracy of the *replication* of an approved design. Testing the replication of software is very simple, and can often be achieved with adequate confidence using a simple checksum. The replication of hardware is much more complicated to test, because of the wide range of possible faults. Consequently, most production testing is aimed at detecting hardware faults. Because production testing is intended to detect errors in replication rather than in design, only dynamic testing methods are appropriate. In non-critical applications production testing might be applied to only selected samples of the production output, particularly where these are being manufactured in high volume. In safety-critical systems, testing is required for all units.

The three categories of testing described within this section may each make use of similar testing techniques, including those described earlier in this chapter. However, the test cases selected for use with these techniques are likely to differ, to reflect the diverse goals of the testing activities.

12.13 Additional information

The material within this chapter provides an introduction to a topic of great breadth. Additional data and guidance may be found in generic international standards, such as the draft of IEC 1508, or appropriate industry-specific standards such as DO-178B. These provide information on appropriate testing and validation methods for the various phases of the development lifecycle, and for systems of different levels of criticality. Standards will be discussed in some detail in Chapter 14.

Further useful information has recently become available as a result of a major research programme carried out in the UK. This work, which went under the title of CONTESSE, was performed by a consortium of major companies and universities, with funding from the Department of Trade and Industry (DTI) and the Science and Engineering Research Council (SERC). The project looked at various aspects of the testing and validation of safety-critical systems, with particular importance being placed on the use of simulation. The findings of the project represent the views of many of the UK's leading companies within this field, and these have recently been published. The *CONTESSE Test Handbook* (1995) provides detailed information on testing methods and includes much of the survey data obtained during the project. It also includes a detailed discussion of the selection of development lifecycle models and the use of environmental simulation techniques.

REFERENCES

BCS (1995). *Standard for Software Component Testing*. Working Draft 3.0, British Computer Society Specialist Interest Group in Software Testing (BCS SIGIST) – standard in preparation

Bologna S. (1993). Real-time requirements specification and animation using extended Petri nets: theory and applications. In *Safety Aspects of Computer Control* (Bennett P., ed.), pp. 76–87. Oxford: Butterworth-Heinemann

CONTESSE (1995). *CONTESSE Test Handbook* (1995). Glasgow: BAeSEMA

Cullyer W.J. and Storey N. (1994). Tools and techniques for the testing of safety-critical software. *Comput. Control Eng. J.*, **5**(5), 239–44

Fagan M.E. (1986). Advances in software inspection. *IEEE Trans. Software Eng.*, **12**(7), 744–51

IEC (1995). Draft International Standard 1508 *Functional Safety: Safety-Related Systems*. Geneva: International Electrotechnical Commission

Leveson N.G. and Stolzy J.L. (1987). Safety analysis using Petri nets. *IEEE Trans. Software Eng.*, **SE-13**(3), 386–97

McDermid J., ed. (1992). *Software Engineer's Reference Book*. Oxford: Butterworth-Heinemann

MoD (1991). Interim Defence Standard 00-55 *The Procurement of Safety Critical Software in Defence Equipment*. Glasgow: Directorate of Standardization

RTCA/EUROCAE (1992). *Software Considerations in Airborne Systems and Equipment Certification*. RTCA/DO-178B; EUROCAE/ED-12B. Washington: Radio Technical Commission for Aeronautics. Paris: European Organisation for Civil Aviation Electronics

Storey N. and Craine J.F. (1994). Environmental simulation in the development of safety critical software. *Proc. 3rd Int. Conf. on Reliability, Quality Control and Risk Assessment*. Washington DC, pp. 89–92

Wichmann B.A. (1993). Why are there no measurement standards for software testing? *Comput. Standards and Interfaces*, **15**(4), 361–4

Yourdon E. (1989). *Structured Walkthroughs*, 4th edn. Englewood Cliffs, NJ: Prentice-Hall

FURTHER READING

Beizer B. (1990). *Software Testing Techniques*. New York: Van Nostrand Reinhold

PROBLEMS

12.1 Explain the difference between verification and validation. To what phase or phases of a project are these processes normally applied?

12.2 Compare module testing, integration testing and system testing in terms of the nature of the faults they tend to locate, and the relative difficulties of rectifying such problems.

12.3 Explain the difference between static testing and static analysis.

12.4 Discuss the relevance of black-box and white-box approaches to dynamic testing, static testing and mathematical modelling.

12.5 Why is it important that test planning is performed early within the development lifecycle?

12.6 What aspects of the implementation of a system are considered by the overall safety validation plan?

12.7 Describe the characteristics of the three major categories of dynamic testing and give examples of techniques that fall within each group. State whether each group corresponds to a black-box or a white-box approach.

12.8 Explain the use of error seeding within dynamic testing.

12.9 Discuss briefly the use of static code analysis in the testing of software. What implications does the use of this technique have on the choice of programming language?

12.10 Explain the roles of performance testing and performance modelling in system validation.

12.11 With reference to Table 12.4, why are some techniques seen to be suitable for highly critical systems that are not judged suitable for less demanding applications?

12.12 Discuss the concept of exhaustive testing and its relevance to coverage-based testing.

12.13 Explain the difference between test coverage and test adequacy.

12.14 Give examples of embedded computer systems that have: no real-time constraints; 'soft' real-time constraints; 'hard' real-time constraints. Why is the process of determining timing constraints not straightforward?

12.15 Explain the meaning and the use of the test cost factor.

12.16 What factors dominate considerations of design for testability? Give some examples of how these requirements may be achieved.

12.17 What problems exist with available software testing tools in respect of their use for real-time testing?

12.18 Why are considerations of tool integrity of importance and concern to the developers of safety-critical systems?

12.19 Discuss the importance of environmental simulation in the development of safety-critical systems.

12.20 Why is it often easier to simulate a constructed environment than one that contains natural elements?

12.21 How does a simple test harness differ from an environmental simulator?

12.22 Explain the characteristics and use of interface simulation.

12.23 What factors determine the fidelity of an environmental simulation? How does this differ from its integrity?

12.24 Discuss the need for independence in the validation of safety-critical systems.

12.25 Describe the varying forms of testing required for the development, validation and production of safety-critical systems.

13 Quality Management

CHAPTER CONTENTS

13.1 Introduction

In recent years the importance placed on achieving 'quality' within all fields of endeavour has increased enormously. It sometimes seems that our goals in life may be encompassed by driving a *quality* car, attaining a *quality* home and spending *quality* time with our family. This use of the term, almost as a synonym for 'good', is often misleading, and certainly tends to impair our understanding of the word when used within an industrial setting.

Over the years many industrialists and academics have attempted to characterize quality, and it is defined in many ways, including:

- fitness for use
- conformance to requirements
- the totality of features and characteristics of a product or service that bear on its ability to satisfy stated or implied needs.

What the last of these definitions lacks in brevity it makes up for in credibility, as it comes from ISO 9000, one of the most respected of the international quality standards.

Quality management aims to maintain and improve all aspects of the quality of the products and services supplied by an organization, and the processes within that organization. This activity may be divided into **quality assurance** and **quality control**, as shown in Figure 13.1.

Quality assurance concentrates on the **process** of manufacture and attempts to ensure that work is performed correctly. Quality control aims to ensure that the **product** is correct, where the term 'product' represents what is

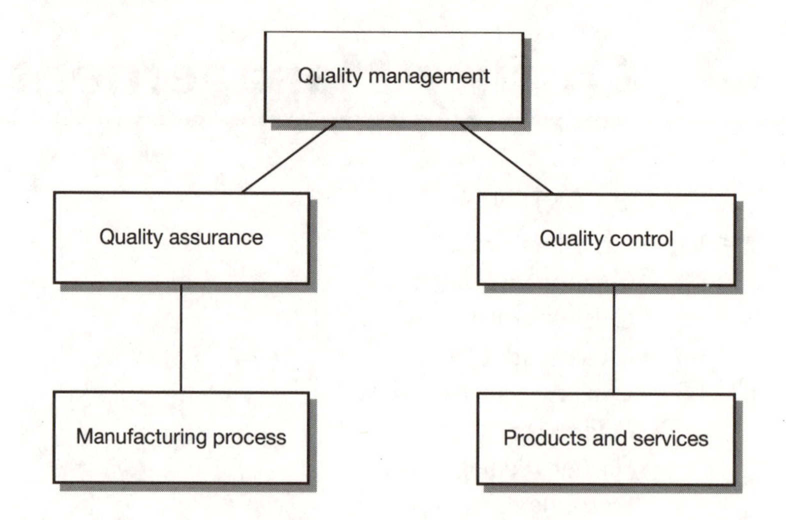

Figure 13.1 Areas of quality management.

delivered to the customer. A product in this context may be some kind of system or component, or some form of service.

The various aspects of quality management are normally realized through what is termed a **quality management system** (**QMS**) or simply a **quality system**. This is defined by ISO 9000 as:

> *'The organizational structure, responsibilities, procedures, processes and resources for implementing quality management.'*

As quality relates to the ability of a product to meet its requirements, it is clearly of fundamental importance to safety. To understand the role of quality in enhancing safety, we need to look at quality systems in a little more detail. Although the objectives of quality assurance and quality control are obviously closely linked, their methods of implementation are very different. In this chapter we will look briefly at the characteristics of each approach and discuss their implications for the development of high-integrity systems. We will also consider some of the various national and international standards in this area.

13.2 Quality assurance

ISO 9000 defines quality assurance as:

> *'All those planned and systematic actions necessary to provide adequate confidence that a product or service will satisfy given requirements for quality.'*

When the 'product' concerned is a safety-critical system, the main objectives of a quality assurance system are:

- to increase the quality of the product;
- to provide a foundation for the safety justification (safety case);
- to improve development and production efficiency.

The relative importance of these factors will vary greatly between projects, with less critical applications placing much emphasis on the last aspect. In contrast, in more critical applications, improvements in efficiency are invariably of less concern than other considerations.

Contributions to the safety justification of critical systems represent a major aspect of quality assurance. As safety cannot be demonstrated by testing alone, a system's acceptance must be based on confidence gained in other ways. Key factors in any safety case are the development and production processes used and the quality methods used to oversee them.

From its definition it is clear that quality assurance covers a number of activities. These may be categorized into the broad areas of:

- defining the production process and the management system;
- management of resources;
- auditing and corrective action.

The management system needs to cover all aspects of the work, throughout its complete lifecycle. Resources in this context includes the provision of suitably qualified staff and would include such issues as training. Auditing is used to ensure that the various activities of the management system are implemented correctly. It should be noted that quality assurance is not concerned with the design and testing of a system, but is involved in ensuring that the design and testing operations are performed correctly. This is an ongoing activity that continuously strives for improvement through a process of iteration. The overall operation of a quality assurance system is depicted in Figure 13.2.

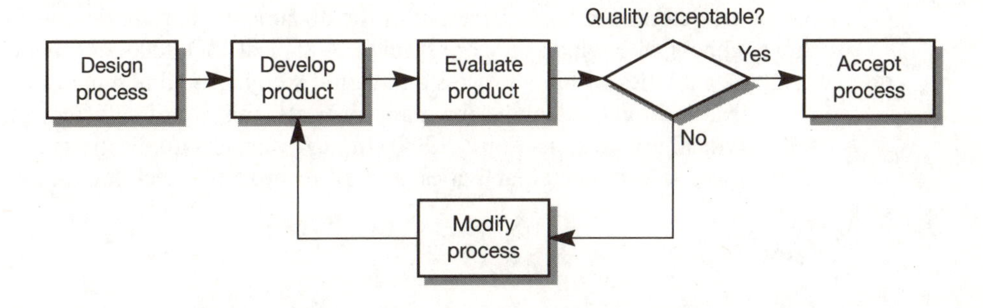

Figure 13.2 The quality assurance process.

Procedures and management structure

A fundamental part of quality assurance involves defining the necessary **procedures** for a given project and the **management structure** concerned. This involves listing the necessary tasks within a project and identifying people to perform them. The flow of information is also documented, so that each member of the team is aware of the requirements for reports and other documentation.

For safety-critical projects the need for a rigorously defined management structure is such that an informal specification of this structure, written in a natural language such as English, may be inappropriate. In Chapter 5 we considered the problems associated with specifications written in natural languages, and noted that these invariably suffer from ambiguity. In that chapter we looked at both formal and semiformal methods of tackling this problem. When defining management structures for critical applications, it is normal to stop short of using fully formal methods but to make extensive use of semiformal techniques. These would typically include diagrammatic tools that rigorously define activities, responsible staff and a reporting structure.

Resources

Each member of the project team defined by the management structure will require an appropriate level of skill and training. Part of the quality assurance function is to establish the levels of expertise required for each element of the team, and to ensure that such human resources are available. In some cases this will require that specialist training is undertaken. In safety-critical projects the competence of the staff involved may be central to the arguments within the safety case.

Auditing

Auditing is used to check whether the various quality assurance procedures are being carried out correctly, and whether they are successful. This is done by a process of data gathering and discussion, which will include looking at samples of the documents concerned. Auditing may be carried out with various degrees of rigour, determined by the fraction of the documents that are reviewed and the thoroughness with which they are studied. A typical ISO 9000 audit would look at all the activities within a process and would study a small number of each type of record. Although adequate for many projects, this is not sufficient for many safety-critical applications (Kirk, 1994). In highly critical applications it might be appropriate to examine all activities, and all records, to check for correctness.

Quality plan

Details of the quality assurance activities associated with a project are normally formalized within a quality plan. This forms the main documentation for the be far from easy. When this approach is applied to hardware components or subsystems, the characteristics to be assessed include not only functionality, but also more complex issues such as reliability, maintainability and safety. We saw in earlier chapters that for highly critical systems the required values for some of these factors are beyond our ability for measurement. With software the situation is even more complicated. First, it is generally impossible to test a program completely to determine its correspondence to the functional aspects of the specification. Secondly, the requirements of the software will include features such as reliability, efficiency or portability, which may be extremely hard to quantify. Quality control depends on our ability to measure parameters within the product that we wish to control. Unfortunately, in highly complex systems this is often very difficult.

Although quality control alone cannot guarantee product quality, it does play an important part in the overall task of producing high-quality systems. In practice, quality management requires a judicial blend of both quality assurance and quality control, to achieve the best results.

13.4 Quality standards

Regulations for quality and safety have existed for more than 150 years, some of the earliest legislation being concerned with railways (Jackson, 1993). In this section we shall look at a few examples of standards that are primarily concerned with quality. We will leave standards relating to other aspects of safety-critical systems until Chapter 14.

ISO 9000

The ISO 9000 series of standards relates to quality management and quality assurance (ISO, 1994). It comprises a number of independent documents that cover different aspects of the topic. In Europe the standards are also known as EN 2900x standards, and within the UK they have been widely used for many years as the BS 5750 standard. The BS 5750 notation is now being replaced in the UK by a BS EN ISO 9000 designation. In the US the ANSI/ASQC Q9000 series of standards is technically equivalent to the ISO series, but uses American spelling and grammar. The main documents within the series are:

ISO 9001	Quality systems: Model for quality assurance in design, development, production, installation and servicing
ISO 9002	Quality systems: Model for quality assurance in production, installation and servicing
ISO 9003	Quality systems: Model for quality assurance in final inspection and test.

quality procedures involved and for the associated management structure. Som
standards, for example Interim Defence Standard 00-55, require that a quali
plan be prepared at an early stage and agreed alongside the project safety pla
The quality plan would also include details of the proposed auditing procedu
to be used to demonstrate conformance.

Implementation of a well thought-out quality plan should result ir
high-quality development and production process that delivers consist
output. However, process quality is a *necessary* but not a *sufficient* requirem
to guarantee the quality of the final product. We therefore need to consider
only quality assurance, but also various aspects of quality control.

13.3 Quality control

ISO 9000 defines quality control as:

> *'The operational techniques and activities that are used to fulfil requirements for quality.'*

Quality control came to prominence in the field of high-volume mecl
manufacture. This often uses techniques of statistical quality control to s
atically reduce the errors associated with a particular manufacturing proce
principles involved are illustrated in Figure 13.3. Here the output of a pr
measured and the results analysed to gain an insight into the characteristic
items being produced. This information is then compared with the spec
for this part, and the difference used to modify the production proc
modifications might be used to improve the tolerance of a component or t
the number of components that fail some form of acceptance test.

When quality control is applied to the production of comput
systems, the basic principles are similar to those described above but t
may be very different. As before, a comparison is made between the c
the process and the original specification, and the performance of the pr
process is then assessed. On the basis of this assessment modification
made in an attempt to fine-tune the operation. Unfortunately, this pr

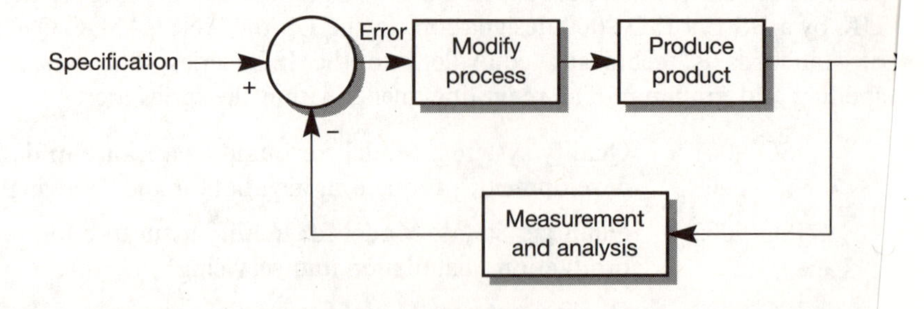

Figure 13.3 The quality control process.

ISO 9001 is intended for organizations that need to assure their customers of the conformity of their products to an international standard throughout their entire development lifecycle. This is important where a contract involves a design element and where requirements are defined in terms of performance. This is the most complete and stringent of the series of standards, and includes all aspects of the quality system.

ISO 9002 is concerned only with the production, installation and servicing elements of a project, and is suitable for work that does not include a design component. It is also less stringent than ISO 9001.

ISO 9003 is the least stringent of the series of standards and covers only those aspects concerned with the inspection and testing of components or systems manufactured elsewhere.

The standards also include a number of guides to assist in their application. Of particular relevance to the material within this book are:

ISO 9000-1	Quality systems: Guidelines for selection and use
ISO 9000-3	Guide to the application of ISO 9001 to the development, supply and maintenance of software
ISO 9004	Quality management and quality system elements.

The second of these two documents provides detailed guidance for organizations developing, supplying and maintaining software. It is directed at bespoke software and is not directly relevant to the production of software products. Among other things, it gives assistance on contractual matters relating to the provision of software. Information within the guide covers three main areas, namely:

- **The quality framework**: Management responsibilities, the quality system, audits and corrective action
- **Lifecycle activities**: Actions that are required during the various lifecycle phases, namely: contract review; requirements; development planning; quality planning; design and implementation; testing and validation; acceptance; replication, delivery and installation
- **Supporting activities**: Actions that are not related to specific lifecycle phases, such as: configuration management; document control; measurement; tools support; purchasing and training.

It should be stressed that ISO 9000 is *not* specifically concerned with computer-based systems. In fact, being primarily concerned with quality *assurance*, the standard may be applied in any industry. Thus, although detailed guidance is given on its applicability to software, its general requirements are equally applicable to all aspects of the production of computer-based systems.

ISO 9000 TickIT is a certification system for quality management systems specially designed to meet the needs of the software industry. This gives detailed guidance on the implementation of ISO 9001 within the information technology area.

ISO/IEC 9126

Unlike ISO 9000, the ISO/IEC 9126 standard is primarily concerned with quality control and is specific to computer software (ISO, 1991). The title of the standard is *ISO/IEC 9126: Information Technology – Software Product Evaluation – Quality Characteristics and Guidelines for their Use*. It defines six characteristics that determine software quality. These are:

- **Functionality**: A set of attributes that bear on the existence of a set of functions and their specified properties. The functions are those that satisfy stated or implied needs.
- **Reliability**: A set of attributes that bear on the capability of software to maintain its level of performance under stated conditions for a stated period of time.
- **Usability**: A set of attributes that bear on the effort needed for use, and on the individual evaluation of such use, under stated conditions.
- **Efficiency**: A set of attributes that bear on the relationship between the level of performance of the software and the amount of resources used, under stated conditions.
- **Maintainability**: A set of attributes that bear on the effort needed to make specified modifications.
- **Portability**: A set of attributes that bear on the ability of software to be transferred from one environment to another.

The document also includes an informative appendix giving details of an 'evaluation process model'. This description does not form part of the standard, but gives guidance on assessing the various characteristics.

The standard permits developers to evaluate software quality in an approved manner, in terms of the specific characteristics described above. This is of particular importance when software is supplied under contract. It also provides a basis for the assessment of software quality as part of the process of independent verification and validation. Unfortunately, the standard does not include the use of quantitative methods for the measurement of the various quality characteristics. This situation reflects the problems associated with defining metrics for many of the factors concerned.

Other civil quality standards

Over the past few years a number of civil standards have appeared in the area of quality. These have been dominated by standards concerned with quality assurance and have tended to concentrate on software issues. Of particular note are those listed below, for which full references are given at the end of this chapter.

ANSI/IEEE (1986)	Std 983-1986 *Guide for Software Quality Assurance Planning*
ANSI/IEEE (1989)	Std 730-1989 *Software Quality Assurance Plans*
ASME (1990)	Standard NQA 2a *Quality Assurance Requirements for Nuclear Facility Applications*

Military quality standards

Various standards exist to define quality requirements for military projects. As with civil standards these tend to be concerned with software, rather than system issues. Standards of importance include:

DoD (1988)	Std-2168 *Defense System Software Quality Program*
MoD (1984)	Defence Standard 00-16: *Guide to the Achievement of Quality in Software*
MoD (1991)	Interim Defence Standard 05-95: *Quality System Requirements for the Development, Supply and Maintenance of Software*
NATO (1993)	Quality Standard AQAP-150: *Requirements for Quality Management of Software Development*

13.5 Quality – an overview

Quality is increasingly being seen as an issue of vital concern to all forms of commerce and industry. Even small businesses are seeing the advantages of becoming accredited by a recognized institution as conforming to an international quality standard – usually ISO 9000 or one of its national equivalents. One of the reasons for this is that larger firms, who are invariably conforming to ISO 9000, will often only employ suppliers and subcontractors who are also operating such a quality system.

Unfortunately, for highly critical projects the quality assurance procedures of ISO 9000 are not sufficiently rigorous and a more stringent quality system is necessary. This will normally require an accurately defined management and reporting structure, and a strict system of auditing.

Although quality assurance is vital in all safety-critical projects, this alone is not sufficient to achieve an adequate level of quality. Quality control methods are also required, to deal with 'product'-centred rather than 'process'-centred issues. Standards such as ISO/IEC 9126 give useful guidance on software quality control, and in particular provide some uniformity to its assessment. However, the absence of the use of metrics in this area is a cause of some concern.

Many of the standards related to quality are concerned exclusively with software. This reflects the general view that it is within software that most problems exist. However, quality, like safety, is a global issue and has implications for all aspects of a system.

REFERENCES

ANSI/IEEE (1986). Std 983-1986 *Guide for Software Quality Assurance Planning*. New York: Institute of Electrical and Electronic Engineers

ANSI/IEEE (1989). Std 730-1989 *Software Quality Assurance Plans*. New York: Institute of Electrical and Electronic Engineers

ASME (1990). Standard NQA 2a *Quality Assurance Requirements for Nuclear Facility Applications*. New York: The American Society of Mechanical Engineers

DoD (1988). Std-2168 *Defense System Software Quality Program*. Washington, DC: Department of Defense

ISO (1991). International Standard ISO/IEC 9126: *Information Technology – Software Product Evaluation – Quality Characteristics and Guidelines for their Use*. Geneva: International Standards Organization

ISO (1994). International Standard Series ISO 9000: *Quality Management and Quality Assurance Standards*. Geneva: International Standards Organization. (Also available in the UK as the BS EN ISO 9000 series of standards, British Standards Institution)

Jackson D. (1993). New developments in quality management as a pre-requisite for safety. In *Directions in Safety-Critical Systems* (Redmill F. and Anderson T., eds), pp. 257–69. London: Springer-Verlag

Kirk G. (1994). The role of quality assurance in high integrity systems. *High Integrity Systems*, **1**(1), 79–82

MoD (1984). Defence Standard 00-16: *Guide to the Achievement of Quality in Software*. Glasgow: Directorate of Standardization

MoD (1991). Interim Defence Standard 05-95: *Quality System Requirements for the Development, Supply and Maintenance of Software*. Glasgow: Directorate of Standardization

NATO (1993). Quality Standard AQAP-150: *Requirements for Quality Management of Software Development*. NATO International Staff – Defence Support Division

FURTHER READING

Kolarik W.J. (1995). *Creating Quality*. New York: McGraw-Hill

Rotherby B. (1993). *ISO 9000*, 2nd edn. Aldershot: Gower

PROBLEMS

13.1 Discuss the distinction between the terms 'quality management', 'quality assurance' and 'quality control'.

13.2 How does quality relate to safety?

13.3 How do the objectives of quality assurance differ when applied to a safety-critical application, as opposed to a system that has no safety implications?

13.4 Describe the form and purpose of auditing, when applied to a safety-critical application.

13.5 Why is the application of quality control more difficult in the case of a computer-based system than when applied to a simple mechanical component? Why does software cause particular problems?

13.6 Describe the differences in content and use of the ISO 9001, ISO 9002 and ISO 9003 standards.

13.7 How does the scope of ISO/IEC 9126 differ from that of ISO 9000?

13.8 Why is the definition of software quality characteristics within ISO/IEC 9126 of importance? How may these characteristics be assessed?

13.9 Why does the use of ISO 9000 not provide a total solution to quality issues within safety-critical systems?

14 Certification

CHAPTER CONTENTS

14.1 Introduction

Certification is the process of issuing a certificate to indicate conformance with a standard, a set of guidelines or some similar document. Any organization or individual may issue a certificate, and its importance will clearly vary with its nature and its issuing body. In some cases a certificate may be required for legal reasons: for example, an airworthiness certificate is required before an aircraft is allowed to fly. In such circumstances the certificate takes on the role of a **licence** from a statutory authority. The need for such licences for safety-critical systems varies greatly between countries.

In areas not covered by legal requirements certification may still be of importance for commercial or other reasons. There is no legal obligation to obtain a validation certificate in order to market an Ada compiler within the UK, but market pressures are such that products that have achieved this certification are likely to have a distinct sales advantage. To sell such a compiler to the US Government, an appropriate validation certificate would be essential.

Certification is often carried out by government bodies, or organizations with a national standing, to indicate 'acceptability' with respect to specific criteria. Examples of non-government bodies that undertake certification include Lloyd's Register in the UK and Underwriters' Laboratories in the US. Certification may also be performed by companies in relation to their suppliers or subcontractors.

Many industries have a regulatory authority that governs all projects within that sector. For example, all civil aircraft systems must be approved by the Civil Aviation Authority (CAA) in the UK and by the Federal Aviation

Authority (FAA) in the US. Other countries have equivalent bodies. Similar regulatory authorities exist in many sectors, including the nuclear, gas supply, rail and mining industries. Military projects are controlled by the appropriate government department, such as the Ministry of Defence in the UK and the Department of Defense in the US.

Certification may be applied to:

- organizations or individuals
- tools or methods
- systems or products.

Of these three groups the last is perhaps the most important, and it is to this form of certification that the majority of this chapter is dedicated.

In order to achieve certification, the developer of a critical product must convince the appropriate regulator of its safety. Given the ethereal nature of safety, this is invariably a very difficult task. The developer must be able to show that all important hazards have been identified and dealt with, and that the integrity of the system is appropriate for the application. Certification may also require evidence of compliance with some particular standard, although such compliance is not in itself sufficient proof of the appropriateness of the design. The developer will need to provide extensive evidence of the development methods used, and the testing performed to investigate the system's behaviour. In addition, it will be necessary to produce a rigorous argument to support the claim that the system is sufficiently safe, and that it will remain so throughout its life. The work involved in achieving certification is considerable and requires careful planning.

We shall begin by looking at the various forms of certification and discussing their relevance to critical projects. We shall then consider the planning and negotiation necessary for certification, and the nature of the safety case needed to support this process. We shall then look at some of the national and international standards in this area.

14.2 Forms of certification

Certification of organizations or individuals

An organization may seek certification from a regulatory authority as a means of establishing its competence in specific areas of activity. This is now relatively widespread in areas such as quality assurance, where many companies have quality management structures that are certified as conforming with BS 5750 or ISO 9000. Testing is another area where certification, or accreditation, is becoming established, and in Chapter 12 we looked at an example of such a scheme in the form of NAMAS.

Certification aims to ensure that accredited organizations meet certain levels of proficiency and that they satisfy agreed standards or criteria. However, this approach is not suited to all areas that are of interest to safety. It is relatively easy to investigate the *procedures* used within a company, but much harder to measure the *competence* with which they are performed. For this reason certification is more often applied to areas such as quality assurance and testing, than to activities such as design.

Certification may also be applied to individuals, and many workers must be certified in order to be allowed to carry out their chosen profession. This is the case in such diverse occupations as doctors, accountants, civil engineers and welders. Engineers working on the development of safety-critical systems often require considerable amounts of skill, training and experience, but at present very few industrial sectors have any form of certification for such people. Examples of industries that *do* have certification mechanisms may be found within the rail sector where, in the UK, a certification scheme is operated by the Institute of Railway Signalling Engineers. Certification does not demonstrate suitability for any given role, but does allow an industry to enforce certain minimum standards. As most sectors do not operate such a system for staff involved in the production of safety-critical systems, these standards must be enforced by the companies themselves through staff selection. It is generally accepted that senior staff should have appropriate professional standing, but this in itself does not guarantee suitability for a given post. In the UK most senior positions would be held by chartered engineers, but this says little about the specific skills or training of the staff concerned.

Some organizations accredit individuals to perform particular tasks, or to work on specific projects. For example, when issuing contracts some companies will insist on nominating key staff to perform the work. Should such an individual leave the project, for whatever reason, the subcontractor would need to seek approval for any replacement. Such nominations are normally applied to only a small number of critical positions, and might include, for example, the project and quality managers.

An interesting example of the certification of individuals can be found in the US civil aircraft industry. The FAA delegates some certification activities to approved employees of manufacturing companies. These designated engineering representatives (DERs) act as agents for the FAA and perform various certification tasks within the company. In Boeing and McDonnell Douglas projects, between 90 and 95% of all certification activities are performed by DERs (Rushby, 1993).

Certification may also be applied to the users or operators of safety-critical systems. Here a manufacturer, or a regulatory authority, may insist that only appropriately trained personnel be allowed to control a system, as the operator is directly responsible for its safety.

Certification of tools or methods

The tools and development methods used in the production of a safety-critical system play an important role in determining its performance. Consequently, several standards place restrictions on the tools and methods that may be used.

Defence Standard 00-55 dictates that several development techniques are mandatory within the development lifecycle and places integrity requirements on all support tools. IEC 1508 gives detailed guidance on the methods and tools that are appropriate for the various phases of a project, for systems of various levels of integrity. DO 178B does not explicitly define the development tools to be used, but gives details of the process of 'tool qualification' required to gain acceptance.

Perhaps the most successful and widely used form of tool certification is the validation process applied to programming language compilers (as discussed in Chapter 9). Here a respected institution certifies that a particular compiler conforms to the international language standard. In the case of Ada, the vendor must also certify that the implementation has no 'extensions'. Unfortunately, this form of certification is not practical for many of the specialist tools used in the development of safety-critical systems.

Certification of systems or products

Manufacturers of safety-critical systems may seek certification of their products because this is a requirement within their industry, or because they believe that it will make them more marketable. Requirements for certification vary widely between application areas and between countries, being voluntary in some cases and compulsory in others. An example of this variability is the medical electronics area, where certification is voluntary within the UK but compulsory in other countries, such as the US and Germany. In areas such as civil aviation and nuclear power generation certification is always compulsory. In most areas certification is applied to complete systems rather than to individual components. However, within some sectors, for example the rail industry, certification is often applied at the component level.

The certification of products containing software poses particular problems for both the developer and the regulator. Because of the difficulties of dependably testing such systems, certification must be based on the process of development as well as the demonstrated performance of the system itself. This will require not only an assessment of the methods used, but also an appraisal of the competence of the staff involved. Inevitably, quality issues will form a fundamental part of this assessment.

14.3 The process of system certification

Although the certification phase of a project comes at the end of the development programme, the planning of this work (as with the verification and validation activities) should be performed at an early stage.

Because certification involves convincing an external organization of the safety of the system, it is essential to hold discussions with this body to see what will be required. This process of **certification liaison** establishes communications, fosters understanding between the parties concerned, and can greatly assist in the certification process.

Initial discussions between the developer and the regulatory body are likely to centre on the overall nature of the system and the development approach to be taken. In some industries specific standards or guidelines are mandatory, and certification will require adherence to such documents. In other industries no particular standard is required, although the adoption of a suitable standard will often make the process easier. For example, in the UK the Civil Aviation Authority (CAA) does not mandate the use of a particular standard but will accept systems developed in line with standards such as DO-178B (described below). A system developer wishing to follow the methods within this standard would initially only indicate this intention to the CAA. However, a company wishing to use a non-standard approach would need to convince the authority of the suitability of each aspect of the development process. In some industrial sectors there are no relevant standards, and developers may decide to model their work on a generic standard (such as IEC 1508 described below) with modifications appropriate to their particular situation.

Having established the overall methods to be used, the developer will then produce a **verification plan** for approval by the regulatory authority. This will give details of the proposed system, the development methods to be used and the documentation to be provided. Where a particular standard is being adopted, the plan will indicate the techniques proposed to achieve conformance with that standard. It will also list any areas in which the developer plans to deviate from the standard, with suitable justification.

Submission of the verification plan will normally be followed by discussions between the two organizations to resolve any areas of misunderstanding or disagreement. Hopefully, at the end of this process the developer will receive agreement from the regulator on the appropriateness of the proposed development scheme. If not, the developer will have discovered problem areas at an early stage, when changes can be made without involving large-cost penalties.

During the project, increased knowledge of the problems involved may prompt changes to the methods used. If such changes influence the verification plan, then prior approval should be sought from the regulator to ensure that certification will not be affected. Thus the process of liaison continues throughout all stages of the project.

As the work progresses the developer will supply the regulator with suitable documentation to show that the provisions of the certification plan have been satisfied. The developer will also provide data produced at various stages of the project, to substantiate this claim. In large projects the documentation required is vast, and represents a massive investment in time and effort. A major part of this submission will be the safety plan, which details the treatment of safety issues throughout the development process. In assessing the material the regulating authority will hold a series of reviews at which the material will be discussed with the development team and any appropriate subcontractors. If the regulator is satisfied that the terms of the certification plan have been satisfied, then a certificate, or licence, will be issued. In some cases this certification may be conditional, imposing certain operational constraints.

14.4 The safety case

In Chapter 2 we introduced the concept of a **safety case** as a means of documenting the safety justification of a system. At that stage in the text many of the components of the safety case had not been discussed, so we now return to look at its content in more detail.

The safety case is a record of all the safety activities associated with a system, throughout its life. This is initially created early in the development process and is then expanded to include details of all aspects of the development work that are relevant to safety. Following development the safety case must be maintained throughout the operational phase, to document any alterations to the system or its use. As requirements change, or the system is modified, it will be necessary to justify such changes in terms of their implications for system safety.

One of the most important uses of the safety case is to support an application for certification. Here the regulatory authority will be looking for evidence that all potential hazards have been identified and that appropriate steps have been taken to deal with them. The safety case must also demonstrate that appropriate development methods have been adopted and that these have been performed correctly. The *CONTESSE Test Handbook* (CONTESSE, 1995) lists a number of items that should be included within a safety case. These are shown in Table 14.1. From the table it is clear that the safety case contains a large amount of data and that its production requires a great deal of effort. Most safety cases are developed using simple tools such as word processors and databases, and rely on manual reviews to ensure their consistency and completeness. In very complex systems this task becomes extremely difficult, and several workers are looking at computer-based tools to assist in this work (Hall, 1992; Forder *et al.*, 1993). These tools do not replace the skill required in the preparation of the safety case, but assist in the *management* of the process. Such tools aim to improve the quality of the safety case by increasing consistency and visibility, and by facilitating analysis of individual aspects of the arguments involved.

One of the problems associated with the production of a safety case is that the issues concerned are always multidisciplinary. It may therefore be appropriate, and necessary, to involve staff with expertise in areas such as computer software; computer hardware; analogue electronics; electrical engineering; mechanical engineering; pneumatics; hydraulics; human factors; and psychology. Input will also be required from specialists related to the

Table 14.1 The contents of the safety case (CONTESSE, 1995).

A description of the safety-related system
Evidence of competence of personnel involved in any safety activity
A specification of safety requirements
The results of hazard and risk analysis
Details of risk reduction techniques employed
The results of design analysis showing that the system design meets all the required safety targets
The verification and validation strategy
The results of all verification and validation activities
Records of safety reviews
Records of any incidents which occur throughout the life of the system
Records of all changes to the system and justification of its continued safety

applications area, such as aircraft engineers in an aerospace project, or biomedical engineers in a medical project. The interaction between these diverse disciplines is often extremely complex, and identifying relevant safety issues is very difficult.

A safety case must include a rigorous argument for the safety of the system, and must demonstrate that it satisfies all its safety requirements. This will involve numerous steps that in some ways resemble the components of a mathematical proof. Each stage of this 'proof' must be carefully justified and any assumptions made explicitly. Any unjustified assumptions represent flaws in the safety argument, and hence the safety case. Unfortunately, identification of unjustifiable assumptions in a multidisciplinary project requires great skill and dedication. For this reason, the production of the safety case represents one of the most difficult and most demanding aspects of the generation of safety-critical systems.

14.5 Guidelines and standards

Certification of a system often requires (or if not, is greatly assisted by) the use of appropriate standards or guidelines. Some of these documents are specific to a particular industry, whereas others are of a generic nature. This section looks at a few of the more important standards and then gives pointers to other documents that are of interest.

IEC 1508 *Functional Safety: Safety-Related Systems*

In the early 1990s the International Electrotechnical Commission produced two documents as a result of many years of effort by internationally constituted working groups. The first of these, designated 65A (Secretariat) 122, dealt with software for safety-related systems and was produced by IEC/SC65A Working Group 9 (WG9) (IEC, 1991). The second, entitled 65A (Secretariat) 123, was concerned with systems aspects of safety and was produced by IEC/SC65A Working Group 10 (WG10) (IEC, 1992). It was intended that these documents would form the basis of two international standards, and in 1992 a draft of each was distributed to national committees throughout the world for comment. These two documents are often referred to as the IEC65A draft standards.

Consultation on the draft standards was completed by the end of 1992, and it became apparent that many reviewers perceived a lack of harmonization between the two documents. In order to overcome this problem it was decided to combine the topics to produce a single international standard on functional safety. The first draft of this standard appeared in 1995 under the title IEC 1508: *Functional Safety: Safety-Related Systems* (IEC, 1995).

The standard has three major and four subsidiary sections. These are:

Part 1: General requirements
Part 2: Requirements for electrical/electronic/programmable electronic systems
Part 3: Software requirements
Part 4: Definitions
Part 5: Guidelines for the application of part 1
Part 6: Guidelines for the application of parts 2 and 3
Part 7: Bibliography of techniques

The standard is primarily concerned with safety-related control systems incorporating electrical, electronic or programmable electronic subsystems. However, it also gives more general guidance that is relevant to all forms of safety-critical systems. It can therefore be used in association with systems that are essentially mechanical, hydraulic or pneumatic. The standard covers not only the control elements of an arrangement, but also any external risk reduction facilities, as discussed in Chapter 5.

The various sections of the standard set out the requirements for achieving functional safety, but do not specify the individuals responsible for carrying out these duties. This is in stark contrast to some other standards (such as Defence Standard 00-55, described below), which set out a required management structure and allocate responsibilities to members of the team.

Great emphasis is placed on the use of a safety lifecycle model, as described in Chapter 5. This is related to an overall system lifecycle model and to individual models concerned with hardware and software development. Safety integrity levels are discussed in some depth, and numerical targets for failure rates are linked to each of the integrity levels. The standard also sets lower limits on the target failure rates that may be claimed for a safety-related system. In applying these limits, systems are divided into two categories, depending on the nature of the demands placed on the system (the difference between these modes is discussed in Chapter 4):

- For a demand mode of operation, the lower limit is set at 10^{-5} failures on demand.
- For a continuous mode of operation, the lower limit is set at 10^{-5} dangerous failures per year.

The standard adopts a risk-based approach to the determination of safety integrity level requirements.

Considerable guidance is given within the standard on all aspects of system development, including the necessary elements of the lifecycle phases; the documentation required; the architectures appropriate for a given system; software and hardware development methods; testing techniques and tool support.

One of the key features of IEC 1508 is that it is a **generic standard**, that is, it is not limited to any specific industrial sector or application area. It is envisaged that the standard will form a basis on which other industry-specific standards will be built. Work is already under way to produce application-specific international standards for a number of areas, including the rail, oil, gas, medical and process control industries (Brazendale and Bell, 1994). Indications are that other industrial sectors will also generate standards in line with IEC 1508, but tailored to their particular needs.

It should be remembered that at the time of writing this book IEC 1508 is still at the *draft* stage, and that its contents may change in subsequent revisions. However, because of the importance of this standard it has been thought appropriate to give an indication of the form that the standard will take when it eventually appears. Similar motivation has prompted those responsible for the development of industry-specific standards to take serious note of the contents of the standard, even in its draft form.

RTCA-EUROCAE DO 178B *Software Considerations in Airborne Systems and Equipment Certification*

This international standard is issued in the US as the Requirements and Technical Concepts for Aviation document RTCA SC167/DO-178B, and in Europe as the European Organization for Civil Aviation Electronics document EUROCAE ED-12B (RTCA/EUROCAE, 1992). Despite its dual designation it is more commonly referred to as DO-178B, even in Europe. The standard is the third in a family of standards dating back to the early 1980s. DO-178 was released in 1981, to be replaced by DO-178A in 1985. The latest standard was released in 1992 and constitutes a major revision.

DO-178B relates to civil aircraft and represents an agreement between US and European manufacturers in this area. It does not cover military aircraft, which are the subject of separate standards that differ from country to country. Despite being an industry-specific standard, DO-178B is widely seen as a model to be followed and has generated a great deal of interest from engineers in a number of industrial sectors. Unlike the above IEC standard, DO-178B is concerned solely with software issues.

The standard is divided into a number of major parts, including sections concerned with:

- system aspects relating to software development
- the software lifecycle
- software planning
- software development
- software verification
- software configuration management
- software quality assurance
- certification liaison
- aircraft and engine certification.

Formal methods are seen as too immature to be included as a normal method of system development, but are included as an 'alternative method' that can be used with the agreement of the certifying body.

The evolution of DO-178B is described by Hawkes and Struck (1993) and a review of the standard has been produced by Wichmann (1994). The latter gives an independent appraisal of its strengths and weaknesses, and also compares it with various ISO standards. The report concludes that DO-178B is a mature standard that has much to recommend it.

MoD Interim Defence Standard 00-55 *Requirements for the Procurement of Safety-Critical Software in Defence Equipment*

The UK Ministry of Defence issued an interim version of Defence Standard 00-55 in 1991 (MoD, 1991), following the issuing of a draft in 1989. The standard has two parts: Part 1: Requirements and Part 2: Guidance. It is concerned with the procurement of military software, and is closely linked with Defence Standard 00-56 (see below).

A major part of the standard deals with safety management issues. It defines a required management structure and allocates specific responsibilities to members of this team. Documentation requirements are also defined for all aspects of the development lifecycle. Hazard analysis, as defined in Defence Standard 00-56, is an essential part of the development process.

Software engineering practices form another major component of the standard, and it is material within this area that has led to 00-55 being seen as one of the most controversial standards of recent years. The use of formal methods is mandated within the standard, in areas such as the production of module specifications. Validation and verification are required to establish compliance with such formal specifications, requiring the use of static and dynamic analysis as well as formal or informal proofs of correctness. The response of the defence software industry to the standard was very mixed, and a debate followed that divided the safety-critical community (Tierney, 1991).

Following feedback on the interim version issued in 1991, a new draft was distributed in August 1995 for comments by December of that year. The revised form suggests that the Ministry of Defence has gone some way towards tackling the concerns expressed about the interim version, while holding firm on many issues that are seen as fundamental to safety. It is expected that the full standard will be issued shortly.

HSE Guidelines *Programmable Electronic Systems in Safety-Related Applications*

In 1987 the UK Health and Safety Executive published a two-volume set of guidelines giving advice on the design and development of safety-critical programmable electronic systems (PESs) (HSE, 1987a, b). The first volume is an introductory guide intended for non-specialists, whereas the second contains general technical information for more specialized engineers.

The introductory guide begins by outlining the basics of PES-based systems, including a discussion of their failure characteristics. It then looks at methods of design that are appropriate to safety-critical applications and introduces a three-point strategy based on reliability, configuration and overall quality. The guide distinguishes between systems that perform control functions and those that act as protection systems. The guide ends with a brief glossary of terms.

The second volume of the guide is divided into three sections. Part 1 presents more technical information on the topics covered in volume 1, and may be sufficient for applications where the hazard level is relatively low. This part considers both hardware and software aspects of a system, and includes material on design and installation. Part 2 looks at safety integrity assessment, including mathematical techniques for hazard analysis and hardware reliability estimation. The final part is a case study based on a chemical processing plant producing explosives.

The HSE guidelines provide a readable introduction for those new to the subject and much practical information for the more experienced engineer. Despite the time that has elapsed since their publication, the guidelines remain essential reading for all engineers working in this field.

Other civil standards

ESA PSS-05-0 *Software Engineering Standards*

A set of guidelines on software engineering methods from the European Space Agency (ESA, 1991). In addition to its general guidance, the document strongly recommends the use of formal methods where practicable.

IEC 880 ***Software for Computers in the Safety Systems of Nuclear Power Stations***
An International Electrotechnical Commission standard relating to nuclear power plants (IEC, 1986). This contains a supplement on 'Software for Computers Important to Safety for Nuclear Power Plant'.

IEC 1131 ***Programmable Controllers***
An IEC standard concerned with programmable logic controllers (PLCs) (IEC, 1993). Part three of this standard relates to programming languages, and was discussed in Chapter 10.

Ontario Hydro ***Standard for Software Engineering of Safety-Critical Software***
This is one of a series of standards produced by Ontario Hydro for use within their atomic energy projects (Ontario Hydro, 1990). It is one of the few civil standards to mandate the use of formal methods. The Canadian Atomic Energy Control Board has itself published a standard in this area (AECB, 1991). This follows closely on the recommendations of IEC 880.

RIA ***Safety-Related Software for Railway Signalling***
This consultative document was produced by the UK Railway Industry Association (RIA, 1991). This organization consists of a number of companies and other bodies interested in railway signalling systems. The document, which is a draft proposal for an industry-specific standard, has close links with IEC65A which evolved into the IEC 1508 standard.

Other military standards

DoD Defense Standard 5200.28 ***Trusted Computer Systems Evaluation Criteria***
A US Department of Defense standard (DoD, 1985). Although this document is aimed at security, rather than safety issues, it includes much that is of relevance to both topics. This includes guidance on the choice of programming languages.

MoD Interim Defence Standard 00-56 ***Safety Management Requirements for Defence Systems Containing Programmable Electronics***
A UK military standard covering hazard analysis and safety classification of computer-based equipment. An interim version of this standard was released in 1991 along with Defence Standard 00-55, with which it is closely linked. A draft of the complete standard was produced in 1993, and a second draft was issued for comment in August 1995 (MoD, 1995a) along with the new version of 00-55. This latest version is split into two parts: Part 1: Requirements and Part 2: General Application Guidance. It is envisaged that the full standard will be issued shortly.

MoD Interim Defence Standard 00-58 (1995) ***A Guideline for HAZOP Studies on Systems Which Include a Programmable Electronic System***
A standard describing the use of hazard and operability studies (HAZOP) within computer-based systems. A draft of this interim standard was issued in 1995 for comment (MoD, 1995b). The use of HAZOP studies was discussed in Chapter 3.

When using any standard it is important to ensure that the most recent version is used. Information on all UK Defence Standards is contained in Defence Standard 00-00 (Part 3) Section 4: Index of Standards for Defence Procurement. This document is published annually, with additional supplements being distributed in *Standards in Defence News*.

14.6 Certification – an overview

The certification of safety-critical computer systems has several aims. These are:

- to improve the safety of critical systems;
- to increase the awareness of the implications of system performance on safety;
- to enforce minimum standards of design and manufacture within the relevant industry;
- to encourage a structure of professional responsibility.

Certification is normally based on the use of some form of standard, although conformity to a standard is not, of itself, a sufficient condition for safety. Regulators look not only at conformance, but also at the details of the system itself. They consider the appropriateness of the design and its treatment of the associated hazards. They will also consider the integrity targets set for the system, and whether these levels have been achieved.

In order to achieve certification the developer needs to convince the regulator that all relevant hazards have been identified and dealt with. Because of the multidisciplinary nature of all safety-critical projects, this is always a difficult task. The required safety case represents a huge investment in time and effort, and will require input from all members of the development team. Certification does not come cheaply!

At present the certification methods and the standards used within different industries vary considerably. This enforces very different working practices on staff within these diverse sectors. This situation limits the exchange of information between application areas, and makes poor use of the limited human resources in this vital area. The development of a widely accepted generic standard in the form of IEC 1508 should help to improve this situation, by allowing industries to produce their own standards while maintaining a common approach to safety. Only time will tell whether this goal will be achieved.

The certification of a product does not prove its correctness and does not remove any of the manufacturer's legal or moral obligations. However, the certification process does promote the use of approved techniques and, hopefully, may lead to safer products.

REFERENCES

AECB (1991). *Proposed Standard for Software for Computers in the Safety Systems of Nuclear Power Stations*. Canada: Atomic Energy Control Board

Brazendale J. and Bell R. (1994). Safety-related control and protection systems: standards update. *Comput. Control Eng. J.*, **5**(1), 6–12

CONTESSE (1995). *CONTESSE Test Handbook* (1995). Glasgow: BAeSEMA

DoD (1985). *Trusted Computer Systems Evaluation Criteria*, DoD 5200.28 – STD. Washington: Department of Defense

ESA (1991). *Software Engineering Standards*, ESA PSS-05-0. Paris: European Space Agency

Forder J., Higgins C., McDermid J. and Storrs G. (1993). SAM – a tool to support the construction, review and evolution of safety arguments. In *Directions in Safety-Critical Systems. Proc. of the First Safety-Critical Systems Symposium, Bristol* (Redmill F. and Anderson T., eds), pp. 195–216. London: Springer-Verlag

Hall B.M. (1992). Safety case structures: issues related to certification of avionics systems. *Safety of Computer Control Systems 1992 (Safecomp '92)*. Oxford: Pergamon Press

Hawkes D.J. and Struck D.J. (1993). An international safety-critical software standard for the 1990s. *Proc. of the Software Engineering Standards Symposium*. Brighton, UK: IEEE Computer Society Press

HSE (1987a). *Programmable Electronic Systems in Safety Related Applications Vol. 1: An Introductory Guide*. London: Her Majesty's Stationery Office

HSE (1987b). *Programmable Electronic Systems in Safety Related Applications Vol. 2: General Technical Guidelines*. London: Her Majesty's Stationery Office

IEC (1986). International Standard 880 *Software for Computers in the Safety Systems of Nuclear Power Stations*. Geneva: International Electrotechnical Commission

IEC (1991). *Software for Computers in the Application of Industrial Safety-Related Systems*, SC65A/WG9 Draft Document. Geneva: International Electrotechnical Commission (IEC reference 65A Secretariat 122)

IEC (1992). *Functional Safety of Electrical/Electronic/Programmable Electronic Systems; Generic Aspects: Part 1, General Requirements*, SC65A/WG10 Draft Document, Version 5. Geneva: International Electrotechnical Commission (IEC reference 65A Secretariat 123)

IEC (1993). International Standard IEC 1131 *Programmable Controllers*. Geneva: International Electrotechnical Commission (within Europe this standard is also available as a normalized European standard – EN 61131)

IEC (1995). Draft International Standard 1508 *Functional Safety: Safety-Related Systems*. Geneva: International Electrotechnical Commission

MoD (1991). Interim Defence Standard 00-55 *The Procurement of Safety Critical Software in Defence Equipment*. Glasgow: Directorate of Standardization

MoD (1995a). Draft Defence Standard 00-56 *Safety Management Requirements for Defence Systems Containing Programmable Electronics* Issue 2. Glasgow: Directorate of Standardization

MoD (1995b). Draft Interim Defence Standard 00-58 *A Guideline for HAZOP Studies on Systems Which Include a Programmable Electronic System*. Glasgow: Directorate of Standardization

Ontario Hydro (1990). *Standard for Software Engineering of Safety Critical Software*. Toronto: Ontario Hydro

RIA (1991). *Safety Related Software for Railway Signalling* (Consultative Document). London: Railway Industry Association

RTCA/EUROCAE (1992). *Software Considerations in Airborne Systems and Equipment Certification*. RTCA/DO-178B; EUROCAE/ED-12B. Washington: Radio Technical Commission for Aeronautics. Paris: European Organisation for Civil Aviation Electronics

Rushby J. (1993). *Formal Methods and the Certification of Critical Systems*. Technical report CSL-93-7, SRI International, Menlo Park, CA. (Also issued as *Formal Methods and Digital System Validation* as NASA CR 4551)

Tierney M. (1991). The evolution of Def Stan 00-55 and 00-56: an intensification of the 'formal methods debate' in the UK. *Proc. of the Workshop on Policy Issues in Systems and Software Development*. Brighton, UK: Policy Research Unit

Wichmann B.A. (1994). *A Review of a Safety-Critical Software Standard*. Teddington: National Physical Laboratory

FURTHER READING

de Neumann B., ed. (1988). *Software Certification. Proc. of the 5th CSR Conference*. London: Elsevier

Wichmann B.A., ed. (1992). Certification. In *Software in Safety-Related Systems* (Wichmann B.A., ed.), Chapter 5. Chichester: John Wiley

PROBLEMS

14.1 What bodies or organizations are responsible for certification?

14.2 What are the aims of accrediting organizations and what factors limit this process? In what areas are the accreditation of companies most common?

14.3 What problems limit the national certification of engineers working on the development of safety-critical systems? Describe the relevance of the certification of individual engineers within critical projects.

14.4 Describe the role of tool and development method certification in the production of safety-critical systems. Give a typical example of tool certification.

14.5 Discuss the special problems faced by the regulators of computer-based systems, as opposed to those concerned with less complex products.

14.6 Describe briefly the liaison process that precedes system certification. At what stage does this occur?

14.7 Explain the form and function of a verification plan.

14.8 How does the system developer seek to satisfy the regulator that the terms of the verification plan have been met?

14.9 Explain briefly the form and purpose of a safety case.

14.10 What aspects of a safety-critical system are encompassed by IEC 1508? To which industrial sector does this standard relate?

14.11 What restrictions does IEC 1508 place on the claims that may be made for the integrity of a system? What is the importance of these restrictions?

14.12 In what fundamental ways does DO-178B differ from IEC 1508?

14.13 How do Def Stan 00-55 and DO-178B differ in their attitudes to formal methods?

14.14 How do Def Stan 00-55 and IEC 1508 differ in their treatment of management issues?

14.15 Discuss briefly the aims of the certification process. To what extent are these aims currently being met?

14.16 How does the process of certification affect the legal responsibilities of the developer of a safety-critical system?

15 Commercial High-Integrity Systems

CHAPTER CONTENTS

15.1 Introduction

In earlier chapters we looked at a number of key topics related to the design and development of computer systems that are used within safety-critical applications. In this chapter we shall look at industrial examples that illustrate several of the points raised and help to place them in a realistic engineering context.

Rather than attempting to cover all the elements of a single project, we shall look at a range of systems and, in each case, highlight areas that are of specific interest. The applications have been chosen to illustrate particular aspects of the development process, and we shall limit our discussions to these parts of each project.

The first application relates to a chemical plant used to produce explosives. Here we shall concentrate on the processes of hazard analysis and risk management, and see how these were used within the safety assessment.

The second project concerns the flight control system of the Airbus A330/ A340 family of aircraft. This uses advanced fly-by-wire techniques that rely heavily on the operation of their various computers. As the aircraft cannot be manœuvred easily by other means, it is essential that the flight control system continues to function at all times. Within this section we shall look in some detail at the fault-tolerant techniques used to achieve continuous operation.

The third and final application relates to the shutdown systems of the Darlington nuclear generating station. This plant was one of the first commercial reactors to use software control in its primary protection equipment, and it consequently produced some novel problems for the regulators during the process of certification. Here we shall look at the various mechanisms used to guarantee safety within the plant, but concentrate on the techniques used to verify the safety-critical software.

15.2 An explosive chemical plant

This study relates to a plant for the manufacture of the explosive pentaerythritol tetranitrate (PETN), which is used in detonators. The factory concerned is situated in Scotland and is run by ICI. In this section we look at the safety integrity of one section of the plant, and consider not only the safety techniques adopted but also the methods used to investigate its characteristics. The information given in this study comes from a more detailed treatment given in Part 2 of the HSE Guidelines (HSE, 1987), and is reproduced with the permission of the Health and Safety Executive.

PETN is made by the nitration of pentaerythritol (PE) in a batch process, as shown in Figure 15.1. Two nitrators operate in parallel within the plant, but

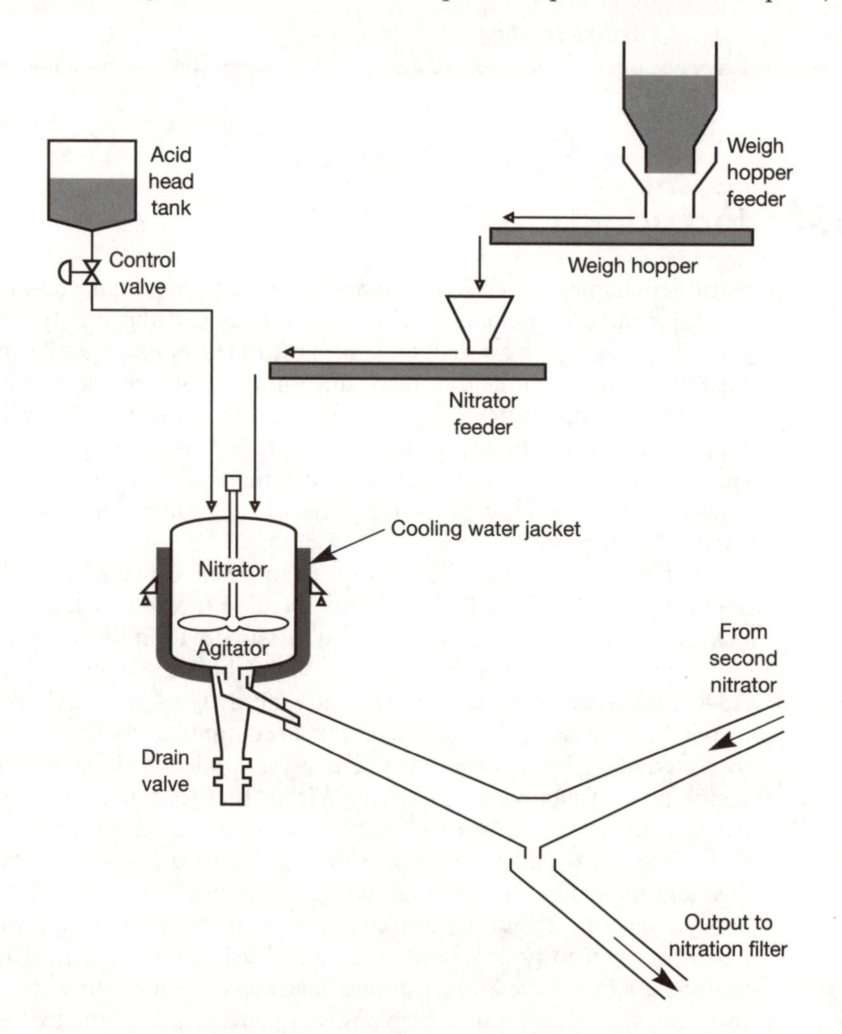

Figure 15.1 The basic nitrator components.

in this study we will consider only a single unit. A predetermined quantity of nitric acid is initially delivered to the nitrator from an acid storage tank. A weighing hopper is then used to measure an appropriate quantity of PE, which is then progressively fed into the nitrator using a vibrating feeder. The chemical reaction within the nitrator is strongly exothermic, and cooling water is fed through an outer jacket to cool the vessel. The rate at which the PE is fed into the nitrator is controlled to keep the contents at a preset temperature. The contents of the vessel are continuously stirred to equalize temperatures and concentrations within the unit.

After all the PE has been added, the reaction is left for a prescribed period of time. Provided that the temperature has dropped below a preset value, the contents of the nitrator are then discharged by opening the drain valve situated at the base of the vessel. This causes the contents to be passed to a nitration filter for further processing.

Potential hazards

If the temperature within the nitration vessel were allowed to rise to an excessive level, this would result in the decomposition of the PETN and the production of toxic fumes. If the condition was not then brought under control, there would also be the risk of fire, which might spread to parts of the building containing the finished explosive. Although several other hazards may also be identified, decomposition represents the main hazard of the process, and within this study we will concentrate on this area. For safe operation the contents of the nitrator must be kept below 35°C.

High-temperature protection

Although the operation of the plant's control system should prevent the temperature within the nitrator from reaching dangerous levels, an additional safety mechanism is incorporated to deal with unexpected situations.

If the temperature within the nitrator exceeds 35°C then its contents are dumped into a drowning tank filled with water. The arrangement used to achieve this function is shown in Figure 15.2. Under normal circumstances the output from the nitrator is fed to the nitration filter via a diverter valve, which can direct its output to the drowning tank. This diverter is arranged so that it normally points towards the tank, and is only directed towards the nitration filter when the control system decides that the nitration process has been completed successfully. If the temperature rises above 35°C during processing, the drain valve is opened and the contents of the nitrator are fed, via the diverter valve, to the drowning tank. Compressed air is fed into the bottom of this tank to agitate the water to stimulate mixing.

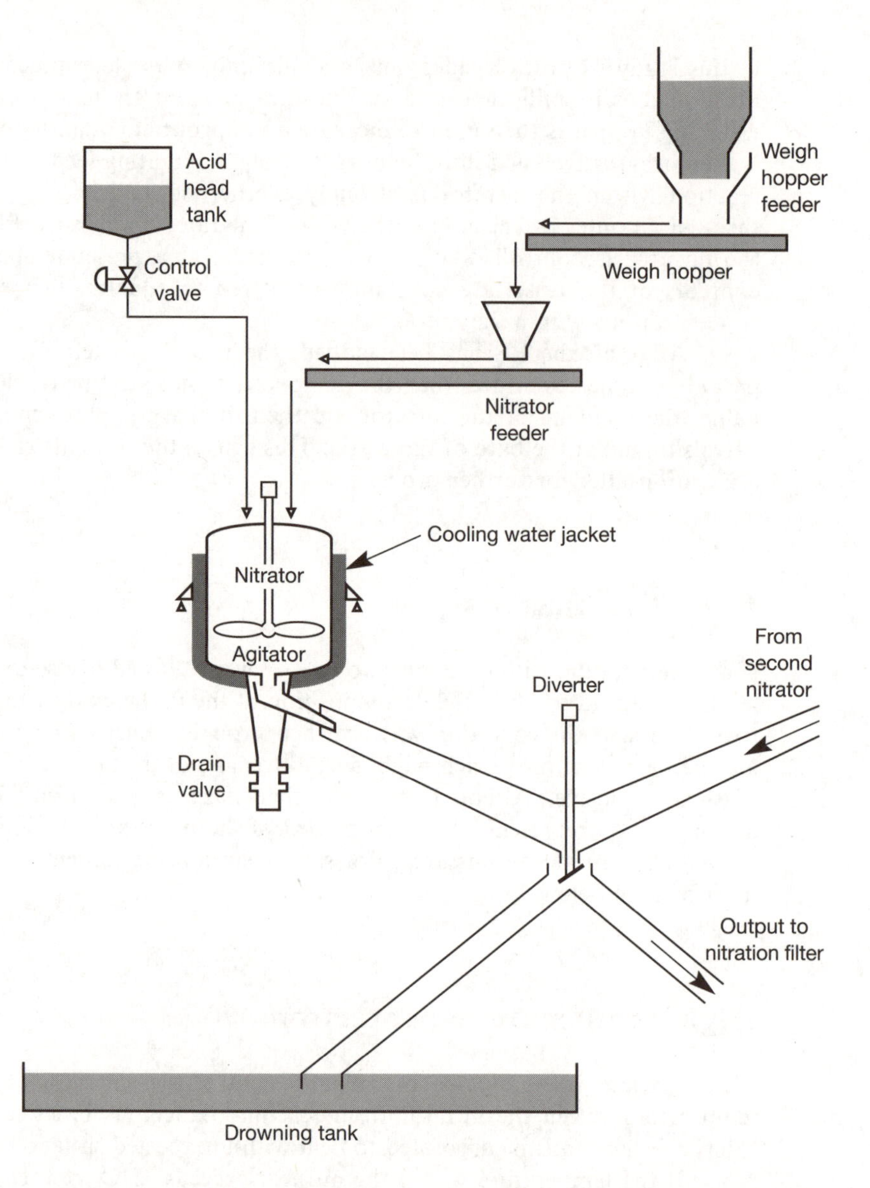

Figure 15.2 Nitrator arrangement, including additional safety components.

Plant control

The various functions of the nitrators are controlled automatically by a minicomputer. This is responsible not only for the nitration process, but also for the operation of other equipment within the factory. The computer takes inputs from various sensors and uses this information to determine the required output signals. In addition, a programmable logic controller is used to monitor the state of the plant and the operation of the computer, and to provide an interlock function. The minicomputer has both control and protection functions, but the PLC is concerned only with protection.

Critical sensors within the system are duplicated, or in some cases triplicated, to protect against component faults. Where appropriate, sensors with different principles of operation are employed to reduce the probability of common-cause failures. Where a critical parameter is sensed by the control computer, a duplicate sensor is used to feed an equivalent signal to the PLC. Operations depending on such parameters then require the agreement of both the computer and the PLC.

Of primary importance to the safety of the plant is the operation of the drain valve, which is determined by the high-temperature control loop. This senses the temperature within the nitrator and opens the drain valve if it exceeds 35°C. The main elements of this control loop are shown in Figure 15.3. The drain valve is arranged so that it is open when de-energized, and is closed by the application of hydraulic pressure. Fluid is supplied to the valve from a hydraulic supply, but two electrically operated valves must each be closed in order for adequate pressure to be applied to close the drain valve. These electrically operated valves are themselves open when de-energized, and are controlled by a relay interlock arrangement involving outputs from both the computer and the PLC. It can be seen that both the computer and the PLC must close their respective relay contacts in order for the drain valve to be held closed. This arrangement provides very good protection against a range of fault mechanisms. Failure of, or disagreement between, the computer and the PLC will result in at least one of the relays being de-energized and will open the drain valve. Similarly, a failure of hydraulic pressure or an electrical power failure will also result in the opening of the valve.

To increase the integrity of this mechanism, three independent temperature sensors are used. Two of these are fed to the computer and the third is fed to the PLC. The high-temperature control loop thus has multiple sensors, multiple processors and multiple actuators. The majority of critical operations require the agreement of both the computer and the PLC before action may be taken. However, if either processor detects a high temperature it can operate the dump mechanism unilaterally.

Self-checking of the computer is provided by the use of a watchdog timer. If this is not reset every second it will 'time-out' and stop the plant by opening the drain valve and dumping the nitrator contents. The PLC also provides a watchdog function that is reset by a signal from the computer every seven seconds. Should the computer fail to reset the PLC timer within 30 seconds, the PLC will act to stop the plant, again by opening the drain valve.

The major sensors and actuators within the nitrator arrangement are shown in Figure 15.4. This also indicates the inputs and outputs from the computer and the PLC, although to simplify this diagram the actual interconnections between the components are not shown. Where duplicated sensors

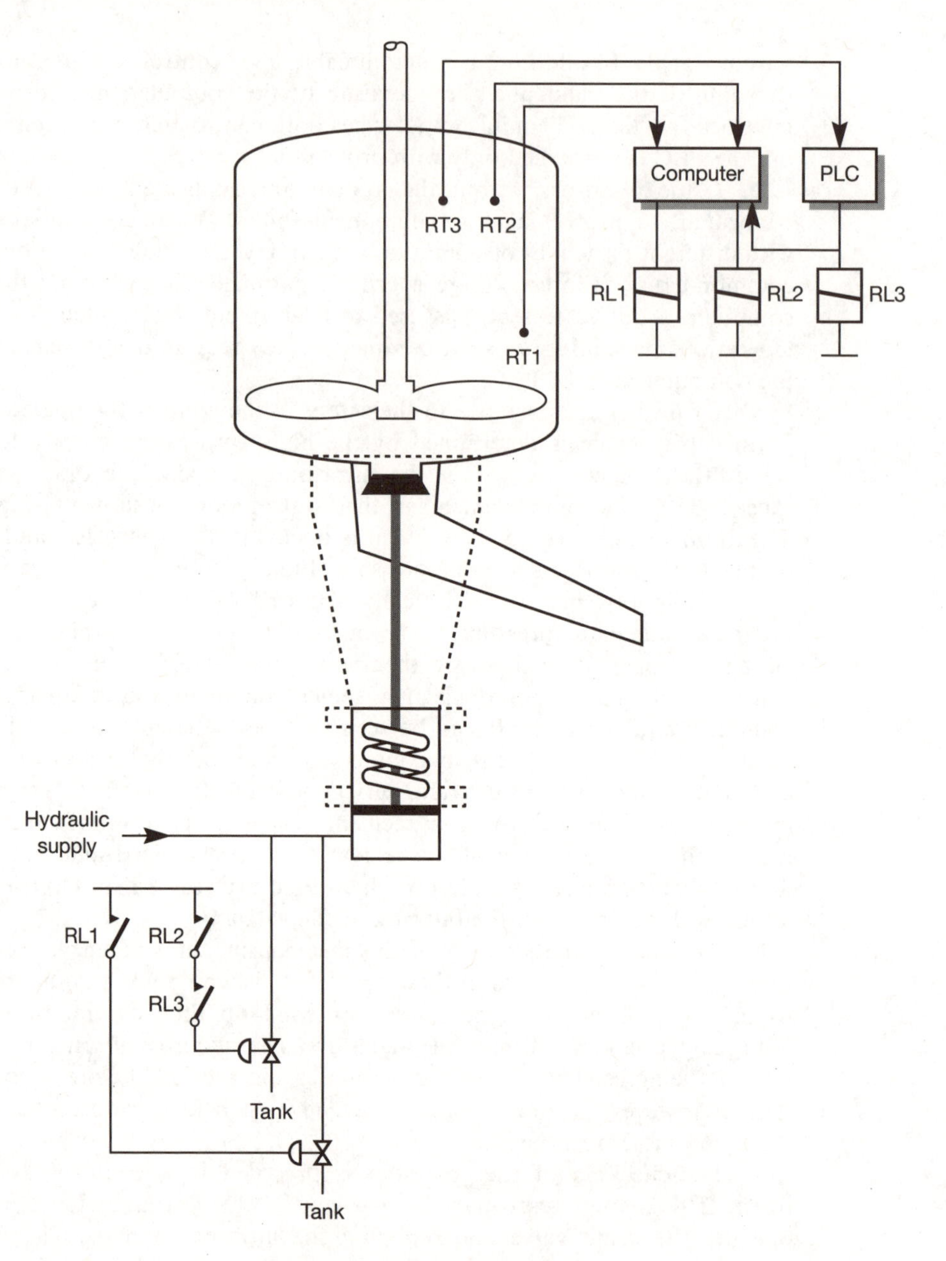

Figure 15.3 Control of the drain valve.

or actuators are used, these are often connected to different processors to provide fault detection and tolerance. It can be seen that the complexity of the plant is somewhat greater than that suggested by the apparent simplicity of the process described in Figure 15.1.

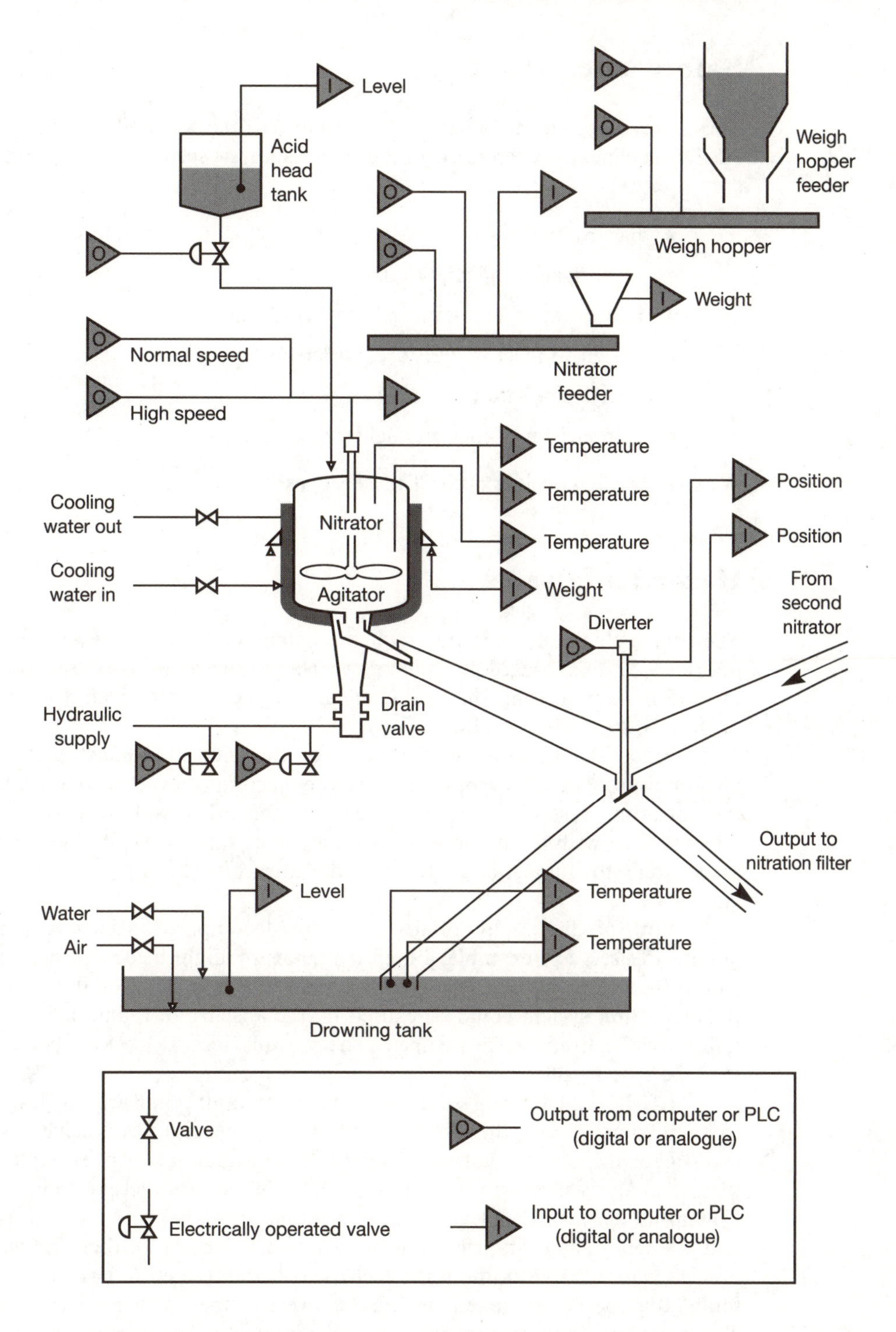

Figure 15.4 Schematic diagram of the nitrator, including safety and control components.

Safety assessment

The safety assessment of the plant followed the methods outlined in the HSE Guidelines and described in the safety analysis section of Chapter 5. These are:

- hazard analysis
- identification of safety-related systems
- allocation of safety integrity requirements
- design to meet integrity requirements
- analysis of safety integrity
- comparison of integrity achieved with that required.

We shall briefly consider each of these stages.

Hazard analysis

The primary hazard associated with the batch production of PETN is decomposition. As this hazard is well known, fault tree analysis is an appropriate method of investigating the characteristics of the plant to identify events that might lead to such a situation.

Figure 15.5 shows the top level of the fault tree constructed for the nitration process. The 'top event' is the decomposition of the contents of the nitration vessel, and it can be seen that this will only occur if the temperature within the vessel exceeds safe limits AND the protection system fails to dump the contents of the nitrator. The top event is given the label A1.

Both of the conditions necessary for decomposition have a number of possible causes. For example, a high temperature might be caused by impurities within the PE, or by having too high a ratio of PE to acid. Similarly, failure of the protection system could be caused by the absence of a dump signal, or the failure of the drain valve to open. The various second-level effects are given the labels B1 to B8.

B1, B3 and B6 represent basic events or faults that are not fully traced to their source. For the other causes it was necessary to delve deeper to investigate the events that can lead to these situations. An example of this further analysis is shown in Figure 15.6, which shows factors relating to B2. This results in a further level, with effects that are labelled C1 to C6. Here C5 and C6 represent basic events, while C1 to C4 require further analysis. This process was repeated until all the factors had been traced to basic events, or to faults that could be taken as inputs, even if their causes were unknown. The complete fault tree consists of nine pages of diagrams and uses levels A to L.

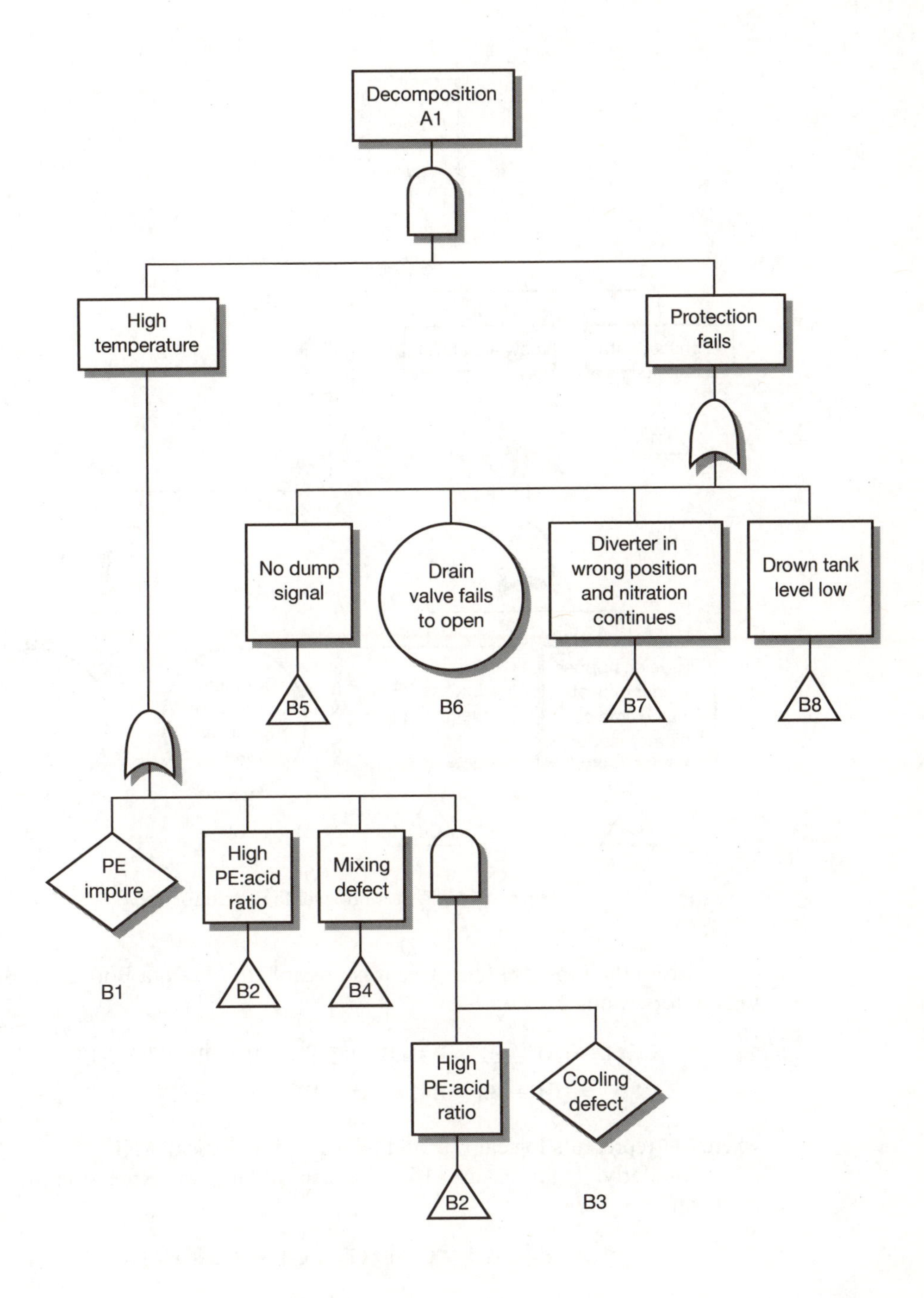

Figure 15.5 The top-level fault tree.

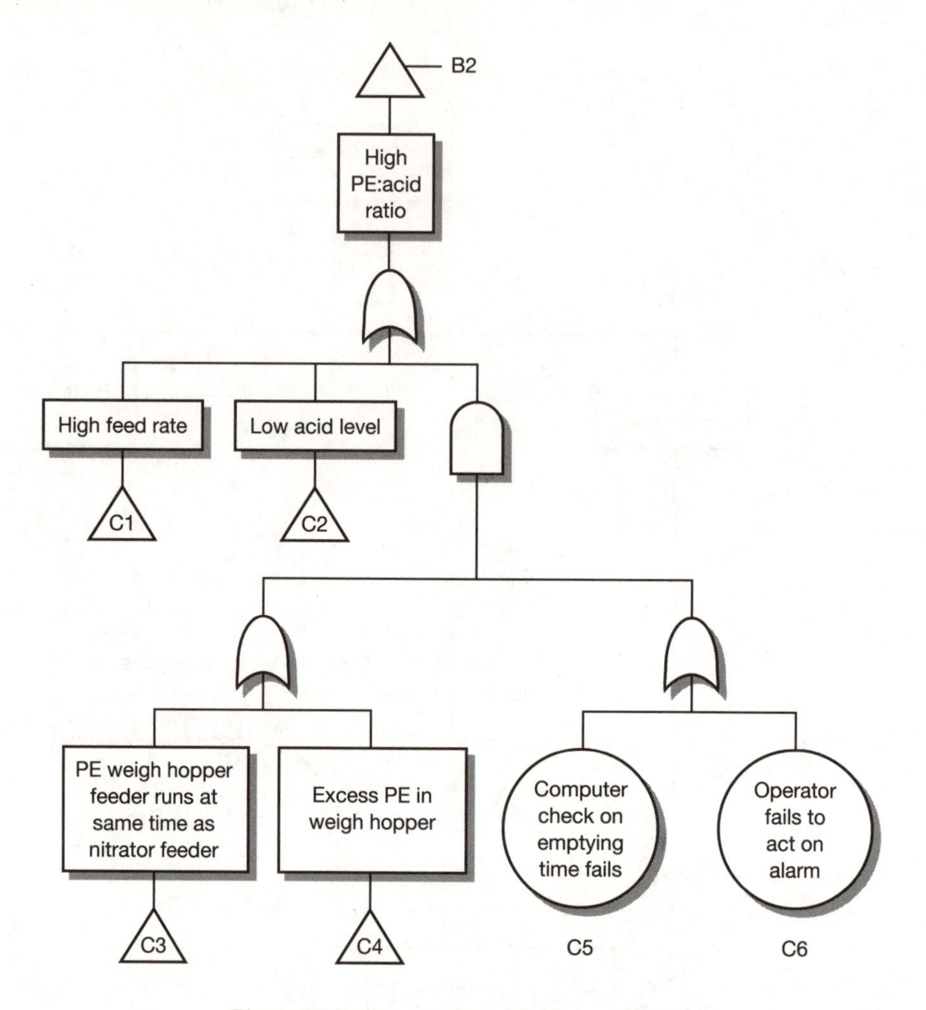

Figure 15.6 A second-level fault tree for B2.

From the top-level fault tree it is possible to obtain a Boolean expression for the top event. This is:

$$\begin{aligned} A1 &= (B1 + B2 + B3 \bullet B2 + B4) \bullet (B5 + B6 + B7 + B8) \\ &= (B1 + B2 + B4) \bullet (B5 + B6 + B7 + B8) \end{aligned}$$

where '+' represents logical OR and '•' represents logical AND.

Similarly, from Figure 15.6 we can obtain an expression for B2 of the form

$$B2 = C1 + C2 + (C3 + C4) \bullet (C5 + C6)$$

In a similar manner we can construct a single expression representing the complete fault tree.

Identification of safety-related systems

From the fault tree it is possible to identify individual failures, or combinations of failures, that could result in an excessive temperature within the nitration vessel. Many of these are concerned with the operation of the control computer. For example, failure of the computer to correctly control the speed of the feeder represents a situation where a single fault could result in a high temperature.

In addition to its role as a system controller, the computer also performs several protection tasks. The computer is therefore part of a safety-related system by virtue of both its control and its protection functions.

The programmable logic controller provides protection to the plant in the event of excessive temperature within the vessel. The PLC is thus also fundamental to the safety of the arrangement. As the computer and the PLC share a common actuator (the drain valve) they are not truly independent but form a single safety-critical system.

Allocation of safety integrity requirements

PETN has been produced by the batch nitration of PE for many years. Conventionally, non-programmable control and protection systems have been used, with a control element that incorporates some protection functions plus an additional protection unit. The control and protection sections have traditionally used separate sensors to guard against sensor failure, but have used a common safety actuator (the drain valve). This basic configuration is shown in Figure 15.7.

The characteristics of existing plants are well understood and there are established standards and procedures for conventional (that is, non-programmable) safety systems. It was therefore decided that the programmable system should have a safety integrity that was at least as good as a non-programmable system.

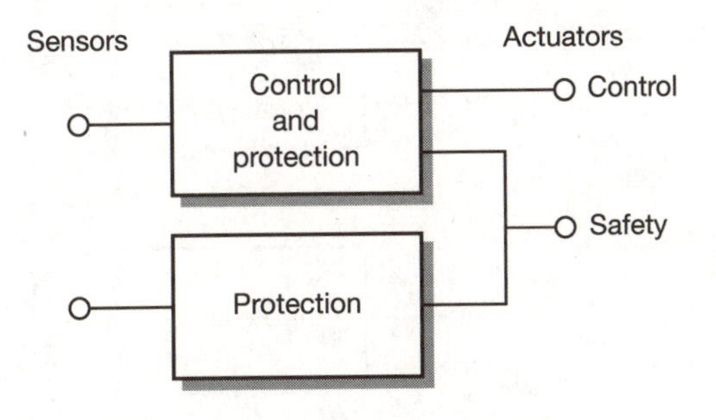

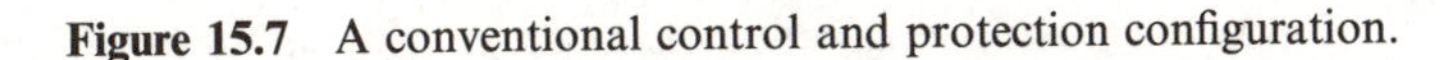

Figure 15.7 A conventional control and protection configuration.

Design to meet integrity requirements

The HSE Guidelines describe three elements to be considered in attempting to satisfy the integrity requirements of a safety-critical system. These are:

- configuration
- reliability
- overall quality.

The **configuration** adopted for the programmable control and protection system is similar to that adopted in non-programmable implementations, as shown in Figure 15.7. As the control and protection element is implemented using a computer, whereas the protection unit is in the form of a PLC, there is comprehensive diversity in both the hardware and the software of these two channels. An additional sensor is also used to increase fault tolerance. The resultant configuration is shown in Figure 15.8.

The **reliability** of the system was assessed by applying quantitative methods to the fault tree described earlier. The probability assigned to each event was determined by a combination of good engineering practice and existing data on failures.

The **overall quality** of the system was assessed with respect to the established standards and procedures used with this area. Although these are concerned primarily with non-programmable systems, many aspects of the programmable system could be judged in a similar manner.

Analysis of safety integrity

The **configuration** adopted within the control and protection system fulfils all the integrity requirements set out in the HSE Guidelines. It includes a level of redundancy consistent with that used in equivalent non-programmable systems,

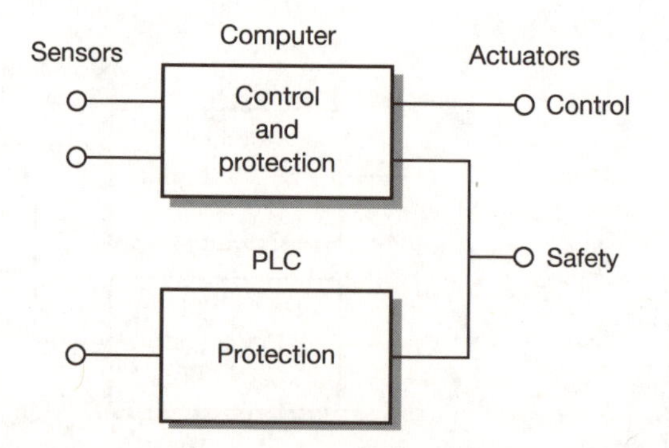

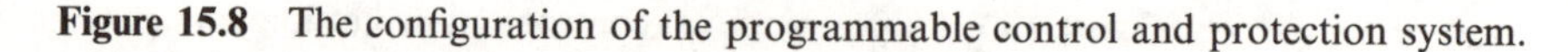
Figure 15.8 The configuration of the programmable control and protection system.

and also provides protection against both random and systematic failures within the programmable elements.

A quantitative analysis of the **reliability** of the system was performed by adding failure rate data to the system's fault trees. This was achieved by replacing the elements within the Boolean expressions discussed above, with their corresponding numerical failure rates. The resulting expressions were then studied to determine the single and combined effects that would lead to the top event. Evaluation of the resulting expressions then gave an estimate of the overall system reliability. The results indicated a dangerous failure rate for the complete system of about 0.10 events per 10^6 hours of operation. This corresponds to about 8.8×10^{-4} dangerous failures per year.

The assessment of the **overall quality** of the system considered a number of aspects. This included an analysis of the quality standards used, the staff involved and the procedures followed. A systematic examination was also carried out following methods outlined in the HSE Guidelines. This involved the use of an extensive set of checklists to examine the hardware and software development process.

Comparison of integrity achieved with that required

It was concluded that the integrity achieved did indeed satisfy the requirements of the system, and that the predicted failure rate of about one dangerous failure in every 1100 years of operation was acceptable. The overall quality requirements were satisfied partly by the use of equipment from established and reputable manufacturers with established quality assurance systems, and partly by the use of competent and experienced staff.

15.3 The Airbus A330/A340 primary flight control system

Electronic control systems have been used in civil aircraft for more than 40 years (Potocki de Montalk, 1993). Early applications were concerned with engine performance, and from the mid-1950s analogue techniques were used to control the hydromechanical actuators responsible for engine fuel and air flow. Some 20 years later, digital methods were introduced to control the variable air intakes for Concorde. Modern engines now make extensive use of microcomputer-based systems to optimize engine performance and fuel economy.

The introduction of Concorde also represented the first use of electronic systems to manipulate the hydraulic controls used to fly the aircraft. In Concorde analogue electronics are used, with a mechanical backup arrangement. Digital systems were first used in such systems in the early 1980s with the introduction of the A310. This uses multiple computers to control the slats,

Figure 15.9 A340 Airbus.

flaps and spoilers (these terms will be explained later) but uses more conventional methods for the primary flight controls. Digital techniques were extended to include the primary flight controls in the A320, which was introduced in 1988. Although this aircraft can be flown using mechanical backup systems, under normal circumstances it adopts a completely 'fly-by-wire' approach, where crew commands are transmitted to the control surfaces through computers rather than by mechanical linkages. In the mid-1990s Airbus introduced the A330/A340 family of aircraft. This also incorporates fly-by-wire techniques and makes extensive use of advanced computer systems. The A330 is a twin-engined aircraft, whereas the A340 has four engines (Figure 15.9). In this section we will look at aspects of the design of the computer systems used for the primary flight controls of these aircraft.

The decision to place such great reliance on the correct operation of a computer-based system was not taken lightly. In this case, the impetus came from a desire to reduce the pilot's workload and to prevent the crew from inadvertently exceeding the aircraft's controllability limits. The primary motivation for both these changes was to improve safety. Statistics suggest that about 60% of all aircraft accidents involve some aspect of human fallibility. This does not imply that such incidents are due to 'pilot error', but does indicate that human characteristics play a significant part in determining aircraft safety. One of the key issues affecting the performance of the aircrew is their workload, and anything that can reduce this is likely to improve overall safety. Advanced computer-based flight control systems aim to reduce the load on the pilot by providing a more intuitive user interface and by performing some functions automatically. Such systems also act to maintain the aircraft within its normal range of operation, and would, for example, prevent the pilot from inadvertently entering a stall condition. This results in both a reduction in crew fatigue and an improvement in flight comfort.

Although the A330 and A340 aircraft can be flown without the use of their electronic flight control system (EFCS), failure of this system would represent a considerable reduction in overall safety levels. The EFCS therefore requires a very high level of integrity and is designed and produced to the stringent standards appropriate for such a system. Because the aircraft relies heavily on its computer system to operate its various control surfaces, it is imperative that the control system remains operational at all times. Fault detection is therefore not sufficient to provide safety and the system must also provide effective fault tolerance to allow the unit to continue safe operation, perhaps for several hours, in the presence of faults. There are several aspects of this system that are of relevance to the material within this book, but here we will concentrate on the architectural features used to achieve this high level of fault tolerance.

Flight control surfaces

The flight of an aircraft is largely controlled by the use of a number of control surfaces that affect the flow of air over the plane's body. The flight control surfaces of the A340 are shown in Figure 15.10 (Airbus Industrie, 1992).

The primary flight control surfaces are the ailerons, elevators and rudder.

- **Ailerons** are movable surfaces on the trailing edge of the wings that control the banking of the aircraft (the roll axis). In a conventional aircraft these are operated by rotation of the control stick or yoke. Turning the yoke to the right raises the aileron on the right-hand side of the aircraft and lowers that on the left. This causes the plane to bank to the right. Rotation of the yoke in the opposite direction will bank the aircraft to the left.

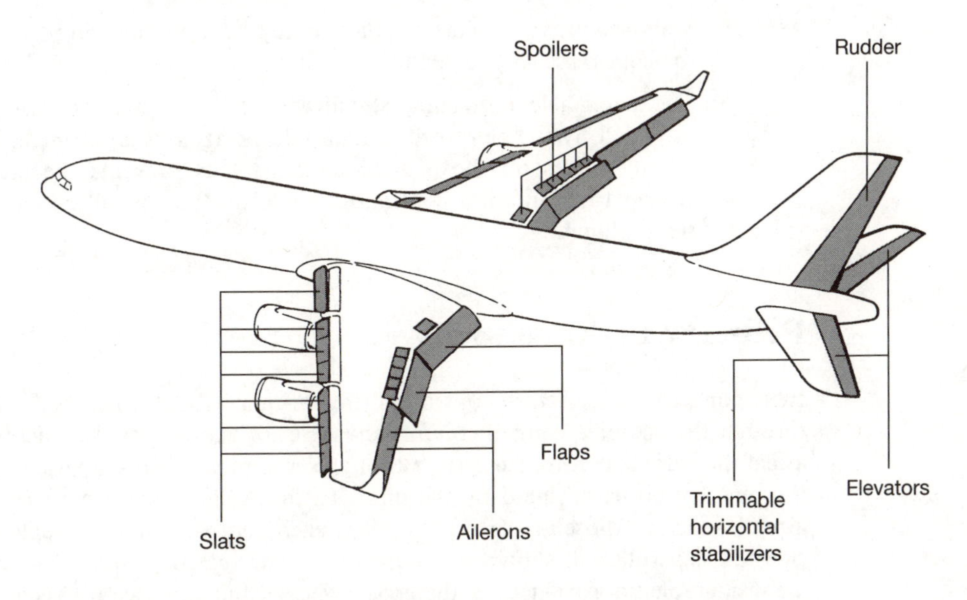

Figure 15.10 The flight control surfaces of an A340.

- **Elevators** are movable aerofoils on the rear edge of the horizontal stabilizer (the rear surface) of the aircraft. They are moved in unison, and are used to control the motion of the aircraft in the pitch axis. In a conventional aircraft the elevators are controlled by moving the control column forwards or backwards. Pushing forward on the column will lower the elevators, causing the aircraft to pitch nose downwards. Conversely, pulling the column backwards will cause the elevators to rise, forcing the nose up.
- The **rudder** is a vertical, movable control surface situated on the rear edge of the vertical stabilizer (the tail fin). Moving the rudder from side to side causes the aircraft to rotate about its vertical axis (the yaw axis). The rudder is normally controlled by foot pedals situated in front of the control column. Pushing the left pedal causes the rudder to turn to the left, forcing the tail of the aircraft to the right. This causes the nose of the aircraft to move to the left. The rudder pedals are also used to steer the aircraft when taxiing.

The aircraft also has a number of secondary flight control surfaces.

- **Flaps** are movable surfaces situated on the inboard trailing edge of the wings. Lowering the flaps increases lift and drag, allowing a slower approach during landing.
- **Spoilers** are situated on the top of the wing, in front of the flaps. Their function is to disrupt the flow of air over the wing and thus to reduce lift and to slow the aircraft by increasing drag. They may be used to allow a steep landing approach at reduced speed.
- **Slats** are movable slots on the leading edge of the wing. Air flowing through these slots helps to prevent stalls.
- The **trimmable horizontal stabilizer** (**THS**) is used to trim the lift provided by the elevators to maintain horizontal flight in the absence of any forces on the control column. This prevents the crew from having to maintain a continuous force on the control column during steady flight.

Primary flight controls

In a conventional aircraft control of the primary flight surfaces is achieved through the use of a control column and a set of rudder pedals. These directly affect the various control surfaces, although servo mechanisms are used to reduce the physical effort required by the pilot. In the A330/A340 aircraft (and other aircraft, such as those of the A320 family) each control column is replaced by a sidestick controller, as shown in Figure 15.11. The sidestick controller represents a considerable improvement in the ergonomics of the interface between the crew and the flight control system. However, the changes to the man–machine

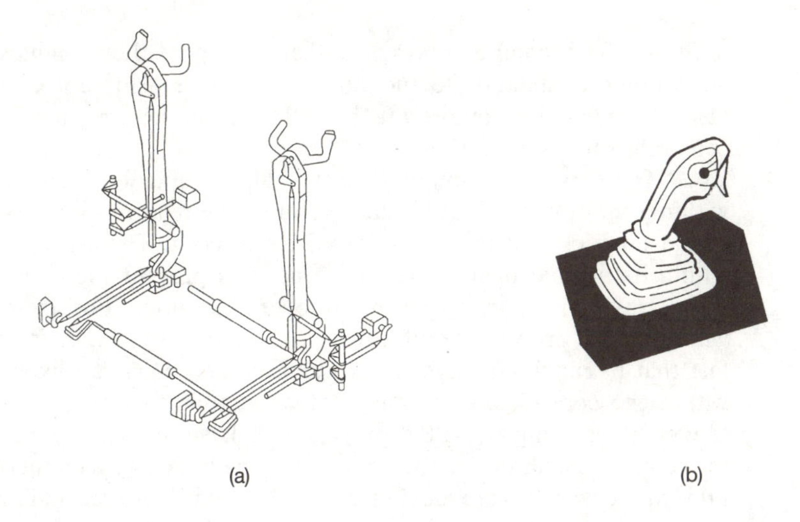

Figure 15.11 (a) A pair of conventional control columns and (b) a sidestick controller.

interface involve far more than an alternative input device, as illustrated in Figure 15.12.

Within a conventional mechanically controlled aircraft, movements of the flight controls are amplified and then applied to the various control surfaces. The power required to operate the surfaces is supplied through the use of hydromechanical servo-amplifiers, but the task of coordinating the various movements is left to the flight crew. In a fly-by-wire aircraft, the pilot provides signals to the flight control computers to indicate what the aircraft

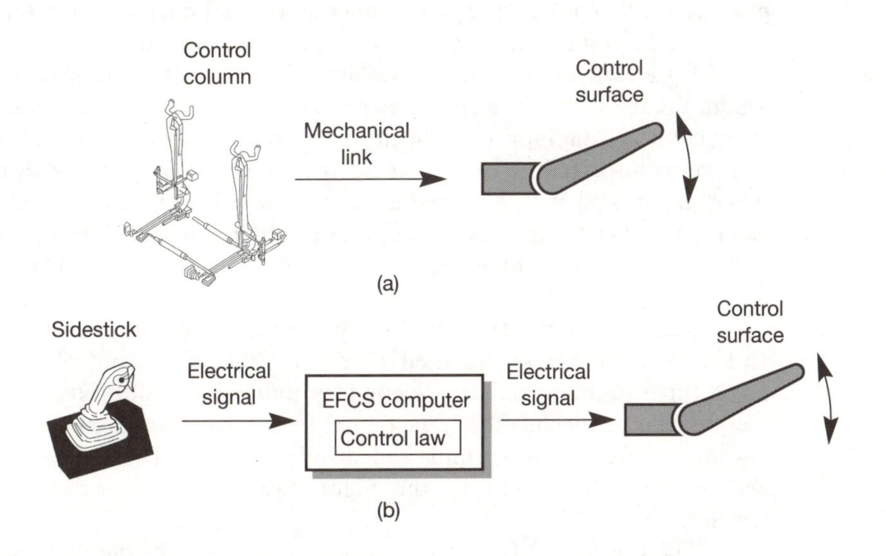

Figure 15.12 A comparison of (a) mechanical and (b) electrical control.

must do. The computer systems then interpret these signals and generate appropriate commands to the various actuators. This not only simplifies the task of controlling the aircraft, but also allows the computer system to apply constraints to its operation.

The constraints imposed by the flight control system are implemented within a set of control laws that determine the relationship between movement of the sidestick and the operation of the aircraft. These act to keep the plane within its normal operational envelope, and prevent the crew from inadvertently straying into an inappropriate operating mode. For example, the system would help to prevent the pilot from stalling the aircraft, or from descending so fast that its maximum safe speed was exceeded. One can liken the constraints within the control laws to those of an automotive antilock braking system (ABS). When using an ABS arrangement a driver may apply maximum pressure to the brake pedal in the knowledge that the braking system will automatically prevent the wheels from locking. Similarly, the pilot of an A340 may request the maximum rate of climb, knowing that the flight control system will help to prevent the aircraft from stalling.

Flight control system architecture

Because of the reliance placed on the flight control systems, and the difficulty of manœuvring the aircraft without them, fault tolerance is of great importance. This is implemented in a number of ways and at a number of levels.

A degree of fault tolerance is provided by the choice of the primary and secondary control surfaces that are connected to the flight control system. In the (extremely unlikely) event of a complete failure of the automated system, the plane can still be flown using the rudder and the trimmable horizontal stabilizer, which are both mechanically linked to the pilot's controls.

Reversion to the use of mechanical backup systems would represent a significant reduction in aircraft safety, and is an ultimate fallback position in the event of a total failure of the electronic systems. However, the system is able to cope with the failure of a great many individual components with no loss of functionality and with little reduction in safety levels. This is achieved by the use of multiple computers, sensors and actuators, in an arrangement that is designed to provide a high degree of protection against a wide variety of system faults.

The computers used in the flight control system are shown in Figure 15.13. Five computers are used to control the flight control surfaces, there being three primary and two secondary units. Two additional computers are used as 'data concentrators', which gather information from the flight control system and feed it to warning and display systems. These data concentrators also supply information to the flight data recorders and to maintenance systems.

The functions of the five computers that control the flight surfaces may be divided into two areas:

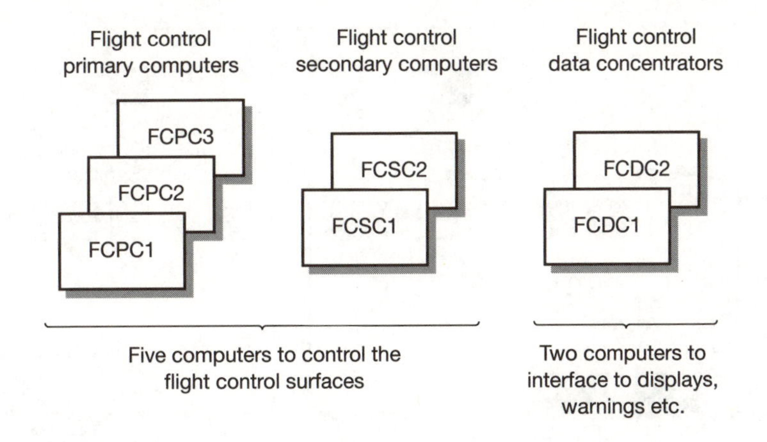

Figure 15.13 The flight control system computers.

- **computational functions**: calculations concerned with the control laws;
- **execution functions**: control of the various servo loops.

Each computer consists of two diverse channels in the form of a command unit and a monitor unit. These channels have independent hardware and different software. Disagreement between these channels would result in the shutting down of that computer, with control being diverted to another processor. Failure of one or more of the processors may be tolerated through the arrangement used to connect the computers to the various actuators. This arrangement ensures that each flight control surface is controlled by multiple independent actuators, which are in turn controlled by different computers. This guarantees that failure of a single actuator or computer will not result in a loss of control of that surface.

As movement of the various control surfaces is achieved using hydraulic actuators, the hydraulic supply represents a key component within the control system. In common with other commercial aircraft, three separate hydraulic supplies are used to prevent the failure of a single supply causing a loss of all the aircraft's actuators. These are designated as the blue, green and yellow hydraulic circuits, and are routed separately throughout the plane to prevent any local event from damaging the diverse systems.

The layout of the various elements of the control system aims to protect the aircraft against failure of any individual computer, actuator or hydraulic supply. In addition, the arrangement provides some protection against multiple faults. The basic layout of the system is shown in Figure 15.14.

Although the flight control system can function correctly in the presence of several forms of single and multiple faults, if additional components become inoperative there comes a point at which some functionality must be lost. In order to maintain safe operation, the system is designed to achieve a graceful degradation of function through a process of reconfiguration.

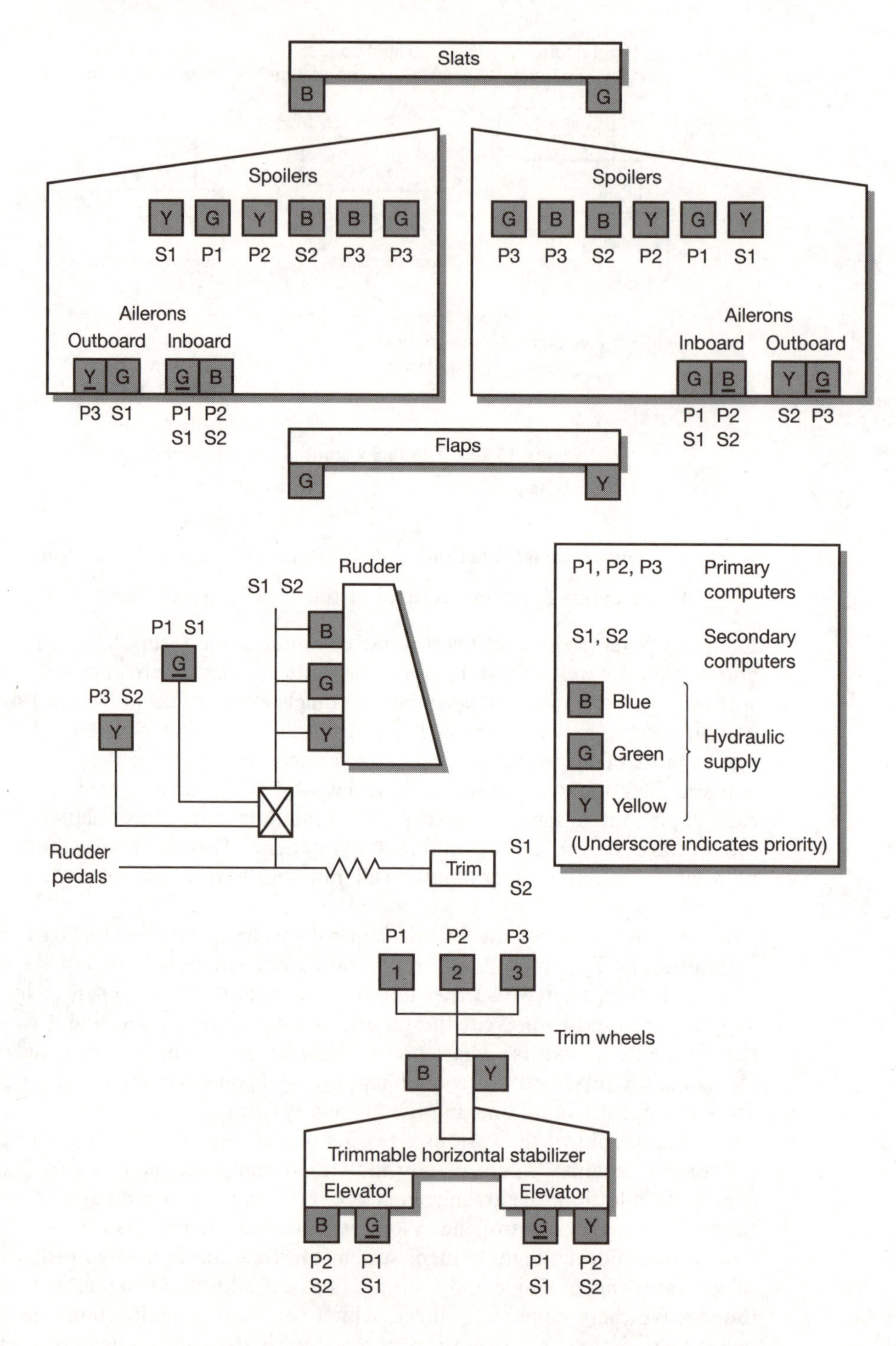

Figure 15.14 The computer and actuator arrangement of the A330/A340.

Fault tolerance through reconfiguration

The flight control system may be reconfigured in two ways to cope with system faults. First, the tasks performed by the various computers can be redistributed according to a preset schedule, to share critical tasks between available resources. Secondly, the system can adopt alternative control laws, depending on the status of system components. This latter approach is illustrated in Figure 15.15, which indicates the system's ability to switch between control laws, depending on system availability.

The flight control system can implement three distinct control laws:

- normal
- alternate
- direct.

Under ordinary circumstances the aircraft operates under the **normal flight control law**. This takes signals from the sidestick and generates appropriate movements of the control surfaces to implement the required actions. This law also provides automatic pitch trimming, gives stabilization against atmospheric fluctuations (gusts of wind) and reduces pilot workload. The normal law also provides flight envelope protection by helping the pilot to avoid stalling the aircraft or exceeding its maximum safe speed. One of the features of this mode is that it gives good protection in the event of engine failure by automatically compensating, in the short term, for the asymmetrical loss of thrust.

In the event of substantial loss of system resources the flight control system may change to the **alternate flight control law**. This provides the automatic pitch control and stabilization features of the normal law, but does not implement most of the envelope protection features. It does, however, provide warnings of imminent stall or overspeed conditions.

If the aircraft were to suffer loss of a large part of its flight control system, it might be necessary to revert to the **direct flight control law**. In this

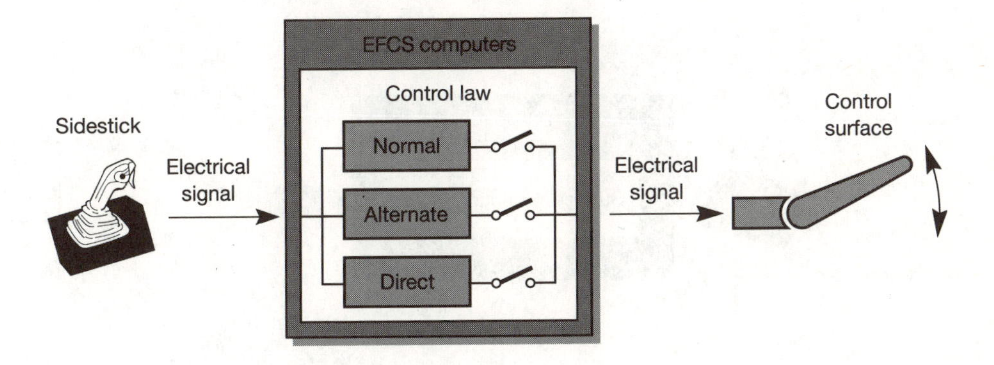

Figure 15.15 The flight control laws.

mode the position of the sidestick controller is used to directly determine the position of the flight control surfaces, and features such as automatic pitch trimming are lost. This mode also provides no envelope protection, but conventional stall and overspeed warnings are given.

Figure 15.16 illustrates the principal differences between the normal and direct flight control laws. In the former, inputs from the sidestick are interpreted as aircraft objectives and are compared with the aircraft's response to determine the required actions of the control surfaces. This law therefore represents a closed-loop control method. When using the direct law, signals from the sidestick are interpreted as direct orders to move the associated flight control surfaces. This method of control is therefore basically open-loop.

No single failure within the flight control system will cause the loss of the normal flight control law. Some double failures will result in the adoption of the alternate law, but at least three components must fail in order to force the system to adopt the direct law. It should be remembered that even when using the direct flight control law the aircraft has a degree of control equivalent to that of a conventional aircraft.

Computer architecture

Each primary and secondary flight control computer consists of two processors, one assigned the role of command and the other that of monitor. These exchange the results of their computations and any disagreement will lead to the combination adopting a fault status, or to the loss of its function.

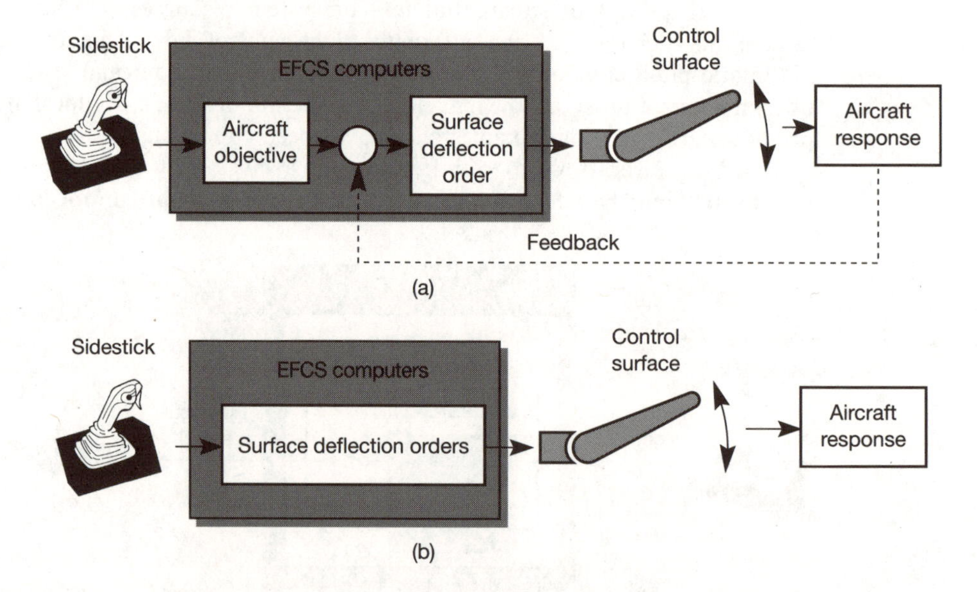

Figure 15.16 A comparison of the normal and direct control laws: (a) normal control law with aircraft feedback; (b) direct control law.

The primary computers employ two Intel 80386 processors operating at 16 MHz. The command channel is programmed in assembler, and the monitor uses PL/M. The combined software amounts to some 800 kbytes. The hardware and software of the computers are supplied by Aérospatiale.

The secondary computers use two Intel 80186 processors operating at 12 MHz. Assembler is again used for the command processor, but Pascal is used for the monitor. The software occupies about 300 kbytes. The hardware of the computers is supplied by Sextant Avionique, and the software is supplied by Aérospatiale.

Fault tolerance

It can be seen that the A330/A340 flight control system provides a high degree of fault tolerance through the use of extensive and diverse redundancy. This includes:

- **Mechanical**: Mechanical linkages to the rudder and trimmable horizontal stabilizer give control in the event of total electronic system failure.
- **Computers**: Five computers of two types are used. Each computer uses two independent processors with diverse software and diverse programming languages. The primary and secondary computers have diverse hardware (including different processors), diverse software and different hardware manufacturers.
- **Sensors**: Multiple sensors (two or three) are used in each case.
- **Actuators**: One, two or three actuators are used for each surface.
- **Hydraulic supplies**: Three independent circuits and eight pumps are used. Hydraulic power can be produced mechanically or electrically from the engines, or by using a ram air turbine.
- **Electrical supplies**: The A340 uses six generators, two batteries and five buses. Four of the generators are driven by the engines, one by an auxiliary power unit and the last by the hydraulic system.

Although fault tolerance cannot in itself guarantee safety, in this case it provides the foundation for a system of very high integrity.

15.4 Darlington nuclear generating station

The Darlington nuclear generating station is situated some 70 km east of Toronto in Ontario, Canada, and produces about 20% of the province's electricity needs (Figure 15.17). As in all nuclear plants, safety is of the utmost importance, and the operators, Ontario Hydro, have incorporated a number of independent

Figure 15.17 Darlington nuclear generating station.

means of protecting their employees and the public. These include what might be seen as primary methods, which aim to prevent the reactor from entering a dangerous state, and secondary techniques that would limit the impact of any incident that occurred. These secondary methods include the use of containment buildings and a vacuum arrangement to prevent radioactive material from reaching the outside world.

The Darlington station contains four reactors, each housed in a separate building and equipped with its own control and safety systems. The output of a reactor is determined by its control system, which can increase or reduce the release of energy. If required, or in the case of an emergency, this control system can shut down the reactor by stopping the nuclear reaction altogether. Each reactor is also equipped with two completely independent shutdown systems which likewise can halt the nuclear reaction. Each reactor therefore has three independent means of achieving a system shutdown.

Whereas the reactor control system implements a complex array of functions, the operation of the shutdown systems is relatively straightforward, allowing fairly simple mechanisms to be used. Traditionally, shutdown systems have been implemented using analogue devices and relays. Such arrangements are well understood and sustain a great deal of confidence. However, such systems are incapable of performing sophisticated checking operations, and in this power station it was decided that safety could be improved by adding programmability. Each reactor therefore employs two computer-based shutdown systems. Because of the relative complexity of the control system, the safety analysis assumes that this is likely to fail often. It is therefore the responsibility of the shutdown systems to ensure safety.

All Canadian nuclear power stations must be certified by the Atomic Energy Control Board of Canada (AECB). Because the Darlington station was the first Canadian reactor to use software-controlled shutdown systems, its certification presented the AECB with some novel problems. As the project neared completion, despite considerable amounts of testing the regulators were uncertain of the adequacy of the software. To resolve these problems they recruited several external consultants to carry out an investigation.

The correctness of the software was investigated through a process of formal review. This involved the retrospective use of formal methods to analyse a system that had already been implemented. The work uncovered several areas of concern, but was eventually able to convince the regulators that the system should be certified. The power station then went into operation in 1990.

The Darlington power generating plant could be used to illustrate several aspects of the material covered within this book. However, here we will look briefly at the general architecture adopted to tolerate faults within the plant, and will concentrate on the methods used to validate its software. At present, this application represents one of the most important examples of the use of formal methods in the verification of safety-critical software.

Nuclear reactor operation

If a neutron, travelling at an appropriate speed, strikes an atom of uranium it will cause the atom to split, creating two smaller atoms. This process releases heat, and also produces from one to three new neutrons which can, in turn, split other uranium atoms. This process is known as nuclear fission, and is shown in Figure 15.18.

Normally the neutrons produced by the splitting of an atom are travelling too fast to themselves split atoms. In order to produce a 'chain reaction' a moderator is used to slow down the neutrons to about 2.4 km per second. A number of moderating materials may be used, including water, heavy water (deuterium oxide) and graphite. This is shown in Figure 15.19.

Heat produced by the nuclear reaction is used to produce steam to drive an electricity generator. The rate of production of heat is controlled by the insertion of neutron-absorbing control rods into the reactor vessel. As these are lowered into the active region they progressively reduce the power output of the unit. The basic elements of a nuclear generating station are illustrated in Figure 15.20.

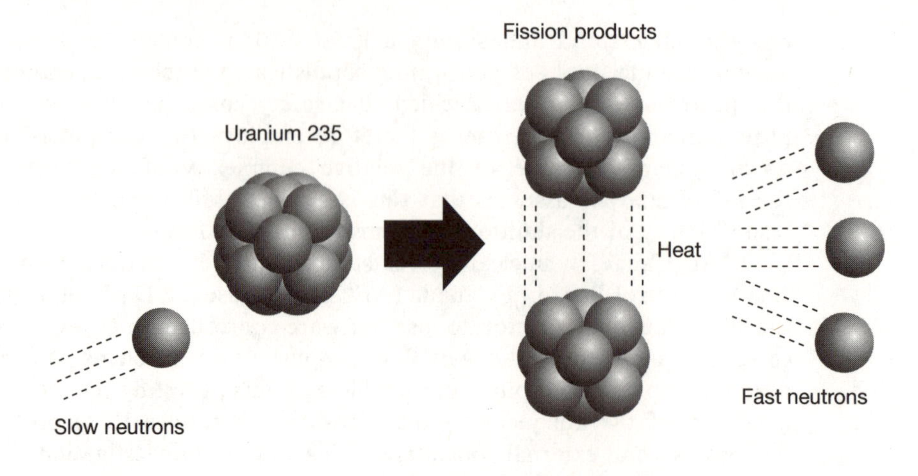

Figure 15.18 The fission process.

The reactors in the Darlington station use natural uranium as their fuel source and deuterium oxide (heavy water) as their moderator. This is a common arrangement in Canada, and such units are referred to as CANDU reactors (CANadian Deuterium Uranium). The station uses four reactors, each capable of producing about 900 MW of electricity. Each reactor is housed in a separate building and has its own generator, control system and shutdown systems.

The central component of the reactor is the calandria. This is a horizontal cylindrical vessel through which pass 480 fuel channels. Uranium pellets are inserted into these channels within fuel bundles. Each channel can take up to 13 bundles, allowing a maximum of 6240 fuel bundles to be inserted. The initial cost of fuelling a reactor is about 30 million Canadian dollars, and the active life of a bundle is about 18 months. The calandria is surrounded by tanks that contain shielding material consisting of natural water and steel balls.

The heat produced within the reactor can be controlled in a number of ways. One of the primary control mechanisms uses control rods that are inserted or removed from tubes within the calandria. Each reactor has

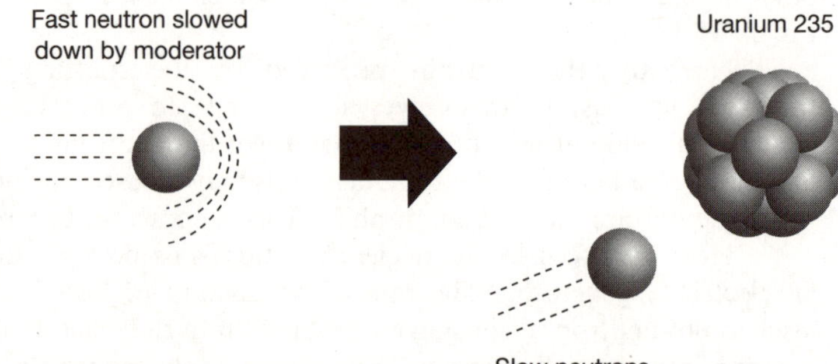

Figure 15.19 The process of moderation.

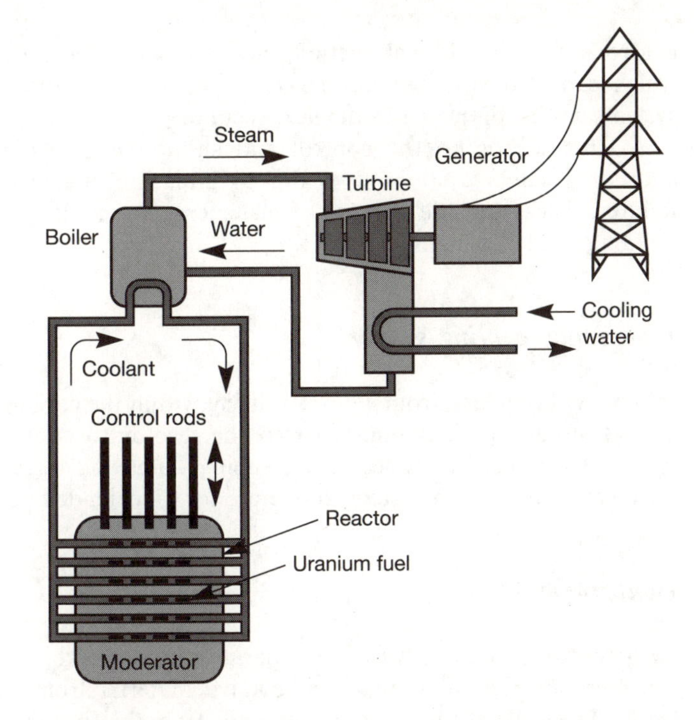

Figure 15.20 The basic elements of a nuclear reactor.

24 stainless steel control rods. Their function is to absorb neutrons and hence to reduce the rate of the fission process. Lowering the rods into the reactor vessel reduces the power output, whereas raising them results in an increase of power.

Heavy water is pumped through the calandria to act as a moderator for the fission process. Heavy water is also used as the primary reactor coolant. This is pressurized and pumped through the calandria to extract heat from the reactor vessel. The coolant liquid reaches temperatures in excess of 300°C. The moderator and primary coolant systems together require about 500 tons of heavy water, with an approximate cost of 300 million Canadian dollars per reactor.

After driving the turbine, steam is condensed using cooling water taken from Lake Ontario. Water is drawn in at a rate of 155 000 litres per second, and is then discharged back to the lake. The warm water is immediately mixed with colder lake water, which limits the temperature difference between the mixed water and the surrounding lake water to less than two degrees centigrade.

Ensuring reactor safety

The safety of the plant is guaranteed through the use of a number of independent safety systems. The reactor control system can stop the nuclear reaction at any time by fully lowering the control rods into the calandria. In the event that the control system should malfunction, there are two independent shutdown systems which can also stop the nuclear reaction. The operation of these shutdown systems will be discussed in the next section.

In addition to the control and shutdown mechanisms there are also additional safety systems that aim to limit the effects of major equipment failures. These include the use of an emergency cooling system, containment buildings and a vacuum system.

Emergency cooling system

In the event of a leak from a pipe or fitting within the cooling system, water from a large storage tank is pumped into the reactor to cool the fuel. A recovery system is also used to collect any escaping water and to recirculate it, allowing the emergency cooling system to operate for an extended period.

Containment

Each reactor is housed within a separate sealed reactor containment building, which is designed to prevent radioactive material from reaching the outside world. The walls of this building are made from reinforced concrete and are over one metre thick. The basic arrangement is shown in Figure 15.21.

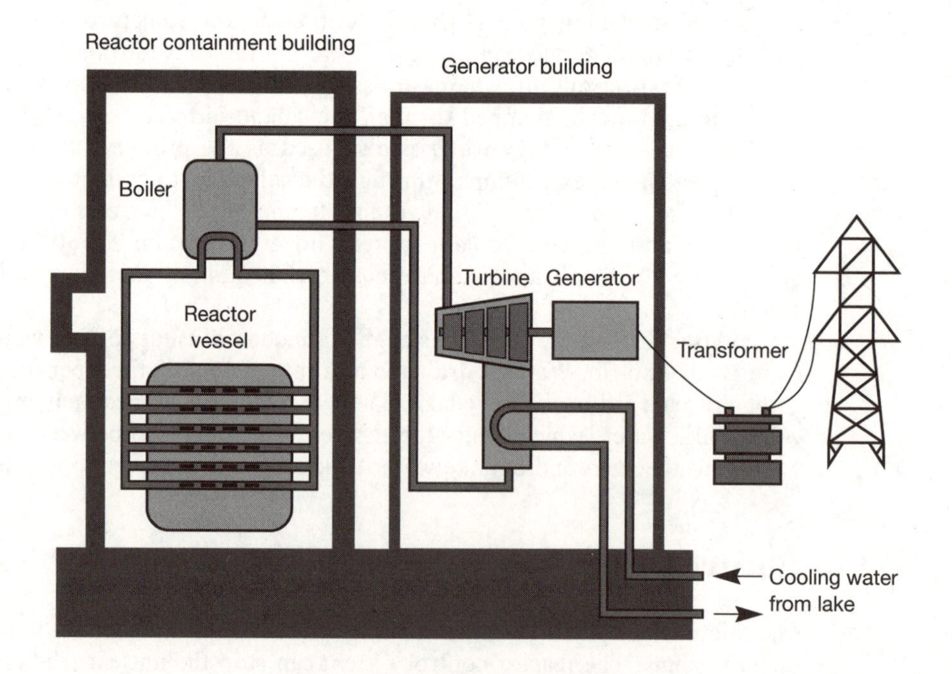

Figure 15.21 Reactor containment.

Vacuum system

Each of the four reactor containment buildings within the Darlington station is connected by a pipe to a nearby vacuum building. If radioactive steam were to leak into one of the containment buildings it would automatically be sucked into the vacuum building, where it would be trapped, condensed into a liquid and contained. Some days after an accident the pressure in the vacuum building might begin to approach that of the outside atmosphere. In this case, operators would vent the vacuum building through large filters designed to trap most radioactive particles. The vacuum building consists of a circular tower over 70 metres high and 50 metres in diameter, with a free volume of nearly 100 000 cubic metres. The vacuum arrangement is shown in Figure 15.22.

The shutdown systems

Each of the four reactors has two independent shutdown systems which can terminate the nuclear reaction in the case of an emergency. The first of these, SDS1, drops neutron-absorbing shutoff rods into the reactor vessel. These function in a similar manner to the control rods, but are used to stop the reaction completely. Each reactor has 32 shutoff rods, which are made of stainless steel and cadmium.

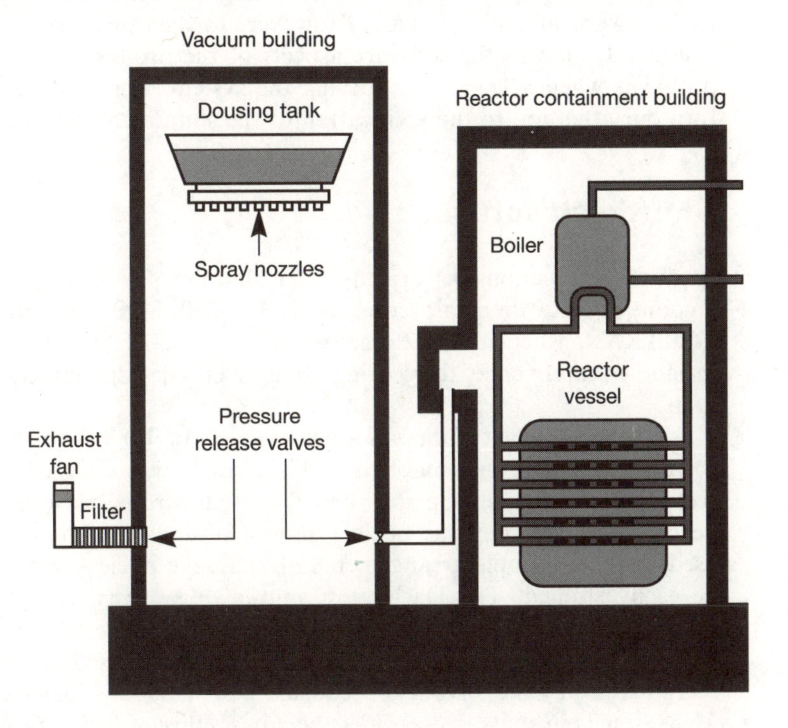

Figure 15.22 The vacuum system.

The second shutdown system, SDS2, injects a liquid poison (gadolinium nitrate) into the moderator. This removes its moderating properties and terminates the nuclear reaction.

The operation of the control system and the two shutdown systems are completely separate, and any one of these can stop the reactor, regardless of the actions of the others. In order to minimize the probability of a common-mode failure, the two shutdown systems incorporate a high degree of independence. They use separate sensors and often measure different physical quantities. They also adopt diverse mechanisms to achieve a shutdown, and therefore have independent actuators. The systems use dissimilar computer hardware and the software was produced using different programming languages, by separate teams (although these teams had a common manager). Because of these measures it is thought that the probability of a common-mode failure is acceptably low.

Considerations of safety alone would dictate that the various shutdown mechanisms should be activated if there is any doubt as to the safety of the plant. However, it must be remembered that shutting down the reactor has considerable financial consequences. While the reactor is offline it is not producing electricity and is thus losing income for its operators. Also, actions such as poisoning the moderator will necessitate an expensive clean-up operation before the reactor can be used again. For these reasons it is essential that the reactor is shut down only when really necessary.

The integrity of the shutdown arrangement is clearly dependent on both its hardware and its software. However, for reasons that were discussed in Chapter 12, it was the software aspects of the project that posed the greatest problems when it came to certifying the system. For this reason, we will now turn our attention to the verification of the shutdown software.

Shutdown software

Because the functions performed by the shutdown systems are fairly simple, the amount of software employed is relatively small. SDS1 uses about 7000 lines of FORTRAN, whereas SDS2 employs 13 000 lines of Pascal. Both systems also include assembly code, there being about 6000 lines distributed between the two units.

Work began on the shutdown system in 1983, and by early 1987 the software was nearing completion. The AECB was charged with the task of certifying the nuclear plant, and held numerous reviews throughout its development. In previous nuclear power stations the shutdown systems had used relatively simple arrangements of analogue devices and relays that could be easily studied. The Darlington shutdown systems, being software based, presented the regulators with a more onerous task. The AECB thought that the software was of sufficient complexity to require outside assistance, and they recruited a number of outside consultants, including David Parnas, now at McMaster University, to consider the advisability of licensing systems based on such software.

As part of the review process several discrepancies were uncovered that raised doubts as to whether the software correctly implemented the system requirements. Also, although the software for the two shutdown systems was written by different teams, an informal analysis performed by Parnas discovered a common design error in the two implementations (highlighting the problems associated with diverse design, as discussed in Chapter 6). Faced with these problems the AECB felt unable to grant an operating licence without further inspection. This resulted in a project involving a team of about 60 people, who performed an inspection of the code over a period of about one year.

The project team included university-based staff who were not specialists in the field of nuclear power generation. Their task was to investigate the software and to see whether this fulfilled its requirements. Therefore the success of the task was critically concerned with the interpretation of the various specifications.

System documentation

The complexity of the processes within a nuclear reactor is so great that a complete comprehension of all aspects of the design and operation of the plant is probably beyond the capability of any single individual. Fortunately, those elements that are directly relevant to the design of a shutdown system represent only a small fraction of this information. In order to make the design task manageable, system requirements documents were used to describe the properties required by each shutdown system. This approach was intended to enable teams of programmers to implement systems to satisfy these requirements, without a detailed knowledge of the operation of the remainder of the plant.

Clearly, the success of this process was affected by the ability of the programmers to correctly interpret the intentions of those responsible for producing the requirements documents. The programmers concerned with the project were often software specialists rather than experts in the field of nuclear engineering. Consequently, they could rely only on their understanding of the requirements documents to determine what the software should do. Some of the programmers did have specialist knowledge of the application area and would inevitably use this knowledge to interpret the various documentation. However, when ambiguities were present this apparent advantage might result in their adopting different techniques from those envisaged by the plant's designers.

Unfortunately, the documents used for the specification of the shutdown systems were based on the use of natural languages. In Chapter 5 we considered the use of natural language specifications and looked at the associated problems of ambiguity. From that discussion it is clear that all documents written in natural languages are subject to diverse interpretation.

In their paper on the assessment of safety-critical software in nuclear power plants, Parnas *et al.* (1991) give an example of possible ambiguities associated with natural language specifications. They consider the simple statement,

> 'Shut off the pumps if the water level remains above 100 metres for more than 4 seconds.'

Such a statement could relate to the control of pumps used to fill a water tank. Although the meaning of this sentence may appear clear, its interpretation is less obvious if we consider the effects of variations in the water level with time. An engineer attempting to implement this statement might reasonably interpret it in a number of ways. For example:

(1) 'Shut off the pumps if the mean water level over the past four seconds was above 100 metres.' This condition may be expressed mathematically as

$$\left[\int_{T-4}^{T} WL(t)\mathrm{d}t\right] \div 4 > 100$$

(2) 'Shut off the pumps if the median water level over the past four seconds was above 100 metres.' This may be expressed as

$$\{\mathrm{MAX}_{(T-4,T)}[WL(t)] + \mathrm{MIN}_{(T-4,T)}[WL(t)]\} \div 2 > 100$$

(3) 'Shut off the pumps if the rms water level over the past four seconds was above 100 metres.' This may be expressed as

$$\left(\int_{T-4}^{T} WL^2(t)\mathrm{d}t \div 4\right)^{1/2} > 100$$

(4) 'Shut off the pumps if the minimum water level over the past four seconds was above 100 metres.' This may be expressed as

$$\mathrm{MIN}_{(T-4,T)}[WL(t)] > 100$$

Of these four forms the last represents the most literal, and probably the most likely, interpretation of the original statement. However, large waves within the tank could cause problems for an implementation based on this function by preventing the pumps from being turned off, even though the water had reached a dangerously high level.

The problems illustrated in this example are typical of those associated with all systems based on the use of natural language specifications. In the case of the Darlington shutdown systems the problems were exacerbated by the complexity of the nuclear processes concerned.

Software evaluation

The software evaluation team initially performed an informal analysis of the software and identified a number of areas of concern. In January 1989 they proposed a formal mathematical inspection of the code as a means of gaining sufficient confidence to allow certification.

Neither Ontario Hydro nor the reactor's designers had had any previous experience of formal methods in such a situation. The application also represented an unusual use of such techniques, as it involved a form of 'reverse-engineering' aimed at validating an existing system implemented using more conventional methods.

In the view of the developers, the use of formal methods was an alternative to completely reimplementing the shutdown systems using non-programmable methods. Faced with these options, in May 1989 they decided to proceed with a formal review of the existing designs, using techniques suggested by David Parnas.

The formal inspection

The method adopted had three main components:

- preparation of formal requirements documents;
- development of program-function tables for the software;
- demonstration that the program functions were consistent with the requirements.

The preparation of the formal requirements took as its starting point the existing informal requirements documents. This work was performed by nuclear engineers who had a detailed knowledge of the plant's operation. The formal documents described each function of the system in a mathematical form, removing any ambiguity. The formal requirements were presented in the form of **requirements tables**, using techniques developed at the Naval Research Laboratory. These techniques were originally used for the A-7 aircraft, and form part of what is called the software cost reduction (SCR) method.

In order to allow a direct comparison between the system described by the formal requirements documents and that implemented by the software, it was also necessary to represent the programs in a mathematical form. The operation of a piece of software may be described by considering the states of the system on entering and leaving the program. The mapping between these states then defines what is termed the *program function*. The relationships between the input and output states of the various software routines were presented in the form of **program function tables** (Parnas, 1994). The form of these tables is illustrated in Figures 15.23 and 15.24. The former shows an example of a simple Pascal program and the latter gives the corresponding program function table (Parnas *et al.*, 1991). An explanation of the notation used in these tables is not within the scope of this text, although an appreciation of its form is useful.

In order to demonstrate consistency between the requirements and the program functions, engineers carried out 'proofs' of equivalence. These were performed almost entirely by hand, there being no automated tools available for the novel methods used.

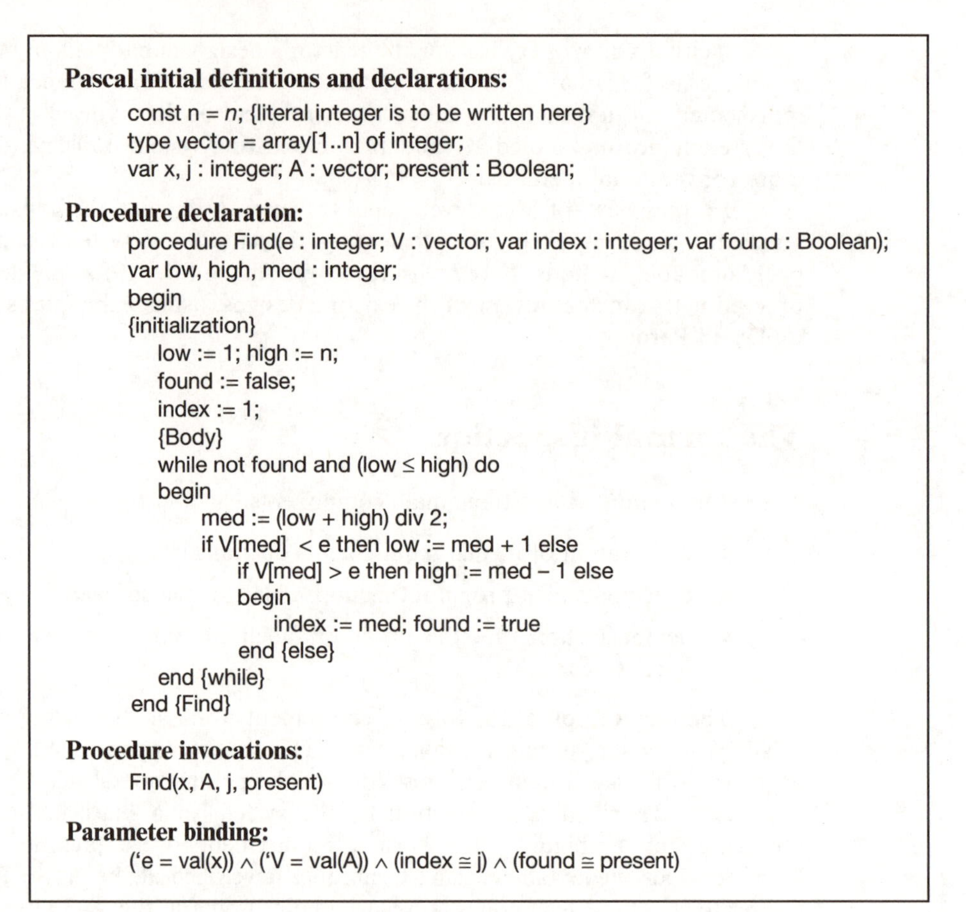

Pascal initial definitions and declarations:

```
const n = n; {literal integer is to be written here}
type vector = array[1..n] of integer;
var x, j : integer; A : vector; present : Boolean;
```

Procedure declaration:

```
procedure Find(e : integer; V : vector; var index : integer; var found : Boolean);
var low, high, med : integer;
begin
{initialization}
   low := 1; high := n;
   found := false;
   index := 1;
   {Body}
   while not found and (low ≤ high) do
   begin
      med := (low + high) div 2;
      if V[med]  < e then low := med + 1 else
         if V[med] > e then high := med – 1 else
         begin
            index := med; found := true
         end {else}
   end {while}
end {Find}
```

Procedure invocations:

```
Find(x, A, j, present)
```

Parameter binding:

$(\text{'e} = \text{val(x)}) \wedge (\text{'V} = \text{val(A)}) \wedge (\text{index} \cong \text{j}) \wedge (\text{found} \cong \text{present})$

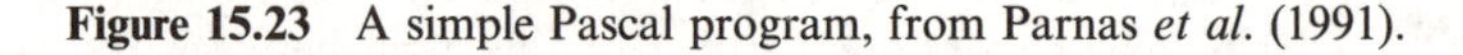

Figure 15.23 A simple Pascal program, from Parnas *et al.* (1991).

Find(x, A, j, present)

$R((\text{'x}, \text{'A}, \text{'j}, \text{'present}), (\text{x'}, \text{A'}, \text{j'}, \text{present'})) =$

$((1 \le n) \wedge \forall i\, [(1 \le i < n) \rightarrow (\text{'A}[i] \le \text{'A}[i+1])\,]) \rightarrow$

	$\exists i\, [\,(1 \le i \le n) \wedge (\text{'A}[i] = \text{'x})] =$	
	true	*false*
j' |	'A[j'] = 'x	*true*
present =	true	false

$\wedge$ NC(x, A)

Figure 15.24 A tabular expression of the function of the program of Figure 15.23, from Parnas *et al.* (1991).

The review process

The formal review was performed by four teams:

(1) A team from Atomic Energy of Canada Limited (AECL), the designers of the CANDU reactor system, prepared the formal requirements documents.

(2) Consultants employed by Ontario Hydro examined the code and produced the program function tables.

(3) A group from Ontario Hydro compared the formal requirements and the function tables, and produced 'proofs' that the latter were correct implementations of the former.

(4) AECB employees and consultants audited the process and reviewed a subset of the 'proofs'.

Any discrepancy was first reported to the second team, who were asked to check the work. They were not told the nature of the problem, but simply asked to review the material. If this failed to resolve the problem it was reported to a group of safety experts for evaluation. This normally uncovered one of the following:

- The requirement tables were wrong. In this case they were corrected and the process repeated.
- The programmers had added material in addition to that set out in the requirements – often in an attempt to improve the system. In some cases this change was accepted as being of positive benefit.
- There was a coding error that did not adversely affect safety. This was allowed to remain.
- There was a coding error that did affect safety. This was corrected and the review repeated.

Prior to the formal review the software had undergone a great deal of testing and it is, perhaps, not surprising that the review uncovered relatively few faults and resulted in only a small number of changes. However, all the modifications made were seen as important.

Formal inspection of SDS1 was completed in November 1989, whereupon AECB issued a licence for 1% power operation. In January 1990 work began on the formal inspection of SDS2, which was completed about one month later. In February 1990 AECB issued a licence allowing full-power operation of the Darlington station. Two of the four reactors became operational in 1990, a third in 1991 and the last in 1992.

An overview of the Darlington project

Although the techniques described in this study represent an important milestone in the use of formal methods, they do not correspond to the most efficient use of these powerful tools. The application is unusual in that formal techniques were used to reverse engineer a system that had been implemented using more conventional methods. The engineers responsible for the verification work considered that their task could have been made much easier if the use of formal methods had been taken into account during the design phase of the project. They also thought that the use of object-oriented design or abstract data types would have greatly simplified the verification task.

The formal review actually resulted in the location of a relatively small number of problems. However, the work should be judged not in terms of the errors located, but in respect of the confidence that it gave in the correctness of the final software. The developers of the software had no previous experience of formal methods and undertook this work very reluctantly. However, they came to the conclusion that this was the only alternative to completely redesigning the shutdown systems using non-programmable techniques.

We noted in Chapter 11 that the use of formal methods is an issue that is currently the subject of much debate within the safety-critical systems community. As a result of such discussions, several groups of researchers have considered the success of such techniques in a range of applications. One study evaluated the Darlington project from a number of viewpoints, including areas such as cost; time to market; customer satisfaction; design; verification and validation; requirements capture; and tool usage (Craigen *et al.*, 1994). This study found that the techniques used had resulted in positive benefits in all of these areas, and concluded that the project had been successful in demonstrating that the code conformed to its specification, and had helped increase assurance.

It is estimated that the software verification process cost about 4 million Canadian dollars, whereas the cost of replacing the shutdown systems with simpler, non-programmable units would have been about 1 million dollars. However, it is likely that a decision to replace the shutdown systems would have resulted in a delay of about one year, at a time when interest charges were costing about 20 million dollars per month. Replacing the shutdown systems with more conventional relay-based units would also have caused problems because of the space required. The area allocated within the reactor buildings was sufficient for the computer-based systems, but could not easily house the much larger relay-based equipment.

One of the factors leading to the high cost of the verification process was the absence of any form of automated tool support. Ontario Hydro and AECL are currently working on the development of tools to assist in this form of verification, with the aim of producing tools for use in the very near future. More fundamental and long-term work on tool development is currently under way at a number of institutions, including McMaster University, the University of Quebec, the University of Warsaw, the Naval Research Laboratory, ORA and SRI.

15.5 Conclusions

In this chapter we have considered three very different safety-critical systems, each illustrating different aspects of the material covered earlier. These examples help to place the various techniques in a realistic engineering context, and illustrate some of their characteristics and their limitations.

It would not be practical to summarize *all* the important points raised by these examples. However, it is perhaps useful to summarize a few of the major points from the earlier chapters which are highlighted in these examples.

(1) Preliminary hazard and risk analyses should be applied to all engineering projects at an early stage. In systems that are found to have safety implications, more detailed hazard and risk analyses should form an ongoing part of the development process. All stages of this work should be extensively documented to produce a substantive body of evidence to support later claims for the system's safety. Hazard and risk analyses may also be used retrospectively to assess the safety of existing systems, as shown in the first commercial application within this chapter.

(2) Safety is most effectively achieved though the use of system architectures that are intrinsically safe. Where this is not possible, the next best option is to use arrangements that have failsafe states, and which rely on only simple, well-understood components to ensure safety.

(3) Because safety is only one of a number of system requirements, often more complex arrangements are used in order to achieve certain functional requirements. In some cases this results in complex components, such as computer systems, being directly responsible for safety.

(4) Complexity is a great barrier to achieving safety. In computer-based systems much of the system's complexity is implemented by the software. This makes the task of designing and verifying the software very difficult. These problems arise because of the *complexity* involved and not specifically because of the nature of software. Implementing the same functions within hardware (were this possible) would not remove these problems.

(5) The overall complexity of real systems is often very high and is generally beyond the comprehension of any individual. This necessitates the *partitioning* of systems into manageable components that can be designed and implemented by a number of people. It is essential that there is clear and unambiguous communication between all members of the development team, which will normally include hardware engineers, software engineers and application area specialists.

(6) The choice of an appropriate system architecture is extremely important in providing an adequate level of fault tolerance. However, redundancy alone is not a solution to all the problems of producing safety-critical systems. Because most of the complexity of computer-based systems lies within the software, it follows that most of the problems of fault management will be software related. As software faults are always systematic, they will not be effectively tackled by the use of redundancy based on identical channels. Redundancy with diversity can be used, but is very expensive and, as is illustrated by the Darlington example, is not guaranteed to remove common-mode faults. For these reasons, the safety of computer-based systems must be assured by the appropriate use of a range of fault management techniques, with great emphasis being placed on fault avoidance and fault removal, in addition to fault detection and fault tolerance.

(7) Often the success or failure of a project is dictated by the quality of the advance planning. In this regard, particular attention should be given to the planning of the independent verification and validation process (IV & V), particularly with regard to the software. This is often *very* expensive, and in some cases projects may be judged impractical simply on the basis of the IV & V costs involved. This is illustrated by the Darlington project, where it is quite possible that the implementation methods chosen would have been different if the full costs of independent verification had been foreseen. It is quite possible that this conclusion is also applicable to other major projects, such as the development of the primary protection system (PPS) for the Sizewell B nuclear reactor.

Perhaps one of the most important points to be made within this text is that many of the issues and techniques discussed are themselves the subject of ongoing debate. Although we have accumulated many years of experience in the use of computers in safety-critical applications, we still have much to learn.

REFERENCES

Airbus Industrie (1992). *A330/A340 Flight Controls*. Document AI/EE-A-441.0011/92. Toulouse: Airbus Industrie

Craigen D., Gerhart S. and Ralston T. (1994). Experience with formal methods in critical systems. *IEEE Software*, January, 21–39

HSE (1987). *Programmable Electronic Systems in Safety Related Applications, Vol. 2: General Technical Guidelines*. London: Her Majesty's Stationery Office

Parnas D.L. (1994). Inspection of safety-critical software using program-function tables. *Proc. IFIP 13th World Computer Congress*, Hamburg, Germany, Vol. A-13, 270–7

Parnas D.L., Asmis G.J.K. and Madey J. (1991). Assessment of safety-critical software in nuclear power plants. *Nuclear Safety*, **32**(2), 189–98

Potocki de Montalk J.P. (1993). Computer software in civil aircraft. *Microproc. Microsyst.*, **17**(1), 17–23

FURTHER READING

Leveson N.G. (1995). *Safeware: System Safety and Computers*. Reading, MA: Addison-Wesley

Appendix A
Acronyms

ABS	antilock braking system
AECB	Atomic Energy Control Board (Canada)
AECL	Atomic Energy of Canada Limited
AEEC	Airlines Electronic Engineering Committee
AGREE	Advisory Group on Reliability of Electronic Equipment
ALARP	as low as is reasonably practicable
ALU	arithmetic logic unit
ANSI	American National Standards Institute
AQAP	Allied Quality Assurance Publications/Procedures (NATO)
ARINC	Aeronautical Radio Inc.
ASME	American Society of Mechanical Engineers
BCD	binary coded decimal
BCS	British Computer Society
BIST	built-in self-test
BITE	built-in test equipment
BS	British Standard
BSI	British Standards Institution
CAA	Civil Aviation Authority (UK)
CAD	computer-aided design
CAE	computer-aided engineering
CAN	controller area network
CANDU	Canadian Deuterium Uranium (reactor)
CASE	computer-assisted software engineering
CEN	European Committee for Standardisation (Comité Européen de Normalisation)
CENELEC	European Committee for Electrotechnical Standardisation (Comité Européen de Normalisation Electrotechnique)
CIA	Chemical Industries Association (UK)
CMOS	complementary metal oxide semiconductor
CPU	central processing unit
Def Stan	Defence Standard (UK)
DER	designated engineering representative
DIN	Deutsches Institut für Normung
DoD	Department of Defense (USA)
DTI	Department of Trade and Industry (UK)

EC	European Community
ECAD	electronic computer-aided design
EEPROM	electrically erasable and programmable read-only memory
EFCS	electronic flight control system
EMC	electromagnetic compatibility
EPROM	erasable programmable read-only memory
ESA	European Space Agency
ETA	event tree analysis
EU	European Union
EUC	equipment under control
EUROCAE	European Organisation for Civil Aviation Electronics
EWICS	European Workshop on Industrial Computer Systems
FAA	Federal Aviation Authority (USA)
FAR	Federal Airworthiness Regulations (USA)
FBD	functional block diagrams
FCC	Federal Communications Commission (USA)
FMEA	failure modes and effects analysis
FMECA	failure modes, effects and criticality analysis
FTA	fault tree analysis
FWC	flight warning computer
HAZOP	hazard and operability studies
HCI	human–computer interface
HMSO	Her Majesty's Stationery Office
HOL	higher-order logic
HSE	Health and Safety Executive (UK)
IDS	interface design specification
IEC	International Electrotechnical Commission
IEE	Institution of Electrical Engineers (UK)
IEEE	Institute of Electrical and Electronic Engineers (USA)
IFAC	International Conference on Automatic Control
IL	instruction lists
ISO	International Standards Organisation
IV & V	independent verification and validation
JAR	joint aviation requirements
LD	ladder diagrams
LSI	large-scale integration
Mil Std	Military Standard (USA)
MMI	man–machine interface
MoD	Ministry of Defence (UK)
MOS	metal oxide semiconductor
MSI	medium-scale integration
MTBF	mean time between failures
MTTF	mean time to failure
MTTR	mean time to repair
NAMAS	National Measurement and Accreditation Service (UK)
NASA	National Aeronautics and Space Administration (USA)

NATO	North Atlantic Treaty Organization
NMOS	*N*-type metal oxide semiconductor
NMR	*N*-modular redundant
NPL	National Physical Laboratory (UK)
OOD	object-oriented design
OOP	object-oriented programming
PCB	printed circuit board
PE	pentaerythritol
PES	programmable electronic system
PETN	pentaerythritol tetranitrate
PHA	preliminary hazard analysis
PHI	preliminary hazard identification
PLC	programmable logic controller
PPS	primary protection system
PSU	power supply unit
QMS	quality management system
QRA	quantified risk analysis/assessment
RAM	random access memory
RIA	Railway Industry Association (UK)
ROM	read-only memory
RSRE	Royal Signals and Radar Establishment (UK)
RTCA	Radio Technical Commission for Aeronautics (USA)
SAFECOMP	Safety in Computer Systems
SCR	software cost reduction
SCS	safety-critical system
SDS	shutdown system
SERC	Science and Engineering Research Council (UK)
SFC	sequential function charts
SIL	safety integrity level
SRI	Stanford Research Institute (USA)
SRS	safety-related system
ST	structured text
STARTS	software tools for application to large real-time systems
TCAS	traffic alert and collision avoidance system
TCF	test cost factor
THS	trimmable horizontal stabilizer
TMR	triple modular redundancy
TTL	transistor–transistor logic
TÜV	Technischer Überwachungs Verein (Germany)
V & V	verification and validation
VDM	Vienna development method
VLSI	very large-scale integration

Appendix B
Test Case Generation

The BCS draft *Standard for Software Component Testing* (BCS, 1995) gives several examples of the generation of test cases for dynamic testing. In this appendix we shall look at two examples taken from this standard, illustrating the generation of test cases for two forms of testing, namely equivalence partitioning and boundary value analysis. These examples are based on a program for grading examination results.

The 'generate_grading' program

The software component *generate_grading* is defined by the following textual specification:

> *The component is passed an exam mark (out of 75) and a coursework (c/w) mark (out of 25), from which it generates a grade for the course in the range 'A' to 'D'. The grade is calculated from the overall mark which is calculated as the sum of the exam and c/w marks, as follows:*
>
> greater than or equal to 70 – 'A'
> greater than or equal to 50, but less than 70 – 'B'
> greater than or equal to 30, but less than 50 – 'C'
> less than 30 – 'D'
>
> *Where a mark is outside its expected range then a fault message ('FM') is generated. All inputs are passed as integers.*

Equivalence partitioning

First the partitions for the two inputs are identified. The *valid* partitions can be described by:

$0 \leqslant$ exam mark $\leqslant 75$
$0 \leqslant$ coursework mark $\leqslant 25$

The most obvious *invalid* partitions are described by:

exam mark > 75
exam mark < 0
coursework mark > 25
coursework mark < 0

Partitioned ranges of values can be represented pictorially thus:

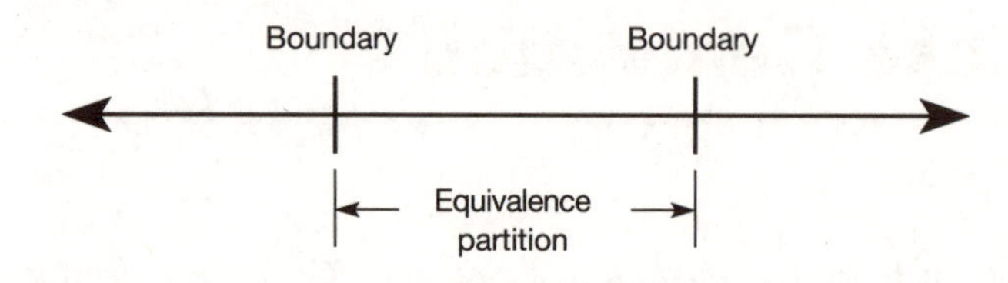

Therefore, for the input 'exam mark' the same notation leads to:

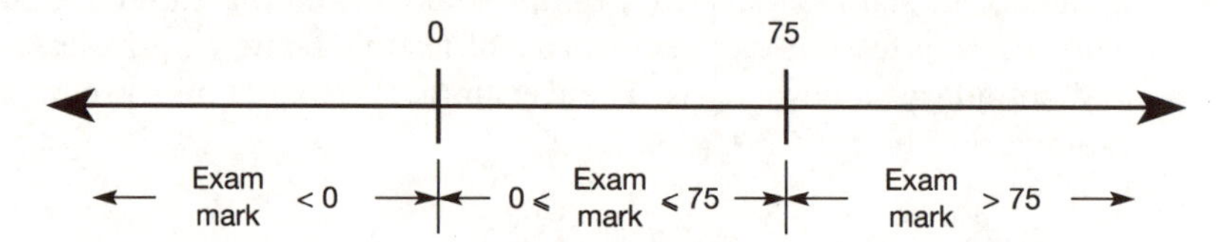

And for the input 'coursework mark' we get:

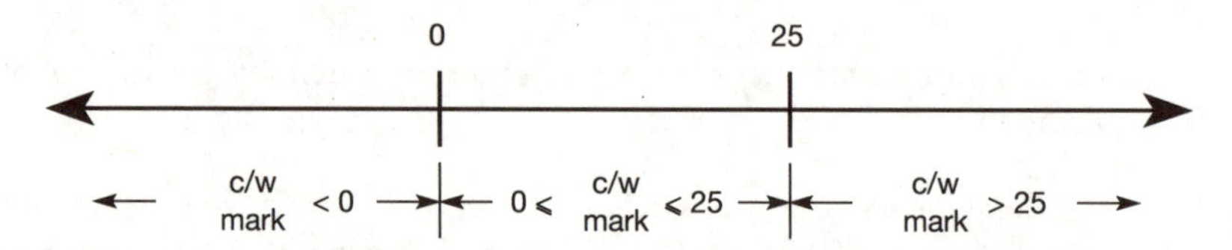

For each partition a single test case is generated to be representative of all values in the partition, as shown below:

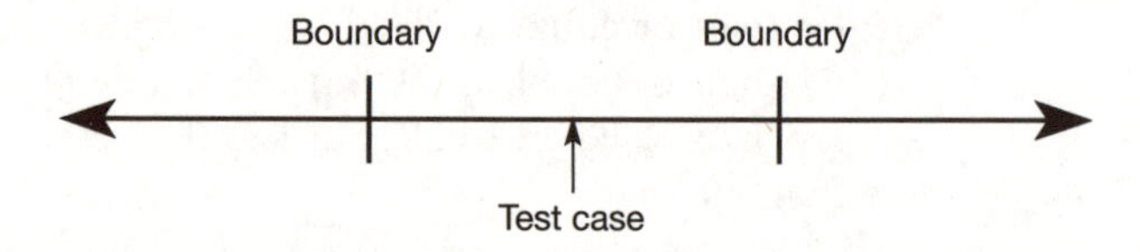

Thus, the three test cases derived from the input exam mark are:

Test case	*1*	*2*	*3*
Input (exam mark)	44	–10	93
Input (c/w mark)	15	15	15
Partition (exam mark)	0 ≤ exam mark ≤ 75	exam mark < 0	exam mark > 75
Expected output	'B'	'FM'	'FM'

Note that the input coursework (c/w) mark has been set to an arbitrary valid value of 15.

The test cases derived from the input coursework marks are thus:

Test case	*4*	*5*	*6*
Input (exam mark)	40	40	40
Input (c/w mark)	8	–15	47
Partition (c/w mark)	$0 \leqslant$ c/w mark $\leqslant 25$	c/w mark < 0	c/w mark > 25
Expected output	'C'	'FM'	'FM'

Note that the input exam mark has been set to an arbitrary valid value of 40.

Less obvious invalid input equivalence partitions would include any other inputs that can occur not so far included in a partition, for instance non-integer inputs or perhaps non-numeric inputs. In order to be considered an equivalence partition those values within it must be expected, from the specification, to be treated in an equivalent manner by the component. Thus we could generate the following invalid input equivalence partitions:

exam mark = real number
exam mark = alphabetic
coursework mark = real number
coursework mark = alphabetic
etc.

The following test cases are thus derived from possible invalid inputs:

Test case	*7*	*8*	*9*	*10*
Input (exam mark)	48.7	q	40	40
Input (c/w mark)	15	15	12.76	g
Partition	exam mark = real number	exam mark = alphabetic	c/w mark = real number	c/w mark = alphabetic
Expected output	'FM'	'FM'	'FM'	'FM'

Next, the partitions for the outputs are identified. The *valid* partitions are produced by considering each of the valid outputs for the components thus:

'A'	is induced by	$70 \leqslant$ total mark $\leqslant 100$
'B'	is induced by	$50 \leqslant$ total mark < 70
'C'	is induced by	$30 \leqslant$ total mark < 50
'D'	is induced by	$0 \leqslant$ total mark < 30
'Fault message'	is induced by	total mark > 100
'Fault message'	is induced by	total mark < 0

where total mark = exam mark + coursework mark. 'Fault message' is considered here as it is a specified output.

The equivalence partitions and boundaries for total mark are shown below:

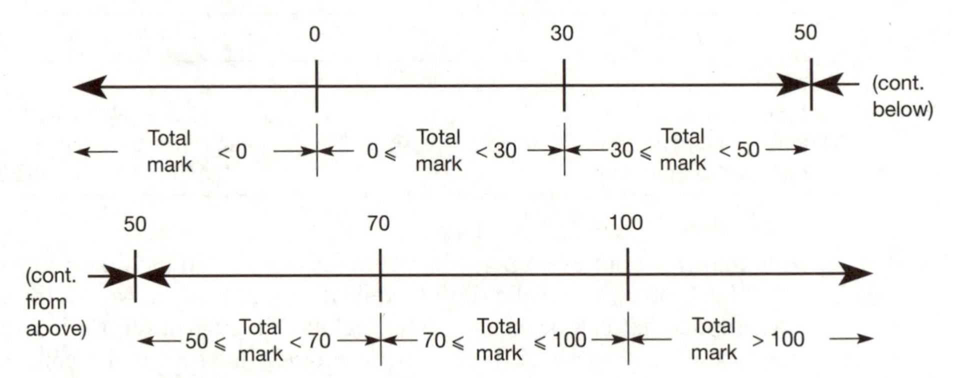

Thus the test cases derived from the valid outputs are:

Test case	*11*	*12*	*13*
Input (exam mark)	–10	12	32
Input (c/w mark)	–10	5	13
Partition (of total mark)	total < 0	0 ⩽ total < 30	30 ⩽ total < 50
Expected output	'FM'	'D'	'C'

Test case	*14*	*15*	*16*
Input (exam mark)	44	60	75
Input (c/w mark)	22	20	75
Partition (of total mark)	50 ⩽ total < 70	70 ⩽ total ⩽ 100	total > 100
Expected output	'B'	'A'	'FM'

The input values of exam mark and coursework mark have been derived from the total mark, which is their sum.

An invalid output would be any output from the component other than one of the five specified. It is not possible to group these possible outputs into coherent *invalid* output partitions, although values from this group must be tested. Thus invalid (non-specified) outputs must be identified and then the corresponding inputs that could *possibly* induce these outputs make up the test cases:

Test case	*17*	*18*	*19*	*20*
Input (exam mark)	85	–10	50	0
Input (c/w mark)	25	0	13	–10
Partition (output)	'E'	'z'	63	'@'
Expected output	'FM'	'FM'	'B'	'FM'

The identification of invalid outputs and the derivation of inputs that can include them are very subjective, and so testers can be expected to differ in this area.

Boundary value analysis

The partitions used in this example are identical to those derived for the equivalence partitioning example given above.

For each boundary three values are used, one on the boundary itself and one either side of it, the smallest significant distance away, as shown below:

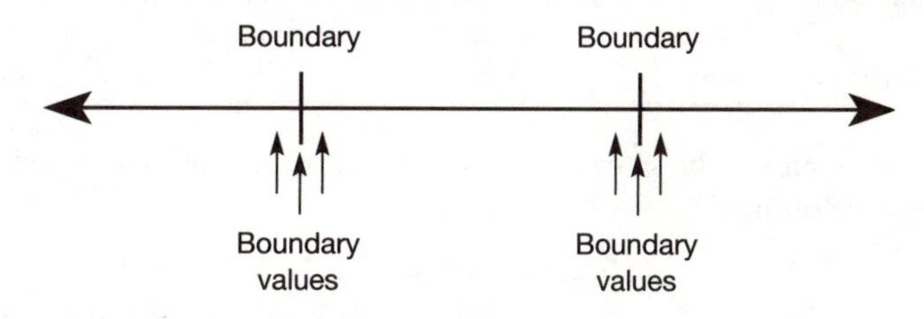

Thus, the six test cases derived from the input exam mark are:

Test case	*1*	*2*	*3*	*4*	*5*	*6*
Input (exam mark)	–1	0	1	74	75	76
Input (c/w mark)	15	15	15	15	15	15
Boundary (exam mark)	0	0	0	75	75	75
Expected output	'FM'	'D'	'D'	'A'	'A'	'FM'

Note that the input coursework (c/w) mark has been set to an arbitrary valid value of 15.

The test cases derived from the input coursework mark are thus:

Test case	*7*	*8*	*9*	*10*	*11*	*12*
Input (exam mark)	40	40	40	40	40	40
Input (c/w mark)	–1	0	1	24	25	26
Boundary (c/w mark)	0	0	0	25	25	25
Expected output	'FM'	'C'	'C'	'B'	'B'	'FM'

Note that the input exam mark has been set to an arbitrary valid value of 40.

Invalid equivalence partitions identified in the previous section include:

exam mark = real number
exam mark = alphabetic
coursework mark = real number
coursework mark = alphabetic
etc.

Although each of these equivalence partitions must be tested (as per equivalence partitioning) there is no real benefit in choosing boundary values for such partitions. Boundary value analysis is an error-based technique that concentrates the test cases on the boundaries where it is known faults are more likely to occur. In the case of these partitions test cases based around the boundaries are no more likely to reveal faults than other values in the partition. The following test cases are thus derived:

Test case	*13*	*14*	*15*	*16*
Input (exam mark)	48.7	q	40	40
Input (c/w mark)	15	15	12.76	g
Partition	exam mark = real number	exam mark = alphabetic	c/w mark = real number	c/w mark = alphabetic
Expected output	'FM'	'FM'	'FM'	'FM'

Next, the partitions for the outputs are identified, as for equivalence partitioning.

'A'	is induced by	$70 \leqslant$ total mark $\leqslant 100$
'B'	is induced by	$50 \leqslant$ total mark < 70
'C'	is induced by	$30 \leqslant$ total mark < 50
'D'	is induced by	$0 \leqslant$ total mark < 30
'Fault message'	is induced by	total mark > 100
'Fault message'	is induced by	total mark < 0

where total mark = exam mark + coursework mark. 'Fault message' is considered here as it is a specified output.

The equivalence partitions and boundaries for total mark are shown below:

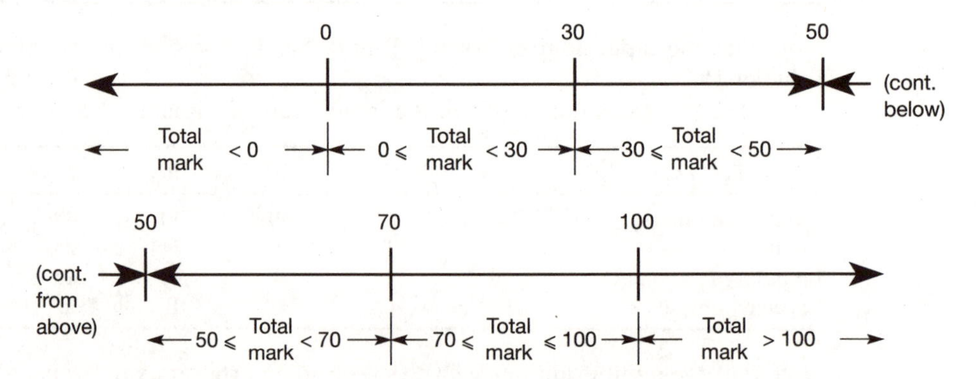

Thus the test cases derived from the valid outputs are:

Test case	*17*	*18*	*19*	*20*	*21*	*22*	*23*	*24*
Input (exam mark)	–1	0	0	29	15	6	24	50
Input (c/w mark)	0	0	1	0	15	25	25	0
Boundary (total mark)	0	0	0	30	30	30	50	50
Expected output	'FM'	'D'	'D'	'D'	'C'	'C'	'C'	'B'

Test case	*25*	*26*	*27*	*28*	*29*	*30*	*31*
Input (exam mark)	26	49	45	71	74	75	75
Input (c/w mark)	25	20	25	0	25	25	26
Boundary (total mark)	50	70	70	70	100	100	100
Expected output	'B'	'B'	'A'	'A'	'A'	'A'	'FM'

The input values of exam mark and coursework mark have been derived from the total mark, which is their sum.

An invalid output would be any output from the component other than one of the five specified. It is not possible to group these possible outputs into coherent *invalid* output partitions although values from it must be tested (as per equivalence partitioning). Thus invalid (non-specified) outputs must be identified and then the corresponding inputs that could *possibly* induce these outputs make up the test cases:

Test case	*32*	*33*	*34*	*35*
Input (exam mark)	85	–10	50	0
Input (c/w mark)	25	0	13	–10
Partition (output)	'E'	'z'	63	'@'
Expected output	'FM'	'FM'	'B'	'FM'

The identification of invalid outputs and the derivation of inputs that can include them are very subjective, and so testers can be expected to differ in this area.

So far several partitions have been identified that appear to be bounded on one side only. These are:

exam mark $>$ 75
exam mark $<$ 0
coursework mark $>$ 25
coursework mark $<$ 0
total mark $>$ 100
total mark $<$ 0

In fact, these partitions are bounded on their other side by implementation-dependent maximum and minimum values. For integers held in 16 bits these would be 32767 and -32768 respectively. Thus, the above partitions can be more fully described by:

$75 < \text{exam mark} \leqslant 32767$
$-32768 \leqslant \text{exam mark} < 0$
$25 < \text{coursework mark} \leqslant 32767$
$-32768 \leqslant \text{coursework mark} < 0$
$100 < \text{total mark} \leqslant 32767$
$-32768 \leqslant \text{total mark} < 0$

It can be seen that by bounding these partitions on both sides a number of additional boundaries are identified, which must be tested. This leads to the following additional test cases:

Test case	*36*	*37*	*38*	*39*	*40*	*41*
Input (exam mark)	32766	32767	32768	–32769	–32768	–32767
Input (c/w mark)	15	15	15	15	15	15
Boundary (exam mark)	32767	32767	32767	–32768	–32768	–32768
Expected output	'FM'	'FM'	'FM'	'FM'	'FM'	'FM'

Test case	*42*	*43*	*44*	*45*	*46*	*47*
Input (exam mark)	40	40	40	40	40	40
Input (c/w mark)	32766	32767	32768	–32769	–32768	–32767
Boundary (c/w mark)	32767	32767	32767	–32768	–32768	–32768
Expected output	'FM'	'FM'	'FM'	'FM'	'FM'	'FM'

Test case	*48*	*49*	*50*	*51*	*52*	*53*
Input (exam mark)	16383	32767	1	0	–16384	–32768
Input (c/w mark)	16383	0	32767	–32767	–16384	–1
Boundary (total mark)	32767	32767	32767	–32768	–32768	–32768
Expected output	'FM'	'FM'	'FM'	'FM'	'FM'	'FM'

REFERENCE

BCS (1995). *Standard for Software Component Testing*. Working Draft 3.0, British Computer Society Specialist Interest Group in Software Testing (BCS SIGIST) – standard in preparation

Appendix C
Answers to Numerical Problems

3.17	0.8379
3.18	0.9441
4.4	0.025 deaths per year
4.5	3.3×10^{-7}, $\sim 3.3 \times 10^{-7}$ deaths per person-year
6.11	200, $\sim 4 \times 10^{-47}$
7.5	0.61
7.6	497.5 years
7.7	1005 hours, 0.995
7.8	0.976
7.9	2.4 failures/hour
7.10	0.504
7.11	0.544
7.12	0.9999
7.13	0.999
7.14	3
7.15	0.9998
7.16	0.9771
7.17	0.972
7.18	0.5
7.19	0.991
7.20	0.993
7.21	1.0, 0.999 76
7.22	1.0, 0.976 85
7.24	State 1: 0.4; 0.6; 0.7; 0.75; 0.775. State 2: 0.6; 0.4; 0.3; 0.25; 0.225.
7.25	P(1) = 0.8; P(2) = 0.2
7.26	0.98, 0.02
11.8	~585 000 years

Index